Latin American
Political Parties

Robert J. Alexander

The Praeger Special Studies program—utilizing the most modern and efficient book production techniques and a selective worldwide distribution network—makes available to the academic, government, and business communities significant, timely research in U.S. and international economic, social, and political development.

Latin American Political Parties

PRAEGER SPECIAL STUDIES IN INTERNATIONAL POLITICS AND GOVERNMENT

329.98
A 377L

131823

Praeger Publishers New York Washington London

PRAEGER PUBLISHERS
111 Fourth Avenue, New York, N.Y. 10003, U.S.A.
5, Cromwell Place, London S.W.7, England

Published in the United States of America in 1973
by Praeger Publishers, Inc.

All rights reserved

© 1973 by Robert J. Alexander

Library of Congress Catalog Card Number: 77-129136

Printed in the United States of America

To Sidney Simon

PREFACE

The origins of this book are to be found in a discussion that I had with my friend Professor Alex Garber of the California State College at Sacramento several years ago. He and I were both fascinated by the "Jacobin Leftists", and he suggested that I write a volume about them. Although a bit skeptical, I was willing to undertake the project if I could have reasonable assurance of finding a publisher. Professor Garber agreed to approach Frederick Praeger with the idea; he was interested, but suggested that the book ought really to deal with all the different kinds of parties that exist and have existed in Latin America. The present volume is the result.

I hope that this book will make Latin American politics somewhat more comprehensible to North Americans—and perhaps to some Latin Americans, too. I also hope that it may become a reference volume, since I have tried to include at least some discussion of all the important parties of recent decades, as well as the outstanding ones of the period since independence.

When one is discussing matters that are to some degree controversial, it is always advisable that the author warn of his prejudices. I am most disposed toward parties of democratic reform, and it is among them that I have most of my closest Latin American friends. However, I have tried to be as objective as possible in dealing with all kinds of parties that are treated.

Many have contributed directly or indirectly to this volume. First, I must mention the thousands of Latin American political leaders and rank-and-filers with whom I have talked during the last quarter of a century. Much of this book is drawn from these discussions.

In the second place, I must thank those who have helped get this book published. These include Ms. John Carman, who typed the final manuscript, and Mary-Stuart Garden, the editor who saw the work through.

Finally, I must thank my children, Meg and Tony, and my wife, Joan, for bearing with me during innumerable evenings and weekends when my attention was centered on Latin American politics rather than on them.

Rutgers University
New Brunswick, N.J.
March 1972

CONTENTS

	Page
PREFACE	vii
INTRODUCTION: THE ROLE OF PARTIES IN LATIN AMERICAN POLITICS	xvi
Nomenclature of Latin American Parties	xvii
The Nature of Latin American Parties	xviii
Role of the Parties in Recent Decades	xx
The Future of Latin American Parties	xxii
Format of the Volume	xxiv

PART I: PERSONALIST AND TRADITIONAL PARTIES

INTRODUCTION	3

Chapter

1	PERSONALIST PARTIES	4
	Caudillo Antecedents of Personalist Parties	5
	Persistence of Personalist Politics	6
	The Partido Dominicano	6
	Peruvian Personalist Parties	8
	The Velasquistas of Ecuador	11
	The Partido Panameñista and Arnulfo Arias	14
	Personalist Factions of Other Parties	15
	Other Personalist Parties	17
2	THE LIBERALS	19
	Liberalism in the 19th Century	20
	The Liberal Parties Since World War I	27
	Honduras	28
	Nicaragua	30
	Venezuela	32
	Colombia	34
	Ecuador	37
	Bolivia	39
	Chile	40
	Uruguay	43
	Paraguay	45

Chapter		Page
3	THE CONSERVATIVES	48
	Mexico	49
	Guatemala	53
	Honduras	54
	Nicaragua	57
	Colombia	59
	Ecuador	64
	Bolivia	67
	Chile	69
	Argentina	73
	Uruguay	77
	Paraguay	78
4	THE RADICALS	80
	Argentina	80
	Origins of the Unión Cívica Radical	80
	The First Radical Government	83
	The Period in the Wilderness	85
	The Radicals in the Perón Period	86
	The Radicals in the Aramburu Period	89
	The Radicals in the Frondizi Administration	91
	The Radicals in the Guido Period	92
	Radicalism Under Illia and the Military Regime	93
	Organizational Structure of the Radicals	95
	Chile	96
	Early Decades of the Chilean Radical Party	96
	The Ibáñez Dictatorship and Afterward	97
	The Radical Regimes	98
	The Radicals After 1952	101

PART II: THE LATIN AMERICAN SOCIALISTS

	INTRODUCTION	105
5	THE SOCIALISTS IN ARGENTINA	107
	Philosophy of the Socialist Party	108
	Early History of the Socialist Party	109
	Socialist Growth and Division	111
	The Socialists in the 1920s	113
	The Socialists During the Era of "Patriotic Fraud"	115

Chapter		Page
	The Socialists and the Perón Regime	118
	The Socialists in the post-Perón Period	120
6	THE CHILEAN SOCIALISTS	123
	The Partido Democrático	123
	The Partido Socialista Obrero	125
	Origins of the Partido Socialista	125
	The Socialists and the Popular Front	127
	The Socialists and González Videla's Regime	132
	Split and Reunion	133
	Recent History of the Chilean Socialists	135
	Strengths and Weaknesses of Chilean Socialists	138
7	THE URUGUAYAN SOCIALIST PARTY	140
	The First Uruguayan Socialist Party	140
	The Second Partido Socialista	142
	The Socialists and the Terra Dictatorship	143
	World War II and After	144
	Ideological Evolution and Decline of the Partido Socialista	146
	Strengths and Weaknesses of the Uruguayan Socialists	150
8	OTHER SOCIALIST PARTIES	151
	Ecuador	151
	Peru	155
	Colombia	156
	Brazil	158
	Venezuela	162
	Panama	164
	Bolivia	166
	Cuba	167
	Mexico	168
	Puerto Rico	171

Chapter	Page

PART III: THE NATIONAL REVOLUTIONARY PARTIES

INTRODUCTION		177
9	THE PARTIDO APRISTA PERUANO	180
	Origins of the Apristas	180
	Establishment of the Party	183
	The Apristas and the Bustamante Regime	186
	The Odría Period	188
	Aprista "Critical Support" of Prado	190
	The Apristas as the Loyal Opposition	193
	Significance of the Aprista Party	195
10	ACCIÓN DEMOCRÁTICA	197
	Origins of Acción Democrática	197
	The First Acción Democrática Regime	199
	The Dictatorship	201
	Acción Democrática and the Provisional Government	203
	The Betancourt Administration	205
	The Leoni Administration	209
	Splits in Acción Democrática	212
	Strengths and Weaknesses of Acción Democrática	215
11	THE PARTIDO LIBERACIÓN NACIONAL OF COSTA RICA	217
	Antecedents of Liberación Nacional	218
	The Civil War of 1948	221
	The Figueres Provisional Government	222
	The Establishment of Liberación Nacional	223
	The Figueres Administration	226
	Recent History of Liberación Nacional	229
	Assessment of Liberación Nacional	231
12	THE MOVIMIENTO NACIONALISTA REVOLUCIONARIO	233
	Origins of the MNR	233
	The MNR and the Villarroel Regime	235
	The "Six Years"	236
	The First Paz Estenssoro Government	238

Chapter		Page
	The Siles Administration	241
	The Disintegration and Decline of the MNR	244
	The MNR Since 1964	248
	Strengths and Weaknesses of the MNR	250
13	THE PARTIDO POPULAR DEMOCRÁTICO OF PUERTO RICO	251
	Origins of the Partido Popular Democrático	251
	The PPD During World War II	253
	Operation Bootstrap	254
	Political Evolution of the Partido Popular Democrático	257
	Schism and Defeat of the PPD	260
	Strengths and Weaknesses of the Partido Popular Democrático	262
14	THE PARTIDO REVOLUCIONARIO INSTITUCIONAL OF MEXICO	263
	Origins of the Revolutionary Party	263
	The Reorganization of the PNR	265
	The Post-Cárdenas Regimes	267
	The Ideology of the PRI	268
	Government by Consensus	271
	Factions in the PRI	274
	The Crisis of the Díaz Ordaz Period	275
	The Future of the PRI	278
15	OTHER NATIONAL REVOLUTIONARY PARTIES	280
	Cuba	280
	Origins of the Auténtico Party	280
	The Auténticos in Office	282
	The Decline of the Auténticos	283
	The Auténticos in the Castro Regime	285
	Reason for the Failure of the Auténticos	286
	The Ortodoxos	288
	The Dominican Republic	290
	Origins of the Partido Revolucionario Dominicano	290
	The PRD After Trujillo's Death	291
	The PRD in Power	293
	The PRD Since 1963	296

Chapter		Page
	Strengths and Weaknesses of the PRD	300
	Guatemala	301
	Haiti	306
	Paraguay	308

PART IV: THE CHRISTIAN DEMOCRATIC PARTIES

INTRODUCTION — 315

16 THE CHILEAN CHRISTIAN DEMOCRATS — 318

The Falange Nacional	318
The Beginning of the Christian Democratic Party	322
The 1964 Election	325
The Frei Government	328
Ideological Trends Within Chilean Christian Democracy	334
The 1970 Election and Thereafter	335

17 THE COPEI OF VENEZUELA — 338

Early History of Copei	338
Copei and the Pérez Jiménez Dictatorship	340
Copei in the 1958 Provisional Government Period	344
Copei in the Betancourt Administration	345
Copei as the Loyal Opposition	346
Victory at Last	347
Reasons for the Rise of Copei	349

18 OTHER CHRISTIAN DEMOCRATIC PARTIES — 352

Argentina	352
Brazil	354
Uruguay	356
Peru	357
El Salvador	359
Guatemala	360
Dominican Republic	362
Bolivia	363
Paraguay	364
Colombia	365
Panama	365
Costa Rica	366

Chapter		Page
	Nicaragua	366
	Mexico	367
	Haiti	367
	Cuba	368
	Puerto Rico	368
	International Organization of Christian Democrats	368

PART V: TOTALITARIAN PARTIES

INTRODUCTION 373

19 THE ORTHODOX COMMUNIST PARTIES 375

    Origins of the Communist Movement in Latin
        America 375
    Ebbs and Flows of Communist Strength 376
    Principal Communist Appeals 379
    Groups to Which the Communists Have Appealed 381
    Communist International Organization in Latin
        America 383
    The Orthodox Communists and the International
        Communist Schism 385

20 SCHISMATIC COMMUNIST PARTIES 388

    The Trotskyites 388
        Chile 388
        Cuba 390
        Bolivia 391
        Mexico 394
        Other Trotskyite Parties 395
    The Right Opposition 396
    The Titoite Heresy 396
    "Dual Communism" 397
    The pro-Peking Dissidents 404

21 THE JACOBIN LEFT AND CASTRO COMMUNISM 410

    Origins of the Jacobin Leftists 410
    The Jacobin Leftists and the Cuban Revolution 412
    Castro and the Orthodox Latin American
        Communists 414
    The Theoretical Positions of Castro Communism 416

Chapter	Page
From Jacobin Leftism to Fidelista Communism	418
The Fidelista Parties and Groups	423
Castro's Abandonment of Independence	426

22 FASCIST PARTIES 428

The Axis and Latin America	428
Ação Integralista Brasileira	429
Partido Nacista de Chile	432
Falange Socialista Boliviana	433
Unión Nacional Sinarquista	437

PART VI: MISCELLANEOUS PARTIES

INTRODUCTION	441

23 THE BRAZILIAN PARTIES 442

Brazilian Parties Before 1945	442
The Reestablishment of Parties in 1945	445
União Democrática Nacional	446
Partido Social Democrático	449
Partido Trabalhista Brasileiro	454
The Dissident Trabalhista Parties	460
The Ideological Parties	461
Partido Republicano	462
The post-1965 Parties	462

24 THE PERONISTA PARTY AND MOVEMENT 465

Origins of Peronismo	465
Establishment of the Peronista Party	468
The Peronista Parties During the Perón Regime	469
The Peronista Parties and Justicialismo	472
The Peronistas in the Immediate post-Perón Years	473
New Trends in Peronismo	476
Nature and Prospects of Peronismo	481

NOTES	483
BIBLIOGRAPHY	504
INDEX OF PEOPLE AND PARTIES	523
ABOUT THE AUTHOR	538

INTRODUCTION:
THE ROLE OF PARTIES
IN LATIN AMERICAN POLITICS

There is a tendency among observers of Latin America to underrate the importance of parties in the politics of the area. Stress is put on the alleged tendency of Latin Americans to follow individuals instead of ideas, upon the propensity of the military to make and unmake governments at will, and, more recently, on the supposed significance of guerrilla armies as spokesmen for the underprivileged.

It is the purpose of this book to discuss the nature, organization, and ideological and programmatic differences of the Latin American parties. Obviously in a work of this length the matters being discussed are of some consequence. It is my conviction that since the early years of these countries' independence, political parties have played a significant role in Latin American affairs, that in the middle decades of the 20th century this role has been of particular importance, and that parties are likely to continue to be an important determinant in the future.

Of course, no one deny that the personality of individual political leaders has been of major importance in the political history of Latin America. The earliest party divisions in many of the states tended to center on the leaders of the independence movement. Caudillos, whose influence was based on their ability to rally sizable groups of followers willing to fight and, if necessary, die for them, were characteristic of the 19th century. Even in recent decades a number of political parties have been organized almost exclusively for the purpose of supporting particular political leaders; a chapter is devoted to these organizations.

However, undue emphasis should not be put upon personalism in Latin American politics; it is a phenomenon not unknown in other parts of the world. One need only think of the careers of Dwight Eisenhower and Charles de Gaulle.

In the second place, from the earliest days of independence, Latin American political leaders disagreed over ideas and programs, as well as over individual ambitions. Such disagreements gave rise to the earliest political parties. In recent decades schisms in parties throughout the hemisphere have centered as much on conflicting ideas as on personality conflicts. Many of those politicians who have shown personalistic tendencies have risen to national fame through a political party.

Nor can the importance of the military in Latin American politics be ignored. However, the military leaders who rose to national leadership during the 19th century more often than not achieved prominence as leaders of an existing political party or a faction of one. More recently military leaders have often worked with a political party in seizing power, or have won the support of a party once they were in control. A successful military leader almost always has felt the need for organizing a political party to rally civilian support for his regime.

Finally, even the guerrilla armies, or would-be guerrilla armies, of Latin America are by no means independent of political parties. As is indicated later in this book, some of these efforts have been launched by political parties, and others have had political objectives and have hoped that military success would lead to the formation of a political party growing out of the guerrilla army.

NOMENCLATURE OF LATIN AMERICAN PARTIES

One factor that makes difficult the analysis of Latin American political parties along ideological lines is the names they have used. These labels are often as meaningless as "Republican" and "Democratic" are for the two major parties in the United States. Frequently the names of Latin American parties are misleading.

During the 19th century the titles "Liberal" and "Conservative," used by a large number of the Latin American parties, were comparatively straightforward. An observer with any political sophistication, and with some knowledge of parties and philosophies then current in Europe, would have no great trouble in judging the parties' general philosophies and programs from these names.

However, with the proliferation of parties in the 20th century, the names that have been widely adopted are more confusing. On the one hand, many parties have appeared whose names give no indication of their political philosophies: Republican, Democratic, National, Unionist, Red, White. On the other hand, the names of some parties are deceiving. For instance, the most conservative party of Bolivia has for years been the Partido Unión Republicana Socialista; and the Partido Social Democrático of Brazil was certainly not Social Democratic in the European sense—in fact, one would be hard pressed to maintain that during most of its existence it had any political philosophy at all.

Furthermore, the same name has often been applied to parties in several countries that are very different. Thus, in recent decades the Liberals of Chile have been the most conservative party in the country, those of Ecuador have been more or less in the center, those of Honduras have been the major party of the Left, and in Nicaragua the Liberal Party has been the private preserve of the

Somoza family, which has ruled the country for more than three decades.

The only way to deal with this problem is by careful analysis of the important parties that have existed since World War I in Latin America. In this book all of the major parties, as well as a fair number of the more significant minor ones, are covered.

THE NATURE OF LATIN AMERICAN PARTIES

In this volume the discussion of Latin American political parties is organized principally around their ideological and programmatic differences. This method of categorization is not unchallengeable, although I feel that it is the most meaningful way of considering these organizations.

In Brazil one frequently hears the complaint that the parties predominant between 1945 and 1965 were not "meaningful," by which the protestor usually means that they were not clearly definable in ideological terms. This is one of the reasons why a separate chapter is devoted to a discussion of the major Brazilian parties of this period.

Professor James Payne has argued against the relevance of ideologies and programs in analyzing Latin American political parties.[1] He has presented an alternative analysis of parties and of politics in Colombia that he thinks adequately explains the situation in that country, and he would tentatively extend his conclusions about Colombia to all of Latin America. Although, within limits that will be indicated in the chapters dealing with the major Colombian parties, I am willing to accept Payne's thesis as shedding much light on the politics of that country, it does not give an adequate description of political behavior in the area as a whole.

The Payne argument is that the leaders of the two major Colombian political parties are not concerned with ideological or programmatic issues but, rather, with the prestige that political activity can bring them. The rank-and-file party members are not in politics because of convictions concerning issues but, rather, for the jobs that can result from supporting a particular leader or faction. He offers extensive evidence to bear out his thesis.

As a corollary to his basic argument, Payne insists that it does not make sense to analyze Colombian politics on the basis of a supposed ideological distinction between the parties. Among the great majority of Colombian politicians there are neither "radicals" nor "reactionaries." There is no basic distinction to be drawn between the Conservatives and Liberals—or, for that matter, among the various subgroups into which these two major parties are divided—on such ideological issues as agrarian reform, industrialization, support of trade unionism, social legislation, and protectionism. Payne maintains that virtually all politicians are "demagogic," willing to support any policy or issue that seems likely to win popular support.

Even if one accepts this analysis as useful to understanding Colombian political behavior, it is not universally applicable even there, and certainly does not explain the nature and functioning of most of the major parties in other Latin American countries. Even in Colombia it was Liberal governments professing an anticlerical philosophy that adopted laws limiting the rights of the Church; it was the Liberal government of Alfonso López that first authorized legal trade unions and enacted much of the nation's labor and social legislation; and it is the Liberal Party that for more than three decades has had firm control over one of the country's major trade union groups, whereas the Conservatives have had no such central labor organization under their direction. As Payne himself points out, the hierarchy and clergy of Colombia are overwhelmingly favorable to the Conservative Party, a fact not completely without ideological implications.

Going beyond the frontiers of Colombia, it would be hard to maintain that there is no ideological distinction among the Liberals, Christian Democrats, and Socialists of Chile; between the PRI and Acción Nacional in Mexico; or between Acción Democrática, the Copei, and the Unión Republicana Democrática (URD) in Venezuela. Likewise, there are important ideological distinctions among the Apristas, Christian Democrats, and Pradistas of Peru and between the Bolivian Movimiento Nacionalista Revolucionario (MNR) and the Falange Socialista Boliviana. The Communists, whether pro-Moscow, pro-Peking, or pro-Castro, have a distinctive ideology wherever they are found in Latin America.

Ideology and program are, then, a significant way of distinguishing the various parties of the hemisphere. They are also a convenient vehicle for bringing some kind of intellectual order out of what would otherwise be the chaos of competing political groups. They will be a basic instrument for analyzing and discussing the region's parties.

However, an analysis based only on ideological or programmatic distinctions is not sufficient for a thorough understanding of these parties. The significance of political groups can also be understood in terms of the elements in the population that they represent or seek to represent. The analyses of individual parties try to give certain emphasis to this aspect.

Some light can be cast on the Latin American parties by noting their forms and methods of organization. Whether they seek to establish local units throughout the country, whether they maintain functional organizations for appealing to special groups in the population, the degree to which their leadership is subject to control or pressure from the rank and file, and the extent to which they maintain contacts with parties in other countries that they consider to be their counterparts give a wider comprehension of these organizations. All of these aspects of the Latin American parties will be covered to some degree.

For some parties tradition is of primary importance. Certainly this is a major factor in determining loyalties of individuals, groups, and even regions of Colombia to one of the two principal parties. It is also an important element in explaining the continued loyalty of the workers of Peru to the Partido Aprista Peruano. Other such instances will be noted in discussing individual parties.

There is no doubt, too, that the yen for office and the material benefits it can bring play a certain role in all of the Latin American parties. Bitter fights have been waged and many parties have been split over who should be the candidate for president, or whether the party should join the incumbent president's cabinet. Some parties have made it almost a matter of principle always to have their members in the government—the Radical Party of Chile for several decades and the Unión Republicana Democrática of Venezuela during the 1960s are examples of this behavior. However, in most cases mere office-holding has not been the principal objective of the major Latin American parties—they have sought positions in the government in order to pursue a program or defend the interest of social or economic groups associated with them.

Finally, the history of the various parties is of considerable importance. The way in which they have behaved in moments of crisis, what they have actually done if they have come to power, and the relations they have maintained with organized labor, the armed forces, the Church, the rural landlord, the peasantry, and other pressure groups and classes shed much light on the nature and role of the Latin American political parties.

ROLE OF THE PARTIES IN RECENT DECADES

Since World War I the role of political parties has been of growing importance. They have carried the burden of the struggle to establish a firm basis for political democracy; some of them have led the process of social change and economic development; others have been instrumental in defending the status quo. Generally the political parties have tried to limit the influence of the military in Latin American politics.

Agitation by national revolutionary, Socialist, Communist, Christian Democratic, and other parties has been instrumental in extending the right to vote in Latin America, through eliminating literacy requirements and giving the franchise to women. These same parties have been in the forefront of campaigns to organize workers and peasants into unions, thus giving them both the economic and the political power necessary to make effective their legal right to the franchise.

The wide adoption of labor and social legislation, to protect the rights and improve the working conditions of the humbler elements, has been due in large part to the agitation of the parties of the Left, and sometimes has actually been carried out by governments controlled by these parties. Fundamental agrarian reforms have been carried out by governments of national revolutionary parties in Mexico, Venezuela, and Bolivia; by a Christian Democratic regime in Chile; and by a Communist one in Cuba. Large-scale efforts to make education available to the great mass of the population have been made by national revolutionary governments in Mexico, Bolivia, Puerto Rico, and Venezuela; by the Colorado (Liberal) administrations in Uruguay; by the Christian Democrats in Chile; and by the Communists in Cuba.

The philosophy of "developmentalism"—the pushing of rapid economic development and particularly of industrialization, as a means of assuring both a greater degree of effective national independence and rising levels of living—has become an integral part of the political program of most of the Latin American parties of the Left. Particularly important in this regard have been the programs of the national revolutionary governments of Mexico, Bolivia, Costa Rica, Puerto Rico, and Venezuela since World War II; the Socialist-Radical government of Chile in the early 1940s; the Colorado government of Uruguay during World War II; the Peronista and Frondizi Unión Cívica Radical Intransigente regimes in Argentina; and the Social Democratic administration of Juscelino Kubitschek in Brazil.

All of this is not to say that only the organized political parties of Latin America have been responsible for the kinds of programs discussed. Some labor codes have been enacted by military dictators, some nonparty governments have paid particular attention to economic development, and some dictatorships have at least formally extended the right to vote to groups that had previously not possessed it. However, the main push for social change and rapid development, for broadening the participation of the masses in national political life, has resulted from the agitation of the Left political parties, and less frequently from the actions of governments controlled by parties of the Left.

Not all Latin American political parties have favored change. In Chile the Liberals and Conservatives long resisted it, as did the Conservatives (National Democrats) of Argentina, the Nationalists of Uruguay, and the traditional parties of Bolivia and Paraguay.

The exigencies of practical politics have not always made it possible for the political parties to avoid cooperation with elements of the military. In various countries civilian political parties have conspired with military men to throw out the regime in power. Usually, although not always, such conspiracies have been provoked by the existence of a military dictatorship. However, on balance, virtually all of the political parties, from Right to Left, have sought to assert the supremacy of the civilians over the armed forces in determining what government should be in power. Whatever success has been achieved in curbing militarism in Latin America during the last half century is due mainly to the influence of the political parties. The development of mass parties with a broad base of support among the civilian population has tended to make military coups somewhat more risky. The loyalty of civilian members of their families to a political party has certainly influenced individual military officers against belief in the "right" of the armed forces to be the ultimate arbiters of government, regardless of the wishes of the civilian populace.

THE FUTURE OF LATIN AMERICAN PARTIES

During the 1960s at least two new menaces threatened the future role of political parties in the area's public affairs. One of these was the threat of guerrilla war. The other was a change of attitude by some military men concerning their own role in politics.

The purpose of most of the guerrilla bands that sought to come to power in half a dozen or more of the Latin American countries after the triumph of the Castro revolution in Cuba was to establish a regime that would suppress all political parties but one—the one arising from the guerrilla struggle. However, more than a dozen years after Castro's victory no other guerrilla army had been able to duplicate his feat; and in the latter half of the 1960s the guerrilla movement in general suffered a number of severe setbacks. Although the possible success of a guerrilla effort could not be completely discounted, by the end of the 1960s the dangers to political parties in Latin America did not come principally from this quarter.

More menacing seemed to be the changed attitude of some military leaders of the area. It had been traditional in Latin American coups d'état that after a certain interval elections would be called to "constitutionalize" a de facto regime set up by the soldiers, and at least a few political parties normally took part in such elections. Furthermore, with the exception of such regimes as the 31-year dictatorship of Rafael Trujillo in the Dominican Republic, military dictatorships have usually not lasted for more than a decade.

However, during the 1960s three military regimes came to power with the announced intention of staying in power indefinitely and of paying little heed to the traditional niceties of government change by coup d'état. After some hesitation following the Brazilian coup of 1964, its military leaders outlawed all existing parties and made it clear that they would stay in power until they felt that they had "carried out the objectives of the revolution"—with no indication as to when this was likely to be. In 1966 the military seized power in Argentina and announced their intention of staying in power "for 10 years." They, too, dissolved all political parties and proclaimed their intention of carrying out a "revolution."

Finally, the military of Peru took power in that country in October 1968. The new dictatorship announced that it had no intention of calling elections in the foreseeable future and dissolved the Supreme Electoral Tribunal on the ground that it was "unnecessary." It, too, proclaimed its intention to carry out a "revolution" and adopted a strongly nationalistic attitude designed to win it wide popular support.

As a result of these events there has been some fear among political party leaders throughout Latin America that military men elsewhere would follow the lead of their Argentine, Brazilian, and Peruvian colleagues in rejecting the role of parties in the nations' political life. They fear that such an eventuality might mean the beginning of a period of generalized military tyranny that would postpone or even end the possibility of the establishment of a firm basis for political democracy in the area.

However, it is by no means certain that such a permanent or semipermanent type of military regime is "the wave of the future" in Latin America. For one thing, in some Latin American countries the political parties and other civil organizations associated with them will be able to prevent such a development. For another, the military of other nations will realize the dangers to the armed forces as an institution that is involved in assuming complete responsibility for the conduct of government on a long-term basis.

The mere seizure of power by the military leaders does not end politics in government. There are still differences of opinion that will undoubtedly arise among the military men themselves and among the civilians who inevitably must be associated with them, as well as in the wider range of the population. If the armed forces are solely responsible for the government, as they were in Argentina, Brazil, and Peru in the late 1960s, these conflicts concerning ideas, ideologies, programs, and policies will inevitably find expression within the military.

Thus the armed forces will be divided into factions along political lines. This will diminish the possibility of their performing adequately the two functions they are supposed to fulfill: national defense and maintenance of internal order. Such risks are traditionally present when the armed forces have taken power for relatively short periods of provisional or pseudo-constitutional government; they will be intensified in military regimes that intend to stay in power indefinitely and to rule in their own name. This is a fact of which many military men are quite aware, and it will help to discourage them from attempting to follow the example of their colleagues in Brazil, Argentina, and Peru.

Civilian political parties are the best instruments so far developed for the expression of the kind of differences of opinion and interest that many military men fear might tear their institution apart. It seems likely that political parties will continue to play an important part in Latin American political life, and that the studies that follow will not have been written about institutions no longer in existence.

FORMAT OF THE VOLUME

This book is divided into six sections, which for the most part are organized in terms of the ideology and programs of the parties discussed. It begins with a survey of the "traditional" parties of the area, which in most cases stem from the early decades of independence, the parties that dominated the political picture in the 19th century and in some cases are still important. Included in this discussion are not only the Conservative, Liberal, and Radical parties but also the personalist ones, those organized for the purpose of enhancing the fortunes of a particular political leader.

Subsequent parts of the book will deal with the kinds of parties that have largely been characteristic of the present century and have reflected the profound political, economic, and social change through which the area has been passing, particularly since World War I. There are separate sections on the national revolutionary, Socialist, and Christian Democratic parties, with individual chapters devoted to the most important groups in each of these categories. There is also a section on the totalitarian parties, discussing the various brands of Communist organizations that have emerged in the area, as well as the few but in some cases significant fascist parties that have existed in recent decades.

Finally, there is a section devoted to parties that do not neatly fit into any of the ideological categories with which most of the book is concerned. It will deal with the major Brazilian parties that existed during the period of relative democracy in that country between 1945 and 1965, and with the Peronista Party of Argentina, which is in many ways unique.

It is hoped that this discussion will make some contribution toward clarifying the admittedly confusing panorama of Latin American politics; that it will not only present an understandable picture of the principal party organizations that have functioned and presently function in Latin American politics but that it will also give some feeling of the social and economic forces that have formed the background for partisan political activity.

PART

I

**PERSONALIST
AND TRADITIONAL
PARTIES**

INTRODUCTION

This section deals with those parties that generally dominated Latin American politics during the first century of the independence of the countries of the area. The liberal and conservative tendencies in Latin American politics originated in many countries during the early postindependence years. In that period the leaders of the new nations divided over the issues of the secular powers of the Roman Catholic Church, whether the countries should be organized along federal or centralist lines, and the role of the government in the economy.

Until World War I most political controversy centered on these issues, and the political forces tended to rally behind parties under the banners of the Liberals and Conservatives. The Radicals arose during the 19th century, at least in Chile, as the left wing of the Liberals, more intransigent than the Liberals in their opposition to the position and privileges of the Church.

Finally, there was an exceedingly strong element of personalism in Latin American politics of the 19th century. Personalist leaders arose within the Liberal and Conservative ranks and often came to dominate these parties. The personalist tradition has endured to some extent into the 20th century and, as will be noted in Chapter 1, there have been various personalist parties in Latin American during recent decades.

Generally the parties dealt with in Part I do not reflect the changes in the economy and society of Latin America since World War I. As will be noted later in the book, they have been to a large degree superseded by parties of different kinds and ideologies. However, since they have been of great importance in the past, and still have their representatives in contemporary Latin American politics, they are important to an understanding of the political scene in Latin America in the second half of the 20th century.

CHAPTER 1

PERSONALIST PARTIES

Casual observers of the Latin American scene, and even some professional Latin Americanists, maintain that most Latin American political parties are "personalist." At first glance there would seem to be considerable justification for such a point of view. It is true that in most Latin American parties, personalism plays a very important role. Some ideological parties and some class parties were first organized around the personality of a particular leader. Even the Communist Party of Brazil gained most of its importance in national politics because of the charisma of its principal figure, Luiz Carlos Prestes. On various occasions parties that were not basically personalist have been split because of the personal ambitions or rivalries of individual leaders.

However, it might be well for North Americans to remember that the influence of personalities is of some importance in their own parties. For example, the influence of Dwight Eisenhower in the Republican Party of the 1950s certainly owed more to his personality than to his strong adherence to a particular ideology, his representing a particular element of the population, or his proved administrative ability. But Eisenhower's emergence as a chief of the Republican Party did not make that group "personalist" in any meaningful sense. Much the same could be said about the impact of individual leaders in Latin American parties. However, it is also undoubtedly true that real personalist parties, of a kind that has little or no parallel in the political history of the United States, have existed and still exist in Latin America.

In order to differentiate between such really personalist parties and those that may appear to be this type of party but are really not, it is essential to define a personalist party. Here it will be identified as a party that is organized and maintained solely to support the ambitions of a particular political leader. Without him the party has no reason to exist; with his disappearance such a party will disappear.

A number of Latin American parties that from their origins or their names would appear to be personalist are not really so. Although they may have started out in this category, they have come to represent particular groups, or to stand for a definite ideological position. Among the parties of this type are the Uruguayan Batllistas, the Peronista Party of Argentina, and the Partido Trabalhista of Brazil.

CAUDILLO ANTECEDENTS OF PERSONALIST PARTIES

The antecedents of the leaders of the present-day personalist parties are the 19th-century caudillos. The caudillo is now virtually a thing of the past, but he has played a very important role in the political history of many of the Latin American countries.

The caudillos often worked within one of the existing 19th-century parties, usually the Liberal or Conservative. However, their followers were devoted to the caudillos much more than to the parties to which they formally belonged.

The typical caudillo was a local leader, usually a sizable landholder, with considerable influence in his part of the country. He had a marked degree of charisma and the ability to mobilize loyal followers for "elections" or for armed conflict with his opponents. A successful caudillo would defeat or absorb his rivals. If he became powerful enough, he would descend upon the capital with his armed followers and become president of the republic, remaining until defeated by a rival caudillo. During his incumbency the national army would in effect consist of the loyal personal supporters of the caudillo-president.

The caudillo was typical of Venezuela throughout most of the 19th century and considerably beyond it. He was also the dominant type of politician in most of Central America, in Argentina before 1852, in Uruguay until the end of the 19th century, and in the Dominican Republic and Haiti until World War I. The caudillo appeared intermittently in various other Latin American countries.

Since World War II the traditional caudillo has virtually disappeared. Economic changes, the development of middle and urban working classes, and the advent of professionally trained armies have helped to destroy the milieu in which the caudillo prospered. Juan Vicente Gómez, the last Venezuelan caudillo, died in December 1935; Tiburcio Carías Andino, the last caudillo of Honduras, died in his nineties in the late 1960s, after having been out of power since 1948. The last caudillos of Guatemala and El Salvador were overthrown in

1944. Rafael Leónidas Trujillo, who represented perhaps a transition between the old-fashioned caudillo and the modern military dictator, was assassinated in May 1961. Today no Latin American country is governed—nor is any likely to be governed in the future—by a figure in the 19th-century caudillo tradition.

PERSISTENCE OF PERSONALIST POLITICS

However, the passing of the caudillo has not meant the extinction of the kind of personalist politics of which he was a classic example. There persist some political parties that are devoted almost exclusively to furthering the interest of a single political leader, rather than to defending the interests of a class or group or representing a particular ideology.

Various factors have stimulated the development of personalist parties in recent decades. For one thing, dictatorial regimes frequently give rise to personalist parties. Dictators organize them as vehicles for "legitimizing" their elections. Not infrequently, too, dictators who have fallen from power organize personalist parties to sponsor their attempts to return to power.

A second important cause for the rise of personalist parties is the rise of popular figures who are not affiliated with any existing party. Needing an organization through which to campaign for high office, they organize a national political party. Sometimes they attempt to give "ideological" content to such parties; and occasionally, as in the case of the Partido Peronista, they succeed in creating an organization that can persist long after they have passed from the political scene and that becomes transformed into an ideological group.

Finally, some personalist parties are formed by dissidents from existing organizations. Although they may have little or no disagreement with the basic political position of the parties to which they have belonged, they find that their personal ambitions are thwarted and therefore organize a rival group to foster their own careers.

The Partido Dominicano

Probably the outstanding example in recent Latin American history of a personalist party organized by a dictator in power was the Partido Dominicano, established in the Dominican Republic by Rafael Leónidas Trujillo, who ruled that country for 31 years. The first step toward establishing this party was taken in 1930, the year in which Trujillo seized power by a military coup, when an "organizing committee" was established to lay the basis for the formal organization of a political group to support the regime. The Partido Dominicano was formally set up in 1932. It continued to exist until some months after the assassination of Trujillo in May 1961.

During most of this 29-year period, the Partido Dominicano was the only party in the Dominican Republic. All public officials, whether formally "elected" or appointed, belonged to it. An impressive headquarters was built for it in Santo Domingo (which had been named by Christopher Columbus but was rechristened Ciudad Trujillo), and it was made a distributor of much of the patronage at the regime's disposal. Any person holding an important post in Dominican society was forced to belong to the party. A youth group sought unsuccessfully to rally the younger generation behind the dictatorship.

In the late 1940s Trujillo allowed the formation of two "opposition" parties, the Partido Laborista Nacional and the Partido Nacional Democrático. He did so to "prove" that his regime was democratic. The falsity of the maneuver was shown by the fact that their candidates for president were also candidates for lesser offices on the ticket of the Partido Dominicano. By the early 1950s nothing more was heard of either of these groups.

Trujillo made the Partido Dominicano virtually a part of the constitutional system of the country. He had the constitution revised to provide that when any member of a legislative body died, resigned, or otherwise vacated his office, his successor was to be chosen by the body to which he had belonged from a list submitted to it by the president of the party to which he had belonged. During most of his dictatorship Trujillo served as president of the Partido Dominicano, and so it was he who regularly submitted the names from which successors of legislators were to be chosen. It was understood that the first name on the list was always the person to be chosen.

This system was reinforced by another rule, unwritten but strictly followed by Trujillo. He required that all officeholders, whether appointed or "elected" submit to him their undated resignations before taking office. He was then free to submit "resignations" to the appropriate legislative bodies, accompanying them with his suggestions for replacements. The dictator's use of this system was carried almost to the point of the ridiculous, so that in one congressional session there was a more than 200 percent turnover in the membership of Congress.[1]

The Partido Dominicano died with Trujillo. By the end of 1961 it was remembered only as one of the most hated institutions created by a most hated dictatorship. Its headquarters in the capital—renamed Santo Domingo—and in the provinces were converted to better uses, and those who had held high office in the party sought only to forget that fact.

Peruvian Personalist Parties

In recent decades two personalist parties have been of some importance in Peru. Both were organized by men who had once been dictators and were seeking to return to the presidency. A third party was organized as a personalist group and, despite efforts to convert it into an ideological party, has remained personalist.

Ever since 1930 Peruvian politics has been dominated by the Partido Aprista Peruano, the pioneer national revolutionary party. Although in the late 1950s several other ideological parties were established, most of the other political groups that have been organized in this period have been designed to support the ambitions of particular politicans.

The first of these personalist parties is the Movimiento Democrático Pradista (MDP). It was established just before the election of 1956 to foster the efforts of Manuel Prado to return to the presidency. Prado had been president and dictator of Peru between 1939 and 1945; and although during that period he had persecuted the Aprista Party, he turned to these old antagonists for support in the 1956 election, knowing that the MDP would not be sufficiently strong to assure his success. He won this support through a promise to legalize the Aprista Party, govern democratically, and assure it a chance—which seemed virtually a certainty—to win the following election in 1962.

During his second administration Prado relied heavily on the MDP. It was the strongest party in parliament, since the Apristas had not been permitted to have candidates for Congress in the 1956 election. Most government positions were held by members of the party, as were many diplomatic posts.

Prado was overthrown by a military coup d'état in July 1962 and was sent into exile, where he died not long afterward. Attempts by his followers to reorganize the party as the Movimiento Democrático Progresista, and to make it a permanent factor of some importance in Peruvian politics, brought meager results. The MDP, whatever it was called, consisted almost exclusively of the friends of Manuel Prado and opportunists who were attracted by his presence in high office. The friends of Prado were relatively few, and the MDP had no attraction for opportunists once he had fallen from power. It was formally dissolved in 1970.

The second Peruvian personalist party of recent years is the Unión Nacional Odriista (UNO). This party was organized after Manuel Odría left the presidency in 1956. During his dictatorship, in 1948-56, General Odría had gained some popularity, particularly among residents of the shantytowns around Lima, whom he had aided considerably in their efforts to convert their squatter settlements into permanent city suburbs.

PERSONALIST PARTIES

Although Odría went into exile for some years after leaving the presidency, he returned to Peru in time to campaign in the 1962 presidential election. Former officials of his regime had in the meantime organized the UNO. Odría became the party's nominee for the presidency, and his wife assumed a major role in the party organization in Lima.

In the 1962 election Odría came in a close third, with 28 percent of the popular votes. However, the military carried out a coup that resulted in cancellation of the election results. When a new poll was held a year later, Odría's percentage of the vote fell by several points.

During the five years of the administration of Fernando Belaúnde Terry, elected in 1963, Odría's followers in Congress formed an alliance with the Aprista Party; and this coalition controlled the legislature. The Odriista Party acted as the principal spokesman for the more conservative elements in national politics, even though most of the party's popular support came from the humble residents of Lima's marginal wards.

In 1968 the UNO was divided. Half of its members of Congress, led by Julio de la Piedra, former president of the Senate, quarreled with Odría and, as a result of this split, the Piedra faction withdrew from the Unión Nacional Odriista and formed the Partido Social Democrático. With the seizure of power by the military in October 1968, and the subsequent cancellation of the elections scheduled for June 1969, it was impossible to determine how much damage this split had done to the Odriista Party. However, it was clear that the UNO had not developed a program or an appeal beyond the declining popularity of Manuel Odría. He declared the party dissolved early in 1971.

The third personalist party established in Peru in the 1950s was Acción Popular. This party, too, came out of the election of 1956. Manuel Prado's principal opponent in this contest was Fernando Belaúnde Terry, dean of the Faculty of Architecture of the Engineering University and a deputy in 1945-48. He was an independent nominee and received strong and enthusiastic support from young professional and university people. Although the Odría government was openly hostile to Belaúnde's candidacy, he came in a strong second to ex-President Prado; and it was not at all clear in the minds of Belaúnde and his followers that he had not been "counted out."

After the election of 1956 Belaúnde decided to capitalize upon the momentum that had been gained and to found a political party that, he hoped, would be able to organize his followers on a permanent basis and assure his election in 1962. Only a few weeks after the poll the founding convention of Acción Popular met and formally launched the new organization.

Acción Popular was quite openly patterned on the Partido Aprista Peruano. Even its initials were the same (PAP), and the organizational structure was identical. The program of Acción Popular also was very similar to that of the Apristas—Indianism, nationalism, developmentalism, political democracy—although Belaunde tended to put less emphasis on social reform and more on economic development and did not attempt to build a distinctive political philosophy as an underlying basis for Acción Popular's program, as the early leaders of Aprismo had done.

During the following six years Acción Popular took its place alongside the Partido Aprista Peruano as one of the country's major parties. It established local organizations in most parts of the country and was particularly strong in the southern regions of Arequipa, Puno and Cuzco. It attracted many young professional people who in an earlier period would have become Apristas. It won some influence among the Indian peasants, the largest element in the Peruvian body politic but largely unfranchised because of literacy voting requirements.

Belaúnde was the party's best advertisement. During 1956-62 he traveled constantly and very widely throughout Peru. He came to know from personal observation the particular problems of even the remoter parts of the country and established contacts with local leaders throughout the republic.[2]

Belaúnde was Acción Popular's candidate for the presidency in 1962. He came in a very close second behind the Aprista nominee, Víctor Raúl Haya de la Torre. A military coup resulted in the cancellation of these elections, and new ones were held in 1963. This time Fernando Belaúnde Terry was elected president, although his party and its allies did not obtain a majority in either house of Congress.

The Belaúnde administration—August 1963 to October 1968—was marked by extensive reform and economic development. An agrarian reform law was passed; a large community development program was organized, particularly in the Indian communities; large public housing efforts were started; new industries were established; and particular emphasis was put upon expanding the country's road system.

However, all of this activity did not serve to consolidate Acción Popular as a political party. It remained very largely a "Belaúndista" party. Its organizational structure continued to be weak, it encompassed a very wide spectrum of political thought, and it did relatively little to train and indoctrinate the very large group attracted to the party by Belaúnde's campaign efforts.

The upshot was a division in the party, which began shortly before Belaúnde was overthrown by the armed forces early in October 1968. His vice-president, Edgardo Seoane, raised the banner of revolt against Belaúnde's personal leadership of the party, with the result that Belaúnde secured the establishment of a committee to reorganize Acción Popular. Following Belaúnde's overthrow Acción Popular split into two rival groups, one following Seoane and the other continuing to accept the leadership of the exiled president.

The Velasquistas of Ecuador

One of the most remarkable and long-lasting personalist political groups in recent Latin American history has been that composed of the followers of José María Velasco Ibarra, five times president of Ecuador. During his 35 years in politics, Velasco was seldom if ever formally associated with a traditional political party; and on several occasions his personal followers were organized to support his return to the presidency, usually succeeding.

One close observer of Velasco, writing in 1964, has underlined his importance in recent Ecuadorian politics: "For the past twenty years, real issues have played second fiddle to Velasco, and the first question about any individual or group has been how does he or it stand on Velasco rather than on, for example, agrarian reform."[3]

Velasco is a formidable demagogue. He has the ability to adapt what he has to say to the audience to which he is speaking; but, as Ashley Hewitt has said, Velasco "can get through a four or five hour discourse without saying anything of substance." His oratorical appeal is principally to large audiences of his humble fellow citizens, and they have been the backbone of his political support.

Velasco's physical appearance is not what one would expect of a popular demagogue. He has been described as ". . . small in appearance, and moves with the jerkiness of a puppet. His face is gaunt, and his prominent teeth, cheekbones, and balding head give him a curious resemblance to a skull."[4]

Velasco first became president on a provisional basis in 1934 and remained in power for about a year. In 1940 he ran for president for the first time, with the support of the Socialist Party, but was defeated by the Liberal Radical Party's candidate, Carlos Arroyo del Río.[5]

As usual in Ecuador, Arroyo did not complete his term. He was overthrown in 1944 as the result of rising discontent over growing economic dislocations resulting from World War II, and over his having signed the Treaty of Rio de Janeiro, which ended the short-lived war of 1942, in which Peru had seized over 300,000 square miles of land claimed by Ecuador.

The leader of the movement that overthrew the president was José María Velasco Ibarra, this time backed by the Conservative,

Liberal Radical, Socialist, and Communist parties. He was chosen constitutional president by the Constitutional Assembly that was elected soon after the coup.

Before this coup Velasco had been candidate for president in elections scheduled for a few days after the date on which Arroyo was overthrown. The ouster of the president was in part brought about by fear that these elections would be rigged.[6]

Although as candidate Velasco had had the backing of the Liberal, Socialist, and Communist parties, united in the Democratic Alliance, apparently he did not entirely trust this heterogeneous group of supporters. Soon after his election by the Constitutional Assembly, Velasco sought for the first time to organize his personal followers into a new political party. This was the Partido Demócrata Nacional, which announced its statement of principles on September 18, 1944, a statement that began with a proclamation of personal loyalty to Velasco.[7]

However, this effort to organize his own followers into a coherent political group was not successful. During most of the rest of his second administration, Velasco depended mainly upon the Conservative Party for his congressional and general support. All of the other parties united against him, and he was overthrown in 1947.

Although Velasco went into exile in Argentina after his second ouster from the presidency, he did not by any means lose all of his popular support. A network of "Velasquista committees" was organized throughout the country. It was these that supported their leader in yet another bid for the presidency, at the end of Galo Plaza Lasso's term of office in 1952.

Lillo Linke has described what happened during Velasco's third bid for the presidency:

> At the beginning of the campaign Dr. Velasco Ibarra's candidacy was not taken seriously. His two previous failures, plus a total of fourteen years in exile, had caused his figure to fade into the background. Or so it seemed. Because no sooner did he set foot again in Ecuador than the old magic began to work. The passionate resistance he stirred up, especially in the capital, among university students, civil servants, and much of the middle class in general, was only proof that he was not really a forgotten man. . . . The results of the June election of 1952 were: 150,000 votes for Dr. Velasco, to 116,000 for the Conservative candidate, and 84,000 for the Liberal candidates together. The total of 351,000 votes was the highest ever registered in the country, and in an honest election.[8]

During this third administration Velasco kept his Velasquista committees in existence. Lillo Linke notes that "these have no programs except that of supporting Velasco Ibarra." The members of these committees included, according to Miss Linke, "lawyers, artisans, small shopkeepers, and humbler people" as well as "some businessmen or bankers who believe in the creative modernizing activities of Dr. Velasco Ibarra."[9]

This time Velasco stayed in office for the four-year term. He turned over the office in 1956 to a former supporter turned bitter enemy, Camilo Ponce Henríquez, candidate of the Partido Social Cristiano, elected with support of the Conservative Party. However, Velasco aspired to return to the presidency.

In 1960 Velasco again ran for the presidency, this time again as an independent candidate against the nominees of the traditional Conservative, Liberal Radical, and Socialist parties. Once again he was victorious; and once again he was overthrown, this time about two years after his election. His successor, Vice-President Carlos Arosemena, was ousted by the military in 1963, at least in part for fear that Velasco might return to office.

Velasco's third ouster, and fourth retirement from the presidency, did not end his popularity. His supporters this time organized a new national party, the Frente Popular Velasquista. Soon after the overthrow of the military junta (which had seized power on the fall of President Arosemena) early in 1966, Velasco returned to Ecuador from Argentina once again and announced his candidacy for a fifth term. When elections were finally held in June 1968, Velasco was elected once more, as candidate of his own party, receiving 280,316 votes. His nearest rival, Andrés Cordova, backed by the Liberal Radical and Socialist parties, received 264,266 votes; Camilo Ponce Henríquez, backed by the Partido Social Cristiano and the Conservative Party, received 259,256 votes; the extreme rightist Agrupación Revolucionaria Nacionalista Ecuatoriana candidate, Jorge Crespo Toral, got 31,983 votes; and Elias Gallego Anda, nominee of the Communist-backed Unión Democrática Popular, polled 16,987 votes.[10]

The nature of the supporters of Velasquismo during the last 35 years is described by Ashley Hewitt, Jr.:

> <u>Velasquismo</u> is a sort of political spectrum by itself, embracing or having embraced from time to time such contrasting figures as Camilo Ponce and Manuel Araujo Hidalgo, the pint-sized extreme leftist who was Velasco's Minister of Government in the last Velasco administration and is now a free-wheeling Jacobin revolutionary. Motives of individuals for supporting Velasco have varied considerably. Some, and especially the <u>chusma</u>, believed

in him without reserve. Some others thought (wrongly) his unusual talents could be turned to a good purpose. It has even been asserted that the extreme left gave him clandestine support with confidence that chaos would follow in his train. The most pervasive motive for joining the Velasco camp, however, has been opportunism. Businessmen, politicians, and military officers on the make flocked to his banner with the conviction that at least they could not lose even if they did not find El Dorado. Velasco proved some of them wrong, but was quite prepared to promise anyone anything that seemed to appeal to them; as with individuals, so with groups....[11]

The Partido Panameñista and Arnulfo Arias

A personalist party not unlike that of Jose María Velasco Ibarra in Ecuador is the Partido Panameñista of Arnulfo Arias. Arias has been president of Panama three times and has been overthrown each time. His unfortunate experience in the presidency has not seemed to dampen the enthusiasm of his followers to return him to this position.

Arnulfo Arias, brother of a former president, was elected chief executive of his country for the first time in 1940 as candidate of the Partido Panameñista. During that first term he carried out a nationalistic program that resulted in the removal of most of the Oriental businessmen and the restriction of the rights of English-speaking Negroes of West Indian descent. This program and the oratorical powers of Arias won him lasting support, although he was removed from office only about a year after becoming president.

In 1948 Arias was once again a candidate for president on the Partido Panameñista ticket. Although he was declared to have lost the election, in 1949 the chief of the national guard, José Remón, overthrew the "victorious" candidate and declared that Arias had been elected after all.

During his two years in office for the second time, Arias was high-handed. Six former presidents were jailed, at least one newspaper was closed, and Congress was dissolved by the president. Although these dictatorial actions did not lessen the enthusiasm of Arias' followers for their hero, they did finally arouse the opposition of the man who had placed Arias in power, José Remón. In 1951 he overthrew Arias once again. Two weeks later Arias was deprived of his civil rights, including the right to be elected president, by the National Assembly that he had previously dissolved.

Despite this political misfortune Arias continued to have widespread support, particularly among the humbler people of Panama City. However, his fellow politicians appeared not to take his possibilities very seriously, and his civil rights were restored. As a result Arias ran once again for the presidency in 1964 but was declared to have lost to the government's nominee, Marcos Robles, although Arias and his supporters believed that he had won.

In 1968 Arias once again ran for the presidency. This time the nominee of the Partido Panameñista was victorious. His margin of victory was sufficient for it to be impossible to deny that he had won. As a result he took office on October 1. However, certain actions of the new president once again made certain civilian elements fear that he was intending to be a dictator and made the leaders of the national guard (the country's combined police force and army) fear that he was going to deprive them of their jobs. As a result, on October 11, 1968, the military once again overthrew Arias, this time only 10 days after he had assumed office. The move had the support of important business elements in Panama City and the interior.

Even those who overthrew Arias admitted that he had the support of the majority of the population of Panama. His hold on the imagination and the loyalty of the people had little to do with positive achievement or a well-defined ideology or program. Arias, like Velasco Ibarra in Ecuador, was popular because he was able in some way to associate himself with the aspirations and the animosities of the common people. There is little doubt that he remained the most popular political figure of Panama, despite his misfortunes the three times he served as president.

Personalist Factions of Other Parties

There have been various examples in recent Latin American history of personalist parties that have been organized by dissident leaders of other parties. Two such instances are particularly worthy of note.

The first example is the various splinter parties that broke away from the Partido Trabalhista Brasileiro (PTB). The PTB was originally organized at the end of President Getúlio Vargas' first period in power, in 1945, as a vehicle for mobilizing his supporters. Subsequently the PTB was converted into the principal party representing the urban working class.

When it was established, the PTB attracted not only people loyal to Vargas but also a considerable range of opportunists, who thought that support of the Partido Trabalhista was the surest way to achieve high office. One of these, Hugo Borghi, an industrialist who had acquired a fortune during Vargas' Estado Novo dictatorship (1937-45) and had held various public posts during that period, became the leader of the PTB in the state of São Paulo and its candidate for governor of that state in the elections of January 1947. However, when he was defeated and concluded that the PTB could no longer serve his purposes, he organized a dissident group, the Partido Trabalhista Nacional. This party continued to exist until the suppression of all political parties in October 1965, but it never became a major factor in national politics.

At least two other parties were established by scissions in the PTB: the Partido Social Trabalhista and the Partido Republicano Trabalhista. The latter gained importance principally as the vehicle through which during the 1950s the Brazilian Communists were able to get their members elected to the national Congress and state legislatures, at a time when the Communist Party itself was officially illegal. The Partido Social Trabalhista was of little significance in the general political picture.

Other examples of personalist parties emerging out of well-established political groups are several of the factions into which the Partido Colorado of Uruguay came to be divided. The energetic reform program of President José Batlle between 1911 and 1915 provoked much dissension within his Partido Colorado. Several leaders who were opposed to the Batlle program broke away to form rival groups. The majority of the party who supported Batlle came to constitute the Partido Colorado Batllista, which remained the country's largest party for more than a generation and was an ideological rather than a personalist party. It continued to exist and be the main vehicle of democratic reform long after its founder had died.

However, the rivals of the Batllistas within the Partido Colorado ranks became purely personalist groups. Thus there persisted for more than 30 years the Partido Colorado Riverista and the Partido Colorado Blancoacevedista, named after two of Batlle's principal rivals. In the early 1940s a group broke away from the Partido Colorado Batllista to form the Partido Colorado Baldomirista, consisting of the followers of ex-President Alfredo Baldomir.

By the 1950s the Partido Colorado Batllista itself had split. The principal division was between the group following José Batlle's son, Cesar Batlle Pacheco, which under the peculiar electoral system of Uruguay came to be known as the Lista 14, and that backing his nephew, Luis Batlle Berres, which bore the name Lista 15. In the 1960s even further splits occurred in both Lista 14 and Lista 15, with each dissident faction supporting a particular political leader.*

---

*Uruguay has a peculiar electoral system under which the two major political parties, the Colorados and the Blancos, can name as

Other Personalist Parties

Several other personalist parties that have appeared in recent years in Latin America are worthy of mention. One of these is the Partido Cruzada Nacional, organized by the supporters of Venezuelan ex-dictator Marcos Pérez Jiménez. He had ruled the country between 1948 and 1958 and had been overthrown as the result of a popular uprising supported by the armed forces.

In 1963 Pérez Jiménez, who had taken refuge in the United States, was extradited to Venezuela, where he was put on trial for stealing some $13 million during his presidential term. The preliminaries and trial took five years; and when the verdict was finally announced, the ex-dictator was sentenced to five years in prison. Since he had spent this time in jail before his conviction, he was released and went into exile in Spain. From there he ran for the Senate in December 1968. His Cruzada Nacional, organized to support him and his friends, succeeded in electing 15 members to the Chamber of Deputies as well as several senators, including Pérez Jiménez himself.

Of some significance, too, was the Partido Social Progresista, which existed in Brazil between 1945 and 1965. It was organized by Adhemar de Barros, who during the Vargas Estado Novo dictatorship (1937-45) had been interventor (appointed governor) of São Paulo for several years and had acquired considerable popular support because of his oratorical ability and his widely scattered public works programs. In 1946 he merged his largely São Paulo party with another party that had been established in the Northeast; and from then on the Partido Social Progresista became his personal vehicle. In 1957 he was elected governor of São Paulo on its ticket, and in 1955 and 1960 he ran for president of Brazil as its candidate. In 1962 he was once again elected governor of São Paulo, in which capacity he was one of the principal civilian architects of the 1964 "revolution" that overthrew President João Goulart. However, in June 1966 he was removed as governor of São Paulo and banned from further political activity for 10 years. Since he was approaching 70, this ended his political career. In any case, his party had been outlawed by President

---

many candidates for president or other posts as there are factions in their midst. Who wins the presidency is then decided by the total vote cast by the various factions of the two parties; the ultimate winner is the candidate within the majority party who has gotten most votes. The rival factions of the various parties, as well as those of minority parties, are allotted numbers. The Batlle Pacheco group was assigned the number 14, while the Batlle Berres group was given the number 15.

Humberto Castelo Branco's decree of October 1965, which abolished all existing political parties.

Another personalist party of considerable importance in the 1950s and 1960s has been the Unión del Pueblo Argentino (UDELPA), which was formed, after his exit from the presidency, to foster the ambitions of Pedro E. Aramburu. He was the second provisional president to rule Argentina after the overthrow of Juan Domingo Perón.

During his period in office, Aramburu developed a reputation as a soldier who felt that the armed forces as an institution should retire from active participation in politics and intervene only when the country's basic institutions were in peril. On the basis of his reputation Aramburu was able to rally considerable support among the civilian population, as well as having considerable influence in the military.

The influence of Aramburu was indicated in the election of 1963. He himself was a candidate for the presidency in that contest, and he came in third—after the Unión Cívica Radical del Pueblo's Arturo Illia and the blank votes cast by Peronistas and other opponents of the status quo. His party elected several members of the Chamber of Deputies.

Aramburu apparently had little to do with the military coup d'état that overthrew Illia in June 1966. He and his party—which was outlawed along with all of the others by the new army dictatorship of Juan Carlos Ongania—were part of the opposition after 1966. Aramburu was kidnapped and assassinated on May 29, 1970.

Purely personalist parties have certainly played a role in Latin American politics in recent decades. They have generally been devoid of any very definable ideology or political program except to advance the aspirations of their founders. They have not infrequently been vehicles of dictators or ex-dictators aspiring to return to power. However, their importance should not be exaggerated, and they have represented only a small fraction of the important political parties of Latin America.

CHAPTER

2

THE LIBERALS

The 19th-century Latin American Liberals borrowed their philosophy and ideas largely from Europe and the United States. Ideologically they were heirs of the American and French revolutions and of the school of Adam Smith.

Three particular issues were of special importance to the Latin American Liberals during the first century of independence. First of all, they were anticlerical, that is, they were strongly opposed to the temporal influence of the Roman Catholic Church. During the colonial period the Church had been virtually a branch of the Spanish and Portuguese administrations. It had been the only recognized religious group, had had the right to levy taxes for its own support, and through the Inquisition had controlled the printed matter that circulated in the colonies. The Church had also owned vast areas of land and had controlled most of the educational institutions, as well as most of the hospitals, orphanages, and other charitable institutions. It also had exclusive control over registration of births and deaths and control of all cemeteries.

Throughout most of the 19th century the Liberals of the various Latin American nations fought to restrict the privileges with which the Church emerged from the colonial period. Although they were not necessarily opposed to the Catholic religion, they sought to strip the Church of its temporal privileges and to limit it strictly to the spiritual realm.

Generally, also, the Latin American Liberals of the 19th century were federalists. They advocated the limitation of the powers of the national governments and the strengthening of the rights of the provinces.

Finally, the 19th-century Liberals were generally Manchesterians. They favored free trade, opposed attempts to establish tariffs and other protective devices for the infant manufacturing industries of Latin America, and generally were opposed to government intervention in the economy.

LIBERALISM IN THE 19th CENTURY

Probably the most famous 19th-century Latin American Liberal Party was that of Mexico. Led by Benito Juárez, it came to power in the wake of Mexico's defeat in what is known in the United States as the Mexican War. During the next two decades it put on the statute books the principal elements of the its program.

The constitution of 1857 contained the principal elements of the Liberal program. In the first place, it was thoroughly anticlerical. It separated Church and state, forbade the existence of religious orders in the republic, deprived the Church of the right to own land or to maintain schools, and even forbade priests to wear their clerical garb in public or to conduct religious services anywhere except in church buildings.

The 1857 constitution established a federal form of government. It gave the states the right to elect their own chief executives and legislatures and granted them extensive autonomy to run their own affairs.

The 1857 constitution was Manchesterian in a thorough-going fashion. It not only forbade the Church to own land but also extended this prohibition to any "corporation," thus outlawing the Indian communities that still owned a sizable part of the arable area of the republic. Ironically this provision, advocated and supported by the Indian leader Benito Juárez, who is one of the "patron saints" of the Mexican Revolution, probably was responsible for more damage to the Indian peasantry than any other single piece of legislation in the country's history.

Juárez died in 1872. After an interim one of the chieftans of his army, General Porfirio Díaz, seized power. During his 35-year regime (1876-1911) much of the constitution of 1857 was converted into a dead letter. Federalism became a myth, and the Church regained much of the power of which it had been deprived by Juárez. However, the "free enterprise" elements of the constitution of 1857 were fully enforced, so that not only the Indian communities but virtually all peasant landowners were deprived of their land. The "Liberal" regime of Díaz came to an end with the Mexican Revolution of 1910.

The victory of the Liberals in Guatemala occurred in 1871, when the caudillo General Justo Rufino Barrios seized power. His regime followed the lead of that in Mexico, separating Church and state, dissolving all religious orders, and forbidding the Church to own

THE LIBERALS

anything except its houses of worship. The Barrios regime also was loyal to the principles of "free enterprise" and sought to induce foreign enterprises to enter the country to begin a rational exploitation of its natural resources. During subsequent Liberal regimes German and Swiss settlers established the coffee industry and the United Fruit Company opened up large banana plantations.

However, neither Barrios nor those who succeeded him and ruled in the name of the Liberal Party until 1944 believed in or practiced political liberalism. Ronald Schneider comments: "In his conduct of internal affairs Barrios resembled his contemporary Porfirio Diaz of Mexico."[1] Much the same could be said about Manuel Estrada Cabrera, who ruled from 1898 to 1920, and Jorge Ubico, who was president from 1931 to 1944 and whose overthrow marked the end of the Liberal era in Guatemala.

In Colombia the division of political forces into the Conservative and Liberal parties had become clear by 1840. Nine years later the first Liberal Party government came to power under José Hilario López. Hubert Herring has described the policies of this first Liberal administration:

> . . . Intensely anticlerical, López evicted the Jesuits, proclaimed full religious liberty, assigned the appointment of parish priests to municipal authorities, transferred state support for the Church from the central government to the provincial authorities, disbanded ecclesiastical courts, outlawed tithes, and legalized divorce. When Bogotá's Archbishop Mosquera and two bishops protested, they were summarily exiled. Slavery, persisting in spite of Bolívar's edicts against it, was finally ended. Trial by jury was provided in criminal cases, freedom of the press was guaranteed, and the death penalty was abolished. Suffrage was extended to all males; and governors and judges were chosen by popular election. All these provisions were incorporated into a new constitution in 1853, which returned to the divisive principles of federalism.[2]

Although the Liberals were ousted from control in 1857, partly because of a split in the party over the issue of free trade, they were able to recapture power in 1861 and continued to rule until 1880. During this period federalism continued, and Manchesterian ideas were reflected in the prohibition of ownership of property by any "corporation." With the exception of 1865-67, when Tomás Cipriano de Mosquera (a one-time Conservative turned Liberal) imposed a dictatorship, the Liberal period was marked by a wide degree of civil liberties and more or less respect for the rules of political democracy.

In 1879 the moderate faction of the Liberal Party supported the election of Rafael Núñez as president. In spite of having been the Liberal candidate, however, Núñez turned quickly toward the Conservatives; and his inauguration marked the beginning of a long era of Conservative rule. The Liberals did not regain control of the government of Colombia until 1930.[3]

In Venezuela the period of so-called Liberal rule was more reminiscent of similar periods in Mexico and Guatemala than of that of Colombia. Liberal forces first appeared on the scene in the period between 1863 and 1870, which Hubert Herring describes as "a chaotic interlude between dictatorships."[4] It was in fact the period of the so-called Federal War, which took on all of the aspects of a social conflict and resulted in the near-extinction of the old aristocratic landed group that had been economically and socially dominant during the colonial period and had maintained considerable power during the first decades of the republic. Herring says of the Liberal leaders during this period: "The Liberal spokesmen were uninformed and unconvincing. Several men of reasonably good intentions held power briefly, but proved incapable of restoring order."[5]

Order was restored by Antonio Guzman Blanco, who seized power, still in the name of the Liberals, in 1870 and exercised a very personal dictatorship until 1888, when he was overthrown during an ill-advised visit to Paris. The Liberals ostensibly remained in power; and Cipriano Castro, the dictator who seized power in 1899, proclaimed his regime the Liberal Revolutionary Restoration. However, Herring comments: "Castro's rule was more corrupt and dissolute than any the country had known."[6] Under the rule of Castro's successor, Juan Vicente Gómez, who seized control in 1908, when Castro made the mistake of going abroad, there was little pretense that the regime was anything more than the personal rule of the "Tyrant of the Andes."

The antecedents of the Liberal Party of Ecuador are to be found in the early years of the republic in those politicians who grouped themselves around Vicente Rocafuerte, whom Hubert Herring describes as "ablest of the agitators, . . . a wealthy young aristocrat who had lived in the United States, England, Mexico and France. . . ."[7] For some years Rocafuerte alternated in the presidency with the founder of the republic, Juan José Flores, who had been one of Bolívar's generals. In 1845 Flores was overthrown by the Liberals and was deported to France, joining Rocafuerte, who had been exiled there by Flores some years before. Of the period following 1845 Herring comments: "Thus rid of the two rivals, Ecuador had fifteen years of anarchy (1845-60): eleven presidents or juntas ruled fitfully, usually under the banner of Liberalism; three new constitutions were adopted; civil wars were frequent, and border wars with Colombia and Peru continued; and the conflict between the clergy and their opponents

THE LIBERALS

became more savage. The one bright spot was the final ending of Negro slavery."[8]

In 1860 the famous Conservative leader Gabriel García Moreno came to power, and for 35 years thereafter the Liberals were in opposition. In 1878 the various elements that had rallied under the Liberal banner formally established the Partido Liberal.[9]

In 1895 a revolution of the Liberals, who were now known as the Partido Liberal Radical, put in the presidency Eloy Alfaro, who dominated the country until his murder in 1912. The Liberals remained in power, with a few interruptions, until the mid-1940s. Of this long period Herring comments: "Under twenty-eight presidents, three new constitutions were drafted, religious orders were banished, and the privileges of the Church were curtailed. However, the Liberals' promises of free elections and honest government proved empty."[10]

Except for their anticlerical measures, the Liberals during their long period of domination did relatively little to put their supposed program into practical effect. They did give certain encouragement to the establishment of the first organizations of workers (mainly artisans' mutual benefit societies) in Quito, Guayaquil, and a few other cities; and they did encourage the entrance of foreign capital to build railroads and to help begin the modern exploitation of the country's agricultural resources along the coast. But there was no move toward federalism, and no effort was made to destroy the semifeudal regime under which the Indians of the highlands lived.

It is difficult to speak of political parties having played any major role in the national politics of Bolivia during the 19th century, in which the country was ruled by succession of caudillo-like military dictators. One of the worst of these, Mariano Melgarejo, who was president between 1864 and 1871, carried out the measure that at about the same time was being put into execution by the Liberal regime in Mexico: he issued a decree in 1866 that declared the Indian communities to be the private property of those living on them, thus facilitating the despoiling of the Indians of their lands by mestizos and whites from the cities.

The Liberal Party of Bolivia emerged in the aftermath of Bolivia's defeat by Chile in the War of the Pacific (1879-81). Alipio Valencia Vega has noted that it had its origins in the "War Party," which urged a continuation of the conflict with Chile after decisive Bolivian defeats in 1880. He adds: "Liberalism in Bolivia arose as a political party when the current of scientific positivism also entered the country. Scientific positivism, based on <u>observation</u> and <u>experimentation</u> at a special moment when the hard reality of the defeat and national mutilation beat strongly against all the negligent <u>idealism</u> hitherto dominant in republican Bolivia."[11]

Valencia has noted that in these formative years, Liberalism "advocated the definitive subordination of Theology to Political

Science, effective individual liberties and particularly freedom of thought, of religion, freedom of teaching, secular education, separation of Church and State, civil marriage, civil registration of births and deaths, secularization of cemeteries, suppression or reduction of convents and monasteries, etc."[12] The Liberals also advocated "full freedom of commerce and industry;" but, as Valencia noted, they never "suggested anything new with regard to the transformation of the feudal economy into a capitalist economy, which is what corresponds to the Liberal period." He concludes that the Liberals "concentrated the aspirations of the middle classes to come to power."[13] The first clearly Liberal government was that of José Manuel Pando, which came to power as the result of a coup d'état in 1899. From then until 1920 the Liberals were in virtually undisputed control of the country. In this period anticlerical laws were passed, as indicated by Hubert Herring: "In 1905, for the first time, toleration was decreed for religious worship other than Catholicism; in 1908 the control of cemeteries passed from the clergy to the municipalities; and in 1911 civil marriage was made obligatory."[14]

The Liberal governments also followed policies consistent with their free enterprise beliefs. As early as 1885 the national leader of the party had said that it would "develop agriculture, mining, commerce, manufacturing, etc., through foreign capital and industries which we shall try to attract...."[15] Once in power they encouraged foreign investment in railroads and in mining, which brought the country an unparalleled period of prosperity, principally as a result of the growth of tin exploitation. In 1920 the Liberals were ousted by the Republican Party in a coup d'état.

The Chilean Liberals emerged during the first confusing years after independence. They grew out of the group that supported the regimes of Ramón Freire and Francisco Pinto between 1823 and 1829. It was during this period that the country had its only experiment with federalism, in accordance with the constitution of 1826, which lasted only two years.

Hubert Herring describes the Liberals of this early period as being "vaguely imbued with French liberalism and British parliamentary ideals, sought government by constitution, talked of reform rather than authority, favored limitations upon the Church (while remaining good Catholics), and argued hazily for land reform."[16]

The first Liberal period came to an end in 1830, when the Conservatives seized power. They held control of the government from 1830 to 1861. For three decades thereafter the two major parties tended to split into various factions, with neither the government nor the opposition being composed exclusively of Liberal or of Conservative elements. However, the influence of the Liberals tended to increase during this period, as was reflected in a substantial body of anticlerical legislation passed during the last decades of the 19th century.

THE LIBERALS

This period was closed with the overthrow of Liberal President José Manuel Balmaceda in a short civil war in 1891. Balmaceda was a new and different kind of Liberal, "not content with baiting the Church and working for popular and representative government." As Hubert Herring notes, his "liberalism took account of the misery of the Chilean masses, the poverty which made the common man the victim of selfish landowners." At the same time his advanced social ideas were combined "with a stern sense of the responsibility of a president to lead the nation. . . ."[17]

Both Balmaceda's social program and his somewhat imperious attitude toward his opponents sparked a revolt in Congress, which completely blocked his legislation, including even the annual budget. The resulting deadlock was finally resolved when the supporters of Congress arose in armed revolt, with the backing of the navy. Although the army remained loyal to Balmaceda, his forces were finally defeated when navy elements seized Valparaíso and Santiago, after 10 months of fighting.[18]

The overthrow of Balmaceda led to the establishment of a congressional regime. Although no constitutional change was made, after 1891 cabinets depended upon the support of Congress, resigning when it voted no confidence. During this period, which lasted from 1891 until 1924, the Chilean regime bore many similarities to that of the Third and Fourth republics of France.

During the era of congressional government, the Liberals were divided into numerous quarreling factions. It was not until the end of World War I that a clear alignment developed in the presidential campaign of 1920, in which the great majority of the Liberal factions supported the candidacy of Arturo Alessandri; the Conservatives constituted the bulk of the support for his rival, Luis Barros Borgoño.

The two traditional parties of Uruguay emerged in the 1830s, around two of the leaders of the independence movement. The Colorado (Red) Party, the nation's member of the Liberal camp, was organized around Fructuoso Rivera, while its opponent, the Blanco (White) Party, supported Manuel Oribe. But in this period Uruguayan politics was not a purely national affair; and for the next three decades the Colorados were generally to be aligned with the Argentine "Unitarios" and with the Brazilians, while the Blancos were to be supported by the Argentine "Federales" and for some time by the Paraguayan dictator Francisco Solano López.

In time the Colorados came to represent particularly the interests of Montevideo. In 1870 the party came to power, and it was to be almost 90 years before it lost control of the national government. However, during the last decades of the 19th century "there were repeated clashes between Blancos and Colorados and between rival factions of the Colorados themselves. Three Colorado despots ruled dictatorially for sixteen years (1875-1890). In the 1890s, making a fine show of constitutionality, two Colorado presidents governed with disregard of democratic niceties and wanton looting of the public treasury."[19]

During this period the thesis that Professor James Payne has applied to Colombia certainly was applicable to Uruguay. Political differences centered largely on the desire to hold office and control patronage, rather than on ideological or programmatic issues. It was not until the inauguration of José Batlle y Ordoñez in 1903 that the philosophical differences between the two parties became sharply defined.

Paraguay was controlled tyrannically during its first 60 years by three dictators: José Gaspar Rodríguez de Francia, Carlos Antonio López, and his son Francisco Solano López. As a result clearly differentiated political parties did not emerge until after the disastrous War of the Triple Alliance (1865-70), which cost the country a large proportion of its adult male population.

In the aftermath of this struggle there emerged the Liberal and Colorado parties. The Liberal Party was established in 1887, under the leadership of Cecilio Báez, a young lawyer and historian. George Pendle has noted of Báez that "he never ceased to demand more and better education; he advocated religious toleration (this policy made it necessary for him to attack the Catholic Church); and he recommended administrative decentralization."[20] The Liberals were finally able to seize power by revolution in 1904, and they continued to control the government until the end of the Chaco War with Bolivia in 1936.

During the latter decades of the Brazilian monarchy, which lasted from 1822 to 1889, Emperor Pedro II ruled through alternating governments of the Liberal and Conservative parties, modeled to a large degree after the two British parties dominant during the same period. Anyda Marchant has described the role of these two organizations:

> ... Two parties—the conservative and the liberal—had crystallized out of the welter of opposing forces that had created such turbulence early in his reign. Theoretically speaking, the conservatives favored a strong central government, a powerful emperor, and no change in the social and economic conditions, of the country, whereas the liberals preferred a stronger legislature, more autonomy for the provincial governments, and the adoption of modern ideas in social and economic matters. But these two parties had no real division of interest on vital issues. Conservatives and liberals alike were landowners or the sons of landowners, with the habits and the point of view of slaveholders and planters, although individuals among them might have ideas in opposition to those of the majority. ....[21]

With the overthrow of the monarchy in 1889 both the Conservative and Liberal parties disappeared. Between 1889 and 1945 there were no nationally organized political parties, with the exception (after 1930) of the Communist and Integralista parties. Until 1930 politics was dominated by so-called "Republican" parties organized on a statewide basis, and after the 1930 revolution other statewide parties were organized around particular political leaders. None of these was in any real sense a Liberal party.

THE LIBERAL PARTIES SINCE WORLD WAR I

Economic and social changes since World War I have seriously undermined the traditional Liberal parties of Latin America. The development of major export products, which had occurred in the generation before the war, was followed by the spread of industrialization. These processes brought into existence powerful middle and working classes. Labor movements appeared, and industrialists and mercantile groups established organizations to defend their interests. More recently even the peasantry, which for centuries has been the most oppressed element in the Latin American population, has begun to organize.

The rise of these new socioeconomic groupings has destroyed the traditional basis of Latin American politics. During the first century of independence, political activity was limited largely to a small group—the landowners, well-to-do merchants of the cities, professional men, the military chiefs, and, to a much smaller degree, artisans and lower middle-class elements.

The new middle-class, worker, and peasant organizations challenged this dominant role of the old aristocracy in Latin American politics. This challenge brought forth new political parties—national revolutionary, Socialist, Communist, and Christian Democratic groups.

The Liberals were more seriously challenged by the rise of the new parties than were the Conservatives. This was because the Liberals were the traditional parties of the Left, and so the new political groups were in direct competition with them.

Many of the Liberal parties disappeared. The traditional Liberal Party of Mexico did not survive the fall of Porfirio Díaz; the Liberal Party of Guatemala has had no place since the overthrow of dictator Jorge Ubico in 1944, an event that ushered in the broader participation of the masses in that country's political life; the Bolivian Liberal Party has played no part since the national revolution begun by the Movimiento Nacionalista Revolucionario in 1952; there has been no Liberal Party of any consequence in Venezuela since the development of mass political parties following the death of dictator Juan Vincente

Gómez in 1935; the Liberal Party of Cuba played no significant role after the overthrow of ostensibly Liberal dictator Gerardo Machado in 1933, and it has disappeared completely since the advent of the Castro regime in 1959. We have already noted the demise of Brazilian Liberalism with the end of the monarchy in 1889.

Those Liberal parties that have survived have done so for one of three reasons. First, they may have been able to persist because of the very strong hold of the two-party system in the country—as in Colombia and Paraguay. Second, they may have survived because they have been able to adapt to the social and economic changes of their nations and to absorb the new middle- and working-class groups, becoming their spokesmen, as in Uruguay and Honduras. Third, they may have persisted because they have been able to become important defenders of the status quo—as the Liberal Party of Bolivia did until 1952 and that of Chile until 1965.

Honduras

Between 1933 and 1949 Honduras was governed by a caudillo dictator of the old school, General Tiburcio Carías Andino, who ostensibly governed in the name of the country' Conservative Party, locally known as the Partido Nacional. However, in 1949 Carías chose a civilian successor, Juan Manuel Gálvez.

During the Gálvez administration the virtual asphyxia of political activity that had characterized the Carías period ended. The Gálvez government permitted the development once again of the opposition Liberal Party.

The Liberals were revived under new leadership and under very different circumstances from those that had characterized Honduran politics before the Carías interlude. A group of young professional people, led by a medical doctor, Ramón Villeda Morales, took the lead in building a party that would appeal to the workers and the middle-class elements of the population. They undertook to advise and to support the new banana workers' unions that suddenly appeared as the result of a strike in the banana regions in May 1954. Subsequently Liberals also helped to stimulate the spread of the organized labor movement into the small industrial center of San Pedro Sula and among the white-collar workers and artisans of the capital, Tegucigalpa.

In the presidential election held at the end of 1954 the Liberals clearly won. However, their Nacional and Reformista (a split-away party from the Nacionales) opponents refused in Congress to recognize their victory, and a constitutional crisis was precipitated. President Gálvez became ill and left the country in the hands of Vice-President Julio Lozano, who dissolved Congress and ruled as a dictator from November 1954 until August 1957.

A military coup by a group of democratically inclined young officers overthrew Lozano. In September 1957 elections for a Constitutional Assembly were held, and the Liberals won a strong victory. The new assembly chose Ramón Villeda Morales, who had been the party nominee in 1954, as president; he took office on January 1, 1958.[22]

During the nearly five years in which the Liberal government remained in power in Honduras, it sought to carry out basic reforms and to stimulate economic development. It enacted a labor code, on the basis of recommendations of a mission of the International Labor Organization, which for the first time provided for general legal recognition of unions and included many specific measures for the protection of workers. The labor movement, which was generally under Liberal leadership, received strong encouragement from the Villeda Morales government. The regime also enacted an agrarian reform law, one of the principal purposes of which was to clarify land titles of many peasants who had been squatters on government-owned land and large private landholdings. A five-year development plan was elaborated, in conformity with the provisions of the Alliance for Progress Treaty of Punta del Este. Finally, civil liberties were firmly protected during this period.

Elections were scheduled for October 13, 1963. There was little doubt that they would be won by the Liberal Party candidate, Modesto Rodas Alvarado. However, on October 3 an army coup, led by Colonel Osvaldo López and supported by the Nacionalista Party, overthrew the government of Villeda Morales and canceled the scheduled election.

In conformity with the tradition of Latin American military coups, Colonel López was subsequently elected "constitutional" president by still another Constitutional Assembly. Although the Liberals had participated in the election of this assembly, they refused to participate in its deliberations, on the grounds that the 35-29 majority of the Nacionalistas over the Liberals had been decided upon by the government before the election was held and did not represent the real decision of the voters.[23]

The Liberals continued to function as the opposition throughout the López administration. Although from time to time leaders of the party were persecuted by the government, the Liberals were generally able to function normally. Their ability to return to power continued to depend more upon the willingness of the army to permit this than upon the support of the voters, which was virtually assured.

The Honduran Liberal Party of the 1950s and 1960s felt a close kinship with the national revolutionary parties of other Latin American countries. Its representatives participated in meetings of the national revolutionary parties on various occasions; and the party helped finance, and sent students to, the political training school that these parties maintained in Costa Rica.

The Liberals reached an agreement with their opponents in the 1971 election. Both parties supported Ramón Cruz for president, and his administration began with a coalition cabinet composed of both Liberals and Nacionales.

Nicaragua

The Liberal Party of Nicaragua was of an entirely different type from that of Honduras. In both countries the Liberals were one of the two traditional parties; but from the mid-1930s on, the Nicaraguan Liberal Party became a major tool of the dynastic dictatorship of the Somoza family.

During the 19th century quarrels between the Liberals and Conservatives in Nicaragua had frequently led to armed clashes. This situation continued during the early decades of the 20th century and was the excuse for two armed interventions by U.S. Marines, during World War I and the 1920s.

The arrangement that ended the second U.S. intervention in 1932 left Juan B. Sacasa, a Liberal, in the presidency and General Anastasio Somoza in the command of the national guard, the armed force that had been organized by the U.S. Marines in the 1920s. Somoza was a man of ebullient personality and soaring ambition. He spoke English quite well, having spent several years in the United States, where he is said to have worked as a car salesman. Undoubtedly his knowledge of English had been of importance in winning him the friendship and confidence of the U.S. Marines.

Sacasa ruled for three years and then was overthrown by Somoza, who officially took over the presidency, after an "election," on January 1, 1937. He continued to rule the country either as president or as the power behind the presidency until his assassination on September 21, 1956.

The key to the continued control over Nicaragua by Anastasio Somoza, and by his sons after him, was their firm grip on the national guard. However, on the civilian front their control over the Liberal Party was almost as important. Through it they maintained an effective civilian political machine.

The Somozas' role as Liberals was also of importance for another reason. Before the advent of Anastasio Somoza to power, Nicaraguan politics had been controlled by a group of wealthy landlords and merchants, some of whom were Liberals but the majority of whom were Conservatives. Somoza was not part of this group, and both he and his sons consistently pictured themselves as representing new middle- and working-class elements. Although the Somoza family came to be the wealthiest in the country and intermarried with the old aristocracy,

THE LIBERALS

there continued to be a strain in the relationship between the "nouveaux riches" Somozas and the older first families of the republic, a strain that the Somozas used to good advantage for political purposes, as a rallying point among the more humble citizens.

In each election after 1936 the Somoza candidate, whether a member of the family or someone selected by them, ran on the Liberal ticket. However, when Anastasio Somoza announced his candidacy for reelection in 1943, a group of Liberals protested, as a result of which they were read out of the party. They formed a rival group, the Partido Liberal Independiente, which from then on was one of the principal elements in the anti-Somoza camp.[24] Subsequently, the Somoza faction of the Liberals took the name Partido Liberal Nacionalista. In the late 1960s the Partido Liberal Independiente had 2 members of the Chamber of Deputies out of 54,[25] and the Somoza Liberals had 36.

In 1956 Anastasio Somoza had the constitution altered to permit him to be reelected for still another term. The Partido Liberal Nacionalista promptly named him as its candidate, and it was at a fiesta to celebrate this event that Somoza was assassinated. The presidency was promptly assumed by Luis Somoza de Bayle, the dead man's son, who had been serving as president of Congress and was constitutionally in line to succeed his father. He promptly named his brother, Anastasio Somoza de Bayle, as commander of the national guard.

Since the constitution had been altered to forbid the immediate reelection of the incumbent president or of anyone closely related to him, the Somoza brothers chose someone outside the family, René Schick Gutiérrez,* to succeed Luis and serve as president until 1967.

No longer being constitutionally barred from the presidency by 1967, Anastasio Somoza de Bayle finally became the candidate of the Liberal Nationalists in 1966. In a turbulent and rather violent campaign he was easily elected and took office early in 1967, the third member of his immediate family to occupy the presidency.

It was widely suspected that when his first term came to an end, "Tachito" Somoza (as Anastasio was widely known) would probably seek to change the constitution to permit his reelection. This was because no member of the third generation of Somozas was yet ready to take his place. His brother Luis had died in 1966. In 1971 he

---

*The German name Schick was a hard one for many of the Somozas' peasant followers to understand or spell. As a result, during his presidential campaign René Schick Gutiérrez came to be known to many rank-and-file Somocistas as Chico Gutiérrez, the name Schick being thus transformed into a good Spanish nickname.

reached an agreement with the Conservative opposition for the election of a new Constituent Assembly, thus postponing the presidential election and making Anastasio eligible once more.

The Somozas owed their long continuation in power to a number of factors besides their control of the nation's armed forces and of the Liberal Party. For one thing, under their rule the country experienced a modest degree of economic development, from which the Somoza family profited very considerably but that also resulted in the improvement of the lot of some segments of the population. For another, the Somozas allowed the development of a trade union movement of sorts, so long as it did not seriously try to unionize enterprises in which the family had a major interest. They also stimulated modest economic development, including industrialization, from which the family benefited considerably.

Finally, the Somozas were blessed with a peculiarly inept opposition. Their Conservative opponents in particular were often willing to reach an amiable compromise that did not endanger the Somozas' rule, or they acted irresponsibly, which tended to engender sympathy for the government rather than for themselves.

Venezuela

The only party in Venezuela in recent decades that has proclaimed itself "liberal" has been the Unión Republicana Democrática. However, whether or not this party should be put in this category, it certainly has differed strongly from most of the Liberal parties of Latin America.

For one thing, the Unión Republicana Democrática (URD) is a relatively new party. It is not one of the traditional groups dating from the early years of independence; rather, it was established in 1946. Nor has the URD taken any position strongly critical of the Roman Catholic Church or been particularly strong in its advocacy of federalism. However, at least on some occasions, it has proclaimed itself in favor of liberal economic policies.

The URD was established a few months after the revolution of October 18, 1945, which placed the Acción Democrática Party in power. The principal leader of the new party was Jovito Villalba, who had been a progovernment senator during the Isaias Medina Angarita government overthrown in October 1945; and it became the principal political vehicle of former supporters of the Medina Angarita regime.

Jóvito Villalba was a member of the "generation of 1928," the group of students who in that year attempted a revolt against the dictatorship of Juan Vicente Gómez. After Gómez' death in 1935, Villalba became the president of the Federation of Students and took

THE LIBERALS

little part in the efforts undertaken by Rómulo Betancourt and other members of the generation of 1928 to establish a revolutionary democratic political party. Once the Partido Democrático Nacional (later christened Acción Democrática) was well established, Villalba was unwilling to join it as a figure secondary to Betancourt.

However, when the Acción Democrática Party came to power and decreed a liberal electoral law, which encouraged the development of new political parties, Villalba took the lead in establishing one. The URD became one of the four principal parties between 1946 and 1948. During this period it was the bitterest opponent of the Acción Democrática regime, perhaps because of the URD's tendency to attract members of the regime that Acción Democrática helped to overthrow.

When the Acción Democrática administration of Rómulo Gallegos was overthrown by the military in November 1948, the URD at first cooperated enthusiastically with the military junta that assumed power. Several of its leading figures assumed state governorships under the junta. However, after the murder of the first president of the junta, Colonel Carlos Delgado Chalbaud, in 1950, the URD went increasingly into the opposition.

In the election of December 1952, called by the military junta to elect a Constituent Assembly to "constitutionalize" its regime, the Unión Republicana Democrática was the bitterest critic of the junta regime. As a result it received the support of the underground organization of Acción Democrática. The upshot was that when the votes began to be counted, the URD was running far ahead of all other parties.

The leaders of the Acción Democrática underground were certain that the military junta, by that time dominated by Colonel Marcos Pérez Jiménez, would not recognize the victory of the URD, if it won, and urged the Unión Republicana Democrática leaders to join in an insurrection to overthrow the dictatorship. The URD leaders expressed their belief that their victory would be honored; and top leaders of the party accepted an invitation to "discuss the matter" at the Ministry of Interior, where they were arrested and deported.

For the rest of the Pérez Jiménez regime, the URD was outlawed. It participated in the Junta Patriótica, which led the campaign inside Venezuela against the Pérez Jiménez dictatorship that resulted, on January 23, 1958, in the overthrow of the regime.

During the provisional government of 1958-59, the URD was the party reputed to have had the closest relations with the administration. In the presidential election of December 1958, it supported the candidacy of Admiral Wolfgang Larrazábal, who came in second, after Rómulo Betancourt, nominee of Acción Democrática.

The three candidates in the 1958 election had agreed that elements of all three major parties—AD, URD, and the Copei—would enter the cabinet of the winner. As a result the URD had three members in the first cabinet of Rómulo Betancourt. The party continued to participate in the Betancourt administration until late in 1960, when the URD ministers resigned. For the rest of the Betancourt government, the URD was in the opposition; and some of its leaders were bitterly critical of the government.

During the election of 1963, the URD nominated its leaders, Jóvito Villalba, for the presidency. However, he came in fourth, after Acción Democrática Raúl Leoni, Copei nominee Rafael Caldera, and independent Arturo Uslar Pietri.

The URD was interested in once again joining the government. However, it was clear that President-elect Leoni was not likely to take into his cabinet members of a party that included some who had indicated their sympathy for the guerrillas who had tried to overthrow the government of his predecessor, Rómulo Betancourt. As a result the URD expelled a number of its left-wing leaders in December 1963.

Although upon his inauguration Leoni formed an all-Acción Democrática cabinet, a few months later he organized the so-called "broad-based government," which included the conservative Frente Nacional Democrático and the Unión Republicana Democrática. The URD remained in the Leoni cabinet until April 1968. When, at that point, they demanded wider control over patronage, Leoni demanded and received the resignation of the cabinet and dismissed its URD members.

When the election of Leoni's successor took place in December 1968, the URD joined with several other parties to back a businessman and former diplomat, Miguel Angel Burelli. He came in third, behind Rafael Caldera of Copei and Gonzalo Barrios of Acción Democrática. However, the URD suffered a severe defeat when it was able to elect only a single senator and 14 deputies.

The election of 1968 reduced the URD from one of the country's three major parties to a minor element. It seemed doubtful that the party could continue to be a significant element in Venezuelan politics. In 1970 it joined a so-called "New Force," together with the dissident AD group, Movimiento Electoral del Pueblo, and the Communist Party.

Colombia

The Liberal Party of Colombia came to power for the first time in half a century in 1930. As the result of a split in the Conservative ranks, Enrique Olaya Herrera, the Liberal nominee, won the election that year. He governed with a coalition of members of the two parties.

It was not until the second Liberal administration, that of Alfonso López, took office in 1934, that the Liberals set about carrying out a markedly partisan program. The López administration gave strong

THE LIBERALS

encouragement to the labor movement, stimulating the establishment of the country's first central labor group, the Confederación de Trabajadores de Colombia, which from its inception was closely linked with the Liberal Party. The President of the CTC usually sat on the National Liberal Directorate.

The López government also enacted a substantial body of labor and social legislation and even passed an agrarian reform law, although succeeding regimes made little effort to put this into effect. The country's tax system was substantially revised, with the result that by the 1940s the Colombian government was one of the few in Latin America that received a substantial proportion of its revenue from income taxes. The constitution was revised, principally to incorporate a number of social measures, in conformity with the tradition established by the Mexican constitution of 1917.

Alfonso López was succeeded by another Liberal president, of a somewhat more moderate bent, Eduardo Santos, whose family owned the large Bogotá Liberal newspaper El tiempo. The Santos administration, faced with the problems engendered by the outbreak of World War II, did not further the reforms inaugurated by López.

López returned to office in the election of 1942. However, ill health and political bickering among his Liberal supporters forced him to resign about a year before his term expired. He was succeeded by Vice-President Alberto Lleras Camargo, also a Liberal.

By the end of the López-Lleras Camargo term in office, the Liberals were badly split. In the early 1940s a leading figure in the Chamber of Deputies, Jorge Eliécer Gaitán, had launched a campaign against what he called "the Liberal oligarchy," accusing the two recent Liberal administrations of having failed to deal with the pressing social problems faced by the worker-peasant and middle-class elements of the country. Although his positive program was extremely vague, his attacks on the "oligarchy" won him wide support, both in the Liberal Party and outside it. For example, Gaitán won over virtually the whole Young Communist League and drastically curbed the fortunes of the Communist Party, which until then had been gaining considerable ground not only in the labor movement but also in the general political arena; dissension within the Communist ranks, arising largely over the question of how to deal with the menace of Gaitanism, led to a three-way split in that party.[26]

When the Liberal Party refused to nominate Gaitán as its candidate for the election of 1946, he undertook to run anyway. As a result the Liberal forces were split; and a Conservative, Mariano Ospina Pérez, was elected. Soon thereafter the Liberals reunited; Gaitán became the virtually unchallenged leader of the party and its presumptive candidate for the election of 1950.

However, Gaitán was assassinated on April 9, 1948, provoking the wild rioting by his supporters that has come to be known as the "Bogotazo." The center of the capital city was converted by the rioters into a scene reminiscent of bombed-out London in World War II.

By this time a virtual civil war had begun in the interior of the country. James Payne argues that such a development was unwanted by the leaders of either of the major parties, but that the struggle for power and position had become so intense that they were unable to curb the animosities of their followers. He would date the "violencia," as it has come to be known, from the aftermath of the 1946 election; it continued at a rising rate until 1953. On a vast scale Conservatives murdered Liberals and pillaged their homes and places of business; and to a lesser degree the same was done by Liberals to Conservatives.

The overthrow of the second Conservative government, that of Laureano Gómez, by the leaders of the army, headed by General Gustavo Rojas Pinilla, in June 1953, was greeted with applause by the Liberals. For a year they worked closely with Rojas Pinilla and cooperated with his call for civil peace and amnesty. However, in June 1954, when he named additional members to the Constituent Assembly that had first been appointed by Laureano Gómez and appointed a group of supposed Liberal representatives without consultation with the National Liberal Directorate, the Liberal Party broke with Rojas Pinilla.

To an increasing degree Rojas Pinilla turned against both of the traditional major parties of Colombia, which threw them together in opposition to him. The result was the so-called National Front Agreement worked out in Spain by Laureano Gómez and Alberto Lleras Camargo, representing the Conservatives and Liberals, respectively. This provided that the two parties would cooperate in trying to oust Rojas Pinilla and that after his downfall they would institute a system by which for a period of 12 years the parties would alternate in the presidency; positions in Congress and other legislative bodies, as well as those that were appointive, would be divided equally between them.

With the overthrow of Rojas Pinilla by the military as a result of a general strike-lockout in May 1957, the National Front Program was put into effect. A constitutional amendment was drawn up containing its main provisions and was adopted by a plebiscite at the end of 1957. Because the Conservatives, who were supposed to have the first president under this arrangement, experienced difficulties in selecting someone, it was decided to extend the National Front for another four years and to have Liberal Alberto Lleras Camargo become the first National Front president. He took office in 1958.

Since 1958 the National Front pattern has been followed. Lleras Camargo was succeeded in 1962 by Conservative Guillermo León Valencia, who in turn gave way to Liberal Carlos Lleras Restrepo in

THE LIBERALS

1966. The last National Front president, Misael Pastrana Borrero, a Conservative, was elected in 1970.

The National Front has been severely criticized both at home and abroad as being undemocratic and tending to perpetuate "oligarchical" control of Colombian politics and government. However, James Payne has argued that such is not the case. He maintains that there has been more real competition for support among the various factions of the two major parties during the National Front period than had ever existed before. At the same time, arguing that the prestige and patronage attached to public office are the main motivations for Colombian politicians, rather than the carrying out of programs and ideological commitments, Payne has pointed out that the perpetual dilemma of Colombian politics—the fear that the victory of Liberals or Conservatives would mean a complete monopoly by the victor of all posts of prestige and power—has been avoided by the National Front system. Hence he argues, elections have in fact been freer and more honest than before.

During the National Front period there has been one major cleavage within the Liberal ranks. Alfonso López Michelson, son of the ex-president, for some years led a group known as the Directorio Liberal Revolucionario, which was ostensibly opposed to the National Front system on the ground that the Liberal Party was the majority party in the country and therefore should have the right to undisputed power. However, in the late 1960s the Directorio Liberal Revolucionario disintegrated; during the administration of Lleras Restrepo the majority of the group was reintegrated in the mainstream of the Directorio Liberal Nacional, and López Michelson became an important member of the Lleras Restrepo government.[27]

Ecuador

The last of the long line of Liberal Party presidents that had begun with the seizure of power by Eloy Alfaro in 1895 was Carlos Arroyo del Río, who was elected in 1940. Hubert Herring notes that Arroyo del Río "brought more tranquility [sic] than the nation had enjoyed for many years." However, he had the great misfortune that during his administration there was a major war with Peru. Victory went unequivocally to the Peruvians; and a settlement contained in the Treaty of Rio de Janeiro, signed in 1942—which was virtually forced on the Ecuadoreans by the rest of the inter-American community—resulted in Ecuador's ceding approximately half of what it had considered to be its territory to its larger neighbor.

This event sealed the doom of Arroyo del Río. His administration was overthrown early in 1944 by a coalition of all parties except the

Liberals: that is, the Conservatives, Socialists, and Communists, under the leadership of the quixotic José María Velasco Ibarra.

Since the overthrow of Arroyo del Río, Ecuador has not had an unequivocally Liberal Party administration. Galo Plaza Lasso, the victor in the election of 1948, was an independent with Liberal sympathies; but he governed with members of various parties. His administration was noted for its quietness and its emphasis on economic development rather than on social change, and it was the first one in many decades both to come into office through an election and give up power to an elected successor.

In the 1950s the Liberals split into various factions; and in several elections there were Liberal factions supporting different candidates, as a result of which the party was unable to win the presidency. Although Liberalism remained one of the major currents of active Ecuadorean public opinion, the party seemed to have lost the possibility of resuming control of the country's affairs.

The Ecuadorean Liberal Party had failed to incorporate within its ranks the new groups that had become active in political affairs in the middle decades of the 20th century. The organized workers of the highlands, for example, tended generally to follow the Socialists and Communists, while those of the coastal region supported these two groups and the Concentration of Popular Forces Party that arose in the late 1940s and was of undefined ideology. Middle-class elements, as well as some workers, tended to be caught up periodically by the demogogic campaigns of the hardy perennial of Ecuadorean politics, José María Velasco Ibarra, who had the remarkable record of becoming president five times.

Nor had the Liberals sufficiently changed their basic outlook and program to take the lead in the social revolution that is long overdue in Ecuador. In the highland areas, where the great majority of the Indian population is concentrated, there is still a state of semifeudalism, in which the land is owned by a relatively small group of holders who trace their tenancy back to the time of the Conquest and the early colonial administrations. Agrarian reform, extension of education to the Indian masses, and incorporation of the Indians into the political life of the country are but some of the measures needed to bring Ecuador into the 20th century. However, even though as early as 1903 the Liberal Party program promised that the party would "initiate an agrarian reform,"[28] successive Liberal regimes did virtually nothing about any of these matters. Since losing control of the country in the mid-1940s, the Liberals have continued to advocate agrarian reform; but they have shown little inclination to campaign on the basis of such issues.

THE LIBERALS

Bolivia

The long period of Liberal domination of Bolivian politics came to an end in 1920, when they were overthrown by the opposition Republicans, who remained in power until the end of the Chaco War with Paraguay, early in 1936. During this long interim the Liberals functioned as the major opposition party.

After the Chaco War traditional party lines were clouded by the rise of new political parties, all of which proclaimed themselves "revolutionary" and all but one of which (the Falange Socialista Boliviana) were of the Left. The Liberal and Republican parties played no role in the military regimes of David Toro and Germán Busch, who ruled between 1936 and 1939. They joined to support the election of General Enrique Peñaranda in 1940, when the only opposition candidate was José Antonio Arze, nominee of one of the new left-wing parties, the Partido de la Izquierda Revolucionaria.

The Liberals were again thrown into the political wilderness by the coup of December 1943, which overthrew Peñaranda's government. The resulting regime of Major Gualberto Villarroel was influenced largely by another new party, the Movimiento Nacionalista Revolucionario.

The Liberals participated in the movement that resulted in the ouster and death of Villarroel in July 1946. In the elections of January 1947, the Liberal Party named as its candidate Luis Fernando Guachalla, who also had the backing of the Partido de la Izquierda Revolucionaria. In a total of about 44,000 votes, Guachalla lost to his opponent, Enrique Hertzog, by only some 400 votes.[29]

The Liberal Party participated in the governments of Enrique Hertzog and Mamerto Urriolagoitia (who succeeded from the vice-presidency when Hertzog resigned because of ill health), since both of the traditional parties were on the defensive during this period in the face of the serious challenge of the Movimiento Nacionalista Revolucionario. However, in the presidential election of 1951 the two traditional parties parted company once again. The Liberals put up their own nominee, Tomás Manuel Elio, whose candidacy was attacked by elements of the MNR as being subsidized mainly by the Patiño mining interest.[30] The Liberals are said to have received only 4,000 votes in the election, the results of which were never officially known, since the counting process was interrupted by a military coup provoked by the apparent victory of the MNR candidate, Víctor Paz Estenssoro.[31]

With the victory of the Movimiento Nacionalista Revolucionario in the revolution of April 9, 1952, the Bolivian Liberal Party virtually passed into history. Although some of its adherents kept up the fiction of the party's existence, it participated in none of the elections held under the MNR regime. Nor did it return as a political force of any consequence with the overthrow of the MNR government in November 1964. The status quo that the Liberals had defended had disappeared, and the Partido Liberal had disappeared with it.

Chile

The election of 1920 was a victory for the majority of the Liberals, behind Arturo Alessandri. His victory has been described by Hubert Herring as having "all of the aspects of social revolution, albeit a bloodless one. The bitter middle class made common cause with laborers in mine and factory to unseat the aristocracy."[32]

Arturo Alessandri, whose popular sobriquet was "the Lion of Tarapaca," was an extraordinary man. He was small in stature, arrogant in nature, had a tremendous flair for popular oratory, and, in this first period in the presidency, a passion for reform. For four years he sought to push through such fundamental items as a labor code, the separation of Church and state, a corporate income tax, a high land tax, and even limited autonomy for the provinces. However, a Conservative majority in the Senate blocked all of these measures.

It was not until they were faced with the threat of a military coup by officers who were outraged at the legislators' decision to pay themselves salaries while military pay was in arrears that Congress finally decided to pass at least some of the legislation demanded by Alessandri. The principal laws passed in the momentous session of September 8, 1924 constituted the basis of the country's famous labor code, the first such instrument to be enacted by any Latin American country.

Despite this action by the Congress, Alessandri was overthrown a few days later. For three months a junta of generals and admirals ruled, but they were ousted by younger officers in January 1925 and Alessandri was recalled. Between March and September 1925, he presided over a process of rapid change. A new constitution, providing for separation of Church and state and the end of the system of parliamentary rule that had prevailed since the overthrow of José Balmaceda in 1891, was enacted. The social laws of September 1924 were put into effect. Other reforms were enacted.

However, Alessandri was overthrown again in September 1925, by Colonel Carlos Ibáñez, one of the leaders in his restoration nine months earlier. From then until 1931, Ibáñez was the real ruler of Chile, occupying the presidency from 1927. During his period of rule, all political parties were kept under close control.

With the overthrow of Ibáñez in 1931, new elections were held. Alessandri once again emerged as candidate of the Liberal Party. He was not victorious and became one of the leading opponents of the short-lived regime of Juan Esteban Montero, a Radical. Alessandri was accused of participating in the plot that on June 4, 1932, overthrew Montero and established a short-lived "Socialist republic," although he denied the charge.[33]

All traces of the Socialist republic had disappeared by September 1932, and in elections two months later Alessandri again ran as Liberal Party candidate. This time he was victorious. During his second administration Alessandri and the party he headed moved markedly to the Right. Although in the beginning he tried to keep the Radicals in his government, they retired from his administration and in 1936 joined with the Socialists and Communists to form the Popular Front.

By the end of the second Alessandri government in December 1938, the Liberal Party—which had been united under his leadership in his second administration—had been completely outflanked from the Left. It had lost whatever support it had had from the urban workers and, like the Conservative Party, depended for its electoral support largely on the ability of Liberal landlords to march their peasants to the polls to vote (largely illegally, be it said, since most of them were illiterate and hence not entitled to vote) for Liberal candidates. However, the Liberals also had considerable support from the new industrialist class, which rose rapidly in economic importance during the second Alessandri administration and the following two decades.

The rise of several parties on the Left tended to drive the Liberals into alliance with their old opponents, the Conservatives. In the election of 1938 they both supported Gustavo Ross Santa María against the Popular Front candidate, Pedro Aguirre Cerda. Three years later, after the death of Aguirre Cerda, although the Conservatives and the majority of Liberals backed ex-dictator Carlos Ibáñez, Alessandri, whose enmity toward Ibáñez was by this time proverbial, led a dissident Liberal group to support Ibáñez' opponent, Juan Antonio Ríos, a Radical, who was victorious. The Liberals and Conservatives also backed different nominees in 1946, when the Liberals ran one of Alessandri's many children, Fernando, and the Conservatives backed Eduardo Cruz Coke.

In the 1946 election no candidate won a majority of the popular vote, so the contest was thrown into Congress for decision. Here the Liberals' attitude was crucial. Alessandri led his party in complicated negotiations with Gabriel González Videla, the Radical nominee, who had also been supported by the Communists and who had gained a plurality of the popular vote. The Liberals threw their support in Congress to González Videla, thus assuring him a majority; in return he agreed to form a cabinet with three ministers each from the Radical, Communist, and Liberal parties. This strange coalition lasted until April 1947, when, on Alessandri's instructions, the Liberals withdrew from the government; González asked for the Communists' resignations and appointed an all-Radical cabinet.[34]

During the rest of the González Videla administration the Liberals generally supported the president, and part of the time they had members in his cabinet. In the 1952 election the Liberals and Conservatives joined to support one of Alessandri's sons-in-law, Arturo Matte Larraín, for the presidency. However, victory went to Carlos Ibáñez, running as an independent. Undoubtedly the fact that Alessandri had died faciliated the participation of the Liberals in some of the later cabinets of Ibáñez.

The Liberals again joined with the Conservatives to support a single candidate in the 1958 election. This time it was another of Alessandri's sons, Jorge, a well-known engineer and businessman, who had served for some time as González Videla's minister of finance. Jorge Alessandri was a political independent and undoubtedly gained some support from being his father's son, as well as from his own reputation as a very good employer and a man of great probity and austerity. He was victorious by a narrow margin. During most of his administration, he drew most of his ministers from the ranks of the Liberal and Conservative parties.

In the election of 1964 there were only two major candidates. One of these was the extreme leftist Salvador Allende, backed by the Socialist and Communist parties; the second was Eduardo Frei, nominee of the Christian Democratic Party. During the early months of the campaign the Liberals joined with the Conservatives and Radicals to put up a third candidate of the so-called Democratic Front, the Radical leader Julio Durán. However, six months before the vote the Democratic Front broke up and Durán withdrew from the campaign. Although he re-entered it as nominee of the Radical Party, the Liberals and Conservatives had by this time thrown their backing to Eduardo Frei, as the lesser of the two evils that had a chance to win the election.

Frei won, but his victory was a catastrophe for the Liberals and Conservatives. The momentum for Frei and the Christian Democrats that had arisen during the September 1964 presidential campaign continued through the March 1965 congressional election. In that poll both Liberals and Conservatives suffered severe defeats. The Liberal Party, which until then had been one of the largest in Congress, received only 7.32 percent of the vote for congressional candidates and elected only six members of the Chamber of Deputies. They did not elect a single senator, although they still had five holdovers whose posts were not at stake in that election.[35]

This catastrophe provoked a unification of the traditional Liberal and Conservative parties. A few months later they joined with a small right-wing party called Acción Nacional to form a new party, the Partido Nacional. With the establishment of this group, the history of the Chilean Liberals as an independent force came to an end.

Uruguay

The story of the Partido Colorado of Uruguay in the 20th century is inseparable from the name of José Batlle y Ordóñez. As candidate of the Colorado Party, he first assumed the presidency of Uruguay in 1903, served until 1907, and after a one-term interval was reelected for a second period in 1911-15. During these eight years in office he set a pattern for his country and his party that survived long after his death in 1928.

During his periods in office, Batlle began the enactment of a series of reforms that gave Uruguay the reputation for being "the Switzerland of Latin America." He pushed through extensive labor and social legislation and strongly encouraged the development of the organized labor movement. He was far ahead of his time in having the government assume control of such essential services as the docks, the electrical network, and the telephone system, with the objective not only of taking them out of the control of foreign firms but also of using them to foster the general development of the economy. Under his inspiration the alcohol and cement monopolies were also created, which established some of the earliest manufacturing enterprises in the country.

As a result of Batlle's initiative a constitutional convention was called in 1917, after he went left office. It wrote a new constitution that separated Church and state and incorporated a number of his reforms.

The writers of the 1917 constitution were not willing to adopt fully one of the basic political reforms that Batlle had been urging for some years. Preoccupied with the Latin American penchant for presidents to become dictators, he wanted to make this very difficult by adopting the Swiss model of a plural executive. He suggested that a Council of State, consisting of representatives of both major parties, be set up in place of the president. He felt that this would make it almost impossible for any single person to seize dictatorial power, and that through becoming involved in the executive branch, the opposition Nationalist Party would be encouraged fully to accept the democratic system of government, instead of continuously plotting to overthrow the established regime.

The constitution makers of 1917 were not willing to adopt this Batllista concept of a plural executive in full. Instead they set up a Council of State that was given executive control over such things as education, health, and public works; but they also kept the president, who was given supervision over internal security, the military, and financial matters.[36]

Batlle's concept of the plural executive brought dissension within the ranks of his own party. During his second term of office, a sizable number of Colorados broke with the president; and for a generation thereafter the party was divided between Batllista and anti-Batllista factions.

José Batle died in 1928; but his party continued in power. In 1933 the Batllista president, Gabriel Terra, led a coup d'état, suppressed the Council of State, and established the only dictatorship that Uruguay has had in the 20th century. However, in 1938 he gave way to another Colorado, Alfredo Baldomir, who during his term of office succeeded in restoring a fully democratic regime.

The Batllista Colorados continued to govern until 1956. In 1952 they finally succeeded in pushing through Batlle's dream of a plural executive. A national plebiscite accepted the idea of having a nine-member Council of State, six of whose members would be from the majority party and three from the largest opposition party. The presiding officer would be chosen each year from among the six majority members.

Since the death of Batlle his successors had largely built on what he left, engaging in few innovations of their own. During World War II the government had energetically pushed the industrialization of the country; and during the administration of Batlle's nephew, Luís Batlle Berres (1947-50), the administration also fostered the development of wheat growing, to free the country from dependence upon Perón's Argentina, in the face of Perón's efforts to blackmail the Uruguayan regime into expelling anti-Peronista exiles who sought refuge there.

However, in the postwar period the country was faced with a series of problems that none of its governments seriously sought to meet. Uruguayan agriculture and grazing lagged behind, technologically, and were increasingly unable to meet the demands for foreign exchange for the nation's mounting imports. The country had gone as far as it could with industrialization through manufacturing enterprises producing consumer goods—at very high prices—and further industrialization was likely only in cooperation with Argentina and Brazil. The social security system established by Batlle had developed to a point where its costs were greater than the economy could afford, in large part because of the system's excessive bureaucracy. Finally, the population continued to increase at a rate that was modest for Latin America, but one that meant that a nearly stagnant economy would force a reduction in the people's relatively high living standard.

This growing complex of problems had political repercussions in 1956, bringing the first defeat for the Colorado Party in almost 90 years. For eight years the opposition Partido Nacional (Blanco) ruled, with the Colorados returning to power only in 1966. In that same election a new plebiscite resulted in the ending of the plural executive system and the reestablishment of the single presidency.

THE LIBERALS

By this time the economic situation of Uruguay had reached crisis proportions. Inflation was increasing at the rate of 100 percent a year, and the economy was wracked by almost interminable strikes and other labor disputes. The government of Jorge Pacheco—who as vice-president had succeeded to the presidency on the death of the victor of 1966, General Gestido, in late 1967—took drastic measures. It instituted an austerity program and, when this provoked strong reaction from organized labor, sternly suppressed the resulting strikes, resorting on several occasions to modified martial law. Meanwhile, it sought to reorganize the social security system and to push forward a program for the modernization of agriculture and grazing that had been started by the Partido Nacional administration in the early 1960s. It also entered into negotiations with both Brazil and Argentina, looking toward a program of further industrialization designed to provide goods needed by its larger and industrially more advanced neighbors. Given time, these programs of the Pacheco government offered hope that the country could survive its economic crisis with the democratic institutions that had been firmly established by José Batlle still intact.[37]

Meanwhile, the Colorado Party had splintered into many fragments. During the 1950s the Partido Colorado Batllista had broken into two competing groups known locally as Lista 14, led by Batlle's son, César Batlle Pacheco, and Lista 15, headed by his nephew, Luís Batlle Berres. However, with the death of both of these leaders in the mid-1960s, Lista 14 and Lista 15 split into numerous subgroups.

Thus the traditional Liberal Party of Uruguay, the Partido Colorado, took the lead under the chieftanship of José Batlle y Ordóñez in carrying through a program of social reform, moderate nationalism, and economic development. Remaining to a large degree the party of Montevideo, it won the loyalty of most of the new urban working class as well as the sizable white-collar middle class. The social and economic changes it brought about made Uruguay for many decades a model of democratic stability and social progress. However, by the latter half of the 1960s, when, after a short period of rule by the Nacionalistas, the Colorados returned to office, they were faced with a new crisis that threatened the gains Colorado regimes had made for the country half a century before.[38]

Paraguay

After 60 years of peace and modest progress between 1870 and the early 1930s (after 1904 under Liberal Party leadership), Paraguay was thrown in 1932 into major military conflict with one of its neighbors. This was the Chaco War with Bolivia (1932-36). Although Paraguay emerged the "victor," the war was a disaster not only for the country but also for the Liberal Party. The last Liberal president, Eusebio Ayala, was overthrown by the military in 1936. During the next three decades the country was thrown into a period of alternating tyranny and anarchy from which it has not yet recovered.

The Liberals constituted the principal opposition to the government of Colonel Rafael Franco, which seized power with military support in February 1936, sought to install a Socialist-type regime, and ultimately gave rise to the establishment of the Partido Febrerista. George Pendle notes of the Liberals that "it is probable that they were implicated in the military rising which overthrew the Franco Government in August 1937."[39]

After almost two years of instability, punctuated by coups d'etat, elections were finally held in 1939. General José Félix Estigarribia, one of the heroes of the Chaco War, was chosen president in an uncontested election in which he was officially the nominee of the Liberal Party. During his short regime, in which the Liberals and the armed forces provided the cabinet members, Estigarribia proclaimed a dictatorship (in February 1940) and brought about the enactment of a new constitution, of which Pendle says: "This Constitution is in the Paraguayan tradition; it is not an alien form imposed upon the country; and so, after its fashion, it serves the purpose for which it was conceived."[40] Soon after the adoption of this constitution in a plebiscite in August 1940, the president was killed in an airplane accident.

His successor was General Higinio Morinigo, chosen "temporarily" by the cabinet but destined to rule for eight years. During the first few weeks of Morinigo's regime, the Liberals continued in his cabinet; but Pendle states that then, "finding that the new President would not be subservient to their wishes, they resigned and were replaced by military officers."[41] Thereafter the Liberals became among the most bitter opponents of the Morinigo regime.

In March 1947 the Liberals joined with the Febreristas and Communists in a short-lived civil war against the Morinigo regime. Colonel Rafael Franco, the Febrerista leader, was the effective chief of this uprising. It was unsuccessful; and since the ancient rivals of the Liberals, the Colorado Party, had supported Morinigo in the conflict, the Colorados thereafter became the government party.

Since 1947 the Liberals have constituted one of the major elements in opposition to the dictatorships of Morinigo, Natalicio González, Federico Chaves, and Alfredo Stroessner, who has been in power since 1954. However, in recent years they have split among themselves over how to carry on this opposition. As a result the party was for some years divided between a wing that was willing to participate in "elections" called by Stroessner, and so enjoyed a small representation in Congress, and a more intransigent wing that refused all cooperation with the dictator.

THE LIBERALS

The principal source of the continuing strength of the Liberals in Paraguay has been the force of tradition. One writer has said: "The Paraguayan masses are either Colorado or Liberal by family tradition rather than private conviction."[42] There is little ideological difference of consequence between the two groups.

By the middle decades of the 20th century, traditional Liberalism had virtually disappeared as a recognizable current in Latin American politics. Many of the 19th-century Liberal parties had disappeared. Of those that had survived, the Liberal Party of Honduras and the Colorado Party of Uruguay had more in common with the national revolutionary parties than they did with the Liberal parties of Bolivia, Paraguay, and Chile. The old issues that had constituted the main points in the program of 19th-century Liberalism had lost all importance. To a greater or lesser degree the Church-state issue had been resolved by depriving the Church of its extensive powers; federalism had disappeared except in Mexico, Argentina, and Brazil, and even in those nations was greatly modified and was no longer considered a major political issue. Virtually no politicians, not even Liberals, any longer supported the ideas of free trade and governmental noninterference in the economy.

By the end of World War II new issues were dominant in Latin American politics. Nationalism, rapid economic development, the enactment of social and labor legislation, agrarian reform, civilian versus military rule, and the incorporation of the masses into active political participation had superseded Church-state, protectionism versus free trade, and federalism against centralization as the questions over which political parties and leaders argued. The Liberals did not react uniformly on these issues. As a result their parties diverged or were entirely superseded by newer political groupings that made these problems the central themes of their ideology and program.

CHAPTER

3

THE CONSERVATIVES

Throughout the 19th century the Conservatives were the great rivals of the Liberal parties in most of Latin America. They stood for the "principle of authority" and, therefore, for a highly centralized form of government. They defended the traditional rights of the Roman Catholic Church against the anticlerical onslaughts of the Liberals. They stressed the need for building up the strength of the nation, and hence stood for protection of industry and agriculture against the free trade ideas of their Liberal opponents.

The Conservatives, like the Liberals, were representatives of the small landholding and commercial elite that dominated the politics of most of Latin America throughout the 19th century. During the 20th century the Conservatives have become the representatives par excellence of this part of society. Although in a number of countries "left wings" inspired by the social teachings of the popes and other Catholic leaders and thinkers have arisen in several of the Conservative parties, these groups have been shunted off in most cases; the Conservative parties have remained true to their names and have been strong defenders of the status quo.

Conservative parties have not always used the name Partido Conservador (Conservative Party). In Mexico in recent decades, the party has been the Partido Acción Nacional, in Uruguay since the 19th century the conservatives have been known as the Partido Nacional or Partido Blanco, and in Honduras they are also the Partido Nacional. In Argentina the one-time Partido Conservador became the Partido Democrático Nacional, while in Bolivia the conservative group is known as Republicano, as it was in Puerto Rico until 1968, when the place of the Partido Republicano was taken by the Nuevo Partido Progresista. Only in Nicaragua, Colombia, Ecuador, and Chile—and in 19th century Mexico and Brazil—is the name Partido Conservador used by the Conservatives.

THE CONSERVATIVES

MEXICO

The Mexican Conservatives dominated much of the early republic, until the so-called Reform Movement gave Liberals control in the 1850's. Perhaps the outstanding figure in Conservative ranks during this period was Lucas Alamán, who was the Conservative leader for 30 years, served as minister several times, and personally dominated the government between 1829 and 1832. Hubert Herring has commented that during this period "Despite provisions of the Constitution of 1824, Conservative-centralist rule was supreme, with the army and the Church as chief allies."[1]

During this period the Conservatives not only sought centralized government and defended the rights of the Church but were also notable advocates of protectionism and industrialization. In looking at this aspect of Alamán's career one is strongly reminded of the role of Alexander Hamilton in the early history of the republican United States. Herring has described this aspect of Alamán's career in the following terms:

> ... He established a national credit bank for agriculture and industry. A trained engineer himself, Alamán had made futile efforts in the early 1820's to restore the mining industry. Later, in a position of power, he continued his efforts, and also sought to establish such industries as textile mills and iron foundries. He anticipated the demand that became articulate in the twentieth century, he dreamed of an industrialized nation freed from economic ties with any foreign land, a nation able to appropriate technical skills from other lands without falling into the hands of alien interests.[2]

The year 1855 marked the beginning of Mexico's Liberal era. However, three years later a Conservative general, Félix Zuloaga, overthrew President Ignacio Comonfort and proclaimed himself president. A three-year civil war followed, with a Liberal government headed by Benito Juárez, who had been Comonfort's vice-president and had been proclaimed president by the Liberals upon Comonfort's resignation. The Conservatives lost this war, and Juárez marched into Mexico City in December 1860.

Defeated at home, the Conservatives sought foreign intervention. The excuse for this was presented in July 1861, when Juárez ordered the suspension of payments on the Mexican foreign debt. Six months later French troops landed in Mexico and, after some preliminary defeats, were able to take Mexico City in June 1863. Juárez first fled north, then succeeded in establishing his headquarters in Vera Cruz, while the French and their Conservative allies installed Austrian Archduke Maximilian as emperor in Mexico City.

Emperor Maximilian proved a disappointment to the Conservatives. He reconfirmed the reform laws that had been proclaimed by the Liberals and did little to hide his disdain for many of the Conservative politicians who dominated his administration. However, his efforts to court the Liberals failed completely; and when French troops were withdrawn in 1865, Juárez and the Liberals returned to power, capturing and executing Maximilian.

The Conservatives collaboration with the French and the victory of the Liberals in 1865-66 brought the virtual end of the Conservative Party. Although some of its leaders remained active in politics until Porfirio Díaz come to power in 1876, the party disappeared in the years that followed.

It was not until 1939 that another national party of conservative orientation began to play a significant role in Mexican politics. In that year, the Partido Acción Nacional was established as the principal right-wing party in opposition to the government's Partido de la Revolución Mexicana (later rechristened Partido Revolucionario Instituctional).

The Partido Acción Nacional (PAN) has been characterized in terms of doctrine and philosophy by particular emphasis on two issues: the role of private enterprise in the economy and the abolition of certain restrictions on the Church, especially in education.

The PAN position on the importance of private property was clearly presented in the principles of doctrine adopted at the party's founding congress. Point 8 of this document started with the assertion "Private initiative is the most vibrant source of social improvement. The State should guarantee it and promote its best and most ordered development. Where private initiative is impossible or insufficient, the State should stimulate the organization of social activities, although in these cases, without killing, disturbing or displacing that initiative . . . ."[3]

Point 9 adds: "Private property is the most adequate means of assuring national production, and constitutes the support and guarantee of personal dignity, and of the existence of the fundamental human community, which is the family." It continues: "The guarantee of property, generally and specifically, has no other limits, insofar as its application to individuals or groups is concerned, than the principles of the common good and the fulfillment of the positive duties of proper use and of social cooperation which are imposed by the principle itself."[4]

Although PAN has strongly insisted that it is not a "confessional party" and has denounced the use of the banner of Catholicism or

Christianity by any political party,[5] it has strongly opposed the traditional anticlericalism of the Mexican Revolution. It has been particularly explicit in its demand that Article 3 of the 1917 constitution, which forbids the establishment and maintenance of Church schools, be abolished. This position was clearly stated in the report of Manuel Gonzáles Hinojosa to the 14th convention of PAN in March 1959:

> ... The PAN, on many occasions and from all points of view, has fought against the official thesis and has formulated the national demand for a total reform of the educational system; recently in the political platform approved in the national convention of 57, it reiterated this demand, making a profound analysis of the problem, with data which the regime itself could not hide or deny any longer and had to confess, with all of its consequences ....
> The derogation of constitutional article three must be demanded as well as the laws regulating it, and there must be instituted a legal regime which guarantees the liberty of teaching and the rights of parents. Nothing justifies the intransigence of the Regime, nor the inertia of the Nation in the face of the consequences of that absurd and obstinate sectarianism.[6]

PAN was established under the leadership of Manuel Gómez Morín, who had been an associate of ex-President Plutarco Elías Calles and was opposed to the leftist orientation of the regime of President Lázaro Cárdenas. Throughout most of its existence, PAN has contained two elements. Howard Cline describes the first of these, "the founding group," which soon came to be led by Efraín González Luna, as urging that "PAN remain aloof in permanent opposition to the Revolution." Those opposed to González Luna "have advised cooperation and participation in national activities as a 'loyal opposition.'"[7]

During its three decades the Partido Acción Nacional has won a well-recognized place in Mexican politics. Around it have grouped the largest number of right-wing opponents of the successive governments of the PRI. Although regarded by many as the rightist "loyal opposition" and by some as being virtually a tool of the government, designed to prevent the rise of more violent and dangerous opposition, PAN has in recent years shown itself capable of offering virtually the only serious conservative opposition to the regime.

PAN did not have presidential candidates of its own in the first two national elections held after its establishment. In 1940 it backed the major antigovernment candidate, General Juan Andreu Almazán, against the government's choice, General Manuel Avila Camacho.

Six years later it backed the other independent opposition nominee, Ezequiel Padilla, against the PRI's Miguel Alemán.

By 1952 the Partido Acción Nacional decided to put up its own nominee and to use the electoral campaign as an instrument for broadening the base of the party. Before that year, according to Robert Scott, PAN "always had been known as a conservative party, representing the interests of the Church, big business, and upper- and middle-class professional people."[8]

However, during this campaign PAN sought to organize a "labor sector," along the lines that the government party had had since the days of Cárdenas. It also organized "alianzas de empleados" to appeal to organized white-collar workers, "some of whom joined because of pressure from their employers and others because of the 'snob-appeal' of belonging to the previously-elite PAN."[9]

The party's candidate in this 1952 election was Efraín González Luna, one of its first leaders. However, he apparently was not satisfied with the meager results that the campaign of 1952 had produced for the party; and, as Scott notes, he "harked back to Acción Nacional's original concept of intransigent and permanent opposition to the revolutionary party and everything it stands for."[10]

The party again ran its own candidate in the 1958 presidential campaign. Its nominee was Luis H. Alvarez, whom Howard Cline refers to as "demagogic" but whom Robert Scott describes as having waged "a vociferous and driving campaign, incorporating sweeping revolutionary-style demands for land reform, labor benefits, social welfare, and other popular causes."[11]

The Partido Acción Nacional had frequently criticized the government party for corrupt electoral processes. After the 1958 election PAN leadership went further in its protests, ordering the six members of the party who had been credited with election to the Chamber of Deputies not to take their seats. However, four of them defied the party leadership and were sworn in.

As a result of disappointment over the 1958 election, the next convention of the Partido Acción Nacional resulted in a violent struggle for power between the doctrinaire followers of González Luna and the moderate faction led by Gómez Morín. The former group, in alliance with a youth element, took control of the party. During the next few years PAN took a particularly militant stand, which led to encounters with the police in various parts of the country. Especially violent clashes took place in Baja California and Chihuahua.

However, the president who was elected in 1958, Adolfo López Mateos, sponsored legislation that assured the opposition parties greater representation in Congress than they had previously been able to obtain. As a result of this legislation, Acción Nacional was able to elect 20 deputies in 1964. In that and subsequent elections Acción

Nacional also made considerable progress in filling municipal and state offices. By 1968 the party had won control of 19 towns and cities, including two state capitals, and had members in several state legislatures.12

In the election of 1970 Acción Nacional ran Efraín González Luna as its nominee for president. He was reported by <u>Latin American Digest</u> of October 1970 as having received 1,945,391 votes as against the 11,923,755 credited to the victorious candidate of the PRI, Luis Echeverria.

Acción Nacional thus remains the largest party in opposition to the Mexican revolutionary regime. However, its chances of ever coming to power are meager. Despite its defense of the Church, which continues to have the loyalty of a large segment of the Mexican population, its chances of becoming the country's majority party are severely hampered by its more or less overt opposition to the Mexican Revolution, which has the backing of an even larger segment of Mexicans, including many who are at the same time loyal to the church.

GUATEMALA

The division of Guatemalan political activists between Liberals and Conservatives took place even before the separation of the Guatemalan province from the Republic of Central America in 1938. During the period of the Central American Republic, led by the Liberal Francisco Morazán, a strong anticlerical, Rafael Carrera, an illiterate Guatemalan Indian, raised the standard of Conservative revolt against the government. With the victory of Carrera the Central American Republic fell apart, and Carrera became the first president of independent Guatemala. He ruled the country from 1838 until his death in 1865.

Hubert Herring has compared Carrera with the Ecuadorean Conservative dictator Gabriel García Moreno and has noted that Carrera sought "to make his nation a living witness to the glory of the Catholic faith."13 Under him anticlerical measures adopted by the Morazán regime were repealed; and the Guatemalan government became the first in Spanish America to sign a concordat with the Vatican, allowed the religious orders to return, and gave the Church control of education.

Carrera also was a strong defender of "private enterprise." As a result, Herring notes, "The creole landowners, the foreigners and the high clergy, while privately deploring his gross ignorance, supported Carrera because of his firm stand on religion and property rights and his firm control of the masses."14

Rafael Carrera died in 1865. Soon after his death the Liberals came to power in Guatemala, under the leadership of Rufino Barrios; and the Conservatives never again ruled the country. A succession of dictators, ruling in the name of the Liberal Party, controlled Guatemala until 1944, when a civilian-military revolution deposed the last of them, Jorge Ubico. Neither the Conservative nor the Liberal Party survived this revolution.

Since the overthrow of Jacobo Arbenz in 1954, several parties have appeared that are pledged to support the economic and social status quo. However, none of these has stood forth clearly as a party in the Conservative tradition, ideologically committed to defense of the Church, support of centralized government, and advocacy of economic protectionism. These issues have been as dead in Guatemala as elsewhere in Latin America. Few have challenged the modus vivendi that has evolved over the years between Church and state, based largely on the reform laws adopted during the Barrios period. Nor does anyone question that Guatemala should be a centralized republic, which it has been in fact, whether under Liberal or Conservative rule. Finally, protectionism is a principle believed in by virtually all politically active elements in the republic.

HONDURAS

The Conservative Party of Honduras, known variously during its history as the Democratic National Party and the National Party, was organized in the last decades of the 19th century as the opposition to the Liberal Party, which had been set up a few years previously. It remained the minority party until the 1920s. John Martz notes that "it was organized on a hierarchic basis in 1911 and, from 1920 on, exercised considerable influence at elections."[15]

The program of the party, as put forward in 1923, was fairly vague. It advocated "strict observance of the constitution, establishment of a Central American Union when feasible, less politics and more administration in government, financial reform, free elections, harmony among the Honduran people, and protection of capital and labor."[16]

By the 1920s the outstanding figure in the Partido Nacional was Tiburcio Carías Andino. He was a man of towering stature for a Honduran—some six feet, four inches tall—was a lawyer by profession, and claimed to be one of two men ever licensed to practice law in all five Central American republics. During periods of exile he actually did practice in El Salvador and Guatemala.[17]

Carías was the National Party candidate for president in 1923. Although he won a plurality of popular votes, more than 50 percent

THE CONSERVATIVES

was required by the constitution, and the Liberal-controlled Congress refused to recognize his election. There followed a period of anarchy, marked by several politicians, including Carías, taking the field with armed groups and by U.S. interference. The Carías army finally was victorious; but as a result of negotiations in which U.S. representatives participated, it was decided to choose as president the vice-presidential nominee on the Partido Nacional ticket, Miguel Paz Baraona.

Five years later Carías again ran for president and this time was narrowly defeated by the Liberal candidate, T. Mejía Colindres. Although Carías still dominated the military, he made no effort to seize power and pledged Mejía Colindres his support, which he was actually called upon to render on inauguration day, when a group of dissident Liberals tried to prevent their party's official candidate from taking office.

The Nacionalistas finally won power in 1932, when Carías was finally elected by a large margin. Although the constitution forbade reelection, Carías remained in power until January 1, 1949, when he turned over the office to another member of the Partido Nacional.

There is little question that Carías was a dictator during his long tenure in office. John Martz, who is generally well disposed toward Carias lists the "negative results of the Carias administration" as "final destruction of municipal autonomy, subjection of Congress to executive whim, neoptism and personalismo, harsh and ostentatious criminal punishment, non-recognition of woman suffrage, smothering of labor organization, suspension of national voting privileges from 1937 to 1949 . . . ."[18]

Carías denied that he was a dictator and insisted that this claim was made only because the opposition was weak during his administration. Quite naturally (in an interview on June 23, 1967) he claimed that his regime had accomplished a number of positive things, including the building of most of the roads existing in 1967, the installation of many water and sewer systems, the maintenance of a good school system—which, he wryly remarked, had deteriorated since his leaving office, because there was not enough "direction of the students in their studies." Carías also claimed to have left the country free of debt.

After 16 years in office, Carías decided to give up power. In Elections held late in 1948, the uncontested Partido Nacional candidate was Juan Manuel Gálvez. Although he seemed to be chosen as a puppet of the retiring dictator, he proved to be nothing of the kind. He began the process of dismantling the Carías dictatorship, allowing the Liberals to return to full political activity and establishing freedom of the press, a central bank, and a national development bank. When, in May 1954, he was faced with a virtually spontaneous general strike in the banana region of the north coast, he handled the situation with supreme diplomacy and tact, refusing to use force to suppress the strike, and in the end used his influence to get the banana companies to recognize the new unions that their workers had formed, even though there was no legislation authorizing trade union organization.

During the Gálvez administration there developed a breach between the ex-dictator and his successor. As a result, when the time came to choose a successor to Gálvez, the Partido Nacional split. The party's official convention nominated Carías; but a group of dissidents closely associated with Gálvez broke away to form a new party, the Partido Reformista, which nominated Carías' old vice-president, General Abraham Williams, as its candidate for the presidency. The Liberals named their new leader, Ramón Villeda Morales.

After a spectacular and sometimes violent election campaign, the voters cast 121,213 votes for Villeda Morales, 77,041 for Carías, and 53,041 for Abraham Williams. Since these results gave Villeda Morales only 48 percent of the popular vote, the final choice was thrown into Congress.[19]

The Liberals were at first credited with 26 of the 56 seats in Congress; but when the body had finally qualified its members, there were only 23 Liberals, together with 22 Nacionalistas, and 11 Reformistas. The result was a deadlock in the choice of a president, which was finally resolved when, after President Gálvez suffered a heart attack, Vice-President Julio Lozano took over and on December 6, 1954, declared himself chief of state, suspending Congress for an indefinite period. The Nacionalistas thus remained in power.

The Lozano regime after a time deteriorated into a personal dictatorship. A number of Liberal leaders were jailed or fled into exile. Lozano organized his own political party, the Partido Unión Nacional (PUN) and entered into a pact with the Reformistas. He called elections for still another Constitutional Assembly; the nature of the poll is shown by PUN's being credited with winning all of the seats.

Despite of this "victory" Lozano was soon out of office. An army revolt led by young officers toppled him and paved the way for elections on September 21, 1958, which gave an unequivocal victory to the Liberals, who won 36 of the 58 seats in a new Constitutional Assembly. This assembly elected Liberal leader Ramón Villeda Morales as president.

The Liberals governed for almost the full constitutional period of five years. However, despite Liberal control of the civilian government during this period, the Partido Nacional continued to be the dominant element in the military, reflecting the still powerful influence of the Carías dictatorship.

The Nacionalista army officers were apparently unwilling to allow a second Liberal administration. Although the Partido Nacional had named a candidate, Ramón Cruz, for the election scheduled for October 13, 1963, his military supporters were not willing to see his fate at the polls, since it was widely expected that Cruz's Liberal opponent would win. They therefore launched a coup d'etat on October 3, overthrew Villeda Morales, and deported him to Costa Rica. The scheduled election was canceled and Colonel Osvaldo López took office as provisional president.[20]

After a period of provisional rule, elections for still another Constitutional Assembly were held on February 16, 1965. While the campaign for these elections was in progress, the Partido Nacional leadership announced that it intended to have the Assembly choose López as president if it won a majority.[21] When the election results were announced as giving 35 deputies to the Partido Nacional and 25 to the Partido Liberal (a number said to coincide with the number that it had been rumored, in the days before the election, the Nacionalistas were "willing" to give the Liberals), the Liberals decided to boycott the Constitutional Assembly.[22]

The administration of Osvaldo López was clearly a government of the Partido Nacional, despite López' claim that he did not belong to any political party. However, there was by no means unanimous support among the Nacionalistas for the regime, and in Congress several Nacionalistas tended to cooperate with the Liberals.

The Nacionalista administration after 1963 showed its conservative inclinations, not so much by reversing the reforms and program launched by the Liberals as by not furthering them. For instance, the agrarian reform law passed shortly before Villeda Morales went out of office still had not been applied half a decade later by the Nacionalista regime. The Nacionalistas were essentially defenders of the economic and social status quo. In 1971 the Nacionalistas made a pact with the Liberals to support moderate Nationalista Ramón Cruz, a civilian, as their joint candidate for president.

NICARAGUA

As in most other Latin American countries, in Nicaragua the Liberals and Conservatives, under the leadership of a variety of caudillos, fought for power throughout the 19th century. The Liberals had the best of it during the first generation of the independent republic's existence, but in 1863 the Conservatives came to power for a 30-year period. Hubert Herring has said of this Conservative era: "They named presidents, put down occasional uprisings, and gave the country a somewhat stable rule. Coffee production increased, bananas were introduced, and the gold mines were worked fitfully. A few Germans and other Europeans entered the country, bought land, and contributed to the moderate prosperity of the era."[23]

This long period of Conservative rule was followed by the 16-year period of Liberal government under José Santos Zelaya, who was ousted in 1909 as the result of U.S. pressure following the execution of two Americans. The fall of Santos Zelya was the occasion for military intervention by the United States, which imposed the Conservative Adolfo Díaz as president.

Díaz has gone down in Nicaraguan history as a "tool" of the Americans because he was maintained in power largely through the U.S. armed forces and because of his approval of the Bryan-Chamorro Treaty, which gave the United States special rights to build a canal through the country. He remained in office off and on until 1928, when an election presided over by the U.S. Marines brought the Liberals back to power under José María Moncada.

The Liberal regime established in 1928 became the dictatorship of the Somoza family when General Anastasio Somoza seized power in 1936. During this regime, which is still in power, the Conservatives have usually played the role of docile opponents. Until his death in 1966, General Emiliano Chamorro, signatory of the Bryan-Chamorro Treaty, led the Conservative Party; and although the party put up opposition candidates to the Somoza nominees in presidential elections, the opposition was usually nominal.

The presidential election of 1966, however, was a harder-fought contest. The Conservative candidate, supported by the Social Christian Party and the Independent Liberals, was Fernando Arguello. The opposition issued fiery proclamations against the candidacy of Anastasio Somoza, Jr., and provoked a major riot in the center of Managua. Despite these pyrotechnics, Somoza won an east victory. In 1971 the Conservative leadership made a pact with Somoza to call a Constituent Assembly, whose deliberations would almost certainly pave the way for Somoza's reelection.

The Conservative Party in the period of Somoza domination has had the great handicap that it has drawn its leadership and much of its support from the traditional landed element. This has been used against it, in order to appeal to the poorer elements of the population, by the Somozas. It has also led to a situation in which, although the Conservative leaders have talked strongly against the Somozas in politics, they have sat with them or their representatives on boards of directors and other bodies controlling some of the country's key economic enterprises, in which Conservative leaders and the Somozas have been partners. This situation has aroused a certain degree of skepticism among many citizens concerning the truth of the Conservatives' protestations of opposition to the Somozas' rule.

COLOMBIA

The division of active public opinion in Colombia between Conservatives and Liberals had become clear by 1840, when the first obviously Conservative administration, under Pedro Alcantara Herrán, was elected. Alcantara took office in 1841 and was succeeded in 1845 by his father-in-law, Tomás Cipriano de Mosquera, who continued in the presidency until 1849. The nature of this first Conservative regime is indicated by Hubert Herring:

> ... the Conservatives gained power as defenders of order, godliness, and strong national government ... the nation prospered from the vigorous alliance of landlords, high clergy and army officers. Their intellectual mentor was Mariano Ospina, able defender of the doctrine of orderliness through Christian discipline. The Conservatives' doctrine of the state was incorporated in the Constitution of 1843, a somewhat Draconian instrument which invested almost absolute powers in the chief executive. The Church regained most of her traditional dignities; her special courts were restored, the schools were extrusted to the clergy, and the Jesuits (banished since 1767) were recalled.[24]

By 1857 the Conservatives were able to regain the presidency with the help of some moderate Liberals, who were particularly opposed to the free-trade program their party's administration had imposed. However, after a short interim the country was plunged into civil war; and in July 1861 Tomás Cipriano de Mosquera, now the major leader of the Liberals, captured Bogotá and installed a Liberal regime that remained in power until 1880.

The figure principally responsible for the Conservative restoration to power in 1880, and the beginning of 50 years of Conservative rule, was Rafael Núñez. He had started his career as a Liberal; and when he was elected in 1880 he was still nominally a member of the Liberal Party, although he was elected largely through the help of the Conservatives. During diplomatic service in Great Britain between 1863 and 1875 he is said to have been much influenced by the ideas of Herbert Spencer and to have returned to Colombia convinced of the virtues of "political centralization, religious tolerance, stringent economic controls, and Catholic morality as the cornerstone of progress."[25] He dominated Colombia politics from 1880 until his death in 1894.

During Núñez' rule the doctrines of the Conservatives prevailed, particularly in the constitution of 1886, which, with amendments, remains in force. It ended all pretense of federalism, converting the provinces into "departments," and restored the full influence of the Church. Catholicism was declared to be the official religion, although freedom of worship was constitutionally assured to other faiths. Church property was to be inviolate, the religious orders were reestablished, and education was made principally a responsibility of the church.

The Conservatives remained in power until a split in the party brought their rivals to office in 1930. The last 20 years of the Conservative rule have been described as showing "a marked advance in realism and cooperation: elections became freer and more honest, and Liberals secured more seats not only in Congress but in most of the cabinets. The press was largely freed from censorship, and political issues were openly discussed."[26]

During the first Liberal Party administration of Enrique Olaya Herrera, in 1930-34, the Conservatives served in the cabinet. However, during the government of Alfonso López, which enacted a number of important reform measures, the Conservatives turned to complete and bitter opposition. At the end of his administration, the Conservatives refused to take part in the election to choose López' successor, claiming that the results would be decided beforehand.

The Conservatives agin boycotted the election of 1942, in which López returned to office. His ill-starred second term, which was completed by his vice-president, Alberto Lleras Camargo, saw a split in the ranks of the Liberal Party, thus opening the possibility for the return of the Conservatives to power.

For their presidential candidate in 1946 the Conservatives chose a prosperous industrialist from the state of Antioquia, Mariano Ospina Pérez, rather than the party's outstanding figure, Laureano Gómez, who had a reputation for being particularly dogmatic in his conservatism, violently anti-Liberal, and of having had pro-Axis sympathies during World War II. Ospina represented the moderate wing of the party, and during the first part of his administration he ruled with a coalition cabinet of Conservatives and Liberals.

However, the coalition broke early in 1948; and in the ensuing reorganization of the cabinet, Laureano Gómez was named foreign minister. This aroused very strong opposition from the Liberals and seemed to preclude any further attempt to maintain cooperation between the two parties.

Soon after Gómez became foreign minister, the Liberal leader Jorge Eliécer Gaitán was assassinated, which led to the popular uprising of his followers in Bogotá that has come to be known as the "bogotazo." While the rioting was at its height, and with only a handful of troops in the capital to protect himself and the regime, Ospina was waited upon by a group of Liberal Party leaders who suggested that the only way to restore order would be for him to resign. Ospina refused, saying that under the circumstances he would leave the presidential palace only as a corpse. Shortly thereafter army reinforcements arrived in the capital, the anger of the crowds burned itself out, and calm returned to the ravaged city.

After the "bogotazo" Ospina once again named a coalition cabinet of Liberals and Conservatives. Meanwhile, Laureano Gómez, against whom much of the wrath of the Bogotá mobs had been directed (his newspaper El siglo was burned down, and the Foreign Ministry was attacked by the Crowd), went into voluntary exile in Spain.

The new coalition lasted about a year. Then, in a dispute over guarantees for the presidential election, the Liberals withdrew. In November 1949 Laureano Gómez was elected president in a contest in which he was the only candidate, the Liberals refusing to participate because of the supposed coercion of the voters by the Conservative regime.

The Gómez administration, which lasted from 1950 until 1953, was the period in which the "violencia," virtual civil war between Conservatives and Liberals, was at its height. Tens and perhaps hundreds of thousands of Colombians were killed in conflicts between members of the two parties, particularly in the rural areas and small towns.[27]

The situation reached a climax in June 1953, when Gómez announced his intention to install a new kind of regime, along corporative state lines, and appointed an all-Conservative Constituent Assembly to draw up the constitution for the new form of government. When the chief of the armed forces, General Gustavo Rojas Pinilla, himself a Conservative, objected, he was dismissed by Gómez. This move was ineffective, for Rojas Pinilla proceeded to depose the president.

The move of Rojas Pinilla was supported by the faction of the Conservative Party led by ex-President Mariano Ospina Pérez, as well as by the Liberals. Throughout most of the Rojas administration the Ospina Conservatives continued to support Rojas Pinilla and to provide members of his cabinet.

After a year's political honeymoon Rojas Pinilla broke definitively with the Liberals; and thereafter his administration was strongly opposed by them as well as by the Gómez faction of the Conservatives, who had been in opposition from the beginning. The regime degenerated into a largely personal dictatorship, although it enjoyed the support of the armed forces and, for a considerable period, of the Ospina Conservatives. The ideological direction of the Rojas Pinilla regime was somewhat obscure, although toward the end he became increasingly vocal in denouncing the "oligarchs" who had allegedly ruled the country and in calling for a political realignment that would destroy the hegemony of the Conservative and Liberal Parties in Colombian politics.

Meanwhile, the leaders of two traditional parties were thrown together by their common dislike of the Rojas Pinilla administration. A series of conferences between Alberto Lleras Camargo of the Liberals and Laureano Gómez, the Conservative former president who had again taken refuge in Spain, brought about the agreement to establish the National Front, the arrangement by which the two parties agreed to alternate members in the presidency and share all legislative and appointive political positions for 12 years (later extended to 16 years).

The Conservatives and Liberals cooperated in the conspiracy that overthrew Rojas Pinilla in May 1957 and in installing the National Front system, made part of the constitution by a referendum at the end of 1957. Although the first president under the new arrangement was supposed to be a Conservative, feuding among different factions of the party made it impossible for them to agree on a candidate; therefore the period of the National Front was extended an extra presidential term, and the first occupant of the presidency under it was the Liberal Alberto Lleras Camargo.

The first Conservative president under the National Front, elected in 1962, was Guillermo León Valencia. During his four years in office, he was much criticized for his failure to push energetically the various reforms and the economic planning and development program that had been started by his Liberal predecessor. Perhaps the greatest achievement of his regime was the success of the army in reducing the activities of the guerrillas. These were largely remnants of the bands that had survived from the "violencia" of the 1940s and 1950s and had been converted into Marxist-Leninist groups representing the three Communist currents (pro-Moscow, pro-Peking, and Fidelista).

The second Conservative government of the National Front period has been that of Misael Pastrana, elected in 1970 in a close and bitterly fought election in which four Conservatives ran against one another, with Rojas Pinilla being at most only slightly behind the victor. The Pastrana regime has tended to be somewhat more concerned than was that of León Valencia with problems of social reform and economic development.

During the National Front the Conservative Party has been split into several factions. Four of these are of greatest significance and have been headed, respectively, by ex-President Mariano Ospina Pérez; ex-President Laureano Gómez (and, after his death by his son Alvaro Gómez); by a one-time cabinet member, Gilberto Alzate Avendaño; and by ex-President Rojas Pinilla. During most of the period the first two of these have been the largest factions; and after the death of Alzate Avendaño in 1960 his followers joined the Gómez

THE CONSERVATIVES

faction. The followers of Rojas Pinilla were at the same time members of his new political group, Alianza Nacional Popular (ANAPO), which, because of the National Front, was not able to present candidates as a separate political party and so presented its nominees within both of the legal parties. Only with the beginning of the dismantling of the National Front was ANAPO recognized as a political party in 1971.

The attitude of the Ospina and Gómez factions toward the National Front changed from time to time, depending on their relative strengths within the Conservative ranks. When the Ospina group was the larger, and thus provided the half of the ministers, governors, and other appointees allotted to the Conservatives under the National Front, they were all in favor of the Front. When they were the minority Conservative group and it was the Gómez faction that held these governmental posts, the Ospinistas spoke against the National Front. The same changes in attitude were characteristic of the Gómez faction. So long as it was an independent group, the Alzate Avendaño element was officially against the National Front. The Conservative followers of Rojas Pinilla were consistently opposed to it.

This variability in the attitude of the various Conservative factions toward the National Front raises the question of the appropriateness of James Payne's belief that in fact little separates Conservatives from Liberals and divides the members of the different factions within the two parties other than the desire for the prestige of public office and the patronage available to those who hold public office. He maintains that not only in recent years but consistently through the history of Colombia there have been no real ideological differences between the Conservatives and Liberals.

Insofar as the period since World War II is concerned, there would appear to be a substantial degree of truth in Payne's analysis. There is certainly little ideologically to differentiate the Conservative Party as a whole from its Liberal opponents, except perhpas some latent anticlericalism among the Liberals. However, this is not the complete picture, particularly if one takes a historically somewhat longer-range point of view.

Certain differences in program and philosophy are certainly discernible between Liberal and Conservative regimes at certain periods during the last century and a quarter. During the 19th century the Liberal regimes curtailed the powers of the Church, and the Conservative ones restored them. In most cases during those decades, too, the Liberal regimes installed federalism, and the Conservative ones ended it. The Conservatives on the whole were much more favorably disposed toward following a policy of protectionism in economic matters than were the 19th-century Liberals.

Even in more recent times there are also some clear differences in policies and philosophies of Liberals and Conservative regimes.

It was the Alfonso López regime, a Liberal government, that enacted most of the country's labor and social legislation and first stimulated the growth of trade unions, as well as imposing the first really appreciable income tax and enacting an agrarian reform law (admittedly unenforced). Even more recently the Liberal regimes during the National Front period have been most forceful in enacting and enforcing agrarian reform, housing, and other social legislation and in pushing planned economic development.

It may be possible to argue that the policies of the López, Lleras Camargo (1958-62), and Lleras Restrepo (1966-70) governments reflect more the personalities and convictions of the three men than they do those of their parties. However, the question still remains as to why these men were leading politicians of the Liberal Party and not of the Conservative.

Certainly most Colombians are not members of either party because they have been converted to a particular political philosophy. They are Liberal or Conservative because to be such is a tradition with their family, or with their part of the country. Also, the issues that originally gave rise to the parties in the earlier decades of the 19th century are largely dead in Colombia, as elsewhere in Latin America. Finally, the Conservative Party of Colombia is much less clearly the defender of the status quo than are some of its counterparts in other Latin American nations. Many—perhaps most, as Payne insists—Conservative politicians are ready to support social and economic changes because they appear to be popular, or out of conviction, while certain numbers of Liberals will oppose such changes. Finally, the position of any politician or faction of either party with regard to a particular measure that is proposed will be strongly, if not decisively, influenced by the effect that measure is likely to have on his or its ability to gain access to power and jobs.

However, on balance, one may conclude that a rough parallel can be drawn with the situation in the United States, where there are also two traditional parties into one or another of which one tends to be born. There is very considerable overlapping from an ideological or philosophical point of view between Democrats and Republicans although, on balance, the Democrats tend to be more favorably disposed to social and economic reform than do the Republicans. Although this differentiation is less marked in Colombia than in the United States, on the basis of the historical behavior of the two traditional parties of Colombia one would seem forced to conclude that it does exist there.

ECUADOR

The forces that were to become the Conservative Party of Ecuador first gathered around the general who had led the separation

THE CONSERVATIVES

of Ecuador from Bolívar's Republic of Gran Colombia, Juan José Flores. He served two terms as president in the 1830's and 1840's, finally being driven out of office and out of the country by a Liberal revolt in 1845. The Liberals remained in power until they were ousted by a revolt led by the devout Catholic Conservative Gabriel García Moreno, supported by the redoubtable Flores, who rushed back from Paris to join the uprising.

However, it was García Moreno and not Flores who took power in 1860 and was to rule, as president or as the power behind the presidential chair, for 15 years. During this period he imposed what is perhaps the most absolutely Catholic regime which any Latin American country has had since independence. Hubert Herring has written: "He proposed to reshape Ecuador into a theocratic state in which the Church would exercise moral and spiritual authority in the name of the Almighty."28

García Moreno imposed two constitutions during his period in control of Ecuador that outlined the nature of the "theocratic" regime. That of 1861 "pledged the government to defend Catholicism as the exclusive religion,"29 and the later one gave citizenship only to practicing Catholics. García Moreno signed a concordat with the Vatican in 1863 that gave the Church complete control of education, allowed it to publish all papal bulls without the state's intervention, and reestablished church courts. He purged the Church in Ecuador of priests deemed immoral and brought in the Jesuits. In 1873 he had Congress dedicate Ecuador to the Sacred Heart of Jesus.

However, the García Moreno regime, which was a rigid dictatorship, abolished freedom of speech and press, and drove opponents into exile, but accomplished many things besides exalting the position of the Church. Herring notes that Garcia Moreno "gave the nation its first efficient treasury, improved its credit position abroad, introduced a uniform currency, built roads, spurred foreign trade, attracted foreign investment and improved agricultural methods. . . . Schools, from elementary to scientific and technical institutions, increased in number, chiefly under the guidance of the Jesuits."30

García Moreno was assassinated in 1875. Only thereafter, as Lillo Linke notes, was it "that the Conservative Party gradually emerged and evolved an organic programme, following the strictly Catholic line laid down by García Moreno." The statutes of the party declared that "the Catholic doctrines are the only true ones which will lead the member to wordly and eternal felicity."31 The Conservatives remained in power until 1895, when they were swept aside by a Liberal revolution.

During the period 1895-1944 the Conservatives remained one of the country's major parties. However, they could not overcome the Liberals, who not only represented the majority of the politically active population, particularly in the cities, but also had the support of the armed forces, which were thoroughly imbued with Liberal doctrines.

Nevertheless, on occasion the Conservatives participated in cabinets of various presidents. This was the case during the second administration of José María Velasco Ibarra in the 1940s. They formed part of the coalition that organized the coup which brought Velasco Ibarra to power in 1944; and during the last two years of this administration, Conservatives constituted virtually the whole membership of Congress and provided most of Velasco's ministers. They also served in his third administration, 1952-56.

It was not until 1956 that the Conservatives returned to power. Strictly speaking, it was not the Conservative Party but an offshoot from it, the Partido Social Cristiano, whose nominee, Camilo Ponce Henríquez, won the election of 1956. However, the bulk of his support came from the Conservatives, and they provided a large proportion of his ministers during his four years in office.

This Conservative-Christian Social interregnum did not see any major change in policies from those of the long Liberal period. There was no attempt to reestablish the position of the Church; and although he gave the country a relatively peaceful and stable government, Ponce Henríquez launched no innovations, in spite of his promise in his inaugural address of an agrarian reform law.

With the end of Ponce Henríquez' term in 1960, the Conservatives again went into the opposition. Velasco Ibarra, elected for the fourth time in 1960, was ousted two years later by an army coup; and his vice-president and successor, Carlos Arosemena, was deposed by still another army mutiny about a year later. For three years thereafter Ecuador was ruled by a military junta, which ousted by a popular uprising early in 1966.

Normal political activity was resumed after the ouster of the military regime. A new Constitutional Assembly was elected, after which presidential elections were held. The Conservative-Christian Social coalition once more named Ponce Henríquez, but the victor was the incomparable Velasco Ibarra, chosen for a fifth time; he took office in mid-1968.

The Conservative Party, in spite of being out of office during most of the last three-quarters of a century, has survived better than the Liberals. It remains the country's single largest political group, it has not been wracked by the constant and violent factionalism that has characterized the Liberals since World War II, and on several occasions it has robbed the Liberals of victory at the polls.

The Conservative Party of Ecuador has not been put in the position of strong defender of the status quo to the degree that has been the case in some other Latin American countries—largely because the status quo has never been seriously challenged. There has arisen no party of major significance that has been firmly committed to trying to end the semifeudal landholding system under which the Indians of the highlands continue to live, nor has any government—with the possible exception of the military junta of 1963-66, seriously sought to carry out such a reform. The party has maintained its strength as principal spokesman for the landed elite of the highland area, who are able to mobilize a sizable vote in the rural areas, and has also had a certain following among more religious elements in the cities.

There have been different currents of opinion within the party in recent years. The group that formed the Christian Social Party broke away, ostensibly inspired by the social teachings of the Church. However, it has remained small and lacking in zeal for reform, and has never become a member of either the hemispheric or the international organization of Christian Democratic parties.

Remaining within the Conservative Party is a current of opinion, representing a certain part of the leadership and rank and file that is more or less Christian Democratic in orientation. Indeed, the president of the party told the author in 1966 that the Conservatives favored agrarian reform, government construction of worker and peasant housing, and the extension of social security to the peasants.32 However, neither it nor any other party has taken measures to put such a program into effect.

Lillo Linke summed up the social composition and sources of strength of the Conservatives thus: "The Conservative Party leaders nearly always belong to the wealthy upper class, frequently with aristocratic pretensions. . . . The Conservatives' main force has always been in the Sierra, the section of the country most remote from outside influences, where the landowners and priests have been preoccupied in maintaining traditions."33

BOLIVIA

The Conservative and Liberal parties emerged after the disaster of the War of the Pacific (1879), in which Bolivia lost its coastal provinces to Chile. The Conservatives assumed power under Gregorio Pacheco. Alipio Valencia has noted; "The Conservative Party was based on the dogmas of Catholicism, believing that the existing economic, social and political order was imposed by God. . . ."34

The apogee of Conservative government came with the presidency of Mariano Baptista, beginning in 1892. Of the Conservative attitudes in this period, Alipio Valencia says: "The demands of the Liberal opposition, such as unrestricted freedom of man and of the citizen, lay education, freedom of religion, separation of Church and State, civil marriage, are subversive propositions, not only against the natural order of nature and society of divine origin, but also against the juridical order of the State, which by virtue of the constitution is a Catholic State."[35]

The Conservatives were overthrown in 1899 by the Liberals, who remained in power until 1920. During this period the old Conservative Party disappeared, but a new opponent of the Liberals was established in 1914, with the foundation of the Partido Republicano. Alipio Valencia has described the group that formed this party as being composed of "discontented Liberals such as General José Manuel Pando, representatives of old Conservatism such as Don Abel Iturralde and Luis Paz; exponents of the landowning aristocracy such as Daniel Salamanca and Domingo L. Ramírez and friends of the artisan "plebe" such as Bautista Saavedra."[36] He comments: "Against the Liberal Oligarchy of the New Rich, . . . the old feudal landlord aristocracy arose in revolt in alliance with the discontented artisans . . . ."[37]

This revolt was successful in 1920, when the Republicans succeeded in winning elements of the military to help them overthrow the last of the Liberal presidents, José Gutiérrez Guerra. The first Republican government was headed by Bautista Saavedra, the paladin of the city artisans rather than of the landed aristocracy. He was succeeded by Hernando Siles, who also represented the more progressive element in the Partido Republicano.

In the election of 1931 a coalition was formed between the more conservative element of the Republicans, now organized in the Partido Republicano Genuino and headed by David Salamanca, and the Liberals, whose leader Dr. Tejeda Solorzano was chosen as vice-president. Hubert Herring has noted that the election of Salamanca was considered a victory of the Patiño mining interests.[38]

Under Salamanca, Bolivia entered the disastrous Chaco War with Paraguay. During this conflict Salamanca was ousted by the military; and his successor, Solorzano, was likewise overthrown by the army soon after the end of the war, early in 1936.

Between 1936 and 1939 Bolivia was governed by two military regimes, those of Colonels David Toro and Germán Busch. These were reform governments, opposed to both of the traditional parties. With the death of Busch in 1939, new elections were called; and in 1940 the Republicans and Liberals joined to back the candidacy of General Enrique Peñaranda.

However, the rule of the traditional parties was interrupted again in December 1943, when Peñaranda was overthrown by a group of young army officers in alliance with the new Movimiento Nacionalista Revolucionario, and Major Gualberto Villarroel was installed as president. There began a process of reform that was interrupted in July 1946, when Villarroel was overthrown and murdered.

THE CONSERVATIVES

In elections early in 1947 the two traditional parties ran rival candidates for the last time. The new Partido de Unificación Republicana Socialista, formed by a reuinfication of the Bautista Saavedra and Salamanca branches of Republicanism together, with the so-called Unified Socialist party, named Enrique Hertzog as its candidate. His opponent was Liberal Party nominee Tomás Manuel Elio. Hertzog won a narrow victory.

The last Republican administration lasted until May 1951. The election held that month resulted in a victory for the outlawed Movimiento Nacionalista Revolucionario, as a result of which Mamerto Urriolagoitia (who had taken over when Hertzog resigned because of ill health) turned power over to a military junta.

With the MNR revolution of April 9, 1952, the traditional parties virtually disappeared. The Partido de Unificación Republicana Socialista remained virtually in suspense during the 12 years rule of the MNR. Although ex-President Hertzog and other leaders continued to speak in its name during this period, the party did not really function. Nor was it possible to revive it as an important political force after the overthrow of the MNR in November 1964.

The Bolivian Republican Party does not exactly fit the pattern of Latin American conservatism. It drew much of its popular support from the artisan class of La Paz and other cities, particularly during the leadership of Bautista Saavedra. However, it also included in its ranks the principal figures representing the landed aristocracy; and in its later years it became the representative of one of the major mining interests, the Patiño Mines. After the Chaco War it was one of the principal defenders of the socioeconomic status quo against the assaults of the MNR, the Partido de la Izquierda Revolucionaria, and other revolutionary groups.

CHILE

Chilean conservatism emerged as a coherent political force during the 1820s, the second decade of independence. Hubert Herring has noted: "The Conservatives, enlisting landholders, high clergy, and the Military, regarded themselves as the party of order and authority. Monarchical in spirit, they sought to continue the social and political traditions of colonial days under a strong centralized republic with a president whom they could control."39

The Conservatives seized power through a rebellion that culminated in the battle of Lircay in April 1830. During the first seven years of the Conservative period, the political life of the country was dominated by Diego Portales, the man who was undoubtedly the most outstanding Conservative figure of the early decades of the republic.

Although Portales was never president, he served in the cabinet and was the dominant figure in the administration of President Joaquín Prieto.

It was Portales who was largely responsible for writing the constitution of 1833, which was to last for 92 years and was to establish the form within which Chile developed one of the most stable regimes of the hemisphere, a kind of aristocratic democracy in some ways similar to that of Britain in the second third of the 19th century.

Alberto Edwards has written: "The majestically simple idea which inspired Don Diego Portales was realizable and capable of organizing real power with appropriate "form" because it was based on an organic spirtual force which had survived the triumph of Independence: the sentiment and the habit of obeying the legitimately constituted Government."40 Portales was capable of carrying out this task because he was "a man inspired with an abstract and grandiose idea, and at the same time as capable in the stratagems and the management of details as the most expert of the professional politicians and agitators . . ."41

On the basis of what had been established by Portales—who was assassinated in 1837—the Conservatives stayed in power until 1861, under Joaquín Prieto, Manuel Bulnes, and Manuel Montt, each of whom served two five-year terms. During most of these three decades the Church enjoyed the greater part of the privileges it had had during the colonial period; and throughout the 30 years Chile lived under a highly centralized administration that spread the jurisdiction of the republic to both the north and the south of the area that had originally declared its independence from Spain. The Conservative governments worked energetically to develop a railroad system and to stimulate the growth of trade and manufacturing, as well as encouraging foreign investment in mining and other activities.

The last clearly Conservative administration, that of Manuel Montt was characterized by sharp conflicts within the Conservative Party. It was followed by the government of José Joaquín Pérez, which marked the beginning of 30 years of party confusion, during which both Conservative and Liberal parties split, with most cabinets consisting of factions drawn from both. However, during 1861-91 the overall influence of the Conservatives tended to decline and that of the Liberals to increase.

This period came to an end with the overthrow of President José Manuel Balmeceda by a navy revolt, backed by the Conservatives and a sizable proportion of Balmaceda's own Liberal Party. This ousting of the president launched the 34-year period in which Chile's government was parliamentary, with the cabinets depending upon their maintenance of a majority in Congress in order to stay in power.

The parliamentary period was marked by frequent rotations of cabinets, and by the formation of "alliances" and "coalitions" in

Congress and in elections that frequently had little relevance to the principles and programs for which the various parties supposedly stood. Ricardo Donoso, speaking only of the administration of President Germán Riesco in the first years of the 20th century, made a comment that would apply equally to most of the period between 1891 and 1920, when he said that these party groupings were "devoid of all program with doctrinal and economic content."[42]

The Conservative Party was one of the major groups inside and out of parliament during these years. It participated in many of the cabinets, but no member of the party served as president during the years of the parliamentary republic. Perhaps the most important event during this period, from the point of view of the Conservative Party, was the virtual disappearance of the Partido Nacional, a group that had originated in the previous period and was composed mainly of dissident Conservatives.

Throughout the period of parliamentary domination, politics continued to be controlled largely by the rural aristocracy, which both the Conservatives and Liberals represented. However, in the presidential election of 1920 this aristocratic control of the presidency came to an end. In the campaign of that year the Conservatives formed part of the Unión Nacional, which backed the candidacy of Luís Barros Borgoño, a Liberal. Aligned against the Unión Nacional was the Alianza Liberal, composed of one faction of the Liberals, the Radical Party, and a faction of the Democratic Party. Its candidate was Arturo Alessandri, a Liberal. The victory of Alessandri, "the first middle-class president," marked the end of the complete domination of national politics by the aristocrats.

However, although they lost control of the presidency, the elements composing the Unión Nacional continued to have Congress securely in their grasp. For more than three years following Alessandri's election, they blocked virtually every measure of reform that he sought to have enacted. The Conservative members of both houses were of key importance in this holding action.

Several of the principal measures advocated by Alessandri were passed in a single hectic session of Congress on September 8, 1924, when the senators and deputies were acting under military pressure. Others, including the adoption of a new constitution that ended the parliamentary system and separated Church and state, were passed in 1925, when, after being overthrown by the military, Alessandri was brought back for six months.

In the period between the second overthrow of Alessandri in September 1925 and July 1931, the country was under the dictatorship of General Carlos Ibáñez. The Conservative Party, like all other political groups, was severely curbed. Some of its leaders strongly opposed the Ibáñez regime, while others cooperated with the dictator.

A few months after the overthrow of Ibáñez, new elections were called for president and Congress. The Conservatives backed their own candidate, Augusto Rivera Parga. He came in behind the two front runners, Juan Esteban Montero and Arturo Alessandri.

The Conservatives remained in the opposition during the turbulent year following the election of Montero. He was overthrown on June 4, 1932, when a "Socialist republic" was formed; this disappeared three months later, and elections were called a few weeks later. The Conservatives again named their own candidate, Horacio Rodríguez de la Sotta, who came in far behind Arturo Alessandri and Marmaduque Grove. However, they elected the second largest number of members of the senate and tied the Radicals for the biggest number of members of the lower house.[43]

During the second administration of Arturo Alessandri, from 1932 to 1938, the Conservatives became one of the major forces supporting the president, who moved distinctly to the Right during this period. In the election of 1938 the party backed Gustavo Ross, President Alessandri's Minister of Finance, and a political independent.

In the 14 years during which three Radical Party members served as president, from 1938 to 1952, the Conservatives were usually in the opposition. However, during the latter part of the administration of the last of these, Gabriel González Videla, who moved considerably to the Right, the Conservatives generally supported the president.

During this period the Conservatives followed different policies in different presidential elections. In 1941, after the death of President Pedro Aguirre Cerda, the Conservatives supported the candidacy of ex-dictator Carlos Ibáñez, who was defeated by Radical Juan Antonio Ríos. When Ríos died in 1946, the Conservatives put up as their candidate Senator Eduardo Cruz Coke. He ran in a four-way race, against the Radical-Communist nominee Gabriel González Videla, Liberal Fernando Alessandri, and Socialist Bernardo Ibáñez; the winner was González Videla. In 1952, at the end of González Videla's term, the Conservatives joined with the Liberals to support Arturo Matte Larraín, a Liberal and son-in-law of ex-President Arturo Alessandri.

Meanwhile, the Conservatives had suffered two splits, brought about by elements inspired by social teachings of the Catholic Church. The first of these took place in the 1930's, when the leaders of the Conservative Youth formed a new group, known as the Falange Nacional, which later evolved into the Christian Democratic Party.

The second split in Conservative ranks occurred in 1949, when Cruz Coke, the Conservative presidential candidate of 1946, led a breakaway group that constituted itself as the Partido Conservador Social Cristiano. Cruz Coke's opponents regrouped as the Partido

THE CONSERVATIVES

Conservador Tradicionalista, which after some time rallied most of the leaders and members of the Conservatives before the split. In 1957 the Partido Conservador Social Cristiano and the Falange Nacional joined with another small group to establish the Partido Demócrata Cristiano. That left the "Conservative" designation in the hands of Cruz Coke's opponents, who adopted the name Partido Conservador.

Neither of these splits significantly reduced the political force of the Conservative Party, which was based largely on the ability of Conservative landlords to mobilize their peasant retainers to go to the polls to vote for candidates favored by the party. However, the victory of the dissident Conservatives regrouped in the Partido Demócrata Cristiano in 1964 signaled the end of the Partido Conservador as an independent party. The victory of Christian Democratic presidential candidate Eduardo Frei in September 1964 was followed by a Christian Democratic parliamentary election triumph in March 1965, which resulted in the Conservatives electing no senators and three deputies.

The disaster of March 1965 drove the Conservative and Liberal parties together. By that time they were the joint defenders of the rights of the aristocratic landowners and of middle-class elements disturbed by the programs of reform and revolution advocated by both Christian Democratic and extreme Leftist parties. The old differences between Conservatives and Liberals were virtually meaningless by the mid-1960s. As a result, a few months after the 1965 defeat, the Conservatives, Liberals, and a small right-wing party joined to form a new group, the Partido Nacional. This ended the history of the Conservatives as a separate party in Chilean politics.

ARGENTINA

Argentine conservatism has differed from its counterparts in other parts of Latin America in at least one significant regard. Argentine Conservatives, as the major political spokesmen for the landed aristocracy of their country, who were concerned principally with export agriculture and feared retaliation from their British customers if Argentina industrialized and began to produce traditional imports, have never been in favor of protectionism and industrialization.

Also, modern conservatism was later in getting started in Argentina than in most of the rest of Latin America, dating only from the last decades of the 19th century. However, it has figured as a supporter of the rights of the Church and the defender of national unity.

During the first half century of Argentine independence, politics was dominated by the conflict between the Unitarios and the Federales. The former were the ideological heirs of the French Revolution in their anticlericalism, but they were not typical Latin American Liberals, since they advocated of a centralized form of government. The Federales were supporters of the Church but at least in theory were also advocates of federalism.

The difference between the two parties was explained in part by the sections of the country from which they drew their principal support. The Unitarios were first and foremost the spokesmen for Buenos Aires and its immediate environs. They were influenced by the role of the port as the principal contact with Europe and its interest in stimulating and controlling trade between the Old World and the Río de la Plata area. They were also influenced by the fact that Buenos Aires was traditionally more permeated by European culture than was the interior of the country.

The Federales, in contrast, represented the interests of the people of the interior of Argentina: the cities and towns that with their immediate environs were largely self-sufficient, with their own artisan industries that would be menaced by a sudden influx of machine-made goods from Europe; the rural folk whose roots were culturally closer to the Indians, who still dominated most of the Pampa and Patagonia regions of present-day Argentina, than they were to Europe.

Until 1832 Argentina was largely dominated by the Unitarios. However, in that year Juan Manuel de Rosas became head ot the province of Buenos Aires, the largest unit of the country. Rosas was the archetype of the caudillo," the landowner able to rally a sizable number of personal supporters for politics or military action, as circumstances dictated. As leader of the Federales, he rallied other caudillos. Although he never officially became more than governor of the province of Buenos Aires, he dominated all of Argentina until 1852.

Rosas is one of the most controversial figures in Argentine history. Although officially a Federalista, he imposed a rigorous dictatorship not only on Buenos Aires but on all of Argentina. His opponents were severely persecuted; and those who could do so, fled into exile. He is generally anathematized by elements in contemporary Argentine politics who oppose not only his dictatorial proclivities but also his anti-European attitudes. However, by others he is revered as an Argentine nationalist who fought off invasions by both the British and the French.

Rosas was overthrown in 1852, when some of his provinical caudillo supporters, led by Justo José de Urquiza, joined with his Unionist opponents. After almost a decade, during which Argentina

THE CONSERVATIVES

was divided into two nations—the Province of Buenos Aires and the Argentine Confederation—unity was restored in 1860, and the development of modern Argentina really began.

During three six-year presidential administrations after 1862, leaders who had come from the Federales camp transformed Argentina. Presidents Bartolomé Mitre, Domingo Faustino Sarmiento, and Nicolás Avalleneda followed policies that encouraged those who had received large lands grants under Rosas, and continued to receive them as land was taken from the Indians, to fence their land (aided by the invention of barbed wire), to develop cattle herds (through crossing British cattle with the native breeds), and to plant large areas to wheat and corn. They also established a virtually universal educational system and encouraged immigration from Europe.

By the late 1880s there existed a well entrenched class of large landholders that had little interest in the ideas of Sarmiento and others for "Europeanizing" Argentina. It was concerned primarily with maintaining its own recently acquired privileges and with the rapidly developing markets for grains and meat in Europe, particularly in Great Britain.[44]

Thus, by the 1890s modern Argentine politics began to take shape. The large landed interest came to be represented by the Conservative Party. The emerging middle class, in both the rural and urban centers, as well as a substantial part of the working class that was developing in Buenos Aires and other cities, came to be represented by the Radical Party; other working-class groups found their political expression in the Socialist Party.[45]

The control of the Conservatives over Argentina was fostered by the lack of free elections and of a secret ballot. Increasingly there arose within the Conservative ranks an element that insisted it would be better for the landlords themselves if there were real political freedom and a system of elections by secret ballot. They argued that this would divert the Radical Party from the position that it had taken since the mid-1890s: it refused to participate in obviously rigged elections and resorted instead to periodic attempts at insurrection.[46]

The more liberal elements in the Conservative ranks won control with the election of Roque Sáenz Peña in 1910. Under his auspices the Ley Sáenz Peña was passed in 1912; this provided for a secret ballot and assured that the majority party in any province would receive two-thirds of the deputies from that province, the runner-up party receiving the other third.

The result of the Ley Sáenz Peña was the victory of the Radicals in 1916 with the election to the presidency of Hipólito Irigoyen, the principal Radical leader. However, the Conservatives continued to control the Senate during most of the first Irigoyen administration. They blocked any attempt to bring about major reforms, with the exception of a law establishing Yacimientos Petrolíferos Fiscales, a government oil firm.

The Conservatives remained in the opposition between 1916 and 1930. In the latter year they cooperated with elements of the army, as well as with dissident Radicals and a breakaway faction of the Socialists, to organize a coup d'état that overthrew Irigoyen, who had been elected president for a second term in 1928.

Between 1930 and 1943 the Conservatives formed part of the Concordancia, which controlled the government throughout this period. Two dissident Radical presidents, General Augustín P. Justo and Roberto Ortiz, were followed (upon the death of Ortiz in 1941) by a Conservative, Ramón Castillo. During this period, although the Conservatives were a minority in Congress, they largely dominated the administration and followed policies favoring the large landholders.

However, the Perón revolution, which began when President Castillo was overthrown by a military coup on June 4, 1943, and was consolidated when Juan Domingo Perón was inaugurated as president on June 4, 1946, decimated the Conservative Party (by then known as the National Democratic Party), as it did most of the country's other political groups. The Conservatives were part of the opposition during this period, being strongly opposed to the antilandlord policies of the Perón administration.

With the overthrow of Perón in 1955, the Conservatives returned to the kind of open political activity that was not possible during the Perón regime. However, the party soon split over the same issue that divided most of the other Argentine parties. One faction, which took the name Partido Conservador Popular, sought to rally support among the supporters of Perón. The other, which formed the Federation of Parties of the Center, was uncompromisingly anti-Peronista, refusing to make any concessions in words or in ideas to the Peronistas.

In the election of 1963, the Partido Conservador Popular formed an alliance with the Peronistas. At one point in the campaign the Peronistas were willing to support the presidential candidacy of the Popular Conservative leader, Vicente Solano Lima, but the military and the government of President José María Guido refused to allow him to run.

The Conservatives of both groups have been reduced to a small minority in Argentine politics. The traditional position maintained by them, that Argentina is destined to be a grain- and meat-producing country and should be ruled by the landowning elite, no longer has any substantial support in the Argentine body politic.

URUGUAY

In Uruguay the Conservatives—that is, the Blancos or Partido Nacional—emerged in the decade after the country achieved its independence in 1828. They centered on one of the leaders of the independence movement, Manuel Oribe. During the following decades the Blancos were allied with Juan Manuel de Rosas of Argentina and Francisco Solano López of Paraguay. The supposed plight of the Blancos served as the pretext that the Paraguayan dictator used in 1865 to begin the War of the Triple Alliance against Argentina, Brazil, and Uruguay, which resulted not only in his downfall but also in the decimation of the male population of his country.

In the latter decades of the 19th century, the Blancos engaged in frequent revolts against the government, controlled by the rival Colorado Party. As the result of one of these insurrections, in 1896, led by one of the last of the old-fashioned Uruguayan caudillos, Aparicio Saravia, it was agreed that the Blancos would have control of 6 of the nation's 18 departments.

This agreement continued until 1903. In that year the Blancos launched their last revolt, which was defeated by the newly installed Colorado government of José Battle y Ordóñez. Batlle ended the de facto division of the country between Colorados and Blancos but took steps to try to convince the Blancos to participate in normal peaceful political activities.

Although the Blancos, who were particularly the representatives of the rural landholding element, were opposed to Batlle's proposal for the substitution of a Council of Government for the president of the republic, after this system was partially adopted in the constitution of 1917, the Blancos participated in the executive power for the first time since 1870, when members of their party served as minority members in the Council of Government. They continued to do so until the coup of Gabriel Terra in 1933, which ended the Councils of Government.

After his coup Terra entered into an agreement with the Blancos, by now known as the Partido Nacional, for the enactment of a new constitution that would assure each of the major parties of half of the members of the Senate. This system continued until 1942, when Terra's successor, Alfredo Baldomir, executed a widely supported coup, as a result of which he ended the constitution of the 1930s. Later in the year elections for both houses of Congress were held, and the Blancos emerged again as the minority party.

The Blancos continued to be the minority party until 1958. Unlike the Colorados, who from the period of World War I had split into several rival factions, the great majority of the Blancos remained united under the leadership of Luís Alberto Herrera, their frequent candidate for president. A small group broke away in the 1920s to form the Partido Blanco Independiente and established itself as a completely separate political party. Only after the death of Herrera in 1959 did the Blancos begin to divide into several rival factions.

The Colorados' continued control of national politics, even though the Blancos under Herrera's leadership constituted for many years the largest single faction in Uruguayan politics, was explained largely by the country's unique election law. This provided for the legal organization of "sublemas," or factions of existing parties, which, although still members of those parties, could name their own lists of candidates in general elections. The decision as to which of the parties had won the presidency and seats in the Congress depended upon the sums of the votes for candidates of the various factions of each party, while the particular individuals elected were those who had received most votes within their particular party. Thus the several factions of the Colorado Party were for many years able to get more votes for all of their presidential and congressional candidates than was the single list of Blanco nominees, although the Blancos received more votes than any single factional list among the Colorados.

It was only in 1958 that the Nacionalistas, although now themselves divided into several competing groups, were able to get more votes than the Colorados. As a result, for the first time they received the six seats in the Council of Government (which since a referendum in 1950 had substituted for the president) allotted to the majority party. The Colorados received the three seats allotted to the minority.

The Blancos controlled the Council of Government for two terms but were defeated in 1966. In that election a referendum resulted in the abolition of the Council of Government and the reinstitution of the single-man presidency. Since then the Nacionalistas have constituted the opposition to the Colorado government.

Although it is still true that the Nacionalistas are the party that particularly represents the rural landed elements, it has also enjoyed support among the urban population, particularly among the packinghouse workers. The differences in ideology and programs that once separated it from the Partido Colorado under Batlle's leadership have become less important since World War II. Differences between the two parties are now as much matters of family and personal tradition as they are of differences in principle.

PARAGUAY

In contrast with the situation in neighboring Uruguay, the Colorados of Paraguay are the party of conservative traditions.

THE CONSERVATIVES

George Pendle has said of the origins of the Colorado Party that it was established "by a war hero, General Bernardino Caballero, who in 1874 founded a Conservative Party—the Colorados—and personally appointed the Governments of the country for the next thirty years."[47]

The Colorados remained in power until 1904, when they were ousted by a Liberal revolution. They did not return to control of the country until 1947. At that time, in a civil war launched by the Liberal, Febrerista, and Communist parties against the government of President Higinio Morinigo, the Colorados, still an important element in national politics despite their more than 40 years out of office, threw their support behind Morinigo. As a result he formed a Colorado cabinet and named a leading intellectual of the party, Natalicio González, as his successor in elections in February 1948, which also provided the Partido Colorado with all of the members of Congress.

Since 1948 the government of Paraguay has been at least nominally Colorado. González was overthrown by a rival Colorado group, led by Federico Chaves; and he in turn was ousted in 1954, when General Alfredo Stroessner, also a Colorado, seized power. He is still in power.

Under Stroessner, the Colorados have split into a pro-Stroessner and an anti-Stroessner wing. The latter has opposed some of the dictatorial actions of the regime, and its principal leaders had to join Liberals, Febreristas and Communists in exile in Montevideo and Buenos Aires.

The Conservative parties of Latin America, which in the 19th century were the advocates of centralized government, the rights of the Church, and the need for protection for industry and agriculture, have in the present century become major supporters of the economic and social status quo against the new parties that have appeared on the scene, particularly since World War II. Although they have continued to be of some importance in a number of the Latin American countries, particularly where the tradition of a two-party system has remained strong, they have generally either disappeared or become a relatively small element in national politics.

CHAPTER

4

THE RADICALS

There have been two parties of some importance in Latin America that have used the word "Radical" in their names: The Unión Cívica Radical of Argentina and the Partido Radical of Chile. Both are "traditional" parties in their respective countries, having their roots well into the 19th century; they have had some sociological similarities; and they have both been parties of the moderate Left. For these reasons it is convenient to discuss them together.

ARGENTINA

Origins of the Unión Cívica Radical

The Argentine Radicals owe their foundation to a rising revolt during the last decades of the 19th century against the domination of the cattle-raising and grain-growing elite that won control of that country following the nation's reunification in 1860. Under the administrations of Bartolomé Mitre, Domingo Faustino Sarmiento, Nicolás Avalleneda, and Julio A. Roca (1862-86), the pampas-based export economy of Argentina was firmly established. The great plains were fenced in, the cattle breeds were improved, the cultivation of wheat expanded rapidly, and Argentina was converted into one of the major producers of grain and meat for the British market. At the same time railroads were extended through much of the pampas-area, the port cities of Buenos Aires and Rosario grew rapidly, and the great stream of immigration from Europe—particularly from Italy and the Iberian Peninsula, which was not to cease until the 1930's—began.

This new economy was firmly in the hands of the great landowners of the pampas. During the Rosas period (1838-52) and subsequently, as the great Argentine plains and the more southerly areas of Patagonia were seized from the Indians, huge land grants were made to soldiers who participated in the anti-Indian campaigns and to favorites of succeeding governments. Except in the northeastern parts of the country, there was little room for a small peasant class; and the raising of cattle and the growing of wheat and other grains was largely in the hands of the large estancieros, who owned estates of thousands and sometimes tens of thousands of acres.

Although the presidents of this post-1860 period were motivated by what they believed to be the best way to develop the resources of their country and to improve the well-being of their people, the upshot of this development process was the establishment of firm economic, social, and political control by a very small group of rural landowners who came to constitute a new aristocracy. They divided their time between luxurious mansions on their estates and even more sumptuous houses in Buenos Aires, Rosario, or other cities. Their sons were often sent to Europe for their education and the whole family frequently went there for extended vacations, their spending habits abroad becoming as famous as those of American millionaires. The pampas-barons became famous for their polo ponies and for their skill at this aristocratic game.

To an increasing degree the landed aristocracy tended to confuse what was best for their personal interests with what was best for Argentina, and they saw the welfare of their country largely in terms of their own continued control over its affairs. Even under such a supposedly democratic president as Sarmiento, democracy was a limited affair. Although there existed a wide latitude for freedom of expression, elections were largely "arranged." There was no such thing as a secret ballot.

Furthermore, this new regime, although based on the exploitation of the country's agricultural resources, was in many ways international and Europeanizing. Successive governments welcomed large European, particularly British, investments in railroads, public utilities, marketing agencies, and banks; and the economy as a whole became largely dependent upon the willingness and ability of the British to buy Argentina's products.

By the late 1880s there began to appear strong opposition to this rule of the landed elite. It was partly a protest against the exclusion of an increasingly large middle-class and working-class element from effective participation in the nation's affairs, and partly a resentment of the growing dependence of the Argentine economy on that of Britain and of the avowed efforts of at least some of the national leaders to convert Argentina virtually into a European country. It was also partly a result of resentment of the provinces against the growing domination of Buenos Aires in all spheres of national life.

This opposition first found organized expression in 1890 in the formation of the Unión Cívica, led by a group of young men, among whom Leandro Alem and Hipólito Irigoyen were the most outstanding, and by a group of older politicians headed by ex-President Julio A. Roca. These civilians joined with an element of the armed forces in July 1890 to attempt a military coup against the government of Miguel Juárez Celman. Although the uprising was suppressed, the president was forced to resign, turning over his office to Vice-President Carlos Pelligrini, the country's first president of Italian extraction.

Soon after the failure of the revolution of 1890, the younger element in the Unión Cívica withdrew to form the Unión Cívica Radical, led at first by Leandro Alem. After Alem's suicide in 1896, the leadership of the new party was assumed by Hipólito Irigoyen, who was to dominate it for a generation.

The Unión Cívica Radical at first sought to participate in elections. However, they soon became convinced that under the existing electoral system they had no chance of being conceded victory, no matter how large an actual majority they might have. As a result, under Irigoyen's leadership the party refused to take any part in the electoral process.

Unwilling to participate in elections, the Unión Cívica Radical had only one way open to power, that of conspiracy and attempted revolution. Upon various occasions during the last decade of the 19th century and the first decade of the 20th, it sought—unsuccessfully— to use this method.

However, there was developing within the ranks of the dominant oligarchy an element, largely headed by ex-President Carlos Pelligrini, that felt reform would permit the Radicals to participate in the normal political process. According to Rodolfo Puiggrós, this element felt that it made more sense to allow the Radicals to participate in honest elections, and even to allow them to win, and then to force them to modify their opposition to the economic and social status quo, than it did to keep them virtual pariahs.[1]

By the end of the first decade of the present century, the Radicals had come to represent a sizable proportion of the nation. They had wide support among the immigrant small middle-class merchants and craftsmen of the large coastal cities, as well as a considerable following among the new working class in the packinghouse, on the railroads, in the ports, and in the small factories that were beginning to appear. Frequently the lawyers, doctors, and teachers in small towns of the interior were Radicals. To a great degree, too, the Unión Cívica Radical represented a deep strain in Argentine national politics, going back to colonial days—the resentment of the interior against the port, Buenos Aires. In contrast with the efforts of the oligarchy to Europeanize Argentina, the Radicals in many areas represent the "American" tradition, the indigenous roots of the national character. In this sense they represented the "barbarism" of which Domingo Faustino Sarmiento talked, in contrast with the "civilization" of Buenos Aires and its foreign influences.

The First Radical Government

As a result of the election of 1910, the element of the aristocracy that favored political reform came to power in the person of President Roque Sáenz Peña. He sponsored and got through Congress the famous Sáenz Peña Law, which provided not only for the secret ballot but also for a system whereby two-thirds of the deputies from any province were allotted to the party getting the largest number of votes in that province and one-third to the party with the second highest vote. Thus in most provinces the Radicals were assured of at least one-third of the members of the lower house of Congress.

The Sáenz Peña Law succeeded in doing what it was designed to do: convince the Radicals to abandon their policy of abstentionism. In 1912 the Radicals began to participate in elections under the new system, with notable success. They not only won seats in the national Chamber of Deputies but also won control of some provinces in the next four years.

In 1916 the Radicals enjoyed their first national triumph. The Unión Cívica Radical leader, Hipólito Irigoyen, was elected president. With him a Radical majority of the Chamber of Deputies took office. However, the Senate continued to be controlled by the Conservatives until 1922.

During his first six years in power, Irigoyen did not succeed in bringing about major reforms. Although he suggested various pieces of labor legislation, little was actually passed. He himself generally had a friendly attitude toward organized labor, although he met fierce opposition not only from employers but also from anarchist elements that controlled a sizable part of the trade union movement.

Perhaps the first Irigoyen administration was most notable for its emphasis on nationalism. This found expression in both politics and economics. In the former, the principal issue was the attitude that Argentina should adopt toward World War I. Although there was very strong pressure brought upon the president to have Argentina formally join the side of the Allies, he resisted and Argentina remained neutral. Irigoyen undoubtedly adopted this position not only because he felt that Argentina's interests would not be served by becoming a belligerent but also because he did not think that it was fitting for a sovereign power such as Argentina merely to follow the path of its principal customer, Great Britain.

The other major manifestation of Irigoyen's nationalism was his sponsorship of the law establishing the Argentine government oil company, the Yacimientos Petrolíferos Fiscales, in 1922. Although this firm was not given a monopoly, and foreign oil companies continued to operate in the country, the establishment of YPF was the first serious effort to bring at least some of the country's subsoil resources under the control of the nation.

Irigoyen was succeeded by another Radical, Marcelo T. de Alvear, a very different type of person. Himself a large landowner, the second Radical president did not feel any great passion for reform, nor was he a strong nationalist. He was content to ride the wave of the prosperity of the 1920s without attempting any notable adventures in terms of government policy.

During the Alvear administration a serious split developed in the Unión Cívica Radical between the supporters of Irigoyen and those of the incumbent. Ostensibly this was a struggle over the continuing efforts of Irigoyen to dominate the Radical Party, but around this issue there also developed important ideological differences. The Irigoyen wing of the party, which soon took the name Personalista, undoubtedly represented the more nationalistic and reform-minded elements; the more conservative groups tended to throw their support behind Alvear's anti-Personalista group.

By the presidential of election of 1928, when Irigoyen was again eligible to run, the Radicals were split into two distinct parties, the Unión Cívica Radical Personalista and the Unión Cívica Radical Anti-Personalista. The nominee of the former was Irigoyen, who won a strong victory at the polls.

The second Irigoyen administration was tragic. Although the president and his party continued to be widely popular, as was indicated by congressional and other elections in 1930, Irigoyen confronted problems with which he was unable to cope. Within months of his taking office, the world was swept by the Great Depression, which hit Argentina with particular violence. No more than other national leaders of the time was Irigoyen able to deal with the problem. Furthermore, Irigoyen was by this time a very old man, and personal idiosyncrasies that might have been annoying before were catastrophic by 1929-30. He had long had the reputation of being distrustful even of his close associates, and this characteristic was accentuated in his second administration. In his attempt to deal personally with virtually all aspects of public policy, Irigoyen created a situation in which many things were left undone. His attitude undoubtedly also tended to intensify another factor that had already become noticeable, the tendency for widespread corruption in the ranks of the Radical government. No one has ever accused Irigoyen himself of being corrupt, but undoubtedly his attempt to do everything himself meant that he did not have time to

THE RADICALS

maintain real vigilance over the sometimes scandalous behavior of some of his subordinates.

The Period in the Wilderness

The upshot of this situation was the revolution of 1930. On September 6, 1930, Hipólito Irigoyen was overthrown by a group composed not only of top leaders of the armed forces but also of leaders of the Anti-Personalista Radicals, the Conservatives, and the dissident Independent Socialists.

The new government of General José Uriburu was exceedingly heterogeneous. The new president was himself an admirer of the semifascist Spanish dictator Primo de Rivera and was closely advised by a group of extreme right-wing Catholic intellectuals and politicians. But much of the military power rested in the hands of General Augustín P. Justo, an Anti-Personalista Radical, who thwarted Uriburu's preliminary attempts to establish a corporative state system and brought constant pressure to get back to an elected constitutional regime.

During this period the Irigoyen Radicals were virtually banned from participating in politics. The new government made one false start in March 1932, when it permitted elections in the province of Buenos Aires and several other areas, elections that were won overwhelmingly by the Personalista Radicals. These election results were cancelled by the national government, and the Personalistas were not allowed to participate in the subsequent general elections of 1932.

With the election of President Augustín P. Justo in 1932, with the support of the three parties making up the government coalition—the Anti-Personalista Radicals, the Conservatives (now called National Democrats), and the Independent Socialists—there begin the period of pseudo democracy that was called by its own advocates "the Patriotic Fraud." The Personalista Radicals, Socialists, and other opposition groups were generally allowed to participate in the subsequent elections, but their right to win was seriously curtailed. The national governments of the period used with great frequency their right to "intervene" in provinces in which the opposition won control, ousting the elected regime and appointing a temporary "interventor" whose job it was to organize elections that would "come out right."

In elections after 1932 the Personalista Radicals and Socialists together usually won control of the Chamber of Deputies, with the Personalistas constituting most of the parliamentary majority. However, in the presidential election of 1938 they were "counted out"; and victory went to Roberto Ortiz, an Anti-Personalista Radical backed by the Justo Government and by the parties participating in it.

President Ortiz apparently intended to return to a more truly constitutional and democratic regime. He ousted a number of the more fraudulent provincial governments, and in subsequent elections the Anti-Personalista Radicals gained considerable ground. However, Ortiz was forced by illness to retire after only about two years. His successor, who became president upon Ortiz' death soon after his retirement, was Ramón S. Castillo, a Conservative, who reverted to the tradition of the "Patriotic Fraud" and was preparing still another "managed" election when he was overthrown on June 4, 1943.

From the point of view of the Radical Party, the most important aspect of the Castillo period was the virtual reunification of its ranks. Most of the Anti-Personalistas, led by ex-presidents Alvear and Justo, rejoined the Personalistas to re-form a single Unión Cívica Radical. In the months prior to Castillo's overthrow the names of both Alvear and Justo were being discussed as possible Radical candidates against Castillo's nominee, Robustiano Patrón Costas.

The Radicals in the Perón Period

The revolution of June 4, 1943, marked the real beginning of the Perón era. Although Colonel Juan Domingo Perón was at first a minor figure in the regime, by the first months of 1944 he had become its most important leader. To gain this position he had begun a policy of courting the organized labor movement from his newly created post of secretary of labor and social welfare. By the end of 1944 he was not only vice-president of the republic but also secretary of labor, minister of war, and head of the Postwar Planning Council.

During the three years of the provisional government (June 4, 1943 - June 4, 1946), the Radicals constituted the largest element in the opposition to the regime. Although there is some evidence that Perón would have liked the support of the Radicals, he did not obtain it. They strongly opposed the dictatorial aspects of the regime and frequently called for free elections and a return to a constitutional government.

When Perón was temporarily ousted from power on October 9, 1945, the Radicals—as well as the other opposition parties—refused to join the government, although the head of the group that had ousted Perón, General Eduardo Avalos, urged them to do so. They demanded the ouster of President Edelmiro Farrel, and the running of the government by the Supreme Court as their price for participation in the new regime. For reasons best known to himself, Avalos refused to pay this price; within a bit more than a week, Perón's labor followers had mobilized in support of their deposed leader, and on October 16-17 he was restored to effective power.

THE RADICALS

This crisis brought to the surface a division of opinion within the Radical Party that was to be of grave consequence in the years ahead. A group of younger politicians, who had begun to call themselves the Intransigentes, strongly opposed the party's position. They urged that it take control of the government and that it announce that the Radicals not only had no intention of undoing the prolabor policies which Perón had followed in the previous two years but also intended to push them further. However, the Intransigentes were overruled.

There was also controversy within the Radical ranks concerning the attitude the party should adopt toward the election of February 1946. Perón was the government candidate for president, and the dominant element within the Radical Party agreed to the formation of a common front to oppose him. Although they insisted that the nominees opposing Perón and his vice-presidential candidate come from the Unión Cívica Radical, they agreed that these nominees should be jointly supported by the so-called Unión Democrática, formed by the Radicals, Socialists, Progressive Democrats, and Communists, with the tacit backing of the Conservatives as well.

The Unión Democrática candidates were old-line Radicals, José P. Tamborini for president and Enrique Mosca for vice-president. They conducted an energetic and high-level campaign; but it concentrated on a discussion of the value of democratic principles and criticized the dictatorial proclivities of Perón, without saying much about the social and economic issues that were the main content of the Perón program.

For campaign purposes Perón organized his own Radical Party. A small group of secondary Unión Cívica Radical leaders, headed by Juan William Cooke and Horacio Quijano, established the Unión Cívica Radical Renovadora and endorsed Perón's candidacy. Upon Perón's insistence Quijano, a man distinguished principally by his walrus-like moustache, became his running mate.

The Perón-Quijano ticket was successful by a margin of 55 percent to 45 percent, and the Peronistas also won almost two-thirds of the members of the Chamber of Deputies and all but two members of the Senate. The Radicals succeeded in winning most of the other seats in the Chamber of Deputies.

During the somewhat more than nine years that Péron was president of Argentina, the Radicals continued to constitute the largest party of the opposition. They continued to be virtually the only party represented in the lower house of Congress; and in the presidential election campaign of 1951 the party's nominees, Ricardo Balbín and Arturo Frondizi, were the only opponents of the Perón-Quijano ticket.

However, during this period the fissures within the party that had become evident during the 1943-45 provisional government became exceedingly acute, and the balance of power shifted within the party. By the end of the Perón period, the Intransigente group had succeeded in taking control of the Unión Cívica Radical.

The element that had controlled the party until the Perón period and advocated support of the Unión Democrática in the 1946 election came to be known as the Unionistas. They tended to criticize virtually everything the Perón government did, including its social and economic program as well as its dictatorial political behavior. They were not noted for their nationalism, and their traditions stemmed largely from the Anti-Personalista Radicals of the 1920s and 1930s.

The Intransigentes were by no means a unified group. During the Perón period there were at least two well-defined wings of Intransigencia. The oldest was that known as Intransigencia Nacional, led by Amadeo Sabattini, leader of the party in the province of Córdoba, and with its strength confined largely to that province. During Perón's presidency the Sabattini group opposed any participation by the Radical Party in elections, on the grounds that there were not adequate conditions for a democratic expression of the will of the voter.

The other major element of the Intransigentes was the so-called Intransigencia y Renovación. Its most outstanding figures were Ricardo Balbín, the party's 1951 presidential candidate; Arturo Frondizi, the Unión Cívica Radical vice-presidential nominee in 1951; and Crisólogo Larralde, a Radical leader with some following among the organized workers.

Within Intransigencia y Renovación there were also several tendencies. One of these centered on Balbín, whose influence was particularly strong in the province of Buenos Aires and who represented the Radical tradition of machine politics, in which personality and strong organization counted a good deal more than ideas and programs.

Another element increasingly centered on Arturo Frondizi, who in 1954 became president of the Radical Party. Frondizi was a most untypical Radical. An intellectual with a somewhat cold personality, he gathered around himself a group of young and ambitious intellectuals who devoted their talents to analyzing the conditions of the country and trying to develop programs for a future Radical government. Of all the Radical factions the Frondizi group had the clearest understanding that Perón's popularity was due to the fact that he had done a great deal for the humbler elements of Argentine citizenry, and they tended to confine their criticisms largely to his dictatorial politics while accepting his social and economic reforms and his nationalism.

With the advent of Frondizi to the presidency of the party, the Intransigentes became increasingly dominant within the Radical ranks. Frondizi used his position to "intervene" in a number of the provincial Radical organizations and thus to reduce the influence of the Unionistas.

THE RADICALS

At the same time he aroused a good deal of resentment even in the ranks of other elements of the Intransigente side of the party, resentment that was to come to the fore in the post-Perón period.

The Radicals in the Aramburu Period

With the overthrow of the Perón regime in September 1955, the factionalism within the Radical ranks became even more bitter. Aside from the question of personal ambitions of various party leaders, who foresaw the chance of election to the presidency in a period during which the Peronistas were virtually barred from politics, there were fundamental issues of tactics and strategy that divided the party. Like every other anti-Peronista political group the Radicals were fundamentally split as to what approach should be taken to the Peronistas. Generally the Intransigentes, and particularly those most closely associated with Frondizi, felt that everything possible should be done to emphasize whatever common ground there was between the Radicals and the followers of the fallen dictator. The Unionistas, on the other hand, were unbending in their opposition not only to Perón himself but also to anything they conceived to be appeasement of Peronismo.

During the provisional government of General Pedro Aramburu (November 1955 - May 1958), the Frondizi wing of the Intransigente Radicals became increasingly critical of and even hostile to the regime. Members of the Frondizi entourage established close contacts with many of Perón's labor supporters; lawyers among them defended many of the Peronistas who were being prosecuted and jailed by the Aramburu government; and the group as a whole took a position favoring the maintenance of a unified central labor body even if this group were to revert to Peronista control.

Meanwhile, there was frantic maneuvering for control of the Radical Party and particularly for the party's nomination for president in elections that the provisional regime promised to hold sooner or later. Only 15 months after the overthrow of Perón, long before the Aramburu government had set a date for elections, the Frondizi wing of the party, in control of its machinery, summoned a nominating convention in Córdoba in December 1956. At that convention Frondizi was nominated for president and a relatively obscure member of the Frondizi faction, Alejandro Gómez, was named nominee for vice-president.

A month after this convention, the results of which outraged not only the Unionistas but also the Sabattini and Balbín wings of the Intransigentes, the Unión Cívica Radical split. The Unionistas and the two anti-Frondizi elements of the Intransigentes withdrew to form what they called the Unión Cívica Radical del Pueblo. Those remaining in the old organization rechristened it the Unión Cívica Radical Intransigente. In due time the UCR del Pueblo named Ricardo Balbín as its presidential candidate.

In the meantime the Aramburu government had called elections for a Constitutional Assembly to revise the admittedly antiquated constitution of 1853, which had been proclaimed to be once again in force—displacing Perón's constitution of 1949—soon after Aramburu came to power. In these elections, in which the blank ballots cast by Perón's supporters were the single largest number of "votes," the UCR del Pueblo ran slightly ahead of the UCR Intransigente. However, the two Radical groups were far ahead of all other parties, indicating that the presidential election campaign was going to be largely a contest between them.

The long-awaited general elections for president, Congress, and all provincial elective offices were finally held in February 1958. As expected, the two major nominees were Arturo Frondizi for the UCR Intransigente and Ricardo Balbín for the UCR del Pueblo. The great unknown in this contest was the mass of Peronista voters, who seemed likely to follow the indications of their exiled chief. Both major candidates sought to get the endorsement of Perón; and Frondizi finally succeeded in doing so, by means of a letter addressed to Peronista voters indicating that Perón urged them to vote for the UCR Intransigente nominee.

Various explanations have been given for Perón's endorsement of Frondizi. The UCR Intransigente candidate was accused of having made a deal with the exiled leader, making various promises in return for his support. This seems unlikely, since Frondizi was already committed to a program of amnesty for Peronista political prisoners, the reestablishment of a single trade union body, a sizable general wage increase, and other things wanted by the Peronistas. Perón's own explanation to this writer for his support of Frondizi was that he felt that Balbín would not be capable of staying in office for very long and that when he was overthrown, Frondizi would remain "as a hope for the people," whereas if Frondizi was elected, whether or not he fell, Perón would remain as "the only hope of the people."[2]

It is questionable whether Perón's support actually was responsible for Frondizi's election. The Intransigente candidate had already gained the backing not only of his own party but also of the Communists, some of the right-wing nationalists, and an appreciable militant Catholic element, and would probably have won in any case. It seems unlikely that all of the Peronistas would have cast blank ballots if they had been told to by Perón—which may be an additional reason for his giving his support to Frondizi—and if they had had to choose on their own between the two major candidates, most of them would undoubtedly have voted for the Intransigente nominee. In any case Perón's endorsement assured Frondizi of a sufficiently large margin of victory that elements in the armed forces hostile to him were unable to deny his right to take office, which he did on May 1, 1958.

The Radicals in the Frondizi Administration

Upon taking office Frondizi felt that he had two major tasks: to get the economy functioning adequately once again and to get the Peronistas reincorporated as active members of the body politic. But before he could do these things, he had to pay off political debts acquired during the campaign. He paid off the Nationalists with diplomatic and cabinet positions; he paid off Catholic supporters with a law authorizing the establishment of Catholic universities; and he paid off the Peronistas with a 60 percent general increase in wages over levels of early 1956.

With these things out of the way, Frondizi set about trying to bring about recovery of the economy, which suffered from deterioration of much of its capital equipment—particularly in transportation and public utilities—from rampant inflation, from decline in agricultural output, and from a variety of other ills that had been accumulating since the Great Depression. At the end of 1958 he launched a program of price stabilization and economic development.

The price stabilization program, which got most international attention, was orthodox, seeking to freeze wages and allow prices to be brought into line through competition while restricting credit and creating a single exchange rate for the peso. By the end of 1961 this program had substantially slowed the increase in living costs and had completely stabilized the international price of the peso.

Frondizi's economic development program included many things. He encouraged extensive foreign and domestic investment in industrialization, resulting in the establishment of a national automobile industry and a heavy chemical industry. He established a new system of service contracts in the oil industry, which allowed foreign firms to seek and exploit oil on behalf of the government firm YPF and in a very short time converted Argentina from a major petroleum importer into a net exporter. He settled an expropriation issue with the public utility firm serving greater Buenos Aires, setting up a mixed company and assuring sizable new investment in expanding electric power resources for the capital. He began a large road building program, financed in part by foreign loans, and a process of reorganization, rationalization, and recapitalization of the railroads.

However, although various aspects of his economic program, particularly the price stabilization effort, aroused strong opposition, it was Frondizi's attempt to bring the Peronistas back to participation in normal politics that proved his undoing. To this end he attempted several strategies in succession. When entering office Frondizi apparently foresaw the possibility of the formation of a new political movement that would incorporate the Peronistas, the Intransigente Radicals, and smaller groups as the new Left party in national politics. However, this proved fruitless because Perón was not at all willing to turn his following over to Frondizi or anyone else, and most Peronistas remained loyal to him.

Frondizi then turned to a policy of allowing the Peronistas to organize so-called neo-Peronista parties on a strictly provincial basis, at the same time pushing through Congress a law for proportional representation that would assure the Peronistas only their mathematically accurate share of seats in Congress and provincial legislatures, instead of running the possibility that under the old Sáenz Peña arrangement they would get from one-third to two-thirds of the seats in the Chamber of Deputies and provincial legislatures. However, when provincial elections late in 1961 seemed to show that Peronistas were voting in large numbers for the UCR Intransigente candidates, he suspended action on the proportional representation law, which never got out of the Senate.

This was perhaps Frondizi's major political miscalculation. Its disastrous nature became evident in March 1962, when elections in 10 provinces, combined with congressional elections, all under the Sáenz Peña Law, gave majorities to neo-Peronista candidates in half of these provinces and gave the Peronistas about one-third of the seats in the lower house of Congress.

In the meantime, during the nearly four years of the Frondizi administration, the Unión Cívica Radical del Pueblo constituted the major opposition group in Congress and in most provincial governments. The UCR del Pueblo leaders were exceedingly hostile to the Frondizi administration, charging the president with being "too clever" and "deceitful" and with "betrayal." They opposed the price stabilization program, the government's oil policies, and other elements of the administration's program.[3]

The Radicals in the Guido Period

As a result of the elections of March 1962, Arturo Frondizi was overthrown by the military. He was succeeded by José María Guido, president of the Senate and next in line to succeed after the resignation of Vice-President Alejandro Gómez in November 1958. Most of

THE RADICALS

the period of Guido's administration was one of immense political confusion, in which rival factions of the military fought for control, the economic situation again worsened, and the future of the country seemed very cloudy.

New elections were finally called for July 1963, and they resulted in a triumph for the UCR del Pueblo and a splintering of the UCR Intransigente. As in the 1958 election, the UCR del Pueblo was the political group most favored by the military element then in power. It named a relative unknown, Arturo Illia, as its candidate for president; and he ran without backing from any other party or group.

The Intrasigente situation was much more complex. Ex-President Frondizi (who during this period was kept under arrest but seems to have had little difficulty in maintaining contact with his supporters) returned to the idea of forming a new broad political movement including the Intransigente Radicals, Peronistas, and others and joined with Perón in establishing the Frente Nacional y Popular. It vainly sought a candidate who would be acceptable to the government; and when all of those it chose were denied the right to run, Frondizi joined Perón in urging his supporters to cast blank ballots.

In the meantime, however, the leaders of the Unión Cívica Radical Intransigente who were free and in control of the party's machinery balked at their deposed leader's maneuvers. They finally held a national convention that nominated Oscar Alende as its candidate for president. This nomination met no opposition from the government.

Elections were finally held on July 7. The UCR del Pueblo nominee, Arturo Illia, received 26 percent of the popular vote, while the UCR Intransigente candidate, Alende, received 17 percent. The blank votes, called for by Arturo Frondizi as well as by Perón, accounted for only 18 percent of the total. Although Illia did not receive enough electoral votes to assure his victory, he subsequently won backing from a sufficient number of electors pledged to other candidates to give him the presidency.[4]

Radicalism Under Illia and the
Military Regime

Illia was inaugurated in October 1963. At first his regime was met with a feeling of relief by much of the population, including the armed forces, tired of the uncertainty and confusion of the Guido period. However, Illia's task was not an easy one. The economy was again in bad shape, with inflation on the rise and economic development leveling off. Furthermore, the government met intense resistance from the Peronista-dominated labor movement, which made no secret of its effort to bring about the overthrow of the regime by harassment and politically motivated strikes.

Illia's technique of government was to do little. With the exception of reversing the Frondizi oil policy, his administration took no very drastic measures. It let various labor situations drag on until the Peronista union leaders grew tired or were forced by their members to order a return to work. No extensive programs were undertaken, the president seeming content to try to hold on until his term of office had expired.

However, Illia was overthrown by the same factor that resulted in Frondizi's ouster: the possibility of a Peronista victory in elections. In March 1967 provincial and congressional elections were scheduled, and the possibility of the Peronista victories of 1962 being repeated seemed very great. The military and many anti-Peronista civilians had made it very clear that they would not permit this, and this time the soldiers moved before the elections rather than waiting until they had been held. On June 28, 1966, Illia was ousted by another coup; and two days later General Juan Carlos Ongania was installed as president.

This time the military leaders were not committed to an early return to constitutional government. On the contrary, they legally dissolved all political parties and indicated that they would remain in power for at least a decade. Among the parties dissolved were both factions of the Radical Party.

In spite of legal dissolution both the UCR del Pueblo and the UCR Intransigente continued to exist. The Radicales del Pueblo continued to be particularly active after the overthrow of Illia, and their meetings were on various occasions broken up by the police and military. Neither Radical faction was willing to accept a legal decree ending its existence.

Ongania was overthrown in mid-1970, with General Roberto Levingston being substituted by the military group that controlled the regime. Nine months later the leader of this group, General Alejandro Lanusse, removed Levingston and assumed the presidency himself. Soon afterward he announced his intention of bringing about the reestablishment of a democratically elected government.

In the face of this situation and the legal reestablishment of political parties, the two major factions of the Radicals were reorganized. The UCR del Pueblo and the Peronistas became the main elements in a coalition known as La Hora del Pueblo, which brought consistent pressure on Lanusse to move forward with his program of redemocratization. The UCR Intransigente also revived, although staying outside of any alliances. Similarly, the group originally organized by Frondizi in 1963, the Movimiento De Integración y Desarrollo, was also reorganized. Naturally the future of all the

THE RADICALS

Radical factions depended upon whether the elections scheduled for March 1973 were actually held.

Organizational Structure of the Radicals

For several generations the Radicals have had local party groups throughout the country. In the larger cities there were Radical headquarters in each ward that housed party clubs, to which local party members belonged, as well as "Ateneos Radicales," subsidiary organizations that have sometimes maintained libraries, have conducted public lectures, and have organized other party functions not directly connected with electoral activities. In the smaller towns and villages the Radical Party headquarters was often the home of the local party "caudillo," to which anyone repaired if he had Party business to transact.

On a national level there were two principal party organizations. One was the National Convention, which met every year (sometimes less frequently) and consisted of delegates elected from local party units throughout the country. Its function was supposedly to set national policy and to name party candidates for president and vice-president.

The other national body of the Unión Cívica Radical was the National Committee, generally chosen by a referendum of party members, with delegates representing every province. The presiding officer of this group, which met periodically throughout the year, was the party president.

On a provincial level the UCR organization was largely the same as on the national basis. Provincial congresses met periodically, and Provincial committees presided over the day-to-day activities of the party.

With the advent of the Perón regime, the national, provincial, and local organization of the party became somewhat more complex. Functional groups were organized that were responsible to the national and provincial committees for their day-to-day activities, and ultimately to the national and provincial conventions of the party. These included a Trade Union Committee and a Women's Committee. Even earlier a Juventud Radical, which was particularly active in the universities, sought to arouse party support among the country's youth. Under Arturo Frondizi's leadership the party also developed study groups to prepare various parts of the program for a prospective Radical government.

With the development of the Unionista and Intransigente factions of the party, the local Radical clubs usually were affiliated with one faction or the other. In a province like Córdoba, where Intransigencia

Nacional was overwhelmingly predominant, virtually only one faction had local clubs. In contrast, in Buenos Aires all existing groups within the party were likely to be represented by neighborhood clubs, each with its own headquarters.[5]

CHILE

Early Decades of the Chilean Radical Party

The Partido Radical of Chile was established in the 1860s by a group of left-wing Liberals disturbed by the apparent willingness of many Liberals to form compromises and alliances with their Conservative opponents. Its major stress was on anticlericalism, the party's opposition to the established privileges of the Roman Catholic Church.

Among the founders of the Radical Party were a number of people who had been associated with the Sociedad de Igualdad, a utopian Socialist group formed in the late 1840s by Francisco Bilbao, a Chilean who had spent a number of years in France, where he had had close contact with the utopians there. They took particular interest in the country's artisans and craftsmen and led in the formation of mutual benefit societies and organizations designed to provide adult education for the country's workers.

The Partido Radical found particular favor among the country's lower middle class. It was also particularly strong among the German immigrants who had established their homes in the southern parts of the Central Valley, most of whom were Protestants. They were particularly attracted by the party's opposition to the Catholic Church.

During the period of parliamentary government, following the revolution of 1891, which overthrew Liberal President José Balmaceda, the Radicals took part in the game of political "musical chairs," in the process of which cabinets were changed every few months. In a number of these cabinets the Radical Party had members.

During the great political crisis surrounding the presidential election of 1920, the Radical Party supported the candidacy of Arturo Alessandri. They constituted a major element in the Alessandri camp; and Pedro Aguirre Cerda, a young Radical leader, became the first prime minister under Alessandri. Although his cabinet was soon overthrown by the Congress, still controlled largely by Conservative and allied elements, the Radicals continued to cooperate with Alessandri until he was overthrown in September 1924.

The Ibáñez Dictatorship and Afterward

During the period between 1925 and 1931, when Carlos Ibáñez presided over the country's only 20th-century dictatorship, the Radicals were sorely divided. Some of them, including Juan Antonio Ríos, were among the supporters of the Ibáñez regime. Other Radical leaders went into exile, along with ex-President Alessandri and leaders of other parties.

President Ibáñez' last minister of interior was Juan Esteban Montero, a Radical, who played an important part in convincing the dictator to give up the reins of power in July 1931. Subsequently Montero became a candidate for president, with the support of the Radical Party, and was successful in the elections held in November 1931. His administration was a turbulent and short-lived one, marked by a naval mutiny and several violent labor disputes. He was finally overthrown on June 4, 1932, by a coup that resulted in the establishment of the so-called socialist republic, headed first by Colonel Marmaduque Grove and subsequently by Ibáñez' former ambassador to the United States, Carlos Dávila.

With the overthrow of the socialist republic by the military in September 1932, presidential elections were again called. In this contest the Radicals once again threw their support behind Arturo Alessandri, who was the nominee not only of that party but also of a faction of the Liberals and various other groups. The Alessandri candidacy was successful.

During the first years of the second Alessandri administration, the Radicals participated in his government. However, the increasingly conservative inclinations of the Alessandri administration, particularly its patronage of the right-wing militia group known as the Milicia Republicana and the financial and economic policies presided over by Minister of Finance Gustavo Ross Santa María, finally alienated the Radicals, who went into the opposition in April 1934.

Once in the opposition, the Radicals gravitated increasingly toward an alliance with the extreme Left, consisting principally of the Socialist and Communist parties. The Left had formed the Frente de Izquierda, which in 1936 was converted into the country's first Popular Front by the incorporation of the Radical Party and the new Confederation of Workers of Chile.[6]

During the last months of the Alessandri regime, the Popular Front won several by-election victories. Its chances of defeating the forces of the Alessandri government, consisting largely of the Conservative and Liberal parties, and backing the candidacy of Gustavo Ross Santa María for president, seemed good.

When the time came to choose a nominee for the Popular Front in the 1938 election, the left-wing alliance faced a crisis. The

Socialists strongly favored the candidacy of their most outstanding figure, Marmaduque Grove, the party's lifetime president. However, the Radicals were equally insistent on the nomination of someone from their own ranks.

The die was cast by the Communists. After first toying with the idea of backing ex-dictator Carlos Ibáñez, the Communists endorsed the candidacy of Radical leader Pedro Aguirre Cerda. As a result the convention of the Popular Front accepted the name of Aguirre Cerda after the Socialists had withdrawn their original suggestion of Grove.

In the election of November 1938, Pedro Aguirre Cerda won a very narrow victory, largely due to the support he received from Carlos Ibáñez and his followers in the last weeks of the campaign. Although there were extensive rumors that Aguirre Cerda might not be permitted to take office, he was inaugurated in December 1938.

The Radical Regimes

The inauguration of Pedro Aguirre Cerda marked the beginning of 14 years of Radical Party rule. By this time the Radical Party was the principal political representative of the Chilean middle class, particularly of the country's government employees. From the point of view of political philosophy the Partido Radical was a heterogeneous group. It included a left wing that succeeded in formally committing the party to a policy of democratic socialism. However, other elements, particularly landlords of the southern part of the Central Valley, had little to distinguish them from their Liberal and Conservative neighbors except, perhaps, their opposition to the temporal influence of the Catholic Church.

During the administration of Aguirre Cerda, the government represented the Popular Front; and both the Radical and Socialist parties were represented in the government. During this period, which ended with the death of the president at the end of 1941, the administration had a number of accomplishments to its credit. The Chilean Development Corporation was established, and the administration launched a large-scale program for the industrialization of the country. The government gave strong support to the unionization of urban workers, and most of them were brought into the labor movement for the first time.

With the death of Aguirre Cerda a new election was necessary. The Radicals named Juan Antonio Ríos, who also enjoyed the backing of the Socialists, Communists, and some of the Liberals, led by ex-President Arturo Alessandri. His opponent was the perpetually hopeful Carlos Ibáñez, but Ríos was the victor and the Radical-dominated regime continued.

THE RADICALS

A new crisis was presented by the death of Ríos early in 1946. Another Radical, Alfredo Duhalde, assumed the acting presidency pending the selection of a new chief executive. However, the Duhalde administration followed policies that resulted in a split in the Radical Party.

Upon assuming the acting presidency Duhalde was faced with a serious labor situation. The last months of World War II and the period just thereafter were marked by a series of wildcat strikes, particularly in the mining areas. Although the government at first took little action, Duhalde decided to crack down on two of the offending mine workers unions. The result was a general strike led by the Confederation of Workers of Chile. Although this walkout was suspended by the Confederation after a few days, a new general strike of unlimited duration would be called if the government did not agree to restore the legal recognition to the two unions that had been suspended.

This new walkout split both the labor confederation and the Radical Party. A few hours before the strike was to begin, Duhalde called in the leaders of the Socialist faction of the Confederation, including Secretary-General Bernardo Ibáñez, and agreed to restore the legality of the two suspended unions and to make several other concessions, as well as to form a new ministry with participation of the Socialists, if Ibáñez would call off the strike. He agreed to do so and made a radio speech from the president's office, urging his followers not to walk out.

Communist opponents of Bernardo Ibáñez within the Confederation refused to call off the proposed general strike. Furthermore, they declared Ibáñez deposed as leader of the labor confederation. At the same time there was strong opposition within the Radical Party to the actions that had been taken by Duhalde.

As a result of Ríos's death a new presidential election was called. The majority of the Radical Party nominated Gabriel González Videla, a party leader who had a long record of cooperation with the Communist Party. His candidacy was endorsed by the Communists, who played a major role in his campaign.

The Radical faction led by Duhalde broke with its party and formed a rival Partido Radical Democrático. It first nominated Duhalde for president, with the support of the Socialists. However, only a short time before the election Duhalde withdrew his candidacy, and the Socialists were forced to put up their own nominee in the person of Bernardo Ibáñez.

González Videla won a plurality of the popular vote. However, he did not gain a majority, and the election was thrown into Congress. There, as the result of an arrangement with ex-President Arturo Alessandri, the Liberals threw their support to González Videla, assuring his election.

González Videla took office early in November 1946. His first cabinet, which stayed in office for approximately five months, consisted of members of the Radical, Liberal, and Communist parties. During this period the Communists gave every appearance of being the dominant element in the regime. They encouraged their faction of the Confederation of Workers of Chile to press the government for increasingly greater concessions and succeeded in using governmental influence to force their Socialist rivals out of control of important unions. They resorted to violence against Socialist and anarchist opponents, even assassinating minor Socialist leaders.

During all of this period, González Videla gave little indication publicly that he had any doubts about the role of his Communist colleagues. However, he was not unaware of the parallels between what was happening in Chile and what was occurring at the same time in several East European countries, where the Communists were using force and threats of force to intimidate their Socialist and Peasant party colleagues in the governments; and he was increasingly afraid that they might begin to use the same tactics against him and his party.

González Videla's opportunity to dispense with his Communist associates came as a result of municipal elections held early in April 1947. These showed serious losses by the Liberal and Radical parties and gains by the Communists, as well as by the opposition Conservative and Socialist parties. As a result, the Liberals withdrew from the government, followed by the resignation of the Radical ministers. González Videla had to request the resignations of the Communist members of his cabinet.

In the weeks that followed, González Videla was convinced that the Communists were attempting to provoke the overthrow of his regime. They launched a series of strikes, particularly in the mines; and the president mobilized the military to break these walkouts. At the same time the Communists called with increasing violence for the ousting of the president.[7]

The Radical president soon moved into virulent opposition to his former Communist collaborators. He sponsored the passage in 1948 of the so-called Law for the Defense of Democracy, which outlawed the Communist Party and imposed extensive restrictions on their ability to function legally in the organized labor movement.

The González Videla administration was marked by a considerable increase in the rhythm of inflation, which had been a serious problem throughout most of the Radical period. The regime was also increasingly wracked by scandals and by rumors and certain proof of corruption in the government. By the end of the term in office of the third Radical Party chief executive, the party had been widely discredited among the Chilean electorate.

The Radicals After 1952

The result of this situation was the ignominious defeat of the Radicals in the presidential election of 1952. The victor was ex-President Carlos Ibáñez, who ran as an Independent, with the backing of only of one faction of the Socialists and a group of minor parties. The Radical nominee, Pedro Alfonso, came in a poor third behind Ibáñez and the Liberal-Conservative candidate, Arturo Matte Larrain.

In spite of this defeat the Radicals remained the largest single party, as indicated in congressional elections through the 1950's. However, it failed to elect its candidate in the presidential elections of 1958, when Radical nominee Luis Bossay again ran a poor third to the victor, Jorge Alessandri (backed by Conservatives and Liberals) and Salvador Allende (supported by the left-wing Popular Action Front.

The Radicals lost their position as the country's largest party in the municipal elections of 1962, when they were surpassed by the rapidly growing Christian Democrats. The Radicals even lost ground in the largely Protestant German municipalities in the southern part of the Central Valley, where they had constituted the almost unchallenged dominant party for several generations.

The 1964 presidential election and the 1965 congressional one constituted debacles for the Radical Party. In the first of these, the Radicals at first formed an alliance with the Conservatives and Liberals, behind a right-wing Radical Julio Durán, as presidential nominee. However, when this coalition suffered a severe by-election defeat, Durán resigned his candidacy and the Liberals and Conservatives shifted their backing to the Christian Democratic candidate, Eduardo Frei. However, Durán subsequently reentered the race, this time solely as the nominee of the Radicals—a move apparently designed largely to prevent Radical votes from going to the left-wing opponent of Frei, Socialist Senator Salvador Allende. Durán came in a very poor third behind the victorious Frei and Allende.

In the Congressional election of March 1965 the Radicals also did poorly. They not only saw themselves displaced as the largest party in Congress but also saw the Christian Democrats do the almost unheard-of thing of gaining an absolute majority in the Chamber of Deputies.

There was some speculation after the election of Frei that he might seek an alliance with the Radical Party. However, both the president's desire to have a totally Christian Democratic regime and the Radicals' reticence to back a government they believed to be Church-oriented militated against this. As a result the Radicals soon rejoined forces with the Socialist and Communists against the Christian Democratic regime.

At the end of 1969 a new left-wing alliance, the Unidad Popular, was established among the Communists, Socialists, Radicals, and a dissident Christian Democratic group. However, the prospect of the new alliance had resulted in a new split in the Radical Party, with more conservative elements headed by Julio Durán withdrawing to form a new party, Democracia Radical.[8]

Unidad Popular won the presidential election of September 1970, its candidate, Salvador Allende, receiving a slight plurality over Jorge Alessandri, nominee of the Partido Nacional, formed in 1966 by the old Liberal and Conservative parties. When Allende took office in November, the Radical Party received three posts in the new cabinet.

However, return to the government did not halt the disintegration of the Radical Party. In September 1971 a new split in the party took place when a number of prominent party leaders, including about a third of the Radical member of Congress, broke with the Partido Radical in protest against what they alleged was a "Marxist" program approved by a party congress. They formed the Partido de Izquierda Radical (PIR). With the reorganization of Allende's cabinet in January 1972, both the Partido Radical and the PIR were represented. However, two months later the PIR withdrew from Unidad Popular and the government, and sought to regroup most of the Radicals in the opposition.[9]

By the early 1970s the Radical Party has been reduced to a relatively minor element in national politics. In the municipal elections of April 1971, the party saw its share of the total vote reduced to only about 8 percent, a bit more than half of their showing in the most recent congressional election. The split of September 1971 would undoubtedly result in reducing the party's standing even more.

The possibility of restoring the Radical Party to a major force in national politics seemed to depend upon two things. First, it would be affected by whether the Allende government maintains its popularity and continues to follow a policy of permitting a multiparty system. Second, it would be determined by the ability of the Radicals to reestablish some degree of unity in their much-divided ranks.

PART II
THE LATIN AMERICAN SOCIALISTS

INTRODUCTION

Democratic Socialist parties, that is, parties that have been ideologically more less closely aligned with the parties of the so-called Second, or Socialist, International, have existed in many of the Latin American countries. The older ones date from the last decades of the 19th century.

Only a minority of these democratic Socialist parties have actually belonged to the Second International, in the various phases in which the International has existed since it was originally established in 1889. However, a sizable number have been adherents of the International's (changing) philosophy.

With one or two exceptions the democratic Socialist parties have not developed into major parties. Furthermore, in recent decades the group as a whole has tended to decline in importance, some of the parties disappearing altogether and others undergoing damaging schisms, and most have lost influence in the labor movement and other groups in which they were formerly important.

As a group the democratic Socialist parties have suffered from several handicaps. Some of them have had their roots in immigrant groups; and as these elements of the population have declined in importance, the Socialists have tended to decline with them, finding it very difficult to adapt their attitudes, organizations, and philosophy to meet the needs of the postimmigrant population. To a greater or lesser degree this was the fate of the Socialists in Argentina, Uruguay, Brazil, and Cuba.

Even more generally the Socialist parties have tended to suffer from an inferiority complex vis-à-vis the Communists. The Socialists have usually considered themselves Marxists and parties of the Left, and have frequently found the competition of the Communists to be embarrassing. On many occasions they have felt that the surest way for them to make clear their own Leftism was to ally themselves with the Communists, whose leftist bona fides was seldom challenged. Such alliances have usually been very damaging to the Socialists, who have generally been more loosely organized and less disciplined than their Communist "partners."

During the 1950s and 1960s several of the democratic Socialist parties tended to be converted, more or less thoroughly, to a Marxist-Leninist philosophy. Even more frequently they were plagued by factions that were pro-Communist, or were even infiltrated by agents of the Communists, and which provoked schisms within the Socialist ranks.

In recent decades the democratic Socialist parties in several countries have been faced with other left-wing opponents, including national revolutionary and Christian Democratic parties. The former are parties that have arisen out of the peculiar circumstances of their respective countries, with little stimulation from outside. They have been frankly nationalist—an attitude that the supposedly internationalist Socialist parties sometimes found it difficult to adopt. The national revolutionary parties in particular have tended to occupy the position in the national political spectrum of several countries that might otherwise have been taken by the democratic Socialists.

Despite the decline of the influence of democratic Socialists in the politics of Latin America, they are worthy of some considerable attention. They were among the first political groups to try to represent the new socioeconomic interests engendered by modern economic development, and particularly to represent the urban working class. They have also been of some continuing significance in a number of countries. Finally, since quite a few parties that have had little in common with democratic Socialism have over the last half century tended to use names that seemed to imply they advocated democratic Socialism, it is perhaps of some value to discuss the parties that have been or still are in the democratic Socialist tradition.

CHAPTER

5

THE SOCIALISTS IN ARGENTINA

The Socialist movement of Argentina had its origins principally among the immigrants from Spain, Italy, and other countries who began to stream into the country in the last quarter of the 19th century. Although there had been native utopian Socialists in Argentina earlier in the century, among whom the most prominent was Esteban Echeverría, they did not leave behind any permanent Socialist organization.

Some of the immigrants who entered Argentina with the expansion of its grazing and grain-growing economy had participated in trade unions and radical political groups in their native countries. Some of them were anarcho-syndicalist followers of Bakunin and Kropotkin; others were Marxists. In both cases, when they settled in Argentina, they sought to transplant the ideas and organizations that they had held and belonged to in their old countries.

The Marxist immigrants established small Socialist circles and groups in Buenos Aires and other cities. They were able to recruit some supporters among native Argentines as well, the most prominent of whom was a young medical doctor, Juan B. Justo. He had begun his political career as a member of the Unión Cívica, which had led the abortive revolution of 1890 against the domination of the country by the landed oligarchy. However, he had become disillusioned in the men and policies of Unión Cívica and its successor, the Unión Cívica Radical (UCR), and felt that a more fundamental program of reform was needed.

It was working-class Socialists, principally immigrants, who were responsible for the first celebration of May Day in Argentina. This took place in 1890, the year after May 1 had been proclaimed the international Labor Day; the immediate result of this May Day celebration was the establishment of the first central labor organization of Argentina, the Federación Obrera de la República Argentina (FORA). FORA led a fitful existence throughout the last decade of the 19th century.

In 1894 Juan B. Justo undertook the establishment of the first Socialist newspaper in Spanish in Buenos Aires. Although the German Socialists of the Argentine capital had published Vorwaerts, and other foreign-language Socialist papers were printed from time to time, Justo's La vanguardia was the first Socialist paper published in the national language of Argentina. Seventy-five years later the paper was still being issued on a regular basis.

The Socialist Party of Argentina was established in 1896, under the leadership of Juan B. Justo. It was formed as a result of the merger of most of the foreign-language Socialist groups and small native Argentine Socialist clubs, and at its inception it had only a few hundred members.

PHILOSOPHY OF THE SOCIALIST PARTY

The new party was formally Marxist. It accepted the materialist conception of history, and proclaimed the "class struggle" and the necessity for the workers to unite to seek control of the state. It proclaimed the need for international working-class solidarity and rejected the conceptions of nationalism and patriotism.

The internationalist philosophy of the Socialist Party, and the fact that much of its support was drawn from the immigrant population, gave the Argentine Socialists a peculiar position in national political life. One of the basic controversies in Argentine politics since at least the first half of the 19th century had been that between the "Europeanizers" and the "Americans." The former group insisted upon the need both for heavy immigration from Europe and for strengthening the European bases of Argentine culture. The latter stressed the uniqueness of the mixed-blood Argentine population and the necessity for strengthening the national interests of Argentina against the economic, political, and cultural influences of Europe.

After the middle of the 19th century the principal spokesmen for the Europeanizing element were the political leaders, including Bartolomé Mitre, Domingo Faustino Sarmiento, and Nicolás Avalleneda who were largely responsible for fostering the grazing and graingrowing economy that characterized Argentina by the 1890s and also had been largely responsible for stimulating railroad construction, a public school system, and mass immigration. Thereafter the Conservative Party, which principally represented the large landowners, became the major exponent of this Europeanizing tradition. The Unión Cívica Radical, on the other hand, became the major exponent of the Americanist view.

Although the Socialists were opposed to the landlord control of the national economy and of politics, they tended to agree with the Conservatives' Europeanizing position. They consistently stressed the need for "educating" the Argentine working class and regarded the class struggle of Argentina as largely an extension of the same phenomenon in Europe. They regarded appeals to Argentine national spirit as demagoguery and reaction.

The Socialists' internationalism was also reflected in their position on certain economic issues. Juan B. Justo, the party's founder, was a particularly eloquent advocate of free trade. He attacked any ideas of establishing tariffs and other protective measures for Argentine national industry as designed only to enrich a privileged group, and as tending to raise the cost of living of the country's workers.[1]

During the first three or four decades of the Socialists Party's history, when a large proportion of the Argentine working class consisted of immigrants, this Europeanizing or internationalist tendency of the Socialists was an aid to their expansion. However, by the 1930s, when the workers consisted mainly of sons of immigrants and of migrants from the interior of Argentina, it was one of the factors that undermined the strength of the Argentine Socialist Party.

EARLY HISTORY OF THE SOCIALIST PARTY

In 1896 the Socialists participated in an electoral campaign for the first time, nominating their first candidates for Congress in an election for half of the members of the Chamber of Deputies. They put up five nominees, headed by Juan B. Justo, all of them in Buenos Aires. Of the 12,793 votes cast, the Socialist Party was credited with 138.[2]

Two years later the Socialists participated once again in Congressional elections in the city of Buenos Aires, this time being credited with only 105 votes, even though they put up 15 nominees. There is little way of knowing how many votes the Socialists actually received, since the whole electoral process at this time was widely recognized to be fraudulent. Jacinto Oddone, the historian of the Socialist Party, cites an editorial in the daily newspaper La nación after the 1898 election that notes: "From the point of view of prestidigitation, the Sunday elections were something which eclipsed all precedents, since it was a grotesque mockery . . . since there could be no struggle or doubt about the result that would be produced at the polls by this unlimited falsification."[3]

It was not until 1904 that the Socialists finally elected their first member to the Chamber of Deputies. In that campaign the party named a brilliant and eloquent young lawyer, Alfredo Palacios, as its candidate in the heavily working-class port sections of Buenos Aires. He was elected, receiving 840 votes and defeating several other nominees, including some who had national reputations.[4]

Alfredo Palacios was a very active member of the Chamber of Deputies. During his first four years in office he was successful in getting a number of the bills he introduced passed by Congress. These included a progressive inheritance tax, a law designating Sunday as a day of rest, prohibition of the establishment of water meters in slum houses, exemption of workers' cooperatives from a 7,000-peso license fee, regulation of work of women and children, and measures against prostitution. Other measures he introduced were not enacted by Congress, such as his bills to establish the eight-hour workday, to eliminate the death penalty, to legalize divorce, and to establish a workmen's compensation system. Palacios was also active in questioning various ministers summoned to appear before Congress, including those of interior, public works and the navy.[5]

However, it was not only in the capital city that the Socialist Party was active in elections. The party put up candidates in more than a dozen municipalities of the province of Buenos Aires, as well as in municipal and provincial elections in Santa Fé, Santiago del Estero, and Entre Ríos.[6]

The Socialists did not by any means confine themselves to electoral activities. They were a major element in the trade union movement during the party's early years. Twice during the 1890s the Federación Obrera de la República Argentina, which had been set up in 1890, was revived. In 1901 still another labor congress established the Federación Obrera Argentina, which the Socialists also controlled. However, in the following year, at the second congress of the FOA, anarcho-syndicalist delegates seized control. They remained in control of the organization, changed its name in 1904 to Federación Obrera Regional Argentina, and in 1905 imposed on FORA a statement of principles that committed the organization to the philosophy of "anarchist Communism."

Even before the Socialists formally lost control of the FOA, a group of unionists who objected to the influence of the anarcho-syndicalists in the federation withdrew to establish a rival organization, the Unión General de Trabajadores. The Socialist periodical, La vanguardia, denounced this move as "sectarian." However, when the anarcho-syndicalists took control of the second congress of the FOA, the Socialist trade unionists generally withdrew from the organization and threw their support behind the constituent congress of the UGT, which met in November 1902.

The predominantly Socialist Unión General de Trabajadores existed until February 1909. In the interim apolitical unionists, who

were influenced by the ideas of the Confédération Général du Travail
of France, gained a dominant position in the UGT, displacing the
elements loyal to the Socialist Party. In February 1909 a congress
called as a result of an attempt to unify the two contending labor groups,
FORA and UGT, established still another union group, the Confederación
Obrera Regional Argentina (CORA). The UGT leaders agreed to merge
with this new group, which was of syndicalist rather than Socialist
orientation.[7]

As a result of the establishment of CORA, the Socialists were
left without any national trade union group under their control. Almost
two decades were to pass before the Socialist Party once again controlled a national labor confederation.

The Socialists were also active in the cooperative field. They
were the most important factor in developing the consumer cooperative
movement, and most cooperatives were usually closely associated
with trade union organizations. The most famous of the cooperative
organizations established during the first decade of the 20th century
under the influence of the Socialists was El Hogar Obrera, a housing
cooperative in Buenos Aires, of which Juan B. Justo was the first
president.[8] For half a century the Socialists remained a major factor
in the nation's cooperative movement.

Finally, the Socialists were active among tenant farmers and
small landholders in the provinces of Santa Fé and Buenos Aires.
These farmers, most of whom were immigrants, organized to resist
excessive rents and low prices for their grain. They went on strike
in 1912, and this walkout was supported by Juan B. Justo and other
Socialist leaders. Out of it emerged the Federación Agraria Argentina,
which for many years was at least partly under Socialist leadership.[9]

SOCIALIST GROWTH AND DIVISION

By the end of the first decade of the 20th century, the Socialists
had established themselves as a significant element in national politics. Because of the Radical Party policy of boycotting elections, on
the grounds that their results were determined by the government
before the votes were cast, the Socialist Party was the only important
group that competed at the polls with the dominant Conservative
oligarchy. They mobilized increasing numbers of workers and
intellectuals behind their program and their candidates.

In May 1910 the Socialists and other left-wing elements suffered
a severe setback. In that month Argentina celebrated the centennial
of the beginning of its war of independence. However, the anarcho-
syndicalists, who were violently opposed to patriotic celebrations,
announced a general strike for the week of the celebration. Nationalist

elements took to the streets to break this strike and carried out armed attacks against headquarters and publications of labor and left-wing political groups. Among those attacked were the Socialist Party headquarters and the building where the Socialist paper La vanguardia was published.

Meanwhile, the electoral support for the Socialist Party continued to grow. In 1913 they elected their first national senator, Enrique Iberlucea, a Spanish immigrant, and also placed four members in the Chamber of Deputies. With the reforms in the electoral law brought about by President Roque Sáenz Peña, they continued to expand their following among the voters even though these reforms brought the Radical Party into full participation in the electoral process.

The Sáenz Peña electoral reforms provided guarantees for a secret ballot and assured minority representation in Congress and provincial legislatures. The Radicals first took advantage of this law by offering slates of candidates in 1914 for state governments and the national Congress. In 1916 the Radicals succeeded in electing their candidate, Hipólito Irigoyen, as president.

Although Irigoyen, who was generally regarded as the first middle-class president of Argentina, had considerable popularity among the urban and rural workers, the Socialists did not support him. They criticized his vague program and attributed his announced sympathies for the workers to his being a "demogogue." They were strongly opposed to the nationalism that was a strong ingredient of his popular appeal.

With the outbreak of World War I, the Socialists declared their support for a policy of neutrality. However, the sympathies of most of the principal Socialist leaders tended to be with the Allies. The Conservative government of Argentina also supported a position of neutrality. With the advent of Irigoyen to power in 1916, the government took an even more decidedly neutral position, even though intensified German submarine warfare was affecting Argentine as well as other neutral shipping.

The National Committee of the Socialist Party adopted a stand in opposition to any interruption of diplomatic relations with the Central Powers. However, the Socialist members of Congress supported a motion in favor of such a break with Germany and its allies. As a result, left-wing elements in the party, who had particular support in the party's youth federation, demanded that the Socialist congressmen resign. However, when the matter was put to a referendum of party members, the position of the deputies and senators was upheld.

As a result of this very strong difference of opinion, an element of the left-wing of the party withdrew in January 1918 and formed a rival group, the Partido Socialista Internacionalista. Among its leaders were Victorio Codovilla and Rodolfo Ghioldi. With the establishment of the Communist International in 1919, the PSI became the Argentine affiliate of the Comintern and changed its name to Partido Comunista de Argentina.[10]

Several years before the party split that gave rise to the PSI, the Argentine Socialists had undergone another schism. This was led by Alfredo Palacios, the party's first member of the Chamber of Deputies. Although the incident that served as the excuse for Palacios' expulsion from the Socialist Party in 1915 was his engaging in a duel over an affair of honor, an action forbidden by the party's constitution, this was not the real reason. Palacios had adopted an increasingly nationalistic position, which conflicted with the internationalism preached by the Socialist Party. When the duel incident arose, the party leadership used it to get rid of Palacios, who withdrew to form his own Partido Socialista Argentino. He returned to the old Socialist Party's ranks after the military coup d'état of 1930.

THE SOCIALISTS IN THE 1920s

The Socialist Party made considerable headway during the 1920s. Its electoral backing increased, and it gained more influence in the organized labor movement than it had had in two decades.

The Irigoyen government remained in power between 1916 and 1922 and was succeeded by another Radical Party administration, headed by Marcelo T. de Alvear. Alvear, himself a large landowner, was a man of much more conservative inclinations than his predecessor. However, neither Radical president, even though they were supposed to favor progressive and reformist policies, had been able to enact any substantial body of social and labor legislation that might have favored the country's working classes. As a result, by the mid-1920s there was a considerable degree of disillusion with the Radicals among the workers.

The Socialists were among the major beneficiaries of this disillusion, as became clear in the congressional election of 1924. It gave the Socialist Party a much greater representation in both houses of the national legislature than it had ever had before. The party had 2 senators (Juan B. Justo and Mario Bravo) and 13 deputies.[11]

The election was notable for other reasons. First, the legislators elected by the Socialist Party included a number of leading trade unionists, including Francisco Pérez Leíros, head of the Municipal Workers Federation. Second, it showed that the Socialists had been able to elect representatives in several of the provinces of the interior, in contrast with previous polls, in which Socialist success had been confined almost solely to the city of Buenos Aires and the province of Buenos Aires.

The Socialists also tended to make considerable gains in the trade union movement during the 1920s. During and immediately after World War I anarchist influence in organized labor tended to decline. Furthermore, significant elements of the labor movement turned away from the "direct action" that the anarcho-syndicalists had practiced and toward collective bargaining. Collective bargaining coincided much better than direct action with the attitudes and practices of the Socialists.

In 1922 the Unión Ferroviaria was organized by the categories of railroad workers who were not employed on the locomotives. Those who worked on locomotives had for several decades been organized in another union, La Fraternidad. It was in Unión Ferroviaria and La Fraternidad that the Socialist strength in the labor movement came to be centered. Socialist influence was also notable among the municipal workers, trolley carmen, and the commercial employees, the unions of which were largely organized by Socialist-affiliated trade unionists.

In 1926 the principal unions under Socialist influence came together to form a new central labor organization, the Confederación Obrera Argentina. It immediately took its place as the second largest group of its kind in the republic. Its rivals were the Unión Sindical Argentina, established in 1922 by trade unionists of syndicalist persuasion, and the Federación Obrera Regional Argentina, still of anarchist orientation.

During the remaining years of the decade there were intermittent negotiations among the COA, USA, FORA and a number of autonomous unions, the most important of which was the Graphic Workers Federation, looking toward the formation of a united labor movement. However, no real approach to such unity was achieved until after the establishment of a military dictatorship in September 1930.

The Socialists' progress in the political and trade union fields was imperiled in 1928 by another split in the party's ranks. This division came about over several issues. There was an element in the party that objected to the internationalist philosophy expressed by Juan B. Justo and other major leaders. This same group tended to be critical of the strong opposition of the majority of the party leaders to the landlords' Conservative Party and to the Anti-Personalist Radical party, established by Marcelo T. de Alvear and other relatively conservative opponents of Hipólito Irigoyen; they urged that the Socialists join the Conservatives and Anti-Personalist Radicals to block Irigoyen's obvious ambition to return to the presidency.

The crisis between the two wings of the Socialist Party developed through 1927 and in the early months of 1928. It finally resulted in the exclusion of the anti-Justo faction from the party and its organization of a rival group, the Partido Socialista Independiente.[12]

THE SOCIALISTS IN ARGENTINA 115

Right after this division the PSI seemed to have seriously damaged the Socialist Party. In the election of 1928, the Socialist Party received only 44,500 votes, as against the 49,000 received by the Partido Socialista Independiente. The PSI elected only two deputies, against the eight deputies won by the Independents.[13]

THE SOCIALISTS DURING THE ERA OF "PATRIOTIC FRAUD"

On September 6, 1930, the armed forces overthrew Hipólito Irigoyen, who had been reelected approximately two years before. The excuses for this coup were Irigoyen's failure to deal adequately with the onset of the Great Depression, his general senility, and the widespread corruption of the Radical regime. However, the real reasons were more fundamental.

The coup of 1930 was not a purely military enterprise. The army leaders who were directly responsible had conspired extensively with civilian leaders of various parties. Participants in the conspiracy included the chiefs of the Conservative, Anti-Personalista Radical, and Independent Socialist parties. The coup had the strong backing of the rural landlord class, which had been removed from power by the election of 1916.

The attitude of the two Socialist groups toward this coup differed profoundly. The Independent Socialists participated fully in the conspiracy; and one of their principal figures, Federico Pinedo, became minister of finance in the new government. The Partido Socialista, on the other hand, immediately expressed its opposition to overthrow of the constitutional government and the installation of a military dictatorship.

Between 1930 and 1943 Argentina was ruled by minority governments. During the first two years there was a frankly military dictatorship, and for the rest of the period the administrations owed their "election" to fraud and rested basically on the support of the armed forces. So clearly was this recognized that apologists defended the situation on the grounds that what was practiced was "patriotic fraud," since honest elections, which would have returned the Radical Party to power, would have been a national disaster.

Throughout this period the Socialist Party was one of the principal elements of the opposition. In 1932, when the Radicals were barred from participating in the national election, the Socialist Party joined with the Progressive Democratic Party (a regional group confined largely to the province of Santa Fé) to put up the major opposition ticket to the official candidacy of General Augustín P. Justo. Lisandro de la Torre of the Progressive Democrats was the nominee for president, and Nicolas Repetto (who had succeeded Juan B. Justo as the Socialists' titular leader upon Justo's death in 1928) as candidate for vice-president.

Also in the 1932 election the Socialist Party won the largest representation in Congress that it had ever received or was ever to win again: 42 members of the Chamber of Deputies and 2 senators. The Socialist candidates were elected from the city of Buenos Aires and from the provinces of Buenos Aires, San Luis, and Córdoba.[14] With the return of the Radicals to the electoral scene later in the decade, the Socialist representation in Congress declined sharply. However, the party always maintained some representation from the city of Buenos Aires and one or two of the provinces until the coup d'état of June 4, 1943.

Although the Partido Socialista Independiente virtually ceased to exist as a separate political party, and some of its members returned to the Socialist Party fold, the Partido Socialista suffered another important schism during the 1930s. This was a reflection of left-wing trends notable throughout the world Socialist movement in the years following the rise of Nazism to power in 1933 and the subsequent destruction of the powerful German Social Democratic Party.

As elsewhere, in Argentina the left-wing group that appeared within the Socialist Party demanded a more militant attitude on the part of the party and an acceptance of at least the possibility of the Socialists' use of violence as a means of seizing power, urged an alliance with the Communist Party, and argued in favor of a more friendly attitude toward the Soviet Union. The leftists had considerable support among the Socialist Youth, and their principal spokesman was the young party leader Benito Marianetti, who was influential in the provincial organization in Mendoza.

The majority of the Socialists were not willing to go along with the demands of the left wing. A leading role in the resistance to the left-wing demands was played by Américo Ghioldi, a rising figure in the Socialist organization in Buenos Aires. The left-wingers withdrew or were expelled and formed a rival group, the Partido Socialista Obrero. By the end of the decade most of the principal leaders of the PSO, including Benito Marianetti, had merged the organization with the Communist Party, while some of those unwilling to become Communists returned to the Partido Socialista.

During most of 1930-43 the Socialists had the largest political influence in the organized labor movement. Several of the largest national trade unions, such as the two railroad workers groups, the trolley car workers union, the shoe workers, the commerical employees confederation, and the municipal workers union, were under Socialist leadership; and the party's influence in some other groups, such as the Printing Trades Federation, the Textile Workers Union, and others was considerable.

Socialist unions had joined with those of syndicalist leadership to form the Confederación General del Trabajo, three weeks after the 1930 coup d'état. As a result the Socialist-controlled Confederación Obrera Argentina and the syndicalist-dominated Unión Sindical Argentina ceased to exist. However, no formal congress of the new CGT was held at this time, a statement of principles and an executive committee for the new organization being agreed upon by mutual consent of the participating unions. The principal posts in the CGT were given to the former leaders of the Unión Sindical Argentina.

The alliance of Socialists and syndicalists in the CGT was an uneasy one. It was finally shattered in 1935, when the Socialist trade unionists accused the former Unión Sindical leaders of trying to prevent the holding of the CGT's first congress. The Socialists thereupon established a rival "headquarters" of the CGT and elected their own slate of officers for the organization, at the same time calling the first congress of the organization. After some bitter polemics between the two groups, the syndicalist leaders reconstituted the Unión Sindical Argentina, which continued to exist until the advent of the Peronista regime a decade later. The CGT remained under Socialist control and constituted the largest segment of the labor movement until 1943.

However, the Socialists, although the dominant force in organized labor between 1930 and 1943, did not always act as a united group within the trade unions. They were severely critical of the Communist tactic of establishing "cells" in all unions in which they had members and trying through the disciplined actions of these cells to gain control of the various labor groups. The Socialist Party itself did not follow this policy, which they were later to regret.

Partly as a result of the lack of unity of the Socialists, a new split in the CGT developed late in 1942. At the congress of the Confederación General del Trabajo in December 1942, two lists of candidates for secretary-general and other top positions were offered, both of which were headed by Socialist Party members. So-called List #1 sought to reelect as secretary-general José Domenech of the Unión Ferroviaria. List #2 supported the candidacy of the head of the municipal workers union, Francisco Pérez Leíros, and was also backed by the Socialist-controlled Commercial Workers Confederation. However, List #2 also had the united backing of the Communist Party delegates to the CGT congress.

As a result of this struggle, the CGT broke into two groups, headed respectively by Domenech and Pérez Leíros. The Socialist Party, although generally more sympathetic to the Domenech group, did not take any official position.

THE SOCIALISTS AND THE PERÓN REGIME

This new split in the CGT preceded by only about six months the military coup d'état of June 4, 1943, which put an end to the governments of "patriotic fraud." This coup was engineered by officers who were generally pro-German and feared the possibility of the election early in 1944 of a pro-British president, with the backing of the large landholder element which dominated the Conservative Party.

However, some of the younger officers associated with the new regime soon turned their attention to trying to develop a popular civilian base for the regime and for themselves within it. The principal leader of this group was Colonel Juan Domingo Perón. After some hesitation they turned to the labor movement as the group most likely to be won over to their side. Their assessment of the situation, which proved to be largely correct, was that the organized workers had at best been tolerated by the previous administrations and had not won any significant labor legislation, so that of the larger countries of Latin America, Argentina was lagging far behind in this field. The officers felt, therefore, that if the military regime would offer to back the organizing efforts of the unions and to support them in their collective bargaining negotiations with employers, as well as to enact by decree much of the legislation the workers had long been seeking, it might well be able to build up powerful backing among the organized workers.

For the most part the trade unionists, both Socialists and others, were noncommittal in their discussions with the military men. However, the latter went ahead with their plans, created a new secretariat of labor and social welfare, and placed Colonel Perón at the head of the new organization. During the months that followed the establishment of the secretariat in November 1943, Perón vigorously supported organizing efforts by a large number of unions, brought strong pressure on employers to make sizable concessions in new collective bargaining contracts, and enacted by decree a large number of labor and social security laws.

In the face of this the labor leaders, particularly the Socialist labor leaders, broke ranks. Most of them cooperated with increasing closeness with Perón and his friends in the military government. Those who did so included such Socialist trade unionists as Angel Borlenghi of the Commercial Workers Confederation, the leaders of the Trolley Car Workers Union, and most of those in the Unión Ferroviaria. However, other Socialists, such as José Domenech of Unión Ferroviaria, Alfredo Fidanza of the Shoemakers Union, and Francisco Pérez Leíros of the Municipal Workers Union, rejected such cooperation.

Whatever the attitude of the leaders, the great majority of the rank-and file-workers became sympathetic to Perón. This was particularly the case with the nearly 2 million workers who were brought into the labor movement for the first time between 1943 and 1945. This attitude can be explained in several ways. In the first place, the nature of the Argentine working class had changed very significantly during the preceding several decades. By 1943 a large segment of the workers consisted of sons of immigrants, not of people who themselves had come to Argentina from Europe. In addition, another very large portion of the working class consisted of workers who had migrated to Buenos Aires and other major cities from the interior of the country, as a result of the rapid industrialization, with the concomitant expansion in industrial and other urban jobs, that had been stimulated during the 1930s.

These new groups of workers were receptive to a figure such as Juan Perón. The children of immigrants, to a certain degree they rejected the Socialist, Communist, syndicalist, and anarchist ideas of their parents as something "foreign" to Argentina and associated with "the old country," from which they were eager to differentiate themselves. On the other hand, the migrants from the interior were politically unsophisticated, in many cases never having heard of Socialism and the other doctrines that had been popular in the earlier decades of the labor movement. For them the Argentine labor movement virtually began with Perón, and they were willing to accept whatever philosophical basis for it Perón wanted to offer.

The net effect of these developments was almost complete destruction of the Socialists' influence in organized labor. From 1944 the CGT (which had been reunited by Perón) and most of its constituent unions were Peronista in their loyalties. Although the Socialists continued to have groups of workers in most of the unions and were able to continue to control a few, such as the garment workers and tobacco workers, for some time, they no longer were the major, or perhaps even a major, political factor in organized labor.

Perón used the force of the government to crush the remaining influence of the Socialists and other groups. The Law of Professional Associations was enacted in 1945, requiring that a union wanting to bargain collectively with employers, or to have any dealings with the government, must have legal recognition from the secretariat of labor. Perón used this law to refuse recognition to some of the remaining unions controlled by Socialists—such as the textile workers and the shoe workers—and to organize rival groups that pledged to support him.15

In the meantime the Socialist Party was strongly opposed to Perón. Both before and after his election as president in February 1946, the party attacked him as a profascist and a demagogue, and denied that he had done anything substantial to help the Argentine working class. They also strongly attacked his nationalistic policies, which sought to industrialize the country and repatriate foreign investments. Finally, they attacked the militarism of the regime and its increasingly dictatorial political behavior.

During the 1946 election campaign the Socialist Party supported the Unión Democrática, composed of the Radical, Socialist, and Communist parties and having the backing of the Conservative Party, which opposed Perón's presidential candidacy. For the first time in 40 years the Socialist party failed to elect a single member of congress, and its elected representatives in provincial and municipal posts were reduced to a handful.

As a result of its opposition to the Perón dictatorship, the Socialist Party was severely persecuted. Its newspaper, La vanguardia, was closed by the government; a mob was incited to burn down the party's headquarters, with its exceedingly valuable library; and many party leaders and members were arrested, while others were forced to flee into exile.

The Socialist experience during the Peronista period brought about several fundamental changes in the party. First, the Socialist Party was transformed from an organization with a wide working-class base into one that was preponderantly middle-class. This shift in its constituency also brought an alteration in the ideas of its leadership. Many of them were disillusioned by the apparent ease with which the Argentine workers shifted their loyalties to Perón and became increasingly skeptical of their traditional argument that the proletariat will and should became dominant—economically, socially, and politically.

Another major change in Socialist attitudes was a profound modification of the party's traditional antimilitarist position. In their efforts to help bring about the overthrow of the Perón dictatorship, the Socialist leaders entered into more or less close contact with those in the military who shared their aversion to Perón. Socialists were involved in various military conspiracies against the Perón regime, including the one that finally overthrew him in September 1955. As a result they tended to abandon the blanket condemnation of the military that had been characteristic of the party. The custom of maintaining close contacts with friends in the armed forces, begun under Perón, was continued in the post-Perón period.

THE SOCIALIST IN THE POST-PERON PERIOD

The Socialists emerged from the Perón period badly divided over the issue of how to deal with the Peronistas and the deposed dictator, a situation faced by all of the parties that had opposed Perón during his dictatorship. One group felt that before a democratic regime could be firmly established in Argentina, it was necessary to win the support of a sizable part of the element that had backed the fallen dictator. The other group felt that the job of the Socialist Party was fundamentally that of teaching the Peronistas that they had been wrong to support Perón.

Immediately after the fall of Perón, the Socialists played an important part in national politics. Leaders of the party formed part of the consultative junta that was established as a substitute for Congress during the provisional governments of Generals Eduardo Leonardi and Pedro Aramburu. Socialists regained control of the Municipal Workers Union, were the major element in control of the post-Perón Commercial Workers Confederation, and worked to build up their following in the rest of the labor movement.

In the elections held in 1957 for a new Constitutional Assembly, the Socialists emerged as the fourth largest political group, behind the Peronistas (who cast blank ballots in the election) and the two factions of the Unión Cívica Radical, the UCR del Pueblo and the UCR Intransigente. The Socialist delegates to the assembly worked to obtain the writing of social legislation into the new constitution and for reinforcement of democratic procedures in the new document.

Later in the year a split occurred in the Socialist Party over how to deal with the Peronistas. The group favoring an attempt to win over the Peronistas established the Partido Socialista Argentino, and the more violently anti-Peronista group set up the Partido Socialista Democrático. Both groups put up candidates in the 1958 election, with Alfredo Palacios the nominee of the PSA and Nicolas Repetto named by the Partido Socialista Democrático. Both parties elected a handful of deputies.

Subsequently the Partido Socialista Argentino split again. An extreme leftist element in the party broke away to form the Partido Socialista Argentino de la Vanguardia. It later adopted a strong position in favor of Fidel Castro and underwent several other splits.

Although both the PSA and PSD were in the opposition to the government of Arturo Frondizi, elected in February 1958, neither played an important role in the overthrow of Frondizi's government in March 1962. When the military-backed provisional government that succeeded Frondizi suspended Congress, although agreeing to pay the legislators' salaries, PSA Senator Alfredo Palacios resigned in protest. In the elections of 1963, finally called to elect a successor to Frondizi, both Socialist parties again ran candidates; but neither was an important factor in that election. The PSA won six seats in the Chamber of Deputies, and the PSD was able to place five of its candidates in the Chamber.[16]

The two major Socialist groups, the Partido Socialista Democrático and the Partido Socialista Argentino, were part of the opposition to the government of President Arturo Illia after 1963; but they played little or no part in the military movement that overthrew that government in June 1966.

The dictatorship of General Juan Ongania, installed in 1966, dissolved all political parties. However, neither the PSD nor the PSA ceased to function. The PSD succeeded in publishing its weekly newspaper La vanguardia regularly and in keeping a skeleton organization alive throughout much of the country. The PSA was much less successful in keeping its hierarchy in tact.

With the advent of General Alejandro Lanusse to power early in 1971, and his promise to reestablish constitutional government, both Socialist groups returned to more intense activity. Negotiations began for a reunification of their ranks, but there was considerable doubt that even as a single group they would be sufficiently large to regain legal recognition as a political party.

By the early 1970s the Socialists of Argentina had been reduced to a minor factor in Argentine politics. The decline of the Socialists was due to a number of factors: their "Europeanizing" attitude, their strongly anti-Peronista position during and after Perón's regime, and their general divorce from the country's organized labor movement. It was also due to personal rivalries among leaders. It is doubtful that the Argentine Socialists will ever again become a significant factor in Argentine politics.

CHAPTER

6

THE
CHILEAN
SOCIALISTS

Socialists have been an important element in the politics of Chile for a longer time than in any other Latin American country. Although there have been several different Socialist parties during the decades since the establishment of the first such group in the 1880s, they have been an element of some importance for more than 80 years.

THE PARTIDO DEMOCRÁTICO

European utopian Socialists had their followers in Chile. The most notable of these was Francisco Bilbao, who returned to his native land after the revolutions of 1848 in Europe, and established a group of disciples, the Sociedad de Igualdad (Society of Equality). Although its one venture into national politics, a conspiracy against the government of President Manuel Montt in 1851, was a failure, the Sociedad de Igualdad gave rise in subsequent decades to a number of workers mutual benefit societies, the first organizations that can properly be called part of the country's organized labor movement.

Middle-class people and artisans who had been associated with the mutual benefit societies were largely responsible for the establishment of the Partido Democrático in 1887. The principal leader of the new party was Malaquias Concha. In the election of 1894 the party had its first success when Angel Guarello was elected to the Chamber of Deputies, and it can be argued that he was the first Socialist ever elected to a Latin American legislative body.

The members of the Partido Democrático played a leading part in establishing the first trade unions in Chile. These included the trolley car workers union of Santiago, which is generally credited with engaging in the country's first strike, in 1886.

During the 1890s the labor movement began to expand beyond Santiago and the country's other major cities, to the nitrate pampas in the northern provinces, which had become part of the republic as a result of the War of the Pacific (1879-84), during which Chile had taken these areas from Bolivia and Peru. There the Partido Democrático shared influence with the anarcho-syndicalists. The party members were also of considerable influence among the miners of the region just south of Concepción and the artisans of Santiago, Valparaíso, and other major cities.

With the establishment of the Socialist International in 1889, the Partido Democrático of Chile became a corresponding member. The party exchanged information with the International on a regular basis.

The Partido Democrático's principal leader in the northern nitrate pampas, Luís Emilio Recabarren, was for some time the party's international secretary, in charge of maintaining correspondence with the Socialist International. He also was a major factor in organizing the workers of the nitrate fields into unions and units of the Partido Democrático. He spent a year in Argentina, where he was active in the Socialist Party there.

In 1912 Recabarren led a split in the ranks of the Partido Democrático. Feeling that the party was not sufficiently militant in defending the interests of the country's workers, he withdrew and led the formation of the Partido Socialista Obrero. Among the workers' leaders who supported Recabarren's split was Manuel Hidalgo, the principal working-class leader of the party in the Santiago region.

The Partido Democrático remained in existence despite the withdrawal of Recabarren and his followers. It continued to have influence among the workers of Santiago and particularly among the workers of Concepción and of the nearby coal mining areas. It supported the candidacy of Arturo Alessandri, the country's first middle-class president, who was elected in 1920.

In the succeeding decades the Partido Democrático underwent many splits and reunifications but gave up all pretense of being a Socialist party. In the early 1960s the party split once again; one faction, known as the Partido Democrático Nacional (PADENA), supported the nominees of the Christian Democrats in the elections of 1964 and 1970. The other group, the Partido Demócrata, backed the candidacy of Salvador Allende in 1964. Following the victory of Eduardo Frei, the Partido Demócrata joined with a dissident faction of the Christian Democrats to establish the Partido Social Democrático, which backed Allende again in 1970. With Allende's inauguration the PSD had one member of his cabinet.

THE PARTIDO SOCIALISTA OBRERO

The Socialist Party established by Luis Emilio Recabarren, the Partido Socialista Obrero, became a major factor in the organized labor movement. In 1909 Chile's first central labor organization, the Gran Federación Obrera de Chile, was established by the railroad workers and some other labor groups. Recabarren urged his followers in the nitrate fields and elsewhere to join. As a result the left-wing elements succeeded in gaining influence in the organization. In 1916 they joined the Gran Federación and in the following year succeeded in gaining control. Two years later they changed its name to Federación Obrera de Chile and reorganized it as a highly centralized structure.

The PSO supported the candidacy of Arturo Alessandri in 1920. In the next year Recabarren and another Socialist were elected to the Chamber of Deputies. In 1924 they were reelected.

Meanwhile, the principal leaders of the Partido Socialista Obrero had been won over to the ideas of the new Communist International. The party's convention in 1921 resolved to affiliate with the Comintern and to change the party's name to Partido Comunista de Chile. In 1922 the Federación Obrera, under Communist control, resolved to join the Red International of Trade Unions, the international trade union federation under Communist control.[1]

With the affiliation of the PSO to the Communist International, Chile ceased to have a Socialist Party. Although a small minority of party leaders refused to accept Communist affiliation, they did not organize another party; and more than a decade was to pass before a major party of this orientation again came into existence.

ORIGINS OF THE PARTIDO SOCIALISTA

President Arturo Alessandri was overthrown in September 1924. Before this there was enacted a body of labor and social legislation that, among other things, provided for the legalization of trade unions. Both the Communists and the anarchists, whose influence had been dominant in the labor movement until then, opposed the idea of organizations under their control seeking legal recognition under this legislation.

However, in the years that followed, many unions were established that did receive recognition from the government. Before the end of the dictatorship of General Carlos Ibáñez (1927-31) these organizations had formed a central body, the Confederación Nacional de Sindicatos Legales. The political orientation of the leaders of most of these organizations was Socialist, and they were to form the major basis for the establishment of a new Socialist party.

After the overthrow of the Ibáñez dictatorship in July 1931, the leaders of the legal unions, as well as various members of the middle and professional classes, formed small Socialist parties, each of which had its own particular leader. The most important of these was the Nueva Acción Política, headed by Emilio Matte Hurtado, a leading figure among the Masons of Chile. Others included the Partido Socialista Marxista, Orden Socialista, the Partido Socialista Unificado, the Partido Social Republicano, the Partido Social Demócrata, the Partido Socialista de Chile, the Partido Socialista Internacional, and the Partido Laborista.[2]

All of these groups, as well as the Trotskyite faction of the Communist Party, supported the "Socialist republic" established as a result of a coup d'état on June 4, 1932. The leader of this regime was Colonel Marmaduque Grove, founder of the Chilean air force and a leading opponent of the Ibáñez dictatorship. However, his regime lasted only about two weeks, after which Grove was deported to Juan Fernández Island, far out in the Pacific. The leadership of the Socialist republic was taken by Carlos Dávila, a former associate of Carlos Ibáñez; but in September 1932 Dávila was deposed by the armed forces.

After the overthrow of the Socialist republic, new elections were called for the presidency and Congress. Most of the groups that had supported the Socialist republic formed the Alianza Socialista Revolucionaria, which sponsored the presidential candidacy of Marmaduque Grove. The victor in this contest was former President Arturo Alessandri, although Grove came in a surprisingly strong second.

However, the Grove campaign did not end the cooperation of the elements that had supported the Socialist republic. Virtually all of them except the Trotskyites joined in 1933 to establish the Partido Socialista. Thus, the new party brought together the great majority of elements of the labor movement that were opposed to the influence of the Communist Party, as well as significant middle-class groups.

During the next five years the Socialist Party developed into one of the major factors in Chilean politics. In 1935 the Trotskyites decided to dissolve their party and enter the new Socialist Party en masse. With their entry the party came to control the great majority of the existing trade unions.

The Socialist Party had a particularly active Youth Federation. It gained special importance because of its role in offering opposition in the streets of Santiago and other major cities to the armed and uniformed squads of the Partido Nacista, a party patterned after the

German Nazi Party and drawing particularly strong support for some time from the country's sizable German-speaking community.

From its inception the Socialists controlled the largest of the country's central labor organizations, the Confederación Nacional de Sindicatos Legales (CNSL), which included most of the nation's legalized labor groups. After the merger with the Trotskyites, the party also had considerable influence among the organized workers groups that had not sought recognition from the government.

For some time the struggle between the CNSL and the Communist-controlled Federación Obrera de Chile was particularly bitter. However, with the change of the Communist International's "line" to favor unified action by Communists with other left-wing parties and the abolition of sectarian Communist trade union groups, the Chilean Communists and the Federación Obrera suggested unfication of the Chilean labor movement.

Long negotiations among the Confederación Nacional de Sindicatos Legales, the Federación Obrera de Chile, and the anarcho-syndicalist-controlled Confederación General de Trabajadores resulted in a trade union congress that met in December 1936. Out of it emerged the Confederación de Trabajadores de Chile (CTCh), which was joined by the unions formerly belonging to the CNSL and the FOCh, the anarcho-syndicalists deciding to retain their own CGT group.

The influence of the Socialists was clearly predominant in the founding congress of the CTCh. The first Secretary-general of the new group was Juan Díaz Martínez, a member of the Socialist Party; a Communist was his assistant. However, by the end of 1939 the Communists had gained considerable ground in the labor movement, and relations between Socialists and Communists had become very bitter. As a result, when the second congress of the CTCh met and elected another Socialist, Bernado Ibáñez, as Secretary-General and named Salvador Ocampo, a Communist, as his assistant, the Communists refused to accept the decision and withdrew to form their own Confederación de Trabajadores de Chile, with Ocampo as its secretary-general. However, after a few months of separation, the Communists decided to accept reunification under the leadership of Ibáñez and Ocampo.

THE SOCIALISTS AND THE POPULAR FRONT

Meanwhile, the Socialists had agreed to participate in the establishment of the Western Hemisphere's only Popular Front. Before the establishment of the Popular Front, the Socialists had formed the Bloque de Izquierda, together with the Partido Radical Socialista, the Trotskyites and the Partido Democrático. After the Alessandri government violently broke a railroad workers strike, the third national congress of the Socialist Party issued a call on February 6, 1936, to the Radical and Communist parties to join with the Bloque de Izquierda in a new opposition front to Alessandri.[3] After some struggle within the Radical Party, that group's Central Committee accepted the idea of the Popular Front on May 6, 1936.[4]

The first electoral test of the Popular Front was the congressional election of March 1937. John Reese Stevenson has commented on this election:

> As a result of systematic bribery and the wholesale purchase of votes, artfully directed by the "wizard of finance," Gustavo Ross, the Right, including the Liberal, Conservative, and Demócrata parties as well as a few small independent political groups, was able to preserve its majority in both houses. However, despite the immense sums expended by Ross and the failure of the Popular Front parties to stage a well organized, unified campaign or to iron out difficulties in their respective electoral quotas, the Left did increase its representation to a considerable extent and the electoral strength shown by the extreme Left, the Socialists in particular, was quite surprising. ...[5]

Following this election the Socialist Party's Central Committee met. It issued a strong call for support of the Popular Front on March 27, 1937: "Workers of the city, of the country, and of the mines, we are faced with a single and great enemy—reaction; let us form the only solid great union—the Popular Front."[6]

As the presidential election of 1938 approached, the Popular Front was faced with the problem of selecting a candidate to run against the nominee supported by the government of President Arturo Alessandri, who by now represented most of the country's right-wing elements. The Socialists moved early; and in a convention in April 1937 they named their principal figure, Marmaduque Grove, as their candidate for the December 1938 election. However, the Radical Party, which was then the nation's largest party, insisted that the Popular Front candidate be chosen from its ranks. The Radical Party held its nominating convention in November 1937 and chose Pedro Aguirre Cerda, a vineyard owner and experienced politician, who had been Alessandri's first prime minister in 1920, as its nominee.

The Communists at first proposed the name of ex-dictator Carlos Ibáñez, who was also supported by the Partido Nacista. However, they subsequently swung their support to the Radical candidate.

The Popular Front held a convention in April 1938 to try to reach agreement on a single left-wing candidate for the presidency.

It was agreed that two-thirds of the thousand delegates' votes were necessary to choose a nominee. Grove had the backing of 300 delegates representing the Socialist Party and 60 of the 120 votes of the CTCh. He could thus block the Radical-Communist coalition behind Aguirre, and for two days there was a deadlock in the convention. Finally the Socialists issued the statement: "The Socialist Party in deference to the unity of the Left has resolved to accept, finally, the reiterated withdrawal of his candidacy which Marmaduke Grove has made. . . ."[7]

Although the election was an exceedingly close one, Aguirre Cerda was finally proclaimed the winner. The new president offered posts in the government to all of the parties that had supported him. However, the Communists refused to join the administration, choosing to remain outside, where they could claim credit for the accomplishments of the Popular Front regime while being free to criticize its shortcomings.

In contrast, the Socialists assumed a major role in the administration of Aguirre Cerda. They had three posts in Aguirre's first cabinet, along with six Radicals and two Democráticos. Most prominent among the Socialist ministers was Oscar Schnake Vergara, who assumed the post of minister of development. He was responsible for the establishment of the Chilean Development Corporation, which undertook the leadership in the process of industrialization. He was the Socialists' major spokesman within the government.

So long as Aguirre Cerda remained president, the Socialists were a major factor in the government. However, their relations with the Communists were sorely strained during this period. In conformity with the position of the Communist International, the Communists of Chile took a position of "benevolent neutrality" toward the Axis Powers during the period from August 1939 until June 1941, during which the Soviet Union was aligned with the Axis in World War II. The Socialists, in contrast, strongly favored the Allied Powers. As a result, the Socialists and Communists became bitter enemies, within the labor movement and within the Popular Front, from which the Socialists finally withdrew. Schnake was particularly violent in his attacks on the Communists.

This split between the Socialists and Communists led to a breakup of the Popular Front. The Communists violently attacked Oscar Schnake as "the slave of Wall Street." Upon returning from the United States, where he had gone as minister of development to try to get American economic aid, Schnake replied to the Communists' assaults upon him and proposed that the Socialists "revive our independent line of action since we do not wish to remain any longer tied to a party which has betrayed us." Some time later the Socialist Central Committee adopted a resolution that the party "will not return to the Popular Front, because it is inspired by the Communist party, whose national and international policy is contrary to the interest of the country."8

Meanwhile, the Socialists had undergone two splits, one of them important. In 1937, even before the victory of the Popular Front, a small group of Socialist members under the leadership of writer Ricardo Latcham had withdrawn to form the Unión Socialista, which supported Carlos Ibáñez in the 1938 election, until he withdrew his candidacy. Although this was the first split in the Socialist ranks, it did not prove to be of major proportions.

However, the second division in the Socialists' ranks was of great significance. John Reese Stevenson has described this split as follows:

> ... There had been steadily mounting tension since December 1939, when Grove defeated extremist Cesar Godoy for the leadership of the party. Godoy had accepted this setback with ill grace and immediately began to criticize both the Popular Front and the party leadership, exclaiming on one occasion that the Socialist party was " a house full of rats, moths, and cobwebs" needing a thorough cleaning. Despite the appointment of a special committee to close this widening breach, all efforts at compromise failed. Then Godoy and his supporters attacked the Popular Front candidate in a by-election on April 7, 1940, he and four sympathetic Socialist deputies were forthwith expelled from the party charged with disloyalty and "Trotskyism" among other things. The Godoy followers responded by holding a congress of their own in May and finally seceding from the Socialist party to form the new Socialist Workers' party.9

The new Partido Socialista de Trabajadores, which was joined by at least some of those who had entered the Socialist Party when the Trotskyite Communists had been dissolved, had two members of the Executive of the Confederación de Trabajadores de Chile and one member of the Santiago regional unit of the CTCh when the party was established. However, the Socialists were soon able to get these people removed from their jobs.10

This split put the Socialist control of the labor movement in considerable jeopardy. However, the Communists generally supported the orthodox Socialists against the followers of César Godoy Urrutia. As a result the Socialists remained the largest element in the Confederación de Trabajadores de Chile. Despite Communist support for the Socialists, many of the leaders of the PST soon joined the Communist Party. Godoy Urrutia soon became a member of the

Communists' Central Committee, and for several decades he was a Communist deputy in Congress.

The principal issues between the two Socialist factions in the PST split concerned whether the Socialist Party should remain in the Popular Front government and whether it should develop closer relations with the Communists. The rebels argued against continued membership in the Aguirre Cerda regime and for closer relations with the Communists. Several years later a second split was provoked by largely the same issues. Lifetime Socialist president Marmaduque Grove insisted in 1944 that the Socialists should withdraw from the government of Juan Antonio Ríos, who had been elected with Socialist support after the death of Aguirre Cerda in 1941, and that the Socialists should rebuild their former alliance with the Communists. Grove was opposed by the majority of the party, led by Senator Salvador Allende and CTCh Secretary-General Bernardo Ibáñez, and finally quit the party to form the Partido Socialista Auténtico.

There is considerable reason to believe that in this period the Communists had infiltrated the Socialist Party and that they played a significant role in both the 1940 and the 1944 splits in the Socialist ranks. In both cases important members of the dissident Socialist group subsequently joined the Communist Party and assumed important positions within it shortly after having participated in the split in the Socialists' ranks.

Certainly a major factor in both splits was the question of the Socialists' relations with the Communist Party. This issue continued to plague the Communists through the 1950s and well into the 1960s. Although the basic reason for the formation of the Socialist Party was to mobilize politically those elements in organized labor opposed to the influence of the Communist Party, there were always those in the ranks of Socialist leaders who favored some kind of an alliance with the Communists.

Certainly another basic element in the continuing splits within the Socialists' ranks was intense rivalry among party leaders. The Socialist Party had been formed by bringing together a group of smaller parties, each of which had a single outstanding leader. These political prima donnas had not learned to work together before the party became part of the winning Popular Front coalition in 1938 and had responsibilities of government forced upon it. The possibility of controlling the Socialist Party thus early came to be associated with having influence in the government and controlling more or less patronage, thus intensifying the existing sharp rivalries for leadership within the party.

THE SOCIALISTS AND GONZÁLEZ VIDELA'S REGIME

The struggle between the Socialists and Communists for control of the labor movement, which had continued since the formation of the CTCh in December 1936, broke into the open early in 1946. In January of that year, the government of acting President Alfredo Duhalde suspended the legal recognition of two nitrate workers unions that had engaged in illegal strikes. As a result the CTCh called a general strike, which won the relegalization of the two unions. However, soon afterward the Communist elements in the CTCh pushed for a second general strike, to protest police firing on a demonstration near the presidential palace. Duhalde, who had taken over leadership of the government when Juan Antonio Ríos took sick, sought to prevent this strike by conceding all of the demands made by the CTCh and offering the Socialist Party participation in the government. When the Socialist secretary-general of the CTCh, Bernardo Ibáñez, accepted these terms and called off the strike by a radio broadcast from the President's office, the Communists insisted on continuing the walkout. In addition, they called a meeting of the CTCh Executive, at which they declared Ibáñez "deposed" and elected a Communist, Bernardo Araya, as his replacement.

As a result the CTCh was split into two rival organizations, each using the name of the old confederation. Acting President Duhalde threw the influence of the government behind the Socialist faction. However, virtually all other political elements in the CTCh, aside from the Socialists and a faction of the Partido Democrático, supported the Communist-dominated faction of the confederation, which probably had a majority of the country's unions in its ranks.

Juan Antonio Ríos died, and a new presidential election took place on September 4, 1946. The old Socialist-Communist-Radical alliance had completely broken up; and the Communists and Radicals nominated a pro-Communist Radical politician, Gabriel González Videla, for the presidency. The Conservatives nominated Eduardo Cruz Coke, a doctor and senator; while the Liberals named Fernando Alessandri, a son of ex-President Alessandri. The Socialists, unable to support any of the other candidates, named labor leader Bernado Ibáñez. He came in an exceedingly poor fourth.

During the first five months of the González Videla regime, the Communists participated in the cabinet, along with the Radicals and the Liberal Party, each of which had three ministers. During this period the influence of the government was thrown strongly on the side of the Communist faction of the labor movement. Both the Communist and Socialist factions of the CTCh held national congresses, and the government largely financed the bringing of numerous delegates to the Communist-led congress.

During this period the Socialist Party was very definitely on the defensive. The Communists carried on a campaign of violence against not only the Socialists in the labor movement but also against their anarcho-syndicalist opponents. Among those assassinated by the Communists was the leader of the Socialist Youth Federation. At the same time the Communists carried on an exceedingly violent press campaign against the Socialists, inside and outside the labor movement. A particular victim of the Communist campaign was Bernardo Ibáñez, secretary-general of the CTCh, who was also serving as secretary-general of the Socialist Party.

However, the attacks of the Communists helped to raise the prestige of the Socialist Party. This was shown in the municipal elections of April 1947, in which the Socialists recovered much of the ground they had lost in the 1946 presidential poll.

This municipal election also led to the downfall of the Radical-Communist-Liberal cabinet. When President González Videla demanded the resignation of the Communist members of the government, the Communist Party turned strongly against him, launching a series of strikes that he felt were aimed at bringing down his regime. As a result he cracked down very strongly on the Communist-controlled faction of the labor movement.

González Videla now turned to the Socialists for support. He asked for and received their backing to break revolutionary strikes launched by the Communists. A few months later he invited the Socialists to join his government. Finally, he asked for and received the Socialists' support for a measure to outlaw the Communist Party, the so-called Law for the Defense of Democracy.

SPLIT AND REUNION

This rapprochement between the González Videla regime and the Socialist Party provoked a new split in the party. The issues over which the new schism took place were whether the party should continue in the González Videla government and whether the Socialists in Congress should vote for the Law for the Defense of Democracy. A dissident faction argued in the negative on both of these questions; and under the leadership of the party's former secretary-general, Raúl Ampuero, it withdrew to form a new group, the Partido Socialista Popular. The old party thereupon took the name Partido Socialista de Chile.

This split in the Socialist ranks continued for almost a decade. The Partido Socialista de Chile continued for several years to represent the general tendency of democratic Socialism, while the Partido Socialista Popular was intrigued by Leninist ideas of a highly centralized party organized on the principle of "democratic centralism", for a while being particularly attracted by the Titoite schism in Communism. For some time the Partido Socialista de Chile remained in the government of González Videla, although in the last two years of his administration no Socialist faction was in his government. The Partido Socialista Popular adopted a position of frank opposition to the regime.

The Partido Socialista de Chile continued to control most of the Socialist faction of the labor movement. Its domination of the Socialist element of the CTCh was virtually unchallenged, and the only important group in which the Partido Socialista Popular had considerable influence was the copper workers' unions.

However, in 1952 the position of the two Socialist parties suddenly shifted, as a result of the presidential election of that year. The Partido Socialista Popular, feeling that ex-dictator Carlos Ibáñez, who was making yet another attempt to return to the presidency, was likely to win, supported him. Their explanation was that the general had no well-defined political philosophy and that the PSP would therefore have a good opportunity to develop the program for an Ibáñez government if it were part of it.

The Partido Socialista de Chile took a very different position. In a quick about-face, the party agreed to a deal with the Communists, which involved the PSCh's naming of Senator Salvador Allende as its candidate for the presidency. Until shortly before his nomination Allende had been a member of the Partido Socialista Popular, but he objected to its backing of Ibáñez. When he withdrew from the PSP, he was approached by the underground Communist Party, which promised its support if he could get the nomination of the Partido Socialista de Chile. In spite of his hitherto strongly anti-Communist position and the similar stance of the PSCh, both Allende and the PSCh agreed to the Communists' proposal. As a result Allende was named as the presidential candidate of the PSCh and agreed to accept Communist backing.

Allende came in a poor third, with Ibáñez the winner. As a result the Partido Socialista Popular entered the Ibáñez administration, in which it participated for about a year. It endorsed the Ibáñez government's efforts to carry out a price stabilization program, although this program imposed serious hardships on the country's working class.

The rapprochement between the Partido Socialista de Chile and the Communists had important repercussions in the organized labor movement. For some months before the PSCh-Communist alliance, the leaders of the Socialist faction of the CTCh had been discussing the possibility of launching a new labor confederation that would include its own affiliates and a number of independent national unions but omit the Communists. Their plan was for this new group to affiliate with the anti-Communist International Confederation of Free Trade Unions and its American hemispheric group, the Organización Interamericana de Trabajadores (ORIT).

However, with the sudden political realignment the violent arguments of the Communists against the proposed new labor group, and in favor of "trade union unity," by which they meant the inclusion of their own unions in the new group, received a sympathetic hearing from the Socialists, who had previously been deaf to the Communists' complaints. The willingness of the PSCh to accept a wider unity in the labor movement was intensified by the victory of Carlos Ibáñez in the 1952 presidential election. Ibáñez was known to be a friend of Argentine dictator Juan Perón, and it was widely rumored that he was going to try to follow in Perón's footsteps and set up a government-controlled labor group. This "menace" was the excuse offered by the PSCh to accept the Communist line on the reorganization of the labor movement.

The result of this situation was the founding congress of the new Central Unica de Trabajadores de Chile (CUTCh). Positions on its Executive Committee were apportioned according to agreement among the various political groups represented. The CUTCh congress accepted the Communist suggestion that the new organization remain independent of any international labor group.

When the PSP joined the PSCh in the opposition, efforts were again made to unite the two Socialist factions. They culminated in 1957 in the reformation of a united Partido Socialista. The new party nominated Salvador Allende for president in the 1958 presidential election. This time he was the runner-up to the Conservative-Liberal nominee, Jorge Alessandri, a son of former President Arturo Alessandri.

RECENT HISTORY OF THE CHILEAN SOCIALISTS

With the reunification of the Socialists the party became part of the Frente de Acción Popular (FRAP), which included the Communist Party and some smaller groups. Shortly before the 1958 election Congress repealed the Law for the Defense of Democracy, over the protests of President Ibáñez. Following the election the Socialists and Communists continued to collaborate in Congress, in the labor movement, and in the general political sphere.

FRAP centered most of its attention after 1958 on attempting to win the 1964 election. From the beginning it made clear that Salvador Allende would be its candidate. The chances of the leftist coalition seemed very good. As time passed, it became obvious that the principal block to FRAP's success would be the Christian

Democratic Party. As the 1964 election approached, the campaign became largely a contest between Eduardo Frei, the Christian Democratic candidate, and Allende.

In September 1964 the voters decided for Eduardo Frei by an impressive majority. In March of the following year the Christian Democrats succeeded, for the first time in a century, in getting a one-party majority in the Chamber of Deputies, although they did not win control of the Senate. Subsequently, Allende was elected by the FRAP plurality in the Senate as president of that body.

By this time the Socialist Party had moved very strongly to the left. After the formation of the PSCh-Communist alliance in 1952, the Partido Socialista de Chile gave up its allegiance to the philosophy of democratic Socialism; and with the reestablishment of a united Socialist Party some years later, the new party was officially committed to Marxism-Leninism. The Socialists did not accept orthodox Stalinism, or even the modifications of it offered by Nikita Khrushchev. However, they criticized these forms from the standpoint of their lack of fealty to Marxism-Leninism rather than from that of democratic Socialism.

There were elements within the Socialist Party that were sympathetic to the Chinese Communists. However, after the advent of the Castro regime in Cuba, and its evolution to Marxism-Leninism, the Chilean Socialists generally associated themselves with the Cuban regime and its governing party.

Meanwhile, severe differences appeared within the Socialist Party. Although Allende and other top party leaders strongly showed their support for an alliance with the Fidel Castro regime, they were faced from the early 1960s with an opposition considerably to their left. Led at first by Clodomiro Almeida, and subsequently by Carlos Altamirano, this Socialist left wing was very critical of the Communists as being too conservative. They endorsed, in principle, the attempt to seize power through a guerrilla war, although they did not make any real effort to do so.

Meanwhile, the Socialists had suffered three more splits. In 1964 a small group broke away, under the leadership of trade unionist Baudillo Casanova, to form the Partido Socialista del Pueblo, which supported the Christian Democratic Party's candidate, Eduardo Frei, in that year's election. It did not survive long afterward.[11]

In 1966 what proved to be a more serious division occurred, when a group of young party members broke away and joined with Oscar Waiss, a former Socialist leader who had been expelled from the party in 1960, to form the Movimiento de Izquierda Revolucionaria (MIR). It soon evolved into a frankly Fidelista party, which undertook to organize urban terrorism and prepare for rural guerrilla activities. By the election of President Salvador Allende in 1970, it had become an element of some importance, particularly among students and some particularly depressed peasant groups, and constituted a serious nuisance for the Socialist Party and the Allende regime. Waiss had meanwhile withdrawn from the group, rejoining the Socialist Party early in 1971

The third split occurred in 1967, when Raúl Ampuero accused Allende and other party leaders of misleading the party and withdrew to form a new group, Unión Socialista Popular. The USP ran candidates in the 1969 congressional election against those of the Socialist Party, but they fared badly. After Allende's election they gave critical support to his regime.[12]

As the 1970 presidential election approached, the leadership of FRAP came to the conclusion that if they were to defeat the incumbent Christian Democrats they would have to broaden their alliance, particularly to include the Radicals. Negotiations to this end led to the formation in 1969 of Unidad Popular. During further negotiations concerning the presidential candidate of Unidad Popular, the Socialists again submitted the name of Salvador Allende. Over considerable objection from the Radicals, he was finally accepted as the nominee.

The election of September 1970 gave Allende a slight plurality but not an absolute majority. He therefore entered into extensive negotiations with the Christian Democrats, whose support in Congress was necessary to assure his election. As a consequence of these negotiations, Allende made extensive promises concerning the maintenance of a democratic form of government, in return for which he received the support of the Christian Democratic Senators and deputies.

Once in office Allende's government undertook an extensive effort to carry out its promise to take Chile "on the road to Socialism." Measures included nationalization of the mining industry and of a substantial part of the manufacturing sector, intensification of the agrarian reform program launched by the Christian Democrats and adoption of a kind of collective farming as the general agrarian reform pattern, and a variety of other steps.

The immediate impact of these was favorable for Allende and the Socialist Party, insofar as the voters were concerned. In municipal elections in April 1971, Unidad Popular rose from 36 percent of the vote to 50 percent, and the Socialist Party was the principal gainer within the government coalition. It emerged as the second party in the country, with only the Christian Democrats being larger.

Despite this victory there continued to be considerable tension within the Socialist ranks. One element supported Allende's proclaimed desire to institute Socialism while maintaining the country's democratic political structure. Another segment of the party leadership quite frankly sought the establishment of what one leading

Socialist official told me would be "not very different from those of Eastern Europe."

STRENGTHS AND WEAKNESSES OF CHILEAN SOCIALISTS

One major source of strength of the Chilean Socialist Party since its inception in 1933 has been its sizable mass base among the urban and mining workers, as well as a considerable following in middle-class and professional circles. It has for three and a half decades been the principal counterforce to the Communist Party in the labor movement—in fact, it was started largely by workers who resented Communist domination of the trade union movement. Although over the years the relations between the Socialists and Communists have changed frequently, the Socialists have always represented the principal center of attraction for those within labor's ranks who did not want to come under Communist discipline.

A second advantage—which, however, sometimes proved an embarrassment—was the relative freedom to dissent from party policy and leadership. This was one of the major attractions for people of the Left who did not like the very rigid discipline of the Communists.

These advantages of the Socialist Party have kept it—in one form or another—one of the major parties since it first appeared on the political scene. However, the party has also suffered from severe weaknesses, which go far to explain why it was never able, until 1970, to come to power. Certainly one of these disadvantages has been the prima donna nature of its leadership.

Bitter personal quarrels among top leaders have been a permanent characteristic of the Chilean Socialist movement. These have usually been couched in terms of either an ideological issue or a difference of opinion over immediate party tactics, but they have usually involved a violent struggle for power between different factions led by individual leaders.

Since the early 1950s the Socialists have also suffered from another grave disadvantage, a deep inferiority complex vis-à-vis the Communists. From 1946 until the early 1950s, when the Socialists were in open and bitter conflict with the Communists, both inside and outside the labor movement, the leadership of the Socialist movement received wounds from which they never fully recovered. They were subject to vituperative attack and violent political abuse at the hands of the Communists, and a large number of the party's leaders of that period had their careers destroyed. Those who remained were forever after willing to pay a very high price to avoid coming under all-out attack from the Communist Party. This price usually involved playing the role of junior partner to the Communists in the trade union movement, even though during most of the time since the early 1950s the Socialists' rank-and-file support in organized labor has been considerably greater than that of the Communists. It has also involved political collaboration with the Communists and purging from the Socialists' ranks of those opposed to such collaboration.

This relationship with the Communists for over twenty years has also had an ideological impact upon the party. Because of their sense of inferiority in relation to the Communists, the Socialist leadership usually felt that it had to be "to the left" of the Communist Party. This desire went far toward explaining the Chilean Socialists' proclamation of themselves as "Marxist-Leninists" and their flirting with a series of Communist groups that had differences with the very Moscow-line Chilean Communist Party, including Tito, the Chinese, and Fidel Castro.

CHAPTER 7

THE URUGUAYAN SOCIALIST PARTY

The Uruguayan Socialists were one of the country's principal minor parties for over half a century. However, they never succeeded in assuming a major role in national politics because of the competition of the Batllista faction of the traditional Colorado Party, and in recent years they have suffered from the same kind of inferiority complex in regard the Communists that has long been the principal handicap of the Chilean Socialist Party.

Marxist ideas were brought to Uruguay mainly by immigrants from Spain and Italy in the last decades of the 19th century. Small groups of adherents of the First International, the International Workingmen's Association, in which both Karl Marx and Michael Bakunin were active, flourished for some years in Montevideo. By the early years of the 20th century there were several small groups of workingmen and young intellectuals who had formed Socialist clubs in Montevideo and a few of the interior cities and towns.

THE FIRST URUGUAYAN SOCIALIST PARTY

Most of the local Socialist groups were brought together in 1910, to form the Partido Socialista del Uruguay. Although the new party had in its ranks both intellectuals and workingmen, including important trade union leaders, its outstanding figure was a young man who had already made some reputation for himself as a poet, Emilio Frugoni. He was a native-born Uruguayan, although many of the rank-and-file members and secondary leaders of the party were immigrants.

The Uruguayan Socialist Party had its first test of fire in the congressional election of 1910. In this poll the principal opposition party, the Partido Nacional (or Blanco, as it was popularly known) abstained, which gave a wider field for the competition of the minor parties. The Partido Socialista joined forces with the small Partido Liberal to enter a joint ticket in the elections, and one of the two victorious candidates of this list was Frugoni.[1]

Despite this apparently promising beginning, the new group immediately ran into serious competition. To the left of the Socialists were the anarcho-syndicalists, who dominated the country's principal trade union group, the Federación Obrera Regional Uruguaya, frequently attacked the Socialists as "yellow trade unionists."

But a good deal more serious, as a long-run competitor of the Socialists, was the faction of the traditional Colorado Party led by President José Batlle y Ordóñez. Batlle, who had first been president of the republic between 1903 and 1907, had returned to this post in 1911 for another four-year term. During both of his administrations, Batlle took a strong position in favor of widespread reforms in the country's economy, society, and political life.

Batlle was a nationalist, he was particularly concerned with social problems, and he sought to establish institutions that could provide Uruguay with a secure basis for political democracy. His program of social legislation, including the eight-hour workday, protection for female and juvenile workers, support for collective bargaining, and a friendly attitude toward immigrant laborers, won much support among workers who under other circumstances might have been attracted to the Socialist Party. His program for using the influence of the state to foster the country's economic development, as well as his strong backing for political democracy, won him support from among many middle-class elements that might otherwise have been sympathetically disposed toward the Socialists.

However, in spite of the popularity of Batlle and his party, the Socialists did succeed in building up their own limited constituency. Particularly during World War I the influence of the Partido Socialista grew among the organized workers. One of the younger trade unionists of the party, Eugenio Gómez, emerged as the principal leader of the port and maritime workers and led several important strikes by this group between 1917 and 1919.

The Socialists generally worked within the anarcho-syndicalist-dominated Federación Obrera Regional Uruguaya. By the early 1920s the Socialists constituted the largest political element within this group, controlling not only the port and maritime workers but various other unions as well.

These Socialist trade unionists became the mainstay of the left wing within the Socialist Party. To a growing degree they were attracted to the Bolshevik Revolution and to the new Communist International, established under Bolshevik leadership in January

1919. As a result the Left-wingers were increasingly involved in conflict with the more moderate elements led by the party's founder, Emilio Frugoni.

This struggle reached its climax in April 1921, when a congress of the Partido Socialista resolved to accept the 21 points that the Communist International had laid down for affiliation, to join the Comintern, and to change its name to Partido Comunista del Uruguay. Eugenio Gómez soon became secretary-general of the Communist Party. Emilio Frugoni and a number of his followers withdrew from what had become the Communist Party and re-formed the Partido Socialista del Uruguay.[2]

THE SECOND PARTIDO SOCIALISTA

Throughout the rest of the 1920s the Socialist and Communist parties were bitter competitors, both in the trade union movement and in the general political field. The Communists had taken with them most of the trade union leadership of the party, and it was some years before the Socialists were again able to win influence in the ranks of organized labor. Only on October 11, 1930, did the Socialists succeed in organizing a labor confederation, the Unión General de Trabajadores (UGT) under their leadership. It had unions of printers, marine engineers, commercial employees, and a few groups of industrial workers.[3] This UGT lasted for only a short time. By late 1930s, the only Uruguayan central labor groups were the small anarchist Federación Obrera Regional Uruguaya and the equally small syndicalist Unión Sindical Uruguaya.

In terms of electoral politics, too, the Socialists did not fare well in the years immediately following the Communist split. Immediately after his withdrawal from the ranks of the party upon whose ticket he had been elected to the Chamber of Deputies, Emilio Frugoni resigned his parliamentary seat, on the grounds that he no longer represented the group that had chosen him. It was 1928 before the Socialists again were able to elect Frugoni to the Chamber, with a vote of 3,000. In the elections of 1932 Frugoni was joined in the Chamber of two other Socialists, Liber Troitiño and Manuel Seoana. In the same election the Communists placed three of their members in the Chamber of Deputies.[4]

The pattern set during these years held through the 1960s. Approximately 85-90 percent of the total vote went to the major parties, the Colorados and the Blancos. The Socialist and Communist parties, together with the Catholic-oriented Unión Cívica, constituted the principal minor parties in national politics. The total percentage of the vote received by these three groups did not vary significantly between the 1920s and the 1960s, and the Catholic party's share of the minor party vote remained relatively stable at approximately half of the total. However, over a period of many years, the Socialist and Communist parties tended to ebb and flow with each election. When the Socialist vote fell, that of the Communists rose, and vice versa. Similarly, within the labor movement, when the influence of the Socialists expanded, this usually occurred at the expense of the Communists, and vice versa.

THE SOCIALISTS AND THE TERRA DICTATORSHIP

In 1933 President Gabriel Terra carried out a coup d'état with the help of the national police force and established himself as dictator. Although this dictatorship was a relatively mild one, it was the only such regime that Uruguay has experienced in the 20th century. The president suspended the existing constitution, thus abolishing the Council of State, which according to the constitution of 1917 shared executive powers with the president. He also dissolved Congress and called elections on June 25, 1933, for a new Constitutional Assembly. The constitution it wrote provided that the second largest party (which in practice meant the Partido Nacional) would be assured half of the membership of the Senate, thus giving the Blancos, who had cooperated with Terra's coup, a veto power over any future president.

A number of opposition political leaders, including Emilio Frugoni, were deported to Buenos Aires. He was not allowed to return until after the general elections of April 1934, in which both he and Liber Troitiño were once more elected as Socialist members of the Chamber of Deputies, although the party had failed to win any seats in Terra's Constituent Assembly.[5] Upon his return to Uruguay, Frugoni resumed the editorship of the party's newspaper El sol, which he had published since the establishment of the party in 1922.[6]

For some months El sol had been suppressed by the government of President Terra. The police occupied the headquarters of the Socialist Party, where the paper was published, and announced that the newspaper would not be allowed to appear again unless its editors would agree to submit to prepublication censorship by government officials. In the face of this, the party leaders decided to issue instead the underground organ Adelante, which appeared for several months. El sol did not appear again until after the return of Frugoni from exile, more than a year after Terra's coup.[7]

During the later years of the Terra dictatorship, the Socialists tended to cooperate more or less closely with the Communists, the Catholic Unión Cívica, and dissident elements from both the Colorados and Blancos, presenting a united front against the government. Demonstrations were organized jointly; and there were some negotiations looking toward unity in the 1938 elections, but these did not bear fruit.[8] The Socialists finally ran Emilio Frugoni as their candidate; he received 26,057 votes, compared with the 121,269 received by the winner, General Alfredo Baldomir.[9]

WORLD WAR II AND AFTER

With the reestablishment of more or less fully constitutional government following the election of Alfredo Baldomir as Terra's successor in 1938, the Socialists participated in the return to normal politics. They supported the policies of Baldomir, which were designed to put an end to the remnants of the Terra dictatorship.

The Socialists played an important role in the late 1930s and the first years of World War II in exposing and denouncing the activities of Axis agents in Uruguay. A young Socialist, Hugo Fernández Artucio, was especially active in anti-Nazi work. He gathered much material on the Nazis in Uruguay, such as the connection of the Uruguayan Nazis and the German Nazi Party, the German view that people of German descent in the country were a "national minority," the activities of the local Nazis and the German consul in trying to get the Uruguayans to recognize such a status, and various other issues. After collecting this material Fernández Artucio prepared a complaint that he submitted to the criminal courts, asking that measures be taken against the Nazis. He published the material, in June 1940, in a book entitled <u>Nazis en al Uruguay</u>, which bore a preface by Socialist deputy José P. Cardoso.[10]

The antifascist attitude of the Socialists aroused strong opposition, not only from the Nazi agents in the country but also from the Right-wing Blancos, led by Luis Alberto Herrera, many of whom were pro-Axis in their sympathies. On December 30 Ramón Viña, a Herrerista deputy, tried to shoot Emilio Frugoni during a debate over the pro-Allied policies of the Baldomir government, which were being backed by Frugoni.[11]

The outbreak of World War II and the resulting shift of the Communists from a violently antifascist position to one of benevolent "neutrality" toward the Axis, brought strong clashes between the Uruguayan Socialists and Communists. The further about-face by the Communists after the invasion of the Soviet Union by Germany in June 1941 did little to mitigate the virulent hostility between the two groups.

This enmity broke into the open late in 1942, during a strike by the packinghouse workers. The Communists, whose current line called for them to oppose any important strike, on the grounds that it hampered the cooperation of Uruguay with the war effort of the Allies, and particularly the Soviet Union, denounced this walkout as the work of Axis agents. In contrast, the Socialists threw their support behind the walkout. As a result the Communists lost the considerable influence they had had among the packinghouse workers, which was of key importance because of the significance of the meat-packing industry in the national economy; and the Socialists won some influence in the group, although they never controlled it, as the Communists had done.

The 1942 packinghouse strike also was of significance because it provoked a split in the Unión General de Trabajadores. The Communists continued to control the organization; but Socialist trade unionists, who controlled the Commercial Workers Federation, the Unión Ferroviaria, and several smaller unions, resigned from the UGT Executive and their unions withdrew from the UGT.

The Socialist-controlled unions, together with organizations controlled by independents and other parties, joined to form the Comité de Relaciones Sindicales, which in 1946 changed its name to Comité pro CNT. A third group, the Comité de Enlace de Sindicatos Autónomos, led mainly by workers of Trotskyite and anarcho-syndicalist orientation, was also established.

Meanwhile the Socialists' most prominent leader, Emilio Frugoni, was playing an unaccustomed role. When, at the urging of the United States, Uruguay renewed relations with the Soviet Union, Frugoni was chosen to be the country's ambassador in Moscow. Another Socialist, young Mario Jaunarena, was named as the embassy's first secretary. They served until shortly after the end of World War II.

Three years after the end of the World War II, the Socialist Party of Uruguay experienced a minor split. A group of younger leaders, including several significant trade unionists, the most important of whom was Juan Acuña, withdrew from the party to form the Agrupación Socialista Obrera. They insisted that the older leadership of the party lacked militancy, concentrated too much on electoral politics, and was unconcerned with bringing about fundamental changes in the national economy and society. Members of this dissident Socialist group were of some importance in the leadership of several strikes in the following period. However, this schism did not cause major defections within the party ranks; and within a few years most of the dissidents had returned to the Socialist Party.

After the war enmity between the Socialists and Communists within the labor movement continued. So long as Stalin was alive, the ideological disagreement between the two groups was very sharp, with the Socialists strongly opposing the aggressive activities of the Soviet Union in Eastern Europe and elsewhere, and the cruelties of the Stalinist regime. The Partido Socialista proclaimed its opposition to the one-party dictatorship on the Stalinist model and its affinity with the British Labour Party and other European Socialist groups. It participated in the meetings that led to the reestablishment of the Socialist International in 1951 and was a member of the International for some years thereafter. When the Socialist International decided to establish a Latin American Secretariat in 1956, an Uruguayan, Humberto Maiztegui, was placed in charge.

The Socialist trade unionists cooperated with the elements in the Continental and world labor movements working against the attempts of the Communists to dominate organized labor. They worked with the representatives of the International Confederation of Free Trade Unions (ICFTU) and its affiliate, the Organización Regional Interamericana de Trabajadores (ORIT), who were stationed in the Río de la Plata area. Largely through the help of the ORIT representative, most of the non-Communist unions of Uruguay were brought together in a congress in January 1951 to establish the Confederación Sindical Uruguaya (CSU), which affiliated with the ICFTU and ORIT. The secretary-general of the CSU during most of its existence was Juan Acuña, who in the early 1950s was again a leading trade unionist of the Partido Socialista. Many of the other major figures in the CSU were also Socialists, although it also had in its ranks unions controlled by Batllistas, Independent Nationalists, and other political groups.

During most of the 1950s the Socialists and their allies in the labor movement constituted the majority of organized labor. The CSU had a majority of the country's unions in its ranks and carried out important leadership training and organizing activities. The Unión General de Trabajadores, still controlled by the Communists, was reduced to a relatively minor factor in the labor movement. Anarcho-syndicalist elements had a still smaller element under their leadership.

IDEOLOGICAL EVOLUTION AND DECLINE OF THE PARTIDO SOCIALISTA

Although the Socialists were highly critical of the Soviet Union and the Communist movement, they were also very insistent on their independence of the Western bloc in international politics. They were particularly critical of the role of the United States in world affairs. As a result of growing insistence on this anti-United States orientation, the Socialists tended to move increasingly away from their traditional position.

For instance, as early as 1954 the Socialist Party issued a decision that no trade unionists belonging to its ranks could accept an invitation to visit the United States issued by the American labor movement or the State Department. When Juan Acuña, secretary-general of the CSU, did accept such an invitation in that same year, he was forced to resign from the party.

By the middle 1950s the Uruguayan Socialist Party had adopted a so-called Third Force ideological position. Its national congress, which met October 25-30, 1955, passed a resolution that read in part:

> Congress reaffirms its repudiation of Stalinist Communism, a system that denies freedom and socialism, rests on police terror and state capitalism, leading to the shameful exploitation of the working masses at the hands of the bureaucracy and a privileged minority of the party. . . .
>
> Congress condemns in particular the capitalist imperialists of North America who are depriving the Latin American countries of their wealth and maintain them in backwardness and poverty, adding to the oppression imposed upon those countries by their own oligarchies and dictatorships. . . .
>
> To recognize the great opportunities offered by peaceful coexistence for the advance of socialism does not mean to be indifferent or neutral toward the totalitarian threat, no matter whether it emanates from fascist, Communist or any other quarters. Nor does it mean neutrality toward capitalist imperialism.
>
> What is does mean is a decisive and historically necessary affirmation of socialism as a third force which can lead the peoples toward freedom and universal brotherhood.[12]

In this period the Socialists still rejected any idea of cooperation with the Communists. When the Communists sent a letter to the National Executive Committee of the Socialist Party urging the establishment of "a common front of struggle" in May 1956, the Executive Committee sent a long reply in which it categorically rejected the idea. It stressed "the suppression of workingclass democracy" in the Communist-controlled countries, "Russian colonialism," and "the dependence of the Communist Party on the Moscow line, which leads to an alliance with the bourgeoisie."[13]

However, the growing drift of the Socialist Party to the left was intensified by the Castro revolution in Cuba. The Socialists joined with the Communists and other left-wing elements to declare their strong support of the Castro government. Many delegations that included Uruguayan Socialists visited the island, not only during the first year of the revolution but also in subsequent years, when the Cuban regime had quite openly taken the Communist path.

Although the Socialist Party of Uruguay had taken part in the establishment in 1956 of the Latin American Secretariat of the Socialist International, along with the Socialist parties of Argentina and Chile, it increasingly diverged from the international democratic Socialist movement during the 1960s. One congress of the Uruguayan Socialists adopted resolutions violently repudiating its supposed sister party, the Mapai of Israel, as well as denouncing the attitudes of the French Socialist Party. At the same time it severed all connections with the Socialist International.

This drift to the left on the part of the Partido Socialista del Uruguay aroused considerable resistance within the party's ranks. Many who had been active for years withdrew, without trying to form any rival group. However, in July 1961, when the National Executive Committee of the party undertook to dissolve the local branch in Montevideo, known as the Centro León Blum, and actually seized the branch headquarters by force, the members of this group took the lead in establishing a rival organization that they called "Socialismo Auténtico." Its principal figure was Ricardo Duran Cano.[14]

For several years the members of Socialismo Auténtico carried on the struggle against the Marxist-Leninist line of the party's leadership, without major effect. However, in 1964 the founder of the party, Emilio Frugoni, by now in his eighties, announced his withdrawal from the party and participation in a new reorganizing junta, to establish a new Socialist Party.[15]

One effect of the Socialists' drift to the left was the almost complete destruction of the party's influence on organized labor. Because during much of the 1950s the Socialist Party became increasingly indistinguishable in ideology from the Communists, it was no longer able to offer very effective opposition to Communist influence in the labor movement. To an increasing degree the Socialist leaders withdrew their support from the Confederción Sindical Uruguaya, which helped seriously to undermine this organization.

As a result of these developments, the Communists' influence in organized labor and Uruguayan politics tended to increase. The Communists endorsed the call of the Castro-dominated Confederación de Trabajadores de Cuba at the end of 1959 to launch a new "revolutionary" confederation of labor in Latin America. Allegedly as a step in this direction, the Communist unionists in Uruguay offered to dissolve the UGT if a new national central labor body was formed.

Such a new confederation, the Confederación Nacional de Trabajadores, was established in the middle of 1960. It brought within its ranks the great majority of the Uruguayan organized labor movement, and its establishment virtually marked the demise of the CSU. The Confederación Sindical Uruguaya was officially dissolved on June 15, 1966.[16] The destruction of the CSU did not result in any increase in the influence of the Socialists in the organized labor movement. They had virtually no influence within the new Confederación Nacional de Trabajadores, which was almost completely Communist-dominated.

However, it was not only in the labor movement that the Socialist Party's influence declined. Its electoral support also largely evaporated. In the election of 1962 the Socialists, in spite of their extremist position, were excluded from the electoral front organized by the Communists, the Frente Izquierda de Liberación (FIDEL); they therefore organized one of their own with several small extremist groups and a dissident faction of the Partido Blanco that was registered for electoral purposes under the name Unión Popular. This was a disaster; the only candidates elected by the Unión Popular were those from the Blanco ranks, and so for the first time in many years the Socialists found themselves without any representation in Congress.[17]

This electoral defeat was repeated in 1966, when the leaders of Socialismo Auténtico challenged the right of the Partido Socialista to use the party's name for electoral purposes. As a result the government authorities decided that both Socialist factions should be treated as were factions within the Colorado and Blanco ranks, each being allowed to run its own list of candidates, with the number of deputies or senators to which they were entitled being decided by the total number of votes cast by both lists and the victors, if any, being those with the highest number of votes. However, the total number of votes cast for Socialist candidates of any description was not sufficient to entitle either group to representation in either house of Congress. The Socialist vote was only 1 percent of the total.[18]

By the late 1960s the Socialist Party was in its ideological position considerably to the left of the Communist Party. The Socialists thus continued to proclaim unqualified backing for the Castro regime when the orthodox Communist parties of many Latin American countries were having polemics with Fidel.

The party's extremist position brought the Socialists into strong conflict with the Uruguayan government. After a violent outburst of strikes and student demonstrations in December 1967, the Socialist Party's weekly newspaper El sol was one of several periodicals suppressed by the administration. At the same time the party's headquarters were taken over by the police and were closed. Thereafter the Socialist Party continued to have a semilegal existence.

In the presidential election of 1971, the Socialists joined with virtually all other elements of the Left to form the Frente Amplio.

It named a retired general, Liber Seregni, for president; and although he aroused a considerable amount of enthusiasm outside the ranks of the parties supporting him, he received only about 20 percent of the total vote. One of the candidates of the Colorado Party, Juan María Bordaberry, supported by outgoing President Jorge Pacheco, was the victor.

STRENGTHS AND WEAKNESSES OF THE URUGUAYAN SOCIALISTS

Throughout their half-century history, the Uruguayan Socialists have faced a serious challenge immediately to their Right in national politics. The Batllista Colorados were during most of this period the principal advocates in the country of extensive social, economic, and political reform. The Batllistas drew most of their support from the urban workers and middle-class elements who might under other circumstances have been attracted to a Socialist Party. In contrast with the Socialists, the Batllistas had the advantage that they represented one of the nation's two traditional parties. They were able to mobilize support on that basis from many who might not otherwise have supported them, and the position of the Batllistas seemed to make it unnecessary for workers or intellectuals who wanted to back reform to break with the party to which their families had long been loyal.

Russell Fitzgibbon has summed up the relationship of the Batllistas and Socialists, saying that the Socialists' "orientation, like that of Colorados and Communists, is toward the Montevideo working classes. A practical program to appeal to those classes has been so much the monopoly of the Colorados, however, that the Socialists have been left little distinctive ground on which to stand."[19]

Even when the prestige and effectiveness of the Batllistas as a reform party began to decline after World War II, the Socialists did not succeed in offering a viable alternative to them. Although in the immediate postwar period they built up a following in organized labor that might have constituted a base for pushing a new reform program to carry forward the process begun by Batlle, the Socialists were not able to use their trade union influence. Instead, they veered sharply to the left and in the late 1960s adopted a romantic revolutionary posture that found little sympathy among the organized workers and lost the party much of the backing it had traditionally possessed in both the working and middle classes.

CHAPTER 8

OTHER SOCIALIST PARTIES

Although the Socialist parties of Argentina, Chile, and Uruguay have been the most important groups of this type in Latin America, similar organizations have existed in most of the other countries of the region. Some of these have had relatively long lives; others have been of short duration or have had a sporadic existence.

ECUADOR

During the late 1920s a group of radical intellectuals organized the Partido Socialista del Ecuador. Most of the leaders of this group were in fact sympathizers with the Communist International, and they established the Socialist Party more as a front group for Communist activity than as a genuine democratic Socialist movement. However, there were also in the first Ecuadorean Socialist Party's ranks a number of believers in democratic Socialism.

The Partido Socialista was accepted as a "fraternal" member of the Communist International at the Comintern's sixth congress in 1928. Four years later the name of the party, which by this time had become a thoroughgoing Communist group, was changed to Partido Comunista.

In the meantime those who had opposed the Communist inclination of the Partido Socialista had withdrawn to form other groups. One of these, with its principal following in Quito, took the name Transformación Social, later changing it to Partido Socialista. Another, with its base in the second city of the country, the port of Guayaquil, adopted the name Partido Social Cooperativista. These two groups joined in 1933 to establish the country's first nationwide democratic Socialist party, the Partido Socialista Ecuatoriano.[1]

During the 1930s the Partido Socialista Ecuatoriano developed into one of the country's major political parties, taking its place alongside the traditional Conservatives and Liberals. It received the support of much of the nascent working class of Quito, Guayaquil, and the smaller cities, as well as from some of the country's intellectuals.

The question of Socialist relations with the Communists continued to be a controversial issue within the Partido Socialista Ecuatoriano. During 1935 the two parties formed a united front in opposition to the first administration of José María Velasco Ibarra, whom they accused of dictatorial tendencies, and contributed to the overthrow of his regime.

Subsequently, when the Communist International had adopted the program of trying to establish Popular Fronts wherever possible, and in some cases even sought to convince Socialist parties to merge with Communist parties, Socialist-Communist relations in Ecuador were affected. In the Constituent Assembly elected after the overthrow of the dictatorship of General Federico Paez, a leftist bloc was formed by members representing the Socialists, Communists, and Vanguardia Revolucionaria Socialista (a small party formed by some of those who had belonged to Transformación Social of Guayaquil) who were looking toward the formation of a single party of the Left. However, little progress was made in that direction.[2]

The Socialists and Communists shared the leadership of the organized labor movement. The trade unions generally were few and small in number because of the rudimentary industrialization of Ecuador during this period. The Socialists had considerable strength among the artisans of Quito and Guayaquil, and Communist strength was centered among the railroad workers and the artisans of Guayaquil. The Communists were also active in attempting to organize some of the Indian peasants of the high plateau and had formed the Federación Indígena, led by Ricardo Paredes, founder of the Communist Party, as early as the mid-1920s.

The Socialists were in the opposition during the administration of Carlos Arroyo del Río, who took office in 1942. With the defeat of the Ecuadoreans in the short war with Peru in 1942, the opposition was augmented by the Conservatives and even the majority of the Liberal-Radical Party, to which Arroyo del Río belonged.

Socialists, Communists, Liberals, and Conservatives all participated in the revolutionary movement, led by ex-President José María Velasco Ibarra, that overthrew the Arroyo del Río government in 1944. All four parties were represented in the provisional government that Velasco Ibarra formed.

In 1944 the Socialists also participated in the establishment of the country's first national trade union organization, the Confederación de Trabajadores del Ecuador (CTE). However, they were

OTHER SOCIALIST PARTIES

overshadowed in this organization by the Communists; and the CTE had Pedro Saad, the principal leader of the Communist Party, as its first secretary-general.

The Socialists participated in the Constitutional Congress called after the overthrow of Arroyo del Río, but soon after the election of Velasco Ibarra as the first president under the new constitution, the Socialists entered the opposition. During the latter part of his second administration, Velasco Ibarra governed principally with the backing of the Conservative Party; and his regime was converted into a dictatorship.

In 1948 the Socialists again participated in a movement against the incumbent administration. Velasco Ibarra was ousted from the presidency for the second time, and the Socialists once again participated in the short interim government that succeeded him. They also participated in the subsequent constitutional regime of Galo Plaza, a Liberal, who was elected at the end of 1948.

In the meantime a conflict developed between the Socialists and Communists within the organized labor movement. As a result of this conflict, Pedro Saad was ousted by the Socialists from his post as secretary-general of the Confederación de Trabajadores del Ecuador. However, in spite of this change in leadership of the CTE, the Ecuadorean central labor group did not withdraw from the Communist-dominated Confederación de Trabajadores de América Latina, as did most other national labor bodies controlled by the Socialist parties in the early 1950s. Although they were formally in control of the Confederación de Trabajadores del Ecuador after 1946, the Socialists lived in constant fear that if they strongly opposed the policies advocated by the Communists, the latter would split the organized labor movement. As a result the CTE remained a member of the Confederación de Trabajadores de América Latina long after the latter had come completely under Communist control.

However, this pro-Communist position of the majority of the Socialists was opposed consistently by a minority within the party. Although at some party conventions the anti-Communist current seemed to have a majority, the leadership of the Socialists continued to follow a policy of more or less active cooperation with the Communists throughout the 1950s.

With Galo Plaza's completion of his presidential term in 1952, ex-President José María Velasco Ibarra was again elected; the Socialists once again joined the opposition and remained there during most of his administration. He was succeeded in 1956 by Camilo Ponce Henríquez, nominee of the Social Christian Party, who won with the support of the Conservative Party, one of the few Conservative-supported candidates to be elected president of Ecuador during the 20th century.

During the Ponce Henríquez administration the Socialist Party split. A left-wing group broke away to form the Partido Socialist Revolucionario, which became increasingly associated with the forces in Latin America following Fidel Castro. As a result of this division, the Partido Socialista Ecuatoriano supported the Liberal Party candidate, Galo Plaza, in the 1960 election, while the left-wing Partido Socialista Revolucionario participated in a left-wing coalition with the Communists and several smaller groups. However, the victor was once again José María Velasco Ibarra, who came to the presidency for the fourth time.

The split in the Socialist Party continued. The PSE participated for a time in both the Velasco Ibarra administration and that of Carlos Arosemena, Velasco's vice-president, who became president when Velasco Ibarra was overthrown in 1962. Within a little more than a year, Arosemena was also overthrown by the country's military and the armed forces established a dictatorship. All of the political parties were in the opposition during this military regime, which lasted almost three years.

The Ecuadorean Socialists emerged from the military dictatorship in 1966 split into three different organizations. The Partido Socialista Ecuatoriano, accused of having cooperated with the military regime, represented the right wing; the Partido Socialista Revolucionario was frankly Fidelista. A few months after the ouster of the junta, a group of Socialists who were discontented with both existing parties issued a call to establish a third group, the Partido Socialista Unificado.[3] All Socialist factions were in opposition in Velasco Ibarra's fifth term, 1968-72.

The Ecuadorean Socialists have suffered, during most of their history, from a feeling of inferiority vis-à-vis the Communists. They have hesitated to challenge them seriously in the organized labor movement and frequently have been allied with them in politics. This has probably hampered their assumption of a more significant role in national politics. However, the principal factor that has handicapped the Socialists, as well as all the other elements of the Left, has been the fact that political activity has been confined to a small proportion of the country's population, composed of the large landholders of the highland area, the middle class, and the artisan and working-class elements of Quito, a few other cities of the highlands, and the Guayaquil region on the coast. Finally, the charismatic figure of José María Velasco Ibarra has hovered over Ecuadorean politics during most of the life of the Socialist Party and has succeeded over and over again in rallying support from exactly those elements of the population to whom the Socialists have sought to appeal.

PERU

The origins of the Socialists in Peru were somewhat similar to those of the Ecuadorean Socialists. In the middle 1920s José Carlos Mariategui, a brilliant young Marxist intellectual, established the periodical Amaúta, which served as a forum for all radical tendencies in Peru as well as for writers from other Latin American countries and Europe. He gathered a group of other young intellectuals and some trade unionists around this periodical, and in 1928 they established the Partido Socialista del Perú. Like its counterpart in Ecuador, this party was oriented toward the Communist International and was accepted at the end of 1928 as a "fraternal" member of the Comintern.

In 1929 Mariategui and other representatives of the Partido Socialista del Peru were delegates to the conference of communist parties that met in Montevideo. There they argued strongly in favor of maintaining the Socialist Party as a "front" from behind which the Communists of Peru might continue to carry out their activities with relatively little governmental interference. They also put forward a thesis that the Indians of Latin America should become a major factor in bringing about the revolution in many of the countries of the area.

However, the positions of Mariategui and his followers were repudiated by the congress. They were ordered to establish an open Communist Party in Peru and to adopt the Comintern's official line with regard to "national minorities," which meant advocacy of the establishment of a separate Indian nation.

Mariategui died before he could decide whether to obey the dictates of the Comintern. However, a group of his followers, led by Eudocio Ravines, who had been secretary of the Aprista cell in Paris, went ahead with conversion of the Socialist Party into the Partido Comunista del Perú.[4]

Others associated with Mariatgui rejected this position. Some of them, led by Luciano Castillo, a young lawyer, reorganized the Partido Socialista del Perú. The new party soon established a base among the oil workers of the northern province of Talara, which they were to maintain for four decades.

However, the majority of the Left in Peru was controlled by two other parties, the Partido Comunista, founded by Ravines, and the Partido Aprista Peruano, established after the overthrow of the dictatorship of Augusto Leguía in 1930 by a group of labor leaders and intellectuals led by Víctor Raúl Haya de la Torre. The latter became the majority party among the country's urban workers and intellectuals.

During the four decades following its establishment, the Partido Socialista succeeded in maintaining certain strength in the province of Talara but was unable to expand into a truly national party. Until 1956 it usually had a small minority representation in Congress, and on several occasions Luciano Castillo served as senator. He also ran several times for president, though never gaining more than a small fraction of the total votes.

The Partido Socialista never joined the Socialist International because of a constitutional provision forbidding Peruvian parties to have international affiliations. However, until the early 1960s it considered itself a democratic Socialist party and maintained informal relations with the International—during the 1950s particularly with its Latin American Secretariat, with headquarters in Montevideo.

With the advent of the Castro regime in Cuba, the Partido Socialista del Perú enthusiastically supported it. Even after the Castro regime's gravitation in the direction of Marxism-Leninism, the Peruvian Socialists maintained considerable enthusiasm for that government. However, the role of the Partido Socialista in the Peruvian extreme Left was overshadowed by several new groups, including the Movimiento de la Izquierda Revolucionaria, formed by a group of dissidents from the Partido Aprista Peruano. In any case the Partido Socialista del Perú has never been a major factor in Peru's politics.

COLOMBIA

Utopian Socialism had its adherents in Colombia. In 1848-50 there existed in Bogotá and other cities so-called Sociedades Democráticas that were allied with the Liberal Party but had a philosophy similar to that of some of the French utopians of the period. At about the same time Manuel María Marieda, a Conservative social philosopher, published a book advocating agrarian socialism that in many ways foreshadowed the work of Henry George. At the turn of the century the great Liberal caudillo Uribe Uribe openly urged the adoption of a Socialist program for Colombia.[5]

At the end of the 1920s a group of left-wing Liberals organized the Partido Socialista Revolucionario, which played a major role in the labor movement of that period. However, with the advent of the Liberal Party to power in 1930 the PSR split into two groups, the larger of which reentered the Liberal ranks, the smaller converting the Partido Socialista Revolucionario into the Partido Comunista.[6]

It was not until the mid-1940s that an avowed Socialist Party was established in Colombia. The leader of this group was Antonio García, an economist and professor at the National University in

OTHER SOCIALIST PARTIES

Bogotá. Under his leadership the Partido Socialista Colombiano (which a few years later changed its name to Partido Popular Socialista) was established by a group of young intellectuals and labor leaders. The party, which was organized in January 1947, included some of the chief figures in the Confederación de Trabajadores de Colombia (CTC).

The chief importance of the Partido Socialista during its first year of existence came from the role of its leaders as close associates of Jorge Eliécer Gaitán, the flamboyant leader of the Liberal Party. A popular demagogue whose program was decidedly vague, Gaitán relied extensively on Antonio García and other Socialist leaders to provide concrete suggestions for reforms and ideas concerning the changes that the Gaintanista movement was trying to bring about in Colombian society.[7]

With the assassination of Gaitán on April 9, 1948, the country was thrown into a long period of civil strife that resulted in the death of several hundred thousand people in the so-called "violencia." For the following five years the Socialist Party struggled to maintain its existence in the midst of the bitter conflict between Conservatives and Liberals. Its influence in the labor movement was virtually destroyed.

With the overthrow of the Conservative government of Laureano Gómez in June 1953 by a military coup, the Socialists threw their support behind the new chief executive, General Gustavo Rojas Pinilla. Antonio García became one of the principal "brain trusters" for Rojas Pinilla, as he had been for Gaitán. When Rojas Pinilla appointed a new Constituent Assembly in 1954, he named Garcia to this body. García also became a member of the National Economic Council. At the same time Luís Emiro Valencia, one of García's principal lieutenants, became a leading member of the Bogotá City Council.

The explanation for the Socialists' support of Rojas Pinilla, even after he had become an avowed dictator, was that they felt that he was seeking to destroy the monopoly of power of the traditional Liberal and Conservative parties and that in his own somewhat befuddled way, Rojas was trying to do away with the "oligarchy," which the Socialists felt still dominated Colombian political, economic, and social life. Shortly before the ouster of Rojas Pinilla in May 1957, García and Valencia were among the authors of a speech that Rojas Pinilla gave, in which he proposed to nationalize the country's banks, carry out agrarian reform, nationalize foreign trade, freeze prices, and institute urban reform.[8] However, these proposals for fundamental economic and social changes came too late to save Rojas Pinilla, who was ousted by the military leaders after a general strike and lockout that had the backing of both the Conservative and Liberal parties.

Following the overthrow of the Rojas Pinilla regime, the Partido Popular Socialista disintegrated. Antonio García went into exile, where he worked for many years for various United Nations organizations. Luís Emiro Valencia, who married Gloria Gaitán, the daughter of Jorge Eliécer Gaitán, became one of the principal exponents in Colombia of the Castro regime after 1959. National politics returned to being a virtual monopoly of the Conservative and Liberal parties, and the Popular Socialist Party remained but a memory. Perhaps its most lasting effect was the several books that García had written during the height of the party's activities, in which he had sketched the nature of a Socialist program for Colombia; these books were widely read by Socialist leaders in other Latin American countries.[9]

In 1969 Antonio García returned to Colombia. Although offered a high position in ANAPO, Rojas Pinilla's political group, he rejected the offer. Instead, he tried to reestablish some kind of democratic Socialist party. However, two years later he had not been able to bring into existence any group of significance in national politics.

BRAZIL

Socialist ideas were brought to Brazil largely by the immigrants who streamed into the country even before the overthrow of the Empire in 1889. In 1890 a Liga Operaria, of Socialist inclinations, was formed in Rio; but it did not last long.[10] After the establishment of the republic, various immigrant groups began to establish Socialist organizations. One of these, set up by Germans in São Paulo, consisted of Lasallists rather than Marxists and undertook to criticize certain measures of the new republican government.[11]

In 1890 a workers party along Socialist lines was established in Rio and began publishing the periodical O Partido operario, edited by Dr. France e Silva. A relatively powerful Socialist Party was established in 1892 in the São Paulo city of Campos under the leadership of Murcio Paixão, a deputy in the national Congress. On August 13, 1892, this party addressed a petition to the Chamber of Deputies that demanded the enactment of an eight-hour workday. On May Day during the 1890s there were frequently demonstrations in São Paulo, Campos, Santos, Pará, Rio, and other cities.[12]

The most significant attempt to establish a Socialist Party in the pre-World War I period took place in 1902, when a congress was held in São Paulo, with delegates (including one woman) from Bahia, Pernambuco, São Paulo, Rio Grande do Sul, Paraná, Pará, and Paraíba. The party called upon the workers to organize, be temperate, and win converts to the cause. It demanded protection for labor, reduction of the work day, socialization of the means of production, and international action and cooperation with other Socialists. A party constitution was adopted that provided for the establishment of regional federations and the payment of annual dues by party members.[13]

This party was of considerable importance for a while and published a daily paper, Avanti. However, most of the members of the party were Italian, Portuguese, and Spanish immigrants who were more interested in events in Europe than they were in Brazilian politics. As a result, the party ended up as a São Paulo branch of the Italian Socialist Party.

In this period the leadership of the Socialist Party came largely from middle-class intellectuals, and the party did not succeed in getting any substantial base in the still tiny organized labor movement. The trade unions were largely controlled by anarcho-syndicalists.[14]

With the establishment of the Communist Party by a group of ex-anarcho-syndicalist labor leaders in 1922, left-wing politics in Brazil came to be dominated by the struggle between this group and their former comrades who were still loyal to anarcho-syndicalism. However, there was a small Partido Trabalhista, which had some contact with the Labor and Socialist International and was headed by Dr. Pedro da Cunha.[15]

It was not until after the revolution of 1930 that another serious attempt was made to establish a nationwide Socialist Party. This effort was undertaken by some of the so-called "Tenentes," military men who had played a key role in the revolution that had put Getúlio Vargas in power and sought to maintain their influence by establishing a national political party. This was the Partido Socialista Brasileiro, which resulted from a so-called Congresso Revolucionario, held in 1933. This party, which was headed for a time by Major Juárez Távora, was ideologically somewhat confused and incorporated in its program corporative state concepts along with more orthodox democratic Socialist ideas.

The Partido Socialista Brasileiro declared its program to be "a general line tending to socialism, subordinated to Brazilian conditions." It stated: "Unionization and representation of classes in parliament are the two fundamental theses which we write upon our banner." It set forth the five principles of the PSB as

1. Socialism—adapted to the times and the national necessities and traditions.
2. The predominance of the Union over the States.
3. The interests of the group above those of the individual.
4. The interests of Brazil above internationalism.

5. All power resting on the wishes of the citizens without any distinctions of any kind.16

The party failed to become a major force in national politics, largely because of its inability to mobilize the backing of the Tenentes, particularly those whom Vargas had named interventors (appointed state governors) and who were mainly concerned, after the 1930 revolution, with organizing the basis for political support that could assure their election as governors once constitutional government had been restored. In most cases these Tenente interventors found the radical name and program of the Partido Socialista Brasileiro a handicap they did not want to assume. As a result the party did very poorly in the Constituent Assembly elections in 1933. Thereafter it merged with the remains of the Partido Trabalhista and participated in the short-lived Aliança Nacional Libertadora (ALN), a sort of Popular Front formed by left-wing opponents of the Vargas regime early in 1935. However, the suppression of an attempted revolt by a faction of the ALN in November 1935 led to the Partido Socialista Brasileiro being driven underground by the Vargas regime. It ceased to exist soon thereafter.17

A new Socialist Party was not organized in Brazil until after the overthrow of the Vargas dictatorship in 1945. A group of Socialist-inclined individuals participated in the broad movement against the Vargas regime that took shape late in 1944 and early in 1945, known as the União Democrática Nacional (UDN). Within the ranks of the UDN, they formed the Esquerda Democrática, which took as its slogan "Socialismo e Liberdade." The Esquerda elected several members of Congress on the UDN ticket in December 1945. Thereafter the Esquerda Democrática was reorganized as an independent party.

In the meantime a group of ex-Trotskyites, headed by Mario Pedrosa, a newspaperman and art critic, had in August 1945 established a periodical in Rio de Janeiro, Vanguarda socialista. This group had members in São Paulo and a few other cities, as well as in Rio de Janeiro. Those in São Paulo were among the founders of Esquerda Democrática in that state.18

Although the leaders of Esquerda Democrática feared what they conceived of as the too-radical stance of the Vanguarda socialista group, the two merged in 1947, when Esquerda Democrática changed its name to Partido Socialista Brasileiro. Vanguarda socialista was published as the official newspaper of the PSB, until it was suspended for lack of funds.

The Partido Socialista Brasileiro continued in existence until the suppression of all political parties by President Castelo Branco's Second Institutional Act in October 1965. However, it never became one of the country's major parties. This was due largely to the polar attractions on the Brazilian Left between the forces of the Partido Trabalhista Brasileiro, led first by Getúlio Vargas and, after his death, by João Goulart, and the Communist Party of Brazil, headed by Luiz Carlos Prestes, and to the inability of the Partido Socialista Brasileiro to assume a position of independence vis-à-vis these two rivals. The PSB tended constantly to be torn between the temptation to cooperate with the Communists and the possibility of merging forces with the PTB.

This attitude was particularly disastrous in the early 1950s. After the return of Getúlio Vargas to power at the end of 1950, his prestige among the country's workers plummeted because of his inability to curb inflation and the confusion and corruption that seemed to mark his regime. At the same time the Communist Party's influence also dropped markedly because of its rash use of the labor movement for partisan political purposes. If the Socialists had at that point assumed an aggressive "third position" on the Left, they might well have been able to rally sufficient working-class support to make them a major factor in national politics.

For a while during the 1950s the São Paulo state branch of the Socialist Party did seem to emerge as a major element in the political life of that state. However, this success was more apparent than real. It occurred because of the support the Socialist Party gave to Jânio Quadros in his successful campaigns for mayor of São Paulo and for governor of the state, and their subsequent participation in his administration. Large numbers of opportunists, hopeful of getting jobs, joined the Socialist ranks at this time.

However, the net result of this experience was not very positive from the Socialists' point of view. The party was soon torn by a factional struggle over whether to continue to support the administration of Governor Jânio Quadros. It finally withdrew this backing, but only at the expense of losing most of the recruits brought to its ranks by its participation in the regime.

The one attempt that the Socialist Party made to assume an independent stance on a nationwide basis came too late and did not greatly enhance the party's position. This was its launching of the presidential campaign of General Juárez Távora in 1955. Early in the campaign the party nominated Távora on a platform calling for nationwide agrarian reform and other measures for fundamental change. However, soon thereafter the general's candidacy was endorsed by several other parties, most importantly by União Democrática Nacional, which had little interest in reform and succeeded in converting the campaign largely into a crusade against the remaining influence of Getúlio Vargas, who had committed suicide in August 1954.

Throughout the 1950s the Socialists had some influence in the organized labor movement in Rio de Janeiro, São Paulo, and a few other centers. The Metalworkers Union of São Paulo, the Printing Trades Workers Union of Rio de Janeiro, and the National Airline Workers Union were a few of the groups in which Socialists held leading positions.

During the 1960s a Socialist leader in the state of Pernambuco, Francisco Julião, was the principal force behind the organization of a Peasant League movement in his own and several neighboring states. Although the organization of the Peasant Leagues was due largely to the personal efforts and charisma of Julião rather than to the work of an organized drive by the Socialist Party, the at least passing success of these organizations served greatly to enhance the importance of Julião himself and to catapult him into national and even international prominence. As a result he was first elected to the state legislature of Pernambuco and, in 1962, to the Chamber of Deputies in Brasília[19]

In the presidential campaign of 1960 the Socialists supported the nominee of the heir of Vargas, Marshal Henrique Teixeira Lott— fearing, as a result of their previous association with Lott's major rival, Jânio Quadros, that Quadros might well become a dictator if he were elected president. In the mounting confusion of the early 1960s, the Socialists cast in their lot definitively with the forces supporting the government of João Goulart, who succeeded to the presidency after the resignation of Jânio Quadros in August 1961. Members of the party served in several of Goulart's cabinets and were to be found among the left-wing members of the Goulart camp.

With the overthrow of Goulart by the military in April 1964, the Socialists were thrown into confusion, as were all elements of the Left. Many of them had been willing to support an attempt by Goulart to establish a dictatorship; but when a military dictatorship was set up instead, the Socialists found themselves among those persecuted by the new regime. Four of their deputies, including Francisco Julião, were removed from Congress and deprived of their civil rights. In the state and municipal elections held in 1965, the Socialists supported opposition candidates. The victory of a number of these candidates served as the pretext for the Second Institutional Act late in October 1965, which resulted in the suppression of all existing political parties, including the Partido Socialista Brasileiro.

VENEZUELA

After the Acción Democrática revolution in October 1945, there appeared two small parties in Venezuela that called themselves

"Socialist." One of these was the Partido Socialista Agrario (PSA), established by a Caracas medical doctor, J. Rojas Contreras, which was organized on October 23, 1945, and immediately announced its support for the revolutionary government headed by Rómulo Betancourt.

Upon hearing the announcement of the formation of the PSA, a group of students and workers in the Caracas area who had been contemplating the establishment of a Socialist Party got in touch with Rojas Contreras. This group was headed by Alejandro Freitas, who soon after the death of dictator Juan Vicente Gómez had taken the lead in organizing the first oil workers union at El Tigre, and who by 1945 was a student at the Central University in Caracas.

These two elements merged for some time, with Ramón Mayora, a close associate of Freitas, becoming secretary-general of the PSA. However, quarrels developed between Rojas Contreras and the Freitas-Mayora group; and in October 1946 Freitas and his friends withdrew from the PSA to form a second Socialist group, the Partido Socialista de Trabajadores.[20]

Neither of the Socialist parties was able to gain much influence during the Acción Democrática government of 1945-48—they were unable to elect representatives to the 1946 Constitutional Assembly or the regular Congress chosen at the end of 1947.

With the overthrow of the Acción Democrática regime, the two Socialist parties seem to have adopted different attitudes. For a short while Rojas Contreras served as minister of health in the government of the military junta, while the PST was in the opposition. Both parties were in the opposition during the administration of Marcos Pérez Jiménez (1952-58).

With the overthrow of the Pérez Jiménez dictatorship, both the Partido Socialista Agrario, which now changed its name to Partido Socialista Venezolano, and the Partido Socialista de Trabajadores resumed activity. However, neither party was successful in winning a post in Congress in the election held in December 1958.

In 1961 the Partido Socialista de Trabajadores merged with supporters of former Acción Democrática Senator Ramón Escovar Salóm to form a new party, the Movimiento Republicano Progresista. Alejandro Freitas became the labor secretary of the MRP.[21] Although at the time this party was established it appeared that the MRP might become a group of some significance, rallying particularly businessmen and lower middle-class people of more or less progressive ideas who did not want to join any of the existing parties, such did not prove to be the case. In the election of 1963 the MRP supported the candidacy of a novelist and business executive, Arturo Uslar Pietri, who came in third; and soon afterward it disappeared in the new party, the Frente Nacional Democrático, that Uslar Pietri organized.

Meanwhile, the Partido Socialista Venezolano also participated in the 1963 election, supporting Jóvito Villalba, the nominee of the Unión Republicana Democrática. It also ran its own list of candidates for Congress and succeeded in electing one member of the Chamber of Deputies, Andrés Agelvis Prato.

At the time of the 1968 election, the Partido Socialista Venezolano, which had meanwhile changed its name to Partido Socialista Democrático, at first sought to participate in a coalition of various opposition parties that were trying to offer a "fourth candidacy" against the front runners—Gonzalo Barrios of Acción Democrática, Luis Beltrán Prieto of the dissident AD party Movimiento Electoral del Pueblo, and Rafael Caldera of the Partido Social Cristiano Copei.[22]

However, when these negotiations failed, the Partido Socialista Democrático decided to name its own candidate, and chose Alejandro Hernández, a well known industrialist who for years had headed "Pro-Venezuela," a group active in lobbying for protectionism and other support for Venezuelan industrialization.[23] Hernández' showing was not encouraging: he received only 26,806 votes, or 0.71 percent of the total, in the December 1968 election. The PSD did not elect anyone to the Chamber of Deputies.[24]

Neither Socialist Party succeeded in gaining any significant influence in Venezuelan politics. Nor did either establish contacts with other Socialist parties in Latin America, or with the Socialist International. Indeed, it was Acción Democrática that affiliated with the Socialist International in the mid-1960s.

PANAMA

The Socialist Party of Panama was founded in 1933 by a group of intellectuals and trade unionists opposed to the influence of the Communist Party who were led by Demetrio Porras, son of a former president and a leading young criminal lawyer. It was first called the Partido Socialista Marxista, but the last word was dropped because it was felt that this constituted too handy a weapon for the party's right-wing opponents.[25] In 1935 the party was joined by a small group of Trotskyites headed by Diógenes de la Rosa.[26]

For a number of years the Socialists and Communists fought for control of organized labor. In 1940 groups under both Socialist and Communist influence established the Organización Sindical, which five years later, on August 14, 1945, sponsored a congress that established the country's first central labor group, the Federación Sindical de Trabajadores de Panamá. It remained united until 1948, when the rival Unión General de Trabajadores was established under Socialist leadership.[27]

Meanwhile, the Socialist Party had been very active in politics. In 1940, soon after the election of Arnulfo Arias to the presidency for the first time, the Socialist leaders participated in a conspiracy to oust him. When this failed, Demetrio Porras and José Brouwer, two of the party's principal leaders, went into exile in Chile. While there they participated in a hemispheric conference of Socialist parties sponsored by the Socialist Party of Chile.[28]

With the overthrow of Arias in 1942, Demetrio Porras was sent as Panamanian ambassador to London, where he remained until shortly before the election campaign of 1948. Despite his absence the Socialist Party elected two members of the National Assembly in the election of 1944: Diógenes de la Rosa and José Brouwer.

Factionalism was rife within the Socialist ranks during much of the 1940s. A group opposed to Porras' influence succeeded in ousting him from the position of chief of the party in 1940. However, three years later the pro-Porras element won control and the group opposed to his leadership withdrew to form a rival party, which soon disappeared.[29]

Factionalism was renewed with Porras' return from his ambassadorial post early in 1948. A number of those who had supported him in the earlier struggle now accused Porras of having used this post for corrupt purposes and challenged his right to lead the party. Partly as a result of this internal conflict, the Socialists did very badly in the 1948 election, obtaining only 3,500 votes throughout the republic and losing their two seats in the Assembly. As a consequence the Socialists lost their official standing as a legal political party.[30]

The Socialist Party did not regain its legal status during the 1950s. During much of this time, Panamanian politics functioned under a new electoral law sponsored by Colonel José Remón, the chief of the National Police, who was elected president in 1952: all existing parties were merged into two, Remón's Concentración Patriótica Nacional and the the opposition Partido Liberal. Even when this system was abandoned, it was several years before the Socialist Party regained its legal standing.

However, during the 1960s the party regained some influence, electing one member of the National Assembly. Demetrio Porras retired from the leadership when, with the party's approval, he accepted membership on the nation's Supreme Court in 1961.

In 1964 the Socialists suffered still another split. Although in the election of that year it ran its own candidate, the peasant leader Florencio Marris, a group of members headed by the party president, Ismael Sánchez, broke away to support the candidacy of the Liberal Party's Marcos Robles, who won.[31]

Meanwhile, the Socialists had lost virtually all of their influence in organized labor, which during most of the 1950s and 1960s was divided between a small Communist group, still organized in the Federación Sindical de Trabajadores de Panamá, and a somewhat larger nonpartisan group, aligned with the International Confederation of Free Trade Unions. In terms of general politics, the party remained small and not very important.

BOLIVIA

Several efforts have been made to establish a democratic Socialist party in Bolivia, but none of them has given rise to an organization that could survive more than a few years. The first such effort occurred in the mining town of Potosí in 1913, when a small group of students and workers set up the first Partido Socialista. Those who organized it had learned their socialism largely from books, principally those from Spain. They established some contacts with the Argentine Socialist Party, particularly with Alfredo Palacios. The party had about 200 members, and it organized a number of unions among miners and city artisans. It lasted for about three years, during which it was severely persecuted by the government.[32]

About a decade later a second attempt was made to establish a Socialist Party, this time by Gustavo Navarro, who was better known by his pen name, Tristán Marof. He had been a member of the Bolivian diplomatic corps in Europe, where he had firsthand contact with the post-World War I revolutionary movements. He began to write books and articles under the name Tristán Marof praising these movements and soon left the diplomatic corps. In 1926 he returned to Bolivia and for the next two years organized the country's second Socialist Party. It was distinctly sympathetic to the Russian Revolution, and Marof for some time served as a correspondent for the Communist International's periodical, International Press Correspondence, although he was never a Communist. He went into exile again in 1928, and his party was a casualty of the Chaco War (1932-35).[33]

During this same period a group of university students in La Paz was attracted by Socialist ideas. Led by Francisco Lazcano Soruco, this group joined the traditional Partido Republicano Socialista of President Bautista Saavedra after the revolution of 1930, hoping to convert that group into a genuine Socialist party. They stayed in the PRS until 1940, when they withdrew to form the Partido Socialista Unificado. They fought strongly for two years against the government of General Enrique Peñaranda, which had been elected in 1940 with the support of the Partido Republicano Socialista. However, in 1942 two members of the Partido Socialista Unificado joined the government of Peñaranda. This provoked a split and the formation of the so-called Partido Socialista Independiente (PSI) by those opposed to cooperation with Peñaranda. After Peñaranda's ouster by a coup of young officers and the Movimiento Nacionalista Revolucionario, the PSI cooperated closely with the government of President Gualberto Villarroel during the first months after that regime seized power in December 1943.

However, both Socialist groups were soon in opposition to the Villarroel regime, and they cooperated with those who overthrew it in July 1946. Soon thereafter both of these rather strange Socialist groups disappeared when they merged with two factions of the traditional Republican Party to form the Partido Unión Republicana Socialista.[34]

None of the Bolivian Socialist parties, with the possible exception of the first, was what one would call an orthodox democratic Socialist organization. Nor did any of them become a major factor in Bolivian politics.

CUBA

One of the apostles of Cuban independence, Diego Vicente Tejera, a well-known poet, was the first prominent advocate of democratic Socialism in Cuba. During the preindependence period Tejera was active among the Cuban migrants and exiles in the United States, seeking to establish a Socialist Party among them. Although this effort did not bear fruit, Tejera did succeed in establishing the country's first Socialist organization, the Club La Gloria in Havana, in 1902, shortly before his death.

Tejera's work was continued by a group of Spanish immigrants and native Cubans and gave rise to the formation in 1905 of the first Partido Socialista de Cuba. At its inception the party had branches in Havana and Manzanillo. In 1912 it absorbed another small group, the Radical Labor Party. By 1914 the Socialist Party consisted of five branches, with a total membership of 2,000. It had an official publication, Verdad socialista, which had replaced the earlier periodical El socialista, the country's first Socialist paper.[35]

The Socialist Party failed to become a major factor in Cuban political life. The labor movement was largely dominated by anarcho-syndicalist elements, although the Socialists had some influence in the Railroad Workers Brotherhood and some small unions. By the 1920s the Socialist movement was reduced to a small group of labor leaders and intellectuals in Havana who continued to publish a monthly magazine, Acción socialista. Late in 1925 they sought to bring together a number of unions to form a Cuban Labor Party, but this effort proved fruitless.[36] With the formation of the Communist Party in the same year, the Socialists faced additional competition.

By the late 1920s the principal figure in Cuban Socialism was Juan Arévalo, a Spanish immigrant, who was a leading figure in the Railroad Workers Brotherhood and was editor of Acción socialista. However, his efforts did not result in the establishment of more than a small Socialist group in Havana. Its members were absorbed in a new left-wing party, Unión Revolucionaria, established in 1937 under the leadership of the well-known poet Juan Marinello. Two years later the Unión Revolucionaria merged with the Communist Party to form the Unión Revolucionaria Comunista.[37]

However, the Socialist elements in the URC were strongly opposed to the Communist position of "neutrality in favor of the Axis" between August 1939 and June 1941. As a result they withdrew from the party in December 1940 and reestablished a Socialist group, the Partido Socialista Obrero. Although this party, which was led by Arévalo and Ramón Léon Rentería, a member of the Chamber of Deputies and leader of the Maritime Workers Federation, claimed 20,000 members soon after its establishment, it soon declined.[38] By the late 1940s the Socialist movement in Cuba was reduced to a small Federación Socialista, with its main base in Havana but with branches in Santiago de Cuba and one or two other cities. This group, which flirted with Fulgencio Batista after his seizure of power in a coup d'état on March 10, 1952, disappeared later in the 1950s.[39]

Thus democratic Socialism in Cuba never was able to overcome the competition from other political tendencies on the Left and in the labor movement. First confronted by the anarcho-syndicalists, and subsequently by the rise of the Communist Party, its role as spokesman for elements of the democratic Left was largely taken over, after the ouster of the Machado dictatorship in 1933, by the Auténtico Party led by Ramón Grau San Martín and others who had participated in his short-lived government of September 1933-January 1934. Except perhaps for a short time before World War I democratic Socialism in Cuba never amounted to much more than a sect.

MEXICO

Democratic Socialism as an organized political force played virtually no role in the Mexican Revolution. The most important group of early revolutionaries to profess democratic Socialism was the Partido Socialista de Yucatán, organized in the first years after the overthrow of Profirio Díaz and headed by one of the most colorful figures in the Mexican upheaval, Felipe Carrillo Puerto. It dominated the state of Yucatán during most of the decade 1914-24. Its leaders had only the vaguest ideas of Socialist doctrine. They had some contact with the Socialist Party of the United States through Robert

Haberman, a New York Socialist who visited the peninsula and stayed to become a close friend of Carillo Puerto. For a short time this party sought affiliation with the Communist International. However, in 1928 it became affiliated with the new National Revolutionary Party, established by ex-President Plutarco Elías Calles; since then it has continued to be the state affiliate of the government party.

The first attempt to establish a democratic Socialist party on a national basis was made in 1912. A group of young men, some of them active in the new organized labor movement, founded the periodical El socialista in January of that year. It served as a vehicle for launching the Partido Socialista Mexicano, which was represented at the 1912 convention of the Socialist Party of the United States.[40]

The Socialist Party, under the leadership of its secretary-general, Adolfo Santibáñez, remained active during the turbulent period of recurring civil war between 1912 and 1920. After the United States entered World War I it attracted a number of Socialists from the United States who had fled to Mexico to avoid the draft. It also recruited a number of other exiles, including M. N. Roy, who later founded the Communist Party of India.

The 1919 convention of the Mexican Socialist Party was the scene of a violent struggle for power, in which the foreigners took a leading part. As a result of this meeting, the party split, with both factions seeking admission to the newly established Communist International. As a democratic Socialist group the Mexican Socialist Party thus disappeared.[41]

Another party that for a while had a vaguely Socialist orientation was the Partido Laborista Mexicano. The PLM was the political arm of the Confederación Regional Obrera Mexicana (CROM), the nation's first major trade union body, and its fortunes rose and fell with those of CROM.

During the administration of Alvaro Obregón (1920-24) the Partido Laborista Mexicano was one of several parties supporting the administration. It had a few seats in Congress, and several of its leaders were given government posts. However, it was in the succeeding administration of Plutarco Elías Calles (1924-28) that the PLM reached the apex of its power and influence.

In the election of 1924, in which the Partido Laborista Mexicano was the principal supporter of the candidacy of Calles, the party won 40 of the 272 seats in the national Chamber of Deputies, as well as 11 of the 58 Senate seats and two state governorships. It also won control of the city council of Mexico City and several other municipalities. Soon afterward, Calles chose Luís N. Morones, chief of both CROM and the Partido Laborista, to be the country's first minister of labor and industry.

Throughout most of the Calles regime, the PLM functioned as the government party. However, late in 1927 the president and the PLM leaders had a falling out about who should be the official candidate in the 1928 elections; as a result Calles withdrew his support. Dissidence within the PLM ranks quickly appeared, and the rapid decline of the party began. Morones resigned from Calles' cabinet several months before the expiration of the president's term.

The decisive end of appreciable influence of the Partido Laborista in national politics came in 1929, when ex-President Calles established a new group, the Partido Nacional Revolucionario, as the official party of the Mexican regime. However, the Partido Laborista Mexicano lingered on, as the political arm of the much depleted Confederación Regional Obrera Mexicana, for another two decades. In that period, however, it gave up all pretense of being a democratic Socialist party.

During the years in which it was the dominant Mexican central labor body, CROM became a member of the largely Socialist-controlled International Federation of Trade Unions. During this same period the Partido Laborista Mexicano maintained friendly relations with the Labor and Socialist International. However, in its decline the PLM no longer maintained any connection with the international Socialist movement.[42]

The final effort to establish a Socialist Party in Mexico came in the late 1930s. At that time an important element in the leadership of the Confederación de Trabajadores de México, CROM's successor as the nation's principal labor confederation, established a group called Grupo Socialista de la CTM. It included the third highest official of the CTM Benjamín Tabón, national committee members Rodolfo Piña Soria and Ruben Magaño, and Carlos Gracidas, who had been a labor member of the 1917 Constituent Assembly.[43] It published a monthly journal, Acción social, which carried on a bitter struggle within the CTM against Communist influence. It supported President Lázaro Cárdenas and for a while backed the secretary-general of the CTM, Vicente Lombardo Toledano, turning against him as he moved closer to the Communists after 1937.

As these labor leaders lost their influence in the labor confederation, they reorganized themselves as the Grupos Socialistas de la República Mexicana, with the avowed purpose of ultimately founding a democratic Socialist Party. They held three national congresses but never established a national political party. From time to time some of their members held positions of importance in the Mexican government; and a few of their leaders were active through at least the 1940s in the leadership of the labor movement, particularly in the Confederación Proletaria Nacional.[44] However, by the early 1960s, the Grupos Socialistas de la República Mexicana had expired.[45]

PUERTO RICO

One of the strongest Socialist parties in Latin America for a number of years was that of Puerto Rico, which was for two decades one of the three largest parties on the island. The organizer, and during most of its history the head, of the Puerto Rican Socialist Party was Santiago Iglesias, a native of Spain who, after spending 10 years in Cuba, migrated to Puerto Rico shortly before the invasion of that island by American troops in October 1898.

During the last year or so of the Spanish regime, Iglesias had been disseminating propaganda in favor of trade unionism and Socialism in Puerto Rico. Five days after the occupation by U.S. troops, he began publishing El porvenir social, a newspaper "to which the island owes the most intensive diffusion of Labor and Socialistic ideals, and which was destined to serve as a guide to the multitude of workers throughout Porto Rico," according to Iglesias' own account. In the following months Iglesias led in the organization of two groups, the Free Federation of Workingmen, which was accepted soon afterward as the Puerto Rican state affiliate of the American Federation of Labor, and the Partido Socialista Obrero. The latter was established at a convention in October 1899 and sent a delegate to the founding convention of the Socialist Party of the United States at Indianapolis in 1901.

During its early years the Partido Socialista Obrero did not enter candidates in elections, "its retirement being due to the exceptional conditions which then existed in the island, and to the lack of legal guarantees...." In 1906 the party, running under the name Federación Libre, presented candidates and obtained 1,345 votes. Six years later, under the name Insular Labor Party, the Socialists gained 2,359 votes in the city of Arecibo alone; and in 1914 it won 4,398 votes throughout the island and won control of the city of Arecibo.

However, the real rise in the political influence of the Puerto Rican Socialists, now using the name Partido Socialista Puertorriqueño began in 1917. In the election of that year they gained 24,468 votes and placed Iglesias in the Senate. In 1920 he was reelected to the Senate, and four Socialist members won seats in the lower house.[46]

The Socialists continued to increase their voting strength throughout the 1920s. They were the political arm of the island's trade union movement, which during World War I had succeeded in organizing most of the workers in the sugar industry. They were also strong advocates of statehood for Puerto Rico, feeling, as they stated in their platform of 1932: "The influence of the people of the United States in the destiny of Puerto Rico, has been, is and will be civilizing, and that the extension of the Constitution to Puerto Rico represents a positive guarantee of the public and political liberties convenient and favorable to the enjoyment of individual rights."[47]

In the election of November 1932 the Socialist Party signed an electoral agreement with the Republican Party, the other group on the island favoring statehood. As a result of this agreement Santiago Iglesias was elected resident commissioner in Washington (member of the House of Representatives with a voice but without a vote) with 100,000 votes on the Socialist line and 110,000 on that of the Republicans.[48] The Socialist-Republican coalition controlled the island's legislature for the next eight years, gaining a second victory in 1936, when the Socialists polled about 145,000 votes and the Republicans 155,000.[49] Iglesias returned to the House of Representatives, where he remained until his death in December 1939, whereupon he was succeeded by his son-in-law Bolívar Pagán, who held the seat until 1942.

The decline and disappearance of the Socialist Party resulted from the growth of the Popular Democratic Party, headed by Luís Muñoz Marín in the late 1930s. Santiago Iglesias and many of the other key leaders of the party came to be separated from the rank and file of their party and of the labor movement after 1932. They were busy in Washington and San Juan with problems of government and paid too little attention to the wishes and needs of their constituents. Iglesias' death in 1939 deprived the party of its most popular figure. In the second place, after 1932 the Socialist Party was invaded by a number of opportunists who were more interested in obtaining government jobs than they were in the principles of the party, and this gave rise to a certain amount of corruption in the ranks of the governing Socialist-Republican coalition.

Finally, there can be little doubt that both the program and the personality of Luís Muñoz Marín aroused a great deal of popular support. His urging that, for the time being at least, the issue of the island's political status vis-à-vis the United States be put into the background while the government concentrated on dealing with crucial social problems and the expansion and diversification of the economy undoubtedly appealed to many voters for whom the issue of statehood versus independence seemed sterile. Furthermore, Muñoz Marín's intensive personal proselytizing throughout the island, between the time he formed his party in 1938 and the time of its first electoral contest in 1940, had certainly won him a very wide personal following.

The emphasis of the Partido Popular Democrático on social and economic issues undoubtedly made it possible for it to draw support from advocates of both statehood and independence in the 1940 election. There is no question that many of the workers favoring statehood, who had traditionally supported the Socialist Party, turned to the Partido Popular Democrático in 1940.

OTHER SOCIALIST PARTIES

In the decade following the 1940 election, which put the Partido Popular Democrático in control of the Puerto Rican legislature, the Socialist Party declined catastrophically. It lost control of the labor movement, and its representation in the island's legislature disappeared. The party formally dissolved in the early 1950s.

In most of the countries of Latin America democratic Socialist parties have existed for longer or shorter periods of time. However, in few of these countries have they been able to become a major political factor for any sustained period. Their weaknesses have been several. In some countries they were at their inception based too exclusively on immigrant elements in the population; and with the decline of immigration, the Socialist parties also declined. In others they suffered a kind of inferiority complex with regard to the Communists and so were too often prone to ally themselves with the Communists, alliances usually counterproductive for the Socialists who were more loosely organized and less disciplined than the Communists. By the late 1960s the Socialists had been reduced to an element of minor importance in all but a handful of Latin American nations.

PART III
THE NATIONAL REVOLUTIONARY PARTIES

INTRODUCTION

The most important group of parties of the democratic Left in recent decades has been that of the national revolutionaries. Although each of these parties developed independently, they have had certain characteristics in common and have recognized a special bond among themselves.

Each of the national revolutionary parties has been indigenous to the nation in which it has existed, owing nothing to the proselytizing from abroad that some of the Socialist and Communist parties experienced. Each has developed out of the particular political situation in its respective country. Thus, the Partido Aprista Peruano grew from the university reform movement of 1918 and the struggle against the Leguía dictatorship of the 1920s; Acción Democrática was formed in the process of the struggle to liquidate the remains of the dictatorship of Juan Vicente Gómez; the MNR of Bolivia grew up as one aspect of a rebellion against the old order that had brought about the Chaco War; the Auténtico Party of Cuba came into being through the experiences of the short-lived revolutionary government of Ramón Grau San Martín in 1933, and so on.

The second characteristic of the national revolutionary parties has been their more or less common ideology. They have all been revolutionary parties in the sense of wanting to bring about fundamental economic and social changes. They have all conceived of themselves as multiclass parties, seeking to speak for the urban workers, the peasantry, and a more or less ill-defined middle class. They have all been nationalistic in terms of wanting to bring the economies of their nations under domestic control; in pushing the economic development, diversification, and independence of their countries; and in wanting their nations to follow a more or less independent foreign policy. They have all been believers in political democracy. Since none of them has been avowedly Marxist in its ideology, they have not suffered, to the degree that some of the Socialist parties have, from a feeling of inferiority vis-à-vis the Communists.

A third common link among these parties has been in their methods of organization. Since they have considered themselves as multiclass, they have established specific groups within their party structures to do propaganda and organizational work among various classes and elements. They have had trade union, peasant, and other similar secretariats with appropriate subsidiary organizations.

They have also sought to maintain a higher degree of party discipline than was customary in traditional parties of their area while trying to avoid the lack of democracy characteristic of the "democratic centralism" of the Communists. They have by no means always been successful in maintaining discipline with democracy, as is evidenced by the fairly frequent schisms that have taken place within their ranks.

Another organizational characteristic that is usual among the national revolutionary parties is their programs for studying the economic, social, political, and even cultural problems of their countries and their equally continuous efforts to train their members and lower-ranking leaders in the principles, programs, and objectives of the parties. Generally the parties have maintained permanent committees to study national problems; and some have established schools on various levels of party organization to fulfill the mission of educating the party members.

The national revolutionary parties have maintained more or less close relationships among themselves. Those in a more fortunate position have sought to give refuge to and help the members of sister parties forced into exile by dictatorial regimes. There have been congresses and conferences of the parties at which they have discussed their mutual problems.* In the late 1960s most of the parties joined the Socialist International, and their delegates took a more or less active part in its deliberations.

The national revolutionary parties have had their successes and their failures. Several of them have had more or less extended experience in the government. The Bolivian MNR, during 12 years of rule, brought about one of the most fundamental social revolutions that any Latin American country has experienced in the 20th century; the PRI of Mexico has governed its nation uninterruptedly since the party was formed in 1928, and whatever positive and negative aspects the Mexican revolution has had during that period have been its responsibility; Acción Democrática, in 10 years in Venezuela (1959-69) brought about a thoroughgoing agrarian reform, executed a program for integrating the interior of the country into the 20th century and laid the basis, for the first time in the nation's history, for a tradition of democratic government. In Costa Rica, in three periods of government (1953-58, 1962-66, 1970- ——), the Partido Liberacion Nacional pushed forward the country's rapid economic development and brought about significant social changes. The Popular Democratic Party of

---

*Boletín del Buro coordinador de la Internacional socialista, 4th Trimester, 1966, p. 256.

Puerto Rico set that island on a path of economic and social development after taking power in 1940 that most observers would have thought impossible before its appearance.

On the other hand, the Auténtico Party government in Cuba from 1944 to 1952 was marked by so much corruption and until the last two years of its tenure did so little to carry out its basic program that it went far to discredit democracy in that country. Similarly, in the Dominican Republic, the Partido Revolucionario Dominicano, after winning overwhelmingly the first election after the death of Rafael Trujillo, was unable to maintain itself in power and subsequently veered sharply away from the democratic Left in its ideology and policies.

The national revolutionary parties remain a major factor in Latin American politics. Their role, particularly since World War II, has been very important insofar as the political, economic, and social development of their various countries is concerned; and these parties seem likely to continue to be an important influence in Latin American politics.

CHAPTER 9

THE PARTIDO APRISTA PERUANO

One of the oldest national revolutionary parties of Latin America is the Partido Aprista Peruano. Since 1930 it has been the largest party of Peru; during most of this period it has been the country's majority party, but never has it been allowed to control the government. Its philosophy and program have set a pattern for a large number of other parties in the region.

ORIGINS OF THE APRISTAS

The Partido Aprista Peruano was not established until 1930. However, its antecedents are to be found in the student movement that arose during World War I and in the labor movement that had begun a decade or more before.

Organized labor had begun during the first decade of the 20th century. The first national central labor organization, the Federación Obrera Regional Peruana, had been established as early as 1913; and during World War I it had made considerable progress, particularly among the workers in the artisan shops and factories that had begun to appear in increasing numbers in Lima and its environs.

In 1918 the second element that was to go into the formation of the Aprista Party had its origins in the University Reform Movement. Starting in the Argentine University of Córdoba early in that year, the movement sought to change the nature of the Argentine universities. The students who led this movement tried not only to alter the structure and curriculum of the institutions of higher learning but also to take the university out into the general community and use it as a primary means of bringing about the social and political transformation of the country.

Victorious in Córdoba, the University Reform Movement soon spread throughout Argentina and into other Latin American countries. In Peru one of the first leaders of the movement was Víctor Raúl Haya de la Torre, a student in the University of San Marcos in Lima but a native of Trujillo, in the northern part of the country.

In his home town Haya de la Torre had belonged to a group of young intellectuals dedicated to studying the Indian origins of their country and had become convinced of the need for rehabilitating the descendants of the Incas, who had inhabited Peru before the coming of Pizarro and his conquistadores.

Once at San Marcos, Haya de la Torre soon became a leader of the University Federation. In 1918 he became its president and undertook to see to it that the university reform, begun in Argentina, should be extended to Peru. He put particular stress on the role of the students in helping the humble segments of the community, particularly in aiding the workers to organize to defend their rights.[1]

The students joined forces with the anarcho-syndicalist leaders of the trade unions to establish the "Popular University," a series of schools in union headquarters where the young university men taught union members a wide variety of subjects, ranging from basic reading and writing to world history and collective bargaining. Haya de la Torre and other student leaders also took a major role in bringing together various organizations to form the Federación Textil, embracing most of the country's textile workers unions.

The regime of Augusto B. Leguía, which came into office by coup d'état in 1919, was highly suspicious of the student movement, particularly of its association with the organized workers. Although from time to time it closed down one or another of the student-worker "university" branches, a showdown between the students and their labor allies and the goverment did not come until May 1923.

At that time Leguía sought to strengthen his regime by allying it with the Catholic Church. He decided to "dedicate Peru to the Sacred Heart of Jesus." However, the students protested vigorously against this demonstration of clericalism; as a result of student protests, Haya de la Torre and other leading figures were arrested and, after a few days' imprisonment, deported to Panama.

During the rest of the 1920s the former leaders of the Students Federation were dispersed in exile. A few of them met in Mexico in 1924 and there established what they called the Alianza Popular Revolucionaria Americana (APRA), from which the Partido Aprista Peruano ultimately took its name.

Although at first the members of the APRA regarded themselves as Marxists, they soon evolved a philosophy that was at very least a variant on orthodox Marxism. Their principal theoretician and leader, Víctor Raúl Haya de la Torre, developed the thesis that "imperialism," far from being, as Lenin had argued, the "highest stage of capitalism," was, from the point of view of Latin America, the beginning of capitalism, since it was the foreign firms that brought modern capitalist ideas, methods, and capital to semifeudal Latin America.

Furthermore, argued the Apristas, the real enemy of popular forces in Latin America was the semifeudal landed aristocracy. Not only did this element keep most of the rural population in a state of semiserfdom, reminiscent of the European Middle Ages; it also tended to ally itself with foreign Imperialist firms. In doing so the landlords were willing to make concessions to foreign enterprises that compromised the national interests of the Latin American countries, since they felt that the presence of the foreign firms would strengthen their own position.

The revolutionaries in Latin America should, therefore, try to rally the widest coalition possible of forces opposed to this landlord-imperialist alliance. This meant that there should be formed in each of the Latin American countries, and in Latin America as a whole, a multiclass party that would bring together the urban working class, the peasantry, and those middle-class elements that had interests opposed to those of the landlord-capitalist alliance.

Haya de la Torre and his associates were anti-imperialists. They felt that it was necessary for Latin America to unite to resist the military intervention of the United States, which was then deeply involved in the "Big Stick" policy. However, Haya maintained that although the foreign firms coming to Latin America came to make the largest profit possible, the capital and know-how they brought was needed by Latin America. Furthermore, the Apristas said, the Latin Americans were in a position to insist on the conditions under which they wanted these foreign enterprises to come to their countries, since the foreign investors needed to come to Latin America to augment their profits at least as much as the Latin Americans needed to have them come. Hence, the Apristas said, the Latin American countries should allow foreign capital to come into their nations but should set stringent conditions that should assure that the companies contributed to the needed economic development of these countries.[2]

Several of the positions adopted by the Apristas brought them into strong conflict with the parties and groups affiliated with Communist International. For one thing the followers of Lenin objected to the Apristas' rejection of Lenin's interpretation of the world role of economic imperialism. As a consequence of this disagreement, the Communists also rejected the Apristas' willingness to admit foreign economic enterprises to the Latin American countries under conditions that would guarantee those nations' sovereignty.

In addition the Communists were strongly opposed to the Aprista concept of a multiclass party. In conformity with Marxist-Leninist theory, they argued that the leadership of the revolution in Latin America should be in the hands of the party of the industrial workers, the Marxist "proletariat." They argued, furthermore, that they themselves had already constituted the "vanguard party" of the proletariat; therefore there was no need for another revolutionary party in Latin America. Classes other than the proletariat that might be useful to the revolution should be mobilized in "Anti-Imperialist Leagues"—which would, naturally, be under the leadership and control of the Communists.

Although the Communist International sought for some years to recruit Haya de la Torre and other Aprista leaders to its ranks—even inviting Haya to Moscow, where he was granted interviews by a number of the top Soviet leaders—these efforts came to a standstill after 1928. In that year the Aprista delegation to the World Anti-Imperialist Congress that met in Brussels strongly opposed the position of the Communists, who controlled the majority of the delegations. After this congress the Communists frankly opposed the Apristas, denouncing them as "social fascists."

ESTABLISHMENT OF THE PARTY

After wandering in exile for more than half a decade, the Apristas were allowed to return to their country after Leguía was overthrown in 1930. Haya de la Torre came back as the recognized leader of a party that now included not only his old student followers but also the former anarcho-syndicalist trade union leaders, all of whom joined to form the new Partido Aprista Peruano.

From its inception the Aprista Party had characteristics that were new in Peruvian politics. In the first place it was from its inception a mass party that brought into its ranks workers, peasants, and members of the middle class. Aprista Party units were found not only in Lima, Arequipa, Trujillo, and other major cities but also in the remotest villages and hamlets.

In the second place the Aprista Party was not an organization that functioned only for electoral purposes. It sought to spread its influence into a wide range of other groups and organized such diverse elements as Aprista dentists, doctors, lawyers, trade unionists, peasant unionists, etc. into party organizations that, although autonomous, functioned under the general leadership of the party's top authorities and attempted to influence or control the various professional and interest groups within which these Aprista units operated.

One of the most original elements of the Aprista organization structure was its Universidades Populares González Prada. A network of party-sponsored schools, usually located in local Aprista headquarters, taught a great variety of different subjects. Students could go there to learn not only Aprista Party doctrine and philosophy but also such things as public speaking, trade union organization, history of Peru, world history, basic economics, and even reading and writing. Party members with the appropriate training, particularly students and professional people, taught without pay in these popular universities.

On a regional and national level the party's activities were coordinated by executive bodies whose members were responsible for one or another of the party's wide range of activities. Thus there was a trade union secretary, a peasant secretary, an electoral secretary (charged with seeing that party members were well-informed on the technicalities of registering and voting), a youth secretary, a women's secretary, etc. in each regional Aprista group as well as on the national level.

The party was very tightly organized, in contrast with most earlier Peruvian parties. It sought to coordinate the political activities of all of its members, thus maximizing the effectiveness of its large membership. It exercised considerable discipline over its subordinate units and its individual members, from time to time expelling dissident members.

The party adopted some of the panoply of politics then popular in Europe, which brought it much criticism from its enemies, including charges that it was "fascist." These features included a party song ("The Aprista Marseillaise"), a party salute (the waving of a white handkerchief), and well-rehearsed party cheers.

Another feature of the party's organization that aroused much criticism was the very dominant position within it of Víctor Raúl Haya de la Torre. He was officially given the title of _jefe_ (chief) of the party, and on most issues the other leaders were willing to defer to his judgment.

These characteristics of the Partido Aprista Peruano became permanent attributes. Subsequently, every time that the party was allowed to function publicly, the same forms of organization and symbols, and prominent position of Haya de la Torre, were revived.

Haya de la Torre was the party's candidate for president in the election of 1931 held to choose a successor to Leguía. During his campaign he traveled throughout the country and was greeted with great enthusiasm by workers, middle-class and professional people, and Indians, who constituted the majority of the country's population. However, despite his energetic campaign, Haya was declared to have lost the election. The victor was Sánchez Cerro, who had led in the overthrow of the Leguía regime.

For less than a year the Aprista Party was permitted to function legally. It had a substantial parliamentary minority and considerable influence in the organized labor movement, where the Communists were its principal rival. However, in 1932 elements of the party undertook an uprising in the northern city of Trujillo, which was suppressed by the army, with bloody retribution being taken on the Apristas who were captured. Many of the rebels were shot in cold blood. This incident created a psychological and political gap between the Apristas and the army leaders that continued for four decades.

In 1934 Sánchez Cerro was assassinated; according to the military the assassin was an Aprista, which deepened the river of blood between the army and the Apristas. As a result General Oscar Benavides took over the presidency. He declared an amnesty, which permitted the Aprista members of Congress to return to their posts and provided freedom for the party for some months. Haya de la Torre, who had been jailed for about a year, was released.

However, the honeymoon between Benavides and the Aprista Party was short-lived, and the Apristas were soon forced into underground activity. Haya de la Torre and some of his fellow leaders went into hiding—where they stayed for a decade—and others fled into exile.

In 1936 Benavides decided that his term of office had come to an end and that his successor should be elected. The Apristas were illegal and thus were not allowed to name their own candidate. However, at the last minute they threw their support to Luis Antonio Eguigueren, nominee of a minor party, the Partido Social Democrático, who had not been given any chance of winning. When the votes began to be counted, it became clear that Eguigueren was winning. As a result Benavides suspended the counting of the votes and had Congress extend his term until 1939.

During the remainder of the Benavides period, the Aprista Party remained deep underground. However, in 1939 new elections were finally called and Manuel Prado, a leading banker and son of a former president, was the government's nominee. His principal opponent was Luís A. Flores, nominee of the Unión Revolucionario, a supposedly fascist-inclined party. The Communists supported Prado as "the lesser evil"; and the leader of the Communist Party, Juan P. Luna, ran on Prado's ticket as a candidate for deputy, winning his election. The Apristas remained neutral in this contest.

Manuel Prado was elected. His six years in office were a continuation of the dictatorship of Sánchez Cerro and Benavides, but the Prado regime was more moderate than its predecessors. Although the Apristas were still kept in illegality, party members were allowed to control some of the country's important unions, notably the Textile Workers Federation, headed by veteran Aprista leader Arturo Sabroso.

However, it was the Communists in the labor movement who were favored by the Prado regime. In 1944 Communist trade unionists, under the leadership of Juan P. Luna, the head of the Chauffeurs Union as well as secretary-general of the Communist Party and member of the Chamber of Deputies, was allowed to lead the establishment of the Confederación de Trabajadores del Perú, of which he became secretary-general.

Peru was at least formally on the side of the Allies during World War II. As victory approached, pressure upon Prado rose to reestablish a democratic regime. As a result, when Prado's term approached its end, the president began to arrange for elections to choose his successor. Pressure from General Benavides and others convinced him to allow the Aprista Party to become legal—under the name Partido del Pueblo—although it was not allowed to name its own candidate for the presidency.

THE APRISTAS AND THE BUSTAMANTE REGIME

Because it could not name its own candidate, the Aprista Party threw its support behind the opposition nominee, José Bustamante y Rivero, a diplomat and scholar. However, the party named its own list of candidates for the Senate and Chamber of Deputies and also backed a list of candidates who ran under the name of the Frente Democrático. Among the latter candidates was a young architect, Fernado Belaúnde Terry.

Bustamante won the election. The Apristas won a majority in the Senate and, with their allies of the Frente Democrático, had a majority in the Chamber of Deputies as well. For the next three and a half years the Aprista Party remained legal and carried on intensive propaganda throughout Peru.

The Apristas used their influence in Congress to try to bring about the enactment of some parts of their program. Harry Kantor has summed up these parliamentary efforts of the Apristas thus:

> ... The Apristas proposed laws which abrogated all censorship and limitation on individual freedom, returning their liberty to all political prisoners. They presented projects to increase salaries of teachers, improve education, industrialize the country, raise wages of workers and bring about other changes. At the same time, the Apristas began to pressure in favor of their maximum program for Peru; reorganize the country in a functional democracy; create a National Economic Congress to bring about the overall planning of Peru; permit the exploitation of the desert of Sechura by foreign oil companies; open tunnels through the Andes to supply with the waters of the Amazon the desert of the coast. These were some of the proposals of the Apristas.[3]

They also used their influence with the administration to bring about improvements in the situation of the highland Indians. Party lawyers worked with the Indian Secretariat of the party to present the demands of Indian communities for the return of lands that over a long period had been stolen from them by neighboring landlords. Numerous Indian delegations came down to the Aprista headquarters in Lima to put their cases in the hands of the Aprista authorities, and there was a special dormitory in the Casa del Pueblo where such delegations were housed. Party leaders reported at the time that they had been successful in a great many cases in getting land restored to Indian communities.

On another level the Apristas had pushed through Congress by the middle of 1947 more than a score of laws providing for the expropriation of individual landholdings that were not being used, or were in an area where the exploitation of the Indians was particularly intense, and the division of these holdings among the Indians. They also drew up a general agrarian reform law, but political difficulties of the last year of the Bustamante administration prevented its being seriously considered in Congress.[4]

During most of the Bustamante administration a virtually impossible political situation existed. Bustamante occupied the presidential palace but was virtually unable to make a move without the support of the Aprista Party, which worked under the close discipline of its principal leader, Víctor Raúl Haya de la Torre, whose office was in the party's headquarters, the Casa del Pueblo. A clash between the constitutional president and the leader of the principal party that had elected him was all but inevitable.

During the three years following the election of Bustamante, the Apristas had members in the cabinet for only some 11 months in 1946-47. This was the only period in the party's history in which it had members in the government. During most of his administration, the president ruled with the help of "independents," including a considerable number of military officers.

By the middle of 1948 relations between the Apristas and Bustamante had almost reached the breaking point. For several weeks a widespread boycott by congressmen made it impossible to gather the necessary quorum. This crisis was resolved by the establishment of an all-military cabinet.

On October 3, 1948, a naval mutiny broke out in the port of Callao, near Lima. It is now clear that some elements of the Aprista Party were among the leaders of this uprising. However, when faced with the choice of supporting this move by their followers or refusing to do so, the top leaders of the Aprista Party took the latter alternative. Within a few hours the mutiny was suppressed and its principal leaders were in jail.

President Bustamante reacted violently to the uprising: he outlawed the Aprista Party. Those party leaders who were accessible were arrested; others, including Haya de la Torre, went into hiding. Constitutional guarantees were suspended under a state-of-siege decree.

Perhaps the principal gain for the Aprista Party during this period was the ability given it by legal recognition and a more or less friendly government to extend its organization throughout the country. The Apristas gained firm control of the labor movement, taking it from the Communists, who had been favored by the Prado dictatorship, and also became the dominant element among the organized students. They were also successful in acquiring backing among the Indian peasants of the highlands because of their defense of the rights of the Indian communities as well as their efforts to help the communities establish self-help and educational projects.

THE ODRÍA PERIOD

The outlawing of the Aprista Party by Bustamante was a prelude to his overthrow. At the end of October 1948 General Manuel Odría, an officer who had been promoted to his general's rank with strong support from the Apristas and also owed his nomination as minister of defense to their backing, led an insurrection that ousted the president. He did not do so because of any love for the Apristas, whom he denounced in the bitterest terms; rather, he used this coup as the instrument to establish a military dictatorship, of which he was the head. He was to remain in power for almost eight years.

The Odría government—which was a provisional regime until 1950, when one-candidate "elections" served to convert Odría into the "constitutional president"—severely persecuted the Aprista Party. Its leaders were jailed, exiled, or driven into hiding. Party organizations were broken up, and the distribution of its literature and its newspaper was suppressed. Membership in the party became a crime.

The most notorious instance of persecution of Apristas was that involving Haya de la Torre. After remaining in hiding for about three months, in January 1949 he took refuge in the Colombian embassy. However, the Odría government would not grant him the safe conduct customarily given to political opponents by Latin American regimes, even by dictatorships, under such circumstances. Instead, the government lodged formal complaints with the Colombians, alleging that Haya was a "common criminal," being "intellectually responsible" for a number of violations of criminal statutes.

The debate between the Peruvian and Colombian governments over Haya de la Torre's right to asylum went on for five years. The

Colombians refused to surrender him, and he remained in the embassy throughout this period. The Peruvian regime had trenches dug around the embassy, searched everyone going in and out of the building, and posted soldiers there 24 hours a day. The Colombians were forced to rent other quarters in which they could conduct their embassy's business, only one embassy official remaining with Haya.

Meanwhile, the case became a diplomatic cause célèbre. It was twice taken before the International Court of Justice at the Hague, but no resolution of the issue satisfied either party to the dispute. After five years the case was settled by compromise, with Haya being formally turned over to the Peruvian authorities but being allowed immediately thereafter to go into exile, where he remained for two years.

Continued Aprista control of the labor movement brought persecution of the trade unions by the Odría regime. At one point the major Aprista trade union leaders were jailed, but international pressure brought their release after several months. Some important unions, such as those on the sugar plantations along the coast, were almost completely destroyed by the government and the employers. Others of a strongly Aprista flavor, such as the Textile Workers Federation, succeeded in maintaining their ranks more or less intact.

The government would not allow the Confederación de Trabajadores del Peru (CTP), the nation's central labor organization, to function. Several efforts were made by labor elements of Peronista persuasion, who were working with the Odría government, to reestablish the CTP, the legal recognition of which had been canceled soon after Odría came to power. However, when it became clear that in any labor congress called to reorganize the CTP the Apristas would constitute a majority among the delegates, the government dropped plans for such a meeting.

As the end of Odría's term of office—due to expire in the middle of 1956—approached, the stringency of the dictatorship relaxed. Late in 1955 a number of the Aprista leaders were allowed to return to the country. These included Ramiro Prialé, one of the party's principal figures, who assumed the post of party secretary-general and undertook the task of reorganizing the Aprista rank-and-file organizations. By the time of the election, the Partido Aprista Peruano had been reestablished in most of the larger cities and towns.

Meanwhile, Odría's ambitions to succeed himself were vetoed by other military leaders. As a result there were three candidates for the presidency. The government-supported nominee was Hernán Lavalle, a well-known engineer; apparently the more popular of the two opposition candidates was Fernando Belaúnde Terry, dean of the School of Architecture, who aroused considerable popular enthusiasm. The third nominee was Manuel Prado, the ex-president.

All three nominees sought the support of the underground Aprista Party. A priori, it appeared that Belaúnde was the candidate most likely to receive Aprista support, since he had been an ally of the party during his career as a deputy from 1945 to 1948 and his program was not unlike theirs. However, the Apristas were skeptical of his candidacy on two grounds: they feared that if Belaúnde were elected, Odría would not allow him to take office; and they regarded the movement that Belaúnde had organized around his candidacy as the most serious popular challenge to their party in the Apristas' quarter century of activity.

The Apristas' basic objective in this election was to obtain the legalization of their party. They therefore offered to back Lavalle if Odría would raise the ban that had been imposed on the Apristas in October 1948. When Odría refused to do so, they negotiated with ex-President Prado, on his past record certainly no friend of theirs. However, he promised that if he were elected, he would immediately issue a decree legalizing the party. On the basis of that promise, the underground Aprista leadership agreed to support Prado. Although at first given little chance to win, Prado was victorious, solely because of the support which he received from the Apristas.

APRISTA "CRITICAL SUPPORT" OF PRADO

During the six years following the reelection of Prado, the Apristas had their eye on one principal objective: winning the election of 1962. For that to be possible, it was necessary for Prado to remain in power throughout his allotted term and to preside over those elections. Therefore the Apristas felt themselves bound to support his remaining in office. Although they were frequently critical of actions of his administration, and of individual ministers who served under him, they consistently made it clear that they not only would not participate in any attempt to overthrow him but, on the contrary, would use their influence to maintain Prado in the presidency.

During the Prado administration the Apristas did not accept a post in the cabinet or in any of the leading independent agencies of the Peruvian government. However, a few did have diplomatic appointments, and there were usually Aprista leaders in the Peruvian delegation to the United Nations General Assembly.

This Aprista backing of the Prado regime, an administration that was essentially conservative and made no fundamental alterations in the country's economic and social institutions, somewhat reduced the party's following. It is doubtful that it seriously reduced the actual party membership, particularly among the country's organized workers and peasants. These tended to agree with the party's leaders on the importance of the party's being able to compete freely in the 1962 election, and they interpreted the party's support of Prado as a tactic for this purpose. However, there were undoubtedly many middle-class elements that had followed the Apristas without formally affiliating with the party and became convinced during the second Prado administration that the Apristas had become a relatively conservative party. Such people tended to turn to the Acción Popular Party of Fernando Belaúnde Terry.

The most serious decline in Aprista backing was among the university students. Even when the Apristas were illegal, they had tended to have a substantial backing from this group, and in the party's short periods of legality it had dominated the student organizations. This was not the case after 1956. The Communists, dissident Apristas, followers of Belaúnde, and even Trotskyites were able to gain among the university students; and they usually worked together against the Apristas, depriving them of control of the students' organizations.

Some of the younger Aprista leaders, including a few who had been in exile before 1956, tried to seize control of the party; when they failed, they withdrew to form a rival group, which first took the name Partido Aprista Rebelde. This group tended to work with the Communists in the late 1950s; but after the advent of Fidel Castro to power in Cuba, they enthusiastically supported him. In the early 1960s they changed their name to Movimiento de la Izquierda Revolucionaria, after a pro-Castro group in Venezuela of the same name. In 1965 they undertook a guerrilla campaign that was defeated by the Peruvian Army, and several of its major leaders were killed in the fighting.

The Aprista Rebelde group did not take any substantial part of the Aprista membership with them. However, they constituted a serious challenge to the party among the students, and they carried on constant and violent criticism of the Apristas in their periodicals that sometimes proved embarrassing to the party.

The Apristas continued to control the organized labor movement. The Confederación de Trabajadores del Perú was reestablished, with legal recognition; and Arturo Sabroso, who had been its president from 1945 to 1949, was elected secretary-general. Most of the national unions were also under Aprista control. Most of the unions that had been destroyed during the Odría dictatorship, including the National Federation of Sugar Workers, were reconstituted and were under Aprista control.

The party was able to reestablish its organizations throughout the country. As in the past, the principal center of Aprista strength was in the north, particularly in the coastal areas. In Lima, where the party had also been particularly strong, its influence was considerably reduced, many middle-class people turning toward Belaúnde's party and many of the residents of the shantytowns supporting Odría's Unión Nacional Odriista in gratitude for his efforts while president to help them establish permanent suburban communities. As in the past, the Apristas continued to be weakest in the southern part of the country, including Arequipa, Puno, and Cuzco, where the Belaúnde party was particularly strong.

Víctor Raúl Haya de la Torre returned to Peru soon after the election of President Prado. However, during the succeeding six years he spent most of his time in Great Britain, where he held a part-time position at Oxford University, and in Europe, returning to Peru only for periodic triumphant campaigns around the interior. There is reason to believe that other party leaders made it clear to him that relations between the Apristas and President Prado would be smoother if Haya was not constantly present as a rival center of power and influence.

The Apristas were not in a position during the Prado regime to try to push legislation through Congress that would put on the statute books elements of their basic program. They had at best a handful of members of the legislature during this period and had relatively little influence in that body.

As the 1962 election approached, the Aprista Party nominated Víctor Raúl Haya de la Torre for president. His principal rivals in this contest were Fernando Belaúnde Terry, backed by his own Acción Popular party, and General Manuel Odría, nominee of the Unión Nacional Odriista. Several minor parties also named candidates.

The Apristas were very hopeful that they would win this election. Although they were not unaware of the attrition of their popular support, they felt that the main danger to their victory would come from the military. The feud between the leaders of the army and the Aprista Party dated from the Aprista revolt in Trujillo in 1932, and for more than a generation army officers had been taught that their greatest enemies were Haya de la Torre and his followers. In 1962 the Aprista leaders were fearful that if their nominee won, the military would not allow him to take office.

The provocation for the military action that the Apristas feared was provided by the fact that although Haya de la Torre was the leading candidate, he did not receive the 33.33 percent required by the constitution. Although the Apristas might have been able to elect their nominee in Congress, where they and their allies, the Christian Democrats, had a majority, they did not take the decision to elect Haya and defy the military to overthrow him. Several weeks of confusion followed the election and was ended by a coup d'état by the armed forces. A military junta took control; but after considerable pressure from the United States, which withdrew its ambassador and suspended economic aid, they agreed to hold new elections within a year.

In 1963 the Apristas definitely lost the election. Fernando Belaúnde Terry, again the candidate of his Acción Popular party, was the undisputed winner, with Haya de la Torre running second and Manuel Odría receiving considerably less than he had received the year before. The military turned power over to Belaúnde.

THE APRISTAS AS THE LOYAL OPPOSITION

During the five years following the inauguration of Fernando Belaúnde Terry, the Apristas played a role unique for them and for Peru. They constituted the bulk of the loyal opposition to the Belaúnde regime, both in Congress and in the country at large. In both the Chamber of Deputies and the Senate the Apristas won the largest number of members in the 1963 election. They formed a somewhat improbable alliance with the followers of General Manuel Odría to control both houses of Congress.

Throughout the Belaúnde administration the Apristas and their allies embarrassed the administration in Congress. They frequently interrogated the president's ministers and forced their resignation. Congress cut the budgets proposed by Belaúnde and limited some of his favorite projects, especially the community development program that he called Acción Popular. The similarity of names of this program and the president's party did not escape the notice of the opposition and certainly had something to do with the Apristas' objections to it.

The Belaúnde regime was a reform administration, and there were many in Peru who objected to the Apristas' frequent opposition to programs proposed by the president. Belaúnde sponsored an agrarian reform law, which was finally passed by Congress after considerable modification. The Apristas prided themselves that they had been responsible for inclusion within the law of a proviso granting to Indian tenants small pieces of land that their landlords had allowed them to use for building their houses and growing crops for their own sustenance. According to the provision inserted into the law by the Apristas, the tenants became proprietors of these small plots the day in which the agrarian reform measure became law.[5]

The opposition majority in the legislature also forced other modifications of the bill on agrarian reform that Belaúnde had sent to Congress. One of the most important was the one exempting the sugar and cotton plantations of the coastal region, which were cultivated as modern semi-industrial enterprises, from the provisions of the land redistribution law. The justification for this was that these plantations were highly efficient enterprises, and their productivity would be greatly decreased if their holdings were divided among the tenants and workers. This modification of the Belaúnda measure was backed by both the Apristas and the followers of Odría.

By the middle of 1968 the opposition's harassment of the Belaúnde government precipitated a constitutional crisis. Rumors were widespread that the leaders of the armed forces were conspiring against the regime; and the Apristas concluded that it was necessary to reach a compromise with the president, so as to assure his continuing in office and his presiding over the election of his successor, which was scheduled for June 1969. As a result an agreement was struck between the president and the Apristas to deal with the financial crisis facing the regime and threatening its stability. It was agreed that a new cabinet, the membership of which was agreed to by the president and Aprista leaders, would take office and would be granted special powers by Congress to enact decrees dealing with the government's financial situation.

As a result of this accord between President Belaúnde and the Apristas, the alliance of the Partido Aprista and the followers of General Odría was disrupted. The general's party was split over the issue of approving this agreement, with a majority of its members of Congress, led by former Senate President Julio de la Piedra, supporting the measure—against the general's strong opposition. The de la Piedra faction soon left the UNO to form its own party, the Partido Social Democrático.

Meanwhile most of the other parties in Peru had also suffered splits. Mayor Luís Bedoya Reyes of Lima broke with his party, the Partido Democrata Cristiano, to form his own party, the Partido Popular Cristiano, early in 1967. In August-September 1968 President Belaúnde's party, Acción Popular, was divided over the issue of who should be the candidate in the 1969 election. When Vice-President Edgardo Seoane was nominated, President Belaúnde sponsored the formation of a reorganizing committee to reassert the president's control over Acción Popular.

As a result of the splits in the rivals of the Partido Aprista Peruano, it appeared almost certain that the Apristas would win the election scheduled for June 1969. The Apristas made it clear that they would nominate Víctor Raúl Haya de la Torre. This nomination was dictated by two factors: the belief that Haya, who had been denied the presidency on a number of occasions when, in the opinion of the party, he had been elected, deserved the nomination; and the fear that if Haya was not nominated, the Partido Aprista Peruano would split in trying to choose a nominee from among several eligible contenders.

The prospect of Aprista victory was the major factor provoking military overthrow of President Belaúnde on October 3, 1968. General Juan Velasco, who then became president, dissolved Congress and dissolved the Electoral Tribunal, on the grounds that it was no longer needed. However, he did not dissolve existing political parties, including the Partido Aprista Peruano, and did not move against organized labor, which continued to be under Aprista control.

The Velasco regime launched a program of substantial reforms, including a sweeping agrarian reform, a project for workers' participation in ownership of industrial firms, and extensive government controls over foreign trade. However, in spite of these reforms, the Velasco government did not gain the support of the Aprista Party, which constituted the core of the opposition.

Although not outlawed, it was allowed to conduct open-air public rallies only very infrequently. With no elections it had no electoral activity. However, the wide range of other activities that the party had had traditionally—such as work within unions and other organizations, extensive educational programs, and training courses for members and sympathizers—continued in its hundreds of headquarters all over the country and served to keep the party alive and very active. Perhaps even more important in keeping the party functioning was a conviction among party members—and even among many of its opponents—that the Partido Aprista Peruano was virtually indestructible and would again be the country's major party once partisan activities were again fully permitted.

SIGNIFICANCE OF THE APRISTA PARTY

The Aprista Party has had importance far beyond the boundaries of Peru. The ideas that the Aprista Party, and particularly Víctor Raúl Haya de la Torre, developed have been widely accepted throughout Latin America.

The Aprista concept of a multiclass party to mobilize workers, peasants, and sizable elements of the middle class to change the traditional class structure has been one of the bases of many of the Latin American political parties that have developed since the 1930s. Similarly, the anti-imperialist position of the Apristas, favoring united action of the Latin American countries against attempts by powers outside the area to dominate these countries, has become an integral part of the programs of various Latin American parties.

Similarly, the Aprista position concerning the role of foreign enterprises in the economic development of Latin America has been incorporated in the programs, statements of principles, and practical policies of a considerable number of Latin American parties. These groups have favored the introduction of foreign capital, but under conditions established by the Latin American governments. Finally, the Aprista argument in favor of Latin American unity against outside elements, particularly the United States, has received at least tacit endorsement by many Latin American parties.

The Aprista Party was the pioneer of the group we have classified as the national revolutionary parties. However, its influence was not confined to them. The Christian Democrats in various countries have borrowed to a considerable degree its multiclass party concept and its ideas concerning how to deal with imperialism, as well as some of its organizational techniques. Even the Partido Peronista harked back to Aprismo in some of its concepts on imperialism and nationalism.

As this is being written, the future of the Partido Aprista Peruano is in doubt, in the light of the attempt of the military regime of General Juan Velasco to "steal the Apristas' thunder" and enact many of the measures they have advocated for four decades. However, there can be little doubt of the impact that APRA has had both in Peruvian politics as the long-time advocate of social and economic revolution and in Latin America as a whole as the ideological and philosophical pace-setter of the parties of the democratic Left.

CHAPTER 10
ACCIÓN DEMOCRÁTICA

The Venezuelan Acción Democrática Party has had more experience in control of the government of its country than any other party in the national revolutionary group except the PRI of Mexico. During its period of control of the government, it launched a process of basic change in the economy, society, and politics of Venezuela and set a pattern for all of the progressive democratic parties of the hemisphere.

ORIGINS OF ACCIÓN DEMOCRÁTICA

Acción Democrática had its beginnings in the period following the end of the dictatorship of Juan Vicente Gómez, known throughout the hemisphere as "the tyrant of the Andes." Many of those who established the party had their first political experience in 1928, when a group of students at the Central University of Venezuela, in Caracas, led a revolt against the Gómez regime. They seized control of the presidential palace for several hours but were finally overcome by the military loyal to the dictator.

The leaders of this revolt were arrested and, after a period of persecution and torture, were sent into exile. Their leading figure, Rómulo Betancourt, spent several years in Costa Rica, where he was one of the founders of the Communist Party of Costa Rica. He broke with the party in 1935, when he opposed the affiliation of the Costa Rican Communists with the Communist International. He argued that the revolutionary parties of Latin America should be independent of any international control and should develop programs that were particularly adapted to their own countries.

When Juan Vicente Gómez died in December 1935, his successor, General Eleázar López Contreras, relaxed the reins of the dictatorship.

He allowed the exiles to return and permitted the development of various opposition parties and groups. Most of these organizations had joined by early 1937 to form the Partido Democrático Nacional. It had within it both the followers of Betancourt, who favored the formation of an independent revolutionary party, and the Communists, who were loyal to the Communist International.

In March 1937 President López Contreras cracked down on the opposition. Most of its leaders were jailed and deported. The principal figure of the Betancourt group who escaped capture was Rómulo Betancourt himself. For about two years he remained in hiding in the country but traveled extensively, establishing local groups of the party in virtually every town and hamlet in the nation. In 1939 he was finally arrested and was exiled to Chile, where he remained for two years.

During this period there was a differentiation between the Betancourt group and the Communists. The latter withdrew from the Partido Democrático Nacional to form the Communist Party of Venezuela. From then on the PDN and the Communists became the bitterest of enemies.[1]

In 1941 the term of President López Contreras came to an end. In his place the president selected another general from the state of Táchira, General Isaías Medina Angarita. With his inauguration the relaxation of the dictatorship gained momentum. The new president allowed the legal organization of the country's two principal opposition parties. The PDN came out into the open under the name of Acción Democrática, while the Communists formed a legal party under the name of Unión Popular.

During the administration of Medina Angarita, Acción Democrática fully developed its ideological position and program. It also emerged as the most important opposition party in Venezuela. The ideological posture of Acción Democrática became clear during the discussion of the revision of the concessions granted to the foreign oil companies exploiting the country's oil resources, the principal source of national income and of foreign exchange for Venezuela during 1943 and 1944. Acción Democrática members of Congress urged the establishment of a formula that would provide the largest possible return to Venezuela from the exploitation of its subsoil resources and the investment of this return in expanding and diversifying the national economy and in raising the standards of living of the poorer segments of the community. This policy underscored the Acción Democrática's nationalist philosophy and its struggle for the improvement of the circumstances of the more depressed elements.

Acción Democrática made particular progress in the organized labor movement during the Medina Angarita regime. In 1944 it took control of the organized labor movement from the Communists for the first time. Although no national central labor body was organized under AD auspices during this period, a majority of the local unions were in AD hands by the time the Medina government was overthrown.

THE FIRST ACCIÓN DEMOCRÁTICA REGIME

In 1945 Medina Angarita's term of office was due to end. Acción Democrática attempted to reach an accord with the president concerning the selection of his successor. It was first agreed that both the administration and the major opposition party would back the candidacy of the Venezuelan ambassador to the United States, Diógenes Escalante. However, when he fell sick, Medina Angarita chose another candidate without consulting Acción Democrática. The president also refused to allow a popular election of his successor and insisted on maintaining the constitutional provision whereby the president was chosen by Congress, which he controlled.

At that point AD entered into negotiations with a group of young officers who were plotting against the Medina regime. These majors and captains had made up their minds to oust the president but sought a civilian group to cooperate in their conspiracy. Acción Democrática, after much hesitation, agreed to work with them, but under conditions that would assure AD control of the new government and would give the party freedom to attempt to put its program into operation.

The coup d'état against Medina took place on October 18, 1945. During the next 37 months control of the government of Venezuela was in the hands of Acción Democrática. From October 1945 until February 1947 the government was a provisional regime, headed by Rómulo Betancourt. From February to November 1948, Acción Democrática controlled the government through the elected constitutional regime of President Rómulo Gallegos.

During these three years Acción Democrática put its program into operation. First it sought to increase the country's return from the oil industry by negotiating new agreements with the foreign petroleum companies that assured the government at least 50 percent of the returns from the industry. This "50-50 principle" was subsequently adopted by most of the other oil-producing nations in underdeveloped countries.

The Betancourt and Gallegos governments sought to use the vastly increased resources that the government received from the oil industry to diversify the economy and to raise living standards. It established the Venezuelan Development Corporation, which undertook an extensive investment program both in agriculture and in industry. As a result of this program the country became self-sufficient in sugar and a number of other products.

Large sums were invested by the Acción Democrática government in expansion of the country's educational system, with particular attention to the establishment of normal schools. The government also spent large amounts on expanding the country's social security system and the hospitals and other health facilities for the poor.

Large sums were also spent on subsidizing the prices of basic items for workers and peasants. At the same time the government threw its full support behind the organization of the labor movement; the number of unions grew from about 200 to some 900, about half of the increase being in unions of rural workers, who had not previously been organized. For the first time a central labor organization, the Confederación de Trabajadores de Venezuela (CTV), was established in 1947. It was under Acción Democrática leadership, although a minority of the unions were controlled by one element of the Communist movement, the so-called "Red" Communist Party.

The Acción Democrática government also sought to establish an independent foreign policy. The main feature of this policy was the refusal of the AD governments to recognize governments that had come to power by force, without having the administration confirmed by popular election, and regimes that were outright dictatorships.

The Acción Democrática regime also hoped to establish political democracy on a solid foundation. It sought to keep the military, which had traditionally dominated the Venezuelan government, under control; and it succeeded so long as Rómulo Betancourt remained president. It enacted a law giving all adults the right to vote, thus for the first time giving the franchise to illiterates. It provided a liberal law for the organization of political parties, and two important opposition parties were formed: the Social Christian Copei Party and the liberal Unión Republicana Democrática. It called elections for a constitutional convention, which wrote a new and very democratic constitution, and scheduled elections for president and Congress, and for state and municipal officials.

The Acción Democrática government also undertook basic social reforms. It started a program of agrarian reform, using for this purpose principally land taken from officials of the Medina, López Contreras, and Gómez regimes. In 1948 the program of agrarian reform was institutionalized with the passage of an agrarian reform law—which, however, was barely put into effect before the Acción Democrática regime was overthrown.

During its three years in power, Acción Democrática was undoubtedly the country's most popular party. In fact the party, through its record in power, was able to establish a hold on the popular imagination that subsequently remained largely intact after more than nine years of its persecution by a brutal dictatorship.

Acción Democrática's popularity was demonstrated in the three elections held during this period. In the election for Constitutional Assembly in 1946, AD received 78.8 percent of the popular vote. In the following year, when the president and Congress were elected, Acción Democrática received 70.8 percent; and a few months later, in state and municipal elections, it received 70.1 percent.

Probably the party made most progress in this three-year period among the peasants. The sympathy of the Acción Democrática government and the activity of the party that largely led to organization of the peasants during this period, and the AD regime's agrarian reform program and long-range agrarian reform law, undoubtedly were largely responsible for the AD's winning the backing of most of the country's rural population during these years.[2]

THE DICTATORSHIP

The Acción Democrática government was overthrown by a military coup late in November 1948. President Rómulo Gallegos proved to be no master of keeping the leaders of the armed forces in order, as his predecessor had been. With the ouster of Gallegos, Venezuela entered a period of dictatorship that lasted for more than nine years.

For the first four years the government was in the hands of a military junta, which, until he was assassinated in 1950, was headed by Colonel Carlos Delgado Chalbaud, one of the leaders of the coup of October 1945 and President Rómulo Gallegos' minister of defense. So long as Delgado Chalbaud was in control, the military dictatorship was relatively mild in its political aspects and continued—although it did nothing to expand—the social and economic programs launched by the Acción Democrática regime. However, after the murder of Delgado Chalbaud, the regime, which thereafter was largely under the influence of Colonel Marcos Pérez Jiménez, became much more violent. Between 1952 and 1956 the Venezuelan dictatorship was the most tyrannical government in Latin America, except for that of Trujillo in the Dominican Republic.

In 1952 the military junta made the mistake of calling elections for a Constitutional Assembly. Acción Democrática was not allowed to participate, since it had been declared illegal a few weeks after the November 1948 coup. However, at the last minute the AD underground threw its support to the list of candidates of the Unión Republicana Democrática. When the votes were counted, the URD slate was running far ahead of the other two principal groups in the field—the opposition Copei list and the progovernment nominations put up by the government's Frente Electoral Independiente, a party organized especially for these elections.

When the results of the election became known, Colonel Marcos Pérez Jiménez seized control of the government, suspended further counting of the votes, and announced that "in the name of the armed forces" he was becoming provisional president. Subsequently the votes were "recounted," this time showing that the government's Frente Electoral Independiente had obtained a majority, with Copei and URD receiving minority representation in the new Constitutional Assembly. Both opposition groups refused to participate in the Assembly and expelled any of their members who accepted positions in it.

At the end of its sessions, the Constituent Assembly elected Pérez Jiménez as first president under the new constitution. He remained in office until January 1958, driving all political parties underground, establishing a concentration camp in the Orinoco Valley, virtually destroying the labor movement, and conducting a general reign of terror.

During the first years of the military dictatorship, Acción Democrática was able to maintain a very strong underground. The party was active in what remained of the labor movement and distributed literature; its support was decisive to the victory of the URD in the 1952 election.

However, after Pérez Jiménez assumed office, Acción Democrática was persecuted by the government with particular ruthlessness. Its leaders were jailed or sent to the concentration camp of Guasina; scores of them were killed; hundreds and perhaps thousands were tortured. Two underground AD secretaries-general, Leonardo Ruíz Pineda and Alberto Carnevali, died at the hands of the police. The government used the full force of its control over news and propaganda to picture the AD as "subversive," "the enemy of Venezuela," and to picture Rómulo Betancourt as "leader of the Communist conspiracy in the Caribbean." Several attempts were made to assassinate Betancourt, presumably by agents of the Venezuelan regime, in the several countries in which he spent his nine years of exile.[3]

As a result of this persecution, the AD underground was considerably weakened during the later years of the dictatorship. It became increasingly hard to maintain contact with the party's exiled leaders, and during the last few years the top figures in the Acción Democrática underground were recruited from among young men who had been teenagers when the party was in power.

Throughout the dictatorship Rómulo Betancourt behaved as the potential head of the government of Venezuela. Although he remained in exile, he maintained a position of dignity and continued to be the unchallenged head of Acción Democrática. He wrote a long book, published in 1955, that recounted the history of Acción Democrática, with particular emphasis on the party's three-year experience in government, as well as discussing the origins and nature of the military dictatorship. Betancourt and other exiled AD leaders also paid special attention to developing close relations with leaders of other national revolutionary parties, particularly those of Bolivia, Costa Rica, and Puerto Rico.

ACCIÓN DEMOCRÁTICA AND THE PROVISIONAL GOVERNMENT

The Pérez Jiménez dictatorship fell over the question of how to continue the dictator in office although the constitution provided for the end of his term. He did not want to run the risk of allowing any segment of the opposition to name a candidate to run against him, since the situation of 1952 might be repeated. He did not even dare to allow the nomination of a purely puppet "opposition" candidate by the government, since there was the outside possibility that even such a nominee might win.

Pérez Jiménez procrastinated for many months before deciding how to secure his reelection. Only a few weeks before his term was due to end, he announced that a "plebiscite" would be held. The voters would be asked to vote "yes" or "no" on the question "Should General Marcos Pérez Jiménez continue as president for the next five-year constitutional term?" No provision was made for what would happen if the voters decided in the negative.

For some reason the plebiscite struck most Venezuelans as making the dictator ridiculous, and this made them lose their fear of the dictatorship. Venezuelans high and low began to demonstrate their repudiation of the regime by printed demands that it leave power and by parades, street meetings, and riots. The psychological hold of the dictatorship on the people of the country was destroyed. As a consequence Pérez Jiménez was overthrown on January 23, 1958.[4]

The dictatorship was succeeded by a provisional government consisting of representatives of the three branches of the armed forces, as well as distinguished civilians, presided over by Admiral Wolfgang Larrazábal. No representatives of the political parties were members of the new regime, although each of the major parties had its friends in the provisional government.

The country's four major parties—Acción Democrática, Copei, Unión Republicana Democrática, and the Communists—were revived immediately. Their underground organizations came out into public activity; and as their exiled leaders returned, each of the parties organized large demonstrations in Caracas to receive them. All of the parties began an intensive effort to rebuild their organizations throughout the country.

There was some conflict in Acción Democrática, as in the other parties, between the returning exiles and those who had led the underground during the dictatorship. The young men of the underground were afraid that Betancourt and others would attempt to take over the executive positions in the reconstituted party. However, seeking to avoid this issue, Betancourt and the other older leaders of the party agreed to allow the underground executive, headed by Secretary-General Simón Saez Merida, to remain in charge of the party's organization until a new national party congress could be called.

It was not clear during most of 1958 to what degree Acción Democrática had been damaged by the more than nine years of persecution. The AD leaders insisted that their party was still the majority political group in Venezuela, a claim challenged by the other parties, particularly the Unión Republicana Democrática, which claimed that its winning of the 1952 election had demonstrated that it had become the nation's largest party.

However, it was soon clear that within the labor and peasant movement, Acción Democrática was the largest, if not the majority, party. This was attested to by the willingness of the other parties to give AD the largest representation on the executive committees of most of the reconstituted unions. In some unions, such as the Peasants Federation and the bank clerks, white-collar workers, transport, and construction unions, the Acción Democrática was given clear majority control.

Nevertheless, in many unions and in the Unified Trade Union Committee, which was set up to head the overall labor movement, Acción Democrática accepted a position of minority, although the largest minority. Copei and the URD, which before 1948 had had virtually no influence in organized labor, were the principal gainers from this move, made in the name of labor unity and of civilian unity in the face of the possible danger of a military attempt to reestablish a dictatorship.

Much of the time of the provisional government and of the parties was taken up with working out the details for an election to reestablish a constitutional regime. The writing of a new electoral law, reasserting the principle of universal adult suffrage that had first been established in the Acción Democrática regime of 1945-48, was relatively simple and not the subject of much disagreement.

However, it was much more difficult to reach agreement on candidates for the election. It was first the hope of the leaders of AD, Copei, and URD that they could agree on a single candidate, so as to avoid a split among the civilians. This proved impossible; and a few weeks before the election date, it was agreed that each party would name its own candidate.

Acción Democrática chose Rómulo Betancourt. It had been decided in the party's August 1958 congress that if the party had its own nominee, it should be Betancourt. In this same congress the major posts of leadership in AD were reassumed by the senior figures in the party, most of whom had spent the largest part of the dictatorship in exile.

Betancourt waged an energetic campaign. He had already traveled throughout the country, helping to rebuild the party organization, and had met an enthusiastic reception from local party members, particularly from the peasants, who still looked upon him as their principal leader because of the support his government of 1945-48 had given to their unionization and that government's first steps toward agrarian reform.

Betancourt was also principally responsible for the so-called Punto Fijo agreement. This was a pact among the three presidential candidates—Betancourt for AD, Rafael Caldera for Copei, and Admiral Larrazábal for the URD—pledging each of them to honor the results of the election no matter who won and to bring representatives of all three parties into the cabinet of the new constitutional government. This agreement sought to maintain civilian unity, even though the three parties were campaigning against one another in the election.

Rómulo Betancourt was the uncontested winner of the 1958 election, receiving slightly more than 49 percent of the popular vote. Admiral Larrazábal came in second; and the Copei candidate, Rafael Caldera, was a rather weak third.[5]

THE BETANCOURT ADMINISTRATION

Rómulo Betancourt was inaugurated as constitutional president on February 13, 1959. He turned over the reins of government on March 11, 1964 to his constitutionally elected successor, Raúl Leoni, and in doing so became the first president in Venezuelan history both to take office as the result of constitutional popular election and to turn over office to a constitutionally elected successor. However, this political achievement was not the only accomplishment of the Betancourt regime, and it was made possible largely by what the administration was able to carry out in the economic and social fields.

Certainly one of the most fundamental programs of the Betancourt government was agrarian reform. Even before the passing of an agrarian reform law, both the provisional and Betancourt administrations distributed land that belonged to the government. Early in 1960 a law was passed that called for generalization of the land redistribution program.

The main provisions of the 1960 agrarian reform law were that large landholdings should be purchased by the government, at prices mutually agreed upon or decided by regular courts. Payments would be principally in the form of government bonds, with a small amount paid in cash. This land would be turned over, without payment, to individual peasant families; the recipients would have provisional title for twenty years, during which time they could not mortgage the land and could resell it only to the Agrarian Institute, which originally gave it to them. After twenty years the peasant was to receive freehold title.

There were other provisions to the law. Peasants were to receive credit from the Agricultural and Grazing Bank and receive technical assistance from the Ministry of Agriculture. The Agrarian Institute was to help the new landholders with programs of local road construction, aid for marketing, and help in establishing electricity, water, and sewer systems.

An appreciable start in land redistribution was made during the Betancourt administration. Approximately 50,000 families were given land during the five years in which Betancourt was president, most of it land that had belonged to private landholders. A minority of the land had belonged to the federal, state, and municipal governments.[6]

The Betancourt government also began a program of providing credit to the beneficiaries of the agrarian reform and other small landholders through the government's Agricultural and Grazing Bank. This institution had until then been used mainly by the large landowners, but during the Betancourt government a majority of its resources were directed toward the smaller farmers.

The Betancourt regime also started a unique program for providing rural housing. This program was carried out through the Malaria Control Department of the Ministry of Health, a government agency that had developed particularly good relations with the country's small farmers. Several thousand homes were built by Malaria Control during the Betancourt administration.

Associated with the agrarian reform, which was part of a broader effort to stimulate the development and raise the standards of living of the interior, was a program for providing basic needs for villages and small towns. By the time Betancourt left office, there was virtually no hamlet in the country that had not received either a new school, running water, a sewer system, a paved main street, a diesel-powered electric generator providing light for its homes, a small clinic, or a combination of these.

A second major social program of the Betancourt regime was its drive to expand and improve education. The number of students in all schools rose from about 1,000,000 in 1958 to 1,659,000 in 1963-64, while the number of secondary school enrollees more than doubled, as did that of university students.[7]

At the same time the school system was considerably diversified. Vocational secondary schools were established in every state. A new technical university, the Universidad del Oriente, was set up in the eastern part of the country, with campuses in several cities. An apprenticeship system for training workers on the job was established in 1961, with the organization of the Instituto de Cooperación Educativa, which worked with both private firms and public enterprises in giving special courses to several thousand workers, to raise their skills and prepare them for higher-graded jobs.

Economic development was another major interest of the Betancourt regime. The Venezuelan Development Corporation, which had first been established by the Acción Democrática government of 1945-48, was revitalized and invested 800 million bolivars in private firms, particularly in manufacturing. At the same time the government went ahead with and expanded projects that had been started by Pérez Jiménez to establish steel and petrochemical industries under government ownership. Large sums were also spent on the development of the country's hydroelectric resources, particularly through the government firm, CADAFE.[8]

Simultaneously the government followed a policy of protecting industry. Although many increases in tariffs were forbidden by a trade treaty that the Pérez Jiménez regime had signed with the United States, the government followed the policy of quotas and embargoes on the importation of foreign-made goods that competed with products made in Venezuela.

Special efforts were made by the Betancourt government to develop the resources of the Orinoco Valley. This had been an area of sparse population, with a reputation for being unhealthy. During the first AD administration the government had begun negotiations with American steel companies to open up iron mines where very large iron resources had recently been discovered. These negotiations had not been completed before AD was ousted from power, but concessions were given to the United States Steel and Bethlehem Steel companies by the military dictatorship. The Pérez Jiménez regime also began work on the establishment of a steel plant in the area.

In 1960 President Betancourt established the Corporación Venezolana de Guyanas. The function of this company was to undertake the general development of the Orinico area. It was to develop the agricultural and grazing resources of the region, its hydroelectric potential, and its minerals and manufacturing. It was also to supervise the construction of Ciudad Guayana, and entirely new city destined to have more than half a million people.

In the years that followed, the Corporación de Guyanas undertook the establishment of a large aluminum plant. It planned for and put into construction the first stage of a hydroelectric plant at Guri, on a branch of the Orinoco, which, when completed, will be the world's largest. It began a project for draining a large potential agricultural area in the delta of the Orinoco. It carefully planned the building of Ciudad Guayana. Betancourt hoped to establish the heavy industry of Venezuela in the Orinoco area. On occasions he referred to it as "the Pittsburgh of Venezuela."

The Betancourt regime followed a nationalistic, but not xenophobic, policy toward the petroleum industry, whihh provides most of the country's foreign exchange. It confirmed the policy that the AD government of 1945-48 had first established (and the Pérez Jiménez regime had reversed) of not granting new concessions to foreign oil companies. At the same time, at the end of 1960, Betancourt established by decree the Corporación Venezolana del Petróleo. Its immediate purpose was to take over parts of concessions of the 1950s, which the foreign companies had to return to the government, and to begin to exploit these— at the same time it was to build an experienced staff. The longer-run objective of the AD regime's oil policy was that this Venezuelan government corporation would take over the existing concessions when they expired in the mid-1980s. Meanwhile, a portion of the domestic market was reserved for this corporation.

In spite of extensive provocation, the Betancourt regime maintained a fundamentally democratic atmosphere. The political parties that operated according to democratic rules and did not seek to overthrow the government by force were allowed to function, to hold meetings and congresses, and to issue their publications. Their members continued to sit in Congress, which during the last year of the Betancourt administration was controlled by the opposition.

The Betancourt regime was a government of coalition. In accordance with the Pact of Punto Fijo, it began with representatives of AD, Copei, and URD in the cabinet. In November 1960 the URD withdrew from the government and joined the opposition, but Copei continued to be part of the administration throughout the Betancourt regime. Positions outside the cabinet, such as directors of independent agencies and governors of states, were divided among the coalition partners.

Part of the opposition to the Betancourt government operated within the bounds of democratic procedure. However, elements of both the extreme Right and the extreme Left went outside these limits and sought to overthrow the regime by force. There were four military mutinies, two of which were backed and led by right-wing elements yearning for the restoration of a Pérez Jiménez-type dictatorship. The other two were inspired and in part led by extreme left-wing elements of the Communist Party and the Movimiento de la Izquierda Revolucionaria (MIR), established by dissidents from Acción Democrática. All of these efforts against the regime failed, the government being able to rally the majority of the civilian population as well as the bulk of the armed forces to its defense.

Early in 1962 the extreme Left, apparently having given up hopes of gaining power by a military mutiny, resorted to terrorism in the urban areas and guerrilla war in the countryside. Major emphasis during 1962 and 1963 was placed on urban terrorism, which involved kidnapping well-known people, robbing banks, blowing up cars in the streets, burning warehouses and stores, and killing policemen. During this period attempts to launch a guerrilla war were thwarted largely by the peasants themselves, who either reported the presence of armed bands to the police or soldiers or went out themselves to round up such bands.

The terrorist campaign reached its peak during the months preceding the presidential election of 1963. The left-wing extremists sought to prevent the elections, going to the extent of announcing that they would shoot anyone found standing in line at the polls. This did not prevent more than 90 percent of the voters from casting their ballots.

The response of the Betancourt government to the left-wing campaign of violence provoked charges from the Communists and members of MIR that he was "a worse dictator than Pérez Jiménez." However, the administration acted with considerable leniency, seeking not to break the rules of democratic procedure. Communist and MIR members of Congress were permitted to keep their seats even though some of them were known to be among the leaders and planners of the terrorist activities; they were arrested only after Congress had held its last session, and only after a particularly violent episode in which terrorists had fired on a holiday tourist train leaving Caracas. Those who did not take up arms against the government had little to complain about.[9]

THE LEONI ADMINISTRATION

The election of December 1963 resulted in the choice of Acción Democrática's candidate, Raúl Leoni. He was a founder of AD, a member of the "generation of 1928," had been a member of the AD government in 1945-48, and had served during most of the Betancourt administration as president of the Congress.

The choice of Leoni revealed some interesting facts about the Acción Democrática. He was certainly not the candidate favored by Betancourt, who wanted a continuation of the AD-Copei coalition in the election and in the succeeding administration and was aware that the Copei would not support Leoni. However, Leoni was the choice of much of the lower-ranking AD leadership, particularly of the Labor Bureau of Acción Democrática. It was the party's labor leaders more than any other group who imposed the nomination of Raúl Leoni in 1963.

Leoni won in a field of seven candidates. Copei named Rafael Caldera once again; the URD put up its leader Jóvito Villalba; Arturo Uslar Pietri, a prominent businessman and novelist, was named by a group of independents; Admiral Larrazábal was candidate of his own party, the Frente Democrático Popular; Raúl Rámos Giménez ran as a candidate of a dissident AD group; and extreme right-wing elements organized as the Movimiento de Acción Nacional supported Germán Borregales.

Leoni won with a considerably smaller margin than Betancourt had received, only about 33 percent of the total vote. Rafael Caldera came in second, followed by Uslar Pietri, Villalba, Larrazábal, Ramos Giménez and Borregales.

The Leoni government continued along broad lines the programs that had been started by the Betancourt administration. It stepped up the pace of agrarian reform, so that by the end of Leoni's period in office more than 150,000 families had received land of their own and a much larger number than formerly were receiving credit, technical assistance, and other services needed to make them efficient farmers. The educational program was further expanded, with several new universities being established; and particular attention was given to improving the quality of education, so that there would be fewer students who dropped out of school, especially during the early years of their education.

Economic development efforts were also continued. The first stage of the mighty Guri dam on a tributary of the Orinoco River was opened a few months before the end of Leoni's term. The aluminum plant that had been planned for in the Orinoco industrial complex was completed, and many smaller projects in that same complex were also brought to fruition.

The nationalist oil policy established in the Betancourt regime was continued by Leoni. Long-pending tax issues with the foreign oil companies were settled to the satisfaction of the Venezuelan government in 1966, and a beginning was made in negotiation of contracts with companies to help the Venezuelan Petroleum Corporation exploit its sizable reserves.

Although basic policies were not different between the two Acción Democrática administrations, the two presidents ruled with a somewhat different combination of political forces in their administration. The formation of President Leoni's first cabinet involved extensive negotiations, an effort first being made to continue the AD-Copei coalition. These efforts failed, however; and Copei entered into what was in Venezuela a unique role, that of the loyal opposition.

In the beginning Leoni named a cabinet composed of members of Acción Democrática and independents. However, by the end of 1964 an agreement was reached with the URD and the Frente Nacional Democratico, a new party formed by Arturo Uslar Pietri and his followers, for the formation of what they called a broad-based government (gobierno de amplia base). This was a somewhat unwieldy coalition, with the Frente Nacional Democrático being basically opposed to Acción Democrática's oil policies and the URD being exceedingly hungry for jobs and patronage. It lasted until 1967.

Thereafter, with the withdrawal of the Frente Nacional Democrático from the coalition, only Accion Democrática and URD remained in the administration. However, when URD provoked a cabinet crisis in April 1968, President Leoni suddenly dismissed it from his government, forming a new cabinet of Acción Democrática members and independents. This group stayed in office until the end of Leoni's term.

The extreme left-wing violence that had begun under Betancourt was almost completely extinguished during the Leoni administration. The first few months of the Leoni regime were particularly calm, the extreme leftists having suffered a severe political and psychological blow in the election of 1963, in which more than 90 percent of the voters cast their ballots and victory went to the candidate of Acción Democrática.

However, the first months of 1964 were used by the extreme leftists to regroup their forces. By the middle of the year they had launched a major effort to stir up a guerrilla war in the rural areas. This effort gained ground for about a year, with the situation being particularly serious in the west-central states of Lara and Falcón. Frequent attacks were made by guerrillas on police stations and small garrisons, and one or two small towns were seized for a few hours.[10]

However, by the last months of 1965 the guerrilla war was definitely being won by the government. The guerrillas had failed utterly to arouse any significant measure of support among the peasantry, to whom their effort was supposedly designed to appeal. The peasants had no intention of helping to overthrow a regime that they had been largely responsible for electing and that was giving them the land and was carrying out a wide variety of other programs beneficial to them. Probably the fact that this guerrilla effort had the support of a foreign power, even if that foreign nation was Cuba, militated against its success among patriotic Venezuelans.

As a result of the defeats suffered by the guerrilla effort, the Communist Party of Venezuela, which had been one of the two principal political groups supporting it, decided to withdraw from the struggle and return to the use of legal methods. A majority of the

Movimiento de la Izquierda Revolucionaria also withdrew from the guerrilla war. Although these actions brought denunciation from Fidel Castro and a major polemic between the Cuban leader and the Venezuelan Communist Party, the guerrilla effort was defeated, at least for the time being. Although Castro subsequently sent into Venezuela small groups of well-trained fighters, who were able from time to time to kill a few policemen and soldiers, they were not able to launch a serious effort to overthrow the Leoni regime.[11]

In December 1968 an election was held to choose a successor to Raúl Leoni. Again there were seven nominees. Acción Democrática chose Gonzalo Barrios, like Betancourt and Leoni a founder of AD, and a member of all three Acción Democrática administrations; Luís Beltrán Prieto Figueroa was the nominee of a dissident Acción Democrática group, the Movimiento Electoral del Pueblo, and also had the backing of several smaller groups; Rafael Caldera again had the nomination of Copei; URD and Uslar Pietri's Frente Nacional Democrático supported a businessman and diplomat, Miguel Angel Burelli; Admiral Larrazábal again ran as nominee for the Frente Democrático Popular; Alejandro Hernández, a leading businessman, ran as the candidate of the small Partido Socialista de Venezuela; and Germán Borregales once more was nominee of the Movimiento de Acción Nacional.

This election was exceedingly close. For several days the results were not known. However, the Supreme Electoral Tribunal finally announced that Rafael Caldera, with about 29 percent of the vote, had defeat the Acción Democrática nominee by less than 1 percent of the total. Prieto Figueroa was third, and Burelli came in fourth. Larrazábal, Hernández, and Borregales trailed with very small votes. Thus, after ten years in power, Acción Democrática was defeated. On March 11, 1969, President Leoni turned the sash of office over to Rafael Caldera.

SPLITS IN ACCIÓN DEMOCRATICA

Undoubtedly the major cause of the defeat of Accion Democrática in the December 1968 election was the split a year earlier, which led to the candidacy of Luís Beltrán Prieto and was the third such schism that the party had suffered during its ten years in power. It is important to note something of the causes and impacts of these divisions.

The first split, which took place during the first months of 1960, was the only one of the three to have an ideological basis. It arose from the circumstances of the last years of the Pérez Jiménez dictatorship, when the AD underground had been largely cut off from contact with its exiled leaders. The students and young professionals who exercised the leadership of the underground had much closer contact during these years with the members of the Communist underground than they had with the exile leaders, and they were greatly influenced by the Marxist-Leninist ideas of their Communist friends.

This situation was complicated after the overthrow of Pérez Jiménez by resentment of some of the younger leaders at the leading positions in Acción Democrática that were assumed by the returning exiles of a somewhat older generation. There was an attempt at the August 1958 congress by these younger leaders to have the party refuse to name Rómulo Betancourt as the Acción Democrática candidate for president.

The rivalry between the former underground chiefs and other leaders of Acción Democrática came to a head in March and April 1960. The conflict centered on the actions of Domingo Alberto Rangel, the one AD leader of an older generation who sided with the young rebels, in denouncing the collective agreement signed by the Petroleum Workers Federation and the oil companies, even though he had played an important role in negotiating it. He was brought up on charges and was expelled from the party. When the leaders of the AD Youth supported him, they also were expelled. Thereupon other younger leaders withdrew, joining Rangel and his friends to form a new party that soon took the name Movimiento de la Izquierda Revolucionaria.

The split in the party resulted in the withdrawal of most of the members of the AD Youth, and Acción Democrática never recovered the position of dominance in the university that it had had in the 1940s and in the first year after the fall of Pérez Jiménez. It also caused the withdrawal of a small number of trade union leaders, particularly those of the Bank Workers Federation. However, the rank and file of the party generally remained loyal; and within a year and a half Acción Democrática had regained its former position, except in the student movement.

The second split in Acción Democrática took place at the end of 1961. It centered on a group who had been the youth leaders of the 1945-48 period. At that time they had had certain disagreements with the party's major leaders, feeling that the AD was not being energetic enough in carrying out its program. During the period of the dictatorship these differences of opinion had been generally suppressed by both groups, and in the struggle with the MIR rebels in 1960 the rebels of the 1940s were the most energetic supporters of the disciplining and final expulsion of Rangel and his associates.[12]

The opening of old divisions was provoked, however, by the prospect of the party's nomination for president in 1963. The rebels of the 1940's strongly supported the nomination of Raúl Rámos Giménez, senator and principal figure in the group, which was popularly known as the ARS. This title came from the name of the leading advertising agency of Caracas, the ARS Agency, which had as it slogan "Leave your thinking to us." It was argued that the ARS within Acción Democrática was trying to tell the rest of the party exactly that.

In maneuvering within the party, which was obviously leading up to a decision concerning the presidential nomination, the ARS group came into conflict with what came to be called the Old Guard, the group of founding fathers of the party, among whom were Raúl Leoni, Gonzalo Barrios, Luis Beltrán Prieto, and Rómulo Betancourt. The ARS leaders, in temporary control of the National Executive Committee of the party, suspended Leoni in his functions as president of the party, whereupon he set up rival party headquarters and in turn mobilized his supporters to "suspend" the ARS leaders.

The upshot of this conflict was two party congresses, each of which claimed to be the "real" congress of Acción Democrática. Rómulo Betancourt, although he first sought to reconcile the two factions, finally attended the congress of the Old Guard. The Supreme Electoral Tribunal recognized the Old Guard group as AD in Government and the ARS group as AD in Opposition. It was agreed that whichever party did better in the 1963 elections would have the definitive title of Acción Democrática.

The ARS split was more serious than that of the MIR. It took out of the party a sizable part of its secondary leadership, although it did not make serious inroads into the AD trade union cadre, which remained almost unanimously with the Old Guard. In fact, the trade unionists were among the strongest backers of the Old Guard in this conflict. The split was not serious enough to defeat Acción Democrática in the 1963 election, although it did contribute considerably to reducing the party's vote from the 49 percent that Betancourt had received in 1958 to the 33 percent that Leoni got five years later.

The third split in Acción Democrática was the most serious. It involved a break within both the Old Guard and the Trade Union Bureau of the party. Like the previous division it centered on the issue of the party's presidential nomination, this time for the 1968 election.

Two potential candidates emerged in the preliminary intraparty discussions. One of these was Gonzalo Barrios, the other, Luis Beltrán Prieto. The latter had the backing of Jesús Paz Galarraga, who for seven years had served as secretary-general of the party and had been allied with the ARS group (but had not broken with Acción Democrática when they did). He was felt by many members of the Old Guard to be trying to seize control of the party for himself and to be using the candidacy of Prieto for this purpose. Prieto felt that he had the right to the Acción Democrática nomination as undoubtedly

ACCIÓN DEMOCRÁTICA

the most popular figure with the party's rank and file, at least after Rómulo Betancourt. He also nursed a grievance that he had not been a member of the government during the Betancourt and Leoni administrations, although he had served as both president of Congress and president of Acción Democrática during these two presidencies.

Most of the Old Guard leaders opposed the nomination of Prieto, not so much because they were against him as because they were against the man whom they thought to be Prieto's sponsor, Paz Galarraga. As a result another bitter fight broke out within the party in the last months of 1967, which resulted in Prieto's withdrawal from the Acción Democrática to form the Movimiento Electoral del Pueblo.

This third schism for a while seemed to divide Acción Democrática almost in half. It split the founding generation of the party and its trade unionists, who had constituted the most loyal and firm element in the party. However, the peasant following of AD seems to have remained largely intact. In the 1968 election Acción Democrática proved to be stronger than Prieto's followers insofar as the country's voters were concerned, even though the MEP received the support of the Partido Revolucionario de Izquierda Nacionalista, which had been established by the old ARS group and the majority of the MIR, as well as the backing of the Communists. However, Prieto's backing was sufficient to assure the defeat of Accion Democratica in the presidential election, although AD continued to have the largest group in both the Senate and the Chamber of Deputies.

STRENGTHS AND WEAKNESSES OF ACCION DEMOCRATICA

Acción Democrática has been one of the most successful of the national revolutionary parties of Latin America. It has governed Venezuela for 13 years and has amply demonstrated that a party of its kind can carry out fundamental reforms of the sort needed in most of the Latin American countries and can use the influence and resources of the government to foster rapid economic development. Its program and its achievements have combined social change, nationalism, rapid economic development, and political democracy. The party succeeded in establishing the beginnings of a tradition of democratic government for the first time in Venezuela.

Acción Democrática has also developed an ideological position that is of major importance in the hemisphere. Although the party has not had any Lenins or even Che Guevaras, in terms of being a fount for political dogma and doctrine, its leaders have written enough in exposition of their ideas to spell out in some detail the position of Acción Democrática and other national revolutionary parties.

In the particular period in which they were in power for the second time, the record and position of Acción Democrática was of key importance for the whole of Latin America. This period covered the first 10 years of the Castro regime in Cuba, and in it AD presented a major alternative to the appeal of the Castro Communist administration. There is little question that the success of the AD regime in carrying out its program has gone far to counteract the Castroite argument that the only way to improve the lot of Latin Americans is through guerrilla warfare followed by a totalitarian dictatorship. Guerrilla war failed in Venezuela; and most available evidence would seem to indicate that the Acción Democratica regime in Venezuela was more successful in fostering rapid economic development and in raising living standards of the average citizen than was Castro's government in Cuba.

One of the major assets of Acción Democrática in comparison with other Venezuelan parties has been its extensive organization. Since the late 1930s, when Rómulo Betancourt first established units of the party throughout the country, Acción Democrática has had groups of members and supporters in virtually every center of population. In spite of recurrent splits, it has been able to maintain this network, which has been of key importance not only at election time but also in helping to maintain the party's influence in the labor movement, among the peasants, and in various professional organizations.

The principal handicap of Acción Democrática has been its tendency to split. Although the party has been famed for its discipline, this discipline has tended to crack whenever the issue of who should be the next candidate for president is raised. Acción Democrática will not fully mature as a modern political party until it demonstrates that it can make such an important decision without splintering. Indeed, the question of whether Acción Democrática can continue to be one of the country's major parties, and whether it will be able to return to power after a period of Copei rule, also seems to depend largely on this issue.

CHAPTER

11

THE PARTIDO LIBERACIÓN NACIONAL OF COSTA RICA

Costa Rica is one of the more fortunate Latin American countries. It has a greater degree of social equality, a wider distribution of wealth, and a more general prevalence of education than almost any of the other countries in the area. Small farmers make up the backbone of its citizenry, and there are relatively few people at the extremes of great wealth or abysmal poverty. As a result there is a more generalized respect among Costa Ricans for the rights of their fellow citizens than is characteristic of most Latin American countries, and political democracy has tended to be the rule rather than the exception.

However, even in Costa Rica there have been significant movements for change in recent decades. These have sought to defend the rights of the weakest members of the community, to fight against the very strong influence of foreign enterprises in the national economy, and to stimulate the more rapid economic development of the country.

In 1929 a young lawyer, Manuel Mora, led in the establishment of the Communist Party of Costa Rica. During the following decade most of the country's politically conscious young intellectuals were attracted to this party, which led in the effort to establish an organized labor movement, both in the cities and in the country's larger agricultural enterprises, particularly the banana plantations belonging to the United Fruit Company.

However, by the early 1940s the opportunism of the Communists and their subservience to the interests of the Soviet Union had alienated a large proportion of those young people who were concerned with politics and favored political, economic, and social reform. The way was paved for the advent of another force in Costa Rican political life.

ANTECEDENTS OF LIBERACION NACIONAL

The first step toward developing a new reformist philosophy appropriate to Costa Rica, and a political vehicle to give expression to such a philosophy, was taken in 1940, when a group of students and young professionals established the Centro para el Estudio de los Problemas Nacionales. The original purpose of this organization, which was established in large part by youths who in 1937 had set up the Cultural Association of Students of Law and in the following year had organized the Federation of University Students, was to study the country's principal problems and try to work out answers to them. It published a monthly periodical Surco, and issued a number of individual studies, the first of which was Rodrigo Facio's Estudio sobre economía costarricense, which the group published in 1942.

The Centro was by coincidence established in the same year that the government of Rafael Calderón Guardia came to power. Although Calderón had a reputation as a reformer and was responsible for enacting the country's most important labor and social legislation, his administration was also widely regarded as being corrupt to a degree unusual for Costa Rica. This was one of the three factors that alienated the young men of the Centro from the Calderón administration, despite that government's apparent reforming zeal. The second factor was the increasingly strong alliance between Calderón and his National Republican Party, on the one hand, and the Communist Party, on the other. Third, the Centro members were turned against Calderón by his administration's obvious willingness to use force against those who attempted to criticize his government.

As a result of their hostility toward the Calderón regime, the young members of the Centro tended to turn toward the opposition, led by ex-President León Cortés, and to establish a particularly close connection with Otillio Ulate, publisher of the country's largest newspaper, Diario de Costa Rica, which was a strong supporter of Cortés. Members of the Centro frequently contributed articles to the Diario; and in February 1944, when Ulate decided to suspend publication of the paper, they convinced him to allow them to take it over on their own responsibility. For about a year Diario de Costa Rica was an informal organ of the young members of the Centro.

Meanwhile, the group had gone beyond mere study of the country's problems and tried to do something about them. They had begun to be active in politics, at first through support of the 1944 presidential election campaign of León Cortés. After Cortés' defeat in an election that most of the opposition believed had been fraudulently administered by outgoing President Calderón, the members of the Centro felt that the time had come to organize a party of democratic reform.

The members of the Centro were relatively new to politics. However, there existed within Leon Cortés' Democratic Party a group of young men who had established an organization known as Acción Democrática. The members of Acción Democrática had ideas very similar to those of the Centro, and it was logical that the two join forces. After long and sometimes difficult negotiations, they merged to form the Partido Social Demócrata.

The new party adopted twelve-point program of principles and objectives:

1. Progress of the Republic within the constitutional framework, with absolute proscription of violence and total respect for the liberal political tradition.
2. A regime of government based on public opinion, through freedom of suffrage and other complementary political liberties.
3. Absolute respect for the religious, philosophical and political convictions of the Costa Ricans.
4. Integral development of the citizen through a public education adapted to the economic and social conditions of the country and technical needs.
5. Increase of national wealth through the protection and planned stimulation of small rural property and small industry.
6. Defense of the national economy through rational and just contracts with foreign capital.
7. A technical and honorable administration through the scientific reorganization of public finances, the establishment of civil service, and the autonomy of technical bodies.
8. The defense of the health of the people through coordinate plans of public health and hygiene, education, public works, and economy.
9. Defense of the peasant population through cooperative organization of agriculture and technical aid to it through autonomous institutions.
10. Defense of the wage earning population through political trade union organization and legal protection of its economic-social interests.
11. Defense of the consumers through cooperative organization and the increase of the effective national income.
12. Maintenance of relations with all those states whose governments really represent the majority will of the nation, and friendship and all possible aid to the movements for liberty and against dictatorship carried out by peoples in every part of the world.

The president of the new party was Antonio Peña Chavarría. Among other members of its Executive Committee were José Figueres, in charge of finances, Rodrigo Facio, one of two secretaries of propaganda; and Francisco Orlich, secretary of political information.[1]

Even by joining forces, however, the members of the Partido Social Demócrata remained a small group with relatively little influence in national politics. They were virtually unknown except among a group of young people, principally in San José and one or two other urban centers. In order for them to be able to make a serious impact on politics, they needed a leader sympathetic to their ideas, somewhat older than they, and with an established national reputation.

The leader this young group of would-be reformers was seeking appeared in July 1942. On the occasion of the July 4 celebration of the independence of the United States, which was participated in by virtually all Costa Ricans who supported the war effort of the Allies, José Figueres, a hitherto relatively obscure engineer and coffee planter, was one of the guests at the American embassy in San José, the Costa Rican capital. This made him the witness of a mob action (supposedly to avenge the sinking of Costa Rican merchant vessels by German submarines) against Italian and German retail businesses in San José. Figueres became convinced that this wreaking of vengeance on innocent merchants of Axis origins was an attempt by the Communists to intimidate their opponents and that it had the acquiescence of the Calderón government.

As a result on the evening of July 8 Figueres bought time on one of the major national radio stations to denounce the demonstration and what he conceived to be the government's complicity in it. He denounced the Axis but also said that opposition to the German-Italian-Japanese coalition in the war did not justify such attacks on innocent parties, which he charged were arranged by the government in order to divert attention from its own inadequacies and to intimidate its opponents. Before he had finished his address, Figueres was arrested and soon afterward was deported. He spent the next several years in Mexico.

The deportation of José Figueres provided the younger professional people and students with a leader. It immediately made him a national figure. From his exile in Mexico, Figueres sent back to Costa Rica a series of political letters in which he outlined a program of democratic humanistic socialism, which he said was appropriate for Costa Rica and other Latin American countries. These documents were widely circulated in Costa Rica, and they converted the hitherto obscure planter into a first-rank political figure.[2]

The young men who established the Partido Social Demócrata threw their strong support behind José Figueres even before his return from exile. He was chosen a member of the first Executive Committee

PARTIDO LIBERACIÓN NACIONAL

of the PSD, and upon his return the members of the PSD became Figueres' strongest supporters within the camp of the opposition.

In preparation for the presidential election campaign of 1948, the PSD joined forces with the much more conservative Unión Nacional, headed by newspaper publisher Otilio Ulate. The opposition held a convention on February 13, 1947, to choose a nominee to run against ex-President Rafael Calderón Guardia, who had the full support of the government of President Teodoro Picado. In this convention the PSD delegates voted for José Figueres; but he came in third, behind Ulate and a well-known businessman, Fernando Castro Cervantes.

Once the choice was made, Figueres and the PSD threw their support behind Ulate. However, Figueres made very clear his belief that the government was not going to allow the opposition to win. He began to prepare for armed resistance to the government's stealing of the 1948 election, such as the opposition was sure had occurred in the 1944 presidential poll and the 1942 and 1946 congressional elections.

Before the election of February 1948 there was a showdown between the government and the opposition. In July 1947, following an incident in which police machine-gunned crowds leaving two movie theaters in the city of Cartago, the opposition declared a national strike. Virtually all businesses closed down and all economic activity was halted for a week, during which the government armed members of the Communist Party and unemployed toughs, who broke into places of business, seeking by force to make them open their doors. However, on August 3 a nine-point agreement was signed between the president and the opposition, one point of which provided for the establishment of the National Electoral Tribunal of three, representing the executive, judiciary, and legislature, to preside over the elections and with final power to announce the results.[3]

The campaign was bitterly fought. However, although on election day there were some protests of irregularities on both sides, the National Electoral Tribunal voted two to one to certify the election of Otilio Ulate. Voting to certify were the representatives of Congress and the Supreme Court, with the nominee of the president asserting that the election had been won by Calderón Guardia.

Under the constitution Congress was to receive the results of the presidential election. Congress, however, chose to judge the decision of the Tribunal and reversed its findings, declaring Calderón the winner.

THE CIVIL WAR OF 1948

José Figueres and the young men of the Partido Social Demócrata were prepared for this outcome. For some time they had been collecting arms on Figueres' estate, "La Lucha sin Fin," in the mountains some 50 miles south of San José. Soon after it became clear that Congress had upset the results of the presidential election, a small group took over the nearby airport, where they seized a Pan American Airways plane that landed there on a scheduled flight. With this small "air force" several members of the rebel group flew to Guatemala, where their plane was loaded with arms provided by Colonel Francisco Arana, then commander of the armed forces in the government of Juan José Arevalo.

With these arms in hand, the rebels under Figueres launched a full-scale civil war. The members of their "army" were mainly students, young professional people, and members of the Confederación Costarricense del Trabajo "Rerum Novarum," the national labor confederation that had been established several years before to compete with the Communist-dominated Confederación de Trabajadores de Costa Rica. They also had the help of the so-called "Caribbean Legion," made up principally of exiles from dictator-run countries in and around the Caribbean.

The rebels made a daring attack on and captured the Caribbean port of Limón. They also won control of most of the central plateau and virtually surrounded San José. In less than a month they were within a few miles of the capital.

Meanwhile, the forces supporting the government were in serious disarray. The small Costa Rican army, of a few hundred men, was badly armed and worse disciplined. In addition there were two forces of "volunteers," consisting of personal supporters of Calderón Guardia and the members and sympathizers of the Communist Party. These three groups quarreled seriously among themselves and offered only faltering resistance to the growing forces led by José Figueres.

With the Intervention of the archbishop of San José, a parley was called between the two sides after more than 1,000 people had died in the fighting. Benjamin Núñez, the founder of the "Rerum Novarum" labor confederation and chaplain of the Figueres forces, represented the rebels in these negotiations with President Picado and ex-President Calderón Guardia. An agreement was finally reached whereby Picado would step down and there would be established a provisional government, headed by José Figueres, which took the name Junta Fundadora de la Segunda República. It was further agreed that after not more than two years in power the Junta would give way to Otilio Ulate, who was duly recognized to have won the February 1948 election.

THE FIGUERES PROVISIONAL GOVERNMENT

The Junta Fundadora remained in power for a year and a half. During this period it carried out a number of reforms but did not succeed in its efforts to begin the process of fundamentally altering the economic and social structure of the republic. During these 18 months the government was largely in the hands of the young men who had founded the Partido Social Demócrata.

The longest-lasting reform enacted by the provisional regime, soon after taking power, was its nationalization of the four private banks that were the country's only financial institutions. The theory behind this move was that the credit resources of the country had been largely misdirected, having been channeled principally into commercial enterprises instead of being used to encourage the growth of manufacturing and the modernization and extension of agriculture.

Another drastic but short-run measure of the government was the imposition of a capital levy, a tax of 10 percent on the capital of all business enterprises. The immediate purpose of the measure was to replenish the national treasury, which had been thoroughly rifled by the departing Picado government. However, its longer-range purpose was to impress the people of Costa Rica with the new regime's intention to bring about basic change in the economy and social system of the republic.

Other changes were also necessary. One of these was a reorganization of the social security system. It, like the treasury, had been severely weakened by the illicit siphoning off of funds to private pocketbooks.

The provisional government also called elections for an assembly to write a new constitution. However, these elections proved a severe setback for the Junta Fundadora. Its more or less "official" party, the Partido Social Demócrata, elected only a fraction of the membership of this assembly, with a majority of the delegates consisting of more conservative elements, particularly those associated with the Unión Nacional of President-elect Otilio Ulate. The Junta's suggestions for fundamental changes in the constitution were rejected by the assembly, which wrote a constitution that did not differ very significantly from the one it replaced.

THE ESTABLISHMENT OF LIBERACION NACIONAL

Soon after the adjournment of the Constitutional Assembly, the Junta Fundadora decided to turn the government over to President-elect Ulate, even though it could have stayed in power for six months more. Ulate governed for the next three and a half years. His was, on balance, a conservative regime, putting primary emphasis on financial orthodoxy although carrying out some important development projects, such as the construction of a new international airport for San José.

Relations between Ulate and Figueres and the young men who had been largely responsible for Ulate's being able to take power were rather strained throughout his administration. It was obvious that the Figueristas were restless about the conservative cast of the Ulate government and were anxious for the chance to elect their leader as Ulate's constitutional successor.

The forces that had supported the Junta Fundadora reorganized during the Ulate period. The Partido Social Demócrata was dissolved and a new organization, the Partido Liberación Nacional, was established. The avowed objective of the new party was to change the pattern of Costa Rican politics, which previously had generally been dominated by personalist parties organized by presidential candidates or incumbent presidents for the support of their leaders' political ambitions. It was the hope of the founders of Liberación Nacional to establish an ideological party, which would take advantage of the popularity of José Figueres in order to build up party support but would not be in any sense a purely Figuerista party.

The ideology of Liberación Nacional was national revolutionary. The party wanted to be multiclass in its membership and program, seeking to represent the interests of the small farmers, the urban and plantation workers, and middle-class and professional elements. It strongly supported trade unionism and collective bargaining, and also urged effective government action to encourage industrialization and to help the small agriculturalists.

A summary of the main outlines of the party's program was published under the title <u>Programa ideológico del partido liberacion nacional</u> soon after the establishment of the party. It lists the eleven points of the program as follows:

> 1. Strengthen and perfect the democratic system of respect for human dignity, effectively basing it on freedom of suffrage, conscientious and universal. The full realization of liberty must consist not only of the enjoyment of traditional civil and political rights but also of the maximum satisfaction of the needs for food, housing, clothing, health, recreation, and education
> 2. Promote and strengthen the honest public administration, juridically responsible, coordinated, technically qualified, and regulated by the norms of Civil Service.
> 3. Support planning of the national economy which will make for better use of the material and human resources of the country, and which will consequently result in a great production of wealth.
> 4. Follow a social policy which contributes to the welfare of all, to seek living conditions which guarantee the full

development of the personality of the individual in the exercise of his rights and in the fulfillment of his duties; to obtain a distribution of product which provides all and every one of the highest living levels permitted by the productivity of the social group.

5. Respect and stimulation of private property while recognizing its social function, and seeking to have its benefits extended to the largest possible part of the population. To give support to individual enterprise as an adequate instrument with which man can exercise his initiative and develop his personality.

6. Support of autonomous state organisms to carry out economic-social activities which are of public utility and to undertake those which have the characteristics of monopoly. Those organisms will tend to stimulate individual initiative, foment reproductive savings and increase the number of proprietors.

7. Aid the economically weak groups to struggle effectively through their democratically constituted organizations to improve their conditions of life, participate in the direction of society and enjoy well-being.

8. Stimulate education of the people to the end of forming better human beings, capable of superior achievements.

9. Efforts to attain a high level of public health and social security, to conserve and improve as much as possible the human resources of the country.

10. Conduct international relations within the strict rule of law which guarantees the juridical equality of states. To stimulate as much as possible the independence and solidarity of people in the common struggle for integral liberation, in accord with the precepts and orientation of the international organisms which promote the material and spiritual welfare of all men, respecting the customs of each people.

11. Combat all doctrines and tendencies contrary to the democratic system and the principles of Christian morality.

Liberación Nacional also urged that foreign investment be encouraged, but that it be directed into those branches of the economy that the government felt to be most important, and that it not be given special concessions not equally available to national investors. In particular, the party urged that the country's dependence upon the United Fruit Co. for the largest part of its foreign exchange be ended as soon as possible, through conversion of the company into a shipper of bananas instead of a grower of them and the transfer of its plantations, schools, hospitals, and other properties to Costa Rican hands as soon as feasible.

The Ulate years were used by the Partido Liberación Nacional to carry out intensive organization. Units of the party were established in virtually every population center in the country. Support was particularly widespread among the peasantry and the lower classes in the cities. In contrast, many of the more well-to-do upper-class Costa Ricans tended to look upon Figueres and his followers as being as "dangerous" as the Communists—or perhaps more so, because they were more influential. This prejudice was shared by some of the people who served during this period in the United States embassy in San José.

The party sought to exploit as much as possible its major popular asset, José Figueres, who had caught the imagination of large numbers of Costa Ricans. During 1949-53 he traveled throughout the country, got to know most of the members and local leaders of his party, and carried its message throughout the country. He also found time to go abroad on several occasions, visiting other Latin American countries, the United States, Western Europe, and Israel.

Intensive work was also done on the specific details of a program, which the party hoped to be able to put into effect after the 1953 election. A kind of "ideological kitchen cabinet" met frequently, often with Figueres present, to study and discuss in detail the major economic and social problems facing the country, and to try to work out programs for dealing with these problems.

THE FIGUERES ADMINISTRATION

In 1953 Jose Figueres ran as the Partido Liberación Nacional candidate for president. He was faced with two opponents: Mario Echandi, candidate of Unión Nacional, the party of President Otilio Ulate, whose relations with Liberación Nacional were at a low ebb by this time; and Fernando Castro, who had the backing of ex-President Rafael Calderón Guardia's Partido Nacional Republicano and of the Communists. Figueres handily defeated both of his rivals, while Liberación Nacional also won 31 of the 46 seats in the National Assembly.[4]

During the four years of the Figueres administration, Liberación Nacional sought to put into effect large segments of its program. One of the first moves in this direction was the negotiation of a new agreement with United Fruit. This agreement, which was enacted into law, provided for a substantial increase of the company's payments to the national treasury, with its income and other taxes being raised from 15 percent of its income to 30 percent. In addition, another major demand of Liberación Nacional was met when United Fruit agreed to turn over its schools and hospitals to the Costa Rican government whenever the government wished.5

The pattern of relations between the government and United Fruit established by the Figueres government was subsequently extended to the other Central American countries in which the company operated. In addition, this agreement was undoubtedly a major factor in convincing the company's directors late in the 1950s of the advisability of the enterprise's progressively getting out of the business of growing bananas on its own plantations and shifting to buying the fruit from local producers, confining its own activities principally to providing technical assistance to growers and to shipping and marketing their fruit. This move, of course, was advocated by the Liberación Nacional and its leadership.

The Figueres government also took important steps toward stimulating industrialization of the country. Its major weapons were a policy of high tariffs to protect new manufacturing enterprises from foreign competition and the resources of the nationalized banking system (established under the Junta Fundadora), which were used to help provide the financial resources for launching a number of new firms. Most of the new manufacturing establishments were in the field of light consumer goods, including such items as textiles, shoes, and processed foodstuffs. By the middle of 1956 more than 400 firms had received loans for expansion of capital equipment from the government banks.6

The government banking system was also used to stimulate the expansion of agriculture. A beginning was made on a program that the party had developed for extending branches of the four banks to even the most remote areas of the country and coordinating their activities with those of the Ministry of Agriculture's extension service and other government entities.

The stimulation of both industry and agriculture, as well as the raising of living standards, particularly in the rural areas, was served by the Figueres government's electrification program. The Instituto Costarricense de Electricidad, which had been established during the period of the Junta Fundadora, started the construction of a number of new hydroelectric projects.

Another major program of the Figueres government was in housing. All of the government's efforts in that field were centered on the Instituto Nacional de Vivienda Urbana (INVU); 12,000 people were provided with rented houses and apartments, and 3,000 families in 64 communities became owners of their own homes through the INVU's program.7

The Figueres government put special emphasis on education. Teachers' salaries were considerably increased. The normal schools were greatly expanded, and the number of classrooms was greatly increased. The president boasted in his 1957 message to Congress that "never before have 350 classrooms been constructed in the four years of any Administration. Now, only in the year 1956, 450 have been constructed."[8]

The foreign policy of the Figueres government conformed to the general lines of the Liberación Nacional program. During this period Costa Rica made clear its opposition to dictatorial regimes in other Latin American countries; and exiles from a number of dictator-ridden nations, including Venezuela, Cuba, the Dominican Republic, and Nicaragua, were given refuge. In 1954 the Figueres government refused to send a Costa Rican delegation to the Tenth Inter American Conference, which was held in Venezuela, on the grounds that it was absolutely inappropriate for a conference that had as one of its major purposes the strengthening of democracy in the hemisphere to meet in a country dominated by such a dictatorship as that of General Marcos Pérez Jiménez, then president of Venezuela.

The foreign policy of the Figueres government also stressed trying to get the large industrial countries to understand the importance to the nations producing basic raw materials and foodstuffs of "just" prices for these commodities. Figueres constantly returned to this theme in public speeches and in articles written during his presidency. Typical was a passage in his speech to the assembled American presidents, who met in Panama in July 1956:

> 1. Just prices for our products which make possible local capitalization. The stabilization of the international market could conform to certain principles, or long-term aspirations. For example:
>> Equal remuneration for the work of the different peoples and for their natural resources.
>> Equal compensation for equal effort, to the degree that the different countries are able to apply the same level of efficiency in their work.
>> This may bring us in time to the maximum social aspiration of America: a uniform minimum wage for all of the Hemisphere.[9]

In spite of a substantial record of achievement by the Figueres government, Liberación Nacional did not win the election of 1957 to choose Figueres' successor. The reason for the party's defeat was that it split its ranks in the face of a united opposition. Although the majority of the party supported the candidacy of Francisco Orlich,

PARTIDO LIBERACIÓN NACIONAL

a former member of the Junta Fundadora, who became the official Liberación Nacional nominee, the minister of finance of the Figueres regime, Jorge Rossi, refused to accept the party's decision and launched his own independent candidacy. Thus, although the votes of Orlich and Rossi together surpassed those of opposition candidate Mario Echandi, a former minister in the Ulate government, Echandi received more votes than either of the candidates originating in Liberación Nacional, and was therefore elected.

RECENT HISTORY OF LIBERACIÓN NACIONAL

Although Liberación Nacional lost the presidency in 1958, it continued to have a majority in the National Assembly. This made it possible to prevent the relatively conservative Echandi regime from trying to undo any of the achievements of the Figueres government.

During the Echandi period, although the split that had led to its loss of the 1958 election was healed, the party suffered another division. This one was provoked, at least in part, by the appearance of the Castro regime in Cuba. Although Liberación Nacional had strongly supported the efforts of Castro's 26th of July Movement and other groups to overthrow the Batista dictatorship, and Figueres himself visited Cuba soon after Castro's victory, to show his endorsement of the new regime there, the great majority of Liberación Nacional opposed the drift of the Castro government in the direction of Communism.

However, there was a small minority in the Partido Liberación Nacional that continued to be favorably disposed toward the Castro government, even when it became clear that it was being converted into a Marxist-Leninist regime. This faction, led by a former deputy in the National Assembly, Marcial Aguiluz, finally withdrew from the party and established a rival group. Although this party did not become a major factor in Costa Rican politics, it was violently opposed to Figueres and Liberación Nacional.

In the election of 1962 two former presidents, Rafael Calderón Guardia and Otilio Ulate, ran against Francisco Orlich, who was again Liberación Nacional's candidate. This time the PLN was successful. The Orlich government had a number of accomplishments to its credit. Martin Kruning, writing in The Latin American Times of August 16, 1965, wrote of its record: "As the party in power since 1962, the National Liberation Party has been primarily responsible for steering through Congress an effective agrarian reform bill; eradicating slum conditions; for expanding social security; for establishing awards in the arts and literature fields; and for publishing the works of Costa Rican artists and writers."

However, during the four years of the Orlich administration, there developed a widespread feeling, not only among the general public but also within the Partido Liberación Nacional, that the party was no longer the advanced reform and developmentalist group it had been a decade earlier. Relatively few innovations were undertaken. In addition, the government was faced with a natural disaster, the eruption of the Irazú volcano, which went on for two years, destroying part of the country's second city, Cartago, and covering San José with a heavy blanket of volcanic ash. Inevitably, in spite of its best efforts, the Orlich government was widely accused of not doing enough to deal with the effects of the eruption.

In 1966 the Partido Liberación Nacional was defeated once again. The party's nominee was Daniel Oduber, who had served for a considerable period as foreign minister. In this election the whole opposition—Unión Nacional of ex-Presidents Ulate and Echandi, the Partido Republicano Nacional of ex-President Calderón Guardia, and the Communists—joined forces to support the candidacy of a single nominee, José Trejos Fernández, a professor of economics who had not previously been active in politics.

This second defeat of Liberación Nacional was a very disconcerting blow for the party. Neither the leaders nor the rank and file had expected to lose. For almost a year the party virtually did not function, the caretaker activities of maintaining a skeleton organization being undertaken by what came to be known as "the troika," the three men who had been the party's candidate for president: Figueres, Orlich, and Oduber.

Finally, in July 1967 Liberación Nacional held its first postdefeat national convention. Great dissatisfaction was expressed by rank-and-file delegates over the way the party leadership had behaved, both during the 1966 election and afterward. There were extensive discussions of the causes of the defeat in that election, and there was wide agreement that one more defeat would in all likelihood result in the demise of the party. There was extensive criticism of "the troika"; and a new leadership was chosen to undertake the work of reorganizing the party, strengthening its rank and file, and preparing for the 1970 election. Luis Alberto Monge, a former secretary-general of the Rerum Novarum labor confederation, as well as a former member of the National Assembly and ex-ambassador to Israel, was chosen as secretary-general of Liberación Nacional.

By this time the principal fears of the rise of a party that might rival Liberación Nacional for the support of the workers and peasants, who had long been its principal constituents, came from the small Christian Democratic Party. Although this party had only recently been established and by 1967 was only a small element in national politics, it pictured itself as being to the left of Liberación Nacional and accused Figueres and his associates of having betrayed the hopes of those Costa Ricans who had looked to them for leadership in social change and rapid economic development. It was feared in Liberación Nacional that a defeat in the 1970 election might result in the disintegration of the PLN and the assumption by the Christian Democrats of the role that Liberación Nacional had held since 1948.

This defeat did not come in 1970. José Figueres was again elected president as candidate of the Partido Liberación Nacional. His new administration did not undertake any major innovations in internal policy, although it did innovate in foreign affairs by recognizing the Soviet Union and entering into a substantial commercial agreement with it.

ASSESSMENT OF LIBERACIÓN NACIONAL

The social, economic, and political conditions of Costa Rica have been substantially different from those of most other Latin American countries. This fact has been largely responsible for the great difference between the program and performance of Liberación Nacional and those of other national revolutionary parties.

Costa Rica has never had the large landholding problem characteristic of most other countries of the area. As a result, Liberación Nacional has never had as a major element of its program large-scale agrarian reform; rather, it has concentrated on providing small landholders with sufficient credit, technical assistance, and other facilities.

The social structure of Costa Rica has been less aristocratic than those of most other Latin American nations. Education has long been available to most children, and most Costa Ricans have felt themselves the social equals of even the most prosperous of their fellow citizens. Hence, Liberación Nacional's governments have not been faced with the problem of drastically expanding the nation's educational system and dramatically seeking to reduce the social chasm dividing the various segments of the country's population. Their efforts have therefore been more modest than those in some of the other countries in which national revolutionary parties have come to power.

Finally, political democracy has been much more firmly entrenched in Costa Rica than in most of the rest of Latin America. Liberación Nacional had its roots in the last great struggle to preserve democracy, in 1948; and since that date the democratic regime has never been seriously in jeopardy. The party has concentrated more on the dangers to democracy arising from corruption and nepotism than from military or other coups, such as those that have been the preoccupation, necessarily, of various other national revolutionary parties.

However, perhaps this lack of dramatic issues has been a serious drawback for Liberación Nacional. There is a real reason to believe that within a decade of the party's foundation, many of its principal leaders had become much more conservative than they had been ten years before. Several had become heavily involved in businesses and prosperous professional practices, which many of their fellow party members felt made them reluctant to see any further social changes.

In addition, several factors were threatening Costa Rica with a serious crisis by the end of the 1960s. The increase in the country's population, which was growing at a rate of approximately 4 percent a year, required a very rapid expansion of the national economy if the standard of living was not to decline, let alone be able to rise. Yet during the later 1960s the national income was not growing rapidly enough to provide much margin for the population increase. The future of Liberación Nacional may depend in large part on its ability to develop and carry out programs that can assure the needed rapid rise in national income and the equitable distribution of this additional income among the populace.

CHAPTER 12

THE MOVIMIENTO NACIONALISTA REVOLUCIONARIO

One of the most fundamental of the 20th-century revolutions in Latin America has been that of Bolivia, which has been under way since 1952. The party that started the change and led it during its first dozen years was the Movimiento Nacionalista Revolucionario (MNR), one of the most important of the national revolutionary parties of Latin America. Like all of the parties of this type, it grew out of the circumstances in its country. Although the MNR has recognized general kinship with the other national revolutionary parties and has borrowed ideas from these groups, particularly from the Partido Aprista Peruano, it owes little to foreign influence in either its inception or its history.

ORIGINS OF THE MNR

The Movimiento Nacionalista Revolucionario traces its roots to the Chaco War, which Bolivia fought with Paraguay between 1932 and 1935, and the effect of that war in shattering the old order. The Chaco War was an almost unmitigated disaster for Bolivia. It resulted in defeat in battle, in disillusioning many of the middle- and upper-class younger generation in the ancien régime, and in arousing discontent among the masses of the Indians who made up the great majority of the Bolivian population.

The immediate effect of the war was the establishment of two consecutive military regimes that assumed markedly left-wing positions. The first was the government of Colonel David Toro, which seized power early in 1936. Among its measures were the expropriation of the holdings of the Standard Oil Co. of New Jersey in Bolivia, the appointment of the first minister of labor (an old printing trades union leader), and the encouragement of general unionization of the urban workers. The second was that of Colonel Germán Busch, which took office a year and a half later and, among other things, enacted the nation's first labor code, encouraged unionization of the tin mine workers, and ordered the tin mining companies to pay all of the foreign exchange they earned to the Central Bank, which in turn would make available to the companies the foreign currency they needed for expenses incurred abroad and for paying dividends to foreign stockholders.

It was in the Busch regime that future leaders of the MNR first came to national prominence. Víctor Paz Estenssoro, a young economist and a veteran of the Chaco War, became an adviser to the president. He was generally credited with having drawn up the decree concerning the mine companies' foreign currency.

With the death of President Busch in August 1939 (officially listed as a suicide), the government passed into the hands of more conservative elements for the next three and a half years. It was during this period that the Movimiento Nacionalista Revolucionario was formally established. In 1941 Paz Estenssorro joined with other young Chaco War veterans, including Hernán Siles (son of a former president), Walter Guevara Arce, and Juan Lechín (a prominent soccer player), to found the MNR. At this time Paz Estenssorro, Siles, and Guevara Arce were all members of the Chamber of Deputies, having been elected as independents in the previous year.

The new party, one of several political groups established at about the same time, was, as its name indicated, nationalistic. Its enemies alleged that it was favorably disposed toward the victory of the Nazis in World War II a charge then and later strongly denied by the MNR leaders. The MNR was strongly opposed to the influence of the tin mining companies in national affairs—there was considerable British capital and a small American element among the shareholders of these firms. Furthermore, the cooperation of the tin companies was much needed by the Allies to augment the output of the tin mines, particularly after the Japanese conquest of the Indonesian, Malayan, and Thai sources of the metal in 1942.

This opposition to the tin mining companies largely explained the pro-Axis reputation of the MNR in the early 1940s. Probably a contributing factor also was the opposition of the MNR to further immigration of German Jewish refugees to Bolivia, on the ground that they had not become agricultural colonists, as they were formally pledged to do by their entry permits, but had gone into business in competition with Bolivians in La Paz, Cochabamba, and other cities. However, it is often forgotten in this connection that Paz Estenssoro and other MNR figures had had a leading role in the government of President Germán Busch, which originally opened the country's doors to the Jewish refugees from Nazi Germany.

The MNR remained a party of secondary importance in national politics until December 1942. In that month there was a major clash between tin miners and the army at the large mine at Siglo XX-Catavi, which came to be known as "the Catavi Massacre." Some unionists who escaped from the scene—where soldiers had fired into a large crowd of men, women, and children—came to La Paz and succeeded in making contact with the MNR deputies, who sharply questioned the members of the government with direct responsibility for this affair and, in doing so, won their party its first strong sympathies among the tin miners.

THE MNR AND THE VILLARROEL REGIME

Just about a year after the Catavi massacre, a coup d'état overthrew the government of President Enrique Peñaranda. This coup was the work of a group of young army officers, organized in a lodge known as Razón de Patria (Radepa), and the Movimiento Nacionalista Revolucionario. The conspirators put in power the leader of Radepa, Major Gualberto Villarroel; and the MNR was given several posts in the new regime, with Víctor Paz Estenssoro becoming minister of finance.

This coup met strong opposition from the United States. Six months earlier the government of President Ramón Castillo of Argentina had been overthrown by a group of military men, and the resulting regime of Pedro Ramírez proved to be exceedingly friendly toward the Axis. The United States government feared that the Ramírez regime had played a part in the Bolivian coup and that the result would be another pro-Axis government in South America. These fears centered particularly on the participation of the MNR in the Villarroel regime, because of the party's pro-Axis reputation.

Interestingly enough, United States support at this point was thrown particularly behind the Partido de la Izquiera Revolucionaria (PIR), which by its own proclamation was "independent Marxist" in orientation. When José Antonio Arze, the leader of this party (from which the Communist Party of Bolivia was to emerge a few years later) was wounded in a political clash, he was hurriedly taken to the United States for hospitalization and care—and stayed to teach in the Jefferson School, run at the time by the Communist Party of the United States.

In the face of this pressure from the U.S. government, President Villarroel conceded to the extent of asking for the resignation of the MNR members of his cabinet, although he refused to bring in PIR members as substitutes. However, this concession was enough to bring U.S. diplomatic recognition for the Villarroel regime.

The Villarroel government, in which the MNR participated again sometime after the United States had recognized the regime, carried forward the reform tendencies of the Toro and Busch administrations of the 1930s. Most notable was the strong support that it gave to the unionization of the tin miners. It also took the first serious steps toward developing a program for helping the Indians, by summoning an Indian congress that President Villarroel and other government leaders, including Victor Paz Estenssoro, attended, to hear complaints and suggestions for reform.

The unionization of the tin miners was most important for the MNR. At a congress of the Tin Miners Federation, held at Pulacayo in July 1945, an MNR leader, Juan Lechín, was chosen as executive secretary and a majority of MNR members were seated on its Executive Committee.

At this congress Lechín and the other MNR mine leaders worked closely with the small but vocal group of unionists belonging to the Trotskyite Partido Obrero Revolucionario. It was the latter who were commissioned to write the "Statement of Principles" of the federation, which became known as the "Pulacayo Declaration." They produced a straight party-line Trotskyite document, which was accepted by the ideologically rather naive Lechín—and caused him to be plagued with accusations of being a Communist for many years thereafter.

The MNR leaders had resigned from the Villarroel government several days before the uprising in July 1946 that resulted in the overthrow of the regime. Therefore, they did not suffer the fate of the president and several of his close associates; being hanged from a lamp post in front of the Presidnetial Palace. Paz Estenssoro was able to flee to Buenos Aires, where he stayed during most of the next six years. Other leading party figures also went into exile or into hiding.

THE "SIX YEARS"

For the 69 months that followed the death of President Villarroel, the Movimiento Nacionalista Revolucionario never ceased in its opposition to the various governments that succeeded one another in power. The MNR was outlawed, but its influence continued and grew during most of this period.

Elections were held early in 1947 to reestablish constitutional government. The MNR did not offer a presidential candidate; but a list of nominees for senators and deputies was presented under the name of Miners' Bloc, which had the support of the MNR and the Trotskyite POR. Elected on this list were two senators, Juan Lechín for the MNR and Lucio Mendívil for the POR, together with a group of deputies. Enrique Hertzog, candidate of the so-called Partido de Unificación Republicana Socialista, was elected president.

However, Lechín and the other Miners' Bloc congressmen were not able to occupy their seats unmolested. Within a few months Lechín and most of the rest were arrested and deported. Thereafter he "commuted" between Bolivia and exile, returning on several occasions and being sent abroad each time the government caught him.

In August 1949 the MNR launched a full-scale civil war against the government of President Enrique Hertzog, who had been elected two years earlier. Harold Osborne, who was in Bolivia at the time, has described this unsuccessful revolution:

> . . . In August 1949 the MNR made its most determined attempt to overthrow the regime and this was a revolution planned on the idea of civil war, the people of the country against the army, the country against the capital. The eastern provinces fell rapidly, including the oil centre of Camiri, and by a series of simultaneous and well-planned coups the revolutionaries gained control in most of the mine centres, in several of which bitter fighting took place before peace was restored. The attempt failed owing to psychological rather than strategic factors. . . .[1]

In 1951 the term to which Enrique Hertzog had been elected, and which was continued by Vice-President Mamerto Urriolagoitia when Hertzog resigned because of ill health, was drawing to an end and an election was necessary. Three candidates who were more or less sympathetic to the regime in power were nominated. For some time the MNR underground and exile forces debated whether they should participate in the election. Their principal leaders were out of the country, and the party was illegal. However, after much discussion the party decided that despite these handicaps, it would test its popularity by putting up nominees for president and vice-president, as well as for the two houses of Congress.

As its candidate for president, the Movimiento Nacionalista Revolucionario named its most prominent figure, Víctor Paz Estenssoro; Hernán Siles was to be his running mate. Neither of these men was able to carry on a campaign; and much of their propaganda was by word of mouth, and by the scribbling of their names on walls.

When the votes were counted, the Paz Estenssoro-Siles slate was running well ahead of the other nominees. The government claimed that they had not received the 50 percent plus one required by the constitution, although the MNR leaders asserted at the time that they had won a constitutional victory and later announced that they had discovered the votes from this election and that a counting of them had confirmed their earlier claims.

The good showing of the MNR candidates precipitated a major crisis. President Urriolagoitia felt that he was not strong enough to confront the situation and so turned the reins of government over to a military junta headed by General Hugo Ballivian Rojas. This group stayed in power approximately eleven months, until it was overthrown by an MNR-organized uprising.

Throughout the "six years" the MNR continued to control the tin miners' unions, which were the strongest and most militant working-class organizations in the country. Efforts by the government to organize rival groups among these workers were futile.

Furthermore, the MNR made significant gains during this period among other union groups. These gains reflected the decline in the influence of the "independent Marxist" Partido de la Izquierda Revolucionaria (PIR). Before 1946 the PIR had been dominant among the railroaders, industrial workers, bank clerks, and commercial employees and controlled the only national labor confederation, the Confederación Sindical de Trabajadores de Bolivia. However, as a result of the PIR's support of the coup against the Villarroel regime in 1946, and their participation for many months in the government of Enrique Hertzog, which was widely regarded as a regime of the mine owners and landlords, the PIR largely lost its labor constituency. In the months preceding the 1952 revolution, leaders of key unions that had been under PIR control repudiated the party and joined the underground Movimiento Nacionalista Revolucionario. As a result, by the time of the revolution most of the labor movement was under the control of MNR.

During these half dozen years the MNR itself underwent an extensive change. In the underground and in exile it became increasingly radicalized. Although before 1946 the party had always been "pro-Indian," exalting in its writings and platforms the importance of the Indian to the nation, it had never gone on record in favor of thoroughgoing agrarian reform. However, between 1946 and 1952 the MNR went on record strongly in favor of a general redistribution of the land; it was to be taken from the heirs of those who had seized it during the Conquest and later be given back to the Indians from whom it had been taken. The party also hardened in its attitude toward the "big three" tin mining companies, promising that when it came to power, it would nationalize them.

THE FIRST PAZ ESTENSSORO GOVERNMENT

On April 9, 1952, an uprising broke out against the junta. This revolt was organized by the MNR and the Carabineros, the national police. Three days passed before the success of the insurrection was assured; and by this time the original chief of the movement, General Antonio Selemé, who had been minister of interior of the junta government, had sought refuge in an embassy, thus making it impossible for him to control the new regime. As a result the new government was completely in the hands of the Movimiento Nacionalista Revolucionario.

The two principal MNR leaders on the spot at the time of the revolution were Hernán Siles and Juan Lechín. They could have remained in control of the new regime but chose to be loyal to their party and to bring back from exile Víctor Paz Estenssoro, whom the MNR insisted had been elected constitutional president the year before. He remained in power for the constitutional four years.

It was during the four years of the first Paz Estenssoro government that the MNR carried out the fundamental reforms that constitute the Bolivian national revolution. In a sense this was the destructive phase of the revolution, the period during which the old institions were torn down and only the beginnings of new ones were put in their place. The process of building the new society made possible by the national revolution is continuing.

The first major change, decreed within a few days of the return of Paz Estenssoro, was the establishment of universal adult suffrage. This ended the system that had given the right to vote only to those who were literate in the Spanish language, thus excluding virtually the entire Indian population. By this decree the Indians suddenly came to constitute the great majority of the national electorate, which was increased five times over.

Even more profound, however, was the agrarian reform. This gave the land back to the Indians from whom it had been taken by force, violence, intrigue, and chicanery. It has been argued that the MNR government was forced into carrying out an agrarian reform by the move of some peasants, particularly in Cochabamba Valley, who seized land on their own initiative soon after the April 1952 revolution. However, this argument is in error.[2]

It is true that the Agrarian Reform Law was not decreed until August 1953, some 16 months after the MNR had seized power. However, this was not because the government did not want to carry out a land redistribution program. Quite the contrary. The MNR regime felt that before a successful agrarian reform could be carried out it was necessary to bring the Indians together in organizations that could take the initiative in asking for the land and that could protect the new landowners from the old once the land redistribution had taken place. Time was also necessary to draw up the Agrarian Reform Law.

Immediately after seizing power the MNR established an entirely new ministry, that of peasant affairs. To it was transferred every aspect of affairs having to do with the Indians. Unionization of the peasants, the establishment of cooperatives, technical agricultural assistance, rural education, and rural health and sanitation were some of the jobs undertaken by the new ministry. It became the one government agency that the Indians came to regard as "their own," to which they could present their grievances, desires, and even demands without fear of being intimidated by middle-class bureaucrats.

The most important job of the ministry was organizing the peasants. Three kinds of groups were established among them. Directly under the supervision of the ministry of peasant affairs were the peasant unions, which were established on virtually every estate in the Bolivian highlands. They entered into collective agreements with the landlords, pending the redistribution of the land; and these agreements brought the peasants large increases in their cash income as well as other benefits.

Along with the peasant unions were established peasant militia groups and local units of the Movimiento Nacionalista Revolucionario. The former were armed with the weapons taken from the army, which had been defeated in April 1952 and then dissolved. The army was not reconstituted for more than a year. In that interim the peasant and worker militia constituted the only armed forces in the republic.

On August 2, 1953, the Agrarian Reform Law was finally enacted. It had been drawn up by a commission representing the MNR and other left-wing political groups, as well as the labor movement, the peasantry, and various government ministries, and presided over by Vice-President Hernán Siles. The law provided for the peasants to become the immediate owners of the small plots of land that their landlords had allowed them to use to grow crops for their own sustenance and to maintain their house and garden, and that the rest of the landlords' land should be divided among the peasants and other eligible individuals as soon as the job of surveying and subdividing it could be carried out.

Agrarian reform was the most fundamental change brought about by the Movimiento Nacionalista Revolucionario. It ended once and for all the economic, social, and political power of the white and near-white landlord group that had dominated Bolivia since the Conquest. At the same time it converted the Indian peasantry into one of the fundamental power groups in Bolivian society and politics. It gave them a base; and as long as they held onto the land, the Indians could never again be the pariahs and semiserfs they had been for more than four centuries.

More controversial, at least on an international plane, was the MNR government's expropriation of the "big three" tin mining companies which took place in October 1952. The Patiño, Hochschild, and Aramayo companies had produced most of the country's foreign exchange for more than half a century; and they had a well-founded reputation for making and unmaking governments. The expropriation of these companies was a basic political necessity insofar as the MNR government was concerned, and it was one of the most popular measures taken by the regime.

Economically, the expropriation of the tin companies was not a success, for many reasons. For one, the old companies withdrew virtually all of the foreigners who had constituted most of the managerial and technical personnel of the mining industry. The companies also took with them most of the geological and other maps and other key documents. Second, the mining enterprises were already in serious decline, most of the richest veins controlled by the "big three" being exhausted. Third, labor discipline broke down almost completely after the Revolution. Union officials called control obrero were installed in each mine and were given veto power over every action of the management; strikes were called to get rid of "insolent" managers or engineers, and all attempts to increase productivity were resisted by the union members. Fourth, all workers who had been fired for union or political reasons in the "six years" were reinstated in April 1952, with the result that the government mining firm Comibol was burdened with a large excess labor force. Finally, the mines continued for many years to sell goods to their workers at prices that were a ridiculously small part of what these same goods cost Comibol.

The MNR government also undertook a program for the economic development of the country. The many projects that the regime started included road building, the construction of sugar and oil refineries, the building of electric plants, the opening up of new agricultural land, cattle raising, and the settlement of colonies in the all but unoccupied eastern two-thirds of the country. Many of these projects were ill-planned, and some may have been ill-advised; but they represented the determination of the MNR regime to try to establish a broader base for the economy than its traditional mining and subsistence farming.[3]

THE SILES ADMINISTRATION

As the government of Víctor Paz Estenssoro approached its end, elections were held in June 1956. In these the great mass of the adult population of Bolivia participated for the first time. Various opposition parties, including the right-wing Falange Socialista Boliviana, the Stalinist-oriented Partido Comunista and Partido de la Izquierda Revolucionaria, and the Trotskyite Partido Obrero Revolucionario took part along with the Movimiento Nacionalista Revolucionario.

As its candidate for the presidency, the MNR named Vice-President Hernán Siles, who was considered to represent the "right wing" of the party. His running mate was Ñuflo Chávez, the first minister of peasant affairs and a member of the left wing of the MNR. The government ticket was overwhelmingly victorious, electing not only its nominees for president and vice-president, but a very strong majority in Congress as well.

Upon assuming office Siles was faced with a serious crisis. One of the negative aspects of the first four years of the MNR regime had been a rapid increase in prices. The rate of inflation was reflected in the black market rate of the national currency, the boliviano, which had fallen from approximately 200 to the dollar at the time of the revolution in 1952 to over 12,000 by the end of 1956. The chaotic conditions created by the inflation had been intensified by the government's maintaining the fiction that Bolivia still had a stable currency, insofar as its international exchange value was concerned. Thus a large number of favored importers were given the right to purchase dollars in order to import goods at the old 200-1 rate at a time when the real market rate was 10 to 20 times as high. The upshot of this was a great deal of corruption in foreign exchange dealings and an artificially low cost of production for many Bolivian goods, which were produced largely to be smuggled into neighboring countries. At the same time large quantities of the U.S. aid that was given Bolivia after 1953, particularly in the form of foodstuffs, found its way into the smugglers' markets in Peru, Chile, Argentina, and Brazil.

By the time Siles assumed the presidency, it was clear that the government had to come to grips with the inflation. Even before he was inaugurated, it had been agreed to have the U.S. aid agency, the International Cooperation Administration, provide an expert who would draw up a stabilization program that the government would undertake to follow. This expert, George Jackson Eder, was already in Bolivia when Siles was inaugurated.

Together with Bolivian officials George Eder elaborated a fairly draconian stabilization program. It received the support of the U.S. government and the International Monetary Fund, which agreed to provide a stabilization fund of $25 million to back the Bolivian government's effort. In December 1956 this stabilization program went into effect.

The stabilization effort involved the ending of price controls, the raising of wages and then freezing them for a year, restrictions on private credit, and an attempt to bring the government budget more nearly into balance. At the same time all exchange controls were ended and a new rate for the boliviano, 7,500 to the dollar, was established—subject to more or less daily variations depending upon the supply and demand for foreign currency.

Both President Siles and George Eder had been careful to consult with all elements of the MNR and all groups supporting the government; but although all of the leading officials of the MNR, the government, and the labor movement had committed themselves to support the stabilization program, its enactment provoked a major political crisis which lasted for about six months. Innumerable groups sought relatively minor exemptions from the operation of the program—exemptions that, if they had all been granted, would have ended the effort entirely. Even more important, the left wing of the MNR, led by Juan Lechín and Ñuflo Chávez, decided to renege on their original endorsement of the stabilization program. By the second quarter of 1957 they were in full-scale revolt against it, were strongly attacking Eder, and were implying that Siles was "betraying the revolution."

However, the left-wing MNR leaders had underestimated the general popularity of the stabilization program. Its enactment had quite suddenly ended the almost universal shortages of goods that had existed during most of 1956. In real wage terms more goods and services, rather than fewer, were available to the average citizen as a result of the program. Although a few groups suffered inequities, its major accomplishments were virtually to end smuggling at least for the time being, to bring relative stability in the international value of the boliviano, and actually to lower prices.

Thus, when in June 1957 Juan Lechín led the Central Obrera Boliviana into an attempted general strike against the Siles-Eder program, it failed entirely. There were several reasons for this, aside from the fact that the left-wing leaders were advocating an unpopular cause. One was that the struggle between Lechín and Chávez, on one side; and Siles, on the other, assumed the proportions of a struggle for control of the MNR itself; and in this struggle several extraneous issues became involved. One of these issues was the long-lasting quarrel between the ex-Stalinists and the ex-Trotskyites inside and outside the labor movement.

We have already noted that even before the 1952 revolution, most trade unionists who had been associated with the pro-Stalinist PIR had joined the MNR. Much the same thing occurred with the Trotskyite trade unionists in 1954. During the first months of the revolution, the Trotskyite POR had had considerable influence in the organized labor movement; and its leaders quite openly proclaimed that Victor Paz Estenssoro was the Kerensky of the Bolivian revolution and was soon to be succeeded by a Trotskyite Lenin. However, when the PORistas sought to challenge the MNR's control of the newly established Central Obrera Boliviana, the MNR's principal labor leader, Minister of Mines Juan Lechín, reacted very strongly and succeeded in virtually removing the Trotskyites from the COB leadership. Thereafter most of the Trotskyite trade unionists became increasingly disillusioned with the stronger resistance to the MNR and the revolution conducted by POR leaders. In 1954 the most important POR trade unionists quit that party and joined the MNR. Some of them were elected to Congress on the MNR ticket in 1956.

In the stabilization fight Siles solicited and received the support of the ex-PIR trade unionists within the MNR. At the same time Lechín had the strong backing of the former members of the POR. The result of this was that virtually all of the unions outside of the mining areas supported Siles against Lechín.

Another factor in the situation was the personal bravery of Hernán Siles. He went to the mining areas, and despite threats that he would be killed if he set foot in the mining camps, he appealed to the rank-and-file tin workers—and in the showdown received their support even against Mine Federation leader Juan Lechín. He was much admired for his hombría, the quality of manhood that still ranks very high in the Latin countries.

Thus, Siles won this showdown. However, he did not push his political advantage. Although some of his supporters organized a COB Executive Committee to rival that controlled by Lechín, the president did not give this group his strong backing. Instead, he compromised with Lechín and prevented a serious breach in the ranks of the MNR.

Meanwhile, the basic program of the revolution went forward. The process of land distribution continued; the mines remained nationalized; and within the limits set by the stabilization program, the effort to broaden the base of the economy was continued. The Siles administration was a period of consolidation and of respite after the stormy period of the first Paz Estenssoro regime.[4]

THE DISINTEGRATION AND DECLINE OF THE MNR

The split in the MNR that was avoided in 1957 took place three years later. It was the first of several divisions that finally resulted in its being ousted from power, and it resulted from a bitter struggle over the MNR presidential nomination in 1960.

Walter Guevara Arce, one of the first MNR members of the Chamber of Deputies in the early 1940s, who had served as foreign minister and in other posts in the first years of the MNR regime, was thought by many of the party leaders to be the indicated candidate to succeed Hernán Siles. However, he was generally looked upon as the leader of the party's right wing, and there was very strong opposition to his nomination.

When Víctor Paz Estenssoro, who had been serving as Bolivian ambassador to London, returned home in 1959, Left and Center elements of the party tended to group around him as a rival to Guevara Arce. This rivalry of two founders of the Movimiento Nacionalista Revolucionario caused a violent struggle within the party. When the MNR convention picked Paz Estenssoro, Guevara Arce withdrew from the party to form his own group, the Partido Revolucionario Auténtico, which promptly nominated him to run against the official MNR candidate. Juan Lechín became Paz Estenssoro's running mate.

Paz Estenssoro won an easy victory, although the Partido Revolucionario Auténtico established itself, at least for the time being, as the country's second largest party. In his second administration Paz Estenssoro felt that his principal job was to put the Bolivian economy on its feet once again. Among other things this meant that the mining industry had to be rehabilitated. Output of the mines had continued to decline throughout the years following the 1952 revolution; and the Corporación Minera de Bolivia, the government firm, which had taken over the holdings of the "big three" mining companies, continued to run large deficits.

Paz Estenssoro entered into negotiations with the U.S. government, the Inter-American Development Bank, and West German mining interests. As a result of these negotiations the so-called "Triangular Agreement" was worked out. According to this the Inter-American Bank and the U.S. government would finance a reorganization of Comibol, which would be carried out largely by German experts and technicians. The Paz Estenssoro government agreed to end the system of control obrero in the mines, and to carry out a phased reduction in the excess labor employed by Comibol.

Vice-President Juan Lechín did not openly oppose this program, despite his position as principal leader of the mine workers. For the first years of the second Paz Estenssoro administration, he served as ambassador to Italy and the Vatican, as well as vice-president, and was out of the country most of the time. However, there is little question that the implementation of the Triangular Agreement tended to cool relations between the president and vice-president.

The Paz Estenssoro government also pushed the more general program of economic development that had been launched in the early years of the national revolution. Special attention during this period was given to colonization efforts in the eastern part of the country. This involved road building to connect the Cochabamba-Santa Cruz Highway, which had been completed during the first Paz Estenssoro administration, with river ports and new agricultural areas. It also involved using the army to interest Indian recruits from the highlands in settling in eastern lowlands. At the same time legislation was adopted to encourage both Bolivian and foreign enterprises to invest in Bolivia.

One aspect of the policy of the Paz Estenssoro government that ultimately proved its undoing was that of building up the armed forces. The army had been abolished immediately after the April 1952 revolution, and there was extensive discussion as to whether it should be reconstituted. After a year the army was formally reestablished, but under conditions designed to keep it out of independent participation in politics by assuring its loyalty to the MNR regime.

During the years immediately following the revolution, the army remained largely in the background, politically speaking. No serious military attempts were made to overthrow the MNR regime. The great majority of the officers, who had been carefully selected, were loyal to the revolution. Furthermore, the government had at its command important counterweights to the army in the peasant and mine workers' militia, and to a lesser degree in the industrial workers' militia. Finally, the army was kept lightly armed, so that its ability to defeat the various militia groups in an all-out struggle was by no means certain.

During his second administration Víctor Paz Estenssoro's relations with the miners deteriorated, and their armed forces ceased to be a reliable support for the government. This was one of the factors that led the president to provide more extensive armament for the army and air force. His willingness to do so was undoubtly reinforced by the eagerness of the American government, which was giving extensive economic aid, to strengthen the country's official armed forces.

Although Paz Estenssoro and other leaders of his administration had some misgivings about thus running the risk that the army would assume its long-held role as the principal maker and deposer of governments, the president undoubtedly felt that he could depend upon the thoroughly loyal peasant militia. Virtually every significant group of Indians in the country had been given arms during the early months of the revolution, and they had been trained to use them. Their loyalty to the government was not in doubt.

However, the building up of the army and air force proved to be more dangerous to the MNR regime than Paz Estenssoro had supposed. This was largely because the Movimiento Nacionalista Revolucionario itself was undergoing a process of disintegration that removed from the regime the principal civilian pillar upon which it had rested since 1952.

The second major split in the party occurred as a result of the presidential election scheduled for June 1964. There is considerable evidence that Juan Lechín had been promised by other party leaders the chance to succeed Paz Estenssoro when he agreed to support the former president for election in 1960. However, by the latter part of 1963, when it came time to choose the MNR candidate, there was considerable resistance within the party leadership and elsewhere to fulfilling this promise.

Juan Lechín had traditionally been the leader of the left wing of the MNR. As such, he was looked upon with suspicion by many party leaders, including at least some of those in the labor movement. There was fear of what Lechín might do were he to become president. In addition, there is no doubt that there was strong opposition from the U.S. government to seeing Juan Lechín as president of Bolivia. Most U.S. officials who had dealt with the MNR regime had misunderstood Lechín, thinking him to be a Trotskyite, a Communist, or worse. There is some indication that the U.S. government threatened that if Lechín were elected president, all further U.S. aid to the MNR regime would cease.

In any case the nomination of the Movimiento Nacionalist Revolucionario for president was denied to Juan Lechín. An attempt was made to get him to agree to postpone his aspirations for one more term, but he refused. As a result those who were united on keeping Lechín out of power saw in Paz Estenssoro the only MNR figure who was likely to be able to beat the mine union leader in the 1964 election. The constitution had been altered in 1962, making it possible for the incumbent president to succeed himself.

When it became clear that Paz Estenssoro was going to be renominated by the MNR, Juan Lechín walked out of the party and formed his own organization, the Partido Revolucionario de la Izquierda Nacionalista. It had the backing of most of the mine workers who had traditionally supported the MNR, as well as support from some other working-class groups and some middle-class figures in the old party. PRIN nominated Juan Lechín for the presidency, but he withdrew before the election was held, arguing that there was no chance for an honest election and urging his supporters to cast blank votes.

Although Hernán Siles had first supported the nomination of Paz Estenssoro by the MNR, as the campaign went forward he apparently had increasing doubts. Some time before the election, he finally came out and urged the president to retire from the race and allow the nomination of someone else. By the time the election was actually held, Hernán Siles was virtually a member of the opposition.

Meanwhile, Paz Estenssoro had had difficulty with the nomination of a running mate. The MNR convention that nominated him nominated for vice-president F. Fortun Sanjines. However, this vice-presidential candidacy aroused a storm of opposition within the party, particularly among the supporters of General René Barrientos.

General Barrientos was commander of the air force and also head of the military cell of the Movimiento Nacionalista Revolucionario. He professed himself to be strongly opposed to the military's acting independently in politics, but he was also very obviously anxious to be on the MNR ticket.

A few weeks after the MNR convention, the candidate for vice-president resigned his nomination. The leadership of the Movimiento Nacionalista Revolucionario immediately named Barrientos to take his place on the MNR ticket. However, before this occurred, an attempt had been made on Barrientos' life; and several more were reported after he became the official MNR candidate for vice-president.

When the election was finally held in June 1964, all other candidates had withdrawn from the contest. As a result Paz Estenssoro and Barrientos were elected without opposition. By that time plotting against the Paz Estenssoro regime had already begun; and among the plotters were Lechín, Siles, and various others who had been leaders of the Movimiento Nacionalista Revolucionario until a few months before. Vice-President Barrientos and other military leaders were also parties to this conspiracy.

However, the military men and their civilian associates hesitated to move against their regime. As a result the new administration was inaugurated in August 1964. In the weeks following, the government had grave difficulties with both the tin miners and the students. Army troops were sent into the mining camps to suppress disaffection there, while peasant militiamen were brought into La Paz to cow the students, who had launched a general strike against the regime.

These events seem to have removed the army's reticence about moving against the Paz Estenssoro government. In order to handle the situation in the mining areas and La Paz, it was necessary for the president to disclose fully to the military leaders the strength of the peasant militia. It proved to be considerably less formidable than the army chiefs had believed. The new information apparently convinced them that they could succeed in ousting the Paz Estenssoro government.

Their attempt to do so took place on November 4, 1964. The army in La Paz and other cities arose in revolt. Their move had the support of the miners' militia and of Juan Lechín and other mine union leaders, as well as of the Communists, the Partido Revolucionario Auténtico, and even of Hernán Siles. President Paz Estenssoro was placed abroad an air force plane and was again sent into exile, this time to Peru. Generals René Barrientos and Alfredo Ovando assumed power as copresidents.

THE MNR SINCE 1964

The ousting of the MNR from power resulted in the further splintering of the party. General René Barrientos and those party members who followed his personal leadership removed themselves from the MNR by their act of rebellion against the MNR government.

Many party leaders and trade unionists were forced into exile. Others went into hiding. Some fell into inactivity. But even those who remained active and continued to consider themselves to be loyal MNR members did not show the unity and strength that had characterized the Movimiento Nacionalista Revolucionario the last time it had been in the political wilderness, between 1946 and 1952. They split into several groups.

These divisions became clear at the time of the election in June 1966. One group of MNR members, under the leadership of Víctor Andrade, who had served during most of the MNR regime as Bolivian ambassador in Washington, declared itself to be the "real" Movimiento Nacionalista Revolucionario. They were recognized as such by the military junta, which legalized them as the MNR. This faction named Andrade as their nominee for president.

A group of much younger MNR leaders formed another group, which they called the Movimiento Revolucionario Pazestenssorista. They claimed that they, rather than the Andrade group, represented the real tradition of the MNR and named a list of candidates for senator and deputy, succeeding in electing one senator. Paz Estenssoro himself urged his followers to boycott the election.[5]

Meanwhile, the earlier factions that had broken away from the MNR continued their independent existence. Walter Guevara Arce and the Partido Revolucionario Auténtico supported the military regime and backed General Barrientos for president. Juan Lechín and the Partido Revolucionario de la Izquierda Nacionalista at first supported the military regime, but by early 1965 they were in open conflict with it. A general strike in the mines, which brought the military into the mining areas and resulted in extensive bloodshed, permanently alienated Lechín and his followers. Barrientos was chosen president in the 1966 election and served until he was killed in a helicopter accident early in 1969. Vice-President Luis Adolfo Siles, conservative half brother of Hernán Siles, succeeded but was ousted before the end of the year by General Alfredo Ovando. After about a year he was ousted; and another general, Juan José Torres, came to office, backed by Lechín and the PRIN as well as by the various factions of Communists and Trotskyites.

Throughout this period the MNR remained divided. However, early in 1971 the elements backing Víctor Paz Estenssoro and Hernán Siles rejoined their forces. They constituted the bulk of the civilian opposition to the Torres regime; and in August 1971 they supported a military revolt led by Colonel Hugo Banzer, that ousted Torres. Paz Estenssoro thereupon returned to Bolivia from exile and undertook a major effort to rebuild the base and hierarchy of the party. The MNR participated, together with its ancient rival, the Falange Socialista Boliviana and the military, in the Banzer government.

STRENGTHS AND WEAKNESSES OF THE MNR

It remains to be seen whether the Movimiento Nacionalista Revolucionario will be reconstituted along the lines it had before it began to disintegrate in the early 1960s. However, there is little doubt that its decline created a vacuum in Bolivian politics; and it is certain that large masses of the people remained loyal to the program and the memory of the MNR at its apogee.

The accomplishments of the revolution launched on April 9, 1952, remained generally intact after 1964, despite the overthrow of the MNR government. The land remained largely in the hands of the Indian peasants, and the Corporación Minera de Bolivia continued to control the large-scale mining industry. The government remained committed to fostering the country's economic development.

The major changes were in the trade unions and politics. The very significant power that the miners' unions had enjoyed during the MNR regime was completely smashed by Barrientos, and the mines were put under virtual military occupation. Also, the civilian domination over the military that had characterized the MNR years was destroyed, and governments once again changed at the whim of ambitious generals.

Most important, however, the effort of the MNR government to incorporate the Indians fully into the economy, society, and political and cultural life of the nation continued to be a major part of the programs of post-MNR regimes, at least so long as General Barrientos headed them. He personally took great interest in the efforts of the ministry of peasant affairs, with the aid of USAID, to bring technical assistance, marketing facilities, and new ideas to the Indian peasants of the high plateau.[6]

During the short-lived regimes of Ovando and Torres, the miners' unions regained a considerable part of their strength. But neither of these governments was greatly concerned with the fate of the peasants, and in both the military still held the balance of power.

Although the post-MNR governments did not attempt to destroy most of the social and economic programs launched by the MNR during its 12 years in power, the political situation between 1964 and 1971 remained uncertain and insecure. The decline of the MNR removed the principal instrument through which the civilian population had controlled national political life. The ability of the MNR to reconstitute its forces and reestablish a firm party structure throughout the country will go far toward determining whether the nation will continue to be subject to recurring military coups.[7]

CHAPTER

13

THE
PARTIDO POPULAR
DEMOCRÁTICO
OF PUERTO RICO

For a century Puerto Rican politics has revolved around the question of the island's political status. There have been three general trends of opinion: assimilationists, who seek to have Puerto Rico become an integral part of the United States; independentistas, who wish to see it become a completely separate republic; and autonomists, who seek to work out a special arrangement that will provide internal self-government without breaking all ties with the "mother country." For more than two decades the Partido Popular Democrático has been the principal advocate of the last of these currents of opinion, and during most of this period it has controlled the government and has executed a program to make autonomy a reality. It has brought an economic, social, and political revolution to the island.

ORIGINS OF THE PARTIDO POPULAR DEMOCRÁTICO

To a marked degree the history of the Partido Popular Democrático is the history of its most outstanding leader, Luís Muñoz Marín. Therefore, an essential starting point for a discussion of the party is knowledge of the background of its principal figure.[1]

Luís Muñoz Marín was the son of Luís Muñoz Rivera, who was the outstanding Puerto Rican political leader of his generation. During the last decade of Spanish rule in the island, Muñoz Rivera was the leader of the autonomist faction in Puerto Rican politics. He reached an agreement with the Spanish in 1897 for the establishment of self-government; elections held early in 1898 established this regime, with Muñoz Rivera as its "prime minister."

However, three months later the Spanish-American War broke out, and as a result Puerto Rico passed from Spanish control to that of the United States—and Muñoz Rivera and his associates had to start all over again. For the rest of his career, Muñoz Rivera sought to obtain some degree of self-government for the island; and although it was passed after his death, the 1917 Jones Law, which provided for a full-fledged legislature and gave Puerto Ricans U.S. citizenship, was due largely to his efforts.

As a result of U.S. control over Puerto Rico, the island underwent important changes. The economy was transformed from a largely self-sufficient one, in which most of the people were subsistence farmers, into one that centered on the growing and export of sugar. The population more than doubled during the first 40 years of U.S. occupation, largely as a result of public health efforts of the American authorities. Educational facilities were also significantly expanded, although by no means all of the children of school age were put in school.

The division of Puerto Rican political opinion continued to be among assimilationists, independence advocates, and autonomists. Luís Muñoz Marín made his political debut early in the 1920s as a member of one of the assimilationist groups, the Partido Socialista, which was the principal spokesman for the island's trade union movement.

Muñoz Marín did not long remain active in politics. He moved to the United States, and during much of the 1920s he was a member of the bohemian colony in Greenwich Village. He did not return to live in Puerto Rico until 1932, when he joined the party that claimed to be the heir of his father and supported independence, the Partido Liberal. In 1932 he was elected to the island's Senate on the Liberal ticket.

Throughout the early years of the New Deal, Muñoz Marín, although officially an advocate of independence, worked closely with the Puerto Rican Reconstruction Administration, the New Deal's principal instrument on the island. The prominence he received brought him into conflict with Liberal Party leaders, and he was expelled from the organization in 1937.[2]

Muñoz Marín used this "political exile" to deepen his roots among the people. He traveled throughout the island and met hundreds of thousands of his fellow Puerto Ricans. He built a solid base among the common people, particularly among the peasants in the mountains, the so-called jíbaros.

In 1938 he moved to establish a new party under his leadership. This was the Partido Popular Democrático, and it took a unique position: it argued that the people should for the time being forget about the island's status and turn their attention to trying to deal with its pressing economic and social problems. In this connection the party promised to carry out an agrarian reform, so as to give many sugar workers their own small bits of land; to create an island-wide electricity network, so as to lay the foundation for an effort to industrialize the economy; and promised labor legislation.

The PPD position on the island's status, together with its emphasis on social and economic issues, brought it recruits from all of the traditional sectors of the Puerto Rican political spectrum. A large part of the membership of the militant Nationalist Party joined the PPD, because they were disillusioned by the insistence on violence and terrorism by the party's leader, Pedro Albizu Campos. Much of the Liberal Party's constituency did the same, as did most of the rank and file of the pro-statehood Socialist Party and large numbers of its secondary leadership, attracted to the PPD because of its emphasis on social issues.

The first electoral test of the Partido Popular Democrático came in the 1940 general elections. To the surprise of everyone but the Populares, the party won a majority in the island's Senate and came only three short of a majority in the lower house.

THE PPD DURING WORLD WAR II

Soon after the victory of the Partido Popular Democrático, President Franklin Roosevelt sent his old friend and associate, Professor Rexford Guy Tugwell, to be governor of Puerto Rico. His task was to cooperate with the Populares in their attempt to change Puerto Rican society. He played a very important role during the next five years, helping to develop the many young professional men and technicians attracted into the government by the PPD victory into a highly skilled group of public administrators. He also coached Luís Muñoz Marín and other Populares leaders in the subtleties of practical politics, particularly in the intricacies of the Washington legislative and administrative scene with which they had to deal.[3]

The PPD sought to put its program into effect during the war years. They launched their agrarian reform program, although it was necessary to carry the question of their right to do so to the U.S. Supreme Court. They bought out the private utility companies on the island and established an island grid under the control of the government's Water Resources Authority. They established the Industrial Development Corporation, which took over two factories established by the Puerto Rican Reconstruction Administration and built four more. They developed expanded programs in the fields of health and education.

All of this was accomplished in the face of very considerable difficulties—and some advantages—created by World War II. Because of German submarine attacks on shipping in the Caribbean, as well as a general shortage of merchant vessels, there were great problems in supplying the island with the goods it was accustomed to importing from the mainland, as well as in getting Puerto Rican sugar and other crops to the United States. On the other hand, because of these same difficulties it was convenient to convert much of the island's sugar into rum and alcohol; and the Puerto Rican treasury profited under the arrangement whereby excise taxes imposed in the United States on Puerto Rican rums were returned to Puerto Rico. Wartime federal expenditures on the island were also a boost to the economy.

OPERATION BOOTSTRAP

However, at the end of World War II, the leaders of the Partido Popular Democrático concluded that the strategy for development that they had used during the war would not serve in the longer run to bring about the desired rapid industrialization and general development of the economy. The Puerto Rican government, they felt, did not have the resources to carry out on its own the establishment of a new industrial sector in the economy while building the infrastructure and social services required.

As a result they launched what came to be known as Operation Bootstrap, a program for spreading the responsibilities for the development effort. The direct investments of the government were to be confined to the building of roads, public utilities, housing, schools, hospitals, and other economic and social overhead. For the actual industrialization program reliance was to be put on private enterprise, particularly on firms from the United States.

For the latter purpose several measures were taken. A law was passed under which firms approved by the government could be exempted from the island's income tax and other local taxes if they established new industrial enterprises, a move of particular importance because neither firms nor individuals domiciled in Puerto Rico had to pay U.S. federal income taxes.

Second, the Economic Development Administration was established. Its functions were several. It was to promote on the mainland the establishment of new enterprises in the island, seeking out likely investors and convincing them to establish branches in Puerto Rico. It was also to facilitate the establishment of new firms by securing or training skilled workers, helping mainland managerial personnel get established in the island, and facilitating the firms' contacts with other government agencies. It was also to carry on a continuous study of the economy, watching for developing bottlenecks and for opportunities for new types of investment.

This program continued throughout the period of Partido Popular Democrático control of Puerto Rican affairs. By the late 1960s more than 1,200 factories had been established on a permanent basis on the island. During this period the nature of manufacturing enterprises established on the island changed. In the earlier years the great majority of the new plants were garment factories, with relatively little fixed capital; many of these left the island when their ten-year exemption had expired. A bit later, more complicated garment enterprises—making bras, corsets, etc.—as well as firms making electronic parts were introduced. By the late 1950s a number of plants to serve the Puerto Rican market, such as a grain and feed mill and a slaughterhouse, were established. By the late 1960s a heavier type of industry, based particularly on several large oil refineries and a petrochemical complex, were being set up.

The continued progress of industrialization was indicated by a survey of the Puerto Rican economy during 1967, prepared by the island's Department of the Treasury. It noted:

> Among the more dynamic sectors, the largest advance in 1967 was in manufacturing industry. Income from manufacturing rose by $66.6 million. Manufacturing of metal products and machinery, apparel and textile mill products, each accounted for more than 20 percent of the increase. Manufacturing of chemical products contributed more than 10 percent, and leather goods, nearly 10 percent. The balance of the increase came from manufacturing industries of food, tobacco, wood, paper and printing, stone, clay, glass and other manufactured goods.[4]

Sergio Camero, then administrator of the Economic Development Administration, thus summed up in 1968 the effects of the first 20 years of Operation Bootstrap, insofar as manufacturing was concerned: ". . . The total number of plants promoted under 'Bootstrap' now exceeds 1,600 and represents a broad spectrum of industry, from apparel and aircraft parts to electronic components and petroleum derivatives. Shipments of products from these plants to the U.S. have risen dramatically from $33,000,000 in 1950 to $926,000,000 last year."[5]

The tax holiday law, which had first been established for a period of 10 years, was extended several times to permit additional firms to come to the island. It was also expanded to provide that an existing firm could get tax exemption on enlargement of its plant, to provide exemptions for firms establishing hotels and other enterprises necessary for the tourist industry, and for those setting up modern commercial enterprises such as supermarkets.

These modifications in the original Operation Bootstrap provisions stimulated the development of other sectors of the economy, notably tourism. Starting with the first large tourist hotel in the late

1940s, the Caribe Hilton in San Juan, the government encouraged the spread of dozens of similar facilities in various parts of the island, as well as many smaller guest houses and other tourist accommodations. As a result in 1967 there were 810,000 visitors to the island; they spent $154.9 million, an average of $191 each, thus making an appreciable contribution to the island's economy.[6]

Only agriculture did not participate fully in this economic development. The traditional sugar industry suffered a constant decline from the early 1950s on. It found it increasingly hard to recruit workers for the arduous tasks of cultivating and harvesting the crop. Other traditional crops, such as coffee and tobacco, after considerable development during the 1950s, were also declining, although less drastically than sugar, by the late 1960s. The dramatic growth of some other parts of the agricultural sector, particularly the dairy industry, by no means offset this decline of the traditional crops.

The previously mentioned report of the Puerto Rican Department of the Treasury summed up the agricultural situation by the mid-1960s thus:

> All major sectors shared the 1967 gain with the exception of agriculture. In this sector, income has fallen without interruption since 1963, although the rate of decline has decelerated. For 1967, the annual decrease was 0.4 percent, as compared to a year-to-year decline of 3.4 percent one year ago, 7.4 percent two years ago, and 9.4 percent three years ago.[7]

Meanwhile, the government made extensive investments in many fields. It built a first-class road network throughout the island; it expanded the electricity network; it built extensive popular housing in the urban centers and developed a self-help housing program in the rural areas; it set up schools throughout the island, and by the mid-1950s most school-age children were in the classroom; it established hospitals and other health facilities that helped to bring the death rate of the island below that of the mainland.

The overall economic development of the Puerto Rican economy during the period of Popular Democratic rule is shown by the following statistics:

> Net income of the economy has increased from a level of $225 million in 1940 to $2,097 million in 1964. Income, measured in terms of 1954 prices, has shown an average of increase of about 6.5% compounded annually and in the year ended June 30, 1964 it increased by 8.9%. Per capita net income is now $830 compared to $121 in 1940.[8]

By 1967 the per capita income was $1,037 and had risen 3.7 percent during the previous year, in real terms.[9]

However, during the 20 years the Populares ruled Puerto Rico there was concern for more than the material advancement of the island. Largely through government help and partly through private efforts, there was a rapid and diversified development of cultural institutions. The two existing branches of the University of Puerto Rico at Rio Piedras and Mayagüez were expanded to the point that they had over 20,000 students by the late 1960s and a third center had been established. The private Inter American University grew so that it had over 9,000 students on two campuses, the old one at San Germán and a second in the San Juan area; and a new Catholic University was established in Ponce, to a large degree through the patronage of Luis Ferré, a leading industrialist and politician. The annual Casals Festival, featuring the famous cellist Pablo Casals and other world-renowned artists, was held at the University of Puerto Rico from the mid-1950s, and the Puerto Rican Symphony Orchestra was established in the early 1960s. Important new art museums were established at the University of Puerto Rico at Rio Piedras and in Ponce; and the government subsidized a number of the island's painters and literary men, even though many of them were political opponents of the regime.[10]

POLITICAL EVOLUTION OF THE PARTIDO POPULAR DEMOCRÁTICO

Throughout the 1940s the Partido Popular Democrático increased in popularity. It received a majority in both houses of the legislature in 1944, and by the 1948 election the party elected every member of the Senate but two and all but one member of the lower house. The Socialist and Liberal parties were so badly shattered by the rise of the PPD that they went out of existence. The Republican Party, which had been the principal representative of the sugar interests and was associated with the mainland Republicans, was reduced to almost a minor party.

Meanwhile, the Populares were finding it increasingly difficult to maintain neutrality on the political status of the island. In 1945 and 1946 those party members who favored independence joined with elements outside the Populares ranks to form the Puerto Rican Congress for Independence, thus offering a direct challenge to the position of the PPD.

However, even many of those who favored independence at the time of the establishment of the Partido Popular Democrático had had second thoughts. These included Luís Muñoz Marín himself. When faced with the challenge from the Congress for Independence, the majority of the party's leadership decided that they must oppose the idea, at least as an immediate demand. As a result, in mid-1946 the party leadership decided that membership in the PPD and the Congress were incompatible, ordering party members to withdraw from the latter or be expelled from the party. On July 25, 1946, the Congress was converted into the Partido Independentista Puertorriqueño.

Meanwhile, the Partido Popular Democrático leaders took steps to obtain a wider degree of autonomy for the island. With the resignation of Governor Tugwell in 1946, both he and the Populares leaders urged President Truman to name a Puerto Rican as his successor. Jesús Piñero, a PPD member and until then the island's resident commissioner (member of the House of Representatives with a voice but no vote) in Washington, became governor of Puerto Rico.

The Populares leaders then made another request of President Truman. They asked his support for a law that would allow the people of Puerto Rico to elect their own governor. He agreed; and with his backing such a law was passed in time for the 1948 election, in which Luís Muñoz Marín, who had been president of the Senate since 1941, was chosen governor.

The Partido Popular Democrático was to win four subsequent gubernatorial elections. During all of this time, until 1968, it maintained undisputed control of the island legislature. During most of this period it had every mayor and a majority of every municipal council. For a long time, the party seemed virtually unbeatable.

In the meantime, the Popular-dominated regime worked out a new constitutional status for Puerto Rico. The island's legislature petitioned Congress to pass a law giving Puerto Ricans the right to write their own constitution, as well as to elect or have appointed by elected officials, all of the executive members of the island's government—before this, several cabinet members were named by the U.S. president and the rest appointed by the governor, himself named by the president.

With President Truman's approval such a law, Public Law 600, was passed. As a result a Constitutional Assembly was elected by the Puerto Rican voters; it wrote a constitution that provided for a democratic government with wide powers and proclaimed the island's new status to be the result of an agreement between the people of Puerto Rico and the people of the United States. This point of view was given some credence by a passage in Public Law 600, which stated it to be "in the nature of a pact" between the two peoples.

The status of Puerto Rico under the new constitution was stated to be that of an estado libre asociado, which was to be translated "commonwealth" in English. After approval in a referendum in Puerto Rico on March 3, 1952, and a vote of the U.S. Congress, the new constitution went into effect on July 4, 1952. The first elections under it were held in the following November.

After the establishment of the commonwealth, Puerto Rican politics was again clearly divided among advocates of assimilation (in this case statehood), independence, and autonomy. The Partido Popular Democrático clearly represented the last of these alternatives, while the Partido Independentista Puertorriqueño was for some time the main advocate of independence and the Partido Republicano (which added the word Estadista to its name) the supporter of statehood.

For the time being at least, it was clear that the great majority of the people favored the maintenance of the commonwealth. Even as late as 1967 a referendum on the subject went overwhelmingly in favor of the status quo. After the election of 1948, during which the PIP received about 20 percent of the popular vote, the popular sentiment for independence declined drastically. In subsequent elections the PIP was never able to get as much as 10 percent of the total vote; and in the late 1950s the party split, with its more extreme faction abandoning electoral action and forming the Movimiento Pro Independencia, which in 1971 took the name Partido Socialista and sent its principal leader on a visit to the People's Republic of China.

Until 1967 the major opponent of the Partido Popular Democrático was the Partido Republicano Estadista. It gained an increasingly large percentage of the popular vote in each subsequent election, although its vote never rose to more than 35 percent.

However, although the autonomist position of the PPD continued to have the support of the substantial majority of the population, it was by no means so clear that the people accepted the interpretation of the island's status put forth by Muñoz Marín and other Partido Popular Democrático leaders. Muñoz' point of view was that the commonwealth status was a new political phenomenon, a sharing of sovereignty between two peoples, something that could and should last indefinitely. It was very clear that the overwhelming majority of the Puerto Ricans—particularly the humbler worker and peasant elements—did not want to break their ties with the United States; but it was by no means so clear that they accepted the idea that the form these ties should take for an indefinite period should be the commonwealth. This failure to convince the people of Puerto Rico to accept the permanency of commonwealth status has undoubtedly been one of the two main failures of the Partido Popular Democrático.

Another aspect of the Partido Popular Democrático during the 1950s and 1960s worth mentioning is the party's relations with fellow parties elsewhere in Latin America. The PPD was considered a fellow organization by the national revolutionary parties in Latin America. Relations were particularly close with the Liberación Nacional Party of Costa Rica and Acción Democrática of Venezuela. Governor Muñoz Marín was a specially invited guest at the inauguration of Costa Rican President José Figueres in 1953 and was given all the honors of a chief of state. The Puerto Rican government gave refuge to Rómulo Betancourt, head of Acción Democrática, when he was in exile from the dictatorship of General Marcos Pérez Jiménez.

Muñoz and other leaders of the PPD participated in the Inter American Association for Democracy and Freedom, to which other national revolutionary leaders, such as Betancourt, Peruvian Aprista leader Víctor Raúl Haya de la Torre, and José Figueres, as well as some Christian Democratic leaders of various countries, also belonged. Muñoz was among the honored guests at the inauguration of President Juan Bosch, leader of the Dominican Revolutionary Party, another participant in the IADF, early in 1963.

In the United States the Popular Democrats' closest associations were with the liberal wing of the Democratic Party, although Muñoz maintained contacts with other elements as well. The Popular Democrats' association with national political leadership in the United States was closest during the Kennedy years, when Muñoz advised the president on Latin American affairs, PPD leader Teodoro Moscoso served as ambassador to Venezuela and then as U.S. head of the Alliance for Progress, and Puerto Rican former Assistant Secretary of State Arturo Morales Carrión served as an important official of the U.S. State Department.

SCHISM AND DEFEAT OF THE PPD

After being governor of Puerto Rico for 16 years, Luís Muñoz Marín decided not to run for reelection in 1964. It was therefore necessary for the Partido Popular Democrático to choose a candidate to succeed him. This situation revealed another major weakness of the PPD, its failure to develop a generally recognized successor to Muñoz Marín. Some of the long-time governor's critics charged him with purposely cutting down the power and influence of anyone who possibly might challenge his role as leader of the Popular Democratic Party. Whether or not this was the case, there was certainly no one in 1964 who was the logical candidate for governor when Muñoz decided that he did not want to run again.

In effect the choice of his successor was largely up to Muñoz Marín. His selection was Roberto Sánchez Vilella, who had long been secretary of state of the island's government. Sánchez had the reputation for being a technician of the regime rather than a political leader, although, as was true of all of the principal leaders of the Muñoz government, he was a member in good standing of the Partido Popular Democrático.

Sánchez Vilella was elected to succeed Muñoz. For some time thereafter relations remained friendly between the new governor and

Muñoz Marín, who, although he was only an island senator after 1964, remained the party's principal leader. However, in 1967, after the governor had divorced his wife and married a much younger woman, an action that brought Sánchez Vilella much public criticism, Muñoz and other PPD leaders became increasingly critical of him.

At this point the quarrel between Sánchez Vilella and Muñoz Marín served to polarize already existing tendencies within the Partido Popular Democrático. A number of relatively young intellectuals within the party, who were inclined toward the idea of ultimate—if not more or less immediate—independence for the island, rallied to the support of the governor, even though until then he had been one of the strongest advocates of the commonwealth. This tended to intensify Muñoz Marín's opposition to Sánchez.

Although Sánchez Vilella announced his retirement from politics soon after his remarriage, he subsequently changed his mind and announced that he would be a candidate for reelection on the PPD ticket. When the influence of Muñoz Marín proved too strong, and the Popular Democrático nomination went to Luís Negrón López, the governor withdrew from the party and established a rival group, called the People's Party.

This split in the party that had dominated Puerto Rico for almost 30 years proved disastrous for the PPD. In the election of November 1968, although Negrón López and Sánchez Vilella together had a majority of the votes, the division of Popular Democrático votes between them brought victory to Luís Ferré. The successful candidate had run several times before as nominee of the Partido Republicano Estadista. However, at the time of the 1967 referendum on the status question, when the Partido Republicano Estadista had decided to abstain, Ferré opposed this position, urged statehood supporters to participate in the poll, and withdrew from the party to which he had always belonged, establishing the Nuevo Partido Progresista. It was as candidate of this new party that Ferré finally won the governorship in 1968.

The defeat of the Popular Democrats in 1968 encompassed much more than the governorship. The party also lost the post of resident commissioner in Washington, the majority in the lower house of the island's legislature, and control over the island's principal cities, including San Juan, where the Populares had appeared unbeatable.

Four years later the Populares had recovered much of the ground lost in 1968. They had reunited their ranks and supported Senate President Rafael Hernández Colón as candidate for governor. However, it seemed doubtful that the party would ever recover the degree of control over island politics that it had enjoyed during the 1940s and 1950s.

STRENGTH AND WEAKNESSES OF THE PARTIDO POPULAR DEMOCRÁTICO

Although defeated after 28 years in power, the Popular Democratic Party had transformed Puerto Rico. The island was converted from a country with an economy that depended almost completely on the production of one agricultural product into one with a diversified agricultural-industrial economy. Dramatic improvements were brought about by the PPD regime in the literacy rate and in public health. Virtually every residence in the island was provided with electricity; tens of thousands of improved houses were built for the rural and urban population; and a new middle class associated with the new industries and with government enterprises was developed. The political status of the island was converted from that of a frank colony to a new arrangement under which the Puerto Ricans were largely in control of their internal affairs.

Most important of all, however, was the transformation in the psychology of the people of the island. Whereas despair and frustration had characterized most Puerto Ricans before 1940, the Popular Democratic regime had been able to give the people of the island a faith in their ability to do things and to achieve improvements in their status. From one of the "poorhouses of the Caribbean" Puerto Rico had been converted into a place that people from all continents came to visit for ideas on to how to bring about their own rapid economic development.

However, the PPD failed in two regards. It was unable to convince the majority of the population of the permanency of the commonwealth status adopted in 1952. In addition, the party had been too much the vehicle of its founder and principal leader, Luís Muñoz Marín. Even when he ceased to be governor of the island, his control over the party remained intact, which proved to be disastrous to the party, at least in the short run.

CHAPTER

14

**THE PARTIDO
REVOLUCIONARIO
INSTITUCIONAL
OF MEXICO**

For more than 30 years Mexico has been governed by the same party. This organization, which has long epitomized the Mexican Revolution, is usually regarded by the national revolutionary parties as their Mexican counterpart. Its general orientation and program have been similar to that of other members of this group. However, the Mexican party has reflected the general tendency of the Mexicans to isolationism and the reticence of Mexican political leaders to associate closely with parties and politicians elsewhere in Latin America.

ORIGINS OF THE REVOLUTIONARY PARTY

What is presently the Partido Revolucionario Institucional was established almost two decades after the beginning of the Mexican Revolution. During the first decade of the Revolution, which began in 1910, there was no serious attempt to organize a political party to lead the process. Much of this period was devoted to military struggles, which made more or less normal political activity virtually impossible.

During the early 1920s two parties served as the principal spokesmen for the revolutionary government. During the administration of Alvaro Obregón (1920-24) the president relied upon the Partido Agrario for his principal support in Congress and in the general public. This party had been organized principally by followers of Emiliano Zapata, the great peasant leader who had made the principle of agrarian reform one of the major planks of the Revolution; Obregón took them under his wing after the assassination of their leader in 1919. The former Zapatistas of the Partido Agrario were largely responsible for enacting the basic legislation for the agrarian reform and getting the process of land redistribution well under way.

During the subsequent administration of Plutarco Elías Calles, the government forces were organized in the Partido Laborista Mexicano. It had its principal base in the country's largest labor organization, the Confederación Regional Obrera Mexicana, and was headed by Luís Morones, who served as minister of labor during much of the Calles administration.

Near the end of his administration, President Calles broke with the Partido Laborista when Luís Morones insisted that he should be the government candidate to succeed the president, instead of ex-President Obregón, whom Calles was backing. As a result the Mexican government was left without an organized national political party.

The country was thrown into a major crisis when President-elect Obregón was assassinated before he was able to take office. During the next six years (1928-34) three different men occupied the presidency, but the real power behind the regime continued to be Plutarco Elías Calles.

Calles felt that it was necessary to organize a new revolutionary party that would be under his direct control and could give a strong civilian base to the government, which at this time depended for its support principally upon the nation's armed forces—themselves not entirely reliable. To this end a congress held under his auspices in March 1929 established the Partido Nacional Revolucionario.

In the beginning the Partido Nacional Revolucionario was in fact a loose federation of state parties, controlled by the revolutionary military leaders who held most of the state governorships. However, Calles began the process of subordinating these groups to the direction of him and the officials of the national group by requiring that all public employees pay "dues" to the PNR. This provided it with a sizable treasury that none of the governors could match. Calles also increasingly channeled government patronage through the Partido Nacional Revolucionario, thus raising its prestige and power.

In preparation for the 1934 presidential campaign, the Partido Nacional Revolucionario nominated General Lázaro Cárdenas, who had served for a time as president of the party, as well as having been governor of the state of Michoacán and a member of the national cabinet. At the same time the party announced a six-year plan, which was in fact a platform for the Cárdenas campaign, stating what his administration proposed to do in its six years in office.

Cárdenas was elected without difficulty. However, his accession to office marked the beginning of another severe crisis in the Partido Nacional Revolucionario and in the government. Although the new president was widely presumed to be little more than a puppet of Calles, he proved to be nothing of the sort. Against the advice of his supposed patron, the new president launched an energetic program to fulfill the promises he had made in his campaign, which essentially amounted to putting into effect the program of the Mexican Revolution. He energetically renewed the agrarian reform, seizing, among other properties, some sizable holdings belonging to foreigners. He also gave vigorous support to the consolidation of the labor movement, which had splintered into nearly a dozen central labor groups after Luís Morones and the CROM had broken with Calles late in 1927.

By early 1936 these steps of the Cárdenas administration had aroused the open and strong opposition of ex-President Plutarco Elías Calles. He denounced as dangerous the strong prolabor and pro-agrarian policies of the administration, and President Cárdenas responded by deporting Calles and Morones to the United States.

Following Calles' deportation Cárdenas went on with his reform program. He nationalized the country's major railroads and in March 1938 expropriated the nation's oil industry. He organized the beneficiaries of the agrarian reform into a strong national organization, the Confederación Nacional Campesina, and supported the establishment of a new labor confederation, the Confederación de Trabajadores de México—which, in the beginning at least, had within its ranks most of the country's major unions.

THE REORGANIZATION OF THE PNR

As part of his reform program, President Cárdenas sponsored the reorganization of the government party. At a congress held in 1938 both its name and the basis of its organization were changed. The party was rechristened Partido de la Revolución Mexicana.

More important than this name change was the restructuring of its organization. The system whereby only government employees were really members of the party was abolished. In its place a form of party structure was established that brought into the Partido de la Revolución Mexicana the principal organizations supporting the government and the Revolution.

The party was reorganized on the basis of four "sectors": the peasant, labor, "popular," and army groups. Each of these consisted of elements from different parts of the body politic and gave a voice within the party to almost all the important pressure groups then active in Mexico. The principal element left out was the Church.

The peasant sector of the Partido de la Revolución Mexicana consisted of only one group, the newly organized Confederación Nacional Campesina. This included within its ranks most of the ejidos, the semicommunal groups of beneficiaries of the agrarian reform, who in the past had been dispersed among the several national labor confederations.

The labor sector was more diverse in its membership. It included not only the largest central labor group, the Confederación de Trabajadores de México, but also several of the smaller confederations and a number of independent industrial unions that did not belong to any central labor body.

The popular sector in the beginning consisted largely of government employees and teachers. According to legislation sponsored by President Cárdenas, these kinds of unions could not belong to any central labor confederation and so could not be part of the labor sector. For purposes of their participation in the PRM they were considered to be "middle-class" groups. A number of organizations were established to represent various groups of businessmen, members of the professions, and independent small and medium-size landholders, which also affiliated with the popular sector.

The army sector consisted of the country's armed forces, and President Cárdenas was severely criticized for "bringing the army into politics" by including it in the government party. His reply was that the army had always been in politics and that all the new form of the party did was to bring this out into the open. As a matter of fact, the establishment of the army sector of the Partido de la Revolución Mexicana was only the penultimate step in withdrawing the military completely from an independent role in national politics. This final move was made in the early 1940s, when the army sector of the PRM was abolished.[1]

During the Cárdenas period the most influential segments of the PRM were undoubtedly the labor and agrarian sectors, although this situation subsequently changed. However, the move that the Cárdenas administration had made to bring virtually every important interest group of Mexico into the government party paved the way for the system of government by consensus that characterized the Mexican regime during the next four administrations.

The national leadership of the PRM consisted of representative figures from its various sectors, together with the principal figures in Congress and the current administration. The PRM leaders cooperated closely with the president, who was the de facto head of the party so long as he remained chief executive of the nation.

On a local basis the government party depended to a major degree on the activity and strength of its sectors. Thus, in some areas the bulk of the party membership was made up of local groups of the Confederación Nacional Campesina; in others its principal support came from the various trade union groups. As time passed, the various groups that composed the popular sector came to be of major importance in an increasing number of areas throughout the country.

The varying degrees of influence of the PRM sectors was reflected in the candidates for public office who were offered by the party. Thus, in the oil field areas of the states of Tamaulipas and Vera Cruz one or more of the party's candidates for deputy were chosen from the oil workers' union. In other areas the party's candidates were chosen from among the ranks of the Confederación Nacional Campesina or from the various groups making up the popular sector. Army officers were not infrequently PRM candidates, although in order to enter upon an active political career they were required to obtain a leave of absence from the armed forces.[2]

THE POST-CÁRDENAS REGIMES

Each of the Mexican administrations since that of Cárdenas has been elected by the revolutionary party. The structure and functioning of the party has remained essentially the same in that period, although there have been some changes. During the administration of Cárdenas' successor, General Manuel Avila Camacho, the army sector was suppressed. In the following administration the name of the party was changed to what it has remained ever since, the Partido Revolucionario Institucional, an alteration symbolizing the phase of construction of new institutions into which the Mexican Revolution had passed.

The center of gravity of the party has shifted considerably during recent decades. The relative influence of the peasant and labor sectors has declined, while that of the popular sector has advanced steadily. This shift in influence among the various elements of the PRI has reflected the growing industrialization of Mexico, the evolution of a more complicated economy, and the rise of the middle class and a new upper class, both of which have found themselves represented more in the popular sector than in the other two.

Each of the administrations of the Partido Revolucionario Institucional has had its own particular flavor and characteristics. The Avila Camacho regime was generally regarded as being rather to the right of that of Cárdenas. It put less emphasis on reform and more on development, and much time and energy were spent by the president and his principal associates in dealing with the problems generated by World War II. Mexico was one of the two Latin American countries that actively participated in this war, sending an aviation group to the Philippine combat zone; it was also a major contributor of raw materials to the Allies.

The government of Miguel Alemán (1946-52) was the first to put major emphasis on economic development. Huge hydroelectric projects, ambitious new industries, large efforts to expand the area in agriculture through irrigation, and large road building programs were some of the aspects of the program of this administration.

After the spectacular and somewhat flamboyant efforts of the regime of Alemán, those of his successor, Adolfo Ruíz Cortines (1952-58), seemed more modest. He too pushed forward the country's economic development, with perhaps somewhat more attention to problems of agrarian and labor reform than had characterized the Alemán administration. At least some effort was made to curb the corruption and nepotism that had reached scandalous proportions in the previous period.

The government of Adolfo López Mateos (1958-64) represented a definite swing back toward social reform and emphasis on the nationalist elements of the Mexican Revolution. More land was distributed under the agrarian reform than in any previous administration, and social security was extended to the ejidos. A large popular housing program was launched. The provision of the constitution of 1917 calling for profit sharing was implemented. At the same time the last privately owned electricity companies serving the general public were nationalized, and an amendment to the constitution was adopted that forbade private firms to own public utilities. Similarly, a law was passed providing for the eventual transfer of at least 51 percent of the stock of all mining companies to Mexican nationals. Despite this more left-wing emphasis of the López Mateos administration, economic development continued apace.

The successor to López Mateos, Gustavo Díaz Ordaz, represented another swing somewhat to the right. Renewed emphasis was placed on economic development, particularly in agriculture; and less attention was given to social reform and nationalism. More serious was the strong overreaction of the Díaz Ordaz government to student unrest in 1968, which seemed to imperil the "government by consensus" that had characterized Mexico for a quarter of a century.

THE IDEOLOGY OF THE PRI

It has frequently been observed that the Mexican Revolution was one of the few great social movements of our time that has had no distinctive ideology or political philosophy. However, this observation is only a half truth. The Mexican Revolution has produced no Lenin, Stalin, Mao Tse-tung, or Che Guevara; but this revolution and its party, the PRI, has had a broadly defined program, whether or not one wants to call that program an ideology or a philosophy.

Throughout its six decades the Mexican Revolution has developed along certain general lines that have been widely understood by most Mexicans and by the leaders of the successive governments. These lines were set forth in the constitution of 1917, which is the nearest thing Mexico has to a clear statement of the ideology of its revolution.

There have been five major planks in the program of the Mexican Revolution: agrarian reform, labor reform and organization, nationalism, economic development, and political democracy.

During the violent years of the Revolution, 1910-20, what started as a mere political revolution to overthrow a man who had been dictator for three and a half decades was converted into an agrarian revolution. The redistribution of the landed estates, which had had their origins in the Spanish conquest of the 16th century, became a major point in the program of the Revolution. This process of land redistribution has continued since the government of President Venustiano Carranza (1913-20). It has evolved into a complicated process, going much beyond mere granting of land to the landless and involving opening new areas to cultivation, providing water for arid areas, and granting credit and technical assistance to the beneficiaries of the reform. Since the early 1920s the program of agrarian reform has been closely associated with the concept of the ejido, a communal institution to which the use rights of the land are actually granted by the state but usually transfers the actual use of the land to the individual families that compose it. This particular institution has come into serious question in recent decades because of its comparatively bad performance in terms of output and productivity.

At about the same time that agrarian reform became a fundamental aspect of the Mexican Revolution, the idea of labor reform and organization was adopted as a basic element of the revolutionary program. Labor unions participated in the civil wars of the first decade of the Revolution; labor reforms were written into the constitution of 1917; the first really national confederation was established in 1918; and the organized workers have since that time constituted a fundamental power group in Mexican politics. At the same time the successive governments have sponsored a vast body of legislation designed to protect the workers and improve their lot, measures that have conformed to the prescriptions laid down in the constitution of 1917.

Virtually from its inception the Mexican Revolution has been nationalistic in tone. In the earlier years nationalism found its expression most frequently in resistance to attempts by the United States to intefere—such attempts involving the use of armed force on two occasions—with the Mexican revolutionary process. In more recent decades it has been most often expressed in economic terms, in general conformity to the principle of "Mexico for the Mexicans." Characteristic of this economic nationalism have been the expropriation of the railroads and oil industry, the buying out of all foreign-owned public utilities, and the program for bringing the mining industry under national control.

Mexican nationalism has also found its expression in the maintenance of an independent foreign policy. The cornerstone of this independent foreign policy has been opposition to the intervention of one nation in the internal affairs of another, a position derived from Mexico's experience with intervention by its powerful northern neighbor. In recent decades this policy has been shown in Mexico's voting pattern in the United Nations and the Organization of American States, which has been determined by what the Mexican government thinks is in the country's best interest in any given case and has frequently seen Mexico aligned against the United States on a wide range of issues. It has also been expressed in the persistence of Mexico in continuing to recognize the Castro government in Cuba, even after the United States and all of the other Latin American countries had broken relations with that regime.

Economic development has been part of the program of the Mexican Revolution since its early years, but it moved to the fore as a major factor only after World War II. Earlier administrations had laid the institutional groundwork for economic development by establishing the Central Bank, the government investment bank (Nacional Financiera), two agricultural development banks, and officially sponsored trade associations. Since 1940 major emphasis by each succeeding administration has been placed on expanding all aspects of the economy.

The Mexican Revolution started as a movement for the reassertion of political democracy, and this has always remained one of its aspirations. This aspiration is set forth clearly in the constitution of 1917; and in recent decades (at least until the Díaz Ordaz administration) there has tended to be a slow but steady growth in government tolerance for dissident opinions, organizations, and activities. Opposition parties both to the Left and to the Right of the PRI have functioned more or less freely; in the early 1960s provision was made for expanding their representation in Congress.

It is doubtful that elections have generally been completely free. Although in the late 1960s the right-wing opposition party, Partido Acción Nacional, was allowed to win control of some 19 municipalities, including two state capitals, in those instances in which the PAN appeared to have won control of state governments the government has interpreted the results so as to give victory to the PRI.

The situation with regard to Mexico's approach to democracy may be summed up thus: the opposition has been allowed to function and has had a certain degree of freedom of press, assembly, and organization, but it has not been generally permitted to win elections. Certainly since the establishment of the PRI there has never been any doubt as to which party would win a national presidential or congressional election.

One of the most significant aspects of this part of the revolutionary program that has been the program of the PRI has been the firm entrenchment of the prohibition of reelection of anyone who has ever been president. This rule was violated only once—in 1928, by Alvaro Obregón, who did not live to take advantage of this abuse of a fundamental revolutionary principle. Since the establishment of the Partido Revolucionario Institucional, the "no reelection" rule has been strictly followed.

GOVERNMENT BY CONSENSUS

During the administrations of Avila Camacho, Alemán, Ruíz Cortines, and López Mateos, the government of Mexico was conducted largely by what might best be described as a process of consensus. This system was complicated and sometimes confused.

In the first place, the Partido Revolucionario Institucional contributed strongly toward providing the basis for establishing a consensus on government policy. As already noted, virtually every important interest group in Mexican politics was represented within the party. In addition the very strong majorities that the PRI had in Congress and other legislative bodies helped to facilitate the process of forming a consensus in the legislative branch and between it and the executive branch.

Most important, laws were passed by Congress as the result of an initiative from the president. However, before the president sent any proposed law to Congress, he submitted it for consideration and comment to representative institutions of the interest groups directly concerned. Characteristic was the case of the profit-sharing law enacted in 1963. Before it was submitted to Congress, it was considered at great length by a commission formed by members of the country's principal employers' organizations and the major trade union confederations; the bill that was finally sent to the legislature was based on what had been agreed on by these interested groups.

Bills coming from the executive were first passed to a standing committee of Congress, where they were generally debated extensively by the committee members, most of whom were PRI members. If there was any significant disagreement with the proposed measure, the PRI committee members would normally take up the matter with the appropriate cabinet member or, in very important cases, with the president himself. Such discussions would generally lead to modifications of the proposal that would be acceptable to all concerned.

The consensus process was also used in the selection of PRI candidates for the presidency. Although the charge was frequently made that the incumbent president freely selected his successor, this was considerably short of the truth. When it became time to consider the party's nomination, an informal committee of perhaps 150 members met. It was the president's right to propose a name from among those generally considered suitable. However, the president's choice was by no means always accepted.

This body, which might be called the presidential selection committee, consisted of representatives of the principal labor organizations, the Confederación Nacional Campesina, the country's principal bankers, industrialists, merchants, all living ex-presidents, the principal PRI leaders in Congress, and the most influential state governors. Each of these individuals was in more or less close contact with his constituency and had widely canvassed it to ascertain which of the possible presidential nominees were most acceptable and which were more or less unacceptable. Because of the nature of this committee, its members were able to reach agreement on a presidential nominee who would be generally satisfactory to all of the principal elements upon which the PRI and the revolutionary government depended for support. No nominee would be accepted who did not receive at least the acquiescence of those making up the committee. On several occasions the president had to submit several successive selections before a PRI nominee was chosen.

Once chosen by the president and his advisers, the nominee's ratification by the Partido Revolucionario Institucional was virtually automatic. It became customary for the Confederación de Trabajadores de México to be the first organization formally to present the new PRI nominee's candidacy; subsequently state units of the party ratified the decision, which was made final by a national PRI nominating convention.

Candidates for lesser offices were also chosen by a process of general consultation. When a nominee for state governor was to be selected, the principal interest groups of the state would be consulted to determine their preferences. In the naming of congressional candidates, there was an attempt to give adequate representation on the PRI slates to all of the elements represented within the party. For both governorships and congressional posts, the PRI candidates were named by the national leadership. Choice of candidates for municipal posts was generally within the province of the state leadership.

This system of government by consensus depended on two fundamental principles. The first was that the leaders of the PRI and the government stayed generally within the limits of the program of the PRI and the Revolution. The second was that the opposition operated within the limitations that made government by consensus feasible.

Furthermore, the maintenance of consensus involved constantly shifting programmatic emphasis. A regime that had laid particular stress on economic development would be followed by one that emphasized other aspects of the program, and vice versa. When any aspect of the general revolutionary program was pushed to the point of creating serious dissension within the party and the forces supporting it, emphasis of the government's policy would be shifted.

Attitudes were as important as programmatic issues. Although it has never been maintained that the PRI governments have been scrupulously honest, some have been more corrupt than others. When one administration seemed to be excessively corrupt, care was taken to have the succeeding president be a man noted for his relative probity.

Also, although complete freedom of expression has never existed in Mexico, the process of government by consensus set definite limits to the degree to which publicly stated opposition could be curbed. Although the major daily newspapers did not find it convenient to clash openly on major issues with the incumbent administration, and generally followed the rule that the president was never to be attacked personally, there was still ample room for criticism, often very severe criticism of the government.

For one thing, members of the cabinet and other officials of the administration were frequently fair game for writers even on the major daily papers. In addition, individuals, businesses, and organizations frequently took paid advertisements in the large dailies to protest some measure of the government or to denounce an abuse by some individual public official.

In addition to these ways of expressing opposition in the large metropolitan press, there were numerous weekly political papers and magazines. The right-wing opposition party, Partido Acción Nacional, long had its own newspaper; and a wide variety of left-wing opposition periodicals appeared from time to time. At least one large Mexico City daily paper in the 1960s generally expressed a left-wing opposition point of view.

In addition to the relative freedom of press, oppositionists also had extensive rights to organize. Small trade union groups outside of and opposed to the PRI traditionally existed. Left-wing activity, which sometimes reached violent proportions, was frequent among the students, particularly those of the National University in Mexico City; and until the administration of Díaz Ordaz, such activity was treated with wide tolerance by the government. In the early 1960s a rival peasant group to the PRI-affiliated Confederación Nacional Campesina, the Confederación Nacional Campesina Independiente (CNCI), was formed and gained significant support among the peasantry of some states.

A government that sought to limit the reasonably well defined rights of the opposition to criticize and attack the regime would violate the concept of rule by consensus. The danger of such a development appeared during the administration of Díaz Ordaz.

The maintenance of consensus government depended as much on the opposition as upon the government. As we have noted, there existed fairly well-defined limits within which opposition was tolerated. However, any group that went beyond these limits was likely to suffer severe consequences, because such action put the whole consensus concept in danger.

An example of such a situation occurred in 1957. A series of strikes by teachers, railroad and electrical workers, and other groups broke out under the leadership of new trade union officials, who were reportedly aligned with left-wing opposition groups and certainly were against the predominant trade union bureaucracy. The government intervened in these walkouts and brought about settlements very favorable to the workers. No reprisals were taken against the labor leaders involved, despite their opposition posture.

However, some of the labor leaders were not satisfied with the results of the strikes and saw an opportunity to capitalize on the situation for the political ends of the parties with which they were affiliated. Within a few weeks of the solution of the walkouts they proceeded to call new strikes with new and much steeper demands. The government stepped in again, arresting the principal leaders of the unions, and broke the new strikes. New leaders, willing to work within the bounds of the consensus system, were elected by the unions involved.

FACTIONS IN THE PRI

Government by consensus has not meant that there have not been factions within the PRI. On occasion these factions have left the party; and in the elections of 1940, 1946, and 1952, the principal opposition candidates were dissident leaders from the PRI.

In the election of 1940, President Lázaro Cárdenas decided to throw his support behind General Manuel Avila Camacho, who had been governor of the state of Puebla and a member of the cabinet for several years. However, another of the revolutionary generals, Juan Andreu Almazán had considerable backing within the PRM. He was one of the most widely respected military chiefs of the civil war days of the Revolution and had held many positions both in the army and in the civil government. When Almazán was denied the official party's nomination, he withdrew to form his own party, the Partido Revolucionario de Unificación Nacional, which promptly nominated him to run against Avila Camacho. Although there was little doubt about who would win, at least some maintained that Almazán had really had more popular support than Avila Camacho. After the election there were threats by Almazán supporters to try to win power by force, but they did not materialize.

In 1946, when Avila Camacho threw the support of the party behind Minister of Government Miguel Alemán to be the first civilian president since the early days of the Revolution, there was again a revolt by some PRM leaders and members. They threw their backing to Ezequiel Padilla, who had been foreign minister during most of World War II and had gained considerable international fame and respect, and formed the Partido Democratico Mexicano. Again, the results were virtually a foregone conclusion, although Padilla waged an energetic campaign throughout the country.

In 1952 President Alemán and his associates chose Adolfo Ruíz Cortines, the minister of government, as the PRI nominee for president. However, one of the last of the revolutionary caudillos, General Miguel Henríquez Guzmán, withdrew grandiloquently from the PRI and established a party of his own. Although his candidacy aroused a good deal of popular support, particularly from more left-wing elements, Ruiz Cortines was easily elected.

However, aside from these dissident elements of the PRI that left the ranks of the party, there existed during the 1940s, 1950s, and 1960s several well-recognized factions that continued to exercise their influence within the party. The best-known of these were the elements supporting ex-Presidents Lázaro Cárdenas and Miguel Alemán. After World War II Cárdenas represented the left wing of the party, was particularly insistent on maintenance of the ejido, and was favorably disposed toward the Soviet bloc (and subsequently toward Fidel Castro) in international politics. Although on several occasions he skirted abandoning the PRI, he never actually did so; and his influence within the party continued to be of some consequence.

In contrast, since leaving the presidency Miguel Alemán has been the recognized leader of the right wing of the PRI. He has had particularly close associations with industrialists and other business elements who prospered during his administration. He himself became one of the larger Mexican entrepreneurs.

THE CRISIS OF THE DÍAZ ORDAZ PERIOD

During the administration of Gustavo Díaz Ordaz, who took office in December 1964, there were some indications that the system of government by consensus might be breaking down. Undoubtedly one of the reasons for this crisis was the nature of the chief executive himself. Before he was selected as PRI candidate in 1963, there was a widespread belief that Gustavo Díaz Ordaz represented the more right-wing elements in the party. Although his predecessor, Adolfo López Mateos, had tended to be aligned with the more left-wing segments of the PRI and perhaps there was some logic in López Mateos' successor coming from the other camp, in the consensus spirit, there were certainly many in the PRI who felt that the swing in the pendulum had been a little too extreme.

Furthermore, in some ways Díaz Ordaz symbolized bureaucratization, and perhaps ossification of the PRI and the revolutionary government in general, which many looked upon with doubt mixed with alarm. Díaz Ordaz was colorless, bordering on ugly in appearance, with little or no charisma—which contrasted rather sharply with the personal attributes of his predecessor. He was seen by many as the typification of the machine politician, who might be efficient as an administrator and have certain adeptness at political infighting but had little mass popularity.

In addition Díaz Ordaz served during a period in which a series of economic and social problems that had been accumulating for a number of years became sharply evident. One of these was the very rapid increase in the Mexican population, which meant that a rising number of people entered the labor market each year. It had become obvious that the industrialization program that had been pursued with great vigor for two decades was not in itself sufficient to absorb this increasing demand for jobs.

The situation was complicated by the fact that the ejido sector of national agriculture had long trailed behind the rural private sector in productivity and output. Partly this was due to the ejido system itself; and partly it was due to the relatively meager government investment for several decades in agriculture, and particularly in the ejido sector, which depended principally on the government for credit, technical assistance, and other inputs.[3]

This situation in agriculture had been reflected during a number of years in the activities of so-called paracaidistas (parachutists), groups of peasants who descended upon private landholdings and seized them without official authorization. Although these activities were undoubtedly given stimulation by left-wing opponents of the regime, they also made clear the existence of a real problem in the rural economy.

Problems in agriculture had also stimulated a large drift of people to the cities, particularly to Mexico City. There were not enough regular jobs there to occupy all of these people, with the result that the living conditions of sizable segments of the urban population were deplorable; and this group was tending to grow. It was the more dramatic because of the extension at the same time of new luxurious upper- and upper middle-class suburbs around most of the larger cities.

One final element undoubtedly played a factor in the situation, the Cuban Revolution. The glamour and romance of the Cuban regime for the young, particularly the students, tended to strengthen the conviction that had long existed among a sizable number of the members of this group that the Mexican Revolution was "old-fashioned"—or, even more extremely put, that it was "dead." Certainly the staid and late middle-aged leadership of the Mexican government contrasted sharply with the young and demogogic chiefs of the Cuban Revolution.

Many of these elements for discontent with the status quo in Mexico found expression within the PRI itself. In the first year of the Díaz Ordaz administration it appeared that the regime was going to make a strong effort to change the situation and to attempt not only to rejuvenate the party but also to come to grips with the economic and social problems that were approaching crisis proportions. The first president of the PRI during the Díaz Ordaz administration, Carlos Madrazo, announced a program for drastically reorganizing the party, to make it more responsive to the rank and file of its various sectors and of the party in general. However, his efforts ran into very strong resistance from bureaucratic elements in the Partido Revolucionario Institucional and the government; and after about a year in office, Madrazo resigned.

The removal of the president of the PRI did not remove the problems facing the party and the Revolution. These were emphasized dramatically after a student strike at the National University in August-October 1968, which culminated in a series of events that raised grave doubts about whether the consensus system of government could survive.

The government strongly overreacted to the student movement. When students seized university buildings, heavily armed troops and riot police were sent against them, in one case reportedly using a small cannon to burst open the door to an ancient university building. These actions only served to reinforce the student movement and to gain it sympathy with the general public. Several weeks later, when a student demonstration was held in the Plaza de las Tres Culturas, troops fired point-blank into a crowd that until that moment had apparently not been acting violently. There were estimates that several hundred people were killed.

This series of events had particular importance because of the adult groups in sympathy with and even helping to guide the movement. Although there was a good deal of talk about "Communist" influence in the student strike, the truth seems to be that dissident elements in the Partido Revolucionario Institucional, particularly politicians associated with former party president Carlos Madrazo, leading intellectuals who had long been closely allied with the party, and politicians associated with the PRI regime, were the principal source of adult support for the movement.

Although the student strike was ended in October 1968 because of the opening of the Olympic Games in Mexico City and the desire of the students not to interfere with an event considered of great symbolic importance for the nation as a whole, the discontent among the younger generation continued and certainly was intensified by the events of the middle months of 1968. Furthermore, grave doubts had been aroused as to whether the government by consensus that had characterized Mexico since 1940 could continue. In August-October 1968 the government had certainly gone beyond the bounds that the consensus government system required in handling these disturbances.

President Luis Echeverría, who succeeded Díaz Ordaz in December 1971, sought to establish a more tolerant atmosphere. He freed most of the political and trade union prisoners in jail when he came to office. However, a year after he came to power, it was not clear whether this softening of the regime would be sufficient to maintain the consensus politics that had for so long been the basis of the Partido Revolucionario Institucional's control of the Mexican government.

THE FUTURE OF THE PRI

Certainly the Partido Revolucionario Institucional of Mexico in many ways has been unique among the parties of Latin America. Although in program it has had marked similarities with the national revolutionary parties, it has differed from them in being originated by an existing government. It has been distinctive, too, in its long tenure in power. It has been singular in its ability over a long period of time to channel the interests and opinions of most major elements in the country.

The kind of system that the PRI has represented since the late 1920s, and particularly since 1940, has depended essentially on the flexibility of the party leadership and upon the willingness of the opposition. The government that it has represented depends on whether or not, after the experiences of the Díaz Ordaz period, the party will be able to resume the flexible and tolerant attitudes that made possible its long rule.

The achievements of the PRI have certainly been many. It has carried forward very fundamental reforms in the country's society, economy, and politics. It has maintained a high rate of economic growth and development unmatched elsewhere in Latin America. It has provided a vehicle through which Mexico has enjoyed for more than a generation a degree of political stability virtually unmatched anywhere else in Latin America. It has succeeded in winning for Mexico a respect among other nations of Latin America and outside of the hemisphere, not only because of the importance of the social revolution it has led but also because of its ability to follow an essentially independent foreign policy.

However, by the late 1960s there appeared some doubts as to whether this record could be maintained much longer. If it is to be continued, the party will have to bend to the forces that are demanding new methods and energetic attempts to deal drastically with the accumulation of economic and social problems facing the nation.[4]

CHAPTER 15
OTHER NATIONAL REVOLUTIONARY PARTIES

Although the Peruvian Apristas, Venezuelan Acción Democrática, Bolivian Movimiento Nacionalista Revolucionario, Costa Rican Liberación Nacional, Puerto Rican Popular Democrats, and the Mexican PRI have been most important and generally the most successful of the national revolutionary parties, there have been a number of other such parties of some consequence. These include the Auténticos and Ortodoxos of Cuba, the Partido Revolucionario Dominicano of the Dominican Republic, the Mouvement Ouvrier Paysan of Haiti, the Febrerista Party of Paraguay, several parties in Guatemala, and the Concentración de Fuerzas Populares of Ecuador. Each of these is worthy of some comment.

CUBA

Origins of the Auténtico Party

The Partido Revolucionario Cubano (Auténtico), popularly known as the Auténtico Party, owes its origins to the Cuban revolution of 1933. For the previous nine years Cuba had been ruled by Gerardo Machado, the worst dictator that the island republic had endured until then. In August 1933 a general strike of students and workers, with the support of most of the country's entrepreneurs and with the help of the U.S. ambassador, Sumner Welles, finally forced the resignation of Machado. In his place Welles worked with the leaders of the country's armed forces to install modest and conservative Carlos Manuel de Cespedes as provisional president. Welles then returned to Washington with the feeling of a job well done.

NATIONAL REVOLUTIONARY PARTIES

However, what neither Welles nor the military men expected happened on September 4. A conspiracy of noncommissioned officers and university students and professors overthrew the new regime. In his place they installed a professor of the University of Havana Medical School, Dr. Ramón Grau San Martín. The new government consisted principally of students and young professors, in addition to Colonel Fulgencio Batista, who until September 4 had been a sergeant and was the organizer of the noncommissioned officers in the coup.

The government of President Grau San Martín remained in office for a little more than four months. During this period it enacted some labor legislation, took over control of the U.S.-owned electric and telephone companies, drew up an agrarian reform law, and gave strong support to the labor movement.

However, the Grau San Martín government had two strong enemies. One was the Communist Party of Cuba—which having made a deal with Machado by which it attempted to call off the general strike that overthrew him, then violently attacked the Grau San Martín government as "social fascist" and sought to form "soviets" in various parts of the island, particularly in rural areas where it had some support among sugar workers. The other was the U.S. State Department, particularly ex-Ambassador Sumner Welles, by then assistant secretary of state for Latin American affairs. It steadfastly refused to recognize the Grau San Martín government, using as one of its principal arguments the activities of the Communist-proclaimed "soviet," which it claimed indicated that the Grau government did not really exercise effective control over the country.

Sumner Welles's successor as American representative in Havana, Jefferson Caffrey, sought to persuade Batista to overthrow Grau San Martín. For several months the colonel refused to take this step; but on January 14, 1934, Batista finally moved, forcing Grau San Martín's resignation and installing in his place Colonel Carlos Mendieta. From then until 1940, when he became president, Batista functioned as the power behind the throne.

After his overthrow by Batista, Grau San Martín became the most bitter opponent of the military dictatorship. He took the lead in founding a political party, the Partido Revolucionario Cubano (Auténtico), which until 1944 constituted the major opposition party.

The program of the Partido Auténtico was adapted to the circumstances of Cuba at the time the party was founded. it urged an agrarian reform that would give land to the landless, particularly the sugar workers. It emphasized the necessity for rapid economic development, designed to assure the island republic a greater degree of economic independence. It advocated extensive labor legislation and strongly supported the rights of the workers to organize and bargain collectively. It urged controls over foreign investment. It strongly supported the reestablishment and maintenance of democratic government in Cuba.

Several other parties merged with the Partido Auténtico during the 1930s. The most notable of these were the Trotskyite branch of the Communist movement, which brought to the Auténticos considerable trade union support, and the small Cuban Aprista Party, which had been organized under the influence of Víctor Raul Haya de la Torre, the Peruvian Aprista leader, in the late 1920s.

In the late 1930s, when Batista was seeking to modify his regime and to become the constitutional president, he approached the leaders of the Partido Auténtico, seeking their support. However, he was turned down and went to the Communists, who co-operated with Batista in one way or another from 1937 until 1958.[1]

The Auténticos named candidates for the elections of 1940, which chose a Constituent Assembly; Grau San Martín served as president of the Assembly. They played a major part in the deliberations of this body and share the credit for writing one of the most progressive constitutions to be adopted by any Latin American country.

The Auténticos constituted the main opposition to the Communists in the labor movement after 1938. Although cooperation with the Batista regime assured the Communists the control of the Confederación de Trabajadores de Cuba established in that year, the Auténticos controlled a number of national unions, including those of hotel and restaurant workers and pharmaceutical workers, and had considerable influence in such key organizations as those of the workers in the sugar and tobacco industries.

The Auténticos In Office

Fulgencio Batista was elected president in 1940. When his term of office approached its end four years later, he decided not to try to violate the constitution by seeking to remain in office, and presided over one of the most honest elections in the country's history. The parties supporting Batista, including the Communists, supported Carlos Marquez Sterling; the principal opposition candidate was ex-President Ramón Grau San Martín, who was victorious. The Auténticos remained in office until March 10, 1952.

The ultimate collapse of the Auténtico Party was due in large part to its failure to carry out its program during the nearly eight years that it remained in power. During the four years of the Grau San Martín administration, although a democratic atmosphere was maintained, virtually no attempt was made to carry out the economic and social apsects of the Auténtico program. Some public housing was built and the social security system was expanded, but little more was accomplished.

A significant development during this period was the assumption of control of the labor movement by the Auténticos. This occurred in 1947, when a congress of the Confederación de Trabajadores de Cuba broke up in fighting between Communists, on the one hand, and Auténticos and independents, on the other. Subsequently a congress was held by each of the two factions, each claiming to be the "real" CTC. The minister of labor, Carlos Prío Socarras, extended legal recognition to the faction controlled by the Auténticos and their allies. From then until the advent of the Castro regime, the Autentico trade unionists who assumed control of the CTC in 1947 dominated the organization, although after 1952 their loyalty to the Auténtico Party became questionable.

In 1948 the Auténtico Party named Carlos Prío Socarras to succeed Grau San Martín, and he was elected. His administration differed considerably from that of Grau and did attempt to put into effect some aspects of the Auténtico program. It sought to win a somewhat greater degree of independence for the Cuban economy by establishing both the Central Bank, which issued Cuban currency for the first time (dollars having been the national currency until then) and the Agricultural and Industrial Development Bank, to stimulate the industrialization and diversification of the national economy. The Prío Socarras regime also undertook a pilot program in the field of agrarian reform, although it did not enact a general agrarian reform law.[2]

During both Auténtico administrations corruption was exceedingly widespread. Fortunes were made by cabinet members, heads of independent agencies, and other government affiliates. Scandals involving members of the government were numerous, and this prevalence of corruption in a party pledged to reform and the support of popular issues brought about a revolt in the Auténtico Party that led to the formation of the Partido Popular Cubano (Ortodoxo), popularly known as the Ortodoxo Party. The corruption of the Auténtico governments also contributed considerably to discrediting both the party and the concept of democratic government in Cuba.

The Decline of the Auténticos

New elections were scheduled for June 1952. However, a coup d'état, engineered by ex-President Fulgencio Batista and his army supporters occurred on March 10, before the election could be held. It was by no means certain whether the Auténtico candidate, Carlos Hevía, or the Ortodoxo nominee, Roberto Agramonte, would have been victorious; but it was very clear that Batista, who was also a candidate, had no chance of winning an honest election.

The coup d'état of March 10, 1952, was successful largely because President Carlos Prío Socarras did not fight to remain in power. Although representatives of the students came to the presidential palace asking for the distribution of the arms gathered there, the Auténtico labor leaders could have declared a general strike if they had been informed in time of Batista's move, and all of the army units in the interior and many of those in Havana stayed loyal to the regime, Prío made no effort to mobilize his supporters until it was too late and Batista had seized control of the radio and television stations and most of Havana.[3]

The overthrow of the Autentico regime led to a decline of the Auténtico Party. Although its trade union leaders remained in the party for about two years, they felt themselves forced to reach a compromise with the new Batista regime that would permit the admission of a handful of Batista's few labor followers into the leadership of the Confederación de Trabajadores de Cuba. When an attempt by ex-President Prío Socarras to organize a military coup against the Batista regime in 1955 failed, a sizable element of the party underground inside Cuba, led by ex-Minister of Education Aureliano Sánchez Arango, withdrew to form a rival underground group, which took the unwieldy name of Frente Democrático AAA.

Meanwhile, the two Auténtico former presidents split over the issue of participating in the election for president, Congress, and local officials organized by Batista late in 1954. Grau San Martín argued that the Auténticos should participate in this election, in the hope that they could win and Batista would repeat his performance of 1944 by permitting them to take power. Ex-President Prío Socarras, on the other hand, maintained that the election engineered by Batista would be a fraud, arguing that the only way to get rid of the dictatorship was by a coup with the help of elements within the armed forces that were opposed to the former sergeant. Two rival Auténtico parties were organized as a consequence, one functioning in such legality as Batista would allow it and the other continuing to conspire in the underground.

During this period the Auténticos lost most of their labor base. The group that had taken charge of the labor movement in 1947, made up principally of Auténticos, continued to maintain a great degree of cohesion. However, after the beginning of open civil war in November, 1956, the group found itself in a very difficult situation vis-à-vis the Batista government. It feared that a showdown between the labor movement and the dictatorship would result in the destruction of the unions; on the other hand, Batista feared that a successful general strike might bring down his regime. Although for a number of years

Batista and the labor leaders had maintained a kind of armed truce, both trying to avoid an ultimate showdown, after the landing of Fidel Castro and his followers the former Auténtico leaders became more committed to keeping Batista in power until he could be replaced legally.

The labor leaders felt that as a group they could not be involved in the conspiracy of the Prío Socarras Auténticos or in the collaboration with the dictatorship of the Grau Auténticos. Thus, as early as 1952 the principal figures in the Confederación de Trabajadores de Cuba withdrew from the Auténtico Party and announced their intention of forming a labor party. Although this project never got well started, most of the leading labor figures were from then on out of all factions of the Auténtico Party. Some of them, including Francisco Aguirre, second figure in the CTC, were secretly partisans of the underground opponents of the Batista regime.

The Auténticos in the Castro Regime

The Auténtico faction of ex-President Prío Socarras and the dissident Auténtico group, the Frente Democrático A.A.A. of Aureliano Sánchez Arango, both took an active part in the military struggle as well as in conspiring against the Batista regime. As a result, once Batista had been overthrown, the Auténticos were allowed to return to open political activity during the first months of the Castro government. The exiles—including Prío and Sánchez Arango—returned. Both the Prío and the Sánchez Arango groups began to establish local units throughout the island. The Prío Socarras Auténticos once again became very active in the labor movement, although they had only a few leaders of national stature, most Auténtico trade unionists having joined the urban underground of Castro's 26th of July Movement. The Prío group also began publishing a weekly newspaper that became one of the most important critics of the Castro government.

The Auténticos saw themselves as the likely heirs of the Castro revolution. They felt that through inexperience, demagoguery, incompetence, and irresponsibility Fidel Castro and his followers would discredit themselves. As a result, they argued, the people would tend to turn back to the Auténtico Party, which had given the country its most democratic regime and in the Prío Socarras administration at least, had begun to put into effect measures designed to bring about basic social changes and rapid economic development.

However, the direction that the Castro regime took after October 1959 thwarted the hopes of the Auténticos, which in any case were probably too sanguine. Within a year the Castro regime was converted from a government that permitted a wide degree of opposition and promised elections into a dictatorship with no intention of allowing itself to be ousted from power. As a result the Auténticos and Frente Democrático AAA found that they could no longer function; by the middle of 1960 their organizations had been suppressed, and all of the important leaders had again gone into exile.

The Grau San Martín faction of the Auténticos played absolutely no role in the Castro period. It had been totally discredited by its collaboration with Batista and had virtually ceased to exist after Castro's accession to power. Although Grau himself made a few public statements, little attention was paid to them; and since he no longer represented a force of any consequence in national politics, the former president was allowed to stay in Cuba unmolested even after the Auténticos of other factions had been forced into exile or been jailed. He died in August 1969.

Reason for the Failure of the Auténticos

The advent of the Castro government to power, and its turn in the direction first of a revolutionary dictatorship of unlimited duration and then of a frankly Communist regime, brought the virtual liquidation of the Auténtico Party. With its disappearance there also disappeared Cuba's principal progressive democratic political organization.

The leaders of the Auténtico Party must bear a large share of the responsibility for the demise of political democracy in Cuba. The discrediting of their party dealt a body blow to the concept of the democratic process as a means through which necessary social change and economic development might be achieved.

At the time the Auténticos come to power in 1944, they enjoyed exceedingly wide and enthusiastic support among the Cuban people. Their decade-long fight against dictatorship, the role that the Auténtico leaders had played in the revolution of 1933, and the program and promises of the party all served to arouse a great deal of hope, particularly among the country's underprivileged.

However, the Auténtico governments failed to fulfill the hopes placed in them. There were two basic aspects to this failure. First, the Grau San Martín government did virtually nothing to carry out the basic social and economic program upon which it had been elected. During the first half of the Prío Socarras administration, the same thing was true. The rather energetic policies of Prío during his last two years in office were not enough to counteract the disillusionment that had developed among broad masses of what had been the Auténticos' constituency. Had the party won the scheduled 1952 elections and had a third period in office, with Carlos Hevía as president, it might well have been able to make up much of the ground that had been lost, since Hevía was determined to build upon the beginnings that Prío had made during his last two years in office. However, the Batista coup of March 10, 1952, eliminated this possibility.

Undoubtedly another factor contributed to the popular disillusionment with the Auténticos. This was the almost unequaled corruption during the two administrations of the party. The extent of this corruption was indicated when President Grau San Martín was indicated for having stolen $180 million during his four years in office. Interestingly, the incriminating documents upon which this indictment was based disappeared mysteriously from the Ministry of Justice files, and the case was never prosecuted.

Corruption had not been unusual in Cuba, but the great mass of the Auténticos' supporters had hoped for something better from their party. When its leaders seemed to be outdoing their predecessors in raiding the public treasury, nepotism, and misuse of patronage, many rank-and-file Auténticos became convinced that the party's leaders had come to power to build up their own personal fortunes rather than to carry out the program that had brought them their popular support.

The disillusionment of many in the Auténtico Party was confirmed and intensified when President Carlos Prío Socarras did not really fight to remain in office on March 10, 1952. At that moment the party still had enough popular backing to give it a good chance to win the elections scheduled for that June. Students, workers, and a large portion of the military were still willing to fight to keep the Prío government in office, as much because it represented a democratic administration as because it was the regime of the Auténtico Party. But Prío did little or nothing to mobilize this support and use it to suppress the insurrection being mounted by Fulgencio Batista. As a result many of those who had backed the Auténticos until that moment were left with the feeling that if the government was not willing to fight for its own existence, the party had little right to return to power.

This experience of the Auténtico government was capitalized upon by Fidel Castro once he decided to take the road toward a long-term dictatorship. When he asked the rhetorical question "Elections for what?", his rhetoric found a considerable echo in the feelings of large segments of the people that the country's one experiment with a democratic regime that promised fundamental reforms had not worked, and that perhaps some other method to achieve these reforms and to push forward the country's economic development should be tried.

The Ortodoxos

The other major national revolutionary party of Cuba was the Partido Popular Cubano (Ortodoxo), commonly known as the Ortodoxo Party. It was founded in 1947 by dissidents from the Auténtico ranks led by a colorful Auténtico senator, Eduardo (Eddy) Chibás.

Chibás had been one of the first important figures in the Auténtico ranks to become disillusioned with the behavior of the Grau San Martín regime. He used both his position in the Senate and a weekly radio program, widely listened to by people both inside and outside the party, to express this disillusionment. He particularly attacked the corruption and scandals of the Grau administration.

Chibás' position naturally caused friction with most of the other leaders of the Auténtico Party, but his attacks upon the policies and practices of the Grau regime were widely echoed by the party's rank and file. As a result Chibás finally led a movement of his followers out of the Auténtico Party and established a rival group, the Partido Ortodoxo.

The five-point declaration of principles that the Partido del Pueblo Cubano (Ortodoxo) adopted in May 1947 was a succinct statement of the national revolutionary program. It read as follows:

1. To revive the program and doctrine of the Cuban Revolution: Nationalism, socialism, and anti-imperialism, developing our activities within the democratic regime established by the Constitution.
2. To form with that objective a party which is profoundly revolutionary in its functional structure, in that it will bring together the social nuclei interested in national liberation: professionals, peasants, workers, youth and women.
3. To fight without quarter against robbery, graft, subornation, cacique-ism and the other vices of traditional politics. Faced with a politics marked by pacts without ideology, we shall maintain with firmness the unadulterated ideology of the Orthodox Revolution.
4. To guarantee the application of the program and the tactical line of the Party and that its structure will not be merely electoral, it is necessary to adopt forms of organization and leadership which imprint upon it the discipline and militancy indispensable to a revolutionary Party.
5. These bases imply a procedure of popular consultation for the creation of the Party, which cannot be the product of a back room formula, but must be the result of popular assemblies.[4]

NATIONAL REVOLUTIONARY PARTIES

Had Eddy Chibás lived, the history of Cuba might have been very different. There is little doubt that he would have won the election of 1952, had it been held; and it is unlikely that, in the face of Chibás' popularity and his willingness to take drastic action, Fulgencio Batista would have been able to overthrow the Prío government by a military coup.

However, Chibás did not live. Although he was a spellbinder and a man of considerable daring and intelligence, his erratic character often led him to do strange things. The strangest of all was his committing suicide early in 1951 during one of his radio broadcasts.

With Chibás' disappearance from the scene, his party was left without any leader who could equal his popularity. When it came time to nominate a candidate for president in the 1952 election, the choice fell upon Roberto Agramonte, a professor of sociology at the University of Havana and a scholar of considerable ability—but completely lacking in charisma and popular appeal. Nevertheless, even Agramonte stood a very good chance of winning the 1952 election before Fulgencio Batista dashed this chance by his coup d'état.

The Ortodoxos were inclined to feel that Batista's coup was aimed more at them than at the Autenticos, because they were confident of their ability to win a democratic election. As a result they became even more bitter opponents of the second Batista dictatorship than were the Auténticos.

One of the younger leaders of the Ortodoxo Party was Fidel Castro. A fledgling lawyer, he had been a candidate for Congress on the Ortodoxo ticket in the 1952 election. When he began to organize his own group of followers after Batista's seizure of power he found most of his recruits within the Ortodoxo Party.

Castro remained more or less officially an Ortodoxo until 1955 even though his spectacular attempt to seize the Moncada Barracks in Santiago de Cuba on July 26, 1953, did not have the endorsement or cooperation of the officials of the Ortodoxo Party. However, when Castro was released from jail in the middle of 1955 and went to Havana to recruit supporters for the armed invasion and guerrilla war that he was proposing as the only feasible method of overthrowing the dictatorship, he established a rival organization, the 26th of July Movement, which from then on had little organic connection with the Ortodoxo Party, although it drew most of its members from the younger ranks of that group.

Throughout the rest of the Batista regime, the Ortodoxos carried on their struggle against the Batista regime. There were few defections from their ranks by those who sought to collaborate with Batista. However, with the launching of the civil war by Castro and his followers late in 1956, the ranks of the Ortodoxos were decimated. The great majority of the party's followers turned to the 26th of July

Movement. A large proportion of the 26th of July underground network in the trade unions, as well as its support in the general population, consisted of people who had been Ortodoxos before 1952.

The upshot of this was that although in the first months of the Castro regime the Ortodoxo Party once again began to function legally, it had only a shadow of its former strength. It had no influence in the reconstituted labor movement, and it had few financial resources and exceedingly limited personnel to undertake the job of reestablishing the grass roots party organizations. Although Roberto Agramonte served for some months as the minister of foreign affairs in the Castro regime, he was there as a distinguished opponent of the Batista dictatorship rather than as a representative of the Ortodoxo Party. With the definite establishment of a dictatorship by Castro at the end of 1959, the Ortodoxo Party disappeared.

THE DOMINICAN REPUBLIC

Origins of the Partido Revolucionario Dominicano

The Partido Revolucionario Dominicano had its origins in the struggle against the 31-year dictatorship of Rafael Leónidas Trujillo. The founder of the party, Juan Bosch, was one of the early exiles of this regime, leaving the country in 1935. Soon thereafter he took the lead in organizing the PRD, which remained for almost a generation the most important group of émigré Dominicans carrying on the struggle against what was certainly in its time the most ferocious dictatorship in Latin America.

Particularly after World War II the Partido Revolucionario Dominicano was able to spread its organization to virtually all places where there was any considerable nucleus of Dominican exiles. It established active groups in New York City and Miami; in San José, Costa Rica; in Mexico City; in San Juan, Puerto Rico; in Havana, Cuba; and in Caracas, Venezuela.

The PRD established close relations with the other national revolutionary parties. During the Auténtico regimes in Cuba, Juan Bosch held a minor post in the government, while his party's secretary-general, Angel Miolán, worked in the Confederación de Trabajadores de Cuba. After the establishment of the Batista dictatorship in 1952, many of the PRD exiles went to Costa Rica and Puerto Rico, where they received considerable help and encouragement from the Partido Liberación Nacional and the Partido Popular Democrático, respectively. After the collapse of the Pérez Jiménez dictatorship in Venezuela, Juan Bosch and other PRD leaders went to Caracas, where they were given considerable aid by Acción Democrática.

NATIONAL REVOLUTIONARY PARTIES

The PRD also had close relations with the Inter-American democratic labor movement. The Organización Regional Interamericana de Trabajadores (ORIT) helped with the establishment of a Dominican trade union center in exile, headed by Angel Miolán; and these Dominican workers played an important role in a conference of exiled trade unionists that met in Mexico City under ORIT auspices in May 1954.

The PRD also established friendly relations with the Inter-American Association for Democracy and Freedom, the Inter-American organization of national revolutionary, Socialist, and Christian Democratic and other Democratic Left politicians, on the one hand, and of liberal politicians and elements of the liberal intellectual community in the United States, on the other. The New York branch of the PRD cooperated particularly closely with the IADF, which had its headquarters in that city.

The PRD After Trujillo's Death

Generalissimo Trujillo was assassinated in May 1961. Even before this event the PRD had been conducting radio programs from Puerto Rico that were easily picked up in much of the Dominican Republic, and the Partido Revolucionario Dominicano was by no means unknown in the land from which its members had come.

Nonetheless, the actual organization of the party on Dominican soil in the weeks and months following the death of Trujillo was an exceedingly difficult and dangerous undertaking. To launch it three of the party's leaders—Angel Miolán, Nicolás Silfa, and Ramón Castillo—returned to the Dominican Republic, on the invitation of President Joaquín Balaguer, a few weeks after the dictators' demise.

The three PRD delegates were assured by Balaguer that they would be free to organize their party in the Dominican Republic. They also had an interview with General Rafael Trujillo, Jr., who was in command of the country's armed forces after his father's death and who gave them similar assurances. However, neither Balaguer nor Trujillo had complete control over the situation in the republic; and the PRD leaders were under constant threat of being injured or murdered by subordinate agents of the regime or by the late dictator's brothers, who were still very powerful and anxious to prevent the undermining of the dictatorship.

Furthermore, it was very difficult to establish a party de novo in a country in which for more than three decades only one man had really been able to play politics. Although some people had heard of the PRD through its radio programs from Puerto Rico, no one had had direct personal contact with its leaders, and the possibility for the PRD to get publicity through the press or other general means of communication was very limited.

The three PRD leaders, plus others who returned in subsequent weeks, traveled widely throughout the Dominican Republic, attempting to establish a rank-and-file base for their party. In each town they talked with local people in restaurants and bars, attempting to determine who among the more distinguished local citizens had the reputation of being honest and socially conscious. They then approached such people and suggested the possibility of their helping to organize a local unit of the PRD. Where they were able to recruit such local leaders, the PRD was able to begin to build a municipal party unit.

During these early months of the post-Trujillo period, the Partido Revolucionario Dominicano sought to avoid open denunciation of President Balaguer, or even of Rafael Trujillo, Jr. (popularly known as Ramfis), being convinced of the sincerity of Balaguer's desire to pave the way for a democratic regime and of his need for the services of Ramfis in order to eliminate the private armed forces of the latter's uncles, who were resisting all moves toward change. In this they differed strongly from the other two major parties that appeared in this period, the conservative-oriented Unión Cívica Nacional and the more left-wing 14th of June Movement.

Juan Bosch did not return to the island until November 1961, after the attempt by Trujillo's brothers to overthrow President Balaguer had been thwarted and all members of the Trujillo family had been exiled. He immediately began a series of radio and television programs, which were of major importance in building up the popular support for the Partido Revolucionario Dominicano.

Bosch had an extraordinary appeal for the common people of the Dominican Republic. For one thing, his appearance on television was striking. With a shock of white hair, a lined face, and a professional if not fatherly aspect, Bosch instilled confidence in his listeners. He spoke to them in very straightforward terms and had a unique capacity for making simple very complicated problems of economics and sociology. He presented a glowing picture of the possibilities for the development of a prosperous economy and a society marked by social justice. He stressed that after three decades of tyranny, it was the responsibility of the Dominican people themselves to bring about this future.

Upon his return Bosch also entered into direct contact with the people of his country, from whom he had been separated for a quarter of a century. He traveled widely throughout the nation, speaking at meetings organized by the PRD and meeting privately with local party leaders and rank-and-filers. When he was in Santo Domingo, he spent much of his time listening to the ideas, hopes, complaints, and aspirations of PRD members and sympathizers.

NATIONAL REVOLUTIONARY PARTIES

Meanwhile, some of Bosch's colleagues in the PRD, and particularly Angel Miolán, the party's secretary-general, worked hard to capitalize on Bosch's new-found popularity. They established local party units throughout the country and sought to impart to the new party members the philosophy and program of the PRD.

The PRD paid particular attention to the peasantry, who made up the great majority of the population. During the latter months of 1962 the party mounted a large campaign in the rural areas to establish a peasants' federation and were successful in organizing units of this group in most parts of the country. Although not formally an affiliate of the PRD, this federation was of great importance in generating sympathy for the party in the rural areas.

The PRD in Power

Elections to reestablish a constitutional government were finally held at the end of 1962. There were two principal candidates for president in these elections. One was Viriato Fiallo, nominee of the Unión Cívica Nacional which controlled the government during most of 1962; the other was Juan Bosch for the PRD.

The 1962 election gave an overwhelming victory to Juan Bosch and the Partido Revolucionario Dominicano. The PRD candidate received 628,495 votes; Fiallo, only 315,873. The PRD also won 25 of the 27 members of the Senate and 52 of the 74 members of the Chamber of Deputies, as well as control of most of the municipalities of the country.[5]

Juan Bosch was inaugurated as constitutional president of the Dominican Republic on February 27, 1963. The swearing-in ceremony was attended by U.S. Vice-President Lyndon Johnson; Presidents Rómulo Betancourt of Venezuela, Francisco Orlich of Costa Rica, and Ramón Villeda Morales of Honduras; Costa Rican ex-President José Figueres; Puerto Rican Governor Luís Muñoz Marín and Jamaican Prime Minister William Alexander Bustamante.[6] The seven months that he remained in office were marked by feverish activity and extensive accomplishment.

The PRD had several objectives toward which they adapted government policy. The first was to establish a solid basis for political democracy. The second was to get under way an extensive program of economic development. The third was to bring about extensive social reforms that had been neglected thus far.

The PRD leaders realized that after 31 years of the Trujillo dictatorship the country was virtually bereft of leaders, particularly on the local and community level, and of organizations through which leaders could arise. Therefore the Bosch government had as one of its principal programs the training of local leaders and the building of various kinds of community organizations. Classes were organized throughout the republic for training leaders of peasant unions, cooperatives, and other kinds of groups, particularly among the lower classes. At the same time the government encouraged the establishment of these organizations.

Another aspect of the work of trying to establish a firm basis for democracy was the Bosch government's practice of democracy. Virtually all political groups were permitted to function; the press was free to criticize—and did with vigor and often with acrimony—and the radio and television networks had the same liberty. It was Bosch's purpose to give the Dominican people actual experience with democracy; and although his opponents charged him with "sowing chaos" and with being "pro-Communist" (because the Communists had the same freedom as other groups, so long as they operated within democratic bounds), these accusations were based principally on the lack of experience of both Dominican leaders and rank and file with political freedom, controversy, and democratic procedures.

Such charges of pro-Communist sympathies on the part of Bosch at that time were patiently absurd. He felt that the Communists out in the open, with freedom to operate, could be much better watched than if they were once again driven underground. Furthermore, he felt that political democracy meant that all should be free to express themselves and organize, so long as they did so within the general rules of democratic procedure.

Actually the Communists were considerably weakened during Bosch's tenure in office. Their control of the Federation of Government Employees was broken when the Bosch administration successfully resisted a largely politically motivated strike by government employees. In addition Bosch reduced to impotence the National Planning Institute, which had been set by his Union Cívica predecessors, who allowed it to be largely staffed by Communists and their sympathizers; he did so by establishing a new planning unit to which he passed most of the old institute's functions.

The PRD government was also very anxious to get the process of economic development started once again. During the year before the election, Bosch and his advisers had worked out a general plan for augmenting and diversifying agriculture, expanding the mining industry, developing tourist facilities and stimulating other parts of the economy. Once in power Bosch established a planning organization to draw up detailed programs in each of these fields and set about trying to mobilize foreign aid and investment for a number of the projects for which more or less detailed plans already existed. He traveled to Europe to interest investors and lenders there in the Dominican Republic; he also received extensive aid from the

Kennedy administration in the United States. However, the Bosch government did not last long enough to get more than a handful of the economic development plans actually started.

Social problems were a pressing item on the agenda of the Bosch government. Of major importance was an agrarian reform law that would make possible the settlement of many landless peasants on land of their own and—it was hoped—would slow the massive drift of the rural population to Santo Domingo and other cities, where there was little employment for them and living conditions were alarming. Such a law was sent to Congress in July 1963, providing for the parceling out of the Trujillo estates to the peasants. It was being debated at the time the Bosch government fell.

Other social issues were also dealt with by the administration. The education system was expanded, a program for building new schools and for training many new teachers was gotten under way, and education was given the largest single budget allotment. As a stopgap measure against unemployment, extensive public works projects were launched.

However, although this program of the Bosch government enjoyed wide popularity among the people, particularly among the peasants and urban workers, it aroused fear and suspicion among many upper-class Dominicans and among the officers of the armed forces. Upper-class people were fearful of the agrarian reform. Both upper-class civilians and military leaders were appalled at the controversy and discussion that arose in the democratic atmosphere of the Bosch regime. The military chiefs were, for the most part, people from the Trujillo armed forces who would in all likelihood have been suspicious of any civilian government that tried to practice democracy; they were particularly antagonistic toward a Left democratic regime of the type of the PRD administration.

Bosch's handling of the military was one of the major political errors he made during his short administration. On the one hand, when he had a chance to carry out a thorough purge of the armed forces, he refused to do so; later, when this chance had passed, he engaged in open polemics with some of the military leaders.

During the week of his inauguration, the principal military chiefs were expecting to be removed from their posts or, at the very least, to be sent as military attachés to distant posts. They were not then in a position to resist any such move, in view of the presence of so many distinguished foreign guests in Santo Domingo. Bosch had a unique opportunity to remove virtually all of the high military leadership left from the Trujillo era.

However, he chose not to do this. Rather, he publicly embraced a number of the top military chiefs and asked them to stay at their posts. However, some months later, when audible grumbling began to be heard in the military ranks, the president publicly denounced those in the military leadership who were making their dissatisfaction known. He thus committed the double error of allowing almost certain enemies to stay in key places of power when he did not have to do so and then, having agreed to try to work with them, publicly quarreled with them, undoubtedly intensifying whatever hostility they had felt for him and his regime.

Another major political error was Bosch's apparent failure to recognize the key importance of his own party to his attempt to establish a firm democracy. At one point, a few weeks after taking office, he is reported to have called together the leaders of the party to announce his desire that the party be abolished, on the grounds that Trujillo had had a government party, which had come to be thoroughly hated by the people, and that he had no intention of the same thing's occurring to the PRD.

Although the other PRD leaders convinced Bosch that the party should not be abolished, his mere suggestion of its dissolution demonstrated his lack of understanding of the key importance of a strong civilian party to democracy, particularly in as unstable a political atmosphere as that of the post-Trujillo Dominican Republic. Particularly in the face of possible military subversion, he needed a powerful instrument such as the PRD to rally support quickly for the regime should it be menaced. However, once in power, he did not attribute sufficient importance to the party.

The PRD Since 1963

The Dominican Republic's short experiment with progressive political democracy under the leadership of the Partido Revolucionario Dominicano came to a sudden end on September 25, 1963. On that day the armed forces overthrew the Bosch government and imposed a government by triumvirate. Although the personnel of this dictatorial regime changed several times, its major figure was Donald Reid Cabral, who had been one of the important members of the provisional administration in power before Bosch was inaugurated. However, despite the civilian leadership of Reid Cabral, the government of the triumvirate was in fact a military dictatorship.

During the 19 months the triumvirate remained in power, the Partido Revolucionario Dominicano constituted the strongest opposition to the regime. Many of its most outstanding leaders were in exile, particularly in Puerto Rico. During this period there took place within the party's ranks a violent controversy over how the PRD should conduct this opposition. Many of the party leaders urged that the party agree to participate in new elections if it received adequate guarantees of the honesty of the poll and of the ability of the winner to take power.

However, Juan Bosch strongly opposed this position. He argued that there was no further hope for political democracy in the Dominican Republic and was reported to have argued privately that "the Dominican Republic must pass through a river of blood to save itself." As a result of Bosch's very strong hold on the loyalty of the PRD rank and file, the party steadfastly refused to accept the idea of participating in new elections and continued to demand that Bosch be returned to power and be allowed to finish out his term.

Meanwhile, the Partido Revolucionario Dominicano, although still legal, suffered considerable persecution within the Dominican Republic. Its national headquarters remained open, and routine activities were conducted from it. However, in the interior of the republic, the headquarters of many of its smaller units were closed and its ranks-and-file members were jailed, beaten, and even killed.

With the return to power through elections closed, in part at least through its own decision, the PRD entered into conspiracy with elements of the armed forces who were opposed to the triumvirate. The result of this conspiracy was the uprising that started on April 24, 1965. Led by Colonel Francisco Alberto Caamaño, it proclaimed its intention of restoring the PRD government to power. Pending the return of Juan Bosch to reassume the presidency, it named his constitutional successor, José Rafael Molina Ureña, president of the Chamber of Deputies, to serve.

The rebels were victorious in the first few days of fighting against the bulk of the armed forces. The members of the triumvirate resigned and went into hiding. Santo Domingo was virtually in the hands of the Caamaño forces when the U.S. government sent in Marines, for the ostensible purpose of "rescuing trapped Americans and other foreigners." However, when all foreigners who wanted to leave had been evacuated, the U.S. troops remained, in a full-scale military intervention, which, it became clear, was designed basically to prevent the victory of the rebels. The U.S. government used as its excuse for this action that Communists were on the verge of taking over the rebel regime, which had proclaimed itself the constitutionalist government. When Molina Ureña refused to continue leading the Constitutionalist forces, Colonel Caamaño was proclaimed provisional president.

The U.S. invasion of the Dominican Republic was "legalized" a few days after it occurred by the formal establishment of an "inter-American force" to which Brazil, Costa Rica, Nicaragua, and Honduras contributed troops. A Brazilian general, Hugo Panasco Alvim, became the official commander, with U.S. Lieutenant-General Bruce Palmer serving as his deputy. The bulk of the troops in the inter-American force continued to be contributed by the United States until the force was entirely withdrawn a year and a half later.

A virtual state of war continued between the inter-American Force (and Dominican troops that had supported the triumvirate government) and the Caamaño forces until August 1965. At that time an agreement was worked out by which Hector García Godoy, who had been minister of foreign affairs in the Bosch government, became provisional president. It was also agreed that elements of the Constitutionalist armed forces would be reincorporated into the Dominican military, and the principal military leaders of both sides would go abroad as military attachés or in other diplomatic posts.[7]

All of the provisions of this agreement were not carried out, particularly the provision for the reincorporation of Constitutionalist military into the regular armed forces. However, the García Godoy regime was able to reestablish some semblance of order and had at least the grudging support of those who had participated in both sides of the 1965 civil war.

The main task of the García Godoy regime was to preside over new elections. There were two candidates in this contest. One of these was Joaquín Balaguer, who had been president at the time of Trujillo's death, had carefully dismantled much of the Trujillo dictatorship, and then had gone into exile when he was overthrown by a military coup early in 1962. He had returned to the island in the middle of the civil war. After the end of the conflict he organized a party of his own, the Partido Reformista.

The Partido Revolucionario Dominicano named Juan Bosch once again. However, during the months of the García Godoy regime the PRD experienced considerable disaffection on the leadership level. Many of those who during the triumvirate period had opposed Bosch's refusal to allow the PRD to participate in new elections, led by party secretary-general Angel Miolán broke entirely with Bosch's leadership. During the 1966 election they sought, without success, to establish a third candidacy against both Balaguer and Bosch.

The election campaign was marked by considerable violence. Fearful of this violence, Juan Bosch virtually did not leave his home in Santo Domingo, limiting his campaign to radio broadcasts. On the other hand, Balaguer, upon whose life several attempts were made, traveled throughout the country.

Because of the threats of violence and foul play during the election, two separate groups went to the Dominican Republic to oversee the poll. One of these was named by the Organization of American States and consisted of observers from several countries. The other was dispatched to the Dominican Republic by an ad hoc inter-American committee, headed by Norman Thomas, the veteran

U. S. Socialist leader. It was composed of people from several countries, many of them students and all of them sympathetic to Bosch's candidacy.

Members of both observer groups agreed unanimously that the elections were, with very minor exceptions, held under honest conditions and that the victor in the poll was Joaquín Balaguer, by a substantial majority. Even Bosch himself admitted that although there was some fraud, it was not sufficiently great to change the results of the election.

During the Balaguer administration, which took office on July 1, 1966, the Partido Revolucionario Dominicano again constituted the largest element in the opposition. Although the PRD proclaimed its determination not to resort to force to overthrow Balaguer, it complained bitterly that his administration was doing little to prevent the campaign of terror being waged by right-wing extremists against not only the PRD but also many other elements that had been associated with the Caamaño side in the 1965 civil war—and even against groups and individuals who had not sided with Caamaño.

The exact origin of this terror, which resulted in the assassination of hundreds of people during the Balaguer regime, was unclear. At least some of the participants wished to take revenge for the end of the Trujillo regime and the death of its dictator. This was indicated by the fact that Antonio Imbert, one of the two surviving assassins of Trujillo and one of the leaders of the "government" set up by invading forces to oppose the Caamaño Constitutionalists in 1965, was one of the victims being severely wounded.

When municipal elections were held early in 1968, the Partido Revolucionario Dominicano boycotted them, on the ground that the democratic process had broke down in the Dominican Republic. The numerous individual leaders of the party who broke away on this issue, and ran as independents in the election, fared universally badly.

Meanwhile, Juan Bosch, who went to live in Spain soon after his defeat in the 1966 campaign, seemed to have given up all faith in political democracy. He argued that what Latin America needed was a "popular dictatorship," since the forces of reaction, the military, and the United States would no longer permit the establishment of democratic regimes with programs of basic economic and social reform.

There was undoubtedly considerable opposition to the Bosch position within the PRD in the Dominican Republic. However, at a meeting with Bosch in Benidorm, Spain, party leaders agreed to accept his point of view. They elaborated with him the so-called Benidorm Declaration. The Socialist International's periodical Socialist International Information, in its March 1, 1969, issue sums up the Declaration thus:

The Declaration defines the PRD, as a party representing a majority of the Dominican people including the workers, peasants, the lower middle classes, the professional classes, and the young. It declares that the PRD will fight to liberate the Dominican Republic from its economic, social and political dependency on the U.S. Pentagon, and to establish a social order corresponding to the true interests of the Dominican people.

It goes on to state that national and local elections would not guarantee the achievement of national independence, although the PRD did not renounce participation under certain conditions in such elections.

Socialist International Information goes on to note: "The Benidorm meeting also requested Juan Bosch to edit his Thesis of Dictatorship with Popular Support, so that it could be presented to the masses of the Party." Subsequently the PRD National Council announced in April 1969 that it would not participate in any further elections and made the Benidorm Declaration part of the party's basic statement of principles.[8]

President Balaguer was reelected in 1970, in an election participated in by a number of smaller parties but not by the PRD, which urged its members to boycott the poll. The Partido Revolucionario Dominicano continued to be the largest opposition party and, despite the Benidorm Declaration, did not make any attempt to seize power by force.

Strengths and Weaknesses of the PRD

The Partido Revolucionario Dominicano was certainly the major popular political party to appear in the Dominican Republic following the death of Rafael Trujillo. Its rapid growth in that period was due both to the personal popularity of its outstanding leader, Juan Bosch, and to the organizing ability of other leaders, such as Angel Miolán. Furthermore, its program for basic social changes, rapid economic development, and political democracy were highly relevant to the needs of the country in the post-Trujillo period.

The PRD failed to maintain power largely as a result of the lack of political experience of the major leaders, particularly Juan Bosch. Faced with strong opposition from conservative elements who feared reform, as well as remnants of the Trujillo dictatorship backed by major leaders of the armed forces, the PRD administration did not know how to use the widespread popular support and the civilian organization of the PRD to curb the reactionary groups anxious to prevent basic change in the country's economic, social, and political life.

Unlike other national revolutionary parties, the PRD gave evidence, after the failure to win the 1966 election, of a tendency to abandon the national revolutionary ideology. However, despite the influence of the inmate pessimism of Juan Bosch, and his adoption of a kind of Jacobin leftist position, it is by no means clear as this is being written that the Partido Revolutionary Dominicano will definitively abandon its traditional support for political democracy in favor of "popular dictatorship."

GUATEMALA

In the years since World War II, Guatemala has seen the rise of several parties of national revolutionary orientation and the fall of all but one of them. These parties have played a major role in the so far abortive revolutionary process that began in 1944 with the overthrow of the dictatorship of General Jorge Ubico.

After the fall of Ubico, three new political parties of some importance made their appearance: the Frente Popular Libertador, the Partido Acción Revolucionaria, and the Partido Renovación Nacional. All of these were of more or less national revolutionary orientation, although Communist elements were active in the first two, particularly in the Partido Acción Revolucionaria. They sought to have the new Guatemalan revolution carry out a program of agrarian reform, labor and social legislation, economic nationalism and development, and political democracy. The differences among them were principally matters of emphasis and of leadership rivalry.

Soon after the inauguration of President Juan José Arévalo, and upon his urging, these three parties, all of which supported his government, merged under the name Partido Acción Revolucionaria, which for about two years was the government party. The national revolutionary orientation of the PAR was demonstrated in its "Declaration of Principles and Fundamental Bases of Political Program," adopted by its national convention on November 16, 1946. In its first point this document stressed the desire to seek an indigenous Guatemalan road to social and economic change. Point One read: "Social reality is the result of a historical process, conditioned by the relations of men to economic phenomena and by the coexistence of spiritual values which orient and give rational sense to life. These relations engender conflicts among social groups which participate in production, which determines human progress. The Partido Acción Revolucionaria recognizes these facts; but given our evolution and the state of our economy, it believes that conflicts can be resolved without appeal to violence and that our revolutionary line should be oriented principally in accordance with our realities."

Point Three of this document asserted: "The Revolution does not consist only of obtaining electoral triumphs; it must culminate in the necessary transformation of our economic, spiritual, political and social structure." Point 8 went on to stress the party's adherence to democratic processes in obtaining these changes: "The completion of the constitutional period of the presidency and the principle of no reelection, as essential civic conquests of Guatemala must be carried out through the free exercise of suffrage and through the right of rebellion only in the case of attempts to continue in office after the legal term."

The PAR document called for a "democratic agrarian reform through collectivization of nationally owned land, the suppression of latifundia, the increase of arable land and the increase of agricultural credit to small proprietors in an individual and collective form." It also strongly supported the right of the workers to organize and called for extensive labor legislation and social security.[9] There remained certain differences among the leadership of the united PAR, and there was particular concern by some over the growing influence of the Communists in the united party. As a result a split took place early in 1948, with the reformation of the FPL, the PAR, and PRN as three separate entities. There was little to distinguish them formally, in terms of their stated programs and objectives, from one another. However, throughout the next few years the Frente Popular Libertador remained the principal party of those who supported the revolution but opposed the influence of the Communists in the revolutionary process. Renovación Nacional was generally identified as the party that had as its principal distinguishing characteristic personal loyalty to Arévalo.

A further split in the Partido Acción Revolucionaria took place in 1950, when most of the avowedly Communists elements withdrew from the party to form an open Communist Party. In the next year one of the major figures in the Frente Popular Libertador, Augusto Charnaud Macdonald, withdrew from that party and established still another national revolutionary-oriented group, the Partido Socialista de Guatemala. For a time it promised to be able to draw within its ranks all of the revolutionaries opposed to the growing influence of the Communists in the government and in the general revolutionary movement. However, with the inauguration of President Jacobo Arbenz early in 1951, the new chief executive was as anxious as his predecessor to have the forces supporting his government organized into a single political party. He may also have been influenced on this issue by the fear of his Communist advisers (including the secretary-general of the Communist Party, José Manuel Fortuny), upon whose word he put great weight, of the dangers to them represented by the Partido Socialista.

NATIONAL REVOLUTIONARY PARTIES

In any case Arbenz' pressure was largely responsible for the formation in June 1952 of the Partido de la Revolución Guatemalteco through the merger of the PAR, FPL, Partido Socialista, and Renovación Nacional. The Communists were not formally part of this group, which some of their leaders hoped could be the rallying point for those who wanted to take the revolution down an indigenous path of social change and economic development.

However, the united PRG was no more successful than the united PAR had been. Due both to personal rivalries among leaders and to influence of Communist fellow travelers or actual members who held high positions in the new party, it split up again within a few weeks. Dissidents withdrew to reform the PAR. Renovación Nacional was soon re-created. Thereafter, until the fall of the Arbenz regime, the government was formally supported by the PRG, PAR, Renovación Nacional, and the Communists, who had changed their name to Partido Guatemalteco del Trabajo. They organized the Frente Democrático Electoral, which during the last year of the Arbenz regime came under the increasingly close control of the Communists. All of these parties were suppressed when the Arbenz administration fell.

The failure of the national revolutionaries to create an effective indigenous party of the Guatemalan revolution had several causes. One was the political inexperience of most of those who were suddenly catapulted onto the political scene in 1944, many of them still university students. Another was the failure of Present Arévalo to use his extensive influence to force a clear differentiation between the real national revolutionary elements and the Communists and his failure to force the organization of the former into an effective party. Third was the open alliance of President Arbenz with the Communists, which effectively undermined efforts made during his term to establish a national revolutionary party, and finally gave the Communists more power than any other organized political group within his administration.[10]

Three years after the overthrow of President Jacobo Arbenz in June 1954, a new attempt was made to establish a national revolutionary party in Guatemala. The leadership in this move was taken by Mario Méndez Montenegro, who had taken an active part in the revolution of 1944 and had elected mayor of Guatemala City on the ticket of the Frente Popular Libertador. As one allied with Colonel Francisco Arana, Méndez Montenegro was in the opposition during the administration of Arbenz, who was elected after Arana had been assassinated in 1949.

However, Méndez Montenegro took no very active role in politics during the Arbenz regime; and it was not until 1957, three years after Arbenz' ouster, that he resumed activity. At that time he took the lead in trying to bring together non-Communist and anti-Communist elements from among those who had supported the Guatemalan revolution and to organize an opposition to the regime of Colonel Carlos Castillo Armas. Their declared purpose was to establish a party that could initiate a "third phase" of the revolution (after the first and second phases represented by the Arevalo and Arbenz administrations) that had been interrupted by Castillo Armas' overthrow of Arbenz.

The elements under Méndez Montenegro's leadership established the Partido Revolucionario. It had one of its first victories in July 1959, when its candidate, L. F. Galich, was elected mayor of Guatemala City. This victory served to establish it as a major contender for power against the anti-revolutionary elements that had taken over the country after the Arbenz regime.

The initial success of the Partido Revolucionario tended to attract elements that were not necessarily sympathetic to its democratic Left position. A number of more extreme leftists joined the party. Over the years most of these elements were expelled and formed small rival groups, including the Partido Revolucionario Auténtico and the Partido de Unidad Revolucionaria. Probably the most important group to be expelled was the Unión Revolucionaria Democrática, headed by Francisco Villagran Kramer, who announced his candidacy for presidency in the aborted election of 1963.[11] The URD did not differ fundamentally in ideology from the Partido Revolucionario, and the split between the two groups seems to have been more a matter of rivalry for leadership than of philosophical differences.

The Partido Revolucionario maintained close contacts with other national revolutionary parties. It was a cosponsor of the Instituto de Orientación Política, which these parties maintained in Costa Rica, and sent a number of younger leaders for training there.

During the early 1960s the Partido Revolucionario was able to extend its organization throughout most of the country. It gained considerable support in the rural areas as the result of its many struggles on behalf of small landowners and tenants being mistreated by large landlords.

The structure of party organization reflected the PR's concept that it was a multiclass party. Within it were specialized groups particularly concerned with workers, peasants, and middle-class elements; and these groups were represented on the party's national directorate.

In 1963 the Partido Revolucionario was preparing to contest the presidential elections scheduled for the end of the administration of Manuel Ydígoras Fuentes. It had named Mario Méndez Montenegro as its candidate and had begun an energetic campaign. However, the election was suspended when the military, apparently fearing the possibility that the victor in the scheduled election might be ex-President Juan José Arevalo, made a coup d'état and suspended the election. For three years thereafter the country had a military dictatorship.

Elections for a new president were not held until 1966. At that time the PR again named Mario Méndez Montenegro as its candidate, but he died only a few weeks before the election. The party leadership then chose his brother, Julio César Méndez Montenegro, to be the Partido Revolucionario nominee. He was a lawyer who had been active in the early years of the 1944 revolution and had been one of the founding members of the Partido Revolucionario, but he had not taken a particularly active role in the party's affairs.

The Partido Revolucionario won the election of 1966 on a platform promising "the third government of the revolution." Julio César Méndez Montenegro was inaugurated as president on July 1, 1966. The first months of his regime were marked by considerable accomplishment, perhaps most notable being the virtual liquidation of the rural guerrilla movement that extreme leftist elements had been carrying on in northeastern Guatemala. This movement, which had drawn much of its support from the university students, was dealt a severe blow by the 1966 presidential election campaign, which tended to draw many of those young men and women who had previously supported the guerrillas.

The Méndez Montenegro government launched a strong campaign against the guerrillas in October 1966. It sent sizable contingents of troops into the region involved and combined military action with a campaign to deal with the problems that had given the guerrillas considerable support. Some large landholdings in the area were given to peasants, and cloudy titles of some small farmers were legally confirmed. A sizable program of building schools, small clinics, and rural housing was undertaken. As a result the Méndez Montenegro regime was able to do in a few months what the military dictatorship of Colonel Enrique Peralta had not been able to do in three years, in terms of wiping out the principal focus of rural insurrection.[12]

However, the side effects of this victory over the rural guerrillas were not so satisfactory. Many of them transferred their activities to Guatemala City and other urban centers, where terrorist attacks on police, politicians, and others by extreme leftists became common. This was answered by even more severe terror from extreme rightist groups, which not only assassinated Left extremists in cold blood but also murdered leaders of the Partido Revolucionario, including members of Congress, and threatened PR trade unionists and lower-ranking political leaders with the same fate.

This terrorism from both extreme Left and extreme Right was one of the major problems that persisted throughout the Méndez Montenegro administration. Even more serious was the blocking of the Partido Revolucionario government's efforts to push a reform program that would start again the revolutionary process that had been suspended in 1954. Particularly bitter struggles between the government and the country's entrenched economic interests took place over the issue of tax reform, designed to make the well-to-do bear more of the costs of government. At least twice the Méndez Montenegro government was forced to back down from quite modest tax proposals by threats to overthrow the regime. Although some progress was made in settling landless peasants on land, and in extending technical and financial assistance to them, and some progress also in public housing, education, and other fields, the Partido Revolucionario government was not successful in launching a really extensive program for reforming the country's archaic economic and social structure. In their blind opposition to change, vested interests showed themselves to be among the blindest and most reactionary ruling groups in all of Latin America.[13]

The upshot was the defeat of the Partido Revolucionario in the 1970 presidential election. The PR nominee, Mario Fuentes Pieruccini, was narrowly defeated by Colonel Carlos Arana Osorio, candidate of the right-wing Partido Liberación Nacional.

HAITI

The Mouvement Ouvrier Paysan was organized in the wake of the democratic revolution in Haiti in January 1946. This uprising upset the dictatorship of President Elie Lescot and, after a short period of provisional government, resulted in the establishment of the administration of President Dumarsais Estimé, who presided over virtually the only democratic government that Haiti has ever had.

During the Estimé administration several political parties were established. These included the (Christian Democratic) Parti Social Chrétien and the Parti Socialiste Populaire, the country's first legal Communist party.

Among these new parties was the Mouvement Ouvrier Paysan. Its major Founder was Daniel Fignolé. He was a teacher who served for a short while as minister of education in the Estimé government, but after a serious disagreement with the president he withdrew from the government and took the lead in organizing the Mouvement Ouvrier Paysan.

NATIONAL REVOLUTIONARY PARTIES

The MOP was closely associated with one branch of the labor movement, the Union Nationale des Travailleurs Haïtiens. This group, which was one of several central labor groups established during the Estimé administration, had particular influence among the country's sugar workers, most of whom were organized in its ranks, and also had a number of small unions among industrial, commercial, and handicraft workers in Port-au-Prince and other cities. Fignolé was both president of the Union Nationale des Travailleurs Haïtiens and head of the MOP.

During most of the Estimé administration, the Mouvement Ouvrier Paysan constituted a major element in the opposition. It supported the wide protest against Estimé's attempt to continue in power when the end of his constitutional administration was approaching, late in 1949.

However, the Mouvement Ouvrier Paysan did not support the military regime that came to power with the overthrow of President Estimé. With the calling of elections that resulted in General Paul Magloire's becoming president, Daniel Fignolé was elected as his party's only member of the Chamber of Deputies. During the Magloire administration, which was a moderate military dictatorship, Fignolé was the only consistent member of the opposition in Congress.

During the Magloire administration Fignolé was a major spokesman in public affairs for the country's lower classes. He urged the extension of the country's meager social legislation and the adoption of an extensive program for economic development, particularly for the diversification of agriculture and especially through the rebuilding of irrigation projects that had existed during colonial times but had disappeared during the first years of independence, early in the 19th century.

During this period the Mouvement Ouvrier Paysan was virtually the country's only legal political party. Both the Parti Social Chrétien and the Parti Socialiste Populaire had been driven underground by the Magloire dictatorship, although Fignolé charged that a number of Communists held high posts in his regime. However, because of his position in the Chamber of Deputies, Fignolé was able to offer some protection and cover to his party. Nonetheless, he lived in constant fear of assassination.

In 1956 President Magloire attempted to continue in power after the expiration of his constitutional period in office. The results were the same as for President Estimé—he was overthrown, after a general strike.

During the six months following the overthrow of Magloire, Haiti experienced frequent changes of government. In one of these changes, Daniel Fignolé was placed in the presidential chair, with the support of the masses of Port-au-Prince and other cities. He stayed in office for only 18 days, during May 1957, after which he was overthrown by the armed forces, which feared his promises for social reform and other changes.

Fignolé was not able to be the MOP's candidate in the presidential election held in September 1957, for he had been exiled to New York on being deposed from the presidency. The only nominee permitted to campaign openly was François Duvalier, who had the support of the military men who really controlled the government. As might have been expected, Duvalier was the victor.

Since 1957 the Mouvement Ouvrier Paysan has maintained an active organization among the numerous Haitian exiles in the United States and other countries. It has published a regular periodical, Construction: Journal haïtien, and has sought to continue an underground organization, for some years being able to do so. However, the ferocious dictatorship that Duvalier established made the existence of any opposition, underground or otherwise, exceedingly difficult.

During the Duvalier period the Mouvement Ouvrier Paysan, which changed its name to Mouvement d'Organisation du Pays, maintained a position of independence with regard to the other elements of the Haitian opposition. It refused to join any united front, either with the supporters of ex-President Magloire, the Communists, or the conservative elements backing Louis Dejoie, one of Fignolé's rivals in the 1957 election. It used the exile period to develop a program for the development of the country, should the future present it with an opportunity to assume power once more.[14]

The MOP of Haiti has maintained only the most tenuous contacts with the other national revolutionary parties. However, its general orientation and program, based on the particular situation and needs of Haiti, make it a member of this particular element in Latin American politics.

PARAGUAY

The Partido Revolucionario Febrerista of Paraguay had its origins in the aftermath of the Chaco War. As in Bolivia, this war seriously undermined the traditional economic, social, and political structure of Paraguay and set new political forces of reform in motion.

A group of young intellectuals became disenchanted with the social, economic, and political system of Paraguay. The land of the country was largely in the hands of large landowners, with a few hundred families holding one third of all of the land. There was no labor legislation and there were few if any legal unions. The

NATIONAL REVOLUTIONARY PARTIES

only road in the country was one from the capital to the airport. Most of the rural workers were kept in semi-servitude.

The professional army was not large enough to provide all of the officers needed in the Chaco War, so many young civilians were drafted. They were in daily contact with the humbler soldiers, of whom some 120,000 are said to have passed through the army during the three years of the war. In the process the young officers became revolutionaries, as did many of the enlisted men.

When the war was over, the civilian officers were mustered out and formed the Asociación Nacional de Ex-Combatientes, a political party. However, fearing this new group, the government changed the electoral law, making it impossible for any groups except the traditional Liberals and Colorados to run candidates. As a result the veterans turned to plotting against the regime. The upshot of this plotting was the revolution of February 17, 1936, led by Colonel Rafael Franco, one of the heroes of the Chaco War.

The new regime carried out a revolutionary program. It established an agrarian reform institute and distributed land to 10,000 families, giving out some 1.2 million hectares. The basis for a complete body of labor legislation was enacted. A total of 77 labor unions were established during the first six months of the regime, and there were 130 functioning by the end of the government's one and a half years. Large landholdings that had been closed to outsiders, and had their own police forces, were opened up. Minimum prices were established for agricultural products, and the Banco Agrario was given a fund to buy commodities if the merchants did not want to buy them at the minimum prices established by the government. Several schools for agricultural foremen were established, as well as two agricultural high schools and an agricultural faculty at the university.

The personnel of the revolutionary government was heterogeneous. It included a minister of interior who was an open admirer of the Axis and issued a decree that those who were to become the Febreristas were to have brought up against them for years afterward. It called for a year's political truce, forbidding activity during this period by any but progovernment elements. Much worse was the preamble, which based the decree on totalitarian principles then being practiced in Europe.

The Associación de Ex-Combatientes held a nationwide meeting soon after this decree was issued and repudiated it. They asked Franco to dismiss the minister of interior, which he did. The decree was canceled.[15]

The government of President Rafael Franco was overthrown by more conservative army elements in August 1937. Soon thereafter the elements that had united behind the Franco government established what they called the Comité de Organización Revolucionaria. For eight years it constituted an active element in national politics, although its ability to exert much influence was strictly limited by the existence during most of this time of a military dictatorship.[16]

Many of the leading Febreristas, including Colonel Franco, were forced into exile, most of those deported going to Montevideo. It was there, in October 1945, that a convention was held under the presidency of Colonel Franco with delegates from exiled groups as well as from the Comité de Organización Revolucionaria in Asunción, to establish the Concentración Revolucionaria Febrerista.[17]

The Febreristas took a major role in a civil war that broke out in March 1947. The leader of the revolt against the government of President Higinio Morinigo was Colonel Franco, and the revolutionary committee established by the rebels consisted of Febreristas, Liberals, and Communists. The struggle went on until August 1947, when Morinigo finally won, with the support of a sizable part of the armed forces and the Colorado Party.[18]

The Febreristas leaders returned to Montevideo, where they remained during most of the next two decades. However, they continued to lead an underground organization of consequence, which was able to exert some influence in the organized labor movement and among the university students.

In 1952 the Febreristas converted their organization into a formal political party. The constitutional convention of the Partido Revolucionario Febrerista was held at Montevideo in February 1952. This meeting adopted a number of basic party documents, including a declaration of principles. It started with the following statement:

> The Partido Revolucionario Febrerista, constituted as the definitive political instrument of the Revolution of February 17, 1936, is the organization representing the manual and intellectual workers of field and city, and of all those who with their agricultural, artisan, industrial, commercial, grazing or general professional activities are disposed to lend their help for concrete efforts in effective and permanent work toward the liberation of the Paraguayan people.

The declaration then elaborated details of the party's advocacy of political freedom and democracy, and its support for social legislation and unionization of both urban and rural workers. It advocated agrarian reform that would "give the land to those who work it." The declaration "repudiates all kinds of imperialism, economic or political" and stated that "all economic policy of the country must be based on the recognition that the Paraguayan people and state are the

NATIONAL REVOLUTIONARY PARTIES

original and exclusive owners of the basic sources of wealth of the soil and subsoil of the nation."

The general economic policy advocated by the Febreristas was set forth in the following terms:

> The Partido Revolucionario Febrerista supports the application of an economic system which, while respecting and stimulating private initiative, proposes the nationalization or socialization, in certain cases, of public services and the basic wealth of the country, whenever the collective welfare, national liberation or social justice demands it and can bring about a better and more equitable distribution of services and benefits for the people and the elements directly producing such services and wealth.

Other parts of the declaration of principles dealt with health and education, religious freedom, international policy, strengthening of the municipalities, and defense of the Guaraní language.[19] The declaration as a whole clearly placed the Febrerista Party in the ranks of the national revolutionary parties of Latin America.

The Partido Revolucionario Febrerista remained in the opposition. In 1959 it formed an alliance with the Liberals and the two parties signed an "Accord for the Freedom of the Paraguayan People." This document pledged the two opposition parties to work together to overthrow the dictatorship of President Alfredo Stroessner and to bring political democracy and social justice to their country.[20]

With a temporary relaxation in the stringency of the Stroessner dictatorship in 1965, the Febreristas took advantage of the situation. Colonel Franco and other exiled leaders of the party returned, and the party agreed to participate in the municipal elections held in that year. The Febreristas had modest success in these elections, even though there was some doubt as to the honesty of the poll. They succeeded in electing members of a number of municipal councils, as in the city of Pedro Juan Caballero on the Brazilian border.[21]

The Febreristas also took part in the election for a Constituent Assembly held in 1967. They won only six seats, however, and the party's participation in these elections aroused considerable controversy within the party's ranks.[22]

The Febreristas have experienced only one serious split in their ranks. This took place in 1964, when a group of left-wingers challenged the leadership. The rebels were expelled and formed their own Partido Revolucionario Febrerista Auténtico. However, their split did not seriously weaken the party's ranks.

The Febreristas have maintained close contacts with other national revolutionary parties. A former secretary-general of the party was long director of the Escuela Interamericana de Educación Democrática, maintained by the national revolutionary parties in Costa Rica.

For more than a quarter of a century the Febreristas have been one of the country's three major political parties, taking their place alongside the traditional Liberal and Colorado parties. Because the country has been under dictatorships during virtually all of the party's existence, there has been little chance to test the party's support among the public. However, that it has the backing of an appreciable portion of the nation's workers, peasants, and middle class seems certain.

PART IV
THE CHRISTIAN DEMOCRATIC PARTIES

INTRODUCTION

As an important factor in Latin American politics, the Christian Democratic parties are of relatively recent origin. Although the Christian Democratic Party of Uruguay was founded before World War I and the Chilean Christian Democrats were established as an independent party in 1938, the rest of the organizations in this category have been established since World War II—several of them only in the 1960s.

There have been Catholic-oriented parties in Latin America since the earliest years of independence, but these are to be distinguished from the more recent Christian Democratic organizations. These earlier parties, the Conservatives, were defenders of the status quo, particularly of the entrenched rights and privileges of the Roman Catholic Church. The Christian Democrats, in contrast, are advocates of basic social and economic change.

Several factors have influenced the growth the development of the Christian Democratic elements in Latin American politics since World War I. Probably the most important element has been the generally "leftward" movement of the Roman Catholic Church in this period. Social encyclicals and pastoral letters by the popes and members of the hierarchy of many of the Latin American branches of the Church have served to emphasize a radical trend in Catholic thinking that was in conflict with the traditional conservative and even reactionary position of the Church in the area. The various pronouncements of Pope John XXIII were of particular importance in this regard.

The writings of a number of European Catholic theologians and philosophers have also had considerable influence upon Catholic intellectuals in Latin America, from whose ranks many of the Christian Democratic leaders have come. Clerical and lay writers in France and Belgium were of particular importance.

The rise of Christian Democratic parties in Europe in the wake of World War II, particularly those of Italy and Germany, was also of great importance in giving prestige to the concept of Christian democracy in Latin America. This was particularly the case in the years immediately after the War.

The evolution of the Church in Latin America during the latter part of the 19th century and the early decades of the 20th centry undoubtedly also contributed to laying the groundwork for Christian democracy in the area. As a result of the extremely conservative position taken by the Church in many countries in this period, Roman

Catholicism and its institution lost the support of a large part of the urban working class and of many intellectuals and professional people, who came to look upon the Church as the sworn enemy of change and of those classes and groups desiring change. This loss of support undoubtedly served to cause soul-searching among many members of the clergy and among elements of the laity who were strongly attached to the Church. They felt the need for a movement based philosophically on Catholic doctrine that would take the side of the oppressed and aspiring elements.

The rise of Christian democracy in Latin America during the last quarter-century has appeared spectacular to some observers. Particularly after the victory of the Christian Democrats of Chile in the election of 1964, there were some who tended to see in this particular political element "the wave of the future" and to feel that there was likely to be a string of Christian Democratic victories in the other nations of the region within a few years.

This prediction has not come to pass more than half a decade after the victory of Eduardo Frei. It is true that the Christian Democratic party (Partido Social Christiano Copei) of Venezuela did win the presidency of that country in December 1968. However, there remain only a few other countries—perhaps El Salvador, the Dominican Republic, Costa Rica—in which the Christian Democratic parties are a factor of sufficient importance in national politics for one to hazard the educated guess that they might be able to come to power within a relatively short time. Elsewhere, although Christian Democratic parties exist in virtually every Latin American republic, they remain elements of minor importance in national political life.

As a group the Christian Democratic parties have had a number of distinctive characteristics. They have generally not sought to obtain a quick victory before an adequate basis was laid. These parties have carried out intensive grass roots organizational work, paying special attention to training their lower-ranking leadership and rank-and-file members in the Christian Democratic ideology and in the techniques of organization, public speaking, party finances, and similar matters. They have also set up special party groups to carry out propaganda and organizational work among segments of the population in which they have special interest, including the urban labor movement, the peasantry, and various professional groups.

Until recently another characteristic of the Christian Democratic parties in Latin America has been the very small number of important splits that they have experienced. Only in 1969, 31 years after its establishment, did the Chilean Christian Democratic party undergo a major division. Few of the other parties have yet suffered such a scission.

However, this immunity from the factionalism and splits that have characterized most other kinds of Latin American political parties may not continue indefinitely. There certainly are very sharp differences of opinion and ideology among Latin American Catholics, even those on the left wing of the political spectrum. The more extreme elements have given up hope of achieving basic social change and rapid economic development through the democratic process, and for many of them Padre Camilo Torres, the Colombian priest who died as a leader of an extreme leftist guerrilla movement, has become a hero and a symbol.

Some of these extreme leftists are to be found within the Latin American Christian Democratic parties. They may well cause more or less serious division within these organizations in the near future.

CHAPTER

16

THE CHILEAN CHRISTIAN DEMOCRATS

The Chilean Christian Democratic Party was the first of its type to come to power in any of the Latin American countries. Its spectacular victory over the opposition of the Socialist-Communist combination in September 1964 led many observers to feel that the Christian Democrats were certain to emerge as the chief answer to the extreme leftist challenge most dramatically presented by Fidel Castro.

THE FALANGE NACIONAL

The Chilean Christian Democrats had their origins in the youth movement of the Conservative Party in the early 1930s. Eduardo Frei, Manuel Garretón, Radomiro Tomic, Bernardo Leighton, and other young Catholic professional men and students participated in the popular struggle that brought about the downfall of the dictatorship of Carlos Ibáñez in 1931. Soon afterward they were recruited into the Conservative Party, and in 1935 they led in the establishment of its Movimiento Nacional de la Juventud Conservadora. The new group was also referred to as the Falange Nacional Conservadora.

Most of the founding leaders of the Falange Nacional had been students under progressive-minded Jesuit priests, particularly Padre Fernando Vives del Solar and Padre Alberto Hurtado Cruchaga. In the early 1930s a number of them visited Europe, where they made contact with various trends within European Catholicism. These trends included the democratic humanist philosophy of Jacques Maritain, whom Eduardo Frei and others came to know personally, and Catholics associated with the various fascist movements then on the rise in Europe. The philosophy and program of the Falange Nacional was influenced by these apparently conflicting tendencies.

The Falange Nacional was committed to democracy. However, the young leaders of the party were deeply impressed with the poverty, misery, and mistreatment of the workers and peasantry that was still widely prevalent in Chile; and they wanted to use the democratic process to bring about basic economic and social changes. In the late 1930s they thought that the organizational form through which such changes might most easily be brought about was the corporate state. This political form—which provided for representation in legislative bodies on the basis of interest groups rather than geographical areas— had been suggested by a variety of Catholic social thinkers and had been put into practice in a perverted way by several of the Fascist regimes of the 1930s. By the early 1940s the Falange had abandoned any idea of a corporative state.

Meanwhile, the social reform ideas of the Conservative youth group had brought it into conflict with its parent body, the Conservative Party. Open confrontations between the two groups occurred in 1938, on the occasion of the presidential election. The Conservative and Liberal parties supported Gustavo Ross, long-time finance minister of the outgoing president, Arturo Alessandri. However, the Conservative youth were unwilling to support Ross, whose principal concern was with fiscal orthodoxy and protection of the status quo.

The Falange Nacional proclaimed its support for Ross's major opponent, Pedro Aguirre Cerda, a leader of the Radical Party, and candidate of the Popular Front consisting of the Radical, Socialist, Communist, and several minor parties, and the Confederación de Trabajadores de Chile. When they refused to withdraw their endorsement of Aguirre Cerda and the Conservative Party leaders moved to discipline them, the leaders of the Falange Nacional Conservadora dissolved its bonds with that party, dropped "Conservadora" from their name, and launched their group on an independent political career.

Throughout the Aguirre administration the congressmen of Falange Nacional supported the government, although the party did not join the Popular Front. When Aguirre Cerda died in 1942, the Falange joined the Popular Front parties and a faction of the Liberals to support Radical Party leader Juan Antonio Ríos against the candidacy of ex-dictator Carlos Ibáñez. Subsequently the Falange had its first cabinet member, when Eduardo Frei joined the Ríos administration.[1]

By this time the Falange had begun to become active in seeking support in the trade union movement. It succeeded in winning control of one small national union federation, that of the flour millers, and had also begun to have some influence in a number of other union groups, particularly those consisting of white collar workers. It had a small representation in the executive committee of the CTCH.

Early in 1946 the CTCH split, one faction remaining under the leadership of the confederation's secretary-general, Bernardo Ibáñez, who was also a Socialist Party member of the Chamber of Deputies; the other group broke away to establish a rival Confederación de Trabajadores de Chile, led by a Communist deputy, Bernardo Araya. The Falange Nacional trade unionists threw their support behind the Communist-dominated labor faction and had representation on its National Executive Committee.[2]

Meanwhile, another trade union group had been established under Catholic influence, the Acción Sindical Chilena (ASICh). It was set up with the help of Padre Alberto Hurtado Cruchaga and succeeded in organizing a few isolated trade unions. It became the Chilean affiliate of the International Federation of Christian Trade Unions. However, despite its Catholic orientation, ASICh was not closely associated with the Falange Nacional, since most of the trade unionists of that party favored working in the general labor movement rather than establishing a specifically Catholic-oriented trade union group. That issue was to cause dissension within the party for two decades.

In September 1946, when still another presidential election was made necessary by the death of Juan Antonio Ríos, there were four candidates. The Radicals and Communists backed Radical Party leader Gabriel González Videla; the Liberals nominated Senator Fernando Alessandri; the Socialists supported Bernardo Ibáñez; and the Conservatives named Senator Eduardo Cruz Coke, a leader of the more progressive faction in that party and author of several important pieces of social legislation. The Falange Nacional supported Cruz Coke, not because of any rapprochement with the Conservative Party but because of their approval of the senator. However, when the popular vote failed to give victory to any of the four and the election was thrown into Congress, as provided in the constitution, the Falange deputies gave their support to González Videla, who had obtained a plurality.

The Falange did not enter the government of González Videla. When, after having the Communists in his cabinet for five months, the president removed them from his government and ended up in 1948 by demanding the outlawing of the Communist Party, the Falange members of Congress voted against the legislation recommended by González Videla, the so-called law for the Defense of Democracy.

After the election of 1946, relations between Senator Eduardo Cruz Coke and his supporters within the Conservative Party became difficult. The more orthodox leaders of the Conservatives were increasingly opposed to his relatively advanced economic and social ideas. This difference of opinion reached the point of provoking a new split in the Conservative Party in 1949. As a result of this schism Cruz Coke and his followers established the Partido Conservador Social Cristiano, while his opponents organized their forces into the Partido

Conservador Tradicionalista, which continued its alliance with the Liberal Party. In their first test at the polls in 1951 the Conservative groups had approximately equal strength.3

The election of 1952 brought to the fore still a third Christian Democratic tendency in Chile. That election saw a four-way contest. The Partido Conservador Tradicionalista and the Liberals backed Arturo Matte Larraín, a son-in-law of ex-President Arturo Alessandri; one faction of the Socialists (the Partido Socialista de Chile) and the underground Communist Party supported Socialist Senator Salvador Allende; the Radical party named Pedro Alfonso. Running as an independent candidate was ex-President Carlos Ibáñez, who had the support of the second Socialist faction, the Partido Socialista Popular, the new Agrarian Labor Party, and several small parties as well as of people unaffiliated with any party.

On this occasion the Falange Nacional threw its backing behind Radical candidate Pedro Alfonso, and the Partido Conservador Social Cristiano supported Arturo Matte. Among the groups supporting Carlos Ibáñez was a small party called Partido Democratico Cristiano, headed by José Musalém Saffie.

Meanwhile, the Falange had continued to be active in the urban labor movement while Catholic elements of the ASICh were undertaking to organize unions in the rural areas as well. In the early 1950s the trade unionists most closely associated with the Falange Nacional organized the Federación Gremial de Chile as a means of penetrating the general labor movement. It undertook to train youngsters for leadership positions in the unions and to coordinate the activities of the Falange members and their sympathizers with the various labor organizations.

After the election of Carlos Ibáñez in 1952 there was widespread fear among labor unionists of all political tendencies that the ex-dictator would seek either to destroy the labor movement or to reduce it to subservience to his government. There was therefore widespread sentiment in favor of ending the divisions into which the Chilean labor movement had fallen since the split of January 1946, which had given rise to the two CTCh's, one under Socialist, and the other under Communist, domination.

The first step in this direction was taken by the Socialist CTCh and some independent unions that had been affiliated with the International Confederation of Free Trade Unions. They issued a call for a labor unity congress, to include every group except those controlled by the Communists. However, when the Communist-controlled unions insisted on being included in the new merger, the Socialist-led groups agreed, although originally they had been strongly opposed to it.

The result of this unity move was the congress in January 1953, which resulted in the establishment of the Central Unica de Trabajadores de Chile (CUTCh). Trade unionists under the influence of the Falange Nacional participated in this congress. In the contest to choose members of the National Executive Committee of the new organization, the Falange trade unionists joined forces with those of the Partido Socialista de Chile; and although this ticket won one member of the new body, he was a Socialist, and so the Falangistas were left without any representative in the executive of the CUTCh.[4]

Meanwhile, the Acción Sindical Chilena, under the spiritual leadership of Padre Alberto Hurtado Cruchaga, was undertaking the job of organizing rural workers into unions. In the early 1950s their only significant success was in the region around the town of Molina in the province of Talca. There they succeeded in organizing a number of workers in the surrounding vineyards; and when the employers refused to recognize and deal with these organizations, the ASICh organized a spectacular march on Santiago early in 1953, which succeeded in firmly establishing the rural union movement in that small area. However, for some years the movement did not spread much beyond the Molina region.

In the early 1950s another movement was established that was to be of considerable significance for the future of Christian democracy in Chile. Under the leadership of Padre Rafael Larraín and with the support of the archbishop of Santiago, the Instituto de Educación Rural (IER) was established. Its purpose was to train future leaders for the rural labor movement. Although with the exception of the Molina area such a labor movement did not yet exist, it was the belief of Padre Larraín and his associates that sooner or later the rural workers were bound to be organized into unions, as their urban counterparts had been. They felt it was imperative, therefore, that bright young peasants of the Christian persuasion be trained to take the lead in organizing such groups when the opportunity presented itself.[5]

THE BEGINNING OF THE CHRISTIAN DEMOCRATIC PARTY

By the mid-1950s the Falange Nacional began to emerge as a more significant influence in national politics than it had been in the previous 15 years. This was reflected in the trend of election statistics. Until that time it had never received as much as 5 percent of the total valid vote in congressional elections. In 1941 it had received 3.4 percent, but in 1945 it had gotten only 2.6 percent; in 1949 the Falange vote rose to 3.9 percent, but in 1953 the total was only 2.9 percent. However, in 1957 there was a significant increase in the party vote, to 9.4 percent.[6]

Certainly one of the reasons for the growth of the Falange Nacional in the 1950s was its strong opposition to the government of General Carlos Ibáñez. From the beginning its senators and deputies made this opposition clear. Although not joining the extreme left-wing Socialist-Communist coalition, the Falangistas generally joined the congressmen of those parties to vote against the government. For example, a coalition of the Falangistas and extreme Left forced the repeal of the Law for the Defense of Democracy, even though President Ibáñez vetoed the repeal measure.

It was in 1957 that the Falange Nacional joined with two other groups to form the Partido Demócrata Cristiano. By that time the forces that had supported General Carlos Ibáñez in the 1952 election had disintegrated; and among the groups that had broken with the president was the Partido Democrático Cristiano of Senator José Musalém. Senator Eduardo Cruz Coke had also retired from active politics; and his party, which had started out with close to half of the membership and support of the Partido Conservador, had been reduced to the status of a minor party.

There were no significant ideological differences among the Falange Nacional, Partido Conservador Social Cristiano, and the Partido Democrático Cristiano. With the entry of the last of these into the forces of the opposition to the Ibáñez regime, where the other two parties had been from the beginning, there ceased to be tactical differences of any importance among the three groups.

As a result the three parties decided to join forces. A congress meeting in 1957 established the Partido Demócrata Cristiano. Although it was still not one of the country's major parties, it was the most important of the parties of secondary importance.

The new party decided to name its own candidate for the presidency in the election of 1958. The logical choice was Senator Eduardo Frei, who was without dispute the outstanding figure in the party. Although Frei was a poor third in the election, he won more than 20 percent of the popular vote, which was much higher than any party of this ideological tendency had ever received before.[7]

The victor in the 1958 election was Jorge Alessandri, son of the late president Arturo Alessandri. He was a political independent but ran with the support of the Liberal and Conservative parties. His major rival was Salvador Allende, the nominee of the Frente de Acción Popular (FRAP, consisting of the newly reunited Socialists, the Communists and the National Democrats).

Although the election of Alessandri was a severe defeat for the extreme leftists in FRAP, it was clear after 1958 that Salvador Allende and FRAP would have an exceedingly good chance of winning in the next election, scheduled for 1964: Jorge Alessandri would not be eligible for immediate reelection, and the Right had no other figure of his popularity within its ranks. FRAP's chances were further heightened because the 1952 and 1958 elections had demonstrated that the hold of the extreme Right on the vote in the rural areas had been seriously impaired, first by the candidacy of Ibáñez and, six years later, by that of Salvador Allende.

However, it also soon became clear that the newly united Christian Democratic Party would offer serious opposition to FRAP in the election to choose a successor to President Alessandri. Its organization efforts and the results of midterm elections soon converted the PDC into a major party.

The Christian Democrats organized on many levels. A major effort was made to establish units of the party in sections of the country where Christian democracy had not previously been represented. This work brought its most remarkable results in the southern part of Chile's Central Valley, where the population of German Protestant origin had traditionally supported the Radical Party because of their strong opposition to the Catholic Church, but in the 1962 municipal election gave considerable support to the Christian Democrats.

Special efforts were also devoted to work in the slum outskirts of Santiago and other major cities. In these callampas, where no government had done very much to aid the people, many of them recent migrants from the countryside, the Christian Democrats began organizing neighborhood committees. Although these groups had the ultimate political purpose of engendering support for the Christian Democratic Party, they were immediately used to conceive and execute small community development projects, to help the callampa residents to help themselves.

The Christian Democrats and other Catholic elements sympathetic to the party also intensified their efforts to organize the rural workers. This part of the population worked on the land for exceedingly low wages and in a state of almost abject dependency upon their employers. A large percentage of them was illiterate. It had been customary for the landlords to mobilize their agricultural laborers on election day and take them to the polls to vote for the Conservative or the Liberal Party, the two major parties favored by the rural aristocrac

Now the Christian Democrats sought to convince the rural workers that they should break their dependency upon their employers. They urged them to form unions, even though these unions almost certainly would be denied legal recognition by the government, and sought to mobilize them into the Christian Democratic Party.

The Christian Democrats also tried to hammer out a program for the government they hoped to lead after 1964. They developed the concept of "Chileanization" of the nation's mineral resources, the major source of exports. They elaborated a program for agrarian reform, as well as the outlines of a law to permit the unionization of rural workers. They talked a good deal about the concept of "communitarianism," which in essence meant reorganizing the economy and society so that individuals would be able, through cooperative efforts, to exercise real influence over their own destinies. They developed ideas for giving a legal basis to the community development program they had begun in the callampas of the big cities.

THE 1964 ELECTION

As had been widely expected, the 1964 presidential election became a contest principally between FRAP and the Christian Democrats. This was foreshadowed by the congressional elections of 1961 and the municipal ones of 1963. The first of these gave the Christian Democratic Party 15.6 percent of the total vote; the 1963 poll resulted in the PDC receiving 22.8 percent of the vote and emerging as the country's largest single party, displacing the Radicals, who had long held this position.[8]

Thereafter several developments in other parties seemed to favor the PDC. A long-brewing crisis within the Partido Democrático Nacional came to a head in 1963. As a result the party split, a majority keeping the party name, withdrawing the party from FRAP, and endorsing the candidacy of Eduardo Frei. An opposition group took the name Partido Social Demócrata, remained FRAP, and supported Salvador Allende.

Among the Socialists also there was dissension. For some time there had been a dissident pro-Chinese Communist element challenging the party's leadership. In 1963 another group broke away to announce its support for democratic Socialism as opposed to the Marxist-Leninist variety endorsed by the Partido Socialista. It formed the Partido Socialista Democrático and also endorsed the candidacy of Eduardo Frei.

Neither the PADENA nor the dissident Socialists brought any large degree of popular support to the Frei candidacy, probably adding a few thousand votes from among their own followers; but their endorsement of Frei certainly had a psychological impact of some consequence to him.

By the early months of 1964 there were four candidates in the presidential race. Besides Eduardo Frei and Salvador Allende, there were Julio Durán, nominee of the Frente Democrático, and an independent candidate, Jorge Prat. The Frente Democrático was an alliance of the Radical, Conservative, and Liberal parties; and Durán was a leader of the more moderate wing of the Radical Party. Jorge Prat had been closely associated with President Carlos Ibáñez and was backed by some extreme right-wing elements.

This alignment of candidates was severely upset in March 1964, when a by-election for deputy in the province of Curicó resulted in a severe defeat for the candidate supported by the parties of the Frente Democrático. As a result the Frente Democrático ceased to exist. The Conservative and Liberal parties withdrew and threw their support to the candidacy of Eduardo Frei as a lesser evil than Allende. Julio Durán first withdrew his candidacy, and then was urged by his fellow Radicals into continuing in the race as nominee of his own party. Durán's reentry did not keep his candidacy from being a minor one during the last months of the campaign. Jorge Prat also withdrew from the contest.

The Christian Democrats flooded the country with electoral propaganda of the most varied types. Pamphlets and throwaways were issued at all levels of sophistication. Characteristic of the more popular type of appeal was the opening of a small pamphlet, <u>Su compromiso con Chile: Síntesis de El programa</u>:

> The Government of Frei will carry out a revolution in liberty, since Chile needs change and because the people hope for profound social and economic reforms.
>
> What does it mean that the Government of Frei will carry out a Revolution?
>
> Frei will carry out in liberty changes in the social and economic structure of Chile to achieve, in the shortest period possible, a better standard of living for all Chileans.
>
> How will this rapid change in the institutions and the social and economic structure of Chile be brought about?
>
> It will be brought about through the support of the people through their organizations, with the cooperation of the social sectors interested in the transformation of the country.
>
> What are the organizations of the people?
>
> The unions, the Neighbors Organizations and the communities, the Federations and Confederations, etc. In general, all of the representative organizations which arise from spontaneous popular initiative. . . .
>
> Why is it said that Frei will carry out a revolution in liberty?
>
> Because it will be a revolution that will develop within democratic legality and will be strengthened by the support of the organized people. The revolution in liberty will not commit abuses or act arbitrarily, will not destroy human rights or fall into physical violence, or choke off the free expression of thought. . . .

Some of the Christian Democratic propaganda material strongly attacked FRAP. For instance, the small pamphlet Ud. decide (You decide) had this to say:

> What is the FRAP? A group of Marxist parties who say that they are popular and "democratic." In the last election, they went all over Chile making promises: they offered land and even showed maps of the distribution which they promised. But the workers and the peasants are not ingenuous children. They have matured and they can no longer be tricked this way. The workers and peasants remember that the parties of the FRAP have often been in the government, and didn't give land to anyone. They were with Aguirre Cerda and didn't let him govern. Then they were with Ríos. They elected González Videla and everyone knows what happened then....
> We see the reality in other countries where the Marxists have taken over the government. Do the peasants of Hungary, Poland, Cuba, etc. have land? Do the workers participate in the management of firms in those countries?
> Is there freedom?
> The Marxists-FRAPistas speak of freedom, but what they want to do is to use the peasant and the workers and manage them for their own purposes.
> In all of the countries where they have come to the Government, the land belongs to the State; the State manages industries; the State is owner of everything, and the workers are obliged to obey, and to those who don't like it, we know well what happens to them....

Frei himself listed the basic reforms that he wanted his government to carry out as agrarian reform, tax reform, reform of labor legislation and laws governing unions, reform of social security, reform of health services, and reform of agricultural marketing. He also listed the establishment of a new basis for relations with the copper and nitrate mining companies and the achievement of price stability. He also wished to bring about full participation by the people in politics and government.[9]

The votes were cast on September 4, 1964, and the result was a strong victory for Eduardo Frei. He received 1,418,000 votes, or 55.6 percent of the total; Allende got 982,000 votes, or 38.5 percent, and Julio Durán obtained 125,000 votes, or 4.9 percent. Frei was particularly strong among the women voters, receiving 63.3 percent of the votes cast by them, while Allende received only 31.9 percent; Frei received only 49 percent of the votes of men, compared with Allende's 45 percent.[10]

Frei's victory was spectacular. He carried working-class areas in the major cities that had long been Socialist-Communist strongholds. He received a large vote in middle-class areas and had the backing of many upper-class groups as well, although the latter elements soon regretted their support of the Christian Democrats.

The success of the Christian Democrats in the presidential election of September 1964 was repeated in the congressional election of 1965. For the first time in 100 years a single party, the Christian Democrats, won a clear majority in the Chamber of Deputies—all of whose members were up for reelection. In the Senate the Christian Democrats also made substantial gains, although since only half of the seats were to be filled, the PDC did not obtain a majority in that body.

THE FREI GOVERNMENT

During its six years in power, the government of Eduardo Frei carried out a considerable part of the program presented by the Christian Democratic Party in 1964. It "Chileanized" the mining industry, established a legal basis for rural unionism and agrarian reform, and pushed through a law for community development. It also stimulated the development of new industries, particularly for export purposes.

"Chileanization" was an alternative to the nationalization of the mines that had been suggested by the Socialists and Communists. It involved establishing new Chilean-incorporated enterprises to take over the holdings of two of the foreign companies in the copper mining industry and eventual full government ownership of the third. The stock in these new enterprises would be divided between the government of Chile and the foreign firms that had formerly controlled the industry; in practice this turned out to be a 51 percent government interest in the former Kennecott copper holdings and a slightly less than 51 percent government share of the former Cerro de Pasco segments of the industry. The agreement finally reached in 1969 with Anaconda provided for eventual full government purchase of that firm's holdings. It was also agreed that the foreign firms would make sizable new investments in Chilean copper, to the end of doubling national production by the early 1970s.

Agreement was reached between the government and the Kennecot and Cerro de Pasco companies few months after the Frei administration took office. However, the enactment of a law for Chileanization took considerably longer, and the necessary legislation was not passed until 1966. In June 1968 the government announced that it was taking similar steps toward Chileanizing the nitrate industry, but that existing legislation was sufficient to authorize such action and no new law would be required. The same legislation was the basis for the argument with Anaconda in 1969.[11]

An agrarian reform law was also one of the major accomplishments of the Frei government. This statute, enacted in July 1967, provided for expropriation of holdings over 80 hectares of irrigated land and comparable amounts of dry-cultivation land. Various other causes for expropriation were also set forth in the law. The owners were to be recompensed, partly in cash and partly in government bonds, which were to be readjusted in value to compensate (at least in part) for inflation during the 20 years for which they were valid.

The land thus expropriated was first to be organized into so-called asentamientos agrícolas. Those who were ultimately to receive the land were to be settled on these asentamientos, which were to last for three to five years. During this period the appropriate government institutions would undertake to train the workers to become independent farmers and would invest considerable funds in improving the land and the capital on the asentamientos. The control of the asentamientos was to be in the hands of committees elected by the settlers.

The question of what form the asentamientos would ultimately take was left open. Several alternatives were possible. The land could be divided into family holdings and granted to the individual workers; the asentamientos could be continued as cooperative farms; or part of the land could be granted as family farms and part organized as cooperative.

Using both this law and an older, more restrictive law passed by the Alessandri administration, the Frei government had seized 645 large holdings, with a total of 1,248,647 hectares of land and 10,284 tenant families on them, by May 31, 1968. By then 366 asentamientos covering 1,036,168 hectares had been established, and some 8,921 families had been settled upon them.

The first distribution of land titles to peasants who had been living on asentamientos for the minimum of three years prescribed in the law was made on November 4, 1968. This took place at Salamanca, in the Choapa Valley, where 225 peasants from four asentamientos were granted 56,224 hectares, receiving both cooperative and individual titles. It was planned to grant titles to 900 additional families, who were to receive 164,614 hectares.[12]

Another important rural change brought about by the Christian Democratic government was the stimulation of trade unionism among the country's agricultural workers. Before the inauguration of

Eduardo Frei the legal organization of rural workers was virtually impossible. However, as soon as the Christian Democrats came into office, there began an extensive campaign to bring the agricultural laborers into unions; and the new government gave a liberal interpretation to the existing laws concerning rural unions, recognizing a number of the newly established organizations.

In addition the Christian Democratic government introduced into Congress a new law covering rural unionization. This law, which was passed early in 1967, provided for the establishment of unions on the basis of municipalities rather than individual plantations, thus allowing workers of different employers in the same municipality to reinforce one another. It also provided—unlike the general trade union law—for the establishment of provincial and national rural workers' unions. Collective agreements on a local, state, or even national level were provided for in the new law.

As a result of the encouragement of the Christian Democratic government, three new national rural workers unions were established, two of them of generally Christian Democratic orientation and the third controlled by the opposition Socialist-Communist combination. By the end of the Frei administration well over 100,000 workers had been brought into the local unions belonging to the three national groups.

The organization of rural workers was even more important than the agrarian reform during the Frei administration. It not only brought about an increase in real wages of as much as 100 percent during the first three years of the existence of these unions but also changed the whole psychology and social structure in rural Chile. It gave large numbers of rural workers an independence of their employers that they had never had, converting them from dependents of the landlords into self-respecting citizens.

Rural unionization also had an important political effect. In the municipal elections of March 1967, the Christian Democratic Party did exceedingly well in the rural areas that had previously been the strongholds of the right-wing Liberal and Conservative parties. This trend was particularly marked in the provinces where rural unionization had made its most extensive gains. [13]

The Frei government also sought to carry out its program for stimulating the further industrialization of Chile, concentrating on four sectors of the economy. First, it undertook a sizable extension of the Pacific Steel Co., which had been established by the government soon after World War II. Second, it encouraged the establishment of an automobile assembly industry. Third, it undertook to expand the nascent heavy chemical industry, based on the country's petroleum and coal resources as well as salts and other resources in the northern desert. Fourth, the government entered into agreements with several foreign enterprises to build three pulp and paper factories to compete with the long-established Cia Manufacturera de Papeles y Cartones.

In the urban parts of the country, the Frei government had some measure of success in its efforts to organize the people of the slums and other poor areas to work to improve the conditions in their neighborhoods. Frei sought the passage of a law that would give legal standing to the "Neighbors' Boards," which had been organized largely under Christian Democratic inspiration, giving them the right to be official spokesmen of their constituents in dealing with municipal governments and the national regime. Another part of the bill sent to Congress provided for the establishment of federations and a national confederation of these organizations, which would also be given legal status.

After a severe struggle in Congress, the Christian Democrats were able to get a law passed that recognized the local groups but not the national and regional ones. The law gave some backing to the neighborhood groups, which carried on an extensive program of local projects for community use.

Although the Frei government scored successes with its Chileanization, rural reform, and industrialization programs, and to some degree with its community development projects, it was less successful in its dealing with the organized workers. This was in considerable degree because the Christian Democrats, and particularly President Frei, did not take seriously enough the potential danger to their party of the continued control of urban organized labor by the Socialist-Communist coalition. As a result they did little, until it was too late, to change the Chilean system of labor relations in a way that might have undermined this left-wing control of the trade union movement.

Thus the Christian Democratic government made no serious effort to push through Congress a revision of the Chilean Labor Code. They might have succeeded in such an attempt in 1965, soon after the strong Christian Democratic victory in the congressional election.

The Labor Code, written in 1924, provided only for plant and local unions and had virtually no provision for establishing national industrial or craft organizations. It also required that elected leaders of legal trade unions continue to work full-time in the factory or office in which they had been employed before becoming union leaders and conduct union business only in their leisure time, imposed extensive government controls over union finances and elections, and provided that there could be only one union in any enterprise.

These provisions tended to strengthen the position of the Communists in the labor movement. It was only they who had sufficient financial support to be able to provide a sizable corps of people engaged in full-time work in the trade union movement. Although these individuals were not officials of the legal unions, they generally intervened in any important labor dispute through the national central labor organizations. Because the Communist labor leaders were the principal element able to serve their fellow trade unionists in labor disputes, their influence far exceeded the number of members their party had among the organized workers.

The Christian Democratic government did little about this situation. Although Minister of Labor William Thayer wrote a general revision of the Labor Code that would have allowed the workers of a given enterprise to organize as many unions as they wished and the establishment of national industrial and craft unions, no serious move was made to get Congress to adopt this bill. There were two reasons for this: President Frei, sure of his party's popularity, felt that he would be able to appeal over the heads of the Socialist-Communist labor leaders to the rank-and-file unionists if he had trouble with the labor movement's leaders; and the Christian Democratic Party itself was divided on the issue, at least one segment in favor of working with the Communists in organized labor instead of against them.

The upshot was that the Christian Democratic Party made no effort during the period when the Frei government was strongest to change the law so as to give its supporters in organized labor a chance to defy the control of the extreme Left. Nor did the Frei government during this period encourage its supporters to organize a new central labor group as a rival to the Central Unica de Trabajadores de Chile.

Such an attempt was made, with the president's blessing, in the middle of 1968 when some Christian Democrats organized the Unión de Trabajadores de Chile. The leadership in this effort was made up largely of Christian Democrats who had been active in organizing peasant unions, but it also had support from heads of a number of other labor groups. In the declaration of principles adopted by the sponsors of the Unión, they declared: "The UTRACH has proposed, with the authority conferred upon it by the desire of the workers themselves, to bring together all those who are outside of the CUT, under humanist and revolutionary principles, and establishing a total independence of political parties and governments. . . ."[14]

However, this attempt to establish a Christian Democratic-controlled central labor group failed completely. The Communists launched a violent attack on the PDC unionists who led the UTRACH effort, and this vituperation served to intimidate most active PDC unionists.[15]

Instead of joining the UTRACH, most Christian Democratic unionists decided to continue to support the Central Unica de Trabajadores de Chile. At the Central Unica's congress in 1969, the majority of Christian Democratic unionists participated, but they were completely outmaneuvered by their Socialist and Communist opponents.

The failure of the Christian Democratic regime in the cities was also due to the party's failure to develop an adequate program for reform in the urban sector of the economy. Although Christian Democratic ideologists had talked extensively about "communitarianism" as their alternative to the capitalism advocated by the Right and the collectivism of the extreme Left, the exact meaning of this concept had never been well defined. For many party members its application to the urban areas was to be found largely in community development efforts in the slum areas, and the Frei government carried out a very ambitious program in this field.

However, many Christian Democrats were not satisfied merely with community development. Nor was it a sufficient program for the country's industrial workers, who were looking for some fundamental change in their relationship with their employers. Center and left-wing Christian Democrats urged in somewhat vague terms the establishment of a system by which the management of industrial and commercial establishments would be placed to a greater or lesser degree in the hands of the workers employed in them, with the workers also sharing extensively in the profits of these enterprises.

However, little effort was made by the Frei administration to put any such program into effect. As a result of this lack of a concrete program to appeal to the urban working class, and of the Christian Democrats' failure to build upon the popularity they had temporarily achieved with the workers during the 1964 and 1965 election campaigns, the PDC made little permanent progress among that segment of the population as a result of the Frei administration.

The failure of the Christian Democrats with the urban Chilean population was also due to the Frei administration's failure to deal effectively with the problem of inflation. Inflation had been plaguing the country since the 1930's, and each regime had promised to stop the continuing rise in prices. The general pattern was for each administration to make progress in curbing inflation during its first two years or so, then for prices to rise rapidly during the latter years of its period in power.

The Frei administration was no exception. During the first two years of the Frei government the rate of price increase fell from 34 percent in 1964 to 25.9 percent in 1965 and 17 percent in 1966. However, in 1967 the rhythm of price increases was stepped up once again, rising to 21.9 percent in that year, to 27.9 percent in 1968, 29 percent in 1969, and about 35 percent in 1970.

Although the Frei administration's agrarian program and its industrial development enterprises could be expected to have an anti-inflationary effect after some years, during the Frei administration these effects were not felt. Furthermore, in 1967 and 1968 the country was faced with the most serious drought in over 100 years, which served to raise prices, particularly those of agricultural products. In addition, the markedly increased government expenditures arising from the Christian Democratic government's ambitious programs had an inflationary effect.

The upshot of this situation was that the Christian Democrats lost much of the support they had received in 1964 and 1965 from the country's middle class. At the same time some manual workers who had backed the Christian Democrats returned to their former Socialist and Communist allegiance.

The effects were made evident at the time of the 1969 congressional election. In that poll the Christian Democratic percentage dropped from 55.6 percent (1964) and 42.3 percent (1965) to approximately 27.9 percent. The number of Christian Democratic deputies fell from 82 elected in 1965 to 55. At the same time the Socialist-Communist coalition maintained approximately the position it had held four years earlier (although the Communists gained somewhat on the Socialists within the extreme Left coalition), and the right-wing Partido Nacional, formed by a merger of the Liberals and Conservatives, regained much ground, winning 20 percent of the popular vote and electing 34 deputies and 5 senators.[16]

IDEOLOGICAL TRENDS WITHIN CHILEAN CHRISTIAN DEMOCRACY

During the Frei administration the conflicting trends that had long existed within the Christian Democratic Party became clearly evident. There were three such major tendencies.

First was the group popularly known as oficialistas, those most closely associated with President Frei and the administration. This element was firmly in favor of Chileanization, agrarian reform, rural unionization, and community development. However, the oficialistas rejected the exaggerated nationalism of some of their fellow party members and firmly opposed immediate nationalization of the copper mines, an idea with which the more extreme elements in the party had toyed. Some oficialistas favored an energetic attempt by the Christian Democrats to wrest the urban labor movement from the hands of the Socialist-Communist coalition, but they did not receive much support from the president for this effort until it was too late. They urged that land taken under the agrarian reform be distributed as family farms. The oficialistas were firmly anti-Marxian and were opposed to any alliance with the Socialist-Communist coalition.[17]

The most strident opponents of the oficialistas were the group known as the rebeldes (rebels). They were strongest among the Christian Democratic Youth and also controlled the labor and agrarian bureaus of the Christian Democratic Party during much of the Frei regime. They fought strongly against any attempt to challenge the Socialists and Communists in the urban labor movement and favored an alliance of Christian Democratic rural unions with those dominated by the extreme Left. They severely criticized the government—in public as well as within the party—for not moving fast enough in the agrarian reform field and urged that the land seized from private landowners be organized into collective farms. Philosophically the rebeldes were much influenced by Marxism-Leninism, and politically they worked in favor of a Christian Democratic-Socialist-Communist alliance.

Between the oficialistas and rebeldes were the terceristas. This group vacillated between the supporters of President Frei and his consistent opponents. During the first years of the Frei administration they generally were more closely allied with the rebeldes, but for a time in 1968 they moved closer to the president. They were most influential in the two organizations that dealt most closely with the agrarian reform, the Corporación de la Reforma Agraria and the Instituto Nacional de Desarrollo Agropecuario.

Throughout the Frei administration there was a constant struggle among the three factions. It reached one high point at the Christian Democratic Party congress in January 1968, when President Frei himself had to appeal passionately to the delegates to win election of his nominee for party president, Jaime Castillo, over Rafael Gumucio, a leading spokesman for the rebeldes. A final split with the rebeldes came in May 1969, when they withdrew from the PDC to form a new party, the Movimiento de Acción Popular Unitaria. They were joined by Jacques Chonchol, former head of the Instituto Nacional, who had been a tercerista. The MAPU quickly aligned itself with the Socialists and Communists and became part of the Unidad Popular, supporting Senator Salvador Allende in the 1970 presidential election.

THE 1970 ELECTION AND THEREAFTER

The election of a successor to President Frei took place in September 1970. The PDC, after some hesitation, named Radomiro Tomic as its candidate. He ran against Salvador Allende, this time backed by a new coalition, Unidad Popular, consisting not only of the Socialists and Communists but also of the Radicals, the MAPU, and two small parties; and Jorge Alessandri, the former president, backed by the Partido Nacional.

Tomic's campaign was a weak one. During most of it he sought to dissociate himself from the Frei administration. By the time, in the last weeks of the campaign, that he realized it was an error to separate himself from his own party's administration and from Eduardo Frei, most popular political leader in the country, it was too late.

Salvador Allende emerged with a plurality of the popular vote— 36 percent—a couple of percentage points ahead of Alessandri. Tomic was a poor third. However, in order to be elected Allende needed the support of a majority in Congress because no candidate had an absolute majority. To win in Congress Allende needed the support of the Christian Democrats.

The PDC was not willing to give this support without conditions. They exacted from Allende both legislation and promises designed to guarantee that he would not destroy the democratic form of government in Chile if he were elected. These concessions made, they threw their votes to him, ensuring that he would succeed Eduardo Frei.

During the Allende administration the PDC has constituted the largest element in the opposition. Its position as the country's largest party was reaffirmed in the municipal elections of April 1971, in which it received 26 percent of the vote. It continued to have the largest representation in Congress.

The Christian Democrats were sharply critical of the president. They strongly censured some of his economic policies and charged elements in his party and the Communist Party with the desire to destroy the Chilean democratic framework. However, they did vote for the constitutional amendment permitting nationalization of the country's mines and sponsored a law defining the three "areas" of the economy proclaimed by Allende—the "social" (government-owned) sector, the "mixed," and the private.

In September 1971 the party underwent a further split. Most of the _tercerista_ faction withdrew to form a new party, Izquierda Cristiana; and it was quickly joined by the principal leaders of the MAPU, which was relegated to the status of a very small group. This exit of the _terceristas_ tended to unify the PDC ideologically and to intensify its opposition to the Allende government.

The rise of the Christian Democrats in Chilean politics was largely due to the creation of a vacuum on the Left as a result of the establishment of the coalition between the Socialist and Communist parties in the 1950s. In the 1933-52 period the Socialists' principal reason to exist had been to present an alternative on the Left to the Communists. When the Socialists joined forces with the Communists in a more or less permanent alliance after the election of 1952, those on the Left who did not want to support the Communists were left with little alternative except the Christian Democrats.

In addition the Christian Democrats owed their success to their determined efforts to build up support among an element that previously had played very little independent part in national politics, the peasantry. In the 1964 and 1965 elections the PDC gained considerable support among this group and thereafter concentrated a large part of its organizational efforts among the peasants.

Once in office the Christian Democratic Party moved to carry out the principal points in its program. It was successful in starting a profound process of social, economic, and political change in the rural sector, in bringing the country's principal export industry under the control of the government, and in stimulating the further industrialization of the economy. However, its neglect of the urban workers, its inability to deal adequately with inflation, and the ineptness of its 1970 presidental campaign brought the defeat of the party at the end of President Frei's term.

The Christian Democratic Party remains the largest party in Chile. Its chances of returning to power depend largely on whether or not the "road ot Socialism" on which President Salvador Allende has embarked the country leads to the destruction of the democratic nature of Chilean politics.

CHAPTER 17

THE COPEI OF VENEZUELA

The Partido Copei of Venezuela was the second Christian Democratic Party of Latin America to come to power. More than 22 years after its establishment, the founder and principal leader of Copei, Rafael Caldera, was elected president of Venezuela on December 1, 1968; he took office on March 11, 1969.

EARLY HISTORY OF COPEI

The roots of the Copei party are to be found in the Venezuelan students' movement of the late 1930s; the immediate reason for the establishment of the party was the revolution of October 18, 1945. Rafael Caldera was a major figure in the leadership of the student generation that followed the death of dictator Juan Vicente Gómez in December 1935. Gómez had ruled the country since 1909, and his regime was one of the last of the caudillo dictatorships of South America. During his long tenure in the presidency, he had treated Venezuela as his personal hacienda and its people as his servants.

Following the death of Gómez, several new political parties, of various ideological tendencies, were established in Venezuela. The two most important were the Partido Democrático Nacional, which in 1941 took the name Acción Democrática and became one of the hemisphere's princiapl national revolutionary parties. Another was the Partido Communista Venezolano, a member of the Communist International—formally established as early as 1931 but taking form for the first time in Venezuela after Gómez' death. It was an orthodox Communist party of Stalinist orientation.

Different political trends were also evident among the students in the post-Gómez period. The first man to emerge as leader of the

THE COPEI OF VENEZUELA 339

student movement was Jovito Villalba, who had been a member of the "generation of 1928" that had made a valiant but futile attempt to overthrow the dictatorship in 1928 and had provided many of the leaders of the PDN, the Communist Party, and various other political groups that appeared in the late 1930s and late 1940s.

Another group was that led by Rafael Caldera. In contrast with most of its competitors in student politics, the Caldera group, the Unión Nacional Estudiantil, was of strongly Catholic orientation and is alleged by many to have sympathized with the Franco side in the Spanish Civil War.

The Caldera group established a political party, Acción Nacional, which elected Caldera and José Lara Lena to Congress. However, the political atmosphere of the time was not propitious for the establishment of new political groups, since after a short period of tolerance, the government of General Eleázar López Contreras cracked down on all independent political goups in the middle of 1937. The leaders were generally jailed or exiled.1

It was not until after the revolution of October 18, 1945, that the way was opened for the establishment of new political parties. That uprising was led by a group of young army officers and the leaders of Acción Democrática, with the principal role in the succeeding government being played by AD, under the leadership of Rómulo Betancourt.

Rafael Caldera was named as solicitor general of the republic by the Acción Democrática government. At that time he was politically independent and was attracted by the promises of reform by the AD leaders. However, within a few weeks Caldera broke with Betancourt and the other leaders of the revolutionary government, and resigned his post.

When the revolutionary regime enacted a new electoral decree providing for the establishment of political parties, Rafael Caldera was one of the first to take advantage of it. Under his leadership the Comité de Organización Política Electoral Independiente (Copei) was established as the organizing committee for a new party of Catholic social orientation. The principal figures in this new organization were the student leaders of the late 1930s who had been officers of the Unión Nacional Estudiantil.

The founding convention of the new party was held in Caracas on January 13, 1946. It adopted the name Partido Copei, capitalizing upon the popularity that the initials of the original founding committee of the organization had already achieved. Rafael Caldera emerged as the party's principal figure.2

The first electoral test of the new party came at the end of 1946, when the Acción Democrática government summoned the voters to elect a Constitutional Assembly to write a new basic law for the republic. Copei succeeded in electing 19 of the 160 members of the Assembly. The party had a majority only the state of Tachira.³

During this period Copei was particularly strong in the three mountain states of Táchira, Mérida, and Trujillo. In the first of these, it received 70 percent of the vote and had extensive support among the urban workers and particularly among the peasantry. Generally the local clergy backed the party in that region, even urging their parishioners to vote Copei. The relatively small support that Copei received in Caracas and other cities outside of the Eastern mountain area came largely from middle-class elements, since at that point the workers and peasantry voted overwhelmingly for Acción Democrática.

There was considerable difference between the national leadership and many of the secondary and local leaders. Rafael Caldera, Lorenzo Fernández, Vicente Giménez Landínez and other major figures in the party were definitely Christian Democratic in their orientation, feeling themselves most closely associated with the Mouvement Républicain Populaire, a Reformist Catholic party influential in France immediately after World War II.⁴ However, the party also tended to attract many of the most conservative elements in national politics. Quite a few of these right-wing elements were of some importance in the state and local organizations of Copei.

Copei's strength in the mountain states was an important factor in determining some parts of the document written by the Constitutional Assembly elected late in 1946, which met during most of 1947. Fear that Copei might win gubernatorial elections in Táchira, Mérida, and Trujillo, and might use control of those state governments as possible bases for conspiracy against the national government, led the overwhelming Acción Democrática majority of the Constituent Assembly to decree that for the first 10 years the new constitution was in effect the governors of all states would be appointed by the president.

Rafael Caldera was the candidate of Copei in the presidential election held at the end of 1947. However, he ran a weak second behind Acción Democrática's nominee, the novelist Rómulo Gallegos. However, Copei won 6 members of the Senate and 19 members of the Chamber of Deputies. Caldera received 262,204 votes, compared with 871,752 for Gallegos.⁵

COPEI AND THE PÉREZ JIMÉNEZ DICTATORSHIP

On November 24, 1948, the constitutional government of President Rómulo Gallegos was overthrown by a military coup d'état. A few days afterward the Copei issued on official statement that it had had nothing to do with the coup and had not participated in the conspiracy that had led up to it. However, for some time the party showed certain willingness to cooperate with the military junta that took power on November 24. One member of the party accepted the post of governor of the state of Táchira, the state in which the party had its greatest popular support.6

However, all willingness of Copei to cooperate with the military junta ended with the assassination of the first president of the junta, Colonel Carlos Delgado Chalbaud, on November 19, 1950. The death of Delgado Chalbaud resulted in Colonel Marcos Pérez Jiménez, another member of the junta, becoming the principal figure in the government. Obviously he was exceedingly ambitious to become president, although a civilian, Germán Suárez Flamerich, succeeded Delgado Chalbaud as president of the military junta.

In 1952 the military regime decided to call elections for a Constitutional Assembly, which would write still another constitution and name a new president and members of a regular Senate and Chamber of Deputies. Copei decided to participate in these elections, although it was fairly certain that the government would not allow the opposition to win. As a result the party had representatives on the National Electoral Board, which presumably was to preside over the voting on a national level, as well as on most state electoral boards. However, in the state of Táchira, where Copei had its most concentrated group or supporters—but the state from which Pérez Jiménez also came, and where he was particularly anxious to have a majority—the government did not name any Copei member to the state electoral board.

During this campaign the Copei took a frankly oppositionist position. As a result it was harassed by the military regime. At one point most of its top leaders were jailed for several days; Edecio La Riva, one of the top figures in the party, was arrested and badly beaten, and many state and local leaders were imprisoned.

The government lost the election. The largest number of deputies to the Constituent Assembly were elected by the Unión Republicana Democrática; the second largest number were chosen under the banner of the government party organized for the occasion, the Frente Electoral Independiente; and Copei came in third. Subsequently the leaders of the party explained the Copei's relatively poor showing on two grounds. First, Acción Democrática, the majority party in the country, had thrown its support behind the URD at the last moment; and second, many of those who wanted to vote for the most strongly antigovernment party voted for the URD, on the ground that it was to the left of Copei.7

However, the government paid little attention to the results of the election. Even before all the votes had been counted, Pérez Jiménez seized power, declared himself provisional president "in the name of the armed forces," and suspended the tabulation of the election results. Subsequently new results were given that showed the FEI as having a majority, with both URD and Copei electing some delegates. Meanwhile, the principal leaders of URD were arrested and deported from Venezuela.

These events caused a crisis within the ranks of the Copei. Some of its more conservative elements were inclined to accept the government's actions as a fait accompli and to take the seats allotted to the party in the Constituent Assembly. However, the majority of the party did not accept this position.

The Copei's first move was to present the provisional president with a list of demands that were the price for its participation in the Constitutional Assembly: strict observation of parliamentary immunity —important because URD deputies had been arrested and deported; "absolute freedom of the press"; release of all political prisoners; a "regime of guarantees" of civil liberties; elimination of political functions of the secret police; immediate reopening of the Central University, which had been closed by the government; and "consecration in the text of the constitution of the principles which motivated the military movement of 18 of October," which had placed Acción Democrática in power in 1945.

These demands by the Copei leadership were turned down by R. Soules Baldo, secretary to the provisional president, in a letter noting that Pérez Jiménez considered these demands "lacking in the serenity required by 'mature reflexion.'" As a result Copei's National Committee decided that those party members named as members of the Constituent Assembly would not take those posts. Subsequently the party expelled four party members who accepted their seats.[8]

As a result of these events, Copei was in open opposition to the Pérez Jiménez government, which remained in power for another five years. Although Copei was never declared illegal by the dictatorship, as Acción Democrática, the Unión Republicana Democrática, and the Communist Party had been, its activities were extensively curtailed. Press censorship prevented the publication of virtually all information on the party's activities and all of its public statements. Frequently its principal leaders were arrested and jailed. Some of the secondary and local Copei leaders were sent to the government's concentration camp in the Orinico delta, and others were exiled. Rafael Caldera was exiled during the last weeks of the Pérez Jiménez regime.

During the dictatorship Copei sought to extend its influence among the country's trade unionists. In this period the Confederación de Trabajadores de Venezuela, which had been organized under Acción Democrática leadership in 1947, was suppressed. The government of

Pérez Jiménez set up its own central labor group, the Confederacion Nacional de Trabajadores; and there were several groups of unions under the leadership of the country's various political parties. The Copei group was known as the Comité Pro-Federación de Trabajadores Organizador de Venezuela; for several years it had control of the Sewage Workers Union and a handful of organizations in the oil fields, as well as scattered other unions. It was severely persecuted by the dictatorship.[9]

As a result of its opposition to the government and the dictatorship's persecution of Copei, the party entered into contact with the underground networks of Acción Democrática and the Unión Republicana Democrática. Exiled leaders of the three groups also collaborated. During 1957, when the dictatorship was faced with the problem of the expiration of Pérez Jiménez' "constitutional" term of office, the three parties agreed to name Rafael Caldera as their joint candidate for the presidency. They felt that since he was the only national party leader still living in the country, he was the logical figure around whom the opposition could rally.[10]

However, Pérez Jiménez decided not to risk the danger of an election. Instead he organized a "plebiscite" in which the voters would be called upon to cast a "yes" or "no" vote on the proposition "General Marcos Pérez Jiménez shall continue in the presidency for the constitution period 1958-63." Naturally the plebiscite produced a resounding "yes" vote.

However, this mockery of an election was the beginning of the end of the Pérez Jiménez regime. Within seven weeks the dictatorship had fallen because of a sudden surge of opposition among all elements of the community. The Church played a particularly significant role in this opposition, with many priests participating frankly in conspiracies against the regime. This position of the Catholic hierarchy had been first indicated in a pastoral letter, issued in May 1957 and signed by virtually all the bishops and archbishops in Venezuela, in which the government had been severely criticized for its failure to deal with the country's pressing social problems.[11]

Members of the Copei were named to serve on the Junta Patriotica, the underground organization that led the struggle against Pérez Jiménez during the last weeks of his regime. It consisted of two representatives each from Acción Democrática, Copei, the Union Republicana Democrática, and the Communist Party. The Junta Patriotica organized the street demonstrations and other actions to rally the populace in the final struggle against the dictatorship.

Meanwhile, Rafael Caldera was in exile in New York City, There he joined with Rómulo Betancourt, principal figure in Acción Democratica, and Jóvito Villalba, main leader of the Unión Republicana Democrática, in a pact whereby the three leaders agreed to work together in the post-Pérez Jiménez period to establish the bases for a return to constitutional government. This pact laid the basis for the cooperation of the three parties after Pérez Jiménez was overthrown on January 23, 1958.

COPEI IN THE 1958 PROVISIONAL GOVERNMENT PERIOD

Rafael Caldera returned to Venezuela soon after the overthrow of Pérez Jiménez. He was greeted, as were the other returning exiles, by a large crowd of his supporters and party members. He was automatically accepted as the leader of Copei and set about the difficult task of rebuilding the party's ranks.

Copei pledged its support to the provisional government, headed by Admiral Wolfgang Larrazábal. It also sought to maintain a united front of the civilian political leaders and parties, in order to pave the way for the reestablishment of a democratic, constitutional government. Caldera joined with Rómulo Betencourt and Jovito Villalba to form an informal interparty junta to advise the government and maintain peace among the most important political parties.

This program of cooperation found expression in the organized labor movement. The trade unionists associated with Copei joined forces with those of Acción Democrática, URD, and the Communist Party to form the Comité de Unidad Sindical. The Copei trade union group that had existed during the dictatorship was dissolved, and the small unions that had been under the influence of the party merged with those controlled by the other political groups to form sindicatos únicos. In elections in these united unions, which were held throughout the year, the four parties with some following in the labor movement—Acción Democrática, Copei, URD, and the Communists—agreed on slates that were more or less automatically victorious. This represented a net gain for Copei in the labor movement, since according to the rules followed during this period, all parties were represented on union executive committees and in a very large proportion of the unions Copei had few if any followers, so it was represented among union leadership far out of proportion to the popular following it then had in the various labor organizations.

Copei early endorsed the idea that the three democratic parties should agree upon a single candidate for the presidency in elections that the provisional government had promised to hold as soon as they could be organized. The Copei leaders were willing to accept, at least in principle, a leader of one of the other parties as this united front candidate.

THE COPEI OF VENEZUELA 345

However, despite extended negotiations among the leaders of the three major parties, there was no agreement on a single candidate for the elections, which were finally scheduled for December 5, 1958. As a result each party decided to name its own candidate. Quite logically Copei chose Rafael Caldera, its founder and secretary-general, as its candidate for president.

Caldera came in a poor third, behind Rómulo Betancourt, the Acción Democrática candidate; and Admiral Wolfgang Larrazábal, who was backed by the Unión Republicana Democrática and the Communist Party. The votes were 1,284,092 for Betancourt; 889,167 for Larrazábal; and 396,293 for Caldera.[12]

COPEI IN THE BETANCOURT ADMINISTRATION

The three presidential candidates had agreed to the so-called Pacto de Punto Fijo, according to which no matter who won the election, he would be recognized by the other two as the victor and would include members of all three parties in his cabinet. As a result three members of Copei—Agriculture Minister Vicente Giménez Landínez, Commerce Minister Lorenzo Fernández, and Minister of Justice Andrés Aguilar became members of Rómulo Betancourt's cabinet.

Copei continued as a coalition partner of Acción Democrática throughout the administration of Rómulo Betancourt (1959-64). When the Unión Republicana Democrática withdrew from the administration in November 1960 and went into the opposition, Copei continued to be part of the administration. In addition, when the Communist Party and the dissident group that had broken away from Acción Democrática and formed a rival party, the Movimiento de Izquierda Revolucionaria, called on the workers late in 1960 to rise in revolt against the Betancourt government, Copei remained loyal to its alliance with Acción Democrática. The two parties succeeded in controlling the Confederación de Trabajadores de Venezuela and defeating the efforts of these subversive left-wing elements. Thence forward the AD and Copei groups continued to control the Confederación.

The Copei undoubtedly capitalized on its participation in the Betancourt administration. Particularly after the retirement of URD from the government, Copei shared governorships and other posts in the public administration with the majority party in the coalition. This facilitated the work of the party in organizing local groups in parts of the country where previously the Christian Democrats had had little or no representation.

The alliance with Acción Democrática also made available to Copei an appreciable amount of patronage. Members of the Christian Democratic Party were given posts in the public administration, and they were able to continue to hold many of these posts even after their party had left the government in 1964.

However, perhaps even more important than the benefits the party gained as a partner in the Betancourt government was the deliberate policy that the Copei followed of organizing grassroots groups in various segments of Venezuelan society. Through the Frente de Trabajadores Copeyanos, the party trained a considerable number of trade unionists, particularly young people, in the strategy and tactics of union leadership. A training school for Christian Democratic trade unionists, sponsored by the Copeyano trade unionists in Venezuela and the Confederación Latino Americana de Sindicalistas Cristianos, established at Caracas in 1962, was of particular use in training Copyano trade unionists.[13]

Copei also was active in other groups. Supporters of the party organized peasant leagues that were part of the Federación Agraria, affiliated with the Confederación de Trabajadores de Venezuela, itself controlled largely by members of Acción Democrática. Copei members in all parts of the Confederación were given representation on the governing organs of the labor and peasant movement.

Copei was also very active in the student movement. During most of the Betancourt administration, its supporters made up the majority of the relatively small element in the student movement that supported the government, since Acción Democrática had lost most of its student supporters in the two splits it suffered—of the MIR in 1960 and the so-called ARS dissidents in 1962.[14]

COPEI AS THE LOYAL OPPOSITION

As the 1963 election approached, a crisis faced the Copei. Although Rafael Caldera and other leading figures in the Copei were inclined to favor the continuance of the AD-Copei coalition, there was resistance within the Copei rank and file to supporting a member of Acción Democrática for president in the next five years. The Copei members demanded that they at least be consulted on which AD leader should be the coalition candidate if an AD-Copei coalition were to be established for the presidential election.

However, Acción Democrática was not disposed to submit its presidential choice to the Copei. As a result AD named as its candidate Raúl Leoni, who was not acceptable to the Copei. In reply the Christian Democrats named their perennial candidate, Rafael Caldera. However, in contrast with his behavior on previous occasions when he ran for president, Caldera did not simultaneously present himself as a nominee for the Chamber of Deputies.

THE COPEI OF VENEZUELA

On December 1, 1963, the Acción Democrática candidate, Raúl Leoni, was victorious, with about 33 percent of the total popular vote. However, Copei's nominee came in second, receiving approximately 20.2 percent of the total vote. At the same time Copei increased its congressional delegation from 3 senators and 19 deputies to 6 senators and 40 deputies.[15]

Before Leoni was inaugurated as Betancourt's successor there were extensive negotiations between AD and the Copei, looking toward the continuation of the AD-Copei coalition in the new administration, but these negotiations did not bear fruit. As a result Raúl Leoni formed his first cabinet completely of members of his own party, Acción Democrática, and independents; and Copei went into the opposition.

The role played by Copei during the Leoni administration was of major importance for the political maturation of Venezuela. Never before had a party that was quite frankly in the opposition not been involved in plotting against the regime in power. However, between 1964 and 1969 Copei fulfilled this role. For virtually the first time in the country's history, Venezuela had an opponent of the government that did not engage in conspiracies to overthrow the regime. The Copei presented the country with its first example of a loyal opposition.

This attitude of the Copei undoubtedly had two bases. In the first place, the leaders of the Venezuelan Christian Democrats were certainly firm believers in the democratic form of government and thus were opposed to using conspiratorial methods to overthrow a popularly elected regime. In the second place, the Copeyanos undoubtedly believed that they had a very good chance of winning the 1968 election and did not want to spoil it by provoking the seizure of power by a military group.

During this period, as during the administration of Rómulo Betancourt, the behavior of the Copei Party was characterized by careful development of grassroots support. Great emphasis was placed by the party on training its younger leadership and its adherents in various organizations, such as the labor and peasant movements, to work within and lead such organizations. The party's attention was particularly concentrated on developing a following in parts of the country where the Christian Democrats had never had appreciable strength, such as the eastern states.

VICTORY AT LAST

As the 1968 presidential election approached, Copei was faced with the question of what policy it should adopt. More than a year before the election date, the party nominated its three-time loser Rafael Caldera. This nomination was not made without reservations or opposition. Many of the younger people in the party felt that Caldera did not have any chance and that one who had lost three times would probably do so again.

The opposition to Caldera and the traditional leadership of the party did not come out into the open. However, there was a widespread feeling within the ranks of the secondary leadership of Copei that if Caldera lost this time, he would have to be replaced in the leadership of the party.

This smoldering rebellion within Copei did not result in an actual split. Throughout Venezuela the party rank and file threw itself into what appeared to be the best chance that the party had ever had of winning the presidency and coming to control the government of Venezuela. To a much greater degree than any other party, Copei used scientific procedures to aid its campaign. Public opinion polls and other methods were used to try to determine the attitudes of the voters and the direction of the campaign. Its progress was aided also by the fact that only about a year before the election, the government party, Acción Democrática, suffered the most serious schism in its history.

The result of the election of December 1, 1968, was the first national victory of Copei, Rafael Caldera being chosen president by the narrowest of margins. The final vote was 1,082,941 for Caldera; 1,051,870 for Gonzalo Barrios, nominee of Acción Democrática; 829,397 for Miguel Angel Burelli, candidate of several smaller parties; 719,733 for Luis Beltrán Prieto Figueroa, nominee of the dissident AD group known as Movimiento Electoral del Pueblo; and lesser votes for several other candidates.[16]

Acción Democrática at first protested the election results, claiming that there had been fraud in several parts of the country. However, these charges were dismissed by the Supreme Electoral Tribunal; and on December 11, 1968, the victory of Rafael Caldera was officially proclaimed. On March 11, 1969, Caldera was inaugurated as president of Venezuela.

Although winning the presidency, Copei elected fewer members of Congress than Acción Democrática; and Caldera could by no means be sure of having the support of a majority in the legislature. Copei won only 16 senators out of a total of 42, and only 50 of the 197 deputies.

In his inaugural speech on March 11, 1969, Caldera outlined the objectives that Venezuela's first Christian Democratic government would seek to attain. He stated: "I will make every effort not only to insure everyone the right to health, work, free expression and a share in the affairs of his own community, but also the right to education, fair housing, social security, welfare, work as a basis for progress, and economy to the service of man, the strengthening of democratic institutions and an inducement for the family to be the fundamental core of society."

Even though Copei did not have a majority in Congress, President Caldera insisted on not forming a coalition with any other party. His cabinets consisted only of members of the Copei and independents. However, for certain measures the government was able to make agreements with Acción Democrática to get them through the legislature. These included a law for reorganizing the universities and one for preparing conditions for the ultimate takeover of foreign oil concessions by the government, scheduled for 1983-84.

Factionalism developed within the Copei during the Caldera administration. One group was closely associated with the president, while two other factions developed that were more or less critical of the administration. In a showdown at the Copei Party congress in August 1971, the elements loyal to Caldera proved to have a majority.

The major issue at stake in this conflict was the party nomination for the 1973 presidential election. The Caldera forces were pledged to support Lorenzo Fernández, contemporary and old friend of Rafael Caldera; Luis Herrera Campins, representative of the second generation in the party's leadership, had the support of many of the leaders and members of the party's youth group, Juventud Revolucionario Copeyano; and Andrés Beaujón, one-time secretary-general of the party, was candidate of the most strongly anti-Caldera elements.

REASONS FOR THE RISE OF COPEI

The success of the Partido Social Cristiano Copei, as the Venezuelan Christian Democrats were known after 1958, was due to several factors. Certainly among the most important were meticulous organizational work, extensive training of party leadership, the maintenance of party unity, and patience.

During the decade that preceded their 1968 electoral victory, the Copei carried out extensive organizational work. Although after the fall of Pérez Jiménez, the party had little if any support in the states east of Caracas, and its principal backing was concentrated in the three western mountain states of Táchira, Mérida, and Trujillo, the Copeyanos slowly and deliberately recruited small corps of supporters in virtually all of the rest of the country. However, they took reasonable care to choose their new recruits, being unwilling to accept people who had been associated with the Pérez Jiménez dictatorship and were seeking "protective cover" in one of the democratic parties. Nor did they put out the welcome mat for mere opportunists who were seeking to use party membership for personal advancement.

Undoubtedly Copei's ability to recruit supporters was aided by the party's participation in the five-year administration of Rómulo Betancourt. Their obvious unwillingness to capitalize on the tremendous difficulties faced by Betancourt, and their loyalty to the ideas of basic social réform and rapid economic development under the auspices of a democratic government during this period, helped to change the attitudes of many who before 1959 had regarded Copei as the country's conservative party.

Copei party members were organized into various functional groups. Workers, for example, became members of the Frente de Trabajadores Copeyanos; and party members in professional, student, and other groups were organized in party units to further the interests of Copei in their respective organizations.

Copei made particular progress in the labor movement, where the party had had few supporters before 1958. Its work there was made easier after the overthrow of Pérez Jiménez when all parties worked together in the unions for nearly three years. This enabled the Copei to obtain positions of leadership in many unions where they had few followers. In many of these organizations the Copeyanos were able to take advantage of this situation to build up an important group of party members. When the extreme Left sought to use the organized workers against the Betancourt regime in 1960-61, the Copei unionists worked with Acción Democrática to assure control of organized labor by the forces supporting the administration. This cooperation with Acción Democrática also paid dividends for the Copei by helping them to recruit supporters in the organized labor movement.

In the Leoni period the Copei did not make the mistake of separating its followers from the bulk of the labor movement, organized in the Confederación de Trabajadores de Venezuela. Although during these years relations with Acción Democrática trade unionists were strained, the Copeyanos proved their loyalty to the concept of labor unity.

In the student movement, too, the Copei was able to make considerable headway during 1958-68. Because most of Acción Democrática's student followers joined the dissident Movimiento de la Izquierda Revolucionaria in 1960, the Copeyano students constituted the bulk of the democratic elements in the universities after 1960. Therefore they were undoubtedly able to gain support and win members among students who otherwise might not have been attracted to the Copei ranks.

The mere recruiting of small groups of followers in various parts of the country would not have been sufficient to assure the sustained growth of the organization. The party added to this continuing membership campaign a program of intensive training of their lower and middle ranks of leaders. Those active in the trade unions and peasant organizations were given particular attention in this regard. The Juventud Revolucionaria Copeyana, the party's youth group, which had its principal following among the students, paid special attention to teaching its members the party's doctrine and political program, as well as techniques for running meetings, working in other organizations, and similar practical matters.[17]

Another factor that worked in favor of the Copei during the decade after the overthrow of Pérez Jiménez was that the party was able to maintain its unity. The other two parties that were consistently of major importance during this period, Acción Democrática and the Unión Republicana Democrática, both suffered severe divisions that tended seriously to weaken them. AD suffered major splits in 1960, 1962, and 1968; the URD expelled its left wing after the 1963 election and suffered another major schism in 1967.

Although the Copei was not completely free of factional discord, particularly during and after the Leoni administration, this did not result in an open division in the party's ranks. This ability of the Copei to maintain party unity undoubtedly meant that energies and talents that might have been devoted to fighting intramural battles could be concentrated on spreading the party's organization and winning its backing among the country's voters.

Finally, Copei owed much of its success to its willingness to build carefully toward a possible future victory, without prematurely trying to obtain power. This attitude was reflected in its consistent support of the Betancourt administration, which was in sharp contrast with the policy of political blackmail followed by the Unión Republicana Democrática. It was shown also in its policy toward the Leoni government, which was one of loyal opposition, and complete refusal to contemplate participation in any movement to overthrow the regime by illicit means. Undoubtedly this consistency of Copei policy for a decade helped to maintain the unity of the party, since it made it unnecessary for Copei leaders to engage in complicated political maneuvering that might have caused dissension within the party ranks.

CHAPTER

18

OTHER
CHRISTIAN
DEMOCRATIC
PARTIES

During the 1950s and 1960s Christian Democratic parties were established in virtually all of the Latin American countries. However, nowhere except in Chile and Venezuela did these organizations become major contendors for power. Most remained relatively small and after a short period of growth and progress tended to decline.

ARGENTINA

The Christian Democratic Party of Argentina arose in the final phase of the struggle against the Perón regime in the early 1950s. It was established by a group of Catholic laymen who were alienated by the dictatorial aspects of the Perón regime but also wanted no association with the right-wing attitudes that had traditionally characterized the old Conservative (or National Democratic) Party. The party received no legal recognition during the Perón regime—indeed, its establishment was undoubtedly one of the factors that provoked Perón's violent attacks on the Church during the last year and a half that he was in power.

With the overthrow of the Perón government, the Christian Democrats emerged as one of the important new forces in Argentine politics. They were represented in the National Consultative Council, which was established as a kind of interim parliament by the provisional government. In the first post-Perón election in 1957, the Christian Democrats made a respectable showing, emerging as the fifth most important element in national politics, behind the Peronistas, the two wings of the Radical Party, and the Socialist Party.

However, the Christian Democrats were riven during the post-Perón period with the same controversy that split virtually all of the

CHRISTIAN DEMOCRATIC PARTIES 353

country's other parties: the attitude that should be taken toward the Peronistas. One faction, led by the the party's first president, Manuel Ordóñez, felt that the best way to deal with the Peronistas was to try to convince them of the error of their ways, making no concessions to them in tactics or ideas. The other faction, led by Horacio Sueldo, argued that it was necessary to deemphasize opposition to Perón and to try to find common ground on the basis of which followers of the fallen dictator could be recruited to the Christian Democratic ranks. This controversy, which raged for several years, finally resulted in the resignation from the party of Ordóñez and most of those supporting him.

The change in the outlook and position of the Christian Democratic Party became particularly clear during the election of 1963. In preparation for that contest, it took part in negotiations for the formation of a Popular Front. The Christian Democrats were joined in this effort by five other legal parties—the neo-Peronista Unión Popular, the Unión Cívica Radical Intransigente, Partido Unión Federal, Partido Federal, and Partido Conservador Popular—as well as by the illegal Peronista organization.

At the first meeting of this rather heterogeneous group, "The PDC put forth a radical economic plan prepared by Guido di Tella. . . . the platform included the cancellation of oil development contracts with foreign companies, an end to relations with the International Monetary Fund (IMF), agrarian reform (including mechanization and expropriation of latifundios), the nationalization of bank deposits, and the creation of an exchange control organ similar to Perón's Instituto de Promoción del Intercambio."[1]

The Christian Democrats officially withdrew from negotiations for the establishment of the Popular Front, which in the end was reduced only to the Peronistas, Arturo Frondizi's fraction of the Unión Cívica Radical Intransigente, and the small Partido Conservador Popular. Soon the Christian Democrats were denouncing the Popular Front "as a Frigerio plot to get his and Frondizi's candidates elected."

However, the Christian Democrats maintained contact with at least some of the Peronistas even after leaving the Front. As a result, after the government had vetoed several nominees put forth by the Front, the Christian Democrats offered to withdraw their candidates for president and vice-president and to support Dr. Raúl Matera, who until shortly before had been head of the Peronista Coordinating Committee, for president. However, this maneuver came to naught both because the government refused to allow Matera to win and because the Peronista trade union leaders denounced Matera as a "traitor."[2]

As a result the Christian Democrats returned to the ticket with which they had begun the 1963 campaign, of Horacio Sueldo for president and Francisco Cerro for vice-president. When the votes were finally cast on July 7, the Christian Democrats came in seventh, with 434,713 votes, about 5 percent of the total. At the same time they elected two senators and seven members of the new Chamber of Deputies.[3]

During the administration of President Arturo Illia (1963-66), the Christian Democrats continued to align themselves with the Peronistas, supporting the "battle plan" of the Peronista leadership of the labor confederation, the Confederación General del Trabajo, frankly designed to imperil the Illia government. At the party's national convention held in August 1964, Horacio Sueldo was reelected its president; and in his acceptance speech he claimed: "The party constitutes the political instrument of spiritual, cultural, economic and social promotion of the working class and the lower middle class."[4]

However, in fact the Christian Democrats had not gained any significant influence in the organized labor movement. It remained one of the country's minor parties, and its possibilities of growth had been shown to be small. After the coup d'état of June 1966, which put General Juan Carlos Ongania in the presidency, the Christian Democratic Party was legally suppressed by the government, along with all of the rest of the country's political parties. It was revived in 1971. when parties were again allowed to function legally; but it was doubtful that the party would again attain the power it had possessed in the mid-1950s.

BRAZIL

The Christian Democratic Party of Brazil was one of several new political groups to emerge after the overthrow of the dictatorship of Getúlio Vargas in 1945. In its early years the party had its greatest strength in the city and state of São Paulo. Jânio Quadros was one of its early candidates for city councilman in São Paulo, and in 1953 he was the party's successful nominee for mayor of the city. However, because of refusal to abide by party discipline and his general disdain for political parties, Quadros was expelled from the Christian Democratic Party during his period as mayor. The Christian Democrats supported one of his opponents, Prestes Maia, when Quadros ran for governor of São Paulo in 1954.[5]

However, the Christian Democrats soon became a national party. By 1955 they had five members of the state legislature of Pernambuco and were represented in the legislatures of a number of other states.[6] In that same year they nominated the old Tenente leader Juárez Távora, who had joined the Christian Democratic Party and later served as its secretary-general, for president. Also endorsed by the Socialist Party, the União Democrática Nacional, and several small parties, he was defeated by the narrowest of margins by Juscelino Kubitschek.

In this period the Christian Democrats were generally aligned with the forces opposed to the influence of Getúlio Vargas, and Távora was generally recognized as the anti-Vargas candidate in the 1955 election. They maintained this position until after the election of 1960.

In the presidential poll of 1960, the Christian Democrats supported the candidacy of Jânio Quadros. As Quadros' running mate they nominated Francisco Ferrari, a young deputy from the state of Rio Grande do Sul who was leader of a dissident wing of the Partido Trabalhista Brasileiro. Because of Ferrari's candidacy the voters who supported Quadros for president split their support for vice-president (the União Democrática Nacional had named Milton Campos as Quadros' running mate), with the result that although Quadros was elected president, João Goulart, the vice-presidential candidate of his opponent, was chosen vice-president.

During the early 1960s the Christian Democratic Party made substantial gains but became badly split over the issue of whether or not to support the government of João Goulart. In the 1962 gubernatorial elections the party won its first state victory when its candidate Ney Braga was chosen as governor of the state of Paraná. It also made substantial advances in a number of other states in this poll.

However, by this time the party was badly divided. There were at least three recognizable factions. On the right was the element led by Juárez Távora and Governor Ney Braga, which was extremely critical of the Goulart regime. On the extreme left was a faction led by Paulo de Tarso, who served for some time as a member of Goulart's cabinet. In the center was a group of young party leaders headed by the vice-governor of Paraná, Affonso Camargo Neto.

In early October 1963, Paulo de Tarso resigned as João Goulart's minister of education.[7] However, when the party's congress met on October 25, the far Left orientation of the former minister came under attack from both of the other factions. As a result the congress adopted a resolution "which disapproved of the political line of action of Sr. de Tarso" and forbade party members to belong to any of the various extreme leftist coalitions then in existence.[8]

At the time of the coup d'état that overthrew João Goulart in April 1964, the split in the Christian Democratic ranks came into the open. Juárez Távora was one of the principal participants in the coup and became minister of transport and communications in the new government of Humberto Castelo Branco; Ney Braga also supported the new regime. At the other extreme Paulo de Tarso was one of the members of the Chamber of Deputies whose election was canceled, and he was forced to flee into exile.

The factionalism within the Christian Democrats reached a climax at a party congress held in March 1965. In that meeting Ney

Braga was defeated for reelection as president of the party by a coalition of the other two factions. He was replaced by André Franco Montoro, who during the remaining months of the party's life energetically tried to reunite the demoralized Christian Democratic ranks.[9] His efforts bore some fruit, and the possibility that the Christian Democratic Party would emerge from the uncertain political situation as the most important spokesman for the democratic Left in Brazilian national politics seemed relatively good.

However, all hope of a return to normal constitutional government and to democratic politics was ended late in October 1965, when Castelo Branco issued the so-called Second Institutional Act, which dissolved all existing political parties. This sounded the death knell of the party, and no serious effort was made to keep the organization alive on an illegal basis.

URUGUAY

The Partido Demócrata Cristiano of Uruguay evolved out of the Unión Cívica, which had been established in 1912, as one of its historians said, for "the defense of Catholic Interest."[10] During the decades that followed, Unión Cívica won a recognized place in national politics, regularly electing a senator or two and a handful of deputies to the national parliament. It was noted for the high quality of its leadership and, particularly in the post-World War II period, had increasingly come to ally itself with the new Christian Democratic parties that were growing up in other Latin American countries. In 1947 Unión Cívica served as host for the first Latin American conference, attended by the Chilean Falange Nacional and small groups from Argentina and Brazil. Dardo Regules, Unión Cívica senator, was named first permanent secretary of the Organización Demócrata Cristiana de América.[11]

However, by the early 1960s younger members and leaders of the party were impatient with what they conceived to be the "confessional" traditions of Unión Cívica and what they felt was its too conservative outlook. They pushed through a move to change of the party's name to Partido Demócrata Cristiano in 1962, and two years later there was a split. The older, more conservative element withdrew to form the Movimiento Cívico Cristiano, leaving the Partido Demócrata Cristiano in the hands of the "young Turks."[12]

The radicalization of the Uruguayan Christian Democrats also brought about a change in the nature of their organization. Somewhat on the pattern of their Chilean and Venezuelan counterparts, they established functional groups to work among particular segments of the population. The Frente Laboral Demócrata Cristiano was set up to try to win influence among the organized workers, and Organización Feminina Demócrata Cristiana to do special work among the women voters; Juventud Demócrata Cristiano was organized to organize the country's youth, particularly in the universities. At the same time special secretariats were organized to handle political problems, finances, propaganda, international relations, and organization, and a special doctrinal secretariat worked out the details of the party's philosophy and program.

Since 1964 the Uruguayan Christian Democratic Party has been aligned with the more radical elements in the Latin American Christian Democratic movement. They sided, for example, with the so-called <u>rebeldes</u> within the Chilean party against the supporters of President Frei.[13]

In 1971 the Partido Demócrata Cristiano served as the fulcrum for a broad alliance of all left-wing elements, the Frente Amplio. As a legally recognized party, the Christian Democrats put forward as candidate a retired general, Liber Seregni; and his campaign was supported by the Socialists, Communists, Trotskyites, dissident left-wing Colorado and Blanco factions, and even by the urban guerrilla terrorist movement, the Tupamaros (Movimiento de Liberación Nacional-Tupamaros). Seregni received about 20 percent of the total vote, which was somewhat better than the leftist parties normally received in Uruguayan elections.

PERU

The Peruvian Partido Democrático Cristiano was established during the last months of the dictatorship of General Manuel Odría (1948-56), when it became obvious that there was going to be a more or less free election to choose his successor. The first unit of the party was set up in the southern city of Arequipa in September 1955, and a branch was established in the following month at Lima. The party's first national congress was held in January 1956.

The Christian Democrats had their first electoral experience in 1956, when they won 4 seats in the Senate and 13 in the Chamber of Deputies. The majority of these were from Arequipa, where the party was strongest. However, some were elected in Lima and elsewhere, at least partly through the support of the country's major party, the Partido Aprista Peruano, which was still illegal and was not able to put up its own nominees.[14]

During its first few years the Christian Democrats maintained close relations with the Apristas. However, with the rise to major influence within the party of Hector Cornejo Chávez, leader of the party's more left-wing elements, relations between the two groups became more strained. In the election of 1962 the Christian Democrats ran Cornejo Chávez as their own presidential candidate. He received only about 50,000 votes, although the party did much better on the congressional level, getting approximately 190,000 votes for its candidates for deputy and senator.

The results of the 1962 election were canceled by a military coup that overthrew President Manuel Prado, and new elections were called for the following year. At that point the Christian Democrats first sought to form an electoral alliance with the Apristas. However, when the Apristas were unwilling to meet the conditions laid down by the Christian Democrats for such an alliance, the latter threw their support behind Fernando Belaúnde Terry, the chief opponent of the Apristas. A formal electoral pact was signed between the Christian Democrats and Belaúnde's party, Acción Popular, whereby the Christian Democrats were given the post of second vice-president on the Belaúnde ticket in return for their support.[15]

Belaúnde won the election of 1963. During most of the next five years, the Christian Democrats had members of the president's cabinet. They were particularly active in drawing up and fighting for the agrarian reform bill that Belaúnde sent to Congress. Although the bill was substantially altered in Congress, an agrarian reform law was passed; and the institute that administered it was to a large degree run by Christian Democrats.

The first municipal elections in 40 years were held in December 1963. In these the Christian Democrats and Acción Popular put up joint tickets in most municipalities; their most spectacular success was in the city of Lima, where a Christian Democrat, Luís Bedoya Reyes, was elected mayor. He proved to be very popular and was reelected in 1967.

However, the meteoric rise in influence of Bedoya Reyes within the Christian Democratic Party caused tensions and an ultimate split in the organization. The left wing of the party, under the leadership of Cornejo Chávez, accused Bedoya Reyes of being too moderate in his administration of the capital city. Also, the mayor of Lima was being increasingly mentioned as a possible candidate of the Christian Democrat-Acción Popular coalition in the presidential election scheduled for 1969, a prospect that did not please the more dogmatic Christian Democrats.

As a result of this conflict, Bedoya Reyes led a split in the Partido Democrático Cristiano in 1967, forming his own party, the Partido Popular Cristiano. It soon outnumbered the older group, particularly in the Lima area.[16]

As the 1969 election approached, each Christian Democratic faction named its own candidate for president. The PDC put up Hector Cornejo Chávez for the second time, while the Partido Popular

Cristiano named Bedoya Reyes. However, the campaigns of both men were cut short by the military coup d'état of October 1968, which installed the government headed by General Juan Velasco Alvarado. The new regime immediately suspended the scheduled elections and dissolved the Supreme Electoral Tribunal as "unnecessary," since the regime had no intention of allowing new elections in the foreseeable future.

When the Velasco government assumed a strong "anti-imperialist" attitude, particularly with its expropriation of the U.S.-owned International Petroleum Corporation, the Partido Democrático Cristiano threw its support behind the regime. The PPC was somewhat more circumspect in its attitude and ultimately joined the opposition.

Hector Cornejo Chávez became head of a new supreme court established by the military regime. In 1971 his close association with the Velasco government provoked a new split in the party's ranks, when most of its youth broke away.

EL SALVADOR

In Central America the Christian Democrats are most influential in El Salvador. The party there goes back to 1954, when a group of university students attended an international congress of Pax Romana, where they were first extensively introduced to the social doctrines of the Church; they returned determined to organize a Christian Democratic Party. However, they first felt the need for a thorough study of Catholic social doctrine and organized themselves into groups for this purpose that soon included a number of professional men.

The actual establishment of the Christian Democratic Party was precipitated by the events following the overthrow of President José María Lemus in 1960. The Junta Cívico-Militar that took over was very much to the Left and included a number of Communist sympathizers. It called new elections and to participate in them organized a new political group, the Frente Cívico, which included virtually all of the country's non-Christian Democratic leftists. As a result the young people who had been planning the establishment of a Christian Democratic Party, but had not intended to do so immediately, decided that they had better advance their schedule and set up their party then, rather than leave the Frente Cívico as the only group participating in the elections.

Meanwhile, a group of military men, worried about the prospect of a pro-Communist government, overthrew the Junta Cívico-Militar on January 25, 1961. They then sought the support of the new Christian Democratic Party for their regime and in the elections they called soon afterward. However, the Christian Democrats had agreed that they would not participate in any military regime. As a result, although the succeeding administration of Colonel Julio Rivera recruited to its ranks a number of people who had originally been allied with the Christian Democrats, the party did not participate in it and in fact became one of the two principal parties of the opposition, the other being the Partido de Acción Renovadora, of more or less Marxist-Leninist tendencies.

Although a new party, the Christian Democrats scored a number of successes in the 1960s. They succeeded in electing Luís Napoleón Duarte, a leading member of the party, as mayor of the capital city of San Salvador; and in accordance with Salvadorean electoral law, which gives all seats in a city council to the party receiving the largest number of votes, also won complete control of the San Salvador council. Duarte gave the city a progressive and energetic administration for two terms, cleaning up the extensive corruption that had characterized municipal affairs, equipping the city with street lights, building a number of new city markets, and generally cleaning up the capital. His efforts won wide support among the city's population.

The strength of the Christian Democrats was centered largely in the central part of the country, around San Salvador. In most of the towns and cities of this area, the party won control of the municipal government.

The PDC came in third in the 1967 presidential election. However, five years later it was the principal challenge to the government's Partido de Reconciliación Nacional. The PDC candidate, Luís Napoleón Duarte, was able to mobilize wide support from more or less progressive and left-wing elements outside his own party's ranks.

In preparation for the possibility of assuming power in the country at large, the Christian Democrats developed a program calling for basic economic and social changes. Their major emphasis in this program was on agrarian reform to end the complete domination of the land by a small handful of powerful families, diversification of agricultural production, and the stimulation of industrialization.[17]

GUATEMALA

The Christian Democratic movement in Guatemala was organized in the wake of the downfall of the pro-Communist government of President Jacobo Arbenz, which occurred in June 1954. During the last year or so of the Arbenz regime a group of young professional men and students, under the leadership of José García Bauer, a labor lawyer and former deputy and labor judge during the administration of President Juan José Arévalo (1945-51), had formed a group to study the social teaching of the Church and lay the basis for the establishment of a Christian Democratic Party.[18]

The Movimiento de Democracia Cristiano (sometimes using the name Partido Democracia Cristiana) was finally organized as a political party in 1955. It was strongly opposed to the reactionary tendencies of the government of Colonel Carlos Castillo Armas, which had succeeded that of Arbenz. Although anti-Communist, the Christian Democrats were favorably disposed to many of the projects the Arbenz government had undertaken, such as an agrarian reform and advanced labor legislation, and were very strongly opposed to the destruction by the Castillo Armas regime of most of the reforms of the Arévalo-Arbenz period.

The Movimiento de Democracia Cristiano was duly recognized as a political party during the Castillo Armas regime, when the requirement for legalization was the presentation of a petition with 10,000 signatures. However, during the military government of Enrique Peralta (1963-66) the party lost its registration when the requirement was raised to 50,000 signatures. Only after the election of 1966, in the last weeks of the Peralta administration, was legal recognition restored to the party.

During the election of 1966 the Christian Democrats sought an electoral alliance with the Partido Revolucionario, headed by Julio César Méndez Montenegro, which proclaimed its intention to return the country to the path of fundamental reform that had characterized most of the 1944-54 period. However, the two groups were not able to reach an agreement; and as a result the Christian Democrats urged their supporters to cast blank ballots. They claimed considerable success for this campaign, with the number of such ballots coming to 15 percent of the total cast.

Like most of the Christian Democratic parties, that of Guatemala undertook extensive grassroots organization and proselytizing among various groups in the community. In the late 1960s it worked closely with the Christian-oriented Federación Central de Trabajadores and the similarly directed Federación Campesina. The party also maintained a research institute to study a wide range of social and economic problems, and to develop programs for reforms and development that might be useful for a future Christian Democratic government.[19]

By the late 1960s the Christian Democrats had become one of the country's three principal parties. They had considerable following in the working and middle classes and were serious contenders for power. The Christian Democrats named their own candidate for president in the March 1970 election. This candidate, Jorge Lucas Caballeros, came in third, with 125,948 votes; 251,135 were received by the winner, Colonel Carlos Arana Osorio, and 202,241 were obtained by Mario Fuentes Pieruccini of the Partido Revolucionario.[20]

DOMINICAN REPUBLIC

In the wake of the assassination of Rafael Leónidas Trujillo in May 1961 and the dismantling of his dictatorship, many new parties appeared in the Dominican Republic. Several of these took names indicating association with Christian democracy. However, the party that emerged as the genuine representative of this political ideology was the Partido Revolucionario Social Cristiano.

During the first year of its existence, the PRSC received considerable aid from the Copei Párty of Venezuela. A number of leaders of the new party went to Venezuela for instruction at the Copei's leadership training school; and officials of the new Confederación Autónoma de Sindicatos Cristianos, the labor movement organized by members and allies of the PRSC, were trained at the trade union leadership school run by the Copei. Several important figures in the Copei visited the Dominican Republic during this period.

The PRSC soon emerged as one of the major factors in the nation's university student movement. For a while it controlled the Student Federation of the National University of Santo Domingo, although in the late 1960s it lost out to the extreme leftists.[21] Its trade union group remained a small but well-organized part of the labor movement.

During the first election after the death of Trujillo, in 1963, the PRSC ran its own candidate, who came in third behind the nominees of the Partido Revolucionario Dominicano and the Unión Cívica Nacional. The party received about 70,000 votes.[22]

Although it had been part of the opposition to the Bosch regime, the Partido Revolucionario Social Cristiano refused to have anything to do with the so-called triumvirate government that came to power after the coup d'état that overthrew Bosch in September 1963. It strongly opposed the government presided over during most of the period September 1963-April 1965 by Donald Reid Cabral.

When the revolution against the triumvirate took place in April 1965, under the leadership of Colonel Francisco Caamaño, the PRSC supported the uprising. Members of the party fought in the armed forces of the "constitutionalist" Caamaño regime; and Antonio Rosario, the president of the PRSC, served for several months as spokesman for the Caamaño government in Washington, D.C.

The civil war started by the Caamaño revolt and marked by massive U.S. military intervention ended in a compromise agreement in August 1965, by which Hector García Godoy became provisional president. In June 1966 elections were held in which Juan Bosch ran as candidate of the Partido Revolucionario Dominicano against Joaquín Balaguer, supported by his own Partido Reformista. The PRSC supported Bosch.[23]

CHRISTIAN DEMOCRATIC PARTIES

In spite of having been aligned with Balaguer's major opponent in the 1966 campaign, the Partido Revolucionario Social Cristiano did not engage in absolute and complete opposition to the Balaguer government. On the contrary, it functioned as the loyal opposition, as a result of which Balaguer on several occasions talked in a friendly fashion about the PRSC, to the great annoyance of its principal leaders.[24]

In the midterm elections of 1968, the PRSC made significant gains, due at least in part to the abstention of the Partido Revolucionario Dominicano. The total votes for the PRSC rose from 60,000 in 1966 to about 125,000 in 1968.[25]

However, the party did not do so well in the 1970 presidential and congressional elections. Although it had its own nominee for the presidency, Alfonso Moreno Martínez, he came in a poor fourth; and the party did not elect any members of Congress. PRSC leaders attributed their party's poor showing to the polarization of the election between President Balaguer and his principal opponent, Francisco Augusto Lora, and to the feeling that even though the PRSC was "a party of the future," a citizen would "throw away his vote" in this particular election by voting for the Partido Revolucionario Social Cristiano.[26]

Throughout its existence one of the outstanding characteristics of the Partido Revolucionario Social Cristiano has been its attention to rank-and-file organization. It has maintained a training school for the instruction of its secondary and tertiary leaders and has spent considerable time and energy in imparting the party's doctrine to rank-and-file members and training them in the problems of organization. Another major characteristic of the party has been its refusal to make opportunistic deals that might have brought about rapid though ephemeral growth of the party.

BOLIVIA

The first party of vaguely Christian Democratic orientation in Bolivia was the Partido Social Democrático, organized in the early 1950s. However, a group of the youth of this party, dissatisfied with its conservative orientation, and particularly with its alliance with the fascist-oriented Falange Socialista Boliviana, withdrew in 1954 to establish the Partido Social Cristiano. This group was one of the smaller opposition parties during the 12-year rule of the Movimiento Nacional Revolucionario (1952-64). Although it sympathized with the military coup that overthrew the MNR government, it refused to ally itself with the forces supporting the subsequent candidacy for president of General René Barrientos. Only 10 days after the overthrow of the MNR government, the PSC held a national convention in which it changed its name to Partido Demócrata Cristiano and adopted a militant program that it described as being of "the Christian Left."[27]

During the short regime of Juan José Torres (1970-71), the PDC underwent a split, with some of its more extremist elements, particularly among the youth, breaking away to form the Partido Democráta Cristiano Revolucionario, which supported the Torres regime. The main body of the PDC, however, was opposed to Torres and participated in the plotting that resulted in the overthrow of Torres in August 1971. But the PDC did not become part of the subsequent government of Colonel Hugo Banzer.

PARAGUAY

The Christian Democratic movement in Paraguay was born in the late 1950s during the long struggle against the dictatorship of General Alfredo Stroessner. Since its establishment in May 1960 at Asunción, the Movimiento Social Democrático Cristiano has constituted one of the major elements in the opposition to Stroessner. As a result it has suffered persecution at the hands of the regime. In December 1962, the vice-president of the MSDC, José María Ronin, and a member of the National Executive Board, Luís Resck, were arrested to prevent their publication of a proposed "Christmas message," in which they planned to denounce the Stroessner government.[28]

The program of the MSDC was demonstrated in a manifesto published by its National Executive Board on May 31, 1960. One passage of this statement said:

> The Movimiento Social D.C. of Paraguay, profoundly preoccupied with the fate of the country and fully conscious that ills that made our national life so precarious are not due only to recent causes or of political origin, today states its firm belief, to pledge its name before history, in the glorious attempt to promote, in loyal collaboration with authentically national political groups, an integral renovation of the fatherland. Because it is democratic and Christian, it aspires to carry out a conception of civic life based on the respect for the eminent dignity of the individual, in social justice and in the continuous and stable maintenance of liberty. . . .[29]

Although in fact a political party, the Movimiento Social Democrático Cristiano was never given legal recognition as one by the Stroessner regime. As a result it did not participate in the few more or less free elections that the Stroessner regime permitted in the late 1960s, and so there has been little chance to gauge (even as inaccurately as this might be possible in one of Stroessner's electoral contests) just how much popular support the Christian Democrats have been able to muster in Paraguay.

COLOMBIA

In Colombia, where the Partido Conservador had long been the principal spokesman for political Catholicism, Christian Democratic ideas had begun to gain some following by the 1960s. A group of young intellectuals known as Testimonio sent a delegation to the international Christian Democratic congress held at Santiago, Chile, in 1955. Those returning from this meeting expressed their hope that a Christian Democratic movement could soon be organized in Colombia.[30]

The Partido Social Democrático Cristiano of Colombia was organized in 1959 by a group of young people, few of whom had been active in any other party. From its inception it was hampered by the existence of the Frente Nacional system, which made it legally possible for only two parties, the Liberals and the Conservatives, to hold public office in the country. (The system is scheduled to persist until 1974.) In the elections of 1964, the party attempted to run a list of candidates under its own name; and when this was not possible, it urged its supporters to cast blank ballots.[31] However, the PSDC leaders went ahead with the work of establishing party organization throughout the country. For instance, late in 1963 a course in party principles was organized at the Antioquia departmental headquarters of the PSDC in Medellín, as well as in the departments of Hila, Tolima, Caldas, Meta, and Atlántico were publishing more or less regular periodicals.[32] By 1968 they had at least a semblance of a party structure in 17 of the 20 departments into which Colombia is divided politically. The party had obtained some influence in the student movement and had a few members in executive positions in the Unión de Trabajadores de Colombia, the country's largest labor group; but most of its support was in the middle class, and particularly among white collar workers.[33]

PANAMA

Christian democracy in Panama traces its origins to the First Week of Christian Studies, which met at Cumbres in March 1957. Those participating in this session and the Second Week of Christian Studies in July 1959 included "intellectuals, professionals and university students, who in one field or another expressed their desire for Social Christian action."

The group that organized these meetings was organized on April 12, 1956, and first called itself Acción Social Demócrata. Subsequently it changed its name to Movimiento Demócrata Cristiano. The first "meeting of leaders" of the group was held in February 1957, and at that session the movement was formally organized.[34]

The Partido Demócrata Cristiano was finally launched at a congress early in 1964. It had its first electoral experience in May of that year, when it named José A. Molino as its candidate for president. He received 9,719 votes, coming in fourth among seven nominees. This showing was considered a success for the new party and was enough to assure its registration as a legal party.[35] In the succeeding years the Christian Democrats continued to be a small but well-organized element in Panamanian national politics.

COSTA RICA

The Christian Democratic Party of Costa Rica was established by a congress at San José in March 1965. This congress represented the culmination of the labors of an organizing committee that had been working for two and a half years to lay the basis for the new party. Although at its inception the Christian Democratic Party remained a small organization in comparison with the nation's three major parties—Liberación Nacional, Unión Nacional, and Partido Nacional Republicano—it was the cause of considerable preoccupation on the part of some of the leaders of these parties, particularly Liberación Nacional. There was fear in the latter that if it were to lose the 1970 elections and continued to move to the Right, the PDC might be able to attract elements that until then had supported Liberación Nacional.

However, these fears did not materialize in 1970. The PLN succeeded once again in electing José Figueres president; and the Partido Demócrata Cristiano's nominee Jorge Monge received only about 1 percent of the total vote.[36] The PDC thus remained a small party whose fate seemed to be linked with the success or failure of the Partido Liberación Nacional.

NICARAGUA

Christian democracy in Nicaragua is represented by the Partido Social Cristiano. It had its origins in the Conservative Youth, which at its fifth congress in July 1957 decided to call itself Movimiento Popular Demócrata Cristiano.[37] It held its first national assembly of leaders on July 14, 1963.[38] In the following year the party was joined by another group of Conservatives, led by Reynaldo Antonio

Tefel, who had been trying for some time to convert the Conservative Party into "a people's party" but had finally concluded that this was not going to be possible.[39]

The Partido Social Cristiano gained its principal support from the lower middle class, and for some years it controlled the student movement at the National University. Although the Conservatives and Social Christians supported the same candidate for president against Anastasio Somoza, Jr., in 1966, the Partido Social Cristiano subsequently conducted the most consistent and principled opposition to the Somoza regime.

MEXICO

In Mexico since the 1930s there has been an opposition party, Partido Acción Nacional, which claimed to gain inspiration from the social teachings of the Catholic Church. However, it was generally considered by Christian Democrats outside Mexico to be too conservative to be recognized as belonging to the Christian Democratic camp. However, in the early 1960s the Movimiento Social Demócrata Cristiano was established, which was accepted as a part of the international Christian Democratic movement. It was not recognized by the Mexican government as a political party, since the country's electoral law forbids the use of religious references in the name of any party.

Like Christian Democratic parties in other Latin American countries, the Movimiento Social Demócrata Cristiano carried out intensive programs of training of its lower-rank leaders and rank and file. For this purpose it established the Instituto de Formación y Estudios Sociales, which held its first classes in November and December 1963. The party also maintained a trade union and peasant training school.[40]

HAITI

The Parti Populaire Sociale Chrétien of Haiti was established by a group of young members of Catholic Action in February 1946, a month after the overthrow of the dictatorship of Elie Lescot. The party published a newspaper, L'action sociale, and participated in elections held later in 1946. Although it claimed to have elected a senator, its victory was not recognized by the electoral authorities. During the government of Dumarsais Estimé (1946-49), the PRSC was one of the major parties in the opposition.[41]

Although driven underground during the dictatorship of General Paul Magloire (1949-56), the PPSC was able to maintain a clandestine organization. It was not so lucky during the tyranny of François Duvalier, who came to power in 1957. In May 1960 the party was invited to send a delegation to the World Congress of Christian Democratic Youth, but Duvalier did not allow them to leave the country. By early 1963 most of the party's leaders were in exile.[42]

CUBA

The Movimiento Demócrata Cristiano of Cuba evolved out of the struggle against the dictatorship of Fulgencio Batista in the late 1950s. Numerous members of the Juventud Obrera Católica fought in the guerrilla forces of Fidel Castro; and during the first months of the Castro regime, they reorganized as the Movimiento Demócrata Cristiano, with the hope ultimately of establishing a Christian Democratic Party. However, as the Castro regime turned toward Communism, the Christian Democrats went into opposition and most were forced into exile. After 1960 the MDC maintained its headquarters and held its regular conventions in Miami, Florida.[43]

PUERTO RICO

The Christian Democratic movement of Puerto Rico took form in the months preceeding the 1960 election, with the establishment of the Partido Acción Cristiana. In that election the candidates of the new party were endorsed by the Puerto Rican bishops, which provoked a serious conflict between them and Governor Luís Muñoz Marín, head of the Popular Democratic Party and candidate for reelection. The PAC did not receive the minimum number of votes required to maintain its registration as a legal party. It continued nonetheless in existence but did not become a major factor in Puerto Rican politics.

INTERNATIONAL ORGANIZATION OF CHRISTIAN DEMOCRATS

The various Christian Democratic parties of Latin America are bound together in both regional and global organizations. On the hemispheric scale there is the Organización Demócrata Cristiana Americana, established at a congress in Montivideo in 1947. On a broader basis the Christian Democratic parties of Latin America belong to the World Christian Democratic Movement, which held its congress at Santiago, Chile, in 1961.

CHRISTIAN DEMOCRATIC PARTIES 369

These international Christian Democratic organizations do not impose any particular discipline on their affiliates. The ODCA maintains an office in Santiago, Chile, and for some time published a monthly newspaper, Dece, which carried news and comment on the activities and ideas of the various parties belonging to the organization. It also holds periodic congresses, at which the principles as well as the strategy and tactics of Christian democracy in the hemisphere are extensively discussed.

In theory, perhaps the only disciplinary measure that ODCA could take against one of its affiliates would be expulsion. However, so far as we know, such an action has never been taken.

Nevertheless, despite lack of actual power over its affiliates, the ODCA undoubtedly exercises considerable influence over them. It helps to create a feeling of community and solidarity among the various parties. Frequent conferences of leaders of the parties belonging to ODCA also help them agree on general lines of policy. Finally, on some occasions—as in the early days of the Partido Revolucionario Social Cristiano—the ODCA and some of the parties affiliated with it are able to give material help to parties that particularly need aid.

The importance of membership in ODCA is perhaps shown by the eagerness of parties to join. This is particularly true of the Acción Nacional Party in Mexico and the Falange Socialista Boliviana in Bolivia, both of which have upon several occasions applied for admission but have been rejected.

PART V
TOTALITARIAN PARTIES

INTRODUCTION

Probably no area of the world has been completely without totalitarian parties during the last few decades. Latin America has had its share of such groups; but, except in the case of Cuba, no totalitarian party has come fully to power, and only in a few countries of the area has this type of political group been a major factor in national politics.

In the discussions in the following four chapters, we have dealt with three different kinds of Communist parties found in the region and have added a chapter on fascist parties, although at the present time these are of little significance. A decade or so ago only two chapters, one on the Communists and one on the fascists, would have been required. However, in recent years there has developed a considerable amount of diversity in the Communist camp, both in the world in general and in Latin America.

Communism as a political movement has existed in Latin America as long as it has anywhere. By the late 1950s there were Communist parties in every Latin American country. The first chapter in this section is devoted to a survey of the orthodox parties that either belonged to the Communist International or would have belonged to it had they existed when it did, and that currently are loyal to the Soviet Union.

However, the Communists of Latin America have been as subject to schism and faction as they have in any other part of the globe. Every division within the Communist ranks that has taken place during the last 50 years has had some degree of repercussion in the Latin American Communist parties. The second chapter in this section is devoted to an analysis of the impact of these splits in the area.

Furthermore, Latin America has had the distinction of having a faction of international Communism based in one of its countries: Cuba. The Castro regime and the party that heads it took the lead for several years in trying to establish a "Third Force" in the world Communist movement; this effort is traced in the third chapter.

Finally, there have been fascist parties in several of the Latin American countries. Although they are now of virtually no significance in the area's politics, they were of considerable importance in the 1930s and 1940s. There are still a few such parties in the region, and perhaps the ideas they fostered are by no means completely absent even in the countries that no longer have fascist parties.

We have confined our discussion of totalitarian parties to the Communists and fascists. Some may argue that other organizations, such as Rafael Trujillo's Partido Dominicano were as absolutist in their demands as any Communist or fascist group has ever been. We would not challenge the absolute nature of the Trujillo regime, which, no less than Communist and fascist parties and governments, tried to control not only the actions of its subjects but also their thoughts. However, there is one major difference between the totalitarianism of the Communist and fascist parties and governments and such phenomena as the Trujillo government and the Partido Dominicano. The former are ideological; they have a philosophy and a dogma that they set up as being the absolute truth and through which they attempt to interpret the past, the present, and the future. Trujillo had no ideology and probably no beliefs and ideas of his own, except concerning his right to govern his island republic.

It is this ideology or philosophy that sets the totalitarian groups apart. It creates a community among the totalitarian parties and justifies our treating the Communist and fascist organizations under the same general heading.

CHAPTER 19

THE ORTHODOX COMMUNIST PARTIES

An orthodox Communist Party exists in every Latin American republic. Some of these parties antedate the Russian Revolution and the establishment of the Communist International. Although a handful of these organizations has participated for short periods of time in governments of various Latin American countries, none of them has succeeded in obtaining complete power for itself.

ORIGINS OF THE COMMUNIST MOVEMENT IN LATIN AMERICA

Several of the Latin American Communist parties existed before the world Communist movement was established. Thus, the Uruguayan Socialist Party, which in April 1921 became the Communist Party of Uruguay, was organized in 1910; the Chilean Socialist Workers Party, which in 1922 was transformed into the Partido Comunista de Chile, was established under the leadership of Luís Emilio Recabarren in 1912. The Argentine Partido Socialista Internacionalista was launched as a left-wing scission in the more moderate Partido Socialista in January 1918, a year before the setting up of the Communist International. The Mexican party was organized in the same year that the Comintern was established.

Several other Latin American Communist parties came into existence during the 1920s. That of Cuba was launched by a group of labor leaders and intellectuals in 1925; the Brazilian party was set up by a number of young anarcho-syndicalist trade unionists in 1922; the parties of Peru and Costa Rica were organized in 1929.

The 1930s saw a number of other Communist parties established. These included the ones in Guatemala, Honduras, and El Salvador, which were subsequently annihilated by dictatorships, and that of Panama. The Venezuelan Communist Party was established in 1931, and those of Colombia and Ecuador were set up in 1930. A handful of parties were organized during the 1940s, including those of Haiti, the Dominican Republic, Nicaragua, and the reconstituted parties of Guatemala and El Salvador. The reconstituted Communist Party of Honduras was probably the last to be established on a permanent basis, in the early 1950s.

During the early years of the existence of Communism in Latin America, the Communist International played an important part in its affairs. Comintern agents played a significant role in establishing the Mexican party. In 1929 the South American Bureau of the Comintern was established, with its headquarters in Uruguay. It intervened actively in the internal affairs of a number of the parties, most notably in those of the Chilean party.

In those early years the Communists organized a variety of "front groups." Thus, as part of the Comintern's crusade against "imperialism," there was organised a string of Anti-Imperialist Leagues, through which the Communist parties sought to mobilize non-Communist elements in their campaign against, in particular, the influence of Great Britain and the United States in Latin America. The various parties set up their own trade union groups, and in 1929 a Latin American labor confederation under Communist control was launched. This was the Confederación Sindical Latino Americana, which had affiliates in all of the Latin American countries in which there were Communist parties.

EBBS AND FLOWS OF COMMUNIST STRENGTH

The Communists have become a major political group in only a handful of Latin American countries. They have been a major party in Chile for a generation; they were a major contender for power in Guatemala during the administration of Jacobo Arbenz between 1951 and 1954; they were an important element in the coalition backing President Fulgencio Batista between 1938 and 1944; they were a major factor in Venezuelan politics for a short while between 1958 and 1960.

However, although not generally reaching a position of major significance in Latin American national politics, the influence of the Communists has varied greatly during the more than half century of their history. During most of the 1920s they slowly gained strength, and by the end of that decade they were of some influence in the organized labor movement of a number of the Latin American countries.

During the so-called Third Period, lasting from early 1929 until about 1935, the Communist International laid down an extremist

ORTHODOX COMMUNIST PARTIES

revolutionary line. The Latin American Communist parties were very loyal to this line. They succeeded in isolating themselves almost completely from virtually every other element in Latin American politics and in destroying much of the influence they had acquired during the earlier period. This was the era of extreme sectarianism, the Communists generally tending to classify all political elements as Communists, or "fascists" (anything from moderate conservatives to real fascists), or "social fascists" (anyone on the Left who was not a Communist). They insisted on the formation of separate Communist-controlled labor organizations that were violently at war with all other elements in each national labor movement.

With the advent of the Popular Front period, the Comintern changed its policy; and this change was obeyed by the Latin American parties. From 1935 until the outbreak of World War II, the Communists sought alliances with the other parties of the Left, and even with some on the Right. They also merged their labor groups with majority trade union movements.

The upshot of this change was the considerable increase in the influence of the Communists, both in trade union affairs and in politics. It was in this period that they were able to form an alliance with Fulgencio Batista in Cuba; to form the Popular Front in Chile with the Socialist, Radical, and several smaller parties; and to become part of the coalition supporting the administration of President Lázaro Cárdenas in Mexico.

It was in this period, too, that the Communists were able to establish the basis for a subsequently spectacular increase in their influence on organized labor. Central labor bodies controlled by the Communists, or in which they had considerable influence, joined with labor groups of other political orientations in the establishment of the Confederación de Trabajadores de América Latina (CTAL). Although at its inception the CTAL was a real united front of trade unionists of every political persuasion except Catholics and anarchists, it later became a completely Communist-dominated group.

For a short while, between September 1939 and June 1941, the period of the Stalin-Nazi pact and the alignment of the Soviet Union with Germany in World War II, the Latin American Communists lapsed again into their previous attitude of isolation from other political groups in the area. They quarreled with their Socialist partners in the Chilean Popular Front, with Cárdenas and his successor Avila Camacho in Mexico, and with groups of the non-Communist Left in other parts of the hemisphere. The period did not last long enough for them to suffer very serious reverses in the organized labor movement, however.

With the attack by Germany on the Soviet Union in June 1941, the Communists of Latin America entered into another period of seeking political alliances. During 1941-45 they showed great flexibility and were willing to support any government or any party that supported the Allied war effort.

It was during this period that the Communists had their first experience in government in Latin America; they had two members of Fulgencio Batista's cabinet in Cuba, during much of his 1940-44 administration. These were Carlos Rafael Rodríguez and Juan Marinello, both of whom later played important parts in the regime of Fidel Castro. Communists also formed part of the junta that governed Ecuador for a short while after the overthrow of President Carlos Arroyo del Río in 1944.

The second part of World War II was the period during which the Communists reached the peak of their influence in Latin American organized labor. They became the dominant influence in the trade unions of Colombia, Peru, Bolivia, Uruguay, Venezuela, Costa Rica, Nicaragua, Panama, and Cuba during all or part of this period. The CTAL also came under their control; and at its Congress in Cali, Colombia, in December 1944, 7 of the 11 men elected to the Executive Committee were avowed Communists. Only one member of the new CTAL Executive was an outspoken anti-Communist.

Communist influence declined rapidly during the postwar period. The very close association with the Soviet Union that the Communists had established in the public mind during World War II rebounded against them when they suddenly turned violently against the USSR's former ally, the United States, in the months following the end of the war; public opinion, even among the Communist-led workers, was generally favorable to the United States at the inception of the Cold War. The Communists also lost their preeminent position in the labor movement, through splits in some Communist-dominated labor groups, through seizure of control by non-Communist groups in some national labor confederations, and by the establishment of new non-Communist trade union centers in several countries. After the founding of the anti-Communist Inter American Confederation of Workers in 1948, the CTAL quickly declined from the majority hemispheric trade union group to a skeleton organization that functioned mainly as the general staff of the Communists within the Latin American labor movement.

By the end of the 1950s the Communists were virtually as isolated in politics and in organized labor as they had been during the Third Period almost a generation before. In few countries would other parties of any significance collaborate with the Communists. Their labor organizations were minority groups in virtually every trade union movement of the area.

However, with the advent of the Castro government to power in Cuba, the Communists were suddenly released from their isolation. They were able to join with a great variety of other groups in

ORTHODOX COMMUNIST PARTIES

expressing enthusiasm for the overthrow of the Batista dictatorship and the advent to power of a regime that promised a new day for the island. They hastened to voice their support and enthusiasm for the new regime, even though in the first months that Castro was in power he gave little or no indication that he would take his regime in a Communist direction.

The Communists were able to make some progress once again in politics and in organized labor in several countries during the first years after Castro's rise to power. However, within a few years the orthodox Communists were faced with two challenges from the left, such as they had not experienced since the decline of the anarchists during the 1920s. These challenges came from pro-Peking dissidents within their own ranks and from the unequivocal supporters of Fidel Castro, throughout his many twists and turns, who by the late 1960s formed a recognizable third force within Latin American Communism.

PRINCIPAL COMMUNIST APPEALS

Throughout the half century history of the Communists in Latin America, they have tended to stress several themes in their propaganda with considerable consistency. Although different emphasis may have been given to these ideas from time to time, they have recurred continuously.

One of these themes is that the Communists are the only true leaders and interpreters of revolution. This was one of their major arguments during the 1920s, when they constantly insisted that their confrères in Russia had made the only successful revolution in this century, and that the local Latin American Communists were the only ones in their countries who held the secret of the Bolsheviks' success. Any other group calling itself revolutionary was in fact composed of "misleaders," "traitors," or "opportunists."

The emphasis on revolution was played down during the Popular Front period, when the Communists were seeking alliances with all sorts of reform groups, but was revived from 1939 to 1941, the time of the Stalin-Nazi Pact. It was again muted during the second part of World War II and was not a major factor in Communist propaganda in the decade and a half after the war, except in countries such as Mexico and Guatemala, where a real revolution was being carried out by non-Communist elements. However, the theme has assumed new importance with the rise of the challenges from the pro-Peking and Havana-oriented Communist groups during the 1960s, the orthodox Communists tending to brand these opponents as pseudo revolutionaries or worse.

A second theme that has been constant in Communist propaganda is the insistence that the Communists are the natural leaders of the organized workers. This claim is consistent with the Communists' belief that they constitute the "vanguard" of the working class and are destined by history to lead it where history intends to take it. Although overt opposition to and contempt for labor groups dominated by other political elements have been somewhat muted during periods in which the Communists have sought to gain the collaboration of these groups, they have never ceased to try to undermine the influence of even supposed allies in the organized labor movement of Latin America.

A third major element of Communist propaganda in Latin America, and the most consistent of all, has been the insistence that the Soviet Union is the model to be followed by Latin Americans. The idea of what the USSR is as a model has changed from time to time, but the concept that it is an example to be followed has been stressed since the early 1920s.

During the 1920s and through the Third Period, the USSR was pictured as the example of revolution. It was shown as having made a successful revolution and of having brought into existence the first classless society, and all Latin Americans who hoped for such an eventuality in their own nations were urged to do as the Soviet Union had done.

During the period of the Popular Front, another image of the Soviet Union was projected by the Latin American Communists. It was argued that the USSR was the one certain bulwark against the growth of fascism and Nazism; and those in Latin America opposed to the spread of these movements were urged to follow the Soviet leadership and to align themselves politically with the Communists, the local group most closely associated with the USSR.

On this issue, as on most others, the Latin American Communists did a sharp about-face during the period of the Stalin-Nazi pact. Instead of being the great opponent of fascism, the USSR was pictured between 1939 and 1941 as the main advocate of peace in a world torn by a "second imperialist war" in which the workers and the masses in Latin America had no interest.

When the Soviet Union was attacked in June 1941, the "second imperialist war" was suddenly converted into a holy war against fascism. As a result the Soviet Union model was presented as the great bulwark in this struggle against the aggression of the Axis powers. The Latin American Communists went to great extremes in expressing their intimate association with the Soviet Union in this struggle, laying special emphasis on the need for the Latin Americans not only to support the Allied war effort but also to accept the Communists as collaborators and allies because of their close relationship with the Soviet Union.

Finally, in the period since World War II, the Latin American Communists have laid stress on the Soviet Union as being the model of two things. First, the USSR has been pictured as the great defender of peace against the allegedly warlike intentions of the United States, even at the risk of provoking World War III. Second, the Soviet Union has been presented as the one country in the world that has found the secret of exceedingly rapid economic development. The Communists have stressed, and overstressed, the transformation of the USSR from a backward agricultural country to "the world's greatest industrial nation" in only a generation. Naturally, they have not talked of the costs of this transformation in economic, political, and human terms; but in the light of the tremendous drive in the Latin American countries for industrialization since World War II, the Communists have felt that this appeal to the example of the Soviet Union would be of particular force in the area.

GROUPS TO WHICH THE COMMUNISTS HAVE APPEALED

Although at one time or another the Latin American Communists have appealed to virtually every significant group in Latin American society and politics, they have tended to concentrate their propaganda on particular elements. A few such groups have been the constant target of Communist efforts, while others have been appealed to only occasionally.

The Latin American Communists have appealed most consistently to the organized workers. This is logical in the light of the Communists' ideology. It is also understandable, since the Communists have consistently had some influence in the trade union movement.

The Communists have also appealed with great consistency to the Latin American intellectuals. There have undoubtedly been several reasons for this. First, the intelligentsia has long been a factor of considerable political significance, generally consisting of members of the upper and upper middle classes, whose importance in national politics has been much greater than their share of the population. Second, the Latin American intellectuals have had a social conscience. They have been concerned over the fate of the lower classes and a priori have been considered elements who might be influenced by the Communist message of social change.

Third, the Communists have not infrequently been able to offer certain material inducements to Latin American intellectuals, particularly since World War II. In an area where writing or painting or composing music has not provided an adequate living to practitioners, the possibility of having works published, paintings exhibited, or music performed in the Soviet Union—and, after World War II, in East Europe as well—has been very attractive. More than one Latin

American intellectual has supported himself to a considerable degree on the royalties or other income received from these sources. In addition, through their patronage by the Communists such artists and writers have achieved worldwide attention that they probably would not otherwise have achieved.

The Latin American Communists have also appealed to the peasants. In 1955 Daniel James argued that the tendency of the Guatemalan Communists to concentrate special attention on the peasants of that country during the early 1950s was an indication that the Guatemalan party was being particularly influenced by the Chinese Communists.[1] However, this assertion was a misreading of the facts.

Until the post-World War II period the peasantry of most Latin American countries was virtually outside the political life of the area. It was largely outside the economy as well, and in some cases did not speak the national language. The peasants were kept in a semiservile state and were suspicious of anyone from the city. As a result the efforts necessary for the Communists—or, for that matter, any political group—to build up support among the peasantry would have been too great to justify the results.

However, long before World War II the Communists did attempt to carry on their propaganda and organizing efforts among the rural population where there was some possibility of success. Thus, during the 1920s the Communists of Mexico built up considerable influence among the peasantry of that country, who had been politically active since the Mexican Revolution. Even in Ecuador, where most peasants still are quiescent, the Communists have sought since the early 1930s to establish a base among the rural Indian population.

Also, in a number of other countries, the Communists were active in seeking to organize rural wage workers on large, relatively modern plantations. Thus, they took the lead in establishing unions among the banana workers of Costa Rica and the sugar workers of Cuba during the 1930s. For some years they had considerable political influence among these groups.

As the peasants and agricultural laborers have become more active and have begun to play a part in politics, the Communists have sought to gain influence among them. This happened in Guatemala during the Arbenz administration (1951-54) and, to a greater or lesser degree, in Peru, Venezuela, Colombia, Brazil, Uruguay, Argentina, and several other nations.

Generally the appeal of the Communists would not seem very attractive to industrialists. However, in Latin America the Communists have from time to time sought to win support among them. They have appealed particularly to national industrial entrepreneurs who have no connection with foreign firms but suffer from competition of firms with such connections and from local branches of foreign enterprises. The appeal to such indigenous businessmen has been on grounds of nationalism and of self-interest. It has not been entirely without success, particularly in Mexico and Brazil.

The armed forces have generally not been very receptive to Communist penetration. Almost by definition, as supporters of law and order and usually as defenders of the status quo, the soldiers have been resistant to Communist influence. However, there have been exceptions.

In Guatemala during the Arbenz administration (1951-54), when both the armed forces and the Communists were supporting the regime, the Communists spent considerable effort on trying to win supporters among the military. A number of important officers were invited to visit the Soviet Union and other East European countries, where they received an elaborate welcome from the national authorities. Communist influence in the government was used to provide the top officers with special benefits, such as cars and extra allowances. However, when the crisis of the Arbenz regime occurred in the middle of 1954, these blandishments did not prove enough to bring the armed forces to the support of the president, and even less to support of the Communists.

In Brazil, too, special circumstances gave the Communists a chance to win some influence among the military, particularly among those who had retired from the service. One of these circumstances was that the man who led the party after 1935 was Luiz Carlos Prestes, a former army officer, who in the 1920s (before becoming a Communist) had led a revolt that had lasted for more than two years and had captured the imagination of many military men. A second factor was the growing nationalistic reaction of many military officers after World War II against the large economic and political influence of the United States in Brazil. At least some of those officers who took a strong nationalist stance were willing to cooperate with the Communists in various campaigns, including that in favor of the so-called Stockholm Peace Petition in the early 1950s. Such willingness was particularly evident during the Goulart administration (1961-64).

During the early 1960s the Communists also had a small measure of success in penetrating the Venezuelan armed forces, particularly the marines. Dissident marines worked with the Communists and their allies in two uprisings in the cities of Puerto Cabello and Carupano in 1962.

COMMUNIST INTERNATIONAL ORGANIZATION IN LATIN AMERICA

Agents of the Communist International took a leading role in the establishment of the Mexican Communist Party in 1919-20. Thereafter

Latin American parties were represented at the various congresses of the Communist International. However, although there were regular reports presented to these meetings on the supposed progress of the various Communist parties in the area, Latin America was not very high on the priority list of the Russians who dominated the Comintern; and they were often criticized for not knowing much about the region.

Nevertheless, the Comintern took extensive action to maintain its control over the Latin American parties. The South American Bureau was established in Montevideo in 1929. It was manned by Russians, East Europeans, and a few Latin Americans during its existence of perhaps a decade. It intervened in an internal struggle in the Chilean Communist Party in the late 1920s, ousting the elected leadership and replacing it with people chosen by the Bureau. In various other countries the Bureau and the Moscow headquarters of the Comintern gave the seal of approval to one group or another in factional fights in parties belonging to the International.

Long after the South American Bureau had supposedly come to an end, the Comintern continued to control the internal affairs of various Latin American parties. In 1940 the leadership of the Mexican party was thrown out by a decision of Communist International delegates who visited the country and chose a new group of leaders.

After the dissolution of the Communist International in 1943, the control of Moscow over the Latin American parties was somewhat more camouflaged. However, with fair regularity delegates of the Latin American Communists attended congresses of the Soviet Communist Party or turned up in Moscow for particular celebrations. Most of the Latin American parties also had permanent delegations at the headquarters of the Communist Information Bureau, established in 1947 to replace the Comintern. They helped to publish the awkwardly named periodical of the Cominform, For a Lasting Peace for a People's Democracy. Others served at the headquarters of international front groups, such as the World Federation of Trade Unions and the World Federation of Democratic Youth.

Numerous secondary leaders of the Latin American Communist parties were sent to the USSR for indoctrination and training. There they were kept under close discipline and were thoroughly instilled with the idea that they should first and foremost be loyal to the Soviet Union.[2]

Throughout the first four decades of the Communist movement in Latin America, its control from the headquarters of the international movement in Moscow was indicated not only by such incidents as have been mentioned but also by the fidelity of the Latin American parties to the twists and turns of the international "line." They obediently purged their ranks of anarchist and Socialist-inclined elements, as directed by the Comintern in the early 1920s, and followed the

Communist International's policy of seeking to penetrate the existing labor movements rather than establishing others under their own control. During the Third Period the Latin American Communists faithfully adopted the sectarian policies ordered by the International, isolating themselves from all other parties, labeling all left-wing opponents as "social fascists," and establishing labor groups under strict party control.

Subsequently the Latin American Communists joined in the Popular Front policy of the late 1930s, shifted again to isolation during the Stalin-Nazi Pact period, and adopted a super Popular Front attitude during the latter part of World War II. In the postwar period they lustily participated in the Cold War on the side of the Soviet Union.

Finally, it may be noted that Latin American Communists played at least some role in the International Communist apparatus. Victorio Codovilla, the founder of the Argentine Communist Party and one of the most loyal followers of Moscow in all of Latin America, served as a Comintern agent for almost a decade during the 1930s. Eudosio Ravines, founder of the Peruvian party, played the same role for a somewhat shorter period and, like Codovilla, was one of the Cominterns' delegation in Spain during the Civil War. Rodolfo Ghioldi of the Argentine Party was dispatched to work with a German known as Arthur Ewert in Brazil during the mid-1930s. Luiz Carlos Prestes, of the Brazilian party, joined the Communists while in Moscow in the early 1930s and served on the Comintern body that oriented the policies of the Latin American parties before returning home in 1935.

THE ORTHODOX COMMUNISTS AND THE INTERNATIONAL COMMUNIST SCHISM

The orthodox Communists of Latin America have wavered little in their loyalty to Moscow in the face of growing schisms within international Communism. None of the orthodox parties of the area has joined the ranks of either the Peking-aligned Communists or those of the Castro-oriented parties. There are various reasons for this.

In the first place, the Latin American Communist parties have a long record of loyalty to the Soviet Union. For several decades their principal reason for existence often seemed to be to defend the Soviet Union and any position it might take in world affairs. Virtually all of the top leaders of these parties, as well as large numbers of secondary leaders, underwent training and indoctrination in Moscow, or under Russian direction in the East European countries after World War II. An appreciable number played important parts in the International apparatus maintained under Soviet control. The leaders of these parties even became used to the idea that their internal disputes were to be settled in Moscow.

A second factor favoring the continued loyalty of the leaders of these parties in the late 1950s and the 1960s, in the face of dissident elements that challenged Moscow's leadership and line, was the age of the parties' leaders. These men were virtually all of middle age, and some of them were old. It was not likely that they would waver from a lifetime of loyalty to the Soviet Union or that they would adopt the line of Moscow's opponents, which called for launching guerrilla wars, an activity not very congenial to men of their age.

In the third place, there was an element of class prejudice in the attitude of the orthodox parties, at least with regard to the Castroite groups. Many of the orthodox parties had a considerable working-class element in the rank and file and even in the leadership. These laboring men or former laboring men tended to look with a certain disdain on the middle- and upper-class origins of the young men who made up the bulk of the most loyal supporters of Fidel Castro, and to regard them as people from whom they had few lessons to learn in what the workers wanted or in how to make a working-class revolution. Not infrequently the Communist workers looked upon the Fidelistas as young men who were sowing their wild oats before assuming posts in their fathers' businesses or entering lucrative professions.

Finally, the orthodox Communist parties had much to lose by the failure of an attempted guerrilla insurrection. They had a certain degree of influence in organized labor, in some cases they had legal recognition for their party, and some even had members in national and local legislative bodies. They had a certain amount of property, in buildings, newspapers, and other forms. They did not care to risk all of these things on a single throw of the dice.

If the other Latin American parties had any reason to doubt the dangers involved in an unsuccessful guerrilla attempt, these were laid to rest by the disaster that befell the Venezuelan Communist Party when it joined in such an effort in 1962-66. It lost virtually all of its influence in organized labor, as well as in various professional organizations; it lost a substantial representation in various legislative bodies; and it passed from being a highly respectable party in 1958-59 to being a group with which no other political party would admit to having any contact. At the same time the membership of the party was reduced to a fraction of what it had been in the 1958-59 period.[3]

The Venezuelan party finally decided to withdraw, allegedly "temporarily," from the guerrilla struggle. This action precipitated a violent quarrel with Fidel Castro, who accused the Venezuelan Communist leaders of "betrayal" and "cowardice." All of the other orthodox Latin American Communist parties came to the defense of the Venezuelan party.

ORTHODOX COMMUNIST PARTIES

As a result of all of these factors, the 19 orthodox Communist parties of Latin America have remained loyal to Moscow in the face of the schisms now wracking the international Communist movement. They have resisted the Peking and Castro elements and have also shown little inclination to follow the "liberal" criticisms of the Soviet party and government that have become a feature of European Communism. Thus, there were no noticeable defections among Latin American Communist parties at the time of the Soviet invasion of Czechoslovakia in August 1968.

In Moscow succeeds in reconstituting a Communist International of sorts under its own leadership and direction, it would seem likely that a sizable proportion of the parties that would join such a group would come from Latin America. All 19 Latin American parties were apparently represented at the world Communist conference called by the Soviet party in June 1969.[4]

CHAPTER

20

SCHISMATIC COMMUNIST PARTIES

During the half century of existence of Communist parties in Latin America there have arisen from time to time dissident groups that have broken away to form rival factions or parties. There have been at least five recognizable groups of schismatic Communist parties. These include the Left (Trotskyite) and Right oppositions that arose in the 1920s and early 1930s as a result of the bitter conflicts within the Communist Party of the Soviet Union; the Titoite heresy of the late 1940s and early 1950s; the Latin American "dual Communist" parties established in the 1940s and 1950s; and the pro-Peking parties that came into existence during the 1960s.[1]

THE TROTSKYITES

During the 1920s there were violent struggles in the Soviet Union for the control of the Communist Party and the government. This situation was reflected in conflicts within the Communist parties in most of the other countries where such parties existed. In Latin America schisms that began with local struggles for power within the parties were often equated with the fights going on within the USSR, and partisans of different groups in the Latin American parties took sides with one or another faction in the Soviet Union.

Chile

One of the most important of these splits in the Latin American Communist parties was the one in Chile. In the late 1920s, because of differences of opinion concerning how to face the dictatorship of General Carlos Ibáñez, the Communist Party split, with the majority of the rank and file electing a leadership headed by Manuel Hidalgo. However, the South American Bureau of the Comintern sided with the opponents of Hidalgo, headed by Carlos Contreras Labarca, even though Hidalgo had been chief of the Communist Party since the death of the party's founder, Luís Emilio Recabarren, in December 1924.

As a result of this conflict, the Communists emerged from the Ibáñez dictatorship divided. Each faction called itself Partido Comunista de Chile and insisted that it was the "orthodox" Communist group. However, the one headed by Contreras Labarca and Elías Laferte, chief of the Federación Obrera de Chile, continued to be loyal to the Communist International and to Stalin. Its opponent, the Communist Party headed by Manuel Hidalgo, gravitated increasingly toward the followers of Leon Trotsky.

In the election of 1931, which followed the fall of the Ibáñez dictatorship, each Communist faction offered its own candidate for president. Elías Laferte ran for the Stalinists and Manuel Hidalgo for the Trotskyites.

In the following year the two parties took different positions once again over the issue of the so-called "Socialist Republic," which came to power on June 4, 1932; it was headed by Colonel Marmaduque Grove, founder of the Chilean air force, and supported by a conglomeration of small Socialist parties and various other political groups, including the followers of Ibáñez. The Hidalgoite Communists backed the Socialist Republic, while the Contreras Labarca-Laferte group violently opposed the new regime, leading a group of students and workers who barricaded themselves in the University of Chile, and vainly called for the establishment of "soviets" throughout the country.

Each Communist group had a following in the organized labor movement. The Stalinist party (Laferte and his followers) revived the Federación Obrera de Chile, which had been the Communist bulwark in the labor unions before the Ibáñez dictatorship. The Trotskyite Communists, under Manuel Hidalgo's leadership, organized "independent" unions that frequently cooperated with the surviving anarcho-syndicalist elements in the Chilean labor movement. The Trotskyites also sought to penetrate the so-called "legal" unions, which had official government recognition. The Stalinists, then deep in the Third Period of extreme isolation, refused to allow their unions to seek government recognition.

In March 1933 most of those groups that had supported the Socialist Republic joined together to establish a new party, the Partido Socialista de Chile. There were then three major elements in the organized labor movement—Stalinists, Trotskyites, and Socialists—with the Socialist Party quickly becoming one of the country's major parties. Although they had not joined the new Socialist Party when it was first established, the Trotskyites decided to do so in 1935. It had by then become the major center of concentration for those groups in organized labor and the political Left that were opposed to the Stalinists. Thereafter ex-Trotskyites, including Manuel Hidalgo, took leading positions in the Socialist Party.

However, a small minority of the Trotskyite Communists refused to join the Socialist Party. They continued to maintain a separate party, which soon took the name of Partido Obrero Revolucionario. The POR never assumed major importance in the labor movement or in politics. The only important trade union group that it continued to influence was that of the municipal workers. However, in the early 1950s Trotskyite control of this group was severely weakened by a split in the party's trade union ranks.

In the early 1960s, when the international Trotskyite movement broke into three rival factions, the Partido Obrero Revolucionario (Trotskista) sided with the group of parties headed by J. Posadas, an Argentine. Although expressing general support for the Castro government and its backing of guerrilla war throughout Latin America, the Trotskyites did not constitute a major factor even among the extreme Left in Chilean politics.

Cuba

Another country in which the Trotskyites originated in the early years of the struggle between the Stalinists and Trotskyites was Cuba. There, during the last years of the bloody dictatorship of Gerardo Machado, which was overthrown in August 1933, a dissident group with considerable influence in the organized labor movement arose within the Communist Party under the leadership of Sandalio Junco. During the hectic period following the overthrow of the Machado regime, this group was expelled from the Communist ranks and, on September 14, 1933, established the Partido Bolchevique Leninista.[2]

During the four months in which the left-wing nationalist regime led by Ramón Grau San Martín was in power (September 1933—January 1934), the new Trotskyite party of Cuba opposed the violent hostility of the Communists toward the government. When the Communists sought to organize a general strike against the Grau regime early in October, the Bolshevik-Leninists used their influence in the labor movement against this walkout.

Although the Cuban Trotskyists were able to function legally during the Grau San Martín government, they were driven underground, along with other left-wing parties, during the succeeding regime of Colonel Carlos Mendieta. Members of the Partido Bolchevique-Leninista took a small but active part in the revolutionary general strike against the Mendieta administration in March 1935.

Relations between the Cuban Trotskyites and the Partido Revolucionario Cubano (Auténtico), organized by ex-President Ramón Grau San Martín, became increasingly friendly as a result of their cooperation in the struggle against the dictatorships of the 1930s that were kept in power by Colonel Fulgencio Batista and because of their common antipathy for the Cuban Communist Party. Finally the majority of the Bolshevik-Leninists joined the ranks of the Auténtico Party. Thereafter a number of them played leading roles in the latter party, particularly in its activities in the organized labor movement.

After the absorption of most Cuban Trotskyites into the Partido Auténtico, the Trotskyite movement on the island was reduced to a handful of exceedingly doctrinaire types with little influence. They were organized in the Partido Obrero Revolucionario. By the time of the Castro revolution in 1959, they were split into at least two bitterly quarreling "parties."

Bolivia

Trotskyism in Bolivia, where it gained more influence than in any other Latin American country, originated in the wake of the Chaco War, which Bolivia fought with Paraguay during the early 1930s. A group of exiles, opponents of the war who were living in Argentina, organized the Grupo Tupac Amaru. They were led by a man who was generally known by the pseudonym Tristán Marof but whose real name was Gustavo Navarro. A member of the Bolivian diplomatic corps in Europe in the 1920s, he had been much influenced by the revolutionary atmosphere of the early years of that decade and had taken a position in favor of a socialist revolution in Bolivia.

Some of the leaders of the Grupo Tupac Amaru (now rechristened the Partido Obrero Revolucionario), including Gustavo Navarro, returned to Bolivia when Colonel Germán Busch took over control of the government in 1937. Navarro became a major adviser to Busch, who governed the country for two years. One of the principal events of this period was the establishment of the first union among the country's tin miners, who worked in the nation's major export industry.

With the suicide of President Busch in August 1939, a conservative regime was installed in Bolivia. Tristán Marof organized his own party, the Partido Socialista Obrero Boliviano. However, most of his former exile associates, who returned to the country following the end of the Busch regime, stayed with the Partido Obrero Revolucionario. Its members had been particularly attracted by the ideas of the exiled Soviet leader Leon Trotsky, and the POR became a member of Trotsky's Fourth International.[3]

For the next few years the POR was a minor factor in the country's political life. It was not until the coup of December 1943, which brought to power a government of young military men in alliance with the national revolutionary party, the Movimiento Nacionalista Revolucionario, that the Bolivian Trotskyites began to acquire some influence in national politics.

As a result of the December 1943 coup, which put Major Gualberto Villarroel in the presidency, the government strongly supported the organization of the country's miners. The miners' unions were principally under the influence of the MNR, but the Trotskyite POR also had considerable support among this group. When the Federación Sindical de Trabajadores Mineros held its national convention at Pulacayo in 1945, the Trotskyites had an important segment of the delegates. MNR union leader Juan Lechín was relatively naïve, politically speaking, and turned over to the POR delegates the writing of the Federation's declaration of principles. It was a purely Trotskyite document, stressing the need for a "continuing revolution," and the MNR leader who dominated the Miners Federation was never able to live it down.[4]

President Gualberto Villarroel was overthrown in July 1946. In the six years that followed, the Partido Obrero Revolucionario strengthened its alliance with Juan Lechín and other MNR leaders in the Miners' Federation and other trade unions. In the election of 1947 a miners' bloc was formed, consisting of MNR and POR miners, which elected MNR leader Juan Lechín and Lucio Mendívil, a POR trade unionist, as senators and a group of MNR and POR leaders as members of the Chamber of Deputies. One of the deputies elected by the miners' bloc was Guillermo Lora, the principal leader of the Trotskyite Partido Obrero Revolucionario.

In April 1952 the MNR seized power in a three-day coup. The new government was strongly supported by the labor movement, and it began a process of fundamental economic and social change that included an agrarian reform distributing the country's large landholdings among the Indian tenants and agricultural laborers, the nationalization of the major mining companies, and a program of extensive economic development.

One of the first results of the April 1952 revolution was the establishment of a new central labor organization, the Central Obrera Boliviana. For the first few months that the MNR was in power, the Trotskyites had a major influence in this new labor group, largely because of the system of representation adopted in the COB. Every regional labor federation, as well as each major industrial union, was entitled to representation in the COB. When a regional or industrial group could not afford to maintain a permanent representative in La Paz, where the COB met once or twice a week, it was entitled to name someone permanently stationed in the national capital to represent it. During the first months of the revolution, the Trotskyites had a number of their members resident in La Paz, named to the permanent body of the COB, to represent provincial federations unable to maintain permanent representatives in the capital.

During this period the Bolivian Trotskyites tended to apply to Bolivia almost automatically the model of the Bolshevik Revolution in Russia. They tended to picture MNR President Victor Paz Estenssoro as the Kerensky of the Bolivian revolution, implying that they, the Bolivian Trotskyites, would play the role of Bolsheviks in the process.[5]

In the COB the Trotskyites tended to challenge the right of the MNR to control the new central labor organization. Although for the first few months the MNR leaders, who in fact controlled most of the nation's labor movement, did not challenge this Trotskyite domination of the COB, they decided to do so when the COB, under Trotskyite leadership, defied the government on the issue of the nationalization of the country's tin mines. The Trotskyites pushed through a resolution opposing the government's nationalization decree and arguing that the government should confiscate the mines without payment instead of agreeing—as it had done—to compensate the former owners of the mines.

When the Trotskyite resolution on the mine nationalization issue passed, the MNR trade unionists reacted violently. Juan Lechín, the miners' union leader who had become minister of mines in the MNR government, mobilized his supporters in the various regional labor groups. The U.S. dissident Trotskyite paper Labor Action of November 3, 1952, told what happened next:

> A session of the Central was thereupon organized with a strong turnout by the Nationalists (who ordinarily do not participate in the sessions); and at this meeting they revoked and condemned the position on nationalization, which had just been published by La Nación, the official government organ. They then formed a new commission to draw up a new Open Letter to the president, with a Nationalist majority on it. . . .

The incident effectively ended the short period of Trotskyite control of the Central Obrera Boliviana. Furthermore, as a result of the dogmatic position the Trotskyites had taken toward the MNR revolution, the Trotskyite party began to lose its influence over its own trade union leaders and rank and file. As a result, early in 1954 most of the more important trade unionists of the POR deserted the Trotskyite ranks and joined the MNR. A number of these trade unionists were elected to Congress in 1956 as MNR candidates.

Meanwhile, the Partido Obrero Revolucionario had split, both factions continuing to use that name. One of these was headed by Guillermo Lora, who had been the party's principal ideological leader; and it continued to have in its ranks most of the Trotskyites among the miners, who for a decade had been the principal source of rank-and-file support. The other group, led by Hugo González Moscoso, maintained the closest relations with the international Trotskyite movement.

By the late 1960s the Trotskyites were split into three factions. The González POR was affiliated with the so-called United Secretariat Fourth International, of which the leading party was the Socialist Workers Party of the United States.[6] One rival group, led by Guillermo Lora and still having the major Trotskyite influence among the mine workers, maintained friendly relations with the so-called "Healyite" faction, or International Committee of the Fourth International.[7] A third element, the Partido Obrero Revolucionario (Trotskista), which had split away from the González POR, belonged to the Posadas splinter of international Trotskyism.

Mexico

Mexico was the only Latin American country with which Leon Trotsky had any personal contact. He fled there in 1937, when he was forced to leave Norway, as a result of the Soviet Union's pressure on that country to get rid of the most prominent Soviet exile. At the time Trotsky was being falsely charged in the famous "Moscow trials" with planning the assassination of Stalin and the undermining of the entire Soviet system.

Trotsky was invited to seek refuge in Mexico through the efforts of his supporters in that country, one of the most prominent being the famous mural artist Diego Rivera. The Trotskyite movement in Mexico had been organized by Communist leaders who were expelled from the Partido Comunista de Mexico in 1929 and afterward because of their refusal to accept the Third Period line of extreme sectarianism, launched in that year.

Refuge was not offered to Trotsky without serious opposition in Mexico. Although they were firm supporters of President Lázaro Cárdenas, the Confederación de Trabajadores de México and its secretary-general, Vicente Lombardo Toledano, violently denounced the arrival of Trotsky. They accused him of undermining the progress and independence of Mexico and urged President Cárdenas to deport him.

Although he soon quarreled with Rivèra, Trotsky continued to have a small group of followers in Mexico. They frequently quarreled among themselves and split into rival organizations. During most of the 1950s there was no Trotskyist group in Mexico. However, at the end of the decade the movement was revived. It split once again into two rival groups during the 1960s, one of which was affiliated with the United Secretariat of the Fourth International, the other with the Posadas faction of international Trotskyism.

Other Trotskyite Parties

In addition to the Trotskyite parties already discussed, the Fourth International had affiliates in several other countries. Until early in 1969 the Trotskyists in Uruguay probably operated in most complete freedom. However, as a result of the growing economic, social, and political crisis facing that country, the Partido Obrero Revolucionario (Trotskista) was officially outlawed in March 1969 and a number of its leaders were arrested.[8]

In Peru the Trotskyists were first organized during World War II. By the late 1960s they were split into two rival groups. The older of these, the Partido Obrero Revolucionario (Trotskista), was affiliated with the Posadas faction of international Trotskyism but was of virtually no importance in organized labor or politics. The other, the Frente Izquierda Revolucionaria, which belonged to the United Secretariat of the Fourth International, launched a guerrilla uprising in the early 1960s, under the leadership of Hugo Blanco. This attempt was quashed, Blanco was arrested, and the FIR became a very minor element in the Peruvian extreme Left.[9]

In Brazil the Trotskyites originated from a split in the Communist Party in the early 1930s. In 1938 the original Trotskyite group was joined by a number of new recruits from the Communist ranks, and the Partido Socialista Revolucionario was established. It was driven underground during the Estado Novo semifascist dictatorship of Getúlio Vargas (1937-45). It was revived after the fall of the dictatorship and was able to gain some very minor influence in the labor movement. By the 1960s the Trotskyists were known as the Partido Operario Revolucionario (Trotskista), and during the government of President João Goulart (1961-64) it had some influence in peasant union movements in São Paulo and the state of Pernambuco.

In general, Trotskyism has never become a major political force in any Latin American country except Bolivia. Even there its importance was limited to a very short period, right after the revolution of 1952. However, the Trotskyites have been able to maintain organizations in more than half a dozen Latin American countries over a considerable period of time. In most nations of the area in which they existed, the Trotskyists were split during the 1960s into

two or more rival parties, usually affiliated with different factions
of the much-splintered international Trotskyist movement.

THE RIGHT OPPOSITION

At about the same time that the left-wing Trotskyite schism
occurred in world Communism and in that of Latin America, there
was also a right-wing breakaway from the Stalinist element that made
up the bulk of the international Communist movement. This consisted
of people associated with the ideas and position of Niolai Bukharin,
who until late 1928 was chairman of the Communist International. In
the United States this element was represented by the followers of
Jay Lovestone, who was personally deposed by Stalin from his post
of secretary-general of the U.S. Communist Party. In Germany the
right-wing opponents of Stalin formed what came to be known as the
Braendler-Thalheimer group, after its principal leaders.

In Latin America the right-wing opposition found few supporters
in the Communist parties. The only group accused by the Stalinists
of belonging to this element was the split-off from the Communist
Party of Argentina led by José Penelón, who for some time had been
secretary-general of the Argentine party and for several years had
been the party's only representative in the city council of Buenos
Aires. The Penelón group founded the Partido Concentración Obrera,
which continued to exist for more than a generation. However, it
ceased to be a Communist party; and after the fall of the Perón regime
in September 1955 it maintained close relations with the right wing
of the Argentine Socialists, the Partido Socialista Democrático. At
no time did the Partido Concentración Obrera represent a significant
force either in national politics or in organized labor.

THE TITOITE HERESY

In the period immediately after World War II the most important
dissidence in the international Communist movement was that centering
on the Yugoslav Communist Party and its break with Stalin and the
Communist Party of the Soviet Union in 1948. Although in Europe,
and particularly in the Communist-controlled countries of Eastern
Europe, the Titoite dissidence had considerable support, evidenced
by the purges in the East European parties shortly after the Yugoslav
break. Titoism had little attraction for the Communists of Latin
America.

The only split in a Latin American Communist Party that had
some relevance to the Titoist heresy was that in the Brazilian party,

led by José María Crispim. As a result of quarrels that Crispim, a Communist trade union leader and former member of the Chamber of Deputies, had with top leaders of the party, he was expelled late in 1952. For some time he published a periodical called Unidade, which reportedly took a somewhat "national Communist" line, similar to that being advocated by the Titoites. However, Crispim never succeeded in organizing a significant party of his own.

Titoism was more attractive to some of the Latin American Socialist parties than to the Communists of the area. This was particularly true in Chile. There a group of leaders of the Partido Socialista Popular, who proclaimed themselves Marxist-Leninists but were in sharp competition with the local Communists, looked to the Yugoslav party as a possible counterpart in the early 1950s. One of these PSP leaders, Oscar Waiss, wrote a book eulogizing the Titoist experiment, entitled Amanecer en Belgrado, which was widely circulated. This interest in the Tito party continued in the Socialist ranks, and the Chilean Socialist Party had a fraternal delegation at the Ninth Congress of the League of Communists of Yugoslavia in March 1969.[10]

However, the pervasive power of Stalin in the world Communist movement, the bitterness of the Cold War, and the long tradition of discipline and obedience of the Latin American Communists prevented any significant group in their ranks from aligning itself with a dissident element in international Communism during the period immediately after World War II. It was not until well after the death of Stalin that, with the signs of a beginning of the disintegration of the monolithic structure of the world Communist movement in 1956, and with the beginning of the public feud between the powerful Soviet and Chinese parties, important schisms began to appear in Latin America that coincided with international Communist splits.

"DUAL COMMUNISM"

Another kind of division in the ranks of a number of Latin American parties that took place in the late 1940s and continued through much of the 1950s had no connection with any international schism. Elsewhere, this writer has dubbed this series of splits "dual Communism."[11]

In Mexico, where the Partido Comunista was thoroughly purged in 1940 during the visit of an impressive group of representatives of the Communist International, there occurred one example of dual Communism. The men who had led the party for 10 years—including Hernán Laborde, Valentín Campa, and Luís Gómez, were expelled from the Communist ranks and their places taken by a new leadership headed by Dionisio Encina, a peasant leader from the northern part of the country. The Laborde group thereupon organized a new party with the somewhat pompous name of Partido Obrero y Campesino de México.

At its inception the POCM took with it a sizable portion of the Communists' trade union cadre. However, in the years that followed, several of these labor leaders withdrew from the party; and at least one of them, Valentín Campa, returned to the Partido Comunista.

In the meantime the POCM did not diverge from the orthodox line of the international Communist movement, and there were no differences of principle between the POCM and the Partido Comunista. The POCM continued to follow the twists and turns of the international line, and the only reasons for the 1940 purge seem to be the decision of the International that the party leadership was not efficacious.

In 1947 a third Communist group was established in Mexico, the Partido Popular (which later became the Partido Popular Socialista), organized under the leadership of Vicente Lombardo Toledano. Lombardo had a long history in the Mexican labor movement, having been a leader of the dominant Confederación Regional Obrera Mexicana in the 1920s; subsequently establishing his own group, the Confederación General de Obreros y Campesinos de México; and in 1936, with the encouragement of President Lázaro Cárdenas, taking the leadership in establishing the Confederación de Trabajadores de México, which at its inception had within its ranks the great majority of Mexican organized labor.

Although Lombardo Toledano was removed as secretary-general of the CTM in 1940, because of his support of the pro-Axis "neutralist" policy of the Communists in the first part of World War II, he remained an important figure in the councils of the Confederación. It was not until 1947, when he announced his intention to launch a new party in opposition to the government's Partido Revolucionario Institucional, which the other leaders of the CTM were unwilling to join, that Lombardo Toledano was finally expelled from the Confederación de Trabajadores de México. His followers then established a small rival trade union group, the Unión General de Obreros y Campesinos de México.

In the meantime Lombardo Toledano had become one of the most important figures in the international Communist apparatus in Latin America, particularly in the trade union field. In 1938, with the support of the Cárdenas government, the CTM under Lombardo's leadership had called a conference of Latin American unions in Mexico City, which resulted in the establishment of the Confederación de Trabajadores de América Latina. Lombardo was elected president of the new CTAL. Although at its inception the CTAL was a united front of Latin American labor, union groups controlled by a wide variety of political elements being affiliated with it, during World

War II it came to be completely Communist-dominated. Lombardo generally sided with the pro-Communist elements within the CTAL and the various national labor groups belonging to it.

After World War II the CTAL became the Latin American regional affiliate of the World Federation of Trade Unions. In 1949, when the British Trade Union Congress, the U.S. Congress of Industrial Organizations, and various other democratic labor groups withdrew from the WFTU because of Communist domination of the group, the CTAL remained as the World Federation's Latin American regional group and Lombardo Toledano remained a member of the WFTU executive committee. In fact, the editing of the Spanish-language edition of its publications was entrusted to Lombardo and his associates.

Thus, by the time that he formed the Partido Popular, Lombardo Toledano was an important figure in the international Communist apparatus, even though he had never joined the Partido Comunista de México. However, at the same time, through his close connections with ex-President Lázaro Cárdenas, he continued to be regarded by many Mexicans as a loyal supporter of the Mexican Revolution, rather than as an international aparatchik.

Hence, by the late 1940s there were three parties in Mexico that followed the general international Communist line. They existed for 15 years, until the Partido Obrero y Campesino de México and the Partido Popular Socialista were merged at the beginning of 1963. However, no unification of the PPS with the Partido Comunista de México has ever occurred.[12]

In Venezuela the establishment of dual Communism took place in 1944, as the result of disagreement among the leaders of the Venezuelan Communists concerning the attitude their party should take toward the government of General Isaías Medina Angarita, then in power. Medina had allowed the Communists to establish a legal party, known as the Unión Popular. In return Unión Popular cooperated closely with the Medina government. However, there were important leaders among the Communists who opposed this cooperation.

Factions were formed in the party around this issue. The group in control of the Unión Popular "front organization," including Gustavo and Eduardo Machado and the trade union leader Luís Miquilena, expelled those leaders who opposed working with the Medina regime. These dissidents established the Partido Comunista de Venezuela, headed by Juan Bautista Fuenmayor as secretary-general.

In October 1945 President Medina Angarita was overthrown by a coup d'état organized by a group of young military officers and the Acción Democrática Party, which until then had been the principal opposition to Medina. The Unión Popular group fought against the coup and, after its success, took a position of unbending opposition to the new government, headed by Rómulo Betancourt, chief of Acción

Democrática. The Fuenmayor group, on the other hand, adopted a position of "critical support" of the Acción Democrática regime.

As a result of the electoral law enacted by the Betancourt government, which provided for universal adult suffrage, each party was required to adopt a color that would identify its list of candidates in elections, thus making it possible for illiterate voters to recognize the competing groups. As a result of this law, the Fuenmayor Communists adopted and were granted by the National Electoral Board the color red, while the other Communists received the color black. As a result the two groups were commonly known as the "Red" and "Black" Communists.

Meanwhile, an attempt to reunify the two Communist parties had as its principal result the passing of the Machado brothers and various other leaders from the former Unión Popular group to the former Partido Comunista faction. Soon thereafter the Black Communists took the name Partido Proletario (Comunista), while the party headed by Juan Bautista Fuenmayor, the Reds, continued to call itself the Partido Comunista de Venezuela.

During the rest of the Acción Democrática regime, the Red Communists worked within the majority labor movement, established under Acción Democrática leadership, and took part in setting up the first national central labor organization, the Confederación de Trabajadores de Venezuela. They also succeeded in electing two members of the Constituent Assembly chosen in 1946, and one senator and three deputies to the regular Congress that was chosen a year later.

The Black Communists and the Partido Proletario (Comunista), in contrast, organized their own Federation of Workers of the Federal District, in rivalry to the group of the same name set up under Acción Democrática and Red Communist leadership. They fared less well than the Reds in the elections of 1946 and 1947, failing to elect a member of Congress on either occasion.

With the overthrow of the Acción Democrática government in November 1948, the two Communist factions again adopted different attitudes. The Black Communists supported the military dictatorship that came to power as a result of the coup overthrowing Rómulo Gallegos. The Reds opposed the coup; and the party was outlawed by the new regime, as was Acción Democrática, a few weeks after the military government took power.

However, during the more than nine years of military dictatorship that followed, the differences between the two Communist parties disappeared. Although the Blacks were permitted to conduct their trade union activities with a wide degree of freedom under the dictatorship—in contrast with the situation facing Acción Democrática and Red Communist unionists, who were severely persecuted—in the

SCHISMATIC COMMUNIST PARTIES

early 1950s the Blacks announced the dissolution of their party, "as a move towards Communist unity."13

Apparently this move succeeded. When the military dictatorship of Marcos Pérez Jiménez was overthrown in January 1958, the Communists emerged as a single united party, again known as the Partido Comunista de Venezuela. Its principal figure in organized labor was Rodolfo Quintero, who had been one of the major leaders of the Black trade union forces; the principal leader of the party as a whole was Gustavo Machado of the Reds.

Dual Communism came to Peru in the wake of the military coup of October 1948, which brought to power the dictatorship of General Manuel Odría. The military regime outlawed the official Partido Comunista del Perú; but in 1950, when the government got around to organizing elections, one of the principal candidates for the Senate on the ticket headed by General Odría was Juan P. Luna, who had been the Communist Party's principal leader in organized labor before the 1948 coup. During the Odría dictatorship, which lasted until 1956, Luna remained a senator and the head of the Chauffeurs' Federation of Peru, one of the country's strongest trade unions. On the other hand, the official Partido Comunista del Perú continued to function as a member of the underground opposition to Odría.

With the end of the Odría dictatorship in the middle of 1956, dual Communism also seems to have ended in Peru. Juan P. Luna retired from politics, although he remained an important figure in the trade union movement. The Partido Comunista del Perú, meanwhile, remained an opposition party to the democratic administration of President Manuel Prado, which succeeded the Odría dictatorship.

The final country in which dual Communism appeared during the 1940s was Argentina. There the difference of opinion within the Communist movement centered on the attitude to be taken toward the military dictatorship, established on June 4, 1943, which gave rise three years later to the government of Perón.

The Partido Comunista Argentino generally took a hostile attitude toward the military regime and the Perón dictatorship. It joined with other political parties, including the Radicals, Socialists, and Conservatives, to support the opponent of Juan Perón in the 1946 election.

However, there was an element within the party, led by Rodolfo Puiggrós, that opposed this position. Early in 1945 Puiggros succeeded in getting the Communist leadership to enter into negotiations with Perón, and he headed the delegation that met the dictator. As a result of these parleys, Puiggrós urged that the Communists support Perón instead of opposing him. However, the bulk of the party leadership, headed by Victorio Codovilla, was influenced mainly by the fact that Perón and his associates had been sympathetic to the Axis in World

War II, at a time when the Soviet Union was associated with the Allied cause; hence they felt that they were bound to oppose Perón at virtually any cost.

The result of this conflict within the Argentine Communist leadership was a split in which Rodolfo Puiggrós and his associates withdrew from the Communist Party and established their own Movimiento Obrero Comunista, which took its place in the ranks of those supporting Juan Perón. During the period of Perón's presidency (1946-55) Puiggrós became an important member of Perón's "kitchen cabinet," allegedly writing some of his speeches. Other members of his group were among those who worked on elaborating a "philosophy" for the Peronista regime, and the Movimiento Obrero Comunista in general was very active in propagandizing for the Perón government.

Meanwhile, the official Partido Comunista de Argentina adopted a somewhat zigzag policy toward the Perón regime. As the Cold War developed, and the Perón regime took an increasingly hostile attitude toward the United States in the late 1940s, the official Communists sought to draw closer to Perón. However, he had little interest in enlisting the backing of the Communists and rejected their overtures.

Despite this disagreement among the Argentine Communists in their perception of the Perón regime, both factions seem to have maintained contact with the world Communist apparatus. The Partido Comunista de Argentina remained in good standing with Moscow. The Puiggrós group also maintained its contacts with Moscow and with its apparatus in Latin America—at least Rodolfo Puiggrós continued to have good relations with Vicente Lombardo Toledano and the Communist international trade union apparatus in Latin America. In its publications the Movimiento Obrero Comunista consistently was friendly and even adulatory toward the Soviet Union.

With the overthrow of the Perón dictatorship in September 1955, dual Communism came to an end in Argentina. The Partido Comunista de Argentina continued to be the recognized Argentine member of the internatinal Communist movement. In contrast, the Puiggrós group took its place as one of the many factions that supported Perón's thwarted aspirations to return to power.[14]

In Cuba dual Communism took a somewhat different form. There the Communist Party (known as the Partido Socialista Popular) had been a close ally of General Fulgencio Batista since 1938. However, when he seized power in March 1952 by overthrowing the democratically elected regime of Carlos Prío Socarras, Batista was in dire need of help and support from the United States and, in the atmosphere of the Cold War, felt it necessary officially to "outlaw" the PSP. From a practical point of view, the Communists were little hurt by this move: their headquarters remained open, and they did not suffer the kind of persecution that real opponents of the Batista dictatorship experienced.

Indeed, cooperation continued between Batista and the Communists through Batista's personal party, the Partido Acción Unitaria. Within a few weeks of the coup of March 10, 1952, labor leaders and others who had been acknowledged members and even leaders of the Partido Socialista Popular—including at least one who had been a candidate on the PSP ticket for the elections of June 1952, which were cancelled by the coup—turned up as prominent figures in the workers' bloc of the Batista party. Through pressure from Batista they were given posts of influence in the Confederación de Trabajadores de Cuba, from which the Communists had been almost totally eliminated a few years before. This kind of dual Communism continued until a few months before Batista was overthrown.

The major characteristic that differentiates the splits in Latin American Communist parties that have been designated "dual Communism" from the other schisms is that those who broke away from the various Communist parties did not completely break their ties with the international Communist movement. Thus, Lombardo Toledano remained an important figure in the international Communist trade union apparatus for more than a decade after establishing the Partido Popular Socialista; Rodolfo Quintero of the Venezuelan Black Communists was after 1948 the principal representative in his country of the World Federation of Trade Unions; Rodolfo Puiggros seems for quite some time to have kept in close touch with the international Communist movement and never criticized the Soviet Union during this period. Juan P. Luna also kept in touch with the Communist world trade union apparatus through his own labor federation after having formally quit the Peruvian Communist Party.

Most of these divisions resulted from struggles for power and differences of opinion on tactics among the leaders. At the time they took place, they did not represent any break with the Stalinist Communist movement. The Moscow leadership, although giving certain recognition to the orthodox party in each case as being the "official" Communist organization, does not seem to have turned upon the dual parties the kind of denunciation and abuse it always used toward ideological deviants.

There is no question that this attitude had its advantages from the point of view of the world Communist leadership and the Soviet Union. It gave them a foot in rival camps, so to speak, in several countries. In Argentina it meant that there were loyal Moscow adherents in both the Peronista and anti-Peronista ranks; in Peru there were Communists both with and against the Odría dictatorship; in Venezuela there were Communists both working with the Pérez Jiménez regime and in the opposition; in Cuba there were people loyal to international Communism supporting the Batista dictatorship and opposing it. Finally, in Mexico there were the Lombardo Toledano group in the government of Mexico and the Partido Comunista de Mexico, which was frankly in the opposition.

However, by the late 1950s the usefulness of this tactic seems to have diminished if not disappeared. For one thing, at least some of the dual Communist leaders seem to have become increasingly alienated from Moscow—this was true of Rodolfo Puiggrós, who became a thoroughgoing Peronista, and of Juan P. Luna, who after the end of the Odría regime in 1956 became a trade unionist. In Venezuela, with the growing unpopularity of the Pérez Jiménez regime, it became convenient for the Black Communists to merge with the Reds and to try to make public opinion forget that the Blacks had ever worked with the dictatorship (an endeavor that was successful to an amazing degree).

Furthermore, with the growing dissidence in the world Communist movement—the widening Soviet-Chinese split and the general centrifugal tendencies that were becoming a scandal within international Communism—there were dangers involved in the dual Communist tactic. There was always at least the latent possibility that the dual Communist group in a given country might seek to join forces with elements in the world Communist movement that were hostile to or at least critical of Moscow. The reestablishment of unity in the Latin American Communist parties and the alignment of these groups firmly behind Moscow came to be of great importance.

THE PRO-PEKING DISSIDENTS

It was probably inevitable that the most far-reaching split in the international Communist movement, the schism between the Soviet and Chinese parties, should have its repercussions in Latin America. When this break came into the open in the early 1960s, the Chinese began to seek sympathizers and supporters among the leaders and members of the Latin American Communist parties; and many dissidents within these parties began to be attracted to the Chinese party and the ideological and tactical positions it took in opposition to those of the Soviet Union.

The first country in which a frankly pro-Chinese Communist Party appeared was Brazil. There in 1961 a group that had long headed the leadership of the Brazilian Communist Party broke away from the party after being defeated in an internal party struggle with the PCB's major public figure and secretary-general, Luiz Carlos Prestes.

SCHISMATIC COMMUNIST PARTIES

The conflict in the Brazilian Communist Party in 1960-61 was not caused principally by the Sino-Soviet feud. During most of the previous dozen years or more, since the Communist Party had been outlawed early in 1947, Luiz Carlos Prestes had been in hiding. The group of leaders that broke away from the party in 1961, headed by Mauricio Grabois, had tended to use the supposed danger that Prestes would be discovered by the police to keep him virtually out of all contact with the rank and file of the party membership and lower-ranking leadership. They tended to speak in his name, with or without his permission.

However, in 1959 Prestes came out of hiding, appeared before a court, and purged himself of the charges of subversion that had been made against him in 1947. When it became possible for Prestes to appear in public and function as party leader without harrassment from the police, he took over active leadership of the party. This deprived the group that had led the party for a dozen years of their positions of dominance and control over the party's activities. Their growing resentment against and conflict with Prestes led to the schism of 1961.

As a result of this conflict, the Grabois group withdrew from the Prestes party, which had changed its name to Partido Comunista Brasileiro, and set up a new group, which took the old name of the party, Partido Comunista do Brasil. The new group immediately aligned itself with the Chinese.[15]

During the administration of João Goulart (1961-64) the pro-Chinese party was in bitter competition with the larger pro-Soviet Prestes party. It had very little influence in the labor movement, in contrast with the Prestes party, although it did have some small success in organizing the new peasant unions of the Northeast.

Together with all of the other elements of the Left in Brazil, the pro-Chinese Communists suffered a severe defeat with the overthrow of the government of João Goulart on April 1, 1964. Since then they have given very little indication of activity or influence except for an occasional pronunciamento supporting a position adopted by the Communist Party of China.

Another of the more significant pro-Chinese splits took place in the Partido Comunista de Bolivia in 1965. Certainly leadership conflicts within the party and the issues of the Sino-Soviet schism brought about the division of the Bolivian Communist Party. The pro-Chinese group took over some of the old party's supporters in the trade union movement, although the pro-Soviet group continued to be the most important Communist element in the Bolivian labor movement. Both Communist parties had control of only a small minority of the Bolivian trade unions.

Both the pro-Chinese and pro-Soviet Communist parties of Bolivia were represented at the Tricontinental Congress in Havana, Cuba, in January 1966. However, only the pro-Moscow party attended the July 1967 conference there, which established the Organización Latino Americana de Solidaridad. At the 1966 congress the Bolivian delegation, on the insistence of the Cubans, chose Mario Monje, the principal leader of the pro-Soviet party, as chairman of their group.

The pro-Chinese party continued to be slighted when the Cubans led by Ernesto Guevara sought to launch a guerrilla conflict in Bolivia. Although Guevara conducted extensive negotiations with the pro-Soviet party and recruited some of his few Bolivian guerrillas from that party, he apparently had few contacts with the pro-Chinese one, which the pro-Chinese leadership bitterly resented.[16]

In Peru the pro-Chinese elements in the Communist Party broke away from the main Communist group in 1966. Both factions formally "expelled" the leaders of the opponent group, and both continued to call themselves Partido Comunista del Perú. The Peruvian pro-Chinese party was of considerable significance in the university student movement. At one time, for example, it controlled the Student Federation at the University of San Marcos in Lima, the country's largest university. By 1971 the pro-Chinese Communists were split into several rival groups.

The Ecuadorean pro-Chinese Communist Party originated, like most of the other splits in Latin America, in large part as a result of dissidence against the entrenched leadership of the national party. Pedro Saad, secretary-general of the Ecuadorean Communist Party for almost 20 years, had served as a senator for much of this period and was a well-to-do merchant in the port city of Guayaquil. By the mid-1960s many of the party's leaders had come to feel that he was too bourgeois. As a result a dissident group broke away to establish a rival organization, which used the same name as the older pro-Soviet party, Partido Comunista del Ecuador.

The Ecuadorean party, unlike most of the other pro-Chinese groups, sought to put into practice its program for fomenting a guerrilla conflict. A delegate was dispatched to China to obtain financial aid for such an attempt, and plans for a guerrilla outbreak were worked out with some Fidelista elements and other groups. However, the whole effort was frustrated when the delegate returning from China was picked up at the Quito airport with $25,000 on his person.

In Colombia the pro-Chinese split in the Communist Party was led by officials of the Communist Youth. They established the Partido Comunista (Marxist-Leninista) and concentrated much of their attention on trying to acquire leadership among the rural outlaw bands that had been operating in isolated parts of the country since the end of the general civil war (known locally as "La Violencia") in 1957. In the late 1960s there were three principal centers of guerrilla activities, one of which was led by the Partido Comunista (Marxista-Leninista).

Chile is one of the few countries in Latin America in which the establishment of a pro-Chinese party was in large part due to direct intervention by the Chinese Communist Party. As early as 1963 the Communist Party of Chile engaged in a polemic with the Chinese party, during which it accused the Chinese of seeking to recruit supporters and to organize them to seize power within the Chilean party. These efforts came to little, and in October 1963 the Chilean party expelled from its ranks a small group of intellectuals, consisting largely of people associated with the Spartacus publishing house in Santiago, which had been specializing in publication of Chinese Communist materials.

The Spartacus group joined with several other small factions to establish the Partido Comunista Revolucionario. This party published an occasional periodical, Revista marxista, which served as a mouthpiece for several of the other pro-Chinese Communist parties of Latin America, as well as republishing Chinese materials from time to time.

The Chinese have given some considerable publicity to the parties in Latin America supporting their general line. In the Peking Review of January 19, 1968, the claim was made that there were "more than ten" pro-Chinese parties in the area. In addition to the parties already noted, there were by this time pro-Chinese groups in Paraguay, Argentina, Mexico, and the Dominican Republic. Subsequently a split in the People's Progressive Party of newly independent Guyana, on the north coast of South America, resulted in the establishment of a pro-Chinese group, led by Brindley Benn, who had been a minister in the PPP government between 1957 and 1964 and had been president of the People's Progressive Party for a number of years.[17]

Note should also be taken of the charges that Fidel Castro has made concerning the activities of the Chinese in the ranks of his Partido Comunista de Cuba. In January 1966 he denounced the Chinese for, among other things, attempting to proselytize among members of the Cuban party. However, these efforts do not appear to have gained many recruits; and so far as we are able to determine, there is no significant pro-Chinese group in Cuba.

The pro-Chinese parties in Latin America have generally been recruited from two groups within the orthodox Communist parties. They have more often than not been led by members of the leadership of the orthodox parties who for largely personal reasons, arising from struggles for power, have found themselves at odds with those who control the orthodox parties. Much of the lower-ranking leadership, and presumably a substantial part of the rank-and-file membership, has been drawn from the ranks of Communist Youth in the various countries.

After the Castro victory in 1959, when the orthodox Communist parties found it possible in a number of countries to break out of the general isolation into which they had worked themselves during the 1950s, they succeeded in a number of countries in recruiting appreciable numbers of young people, attracted as much by Communist support for the Castro regime as by the principles of Marxism-Leninism. When it became clear that, despite their verbal enthusiasm for the Castro regime, the orthodox parties generally had little intention of launching guerrilla struggles, many of these young people became disillusioned. Many of them were attracted to the Jacobin Left groups that became the bulk of Castro's supporters, but some were influenced by the position of the Chinese and their opposition to the alleged "revisionist" stance of the Soviet Union and the Communist parties that continued to follow the lead of the Soviet Communist Party.

However, in no country of Latin America did the pro-Peking elements get control of the majority of leaders and members of the orthodox Communist parties. Although they continued to stress the importance of work among urban labor, as well as among peasants and agricultural wage earners, they did not amass any substantial influence in the organized labor movements. They did not attempt to engage in electoral politics, and so it was difficult to test their general popular backing in comparison with that of the orthodox pro-Soviet parties. However, it is clear that they generally represent only a minority of the Communist movement in countries in which, for the most part, the Communists of whatever tendency are only a small minority of the body politic.

By the late 1960s in a number of countries the pro-Chinese Communists were engaged in bitter polemics with the new pro-Fidelista Communist groups. In Chile the two engaged in violent controversy, and the Bolivian pro-Chinese party launched a strong attack early in 1969 on Fidel Castro himself.

The reasons for this are not difficult to find. The Maoist parties in Latin America found it much more difficult to "differentiate their product" from that of Castro than did the orthodox parties. Whereas the latter could generally afford to ignore Fidel unless he engaged in an open attack on them, this was not the case with the pro-Chinese.

The pro-Chinese parties, like those groups that looked to Havana for leadership, urged that the principal revolutionary force in Latin America was the peasantry rather than the urban workers. They also expressed belief in the eventual need for a guerrilla war, as did the Fidelistas, and supported the idea that in Latin America this was the only feasible way for Communists to obtain power.

However, the pro-Chinese differed from the Fidelistas on two essential points of doctrine. First, they objected that the Castro-Guevara-Debray thesis that it would be possible for Communist revolutionaries to create the "objective" conditions for a guerrilla-led revolution was wrong. They argued—in contrast with the Fidelistas—that before a guerrilla war could be organized it was necessary to develop a considerable degree of support among the peasantry whom the party hoped to lead in a guerrilla uprising.

Even more fundamentally, the pro-Chinese differed with the followers of Castro in their concept of the role of the Communist Party in such a revolt. They were orthodox Marxist-Leninists in this, arguing that any guerrilla war must be organized and led and strictly controlled by the Communist Party, and therefore they rejected the Fidelist idea that the party could develop out of the guerrilla army itself.

Hence, the pro-Peking Communist parties in Latin America felt it necessary to stress their differences in doctrine with the Fidelista groups. As noted, this led them into some bitter polemics against the Cuban leader and his followers in various Latin American countries.

CHAPTER

21

THE
JACOBIN LEFT
AND CASTRO
COMMUNISM

In the late 1950s there arose a new element on the extreme Left of the Latin American political spectrum that is best described as the Jacobin Left. In the following decade the group of parties and factions became the followers of Fidel Castro and the main supporters of his attempt to organize a "third front" in world Communism.

The phrase "Jacobin Left" describes these extreme leftist elements because in many ways they are similar to the Jacobins of the French Revolution. They are jingoistic nationalists; they favor basic social changes at whatever cost in lives and fortunes; they at best distrust democracy and at worst despise it.

ORIGINS OF THE JACOBIN LEFTISTS

The Jacobin leftists arose in the late 1950s as a result of conditions in the Western Hemisphere. First, the overthrow of a series of dictatorships seemed to some people, particularly among the younger politicians of the parties of the democratic Left, to bring too little social change. Second, the latter part of the 1950s was marked by a disastrous fall in the prices of the principal export products of the area. Third, the policies of the U.S. government toward Latin America during the 1950s seemed to encourage the spread of military dictatorships and to take little account of the needs of the area for rapid economic development.

All of these factors tended to convince many young politicians that rapid social change and economic development could not be achieved through the democratic process. They also became convinced that the United States was little concerned with the economic needs of Latin America was interested in the area only as a pawn in the Cold

JACOBIN LEFT AND CASTRO COMMUNISM

War, and felt that military regimes were the best way of keeping these nations "safe." The United States had thus made itself the major enemy of social change in the rest of the hemisphere, they believed.

Jacobin Left elements arose principally in the democratic Left parties. In Venezuela they appeared among the youth of Acción Democrática; in Peru among certain elements of the Partido Aprista Peruano; in Costa Rica among members of José Figueres' Partido Liberación Nacional; in Argentina among elements of the Partido Socialista.

Sociologically the Jacobin leftists were members principally of the middle and upper classes. Young people of these groups, particularly among the university students, were especially attracted to the extremism and calls to violence of the Jacobin Left parties. However, they found little response in the labor movement, whose members generally remained loyal to the democratic Left parties or to the orthodox Communists. The workers felt the need for political democracy if their organizations were to be able to function effectively, and they realized that gains they had made over several decades in terms of social legislation and collective bargaining contracts would be jeopardized by any rash attempt to overthrow the status quo through violence or civil war. Nor did the Jacobin leftists gain influence among the peasants, who to a growing degree were forming their own unions and cooperatives, principally under the leadership of elements loyal to the democratic Left.

Thus the Jacobin Left failed to rally support among exactly those lower-class elements of the population it claimed to represent. The only politically significant group among which it gained influence was the student movement. As the student radicals failed to win support among the workers and peasants, they became increasingly frustrated and moved more to the Left, toward a systematic appeal to violence.

The failure of the student radicals to gain support among the workers and peasants—in contrast with the older student generation that had founded most of the democratic leftist parties and some of the orthodox Communist parties—had a historico-sociological explanation. In the 1920s, 1930s, and the early 1940s, the student leaders could claim with some justice to be the spokesmen for groups that had no one else to speak for them. They could help to organize the labor movement, as the early national revolutionaries did in Peru and Venezuela, and the Communists in several Central American countries and Cuba. They could begin the organization of the peasantry, as in Costa Rica.

However, by the late 1950s the student radicals could no longer play such a role. There were trade union movements in virtually all of the Latin American countries, and the peasant movements were growing in number and influence. As a result the lower classes had spokesmen of their own, and they found little need to seek leadership from the upper and middle classes. Hence they turned a deaf ear to the appeals of the Jacobin leftists, more often than not regarding them as scions of the upper classes who were having a few years of irresponsibility before settling down to comfortable positions in business or the professions.

THE JACOBIN LEFTISTS AND THE CUBAN REVOLUTION

Until the success of the Cuban revolution of January 1, 1959, the Jacobin leftists remained isolated and dispersed. However, the victory of Castro served as a catalyst to bring together all of these groups in support of the new Cuban regime. They became very active in organizing groups to support the Castro government and sent delegations to Cuba to seek help for their own struggles. Because of the initial popularity of the Castro regime, the Jacobin leftists gained a new importance and respectability as its strong supporters.

In the beginning the Castro regime did not pay special attention to the Jacobin leftist elements in other Latin American countries. Between January and October 1959 the Castro government did not have any particularly clear ideology, and there was a violent struggle within Castro's 26th of July Movement to determine whether the new regime would follow a democratic leftist path or a Marxist-Leninist one. During this period Castro tended to support any group in Latin America that seemed to be dedicated to overthrowing military regimes or other dictatorships.

During October 1959, with the arrest of Huber Matos, Fidel Castro gave his approval to the Marxist-Leninist group among his supporters. As a result the Cuban regime moved quickly in the direction of a Marxist-Leninist society. Virtually all of the urban economy was nationalized; most of agriculture was organized in collective and state farms; and the revolutionary dictatorship made it clear that it intended to stay in power indefinitely. At the same time the Castro regime cut virtually all economic and other ties with the United States and moved close to the Soviet bloc. In April 1961 Castro officially proclaimed Cuba a "Socialist" country.

These actions of the Castro regime deprived it of most of the backing it had originally received in other Latin American countries. At its inception Fidel Castro's government had the enthusiastic support of virtually all democratic elements in Latin American politics, from the moderate conservatives to the national revolutionaries and Christian Democrats, as well as the backing of elements of the extreme

Left, including the Communists and the Jacobin leftists. However, as the Cuban regime moved with increasingly clarity into the Marxist-Leninist camp, it came to be opposed by all elements in the Latin American political spectrum except the Communists and the Jacobin leftists.

However, although the Castro government had by early 1961 become a clearly Marxist-Leninist regime, it was by no means clear exactly what its posture would be within the Communist camp. On July 26, 1961, Castro announced the formation of a single party of the Cuban revolution through the merger of the remains of the 26th of July Movement with another anti-Batista group, the Directorio Revolucionario, and the orthodox Communist Party (Partido Socialista Popular). From then until March 1962 the organization of this new party was in the hands of a top leader of the PSP, Anibal Escalante, and its local, regional, and provincial committees were manned largely by orthodox Communists. At the same time members of the PSP took over key positions in the regime, including the presidency of the powerful National Institute of Agrarian Reform (INRA), the secretary-generalship of the Confederation of Workers of Cuba, and the rectorship of the University of Havana.

However, in March 1962, Fidel Castro turned violently against the former leadership of the Partido Socialista Popular, ousted Anibal Escalante (who fled to Czechoslovakia) from the leadership of the new official party, and denounced the orthodox Communists as having tried to take over his regime. All but a few orthodox Communists were removed from the leadership of the new Partido Unificado de la Revolución Socialista Cubana, and in the next two years all but a handful of ex-PSP members were removed from key positions in the government. It became clear that although the Castro regime was going to be Communist, its leadership and orientation were to be firmly in the hands of Fidel Castro and his closest personal supporters.

In the years that followed, the orthodox Communists, most of whom remained firmly loyal to the Soviet Union, were submitted to a series of humiliations. One of these occurred in March 1965, when a former member of the PSP's Young Communist League was accused of having betrayed student leaders who had tried to assassinate Batista in March 1957 and top figures in the PSP were implicated in his activities.[1] Another took place in late 1967, when Anibal Escalante (who had returned a year before from Europe) and several other ex-PSP members were accused of having formed a "microfaction" within the government party and were sentenced to long terms in jail.[2]

Castro's relations with the Soviet Union varied considerably over the years. In 1962 and 1963, after the missile crisis, they were exceedingly strained. During the following two years Castro seems to have made a real effort to improve his position vis-à-vis the USSR, increasingly supporting their position against that of China in international Communist meetings and yielding to their insistence that he return to a major economic emphasis on the growing of sugar. This turn by Castro seems to have been a major factor in his expulsion of Che Guevara from the government and from Cuba.[3]

The end of this pro-Soviet turn by Castro seems to have come at the Tricontinental Congress, held at Havana in January 1966. At that time Castro laid the basis for the independent stand within the Communist camp that was to mark his policy for the succeeding two and a half years. During that meeting he both denounced the Chinese for "Big Power chauvinism" and humiliated the Russian delegates.[4]

CASTRO AND THE ORTHODOX LATIN AMERICAN COMMUNISTS

The zigs and zags of Castro's relations with the Soviet Union were mirrored in his attitudes toward the orthodox Communists of Latin America. As noted, the Latin American Communist parties announced their support for Castro immediately after his seizure of power in January 1959. Communist delegations joined those of Jacobin leftists and democratic leftists that visited the island during 1959.

In the years that followed, Castro's relations with these parties followed an unsteady course. During 1962 and 1963 there were strong polemics between the Chilean Communist Party and Castro, the former making it clear that it needed no instructions from the Cuban leader concerning its policies or programs.[5]

However, as a result of Castro's rapprochement with the Soviet Union, his relations with the Latin American Communist parties improved in 1964. At the end of that year a meeting of all of the pro-Moscow Communist parties of Latin America was held in Havana, and Castro agreed to work through these parties, rather than through Jacobin leftists and other elements, in his relations with Latin America. This promise was kept until the Tricontinental Congress of January 1966.

Nevertheless, Castro made it increasingly clear that he saw only one true road to revolution in Latin America, that of guerrilla warfare. He urged this road on the orthodox Communists of the area, and two parties accepted his advice: those of Guatemala and Venezuela. Starting in 1962, the Venezuelan Communist Party joined with the Jacobin leftist Movimiento de la Izquierda Revolucionaria in launching a rural guerrilla war and a campaign of urban terrorism against the democratic Left government of Rómulo Betancourt. It continued this policy for almost four years. However, at the end of 1965 the Venezuelan Communists began to maneuver for an end to the guerrilla conflict, and by early 1967 it had completely abandoned guerrilla war.

The withdrawal of the Venezuelan Communist Party from the guerrilla conflict threw it into a direct confrontation with Fidel Castro, who continued to support the dissident Communists and MIRistas who wanted to continue the war. The two parties engaged in violent polemics, during which the Venezuelan Communists accused Castro of interfering in Venezuelan affairs and of being a supreme egotist. Castro accused the Venezuelan Communist leaders of cowardice, although they had withdrawn from the guerrilla conflict because of the disastrous effects of that struggle on the party.[6]

The Guatemalan Communist Party also participated for some years in a guerrilla conflict. Forces supported by the Communists waged war with some success against the military regime of Colonel Enrique Peralta. However, with the election of Julio César Méndez Montenegro, candidate of the Partido Revolucionario, as president in 1966, popular support for the guerrilla conflict declined; and early the following year the Guatemalan army was largely able to eliminate the main focus of guerrilla activity.[7]

As a result of the defeats of the guerrilla movement in 1967, the Communists became increasingly disenchanted with this method of trying to gain power. Early in 1969 the Communist Party officially withdrew its support from the guerrilla war and, quite predictably, brought down upon itself the denunciation of Fidel Castro, who threw his backing behind dissident Communists and others who announced their intention of continuing the conflict.

Meanwhile, the relations of Castro with the orthodox Communists throughout Latin America had become exceedingly touchy. Although a number of orthodox Communist parties were represented at the Tricontinental Congress at Havana in January 1966, most of the delegations to the subsequent founding congress of the Latin American Solidarity Organization at Havana in August 1967 were composed of representatives of Jacobin leftist groups.[8]

Castro and the Latin American orthodox Communists disagreed strongly over the relations of the Soviet Union with the governments of the other Latin American countries. Throughout the 1960s the USSR was seeking to increase its diplomatic and commercial contacts with Latin America, and the Latin American Communists strongly supported this effort. However, Castro denounced the resumption of diplomatic relations between the Soviet Union and Chile and Colombia, and the prospect of such a move between the Soviet Union and Venezuela. His attacks on the Latin American Communists on this matter contained only lightly disguised attacks on the Soviet Union itself.

THE THEORETICAL POSITIONS OF CASTRO COMMUNISM

After the Tricontinental Congress of January 1966, Fidel Castro was intent on establishing for himself a "third position" in international Communism. He took the lead in organizing such groups as the Tricontinental Congress and its continuing organization, and the hemispheric Latin American Solidarity Organization; he also sought to establish a theoretical differentiation between his position and that of both the Soviet and the Chinese Communist camps.

The theoretical position of Castro Communism was fundamentally based on two issues: the guerrilla road to power and the concept of "moral" as opposed to "material" incentives in an established Communist regime. The contrast on these issues with the position of the Soviet Union was very obvious, the differences with the stand of the Chinese somewhat more subtle.

Probably the most authoritative statement of the Castro Communist position on the road to power in this period was Régis Debray's well-known pamphlet Revolution in the Revolution? Published by the Cuban regime and distributed in hundreds of thousands of copies all over Latin America, this document obviously had the endorsement of Castro and his government and can be taken as the position of the Castro faction in world Communism.

Debray made a number of basic points in his study. From time to time, in speeches and polemics, Fidel Castro and other leaders of the Cuban regime reiterated and elaborated on these points. Debray's first argument was that the revolution will be brought about only through guerrilla warfare. Subsequent to the publication of Revolution in the Revolution?, Fidel Castro made it clear that this doctrine applied not only to Latin America and other "underdeveloped" areas but to the great industrial countries as well. He publicly speculated on the possibilities of guerrilla war ultimately breaking out in West Germany and the United States, for example.9

Having established to his own satisfaction that guerrilla war was the only road to power, Debray went on to insist that a guerrilla war can be successful only if its political and military leadership is combined and is located in the rural areas in which the armed conflict occurs.

Third, Debray presented the famous "focus" theory of guerrilla revolt, first elaborated in some detail by Ernesto Guevara. He argued that it is not necessary to wait until the "objective conditions" are ready for an armed uprising. On the contrary, it is possible for a group of middle-class young men from the cities to go out into the remoter parts of the countryside and establish a "focus" of rebellion.

The first job of this focal group is to undermine the authority of the established government by constant attacks on its police and soldiers, which demonstrate the government's inability to wipe out the focus of rebellion. Only when this has been accomplished, said Debray, will it be possible to begin to mobilize the support of the peasantry, and subsequently of other groups.

On this point the Castro theory of revolution differed markedly from that of Mao Tse-tung, as had been made abundantly clear in polemics between Latin American supporters of Castro and of Mao. The pro-Chinese Communists in Latin America and elsewhere, while professing belief in the ultimate necessity of guerrilla war, argued that such an effort could not be launched until a great deal of political "softening up" of the rural areas had been accomplished—until a wide degree of support for the coming revolution had been built up among the peasantry, as well as among urban workers. The pro-Chinese Communists also differed profoundly from the Fidelistas' belief that middle-class youth could be the catalytic agents for launching the revolution.

Debray's fourth argument also differed profoundly from the traditional position of the Communists, whether pro-Soviet or pro-Peking. He argued that no deep theoretical training was necessary for the guerrillas. He ridiculed the Communists' classical emphasis on study of the Marxist-Leninist classics and indicated that more often than not this was a substitute for revolutionary action, not a preparation for it. Debray argued, in a somewhat mystical vein, that the lessons of class-consciousness and class solidarity would be learned through the experience of the guerrilla war itself, and that all elements participating in it would be "proletarianized" by the common experiences and common struggles of the civil war.

Fifth, Debray, and through him the Castro Communists, repudiated the fundamental Leninist thesis that the struggle for the revolution must be led by a highly disciplined and highly organized party. On the contrary, he argued, the revolutionary party will emerge out of the guerrilla army; through their struggle the various groups and individuals who have launched the civil war will be forged into a single political unit; and the cream of these guerrilla fighters will form the party which, after the triumph of the revolution, will give leadership to the "building Socialism" phase. Practical success in the revolutionary war will be a much more important credential than thorough knowledge of Marxist-Leninist theory for membership in this new elite.

Finally, Debray argued that all of the traditional revolutionary or would-be revolutionary elements in Latin American politics had failed. He strongly attacked the pro-Moscow Communists for their unwillingness to undertake guerrilla activities but did not spare the pro-Peking ones either, arguing that they have merely reproduced on a smaller scale the bureaucratic inertia long characteristic of the older groups, while the Trotskyites were a sect rather than a true revolutionary force.10

Fidel Castro frequently echoed Debray's arguments. He did so in his famous dictum "Revolutionists make revolutions" and in his frequent attacks on the "pseudo revolutionaries," "traitors," and "cowards," whom he accused explicitly or implicitly of leading the Latin American Communist parties.

The second major theoretical position of the Castro Communist group was its emphasis on "moral" as opposed to "material" incentives in the building of Socialism. On this issue the Fidelistas seemed to have much in common with the followers of Mao Tse-tung, particularly during the Cultural Revolution.

Ernesto Guevara was the great protagonist of the primary role of "moral" incentives. He argued that one of the fundamental tasks in the period of transition to Socialism was the forging of a new kind of human being, one who was self-sacrificing, who would put the interests of the community above his own. It was fruitless to try to reorient an individual in this way if one continued to appeal to him with the same incentives—the improvement of his material well-being—that had been characteristic of capitalism. To continue to do so, furthermore, was to violate "Socialist morality."11

On this point, as on most others, Fidel Castro was not always consistent. There seems little question that one of the issues over which Castro and Guevara had strong disagreements shortly before Che disappeared from the Cuban scene was this question of motivations. At that point Fidel, in the general orientation of trying to get along as well as possible with the Russians, which characterized his policies in 1964-65, was stressing the use of material incentives to get the Cuban workers to labor more diligently and longer.

However, with the decision to launch a third camp in international Communism, which seems more or less to have coincided with the Tricontinental Congress of January 1966, Castro adopted the position that Guevara had so long urged. Thereafter he increasingly emphasized the priority of moral over material incentives, and his speeches contained the same tone of moral condemnation of materialism that was characteristic of Guevara.12

FROM JACOBIN LEFTISM TO FIDELISTA COMMUNISM

After January 1966 Fidel Castro increasingly cut his ties with the orthodox Communist parties of Latin America and recognized the

Jacobin leftists in the other Latin American countries as the counterparts of his Communist Party. As a result the Jacobin leftists were converted into the adherents of the Fidelista "third camp" in world Communism.

This transition was not a difficult one for the Jacobin leftists. Virtually from their inception most of the Jacobin leftist groups had proclaimed their loyalty to Marxism-Leninism. Their belief in the violent road to power seemed to have its greatest vindication in the success of the Cuban revolution. They shared Castro's disdain for the orthodox Communist parties, which they believed to be essentially conservative, bureaucracy-ridden, and tied more to serving the interests of the Soviet Union than to bringing about revolution in Latin America.

The Latin American Solidarity Organization (OLAS) served as a kind of Comintern for the pro-Fidelista Communist groups in Latin America. (The Spanish initials of this group, OLAS, involve a sort of double entendre. The word "olas" in Spanish means "waves," and it can hardly have been a coincidence that the name of the Fidelista Communist group in the area has the implication that it is bringing "waves of Revolution" to Latin America.) Although a handful of orthodox Communist parties sent representatives to the founding Congress of OLAS, the great majority of the delegations were made up of Jacobin leftist groups. After its founding congress the orthodox Communist parties had relatively little contact with OLAS and virtually no voice in running it.

The basic purpose of OLAS, and the fundamental policy of the Castro regime in the hemisphere, was to stimulate, encourage, and aid guerrilla movements in Latin America. After 1966, at least, these movements tended to follow the general pattern put forth in Régis Debray's treatise.

Certainly the most serious and sustained guerrilla effort supported by the Castro government was that in Venezuela, maintained against the Betancourt, Leoni, and Caldera governments. Starting in 1962 as both a rural guerrilla and an urban terrorist movement, it had at first the support of both the orthodox Partido Comunista de Venezuela and the Fidelista Movimiento de la Izquierda Revolucionaria. During 1962 and 1963 it concentrated a large part of its efforts on terrorist activities in the major cities, seeking to provoke a coup d'état by the military, which would substitute a barracks dictatorship for a constitutionally elected popular regime, thus facilitating the extreme Left's efforts to launch a serious rural-based civil war. These efforts failed, as did the attempt of the terrorists to prevent the holding of the general election of December 1963, which constituted a major defeat for the guerrillas when almost 95 percent of the voters turned out and chose a member of outgoing President Rómulo

Betancourt's Acción Democrática Party, Raúl Leoni, as Betancourt's successor.

After some months of regrouping their forces, the Castro-backed forces launched a new offensive by the middle of 1964, concentrating this time on rural guerrilla activity. For about a year these efforts, which were marked by the dispatch of some Cuban army officers (several of whom were captured) to help the Venezuelan rebels, constituted a serious nuisance for the Leoni regime, although they did not fundamentally imperil it. However, by the last months of 1965 it became apparent that the guerrilla efforts had been largely contained and that the prospects of success were at best very remote.

As a result of this situation, and of the terrible reverses that resorting to guerrilla activity had brought to it in the trade union movement and in politics, the Communist Party of Venezuela began to withdraw from the guerrilla activities. By early 1967 it had announced its intention of returning fully to legal political activity and of participating in the 1968 general election. A Communist front party was organized for this purpose, the Unión para Avanzar, which won one Senate seat and six posts in the Chamber of Deputies in the December 1968 election. The complete retirement of the Communists from the guerrilla conflict was confirmed when President Rafael Caldera fully restored the legality of the party, under its own name, soon after taking office in March 1969.

This reversal of policy by the Venezuelan Communists brought them into violent conflict with Fidel Castro and with the Fidelista Communists. Castro announced his firm support for the group of dissident Communists, led by Douglas Bravo, and the part of the leadership of the Movimiento de la Izquierda Revolucionaria who pledged to continue the guerrilla efforts, under the aegis of the so-called Fuerzas Armadas de Liberación Nacional.

The guerrilla activities continued during the early months of the Caldera administration, despite the new president's offers of amnesty for all guerrillas who would lay down their arms. However, the few hundred people involved—reinforced occasionally by small shiploads of Cubans and Venezuelans from Cuba—constituted no menace to the Venezuelan democratic regime, despite an occasional spectacular descent on a small town or robbery of a bank by the extremists.

The Guatemalan guerrilla movement began at about the same time as that in Venezuela. As in Venezuela, for some years it had the support of the orthodox Communist Party. Those participating included a handful of former army officers, university students, and a few peasant recruits.

For several years the Guatemalan guerrilla forces were divided into two groups. One of these, led by Lt. Marco Antonio Yon Sosa, was in 1965-66 somewhat influenced by a group of Trotskyites, mainly Mexican followers of the Argentine Trotskyite leader J. Posadas. It was this group that originally had the support of Fidel Castro.

The second element of the Guatemalan guerrillas was led at first by Lt. Luís Turcios, and its members were recruited largely from the country's Young Communist League. Known as the Fuerzas Armadas Revolucionarias (FAR), it was closely associated with the country's orthodox Communist Party, the Partido Guatemalteco del Trabajo. In January 1966 Castro announced that he was switching his backing to the FAR, at the same time denouncing the Yon Sosa group for its Trotskyite connections.

For several years the guerrillas had some modicum of success in mountain regions near the Caribbean coast. However, with the election in 1966 of the moderate leftist Julio César Méndez Montenegro of the Partido Revolucionario, both guerrilla groups lost much of their student backing. Early in 1967 the Guatemalan army launched a major offensive that largely liquidated the guerrilla mountain bases, and the government's civilian authorities moved into the affected area with extensive programs of medical aid, land grants, and school construction, to try to deal with the social problems that had caused the rebels to have a modicum of support among the local peasantry.

As a result of this defeat, the rebels turned principally to urban terrorism. Although a few groups remained in the mountain fastnesses, the main force of the guerrillas was turned to a campaign of assassinations and other armed forays in Guatemala City and other urban centers. These attacks were met with even more ferocious terrorism by elements of the extreme Right, supported by powerful economic interests and at least some parts of the army. Few terrorists of either side were brought to justice before the courts.

Meanwhile, the Communists had become increasingly disenchanted with the guerrilla campaign. They had been at least mildly sympathetic to the electoral efforts of Méndez Montenegro; and after the guerrilla defeats of early 1967, the party moved cautiously to withdraw from the campaign of violence. There came a final break between the FAR and the PGT late in 1968, with the expected recriminations between the Guatemalan orthodox Communists and Fidel Castro and his Guatemalan supporters.[13]

Subsequently both leaders of the guerrilla conflict were killed. Turcios died in an automobile accident, and Yon Sosa was killed in a clash with Mexican soldiers on the Guatemalan-Mexican frontier. However, the problem of mutual killing by elements of the Left and Right in Guatemalan politics continued.

The most spectacular guerrilla effort was certainly that led by Ernesto Guevara himself in Bolivia. This attempt to put into practice

Guevara's own theories of guerrilla war, and those of Debray, involved a number of high officers of the Cuban army besides Guevara. Within Bolivia they had cooperation from some unattached radicals, and for a while the pro-Moscow Communist Party offered to participate in the guerrilla movement. However, when Guevara made it clear that he, and not the Bolivian Communist Party, was going to command the campaign, the Communists withdrew their backing.

For almost a year Guevara and his small band of Cubans and Bolivians wandered extensively in the heavily forested area of the department of Santa Cruz, in the general vicinity of the Camiri oil region. They fought a number of engagements with the Bolivian army, and temporarily seized several hamlets, but they never constituted a major threat to the Bolivian government.

Certainly Guevara was influenced in this campaign more by geopolitical concepts than by his own theories of guerrilla war. The Bolivian campaign seems to have been conceived of as one to establish a guerrilla base in the heart of the South American continent, from which support could be given to similar efforts elsewhere in Bolivia, as well as in neighboring Argentina, Peru, and perhaps in Paraguay, Chile, and Brazil.

Guevara seems to have failed for at least three reasons. First, his expedition was too much in the nature of a foreign invasion—by Cubans—and facilitated the government efforts to arouse hostility against "foreign intervention" in Bolivian affairs. Guevara also violated one of the postulates he had laid down in his own treatise on guerrilla warfare when he sought to mount a campaign against a government considered by the great majority of peasants as a defender of their rights to the land, which had been given to them in an agrarian reform more than a decade before. In his Diary, Guevara complains repeatedly and bitterly about the guerrillas' failure to win any support among the few peasants with whom they came into contact. Finally, Guevara was faced with some of the most hostile territory, from a physical point of view, to be found in South America: sparsely populated hilly jungle, which made it very difficult for the guerrillas to live off the land.[14]

Guevara was captured and killed in October 1967. Although subsequently some efforts were made to revive his guerrilla band, these had no notable success.

Other guerrilla efforts with at least some Cuban backing have taken place in Argentina, Peru, Colombia, and Nicaragua. In Argentina they proved a disastrous failure and were fairly quickly and easily dealt with by the armed forces in 1965-66.[15] In Peru, after some initial successes among the peasants of the High Andes, the guerrilla efforts, largely mounted by the Fidelista Movimiento de la Izquierda Revolucionaria and the pro-Chinese Communists, were crushed by the

Peruvian army in July and August 1965. In Colombia some of the outlaw bands that had plagued certain parts of the country since the late 1940s were brought under Fidelista political leadership; but although the Fidelistas were able to maintain a certain small base of operation, they were largely contained and isolated by the Colombian army after 1965. In Nicaragua several small groups landed in the northeastern part of the country, but they were not able to establish any firm base of operations.

THE FIDELISTA PARTIES AND GROUPS

The Fidelista faction of Communism in Latin America remained small and diverse. In only a few countries were more or less well organized parties of this persuasion established. In a few others the Fidelista Communists were represented by guerrilla groups. In still others the Fidelista supporters remain dispersed and unorganized.

Probably the most substantial Fidelista party outside of Cuba was the Movimiento de Izquierda Revolucionaria of Venezuela. It had its origins in 1959-60 in the youth movement of Acción Democrática. The young people who had been the leaders of the underground organization of Acción Democrática in the last part of the Pérez Jiménez dictatorship were exceedingly unhappy with the return to control of the older party leaders. Furthermore, they had serious ideological differences with the older leadership. Through close contacts with the Communists in joint underground activity, they had been thoroughly indoctrinated in Marxism-Leninism at a time when it was virtually impossible to obtain the publications of and discuss the party's basic philosophy with the older men who had given Acción Democrática its structure and philosophy.

The discontent of the younger group was obvious during the first year after the fall of the dictatorship. At the AD convention in August 1958 that chose Rómulo Betancourt as the party's presidential nominee, the youth tried to block this choice. With Betancourt's assumption of office early in 1959, they became increasingly critical of his "hesitancy," "failure to carry out the party's program," and other alleged sins. This conflict finally came out into the open in the early months of 1960, when most of the leadership of the party's youth was either expelled from Acción Democrática or voluntarily withdrew.

The AD dissidents organized into a new party, the Movimiento de Izquierda Revolucionaria. They proclaimed themselves Marxist-Leninists and criticized the Communist Party for being too conservative and unwilling to take drastic revolutionary action. However, through their contacts with the youth wing of the Communist Party, they were soon able to pressure that group into cooperation in a campaign of violence and guerrilla activity early in 1962, apparently against the better judgment of many of the older Communist leaders.

The MIR constituted a major force in the nation's student movement. It was largely from this group that the party recruited both its own leaders and its guerrilla cadres. When in 1965-66 some of the older leaders of the MIR, headed by its best-known figure, Domingo Alberto Rangel, urged an end to the guerrilla campaign, they were expelled from the party and the MIR continued along the guerrilla road to power.

After the withdrawal of the Communists from guerrilla activity, the MIR came to constitute the principal element among the rebels. It also continued to have considerable influence among the students. However, it remained outlawed, as it had been since its participation in two unsuccessful military uprisings in 1961; and it made little or no effort to recruit followers among the trade unionists or organized peasant masses. The MIR remained loyal to the idea of putting all of its efforts into seeking the violent overthrow of the constitutional regime, sacrificing any chance to obtain even a minimum of influence in the more general political arena.

A second MIR was established in Peru. This group originated among dissidents of the Partido Aprista Peruano. A number of Apristas, particularly among the youth, were disenchanted with the party's support of the government of Manuel Prado between 1956 and 1962—support that the party leaders hoped would bring them the opportunity to win free elections at the end of Prado's term. This dissident element withdrew to form what they first called the Apra Rebelde. It had considerable influence among the nation's university students and for some time carried on propaganda work among the general population.

With the outbreak of guerrilla activity in Venezuela, the Apra Rebelde changed its name to Movimiento de Izquierda Revolucionaria and began to prepare for launching its own guerrilla campaign. By early 1965 the MIR had established a limited guerrilla front and had recruited some support among the highland Indians. However, the army's successful campaign in the middle of 1965 completely overran this front; several of the MIR's major leaders were killed, others were captured. Since 1965 the MIR has played little part in Peruvian politics.

In Costa Rica a group of Castro-oriented young people, headed by a middle-aged, middle-rank leader of Liberación Nacional, broke away from that party in 1960 to form the Partido Socialista. They objected to the strong anti-Castro position assumed by José Figueres and other PLN leaders. This party participated unsuccessfully in the 1962 elections and made no serious subsequent effort to launch any kind of guerrilla activity.

Still another MIR was established in Chile by a group of dissidents from the Partido Socialista de Chile. It gained some influence in the student movement, coming to control the student organizations at the University of Concepción. During the Frei administration it carried out various urban guerrilla activities, including bank robberies, kidnappings, and other acts of violence. With the election of Salvador Allende as president in 1970, the MIR was split, some supporting the Unidad Popular candidate while others continued to carry out urban guerrilla activities and organize seizures of rural landholdings. It constituted the principal left-wing opposition to the Allende regime.

In the Dominican Republic the pro-Castro Communist faction was represented chiefly by the 14th of June Movement. This group was established during the last years of the Trujillo dictatorship by a band of university students and young intellectuals. During the first year or so after Trujillo's assassination, it emerged as one of the country's three major parties. In 1961-62 it was not particularly pro-Castro, because many of its leaders felt that he had betrayed a move by Dominican exiles to invade the country and overthrow Trujillo in 1959. They also resented the rapprochement that had taken place between Castro and Trujillo in the months preceding the death of the latter.[16]

However, the 14th of June Movement was subsequently radicalized. This was in part because most of the leaders who had founded the party had been killed in 1963 when, after the fall of the government of Juan Bosch, they had tried to launch a guerrilla uprising against the so-called triumvirate government that succeeded him. The 14th of June participated on the "constitutionalist" side in the civil war of April-July 1965, which also served to drive it to the left. As a result, in recent years the 14th of June has constituted the major element in the Dominican Republic allied with the Castro Communist faction. In the late 1960s it was split into several factions.

Aside from these political parties the Fidelista current of Communism in Latin America is represented by a number of guerrilla movements already noted. These include the FALN in Venezuela, the FAR in Guatemala, the so-called Ejército de Liberación Nacional of Colombia, and the remnants of Che Guevara's band in Bolivia.

By the late 1960s the only guerrilla groups having any success were those operating in cities, most notably the Tupamaros in Uruguay. However, these were not following the Guevara-Debray thesis of rural guerrilla war; and their connections with the Castro regime were certainly not as close as those of the ill-fated rural guerrilla movements.

CASTRO'S ABANDONMENT OF INDEPENDENCE

Castro persevered in his efforts to establish a third force in world Communism from January 1966 to August 1968. However, his reaction to the Soviet invasion of Czechoslovakia provided the first major indication that he had given up this attempt, at least for a while. Immediately after the invasion he made a curious televised speech in which he repeated virtually all the charges made against the Soviet Union—interference with self-determination of a small country, interference in internal affairs of a sister Communist party, and so on—asserted that all these were true, but ended by saying that despite this, the invasion was justified and he supported it.

Soon thereafter a clear change in policy toward the Soviet Union occurred. The Cuban Communist Party's newspaper Gramma, which for two and a half years had virtually ignored the Soviet Union, except to attack it by innuendo, suddenly began to carry long and laudatory articles about the USSR. Wide publicity was given to visits of a long line of guests from the Soviet Union and other East European countries, including Soviet Minister of Defense Grechko.

Subsequently the rapprochement with the USSR became even more obvious. The annual trade and aid agreement signed early in 1971 provided for an increase of approximately $100 million in aid to Cuba. It also provided for establishment of a joint Soviet-Cuban commission to study the Cuban economy, make suggestions for its improvement, and orient Soviet aid. In effect this joint commission submitted Cuba's economy to a higher degree of foreign supervision than had existed during most of the long period of Cuban association with the United States.

Elsewhere in Latin America this change in Cuban policy also became noticeable. The curtailment of aid to guerrilla groups provoked an open and violent break with Douglas Bravo, leader of the small group still trying to conduct guerrilla operations in Venezuela. On the other hand, in an abrupt about-face from his position of 1966-68, Castro welcomed the electoral victory of Salvador Allende and the Unidad Popular in Chile late in 1970. He even expressed approval of the reform program of the military regime of General Juan Velasco in Peru.

In December 1971 Castro made a state visit to Chile. Spending three weeks there, he traveled throughout the country; and the theme of his numerous speeches was that guerrilla war was not the only way to power, that the peaceful road represented by the Allende regime had his firm approval. One of his principal tasks on this trip seemed to be to counsel his supporters in Chile to support the Allende regime rather than oppose it from the Left, as many of them had been doing.

On his way home Castro stopped for short visits with General Velasco in Lima and President José María Velasco Ibarra in Ecuador.

During the 1960s the Jacobin Left of the late 1950s was converted into a new branch of international Communism, with its headquarters in Havana. Particularly during the period 1966-68, Fidel Castro quite clearly sought to bring together these groups, which had never been part of the official Communist movement, to form a third force within world Communism. In so doing he put forth a theoretical line distinct from those of the Moscow and Peking camps, and he gave extensive moral and material aid to those adhering to his position elsewhere in Latin America.

However, by the latter part of 1968 Castro had apparently concluded that, for the time being at least, he had failed to create a viable third force. He veered back to close alignment with the Soviet Union, both in state-to-state relations and in party contacts. This left his followers elsewhere in Latin America in great disarray — largely abandoned by their supposed chief and defeated in their efforts to put into effect in their own countries the theory and practice he had formerly advocated so strongly. The only guerrilla groups that still showed some signs of life were those operating in the cities of some of the Latin American countries, whose connections with Castro had always been somewhat tenuous.

CHAPTER 22
FASCIST PARTIES

Latin America has had more than its share of parties and individual political leaders of reactionary and authoritarian orientation. Many of these have been noted elsewhere in this volume and are not discussed in this chapter. Here we are concerned with those parties in Latin America that have had a definite fascist ideology: belief in the corporative state, the "leadership principle", exaggerated nationalism, and the "chosen" role of their parties to rule as a self-selected elite, without competition.

THE AXIS AND LATIN AMERICA

The rise of fascist parties in Latin America was a reflection of the upsurge of fascism in Europe, particularly during the 1930s. Fascist Italy, Nazi Germany, and Falangista Spain sought to spread their influence in Latin America, spent large sums on propaganda in the area, and maintained contacts with parties and individual politicians whom they considered to be friendly. As the fortunes of fascism in Europe seemed to be improving, fascist ideas and, to a certain degree, fascist parties prospered in Latin America. When fascism collapsed in Europe, it tended to collapse in Latin America as well.

The European fascist parties sought to extend their organizations to Latin America. Branches of the Fascist Party, the National Socialist German Workers Party, and the Falange Española Tradicionalista were established to work among the millions of Italian, German, and Spanish immigrants. These branches of European parties had as their purpose the mobilization of support for the regimes ruling Italy, Germany, and Spain; the reinforcement of the loyalty of these immigrants to their native countries (and the consequent

FASCIST PARTIES

weakening of their loyalty to their adopted nations); and the organization of political and military espionage for the Axis Powers.

These branches of foreign parties aroused widespread resistance in Latin America, even though they attempted generally to operate more or less in secret. In Argentina the Chamber of Deputies organized a special Anti-Argentine Activities Committee to investigate their activities; in Brazil Getúlio Vargas submitted them to close surveillance by his extensive secret police and military intelligence apparatus.

The branches of the Italian Fascist, German Nazi, and Spanish Falangista parties operated almost exclusively among the immigrants and had very little direct impact on national politics. They were probably counterproductive insofar as spreading the popularity of fascist ideas in these nations is concerned.

It is not these branches of European parties with which we are principally concerned in this chapter but, rather, with the indigenous fascist parties that appeared in several of the Latin American countries during the 1930s. The most significant of these were the Brazilian Integralistas, the Chilean Partido Nacista, the Bolivian Falange Socialista Boliviana, and the Sinarquista Party of Mexico.

ACAO INTEGRALISTA BRASILEIRA

The Brazilian fascist party, Ação Integralista Braileira, was one of the two parties in the country that were able to establish nationwide organizations during the early 1930s, the other being the Communist Party. It was established by Plinio Salgado, a poet and novelist of strong Catholic inclinations, at São Paulo in 1932 and during the next few years spread rapidly throughout the country.

The early 1930s was a period of great political change and instability in Brazil. In October 1930 Getúlio Vargas came to power as the result of a widely popular revolutionary movement. He governed for three years as a provisional president and enacted a program of extensive social legislation and encouragement of legally recognized trade unionism, which was designed to build up wide popular support for Vargas. However, many of those who had originally supported the revolution that put him in power felt that Vargas was seeking to establish a personal dictatorship and that many of his policies were designed to bring organized labor under government control; and they accused him of carrying out other measures they considered reactionary.[1]

A widely supported revolt against the Vargas regime broke out in the state of São Paulo in July 1932 and lasted three months before it was suppressed. In 1933 a new constitution was written and Vargas was elected to a full term by the Constitutional Assembly.

But opposition to Vargas continued to grow. Late in 1934 the left-wing opponents of the president united in the so-called Aliança Libertadora Nacional; and by this time Ação Integralista Brasileira was the other major opponent of the Vargas regime.

The Integralistas had most of the trappings that had become familiar in European fascist parties: a green-shirt uniform, a "leader" in the person of Plinio Salgado, the Greek letter sigma in place of the Nazis' swastika, a party anthem, and a party militia.

The program of Ação Integralista Brasileira stressed the need for Brazilian national unity, the reorganization of the economy and political structure on the basis of a corporative state, and the importance of Catholicism as part of the Brazilian tradition. The racism of the Nazis was not part of the program of the Integralistas, who called for the integration of the various Brazilian ethnic groups. The Integralista leadership was split on the issue of anti-Semitism, some being as anti-Jewish as the Nazis, but this attitude never became an official part of the party's program.

The Integralistas won wide support in various segments of the Brazilian population. Integralismo was particularly popular among the middle class, including government employees and other white collar workers. It won the allegiance of an impressive number of army and navy officers, and it had powerful organizations among the German-speaking population of the southern states of Santa Caterina and Rio Grande do Sul. Even high officials of the Vargas administration made little secret of belonging to Ação Integralista.

The Integralistas, following the model of their Italian and German counterparts, sought to capture control of the streets. Integralista gangs marched frequently through the streets, attacked political opponents' meetings, and in other ways tried to impress the general populace and the government with their power.

Probably the high point in the history of Ação Integralista Brasileira was the spectacular march through Rio de Janeiro in the middle of 1935. The marchers, who were said to number several hundred thousand, passed the presidential palace to "honor" President Vargas, who observed them from an upstairs window. Vargas' daughter Alzira is authority for the statement that he was shocked to discover the numerical strength of the Integralistas and the number of high government officials and military officers who were marching in this show of force.[2]

Certainly between 1935 and 1937 Plinio Salgado and his followers were convinced that it was only a matter of time until their party took control of the government from Getúlio Vargas. Their optimism was strengthened by the fact that in several months of 1937 Salgado himself consulted with Vargas at meetings the president was holding to discuss his own plan to subvert the constitution he had sworn to uphold. These conferences, which were attended by the president; his close adviser Francisco Campos, who was considered by many to be a sympathizer with the Integralistas; and General Goes Monteiro, as well as (occasionally) by Salgado, elaborated a new corporative state constitution and plans for ending the democratic regime still in force. It seems certain that Plinio Salgado was given to believe that the Integralistas would play a major role in the semifascist regime being planned by Vargas and his closest associates.

The actual coup d'état by Vargas took place on November 10, 1937. He sent military police to close down Congress and later in the day went on the radio to announce the change in government. There was virtually no immediate public reaction.

Although Vargas had instituted what, on paper at least, was a semifascist regime, he had no intention of sharing power with the Integralistas. He is said to have offered Plinio Salgado the post of minister of education; but he gave them no further indication that he planned to give the Integralistas a major position in the new regime, which he intended to be a quite personal dictatorship. On the contrary, early in December 1937 Vargas issued a decree dissolving all existing political parties—with no exception for the Integralistas.

The leaders and members of Ação Integralista Brasileira were furious with Vargas, whom they now classed as a traitor. Their reaction against his supposed betrayal was not long in coming. On May 11, 1938, a small group of Integralistas, including members of Vargas' personal bodyguard, sought to capture the presidential palace. For reasons still not adequately explained, they did not make their final assault, although only Vargas, a few members of his family, and one bodyguard were defending the palace and the army took several hours to come to the president's rescue.[3]

Following the failure of the Integralista coup against him, Vargas took vengeance. Hundreds of leaders of the party were arrested and many were kept in jail for several years; while Plinio Salgado was exiled to Portugal, where he remained until after the overthrow of Vargas in October 1945. Many Integralistas, including some of the top leaders, in time became close associates of Vargas.

With the ouster of the Vargas dictatorship and the return to a more or less democratic constitutional government in 1945, the Integralistas reorganized. However, they had lost virtually all of the popular support they had had a decade before. Their new party, the Partido de Representação Popular, sought to make it appear not only that it was not a fascist organization but that it never had been one. Instead of stressing the ideas of a corporative state, extreme nationalism, and the leadership principle, the Partido de Representação Popular largely emphasized the need for strengthening municipal government.

During the 1945-65 period the ex-Integralistas had a modest representation in the national Congress, and Salgado was a member of the Chamber of Deputies. He also ran for president in 1950, 1955, and 1960. The party was also represented in small numbers in several state legislatures, and some of its members served in state cabinets. However, the Integralistas were never able to regain the status of a major party they had had in the 1930s.

PARTIDO NACISTA DE CHILE

The Partido Nacista de Chile never reached the stage at which it could make a serious bid for power. However, for half a dozen years in the late 1930s and early 1940s it was an important factor in Chilean politics, playing a particularly important role in the presidential election of 1938.

The Partido Nacista was established under the leadership of Jorge González von Maree in the early 1930s. It made a particular appeal to the Chileans of German descent in the southern part of the Central Valley, although it also gained support among some middle-class elements in Santiago and other parts of the country. In the election of 1937 it succeeded in electing two members of the Chamber of Deputies, one of them being González von Maree himself.

Like most parties of its kind, the Partido Nacista had its groups of young storm troopers. These groups sought to gain control of the streets in Santiago and other cities, and to a certain degree they did so in some of the predominantly German areas. However, in the capital and other major cities, the young Nacistas ran headlong into the militia organized by the Socialist Party, with whom they several times fought pitched battles in the streets.

The Nacistas assumed considerable importance during 1938. They endorsed the presidential nomination of General Carlos Ibañez, an ex-dictator, who had been overthrown in 1931. Together with the Unión Socialista, a group that had broken away from the Socialist Party in 1938, they formed the Popular Liberating Alliance, which described itself as "antioligarchical, antifascist and anti-imperialist," to support the general's candidacy.[4]

The Nazis and their allies concentrated most of their fire during this campaign against Gustavo Ross, the nominee of the right-wing Conservative-Liberal coalition, backed by outgoing President Arturo Alessandri. Ross's major opponent was Pedro Aguirre Cerda, candidate of the Popular Front formed by the Radical, Socialist, Communist, and several minor left-wing parties.

On September 4, 1938, the Nazis organized a "march of triumph" in Santiago, in support of Ibáñez' candidacy. Some 12,000 marchers

FASCIST PARTIES

were said to have participated, and John Reese Stevenson has commented: "The Santiaguinos were impressed by the good order and discipline shown by the Nazis, but passed off the demonstrations as the dramatic last gasp of a lost cause."[5]

On the following day the Nacistas made an abortive attempt to seize power, but they took control only of the main building of the University of Chile and the Social Security Building, two blocks from the university and across the street from the presidential palace. Army elements supposed to join the Nacistas' revolt failed to do so; and it was easy for the members of the national police, the carabiñeros, to recapture the buildings seized by the Nacistas. However, in taking the Social Security Building the carabiñeros obeyed an order from higher authorities that no one must leave alive. President Alessandri, who was watching the battle from across the street, was accused by the Nacistas of issuing this order, a charge he strongly denied. Jorge González von Maree and Carlos Ibáñez were both jailed as a result of this insurrection.[6]

The events of September 5 brought the Nacistas to firm support of the candidacy of Pedro Aguirre Cerda. Carlos Ibáñez withdrew from the race, since his supporters felt that their first job was to defeat the presidential candidate backed by Alessandri, who they felt, was responsible for the death of the young Nacistas in the Social Security Building.

Although Nacista support of Pedro Aguirre Cerda helped to gain him a very narrow victory, the election of the Popular Front government helped to bring an end to the Partido Nacista. For some time the Aguirre Cerda regime enjoyed wide popularity, and the growing attacks that González von Maree, from the Chamber of Deputies, and other Nacistas, from the streets, made upon the president and his government helped to undermine the support of the Partido Nacista.

Furthermore, with the outbreak of World War II and the general sentiment in Chile in favor of the Allied cause, the Nacistas decided that the close association that their name gave them with the German Nazis was a handicap. In 1940 they changed it to Vanguardia Socialista, but this mere change in name was not enough to end the decline in the fortunes of the party. It was formally dissolved in the early 1940s, and its former members were scattered among the various Chilean parties. González von Maree joined the right-wing Liberal Party.

FALANGE SOCIALISTA BOLIVIANA

The Falange Socialista Boliviana was established by a group of Bolivian exiles in Santiago, Chile in 1935. In name and in program it was closely modeled on the Spanish Falange, which had been established by José Antonio Primo de Rivera, son of an ex-dictator of Spain, several years earlier.

The ideological fraternity between the Bolivian Falange and its Spanish counterpart was made clear in the program of principles of the Bolivian party. It stressed the importance of establishing a "New Bolivian State," which it described in the following terms:

> An eternal and supra-individual organism which totally represents the Nation whose supreme mission is not sporadic in time and in history, but which has the responsibility of uniting a harmonic continuity of the past, present and future generations; which excludes the social indiscipline by two political forms: anarchic disorganization produced by relaxation of the principle of authority, and the enthronement of oligarchic and caudillistic tyrannies.
>
> The hierarchical system will suppress class or group privileges, giving the option to each Bolivian to occupy the place which his capacity assigns him.[7]

The Falange Socialista Boliviana called for the reorganization of the economy on the basis of corporativism. In Point 6 of the program of principles this idea was stated thus:

> Labor of all under an Organic Regime: Our Fatherland will be for all Bolivians, without class privileges. Every Bolivian will feel himself a participant in the task of creating a Fatherland and in the happiness and feeling of nobility which this will afford. The individual will participate in the organic unity of the State by means of a corporative regime in which each will have his function in accordance with his labor specialty.[8]

In its emphasis on the sociological and political importance of the family, the Falange Socialista Boliviana also followed the ideas of its Spanish counterpart. Point 12 of the program of principles presented this idea:

> The Family Regime: The family is the cell group of social organization. It constitutes the basis of the integral formation of the human personality, of public morality and health, and of the perfecting of the Nation.
>
> The New State will assure respect, welfare, stability and improvement to the Bolivian family.[9]

Finally, the general fascist belief that the interests of the fascist party are coterminous with the interests of the nation, and under its control there is no room for any other political organization, is expressed in Point 5 of the program of principles of the FBS:

> Falange as a Social Movement: We do not constitute a mere political party. We shall mobilize and fortify all of the spiritual, cultural and economic energies of the nation. Our social vision makes us conceive of Bolivia in its authentic expression, with the flourishing of all of its possibilities.[10]

The Falange Socialista Boliviana also followed the Spanish fascist model rather than the German one in its lack of racist elitism. On the contrary, the program of principles of the FSB sought the incorporation of the outcast Indian into the nation. Point 9 referred to the Indian as "the root of our nationality" and promised an agrarian reform to give him "economic liberation" and an educational system to give him "human quality and dignity."[11]

During the first 17 years of its existence, the Falange Socialista Boliviana remained a very minor part of the Bolivian political spectrum. It formed a relatively inconsequential part of the opposition to the regimes in power from 1936 to 1952.

However, after the Revolution of April 9, 1952, which put the Movimiento Nacional Revolucionario in power, the Falange was suddenly catapulted to first-rank importance. This was because the principal old-line parties opposed to the MNR—the Partido Liberal, the Partido Unión Republicana Socialista, and the Partido de la Izquierda Revolucionaria—had been thoroughly discredited by participation in the conservative governments that had been in power during the six years preceding the MNR revolution. The Falange, on the other hand, had remained in opposition during that period and so could not be held responsible for the sins of omission and commission alleged against the governments of 1946-52.

As a result the Falange Socialista Boliviana became the rallying point for the right-wing opponents of the MNR government. The Liberal and Unión Republicana Socialista parties were virtually dormant through most of the 12 years of MNR rule, but the Falange Socialista Boliviana was the most militant opponent of the revolutionary regime.

In the election of 1956 the Falange won a majority in most of the country's major cities, although it was overwhelmed by the MNR support from the peasants and the miners. During the administration of Hernán Siles (1956-60) the Falange served as the major opposition group in Congress and in the country at large.

The Falange's attack on the MNR government frequently stressed the lack of "order" in the country and the alleged "Marxist" nature of the revolutionary regime. Typical was a document issued in March 1957 by Mario R. Gutiérrez Gutiérrez, president of the National Executive Committee of the FSB, headed "To the People of Bolivia," which read in part: "For another thing, what is in play is not the cause of a man, of Siles Suazo, but the cause of Order, Liberty, Justice and Law, in the face of the devastating action of a party, of a 'revolution' that, with disguised Marxist principles, was begun in 1952 and that has brought the Nation the most complete disaster, the magnitude of which certainly has never been surpassed in the history of the American peoples."

Although during the MNR regime the Falange Socialista Boliviana succeeded in winning the support of an appreciable part of the country's small middle class, it never was able to gain any influence among the peasantry or the organized workers. Although large segments of the latter group became disenchanted with the MNR government, they tended to throw their support to groups that broke away from the MNR or, to a lesser degree, to the Communist Party. Despite considerable increase in importance during the 12 years of the MNR government, therefore, the Falange was not able to make a serious bid for power.

Meanwhile, the Falange sought to dissociate itself publicly from fascism and stress the supposed Christian inspiration of its ideas. However, it was not recognized by the international Christian Democratic movement, the Bolivian affiliate of which was the Partido Social Cristiano—which, although opposed to the MNR government, did not cooperate with Falange.

The Falange participated in the conspiracy that overthrew MNR President Víctor Paz Estenssoro on November 4, 1964, but did not become part of the new government or of the regime of President René Barrientos, elected in 1966. In that election the Falange ran as an opposition party and received the largest anti-administration representation in Congress.

Nevertheless, in spite of this apparently good showing, the Falange still did not constitute a major competitor for power because it had never achieved a broad base among the peasants and urban workers and had failed to develop any substantial support in the armed forces. In 1969, during the government of General Alfredo Ovando, the Falange split, a "revolutionary" faction supporting the new regime.

The bulk of the Falange, however, continued to be part of the opposition to both the government of General Ovando and that of his successor, General Juan José Torres. In August 1971 it participated in a conspiracy to overthrow Torres, together with elements of the army and with the Falange's old enemy, the MNR. With the success

FASCIST PARTIES

of this conspiracy and the establishment of a new government under Colonel Hugo Banzer, the Falange for the first time entered the government. Together with the MNR it provided the civilian contingent in the new government of Colonel Banzer.

UNION NACIONAL SINARQUISTA

During the 1930s several fascist-oriented political groups appeared in Mexico, including the Camisas Doradas, or Gold Shirts, organized by a former general, Nicolás Rodríguez, which was dissolved by President Lázaro Cárdenas in August 1936.[12] However, the most important such group to appear was the Unión Nacional Sinarquista.

The Sinarquista movement was established in 1937. Left-wing critics long asserted that members of the Spanish Falange as well as of the German Nazis participated in the organization of the group.[13] There seems little question that before and during World War II the Axis Powers gave the Sinarquistas moral and financial support.

Howard Cline has described the philosophy and background of the Sinarquista movement in the following terms:

> Sinarquismo—Sinarchism—is the opposite of anarchism; the word means "with order." Sinarquistas are believers in "order."
>
> The particular "order" involved is a variant of Catholic Socialism. In Mexico it borrowed totalitarian trappings and ideology to revitalize long-standing Hispanidad tendencies. Sinarquismo appealed especially to peasant groups in the marginal regions of Mexico by stressing the excesses of the Revolution and its failure to better their status; the anti-clericalism of the Northern Oligarchy and its modified but virulent continuance under Cárdenas gave the Sinarquista organization a ready-made force of old Cristeros. [The Cristeros were a group of extremist Catholics who led a widespread peasant revolt against the government of President Plutarco Elías Calles in the mid-1920s.] Though all Sinarquistas are rabidly Catholic, the Church consistently denied any official connection with the movement. . . .
>
> The leadership of the movement was conservative, Mexican, and often extremist. Ultra-reactionary leaders stressed their hatred of Communism, openly disparaged the Reforma and the Revolution, but lauded the glories of Mexico under the Hapsburgs, when the Church and State were coordinate arms of Catholicism. The ideology

emphasized martyrdom, self-sacrifice, and evolved an elaborate jargon, as well as a set of symbols and militant slogans.[14]

In the early 1940s the Sinarquistas were reported to have established their own trade union group, the Federation of Guadelupan Workers. This effort caused sufficient concern among the leaders of the country's largest trade union group, the Confederación de Trabajadores de Mexico, for them to denounce it.[15]

In June 1944, President Manuel Avila Camacho issued a decree forbidding the Unión Nacional Sinarquista to hold any public meetings. However, a much more serious setback to the Sinarquistas during World War II was their splitting into several competing factions. The largest of these decided in 1945 to organize as a legal political party, and for this purpose it established the Partido de la Fuerza Popular. They won a number of seats in municipal councils and state legislatures and one member of the Chamber of Deputies in the election of 1946.[16]

However, the Sinarquistas brought the wrath of the government upon themselves once more when, in December 1948, they held a meeting in front of a statue of Benito Juárez on the Alameda in Mexico City, during which they draped the statue with black crepe and one of the participants was reported to have spat in the face of the statue. This event brought the banning of the Partido de la Fuerza Popular by President Miguel Alemán on January 28, 1949.[17]

In preparation for the 1952 presidential elections the Unión Nacional Sinarquista formed an alliance with the right-wing opponent of the government, the Partido Acción Nacional. It contributed much of the vote received by the PAN nominee, Efraín González Luna.[18] However, in the presidential campaign of 1958, the Unión Nacional Sinarquista, which still claimed some 150,000 members, ordered its followers to cast blank ballots.[19]

Since the 1958 election the Sinarquista movement has continued to decline. Several years before this, Howard Cline had offered an explanation for the dissipation of Sinarquista strength when he commented: "Sinarquism, like Communism, has withered on the vine as moderation and visible material benefits enveloped the countryside: Mexicans _are_ better governed, better fed, better housed."[20]

Fascism did not survive as a serious political force in Latin America after the disasters that World War II brought to fascism in Europe. This was not surprising. Perhaps the really interesting thing about fascism in Latin America is that so few parties of this orientation developed even in the heyday of the movement in the Old World.

PART VI
MISCELLANEOUS PARTIES

INTRODUCTION

In this volume the discussion of the political parties of Latin America has generally been organized in accordance with ideological or philosophical orientation. However, there are some parties in the area that do not fall neatly into any of the categories established in this book. Some of these are presented in the two chapters that follow.

With the exception of the Socialist, Christian Democratic, Communists, and fascist parties, the political groups that have existed in Brazil since the end of the Vargas dictatorship in 1945 are among those that do not fit neatly into ideological categories. Therefore a chapter has been devoted to the discussion of the country's major parties of 1945-65: the Partido Social Democratico, União Democrática Nacional, and Partido Trabalhista Brasileiro.

The movement that was started between 1943 and 1945 by Colonel Juan Domingo Perón, and resulted in 1946 in the founding of the Partido Peronista, also does not fit into any neat category. The Partido Peronista started out to some degree as a personalist group; but from its beginning it represented much more than most of the personalist parties that have existed traditionally in Latin America. From its inception the Peronista movement has represented a large part of the Argentine urban and rural working class. The evolution of the Peronista movement since the overthrow of Perón in September 1955 has emphasized the role of the movement as the spokesman for the majority of the lower-class elements.

Although the Perón regime gave some indication in its last years of evolving toward a corporative state, the political movement that Perón left behind was certainly not fascist in orientation. Increasingly it has become a political movement that is truly representative of most of the country's organized workers. However, it does not fit into any of the other categories used in this volume. It is certainly not Socialist in any orthodox sense. It is not Communist. Nor is it, in view of its origins and outlook, either national revolutionary or Christian Democratic. Therefore the Partido Peronista (in its various forms) has a separate chapter in this section.

The parties treated in this section are important because they are the political groups that have dominated the politics of the two largest countries of South America during the quarter century since World War II. With a discussion of these parties we have, hopefully, completed a survey of the important political parties of Latin America.

CHAPTER

23

THE BRAZILIAN PARTIES

The most important parties in Brazil since World War II have not fitted the categories generally used for analysis of Latin American political groups in this volume. Although there have been some groups with more or less well defined ideologies in Brazil since 1945, the more important ones have not been of this kind.

BRAZILIAN PARTIES BEFORE 1945

During the period of the Brazilian Empire (1822-89), Brazilian parties did not differ particularly from those of the other Latin American countries. Most active politicians were organized into the Liberal and Conservative parties. As elsewhere in the hemisphere, these were parties of the small elite that owned most of the property in the country—including the slaves—and was the only element of political consequence.

During most of this period, the Conservatives and Liberals alternated in power. The differences between them were not particularly great, the Liberals tending to be somewhat more in favor of free trade and somewhat more critical of the secular role of the Church than were the Conservatives. The tenure in office of either party depended principally on the exercise of the so-called "moderating power" by the emperor.

This moderating power was a unique aspect of Brazilian constitutional law and political practice. According to the constitution the emperor was defined as being "above politics" and was given the power to remove the government when he felt that it had lost the support of the voters, or when he felt that a change of administration would be in the country's best interest.

BRAZILIAN PARTIES

To a marked degree government during the period of the Empire was carried on by a process of consensus. Although there were small groups that favored republicanism, abolition of slavery, and other basic changes in the status quo, these elements were generally kept out of power, as were the advocates of absolute monarchy and a very strong Church. When such basic changes as the abolition of slavery and the substitution of a republic for a monarchy came, in 1888 and 1889 respectively, they occurred because those who constituted public opinion had generally become convinced of their desirability.[1]

With the overthrow of the Empire, the Liberal and Conservative parties virtually disappeared. Leadership in national politics was taken by the Republican Party. It had been a minor element in pre-1889 Brazil but assumed major importance during the 41 years of the "Old Republic" (1889-1930).

However, significant changes in the national political scene were brought by the republic, and they caused a marked difference in the nature of the political parties. A federal constitution, which established what might more nearly be called a confederation than a true federation, was adopted for the new regime. The states had extensive powers, and each state tended to be governed by a tightly organized sociopolitical oligarchy, which generally worked through the state Republican Party. For all practical purposes there was a single party in most of the states during most of the Old Republic era.

Each of these state Republican parties functioned through a series of powerful local political machines. The typical leader of such a machine was popularly known as a coronel, or colonel. He served as a liaison between the landlords, who still dominated the economies of the various states, and the state governments. Together the coroneis made up the state leadership of the Republican Party.[2]

The functions of the federal government were limited during this period. Generally the control of the national administration was in the hands of those who dominated the Republican parties of the states of São Paulo and Minas Gerais, economically and politically the most important states during the Old Republic. Frequently the governors of these two states alternated in the presidency.

During the last decade of the Old Republic, dissident parties opposed to the rule of the Republican Party arose in several of the states. The most important of these divergent groups was the Democratic Party, established in the state of São Paulo. It did not represent any major ideological or sociological opposition to the Republicans but was formed as a result of a struggle for power among different politicians within the dominant elite. Democratic parties of less consequence were formed in several other states.[3]

In only one state were there two strong rival parties throughout the period of the Old Republic: Rio Grande do Sul. In many ways politics was a more intense phenomenon in that state than in most of the rest of Brazil. The traditional occupation of the gauchos, as the residents of the state were known, was the herding of cattle and horses. It was these grazers who had fought border skirmishes with the Spaniards and then with the Argentines and Uruguayans throughout much of the colonial and Empire periods. They were more prone than most Brazilians to settle their differences by force.

During the monarchical era the differences between Conservatives and Liberals were more deeply felt in Rio Grande do Sul than in most of Brazil. This rivalry continued during the Old Republic but under a new guise, most Conservatives having become members of the Federal Party and most Liberals gravitating to the state's Republican Party.

Throughout the Old Republic the government of the state was in the hands of the Republicans. Two governors dominated most of this period, Julio de Castilhos and his successor, Augusto Borges de Medeiros. It was only in 1928 that a third governor, Getúlio Vargas, was named.

Despite the continual dominance of the Republican Party in Rio Grande, the Federal Party remained a factor of major importance. In 1893 and 1923 it launched bitter and bloody civil wars to overthrow the Republican government. It was at the end of the second of these conflicts that Borges de Medeiros, who had been governor of the state for more than 20 years, agreed to retire at the end of the term he had just begun.[4]

Borges de Medeiros' successor, Getúlio Vargas, appeased his party's traditional opponents. He brought the Federal Party into the state government; and both the Republican and Federal parties of Rio Grande do Sul supported his bid to be elected president of the republic in 1930, as they also supported his successful attempt to overthrow the federal government by force in October of the same year.

During the 15 years of Getúlio Vargas' first period as president of Brazil, the country's parties continued to be organized principally as state groups. In the years following the revolution of 1930, the "interventors" whom Vargas named in place of the governors used their influence to organize new state parties that would support their own ambitions to become elected governors. Usually these parties were based, like the parties of the Old Republic, on the coroneis, although some elements of the urban working class, whose unionization was encouraged by the Vargas provisional government and who had played no significant role in national politics before 1930, played a part in a few of these groups.

Some attempts were made to launch national parties during 1930-37. One of the most notable was the effort of some of those who had carried out the revolution of 1930 to establish a Socialist Party. The most successful such effort was the establishment of

Ação Integralista, a fascist party that during the mid-1930s established an organization with branches in most of the country's important cities and towns. The Integralistas set up a lasting national party. The Communist Party, which had been organized in the early 1920s, considerably expanded its influence during 1930-37 and also became a national party, althugh it remained small.

In November 1937, Vargas scrapped the constitution of 1934 and established a personal dictatorship, with fascist overtones, that lasted until 1945. In December 1937 he dissolved all existing political parties. There were no legal parties in Brazil again until 1945.

THE REESTABLISHMENT OF PARTIES IN 1945

With the approach of the end of World War II, in which Brazil played the most significant role on the Allied side of any of the Latin American countries, President Vargas found himself forced to promise an end to his personal dictatorship. Early in 1945 he announced that elections would be held before the end of the year. This promise made it virtually inevitable that political parties would be reestablished.

The forces opposed to the Vargas dictatorship had formed a political movement even before Vargas' agreement to hold elections, known as the União Democrática Nacional. Early in 1945 the UDN was converted into a political party that was destined to remain one of the largest such organizations for more than two decades.

Under the aegis of the Vargas government, two parties were organized, the Partido Social Democrático and the Partido Trabalhista Brasileiro. These two groups also continued to be among the nation's major parties for 20 years.

Various other parties were established in 1945 and in the years immediately following. Several of these resulted from minor splits in the Partido Trabalhista Brasileiro, including the Partido Social Trabalhista, the Partido Republicano Trabalhista, and the Partido Trabalhista Nacional.

Other parties included the Partido de Representação Popular, set up by elements of the old Ação Integralista Brasileira; the Partido Socialista Brasileiro, organized by dissidents from the UDN; the Partido Comunista, reorganized and legalized between 1945 and 1947 and semilegal thereafter. The old Federal Party of Rio Grande do Sul was established on a national basis as the Partido Libertador, and elements of the old Republican Party of Minas Gerais took the lead in organizing a national Partido Republicano.

All of these parties were of some significance in 1945-65, during which period real political parties were legal and active. Most of them will be discussed below.

During the years in which these parties were active, there were frequent complaints from Brazilian political scientists, foreign commentators, and many rank-and-file Brazilian citizens that the country's parties were "meaningless." It seems that the real significance of such comments was the complaint that most of these parties had no particular ideological identification. This was true enough. However, they did have more real "meaning" than they were usually given credit for, in terms of representing particular class and sociological groups that were of some significance in Brazilian political life.

UNIÃO DEMOCRÁTICA NACIONAL

The União Democrática Nacional (UDN) had its origins in the struggle against the Vargas dictatorship. It brought together in 1944-45 leading pre-1937 politicians, trade union leaders who were antagonistic to the Vargas regime, the remnants of the Communist Party, young people who had grown to maturity during the dictatorship, leading intellectuals, and distinguished figures among the nation's military leaders. One of the last group, Brigadier General (Brigadeiro) Eduardo Gomes, the principal organizer of the Brazilian air force, became the head of the UDN.

During its early months the UDN devoted itself principally to propaganda against the dictatorship and in favor of the country's military efforts on behalf of the Allies in World War II. It received particularly strong support from the veterans of the Brazilian Division in Italy as they began to return during the first months of 1945.

When the prospect of elections began to grow early in 1945, the leaders of the UDN converted the organization into a political party. However, it was faced with a crisis in May 1945, when the Communists unexpectedly turned against the União Democrática Nacional, withdrew from it, and announced their support for Getúlio Vargas' remaining in power at least until after a Constitutional Assembly could be elected and write a new constitution.

As the electoral campaign proceeded, the UDN nominated Eduardo Gomes as its candidate to succeed Vargas. "O Brigadeiro," as he was popularly called, campaigned throughout the country and aroused wide enthusiasm with his strong attacks upon the Vargas dictatorship.

Late in October, when the opposition leaders and the military chiefs became convinced that Getúlio Vargas was maneuvering to cancel the elections scheduled for six weeks later, Gomes joined with his principal opponent, General Eurico Dutra, and with General Pedro Goes Monteiro, chief of staff of the armed forces, to lead a military coup that ousted Vargas and installed his constitutional successor, supreme court president José Linhares. It was under Linhares' aegis that the election was finally held early in December 1945. To the surprise of most foreign observers and of the UDN leaders, the União Democrática Nacional did not win the election. Gomes ran behind Dutra; and Yeddo Fiuza, who had the backing of the Communist Party, ran a distant third.

During the 20 years following the 1945 election, the UDN remained one of the country's three major parties. Its electoral strength slowly declined, but it continued to be one of the truly national political organizations. Although its support varied from state to state, it had considerable following in virtually all of them. During at least part of this 20-year period, it controlled the administration of Pernambuco and Bahia in the Northeast, Minas Gerais and Guanabara in the Center-South, Paraná and Santa Catarina in the South, and Mato Grosso in the West. Its representation in both houses of Congress was one of the largest party groups throughout the period.

However, even though the UDN was one of the country's major parties for 20 years, it was unable during this period to elect one of its members to the presidency. In the election of 1950 it again ran Gomes, who was this time defeated by Getúlio Vargas. In 1955 the UDN supported the candidacy of General Juárez Távora, a leading figure in the Christian Democratic Party; but he came in second to Juscelino Kubitschek, who had the support of the Social Democratic and Trabalhista parties.

In 1960 there was a bitter controversy within the UDN as to who should be its presidential candidate. A strong faction felt that the nomination should go to Juracy Magalhães, one of the party's founders, its long-time president, and at the time governor of the state of Bahia. However, a majority of the delegates to the UDN convention accepted the thesis of Carlos Lacerda and José Magalhães Pinto, prominent União Democrática Nacional leaders in Congress, that the politically independent ex-governor of São Paulo, Jânio Quadros, was likely to win the election anyway and the party would suffer a major defeat if it did not endorse him. Quadros was the victor, more because of his personal popularity than because of the support of the UDN, Socialist Party, Christian Democrats, Republicans, and National Labor Party. During his seven months in office, the UDN constituted the bulk of the administration's official support in Congress.

However, many of the UDN leaders quickly turned against the president they had helped to elect. This was particularly the case with Carlos Lacerda, who was by this time governor of Guanabara (the city of Rio de Janeiro), and it was a polemic by Lacerda against Quadros that was the immediate provocation for Quadros' resignation from the presidency in August 1961.

It would be difficult to define the ideology or political philosophy of the UDN. It has variously been described as being "liberal," "conservative," and "reactionary," but none of these descriptions is particularly appropriate. For one thing, there were certainly different ideological elements within the party's ranks. For instance, in the North and Northeast there were important leaders of the UDN (known popularly as the bossa nova of the UDN) who were closely aligned with the left-wing nationalist trend that became prominent during the latter part of the Kubitschek administration and in the early 1960s. In other states, such as São Paulo, its leaders and followers were generally to be found in the right-wing part of the political spectrum.

It is probably more fruitful to analyze the UDN in terms of the groups it represented and the attitudes it reflected than in terms of any ideological commitment. More than any other party in Brazil, the UDN was the spokesman for the middle class, including such groups as small businessmen, teachers and other professional people, white-collar workers, and government employees. In some areas it had a strong element of the old coroneis in its secondary leadership. In São Paulo and some other areas it had the support of important elements among the industrialists.

In terms of attitudes, the UDN was throughout its career the most clearly anti-Vargas party in Brazil. For two decades after the overthrow of the Vargas dictatorship in 1945, the most important single dividing line in Brazilian politics continued to be one's attitude toward the ex-dictator and what he was deemed to stand for. It was the UDN that tended most clearly to group those who were against Vargas and all of his works.

Other attitudes, not unconnected with its anti-Vargas position, were also persistent themes of UDN propaganda and action. The party tended to make a fetish of opposition to governmental corruption. The UDN leaders also were quick to accuse their political opponents of "subversion," frequently indicating their fear that the pro-Vargas elements would like to see the restoration of the kind of dictatorship over which Vargas had presided from 1937 to 1945.

Throughout its career the UDN proclaimed itself the most stalwart defender of political democracy. However, this position did not prevent it from opposing the extension of the right to vote to illiterates. Nor did it prevent important UDN leaders from becoming involved in numerous military coups and attempted coups against the governments in power between 1945 and 1964.

Although the anti-Vargas position, the insistence on purity of governmental administration, and opposition to "subversion" were generally characteristic of the UDN, the party leaders were not always completely consistent. Some UDN leaders, for instance, served in the cabinet of Getúlio Vargas during his 1950-54 presidency; no

UDN state administration was noted for its pristine purity and lack of corruption and nepotism; and important UDN leaders were themselves guilty of subversive activities. However, lack of consistency was a general characteristic of Brazilian politics during this period and was by no means confined to the UDN.

As a whole the UDN gave enthusiastic support to the "revolution" that overthrew João Goulart on April 1, 1964. During the following year and a half the party was generally considered to be the group most closely associated with the government of Humberto Castelo Branco. Immediately after the coup the UDN leaders appeared to believe that the action of the military men against Goulart had paved the way for the UDN to elect a president from its own ranks, and they hastened to ratify by national convention the candidacy of Guanabara governor Carlos Lacerda for the elections scheduled for October 5, 1965.

However, as it became increasingly apparent that the military men were in no great hurry to turn control back to civilians, even to those of the UDN, important leaders of the União Democrática Nacional became increasingly opposed to the Castelo Branco regime. This was particularly true of Lacerda, who by the middle of 1965 was in frank opposition to the national administration. This alienation of much of the UDN leadership, and the UDN's refusal to support complacently all of the programs and legislative measures suggested by the president, were major factors in provoking the coup of October 1965, as a result of which Castelo Branco assumed semidictatorial powers through the Second Institutional Act, which dissolved all existing political parties.

PARTIDO SOCIAL DEMOCRÁTICO

Carlos Lacerda is generally credited with the witticism that the Partido Social Democrático was neither a party, nor social, nor democratic. Whatever the truth of the remark, during 1945-65 the leaders of the PSD were regarded to be the country's most talented political operators. Like the UDN and the Partido Trabalhista, the PSD represented recognizable classes and groups.

Throughout its life the Partido Social Democrático was a Vargas party. It was originally organized in the early months of 1945 as a support for the Vargas regime when it appeared likely that the dictator was going to have to hold presidential and congressional elections.

The manner in which the Partido Social Democrático was established was very simple. The Ministry of Interior informed the "interventors" in each state (the officials appointed by the president to substitute for elected state governors) that the president wanted the establishment of a pro-Vargas party and that they were to see to it that such an organization was set up within the state. The interventors then notified the officials they had named to run the various municipalities that local conventions were to be called to establish the "grass roots" organization of the new party. Once these local conventions had been held, and had named delegates to a state convention, the latter met to set up the state organization of the new group. The state conventions chose delegates to the national founding congress of the Partido Social Democrático, which met in Rio de Janeiro.

At its inception the PSD consisted principally of the pro-Vargas <u>coroneis</u> and their followers, government officials, and employees of the local, state, and national administrations. However, from the beginning the Partido Social Democrático also received considerable financial and political backing from industrialists who had prospered under the Vargas regime and whose sympathies—add pocketbooks— were with the president, as well as from some middle-class groups sympathetic to Vargas.

Most of those who took the lead in organizing the PSD were politicians who had first risen to national prominence in the years just before and immediately after the revolution of 1930. Typical was the group that led the party in the state of Minas Gerais. It included Benedito Valadares, who had served as elected governor of the state from 1934 to 1937 and was Vargas' interventor for some time thereafter, and Gustavo Capanema and José María Alkmin, who had also been important figures in state politics before and during the Vargas dictatorship period. Another typical leader of the party was Pedro Ludovico, who had been in control of the government of the state of Goias throughout virtually all of 1930-45.

As soon as it was established on a national basis, the Partido Social Democrático nominated General Eurico Gaspar Dutra, who had been minister of war for the previous seven years, as its candidate for the presidency. In this situation Dutra was generally regarded as the "official" candidate, but neither he nor many of those who supported him was certain that Vargas intended to have an election at all. When it appeared to Dutra and other army leaders that Vargas was maneuvering to cancel or at least postpone the presidential election, Dutra cooperated in ousting the dictator, even though he was supposedly a "government man."

In the election of December 1945, Dutra was chosen president. At the same time the PSD emerged as the largest of the country's political parties, winning more seats in both houses of Congress than any other party. Its success, particularly that of Dutra, was generally considered to have been due to the last-minute endorsement that Vargas gave to the PSD's presidential nominee.

For the next five years the administration was largely in the hands of the members of the Partido Social Democrático, although there were some ministers of other political persuasions. The Dutra regime was a colorless but industrious administration that did nothing spectacular but did get the process of constitutional government working again. Fears concerning the supposed profascist proclivities of General Dutra proved to be largely unfounded, at least insofar as his behavior in office was concerned.

When it came time to chose a successor to Dutra, the PSD was presented with a quandary. It had been established as a Vargas party and was generally regarded as such by the voters. However, when Vargas announced that he would be a candidate in the 1950 election, he chose to run not on the PSD ticket but on that of the other major pro-Vargas group, the Partido Trabalhista Brasileiro, whose senator he had been between 1945 and 1950 (although he actually took very little part in the Senate's deliberations). As a result there was strong resistance within the PSD to endorsing the candidacy of Vargas. This resistance resulted in the PSD's putting up its own candidate, Christiano Machado, a rather colorless figure who was no match for either Vargas or the stern Eduardo Gomes, his two principal rivals. Political wits commented that this was an "attempt to Christianize the PSD," but it was not successful. Machado came in a bad third in the presidential race, and the PSD's reputation for moral probity was not improved by its independent campaign in this election. Important elements of the PSD backed their old chief, Getúlio Vargas.

The Partido Social Democrático cooperated with the new Vargas administration. Several of its leaders served in his government and the PSD contingent in Congress, together with the members of the Partido Trabalhista, usually formed a majority favorable to the administration. The PSD also shared in the considerable patronage at the disposal of the president.

However, following the suicide of Vargas in August 1954, the Partido Social Democrático was thrown into the opposition during the short term of Vargas' successor, João Café Filho. During this period, from August 1954 until the election of October 1955, the PSD devoted most of its attention to trying to win back the presidency for a member of the party.

Certain factors favored the PSD's new bid for national power. Although President Café Filho adopted a frankly anti-Vargas, and therefore anti-PSD, position, there had been a marked turnabout in public opinion that favored those who were known as disciples and former associates of the "martyred" president. By committing suicide, and particularly by leaving a suicide note that pictured himself as the victim of vague but nefarious interests who had sought to thwart his efforts on behalf of the humble people and the national honor of Brazil,

Vargas had brought about a resurgence of sympathy for everything for which he stood.

The Vargas element in national politics took advantage of this situation by forming a coalition between the two parties he had founded. The PSD, which was still considerably larger than the Partido Trabalhista, was given the presidential nomination, which went to Minas Gerais governor Juscelino Kubitschek. The vice-presidential candidacy was given to João Goulart, who had been minister of labor under Vargas in 1953-54 and was his successor as leader of the Partido Trabalhista Brasileiro.

The Kubitschek-Goulart ticket won a very narrow victory over General Juárez Távora, backed by the UDN and several smaller parties, and over two other candidates of less importance. It was not able to assume office, however, until the army leadership, under the command of General Henrique Teixeira Lott, had ousted both President João Café Filho and his successor, Carlos Luz, on charges that they were attempting to prevent the inauguration of Kubitschek and Goulart.

The Kubitschek administration was in many ways the high point in the history of the Partido Social Democrático. The party was most clearly in power during his five year period, and the Kubitschek experience very importantly changed the nature of the PSD.

Juscelino Kubitschek preached what approached being an ideology. He was the enthusiastic and even bombastic advocate of what came to be known as "developmentalism." It was his creed that the resolution of most of the ills plaguing Brazil was to be found in the country's achieving a very rapid rate of economic development, which would convert it into a strong industrial nation that could take its place among the other important countries. The great symbol of this philosophy was Brasília, the new national capital built in what had been a wilderness, in the record time of four years; but its immediately more practical results were the establishment of a national automobile industry, the doubling of electricity output, the great expansion of the steel industry, and the development of a shipbuilding and a large machine tool industry.

The enthusiasm, optimism, and solid accomplishments of Kubitschek and his administration made developmentalism a part of the creed of a large number of politically literate Brazilians; and from his administration on, local and state governments, as well as the national one, tended to be judged to a considerable degree in terms of economic development. Furthermore, the Partido Social Democrático became, more than any other party, the advocate of this new ideology.

However, Kubitschek and the PSD were not successful in electing another PSD candidate to the presidency at the end of Kubitschek's term. To some degree, at least, this was the result of the nature of the candidates offered by the government party and the major opposition groups. The PSD, supported by the PTB and the Communist Party, named the same Marshal Lott who had facilitated Kubitschek's taking office. He was an uninspiring candidate who frequently embarrassed his own supporters by maladroit statements and actions. Running against him was Jânio Quadros, who had wide popular appeal and considerable personal magnetism.

With the victory of Quadros and his inauguration as president late in January 1961, the PSD became part of the opposition. Together with the Partido Trabalhista, the Partido Social Democrático continued to control Congress. Although the leader of the PSD in Congress offered to help the president get through the legislature the most essential elements of a very long program, Quadros would have nothing to do with the parties that had supported Kubitschek. Indeed, he roundly denounced his predecessor and set up investigating committees to look into alleged malfeasance of the Kubitschek regime.

When Quadros suddenly resigned in August 1961, the country faced a major constitutional crisis. The three military ministers sought to prevent the inauguration of Quadros' legally constituted successor, Vice-President João Goulart. PSD members of Congress, led by José María Alkmin, took the lead in pushing through a compromise, which allowed Goulart to take office but reduced his powers considerably by establishing a parliamentary system of government, with the prime minister and cabinet depending upon Congress.

The first prime minister under this new system was Tancredo Neves, a PSD leader from Minas Gerais, He stayed in office somewhat less than a year, and his dismissal by President Goulart marked the beginning of a deep split between Goulart and the PSD. Although some PSD members served in the cabinet after full presidential powers were restored to Goulart by a referendum in January 1963, by the latter part of that year the PSD had virtually withdrawn its support from the president.

Although UDN leaders were most prominent among the civilian politicians who supported the military coup against Goulart on April 1, 1964, it seems likely that leaders of the Partido Social Democrático were also part of the conspiracy. José María Alkmin was elected to the vice-presidency under Castelo Branco, and PSD members of Congress generally cooperated with the regime.

However, the Castelo Branco regime, which adopted a posture of opposition to everything represented by the Vargas tradition, purged a number of prominent PSD leaders, removing them from their public offices and forbidding them to participate actively in politics for a decade. The victims of these measures included Juscelino Kubitschek (who was by this time a senator) and other members of Congress, as well as Governor Mauro Borges of the state of Goiás and other leaders of less importance.

Relations between the Castelo Branco government and the Partido Social Democrático remained ambiguous during the first year and a half of the military regime. This was evident in the elections of October 1965, when 11 of the country's 22 states chose new governors. In most states the candidates of the PSD were pictured by the press as being the nominees of the opposition, and to some degree this was true. However, in at least two states—Minas Gerais and Guanabara—there were widesread rumors that Castelo Branco was quietly supporting the PSD nominees, Ismael Pinheiro and Negrão de Lima.

In any case Pinheiro and Negrão de Lima defeated nominees of the União Democrática Nacional, who were generally regarded as government candidates. PSD-backed candidates also won in four other states. The so-called "hard liners" in the armed forces regarded these PSD victories as defeats for the military regime. Although President Castelo Branco resisted the demands of the "hard liners" that the PSD victors not be allowed to take office, he was forced three weeks after the election to decree the Second Institutional Act, which established a semidictatorial government and dissolved all existing political parties.

PARTIDO TRABALHISTA BRASILEIRO

Like the PSD the Partido Trabalhista Brasileiro was established by the Vargas dictatorship shortly before it was overthrown. Throughout its 23 years of existence, the PTB remained the party most closely connected with Getúlio Vargas and his tradition.

Soon after the establishment of the PSD, Vargas became aware that it was not attracting the support of the urban workers among whom he was personally very popular. They tended to regard it as an upper class party. Furthermore, the Communist Party, which Vargas had legalized as part of his attempt to "democratize" his regime, was rapidly gaining adherents among the urban workers. As a result, Vargas felt that it was necessary to establish a second administration party that would appeal specifically to the workers.

The task of organizing such a party was given to the director general of labor, the second highest official of the Ministry of Labor, José Segadas Viana. He used the machinery of the Ministry to mobilize the officials of the country's several thousand trade unions, most of them dependent on the goodwill of the Ministry for keeping their positions, to form local branches of the new Partido Trabalhista Brasileiro.

During the first months of its existence, the PTB devoted most of its activity to organizing meetings to insist on the need for Getúlio Vargas to remain in power, despite his promise to call elections for a successor. The crowds attending these meetings usually chanted

"Queremos Vargas" (We want Vargas), as a result of which the members of the PTB came to be popularly known as the "Queremistas."

Vargas did nothing to discourage this campaign. Quite the contrary, he addressed some of the new party's meetings. These facts contributed a great deal to the conviction of oppositionists as well as of the leaders of the armed forces that Vargas did not intend to permit the election of a successor. They helped to harden the belief of the military that Vargas had to be removed from office.

After the overthrow of Vargas, the election campaign went forward. The PTB threw its support behind the candidate of the Partido Social Democrático, Eurico Dutra, who had been Vargas' "official" candidate before he was ousted. At the same time it fielded lists of candidates for Congress. The Brazilian electoral law made it possible for Vargas to be listed at the head of the PTB ticket in several states. He also ran for Congress as a PSD nominee in some states. He won in several cases and chose to take office as a PTB senator from his home state of Rio Grande do Sul. However, Vargas attended only a few sessions of Congress during his five years as senator.

During the Dutra government the administration's relations with the Partido Trabalhista Brasileiro became strained. PTB supporters in the organized labor movement frequently worked with the Communists against those trade union leaders who remained under the influence of the Ministry of Labor. As a result, in 1949 the Ministry of Labor suspended all further elections in the trade unions and removed officials of those organizations most clearly under Communist and Trabalhista control, appointing persons of its own choosing to take their places.

As the end of the Dutra administration approached, PTB leaders urged their party leader, Getúlio Vargas, to run for the presidency. He finally decided to do so, and was nominated by the Partido Trabalhista Brasileiro. However, because of the ill feeling between the PTB and the Dutra government, Vargas was not able to obtain the support of the PSD for his candidacy.

The Vargas presidential race was menaced by the fact that another figure who might be expected to draw considerable support from the pro-Vargas ranks was threatening to run. This was Adhemar de Barros, the governor of São Paulo. He had held office during the dictatorship as interventor in São Paulo and had gained considerable popular backing. In 1945 he had organized his own party, the Partido Social Progresista, and had been elected governor on its ticket. He made little secret of his desire to become president.

Vargas moved to "buy off" Adhemar de Barros. He offered the position of candidate for vice-president on his ticket to a member of the Partido Social Progresista, João Café Filho, who had been a longtime opponent of the Vargas dictatorship and, after 1945, had made a considerable reputation as a fighter for popular causes in the Chamber of Deputies. Barros was apparently given to understand that if he would step aside in 1950, Vargas would support his presidential ambitions in the following election, scheduled for 1955.

During the election of 1950 almost the whole labor movement supported Vargas. Even those trade union leaders who had previously been allied with the Ministry of Labor joined the Vargas campaign. For his part Vargas promised the labor movement that he would relax the governmental restrictions, some of which were holdovers from his own dictatorship and others of which had been imposed by the Dutra administration, which hampered the free functioning of the labor movement.

Getúlio Vargas was elected president once again. Most of those who served in his second administration were members of the Partido Trabalhista, although there were also some ministers from the Partido Social Democrático and even a few who had belonged to the União Democrática Nacional, although the UDN never officially gave its approval for members to participate in the Vargas government.

One new figure played a significant role in the second Vargas administration. This was João Goulart, a young man from Rio Grande do Sul whose fazenda (plantation) adjoined Vargas' ancestral home, where the deposed dictator had spent most of the five years after his overthrow. The two men had become firm friends during this period; and when Vargas returned to political activity, he invited Goulart to become a candidate for the Chamber of Deputies on the PTB ticket. Goulart, like Vargas, was elected in 1950.

In one of many cabinet changes, in 1953 Vargas invited João Goulart to become minister of labor. In that post Goulart worked hard to build up a personal following in the labor movement and in the PTB, with the apparent approval of the president. He launched fiery verbal attacks on the pelegos, those trade union leaders who owed their posts more to the Ministry of Labor than to rank-and-file support. However, his real purpose was to build up a group of trade unionists loyal to himself, and he worked closely with pelegos who were willing to accept his leadership and against those who were not.

At the same time Goulart followed a policy of encouraging strikes in strategic industries. He then stepped into the situation as minister of labor to "mediate" these disputes, generally assuring a solution highly favorable to the trade unionists.

These efforts by Goulart aroused widespread suspicions among the Brazilian military leaders. They finally convinced President Vargas to "accept João Goulart's resignation" early in 1954. However, when Goulart left office, many of Vargas' followers were convinced that he had chosen Goulart as his political heir.

With the suicide of Vargas in August 1954, Goulart emerged as the leader of the PTB. He quite logically became the party's nominee for vice-president when the Partido Social Democrático proposed that the PTB name a running mate for a pro-Vargas ticket, to be headed by PSD leader Juscelino Kubitschek.

The Kubitschek-Goulart ticket won the election of 1955. In the new administration, which took office in January 1956, Vice-President Goulart was given extensive control over patronage in the Ministry of Labor and the social security system. However, he was not allowed to choose the top officials of the Ministry. The governmental influence that Goulart enjoyed during the Kubitschek administration permitted him to extend his influence in the labor movement.

Nevertheless, Goulart's control of the PTB did not go unchallenged during the Kubitschek period. First, Senator Alberto Pasqualini of Rio Grande do Sul sought to bring about reforms in the PTB that would give it a well-defined political ideology aligning it with democratic Socialist parties in other parts of the world. When Pasqualini was killed in an airplane accident, the leadership of this reform movement was taken up by Francisco Ferrari, a deputy from the state of Rio Grande do Sul. However, the efforts of Pasqualini and Ferrari were not successful, and in the 1960 election Ferrari ran against João Goulart for the vice-presidency with the support of the Christian Democratic Party. Soon after that election Ferrari withdrew from the PTB to form his own party, the Movimento Trabalhista Nacional.

There was some sentiment in the PTB to have Goulart run for the presidency in the 1960 election. However, since his candidacy would have split the parties of the Vargas tradition in the face of the strong opposition nominee, Jânio Quadros, the PTB leaders agreed that Goulart should be a candidate for reelection as vice-president on a ticket headed by General Henrique Lott, the PSD's nominee for president.

However, the PTB won a concession from its coalition partner. With the help of the PSD a change in the electoral law was passed that separated the election of president and vice-president, thus making it possible for the presidential candidate of one ticket to win at the same time that a vice-presidential nominee running on a rival ticket was victorious. This law was designed to help Goulart's victory in the face of two opposition vice-presidential nominees, both claiming to be supporters of Quadros—the UDN's Milton Campos and dissident PTBista Francisco Ferrari.

Jânio Quadros and João Goulart won the election of 1960. Relations between the president and vice-president were very strained during the seven months that Quadros remained in office. The new president appointed a number of investigating commissions to inquire into the behavior of the preceding administration, and one of these accused Goulart of having been corrupt during the administration of Kubitschek, a charge that brought a bitter reply from the vice-president.

With the resignation of Quadros in August 1961, João Goulart should have become president without question. However, the three military ministers announced their intention of blocking his accession. This precipitated a major constitutional crisis, which brought to the forefront of national politics another PTB leader, Leonel Brizola, brother-in-law of Goulart and governor of Rio Grande do Sul. Brizola announced his support for Goulart and convinced the commander of the Third Army, stationed in Rio Grande do Sul, to take the same position.

Faced with the threat of a civil war, the national military leaders accepted a compromise. The constitution was ammended to set up a parliamentary system, which would strip the president of many of his powers and transfer these to a prime minister who was to be nominated by the president but dependent upon Congress for his tenure in office. Although Goulart agreed to take office under, and took the oath of allegiance to, the revised constitution, it was clear virtually from the beginning that he did not accept the new situation.

Between his inauguration in September 1961 and January 1963 Goulart devoted most of his efforts to seeking the restoration of full presidential powers. He finally succeeded in a referendum in January 1963, in which the vote was overwhelmingly in favor of the return to presidential government.

There was widespread hope that once restored to full powers, Goulart would genuinely seek to deal with the problems of rapidly mounting inflation, the slowing down of economic development, and enactment of basic reforms, with which his administration was beset. However, during the last 14 months of his tenure in office, the president showed utter inability to adopt any definite line of conduct and follow it. He sought to play the game that had been so successful for his mentor, Getúlio Vargas, of setting one group against another. The upshot was that virtually every important element in Brazilian politics lost confidence in Goulart.

During his last few months in office, Goulart seemed to veer to the extreme Left. He bypassed Congress to enact a number of measures that the legislature refused to pass; and he encouraged mutiny in the armed forces by enlisted men and noncommissioned officers. Largely as a result of his actions, a prerevolutionary situation was created, which made it almost inevitable that there would be a coup.

During the Quadros-Goulart period several currents of opinion became evident within the Partido Trabalhista Brasileiro. One of these was headed by San Thiago Dantas, who served as minister of finance and as minister of foreign affairs in Goulart's cabinet. Particularly during the last months of the Goulart regime, he sought

to organize a group that would follow the line formerly advocated by
Pasqualini and Ferrari, turning the PTB into a democratic Socialist
Party. A second group had Sergio Magalhães and several other
congressional figures as its principal leaders and sought to implant
a radical nationalist coloration on the PTB. Allied with this group
but operating on his own was Leonel Brizola, who was elected to the
Chamber of Deputies in the 1962 election and waged an exceedingly
demagogic campaign, urging his followers to arm themselves "to defend"
the Goulart administration against any attempt to overthrow it from
the Right.

Finally, there were the personal followers of Goulart. They
were largely opportunists who were willing to follow the president
in whatever zigzags he made, so long as these served to keep him in
office, but had no loyalty to any particular ideological point of view.

When the blow against the Goulart regime came, it came from
what is usually described as the Right. The president was overthrown
by the military—backed by wide elements of the civilian population,
particularly the middle class—on April 1, 1965. Thereafter the Partido
Trabalhista Brasileiro was the principal sufferer from the government
of Humberto Castelo Branco. Most of its top leaders—including Goulart,
Brizola, and Magalhães—were removed from their posts and were
forbidden to participate in politics for a decade. Its membership in
Congress was decimated, and PTB governors were removed from office.

The party was largely demoralized. Its opportunistic element
threw its support to the Castelo Branco regime, hoping not to be
removed from active politics. When elections were held for 11 state
governorships in October 1965, the PTB had little choice but to support
PSD candidates and was not able to offer any of its own. The PTB
suffered the same fate as the other Brazilian political parties. Late
in October 1965 President Castelo Branco outlawed all existing parties.

Throughout its 20 years of existence, the Partido Trabalhista
Brasileiro was the party to which the typical Brazilian urban working-
man owed his allegiance. Its electoral support grew regularly, and
it moved from the third largest party in 1945 to competitor with the
PSD for the position as the country's most popular political group by
the early 1960s.

The support the PTB received from the workers can be explained
by several factors. First, it was the party par excellence of Getúlio
Vargas after 1945, and a sizable part of the Brazilian working class
remained loyal to Vargas and to his memory after he committed
suicide in 1954. Second, it was originally organized by the country's
trade union officials, and they continued to play a major role in its
leadership until 1956—at the first convention held after João Goulart
assumed control of the party, most of the trade unionists still on its
executive committee were removed and were replaced by opportunist

professional politicians. Third, the party continued to agitate in favor of measures that workers considered to be in their interest, such as extension of the social security system and raising of the minimum wage. Finally, many workers got into the habit of voting for the PTB and did not see any other party that they felt adequately represented them.

In addition to the support it received from the urban workers, the PTB had some backing from intellectuals. Such people as Hermes Lima—who served as prime minister under Goulart and was named by him to the Supreme Court—and Sergio Magalhães were attracted to the party largely because they felt that the smaller, more clearly ideological groups had little chance of coming to power and thus being able to carry out a program, whereas the PTB, for all its faults, was a major contender for control of the country and was thus the appropriate group with which to work.

THE DISSIDENT TRABALHISTA PARTIES

During the 20 years between the founding and extinction of the Partido Trabalhista Brasileiro, several groups broke away to form small dissident Trabalhista parties. Several of these are worthy of some comment.

The Partido Social Trabalhista was probably the first such group to split from the PTB. It was led in the beginning by trade unionists who disagreed with the leadership of the PTB and broke from it early in 1946. The party never grew to major proportions, although it usually had a handful of members in Congress and in some of the state legislatures.

The Partido Republicano Trabalhista acquired some importance for a few years, although it, too, never became a major force in national politics. Its significance resided largely in the fact that for some time it was the principal group willing to nominate known Communists on its ticket, thus providing a vehicle through which the Communist Party, which was outlawed by the Dutra government in 1947, was able to place a handful of representatives in Congress and other legislative bodies. By the early 1960s the usefulness of the PRT to the Communists had largely disappeared, since by then they were able to use the cover of some of the larger parties, particularly the PTB, for electoral purposes.

The Partido Trabalhista Nacional was organized originally as the personal vehicle of a PTB leader of São Paulo, Hugo Borghi. He was a businessman who had prospered considerably during the Vargas dictatorship, and he spent a sizable part of his fortune in an unsuccessful attempt as the PTB candidate for governor of São Paulo in the

BRAZILIAN PARTIES 461

election of 1947. When he failed, he withdrew his supporters from the PTB to form the Partido Trabalhista Nacional. It remained a small but active party, with its principal strength in the state of São Paulo. In 1959 it gained notoriety as the first party to nominate Jânio Quadros for president, a move subsequently seconded by the UDN, the Socialist Party, the Christian Democrats, and the Republican Party.

The Movimento Trabalhista Nacional was organized in 1961 by Francisco Ferrari, who had unsuccessfully sought to challenge João Goulart's control of the PTB. The party did comparatively well in the congressional election of 1962, and its candidate for governor of Rio Grande do Sul won more votes than the official candidate of the Partido Trabalhista Brasileiro, backed by the outgoing governor, Leonel Brizola. The party supported the "revolution" of 1964 but received little backing from the regime.

THE IDEOLOGICAL PARTIES

During 1945-65 five Brazilian parties were generally considered "ideological." Four of these—the Partido Socialista Brasileiro, the Partido Democrático Cristiano, the Partido de Representação Popular (ex-Ação Integralista Brasileira), and the Partido Comunista are dealt with elsewhere.

The fourth party was the Partido Libertador, the successor of the Partido Federal of Rio Grande do Sul of the pre-1930 period. Since the election law in effect after 1945 forbade the organization of purely statewide parties, the leaders of the Partido Federal extended their party to other states. Although the new Partido Libertador continued to have its principal strength in Rio Grande do Sul, it had organizations in other states; and in a few of these it elected national deputies and state and local officials.

As a national party the Partido Libertador had virtually a one-plank platform. It was the principal advocate in national politics of the parliamentary form of government. Its leaders, including Raúl Pila, a veteran gaucho politician who was the party's principal figure, argued that only through a government responsible to Congress could the country avoid the dangers of the kind of dictatorial government it had between 1937 and 1945.

Ironically, when the proposal for the establishment of a parliamentary form of government was actually adopted as a constitutional amendment by Congress in 1961, Pila and other Partido Libertador members of Congress voted against it. They felt that the proposal before Congress was too serious a dilution of the principle of parliamentary government for them to support it.

In the period after the "revolution" of 1964 the Partido Libertador leaders were more principled than the leaders of most of the other parties. Although they supported the coup, they objected strongly to the limitations on democracy imposed by the Castelo Branco government. After the state elections of October 1965, and the resulting Second Institutional Act, by which what was left of Brazilian political democracy was still further curtailed, Raúl Pila announced that with the end of his current term in Congress he was going to retire from politics, in protest against what had happened to the Brazilian democratic system. Some of his fellow party members accompanied him in this gesture.

The Partido Libertador was principally a party of the middle class. Some gauchos of other classes had sentimental loyalties to the party, but most citizens of Rio Grande do Sul were loyal to the new parties—Partido Trabalhista Brasileiro, Partido Social Democrático, and União Democrática Nacional—after 1945. Outside of Rio Grande the Partido Libertador found its principal supporters among the middle class.

PARTIDO REPUBLICANO

The only other national party of some importance during 1945-65 was the Partido Republicano. Like the Partido Libertador, it was principally a one-state party, with its principal following in Minas Gerais. Its principal leader was Arturo Bernardes, who had been head of the old Partido Republicano of that state and had served both as governor of Minas Gerais and as president of Brazil (1922-26). He died in the early 1960s and was succeeded by his son, Arturo Bernardes, Jr.

Although the Partido Republicano had its principal strength in Minas Gerais, it had some strength in other states. It was never a major party in 1945-65 and usually served as an ally of the União Democrática Nacional. It supported the UDN nominees in all of the elections between 1945 and 1960.

The Partido Republicano was also principally a middle-class party. It had no recognizable ideology but, like the UDN, stood for governmental honesty and professed a belief in democratic government. Its support of the coup of 1964 did not prevent it from being extinguished with all of the other existing political parties in October 1965.

THE POST-1965 PARTIES

The Second Institutional Act, decreed by President Castelo Branco in October 1965, provided not only for the dissolution of all existing parties but also for the formation of two new ones. Although in theory it might have made three parties possible, this would have required an even distribution of political support among three tendencies—which was not practicable.

What took place after the Second Institutional Act was a regrouping of the members of Congress into two unequal groups, one of which supported the government and the other officially opposed to it. The Third Institutional Act, which President Castelo Branco decreed within a few weeks of the Second, provided that the initiative for the formation of new parties must come from the membership of Congress.

The great majority of the members of Congress rushed to sign the founding document of the new government party, Agrupação Renovadora Nacional (ARENA). These included the great majority of the former UDN members, the majority of the PSDers, and a sizable contingent from the Partido Trabalhista Brasileiro. There was also a scattering of members from the Partido Democrático Cristiano and other minor parties.

The former members of the PTB formed the bulk of the membership of the new opposition party, the Movimento Democrático Brasileiro. They were joined by many of the PDC deputies, a few from the PSD, most of the Socialists, and members of other minor parties.

The full support of the Castelo Branco government was thrown behind the ARENA. However, as the elections of late 1966 approached, the natural tendency of politicians to gravitate toward the government party was not sufficient to assure the ARENA a victory in several of the key states. As a result the Castelo Branco government used the power it had taken for itself in the Second Institutional Act to cancel the civil rights of political leaders in order to remove certain state leaders of both ARENA and the MDB, including Governor Adhemar de Barros (who had been one of the principal civilian supporters of the 1964 coup) and leaders of the MDB and the ARENA in Rio Grande do Sul, who were threatening to help elect an oppositionist as governor of that key state.

The presidential election of 1966—which, in conformity with the Second Institutional Act, was carried out by Congress instead of the general electorate—had only one candidate. The ARENA nominated General Arthur Costa e Silva, who had been Castelo Branco's minister of war; the MDB refused to name anyone to oppose him. "Election" of Costa e Silva in October 1966 was thus a pure formality.

The two new parties created as the result of the Second Institutional Act lacked real vitality. They had little grassroots organization, and most of the voters regarded them as frauds. However, even the faint semblance of party organization that persisted during the administration of Costa e Silva proved too much for the military men who really controlled the government of the republic after April 1964.

The Costa e Silva regime put an end on December 13, 1968, to even the faint resemblance of political parties that had persisted since the Second Institutional Act of October 1965. Because even ARENA deputies and senators refused to vote for the cancellation of the parliamentary immunity of several MDB deputies who had severely criticized the government on the floor of Congress, President Costa e Silva decreed yet another Institutional Act on December 13, 1968, by which Congress was recessed and the government assumed full dictatorial powers.

Congress was not reconvened for ten months, when it was summoned to elect a successor to President Costa e Silva, who had died of a stroke. The new choice, already decided upon by the leaders of the armed forces, was General Emilio Garrastazu Medici. It was obvious that the military dictatorship would continue for a number of years and that the future of political parties in Brazil would depend on how long the army leaders felt that they must (or wished to) stay in power.

The charge frequently leveled against the Brazilian political parties of 1945-65 that they were not "meaningful" is not true. The principal parties of this period represented recognizable elements in the Brazilian body politic; and although they did not have any particular ideology, they were spokesmen for the principal classes and segments of the population during these two decades.

However, it must be recognized that the political parties failed to establish a solid basis for political democracy. They were unable to break through the division of Brazilian public opinion between supporters and antagonists of Getúlio Vargas, whose dictatorship had created an unbridgeable gap between different groups of Brazilian citizens.[5] The parties established after the dissolution of all existing ones in October 1965 certainly have no ideological principles, nor do they represent any particularly well defined elements of the population.

CHAPTER 24

THE PERONISTA PARTY AND MOVEMENT

The Peronista movement, which has been the most important single political force in Argentina during the last generation, defies easy description and categorization. It began with many of the attributes of a personalist party but was never purely one, representing from the beginning very definite classes and groups within the country. Since the fall of the regime of Juan Domingo Perón, which gave birth to Peronismo, the movement has been seeking a clear ideological identity and legitimacy, neither of which it has yet achieved. It is doubtful that the exact position of Peronismo in the Argentine political spectrum is likely to emerge until after the death of Perón.

ORIGINS OF PERONISMO

Peronismo arose as a direct consequence of the so-called revolution of June 4, 1943. On that day the leaders of the Argentine armed forces ousted President Ramón Castillo and replaced his administration with a military dictatorship. Although this coup d'état was largely motivated by the fear of the pro-German Argentine army leaders that President Castillo was going to name as his successor a pro-British landowner and politician, Robustiano Patrón Costas, the new military regime very soon took on an unexpected reformist coloration that was to have far-reaching results.

This turn of the "revolution" of 1943 was due largely to the efforts of Colonel Juan Domingo Perón and his close associates in the military hierarchy. These younger officers were anxious to gain civilian support for the new regime, which it almost completely lacked at its inception. With this in mind, they turned to the organized labor movement and sought to reach an agreement with its leaders.

Perón and his friends were aware that the trade unions had received little encouragement from previous Argentine governments; and they felt that by adopting an apparently prolabor attitude, they might be able to win the cooperation, if not the allegiance, of the leaders and rank-and-file members of the labor movement. Although the trade unionists were at first hesitant to enter into negotiations with the leaders of the armed forces, to whom they had been traditionally opposed both politically and ideologically, they were willing to adopt a wait-and-see attitude and to give their support to specific measures that favored the workers and the trade unions.

The military regime established a new post of cabinet rank, that of the Secretariat of Labor and Social Welfare, and Colonel Perón was named as the first secretary to head the new organization. He then began a two-year campaign to build up labor support for the regime, and more particularly for himself.

Perón used various devices to appeal to the workers. He put the influence of his office and his power within the military government behind the trade unions' organizing efforts. In 1943 there were probably not more than 300,000 workers in the organized labor movement, and union strength was concentrated largely in the railroads, commercial establishments, municipal workers, and printing trades. The nation's manufacturing industries were virtually unorganized, as was the country's agricultural sector.

Perón encouraged the establishment of strong labor organizations among the packing-house workers, textile employees, metallurgical workers, millers, and other urban groups, as well as among the sugar plantation and mill workers in the province of Tucumán, the vineyard and winery laborers of Mendoza and San Juan, and the employees of the great grain and meat estancias of the broad plains of central Argentina. Also, where there were rival unions of different political orientation, as among the trolley car and bus drivers, he encouraged them to form a single union and threw his support behind the organizing efforts of these newly united groups.

Perón's encouragement of the spread of unionism was often dramatic. He personally went to the packinghouse towns near Buenos Aires and conferred with labor leaders who had long been persecuted by the employers and the government, thus giving these leaders legitimacy and making it clear to the employers that they must deal with the unionists in good faith. He did much the same thing for the even more oppressed and exploited sugar workers in Tucumán.

Besides encouraging union organization, Perón used the prestige of his office to convince the employers generally to make liberal concessions to the unions in collective bargaining negotiations. Increasingly, too, he sought to centralize such negotiations in the Secretariat of Labor, frequently taking part in ceremonies marking the signing of new collective agreements.

Perón also took advantage of the existence of a de facto government to enact a great deal of labor and social legislation by decree. These laws included a full-scale social security system, the establishment of paid vacations, improvement of workmen's compensation, and the enactment of an eight-hour day for rural workers as part of a general law fixing labor conditions for agriculture.

The response of the Argentine workers to Perón's efforts was probably a great deal more enthusiastic than even he expected. Certainly it far surpassed anything the trade union leaders had thought likely. As a result, many of the trade union leaders who had been skeptical of Perón, or who had agreed to work with him cautiously, found that their rank-and-file members were tending to look more to Colonel Perón to improve their lot than they were to their union leaders. Whatever their own skepticism toward Perón, these labor leaders had little choice but to support him if they wanted to continue to control their organizations.

The explanation for this peculiar turn of events was to be found in changes in the Argentine labor force, and in the labor movement itself, in the decades preceding 1943. The urban working force, which a generation before had consisted largely of immigrants from Spain and Italy, who had brought with them anarchism, Marxist Socialism, and even Communism, had been much altered. By 1943 many of the workers were children of immigrants who, although favorable to trade unionism and generally of a radical social outlook, tended to reject the specific ideologies of their parents, particularly the antipatriotic and internationalist prejudices of their immigrant fathers, as being part and parcel of their parents' "foreignness."

Furthermore, as a result of the two world wars and the Great Depression, which had made it difficult for Argentina to import manufactured goods from Europe, the country's industries had grown tremendously in number and size. Since immigration from Europe had virtually ceased by 1930, it was necessary to recruit many of the workers for these new factories from the interior of Argentina. The migrants from the countryside had had little or no contact with the early labor movement, which had been largely anarchist, Socialist, or Communist in its orientation. Indeed, to many of them, it seemed as if trade unionism and the benefits it brought were an invention of Juan Domingo Perón.

The upshot of all of this was that Perón had gained a very wide backing among the country's manual and white-collar workers within two years of having entered the Secretariat of Labor. This was made clear in October 1945, when rival military men forced Perón's resignation from his many posts (he was then vice-president, minister of war, secretary of the Postwar Council, and secretary of labor) and even jailed him for a few days. He was brought back to power, if not to office, by a mass movement of his labor supporters, largely organized by some of the nation's leading trade unionists.

ESTABLISHMENT OF THE PERONISTA PARTY

When Perón returned from his short incarceration on October 16, 1945, he launched his presidential campaign. The poll was scheduled for February 1946, and the new chief executive was to take office on the third anniversary of the "revolution," June 4, 1946.

Perón's major problem was that although he had wide popular support, he did not have an organized political party to back his ambitions. All existing parties were united in opposition to him, and so he set out to organize new groups to carry on his campaign. To establish the most important of these, he turned to his trade union friends; under their aegis the Partido Laborista was launched, with Luis Gay, head of the telephone workers, as its president and Cipriano Reyes, chief of the packing-house workers, as its vice-president. Most of the rest of the party leadership was composed of important figures in the trade union movement, and it drew the bulk of its support from rank-and-file workers.

Besides the Partido Laborista, Perón brought about the establishment of two other parties. One of these was led by secondary figures who had broken away from what until then had been the country's largest party, the Unión Civica Radical (UCR), and they established the UCR Renovadora. As a vehicle for the other scattered supporters of the Perón candidacy, the Partido Independiente was established.

At the end of a bitter campaign, Perón defeated José Tamborini, the choice of his united opposition. At the same time his supporters won almost two-thirds of the seats in the Chamber of Deputies and all but two in the Senate. The Partido Laborista by itself had a majority in both houses of Congress.

It soon became clear, however, that despite his very strong position in Congress and his wide backing in the community at large, Perón was not satisfied with the dispersion of his forces in three separate and potentially competing parties. This situation had caused him some embarrassment during the election campaign, when the Partido Laborista leaders wanted Perón's vice-presidential running mate to be chosen from their ranks; Perón insisted on the nomination of Horacio Quijano, an oldtime Radical leader. Although the Laborista leaders accepted Perón's decision, they felt considerable resentment over it, considering quite rightly that it was their party that represented the bulk of the colonel's supporters.

With all of this as background, Peron announced suddenly in a radio speech, a few weeks before taking office, that the three parties that had supported him would be merged into a single group, to be known as the Partido Unico de la Revolución. He apparently took this step without consulting the leaders of the three parties, and most particularly without consulting the chiefs of the Partido Laborista.

In the beginning there was widespread resistance within the Partido Laborista ranks to the disappearance of their party as a distinctive group. This resistance was led by Laborista vice-president Cipriano Reyes and at first mobilized the support of many of the newly elected Laborista members of Congress. However, by means that still remain unclear, Perón soon convinced all but a handful to accept the establishment of the Partido Unico. Among those who remained unconvinced was Cipriano Reyes, who had been elected to the Chamber of Deputies in February. He took the lead in establishing a new Partido Laborista (indeed, maintaining that it was the <u>original</u> Partido Laborista), and he and one other deputy constituted the Laborista Bloc in the lower house until the expiration of his term in 1948. When his parliamentary immunity from arrest expired, Reyes was promptly clapped in jail, where he remained until the end of the Perón presidency.

Meanwhile, the president and his associates had had second thoughts about the name of their new united party. They were convinced that Partido Unico, even when "de la Revolución" was appended to it, sounded too much like the "single parties" of the recently defeated fascist regimes in Europe. So, since Perón was going out of his way at the time to dissociate himself completely from the idea that he was an adherent of fascism, it was decided that a new title must be adopted for the party. In the end Perón and his followers could come up with nothing more satisfactory, or more descriptive, than Partido Peronista; and it was by this name that the organization was finally launched.[1]

THE PERONISTA PARTIES DURING THE PERÓN REGIME

The Partido Peronista remained one of the two government parties throughout the rest of Perón's time in power. Perón was its official leader, and its stated purposes were to support the regime and to obey its leader.

The partner of the Partido Peronista was the Partido Peronista Feminino, established principally through the efforts of the President's wife, Eva Duarte de Perón. During the first years of his administration she carried on an energetic publicity campaign in favor of granting women the right to vote, which was finally achieved in the Peronista constitution adopted in 1949 to replace the constitution that had been in effect since 1853. At the same time Evita, as she was popularly known, devoted part of her seemingly limitless energy to establishing the party through which the supposedly grateful female population could express its support for the government that had given it the full rights of citizenship.[2]

The separate organization of women for political activity was an old tradition in Argentine politics. The Socialist Party, for example, had for many decades had a parallel group, the Unión Socialista Feminina, through which the women supporters of the party had been able to carry on political activity even when they did not have the right to vote.

Although the two Peronista parties were apparently the principal political groups supporting the regime so long as Perón remained in power, they did not constitute one of the major power factors in that regime. They were convenient vehicles for organizing Perón's supporters for particular purposes rather than participants in the decision-making processes of the government.

The two Peronista parties were the instruments through which progovernment candidates for offices were nominated. They were also, at least in theory, the bodies that organized the campaigns for these nominees. In Congress, provincial legislatures, and municipal assemblies the members elected by the Partido Peronista and Partido Peronista Feminino were grouped together as the Peronista bloc; and their automatic support of the wishes of the president, governor, or mayor (as the case might be) was taken for granted.

The Peronista parties also maintained headquarters throughout the country. Meetings were held in these headquarters and party members came there to lodge complaints, seek jobs, and express their loyalty to Perón, his wife and "the revolution." The bureaucracy of the parties was also used to help mobilize the rank-and-file members for meetings and demonstrations on party holidays such as June 4 and October 17 (celebrated as the day in 1945 when Perón was restored to power), or in moments of crisis when the regime was, felt itself to be, or pretended to be, in danger.

The two Peronista parties were mass organizations rather than elite groups. Millions of the president's supporters were enrolled in the two parties, and little or no attempt was made to screen the membership or to keep out "undesirables." Nor was there great effort to develop a highly trained, indoctrinated, and disciplined core.

Quarrels among Peronista members and lower-ranking leaders were frequent. Sometimes a group of Partido Peronista or Partido Peronista Feminino members of a provincial legislature would defy the party leadership on a particular issue; this might bring expulsion from the Peronista bloc in the particular legislative body and expulsion from the party, which usually meant political oblivion so long as the regime remained in power. A handful of Peronista members of the national legislature suffered the same fate.

However, the role of the two Peronista parties was to render services to the regime rather than to have a vital role in running it. Throughout Perón's period in office, the two principal elements of his power were the organized labor movement and the armed forces. Although most trade union supporters of the regime belonged to the Peronista Party and trade union leaders were frequently members of the Cabinet, Congress, and state and municipal legislatures, their power base was their trade union affiliation rather than their membership in the Partido Peronista or the Partido Peronista Feminino.

During this period the trade unions constituted the highly disciplined group of civilian supporters upon whom Perón counted if he found himself in difficulties. Within the unions there were small groups of armed men who performed certain specialized services for the president and his administration. Perón counted heavily on the ability of the unions to mobilize their members for a general strike, or for massive street demonstrations, should the regime feel itself menaced. They, rather than the two Peronista parties, were the principal vehicles for carrying on intensive propaganda in favor of the regime among the humbler citizens. It was powerful trade union figures such as Angel Borlenghi and Andrés Framini who were confidants of the president and were consulted on important decisions, decisions that would be communicated to the two Peronista parties after they had been made.

The other major power group in the Peronista regime was made up of the leaders of the armed forces. Of course Péron himself had risen to power out of the army's ranks, and he continued to have people in the top leadership of the army whom he could trust. He knew that the loyalty of the armed forces was essential if his regime was to stay in power.

However, even with these two basic pillars of support, Perón seldom took chances. Through his wife, who was given general supervision of labor affairs until her death in 1952, he thoroughly purged the leadership of the labor movement. By the end of the Perón regime almost none of the union leaders who had played an important role in getting him to power were left, their places having been taken by men and women chosen by the President and his wife and uncompromisingly loyal to them. Similarly, in the army Perón changed commands frequently, purged doubtful officers, and sought to build up support among the noncommissioned officers. He continually threatened the army with vengeance from the labor movement if it stepped out of line (using the events of October 1945 as evidence of organized labor's power); at the same time he chastened the labor leaders with the possibility of being able to resort to the power of the military should the trade unionists get too far out of line. In all of this complicated maneuvering, the two Peronista parties played at best a secondary role

THE PERONISTA PARTIES AND JUSTICIALISMO

Perón was acutely conscious of his role in the history of his country and—he hoped—of the world. He did not want to go down in history as "just another Latin American military dictator." As a result he sought to legitimize his regime and to give it continuity by developing a doctrine or ideology for it.

Although Perón had the audacity to address a congress of philosophers on one occasion, he was admittedly not a philosopher, political or otherwise. He therefore confided the job of working out a suitable ideology for his movement and his government to some of his more scholarly advisers. They came up with a doctrine that came to be known as Justicialismo (almost untranslatable in English; perhaps "social justicism" is as close as one can get).

The ideology of Justicialismo was complicated and remained vague. The essence of it was that Peronismo was a "Third Force" movement, opposed both to capitalism and Communism, that sought to balance the forces of acquisitiveness and social justice in such a way as to reach a happy mean that would be able to bring material benefits to all without destroying the individual rights of any.[3]

The two Peronista parties used the banner of Justicialismo. However, there was little serious attempt to indoctrinate the members of the parties in all of the details of this supposed philosophy—which was really of very little interest to the workers, peasants, and white-collar workers who made up the bulk of Perón's supporters.

Perón himself often seemed not to understand Justicialismo clearly. In the early years of his political career he made speeches that seemed to reflect a belief in the elite role of the armed forces in Argentina and in modern society in general, although as time went on he lost his confidence in the political ability of military men.* On the other hand, in the last years of his administration, he seemed in many of his speeches to be veering toward some kind of syndicalist concept of a state and society organized on the basis of the trade unions. Needless to say, these zigs and zags in the president's political thinking caused few ripples within the two Peronista parties, which were committed to the man and his regime rather than to any political philosophy.

---

*Seldom has the writer heard any Latin American political leader talk so disparagingly of military men in politics as Perón did in an interview, Madrid, September 1, 1960.

THE PERONISTAS IN THE IMMEDIATE POST-PERÓN YEARS

One of the first acts of the government of General Eduardo Leonardi, which came to power upon the overthrow of Juan Peron in September 1955, was to outlaw the two Peronista parties. The property belonging to the two organizations was confiscated, and it officially became a crime to try to reconstitute the two banned parties.

During the term of office of Lonardi's successor, General Pedro Aramburu (who came to the presidency in November 1955 and left it on May 1, 1958), the Peronistas were severely persecuted. Hundreds of former Peronista members of Congress and provincial and municipal legislatures (all of which had been dissolved on the overthrow of Perón) were jailed. In some instances serious charges of bribery and worse were brought against them; in other instances they were kept in jail for many months without any formal allegations being made. The same fate befell many of the principal Peronista trade unionists. Many leading Peronistas followed their leader into exile.

As such, the Peronista parties ceased to function. However, the followers of the deposed president continued to be active in the labor movement, and there continued to exist a "Comando Supremo" of the Peronista movement, apparently consisting principally of trade unionists who succeeded in avoiding the police network seeking to capture them. This group maintained surreptitious contacts with the deposed president and transmitted his ideas and orders to the rank and file.

In the first few months after the overthrow of Perón, there was widespread disillusionment among his followers. There had already been a good deal of discontent during the last years of his administration because of the increasingly rampant inflation and his obvious attempts to check wage increases as a means of combatting price rises. Immediately after Perón's overthrow the efforts of the Lonardi regime to expose the corruption of not only the Peróns but also leading Peronista trade union leaders (efforts that reached a high point in a public exhibit of Evita's hundreds of dresses and pairs of shoes, the many fur coats, and vast collection of jewelry) affected the thinking of many who had been Peronistas.

However, this trend of opinion against Perón among his former followers was reversed by the very erroneous labor policies followed by the Aramburu government. He "intervened" in virtually all of the country's important labor unions, removing their elected officials and generally appointing military officers as temporary "leaders." Most of these officers had no experience and little sympathy with the workers or their problems. In addition, the higher posts in the Ministry of Labor during this period were largely staffed by "bright young men" from the country's largest corporations.

The upshot of this was that the workers saw the two organizations that during the Perón regime they had come to look upon as their principal defenders—their unions and the Ministry of Labor—in the hands of their enemies. In addition, the incarceration of many trade unionists and former legislators, many of whom were proved to have been guilty of nothing more serious than having been Peronistas, confirmed the feeling among many workers that Perón had been right when he had pictured himself as the workers' only friend in Argentine national politics.

This situation has profound effects on the political future of Argentina. Another kind of policy toward the workers and the organized labor movement in the crucial two and a half years after Perón was ousted might well have won many of his former supporters permanently away from the ex-dictator. However, the policy that was actually followed served to make hundreds of thousands, and perhaps millions of those who had wavered in their loyalties toward Perón, just before and right after his overthrow, turn their loyalties back to him.*

The upshot of this was that after the first shock of their leader's disappearance, the Peronistas were able to reconstitute their forces, although they were obliged to work more or less underground. By the time union elections were finally held during the final months of the Aramburu regime, a very large part of the labor movement returned to the leadership of Perón supporters, although most of the new officials chosen had not played a major role in organized labor when Perón had been president.

This trend back toward Peronism was notable in the elections for a Constitutional Assembly, held in mid-1957. On this occasion Perón sent orders through the "Comando Supreme" that the Peronistas should cast blank ballots. As a result the largest group of votes cast were blank, indicating that although by no means a majority, the Peronista movement was still the largest political group in Argentina.

When it came time to elect a new president in February 1958, Perón changed his tactics. It has been argued that he was forced to do this, since his supporters were anxious to cast their votes for someone and not to adopt an abstentionist policy, such as they had followed in 1957. Perón himself has argued that he decided to throw his support to the candidate of the Intransigente Radical Party (UCRI), Arturo Frondizi, because he felt that if Frondizi's principal opponent, Ricardo Balbín, nominee of the People's Radical Party (UCRP) won, Frondizi would remain as a widely popular figure: but that if Frondizi were

---

*In an interview on June 7, 1968, General Aramburu admitted to the writer that his government's greatest failure had been its labor policy.

elected, he would inevitably fail in office, leaving Perón as the only really popular figure in Argentine politics.

Whatever the reasons, Perón supported Frondizi in the 1958 election. As a result Frondizi won with such an impressive majority that it was impossible for the considerable group of military men who did not want him to be president to block his taking office.

Although Frondizi had been one of the principal figures in the opposition to Perón as long as Perón remained in office, he and some of his close supporters had developed friendly relations with some of the underground Peronista leaders during the Aramburu period. Frondizi therefore hoped that the support the Peronistas had given him in the election would be continued by much of the Peronista Movement once he took office. This hope was reflected in Frondizi's suggestion of the need to reorganize national politics by forming a new party, composed of his own UCRI, the Peronistas, and some smaller groups. It was also shown in his well-known position in favor of allowing the Peronistas to resume participation in the national political life.

However, such was not to be the case. Within six months of taking office, Frondizi was faced with such a serious inflation that he felt a determined price stabilization policy was necessary. Inevitably one of the elements of such a policy was an attempt to check wage increases, and this measure led him directly into conflict with Peronista labor leaders. By the end of 1958, Frondizi's honeymoon with the Peronistas was at an end.

Although during his last three years in office Frondizi faced strong opposition from the Peronistas, his overthrow in March 1962 was precipitated by his efforts to make it possible for them to return to legitimate political activity. This he sought to do in provincial elections held during the last months of 1961 and in the congressional and provincial elections of March 1962.

Frondizi could not go so far as to allow the legal reestablishment of the Peronista Party on a national basis. However, his administration did authorize the legalization of a series of so-called neo-Peronista parties on a provincial level. These took a wide variety of names, although none was permitted to use either Peronista or Justicialista in its title. Although some had been organized originally by Peronistas who had quarreled with the Perón regime before it was overthrown, others were entirely new, being established by people who had never broken their ties with the main Peronista movement.

The results of several provincial elections in which such neo-Peronista parties participated during the last three months of 1961 did not show as large a vote for these groups as had been generally expected. On the contrary, the UCRI of President Frondizi did much better than had generally been predicted; and it appeared that many Peronistas had cast their ballots for Frondizi's party, as at least the lesser evil.

However, the elections of March 1962 were quite different. At stake were the governorships of 10 provinces, including the largest, that of Buenos Aires, as well as the entire membership of the Chamber of Deputies. When the votes were finally counted, the neo-Peronista parties had won half of the gubernatorial elections, including that of Buenos Aires, where Andrés Framini, the well-known Peronista trade union leader, had been elected.

This success by the Peronistas precipitated a major crisis. The election was widely interpreted as meaning that in the presidential election scheduled for 1964, the Peronistas might stand a good chance of winning. Since they were still committed to the thesis that, if they won, they would immediately allow Perón to return to Argentina and assume command of his political forces—and this the anti-Peronistas were not willing to permit under any circumstances—Frondizi's administration was put in immediate danger. After a crisis lasting two weeks, Frondizi was finally overthrown by the armed forces and was replaced by José Mariá Guido, president of the Senate.

NEW TRENDS IN PERONISMO

With the overthrow of Frondizi, national politics was thrown into a period of unequaled chaos. For some months there was a bitter struggle within the armed forces, between the so-called Azules (Blues), who argued in favor of holding new presidential and congressional elections and working out means for allowing the Peronistas to participate but not win, and the Colorados (Reds), who advocated the establishment of a frank military dictatorship "until the armed forces had straightened things out." After military clash between the two groups, the Azules, under General Juan Ongania, won and made preparations to hold new elections.

In the campaign of 1963 the Peronistas found new allies in their attempt to play an independent role. Ex-President Frondizi threw his support behind the formation of a bloc of his followers and the Peronistas. So did the small Conservative group, the Partido Conservador Popular, and the Christian Democratic Party.

However, the government, although promising elections, had no intention of allowing the Peronistas and their allies to win. It first refused to register the Unión Popular, a neo-Peronista party that the Supervisory and Coordinating Council of the Peronista movement (the semilegal high command of the Peronistas) had hoped to use as its vehicle.

With the banning of the Unión Popular, the Peronistas next sought to form an alliance with other parties to name a candidate who might be acceptable to the government. Although six parties at first participated in the negotiations for this Frente Nacional y Popular, it finally came to consist of the Peronistas, the Frondizi faction of the Intransigente Radical Party, and the Partido Conservador Popular. Raúl Matera, president of the Peronista Supervisory and Coordinating Council, opposed the formation of the Frente and resigned when the Peronistas decided to participate in it. The subsequent offer of the Christian Democrats to run Matera as their presidential candidate was also vetoed by the government.

The Frente finally decided to name Vicente Solano Lima, head of the Partido Conservador Popular, as its nominee for president and a Frondizi Radical, Carlos Sylvestre Regnis, as its candidate for vice-president. The Hispanic American Report noted at the time that the Peronista unions "were forced to support the Frente, but they had no enthusiasm for its candidates." They need not to have worried, for early in June the government refused to allow Solano Lima and Sylvestre Regnis to be registered as candidates.[4]

In the face of this refusal by the government to permit the candidacy of anyone who might be favored by the Peronistas, Perón sent instructions (reportedly through José Alonso, secretary-general of the Confederación General del Trabajo, who stopped in Madrid to see him on the way back from attending a meeting of the International Labor Organization in Geneva), that his followers were to cast blank ballots. This position was made public by Augusto Vandor, head of the Metal Workers Union, for the Peronista trade union leaders and by Delia de Parodi, who had succeeded Matera as president of the Supervisory and Coordinating Council of Peronismo, for the nonlabor Peronista politicians.

This appeal for blank ballots, which also had the backing of Frondizi and Solano Lima, was not as successful as had been anticipated. Only about 18 percent of the voters followed the urging of Perón and his allies.[5]

The victor was Arturo Illia, the candidate of the Unión Cívica Radical del Pueblo, the faction of the Radicals most bitterly opposed to Frondizi, who received 28 percent of the total vote. Frondizi's party abandoned him and named its own candidate, Oscar Alende, who came in second.

During the Illia administration important developments took place within the Peronista ranks. As a result of the poor showing the Peronistas had made in the 1963 election, the Supervisory and Coordinating Council of Peronismo was widely discredited among its followers. With Perón's approval, therefore, a move was made in 1964 to reorganize the Peronista forces in a new party, the Partido Justicialista. Local conventions held during the early weeks of July 1964 chose delegates to the national convention of the new party, which opened on July 28. This convention, which heard a recorded speech by Perón, was dominated by the Peronista trade unions led by Augusto Vandor of the Metal Workers Union.[6] Needless to say, the Partido Justicialista did not achieve recognition as a political party.

After the founding of the Partido Justicialista, its leaders went to Spain to report to Perón. They brought back with them a recorded talk by Peron, which pledged support to the Partido Justicialista and specifically repudiated two other groups claiming to speak in his name, the Movimiento Revolucionario Peronista, led by Hector Orlando Villalón and of pro-Castro tendencies; and the group of former extreme right-wing supporters of Perón led by Guillermo Patricio Kelly.[7]

However, despite the support that Perón seemed to give to the Partido Justicialista, he in fact continued to play the game he had played ever since his ouster from power—dealing with different groups among his followers in such a way as to make sure that none of them could develop its own power base. When, late in 1965, Augusto Vandor, head of the Union of Metal Workers, announced that he was going to take the lead in establishing the Justicialista Party on an open and legal basis, Perón made it clear that he was opposed to the idea. The Peronista trade unionists thereupon split, with José Alonso, secretary-general of the Confederación General del Trabajo, leading the dissident faction, which called itself Peronistas at the Feet of Perón.

Vandor's motives for wanting to organize a party more or less independent of Perón but committed to what he conceived to be the principles of the Peronista movement, were several. First, he felt that the Peronista movement had a permanent place in Argentine political life and should be organized so that it could continue as the chief spokesman for the workers of Argentina long after Perón had passed from the scene. Furthermore, he argued that there was need for the emergence of an open political leadership that could make the day-to-day decisions concerning the functioning of the movement, reserving to Perón only the role of court of last resort and molder of the broadest and most general party policy.[8]

Presumably the reasons for Perón's opposing this effort of his followers to obtain a legitimate place in the Argentine political spectrum were the same as Vandor's reasons for wanting to do so. Perón did not relish contemplating what might happen after his death; neither did he welcome the establishment of any authorized Peronista leadership in Argentina that would not be receptive to his minute regulation of its affairs and might succeed in establishing a "Peronismo without Perón."

Although Vandor succeeded in dominating the Confederación General del Trabajo and the Peronista faction of the labor movement, and ousted Alonso as secretary-general, there was only one opportunity for the two groups of Peronistas to test their popularity with the rank and file of the movement's voters. This came in a provincial election in Mendoza in March 1966. The Vandor group put up a candidate for governor who seemed likely to get the support of most of the Peronistas in the province. However, only 10 days before the election the Alonso forces entered a rival nominee. The government, hoping to encourage the split among the Peronistas, allowed the widespread broadcasting of a recorded statement by Perón urging his followers to vote for the Alonso candidate.

Although neither Peronista faction was successful, the victor being a Conservative, the Peronistas at the Feet of Perón received more votes than did Vandor's Peronistas without Perón. This result undoubtedly contributed to precipitating still another military coup d'état in late June 1966.

The Mendoza results convinced many anti-Peronistas that the Peronistas would win the gubernatorial and congressional elections scheduled for March 1967. They foresaw virtually a repetition of the situation of 1962, in which the Peronistas won in many provinces and in the congressional poll. However, the military was not willing to allow elections to be held that they would then feel forced to cancel. This time they saved themselves that embarrassment by overthrowing the president before the elections were held. On June 28, 1966, the armed forces deposed President Arturo Illia, and established a military regime headed by General Juan Carlos Ongania.

Despite the reasons lying behind the 1966 coup, both factions of the Peronista trade union group tried to establish good relations with the Ongania government. Both Augusto Vandor and José Alonso were present at the inauguration of President Ongania. For some months thereafter labor relations were calm, with no serious strikes and with the labor movement generally expressing its willingness to support the new regime.

However, by early 1967 this honeymoon was over. When the Metal Workers Union and several other important Peronista-controlled groups sought large wage increases that the government was not willing to see granted, the unions involved went on strike. As a result the Ongania government clamped down on the Peronista unions. Legal recognition was withdrawn from the Metal Workers Union and several other groups, and their funds were impounded. This move broke the strike.

The advent of the Ongania government to power at first contributed to restablishing unity in the Peronista movement. In the Ongania regime the Peronistas were faced with a group of military men who spoke about the need for the soldiers to stay in control of the government for at least a decade. Some of the leaders of the administration talked of remaining in control until after the death of Juan Perón. As time went on, it became increasingly clear that the military had decided that they would not risk the reestablishment of a constitutional regime so long as this meant the outside possibility that the Peronistas might win an election under conditions that would oblige them to allow Juan Perón to return to Argentina.

Vandor's Peronistas Without Perón and Alonso's Peronistas at the Feet of Peron reunited. However, early in 1968 a further split occurred in the labor movement that involved a new kind of dissension within the Peronista ranks. A regularly scheduled convention of the Confederacion General del Trabajo in March 1968 resulted in a split in the organization when a relatively left-wing group seized control of the meeting. This element consisted of left-wing Socialists, Communists, and some dissident Peronistas. Other delegates, representing the Vandor and Alonso wings of the Peronistas as well as moderate Socialists, old-line syndicalists, and other elements, withdrew from the meeting and held their own convention shortly thereafter.

Thus two CGT's were constituted. One, led by Vandor and Alonso, had within its ranks most of the big industrial unions in which the bulk of the Peronista labor strength was concentrated. The government granted it the use of the CGT headquarters on Calle Azopardo in Buenos Aires. Although neither group was given recognition as the legal CGT, the Vandor-Alonso faction undoubtedly was the larger of the two. Its rival established its headquarters on the Paseo Colón. The two CGT's were usually referred to in the press and in conversation as the CGT Azopardo and the CGT Passeo Colón.

The seriousness of this development in terms of the Peronista movement lay in the fact that both labor factions were headed by avowed Peronistas and that the leadership of the CGT Paseo Colón represented a version of Peronismo that had previously found relatively little support among Perón's followers. Raimundo Ongaro, secretary-general of the CGT Paseo Colón, belonged to a group of left-wing Peronistas who had been more or less outside the mainstream of the movement, a group willing to work closely with Communists and other extreme left-wing groups. The role of Ongaro and his group in the leadership of the CGT Paseo Colón gave that element of the Peronistas a prestige it had never enjoyed before.

The Ongaro element differed from the Vandor-Alonso Peronistas not only in its willingness to collaborate with the Communists but also in its international associations, developing as it did contacts with the bombastically left-wing Confederación Latino Americana de Sindicalistas Cristianos.[9]

This was not the first time the extreme left wing had appeared in the Peronista ranks. Several years earlier, after the Peronista defeat in the 1963 election, a left-wing extremist challenge to the Vandor-Alonso leadership among the Peronista trade unions was mounted by Rubén Sosa, who was backed by some nonworker Peronistas who had ties with the government of Fidel Castro. For a short time Sosa's group had the support of Andrés Framini, one of the few remaining Peronista union leaders from the pre-1955 period. However, Framini soon withdrew his backing from the Sosa forces, and the Vandor-Alonso leadership was able handily to beat back this challenge from the Peronista extreme Left.[10]

The old-line Peronista leadership of the CGT Azopardo received a serious setback when Augusto Vandor was assassinated on July 1, 1969. This event provoked a wave of violent protests by workers who had supported Vandor, and the government immediately arrested Raimundo Ongaro "to protect him from possible attack." Ongaro remained in jail for several years. José Alonso was murdered about two years after Vandor.

Peronismo remained underground—along with all other parties—until General Alejandro Lanusse seized the presidency in April 1971. The new president announced his intention of calling new elections early in 1973 and made overtures to the Peronistas, and even to Perón. The Peronistas joined with the Unión Cívica Radical del Pueblo and several minor groups to establish a coalition known as La Hora del Pueblo. Its main function was the bring pressure on the Lanusse government to fulfill its promises concerning elections and to help prepare the way for this return to constitutional government.

Perón meanwhile continued to play a complicated game with the many groups that claimed to be his supporters. By the advent of President Lanusse to power, these had come to include not only labor supporters but also a sizable element among the students. They also included elements seeking to launch a guerrilla campaign against the military regime. Perón did not repudiate any element among his supporters or give official authorization to any of them.

NATURE AND PROSPECTS OF PERONISMO

By the end of the 1960s the Peronista movement remained a major factor in Argentine politics. Although suppression by successive governments had made it difficult to maintain a single functioning political organization or party to represent the Peronista movement, it had continued to have a solid basis of organization and support in the country's labor movement. After the advent of the Ongania government, and until Lanusse became president, the political wing of Peronismo shared its position of illegality with all of the other political parties of the country.

It was clear that by the early 1970s the Peronista movement still represented their own particular political party for most workers. Virtually all of the labor movement was controlled by Peronistas. To most workers Peronismo stood for the struggle for better working conditions, improved social security, and a better level of living for the humbler citizens. It was the political group that had first made the workers of Argentina a major power in national politics—which they remained in the early 1970s, despite the temporary set-backs administered to the labor movement by the Ongania government.

Although there were middle- and upper-class elements in Peronismo, its base was in the labor movement; and its most outstanding leaders were trade union officials. In view of the disintegration after 1955 of most other political groups that had traditionally had some following in organized labor, it seemed likely that after the death of Perón had removed the main element still separating the Peronistas from their long-time opponents, the Peronistas and most anti-Peronista elements in organized labor would join forces in the political arena. It also seemed possible that important nonlabor elements, particularly those led by ex-President Arturo Frondizi, might form part of such a new party, which would have as its core the quarter-of-a-century-old Peronista movement.

NOTES

INTRODUCTION
   1. See James Payne, Patterns of Conflict in Colombia (New Haven: Yale University Press, 1968).

CHAPTER 1
   1. For a more thorough discussion see particularly Jesús Galíndez, La era de Trujillo (Santiago, Chile: Editorial del Pacífico, 1957); Robert Cressweiler, Trujillo: The Life and Times of a Caribbean Dictator (New York: The Macmillan Co., 1966); and Germán E. Ornes, Trujillo: Little Caesar of the Caribbean (New York: Thomas Nelson & Sons, 1958).
   2. For information on Belaúnde's ideas about the nature of Peru's problems and its development and reform, see Fernando Belaúnde Terry, Peru's Own Conquest (Lima: American Studies Press, 1965).
   3. Ashley Cooper Hewitt, Jr., "Ecuadorean Political Parties," unpublished manuscript (1964), p. 48.
   4. Ibid.
   5. New York Times, January 11, 1940.
   6. Ibid., May 30, 1944.
   7. Daily Information Bulletin of Office of Coordinator of Inter American Affairs, Washington, D.C., September 19, 1944.
   8. Lillo Linke, Ecuador, Country of Contrasts (London: Royal Institute of International Affairs, 1954), p. 32.
   9. Ibid., p. 41.
   10. El mercurio (Santiago, Chile), July 14, 1968.
   11. Hewitt, op. cit., p. 50.

CHAPTER 2
   1. Ronald Schneider, Communism in Guatemala 1944-1954 (New York: Frederick A. Praeger, 1959), p. 5.
   2. Hubert Herring, A History of Latin America (New York: Alfred Knopf, 1964), p. 454.
   3. Miguel Urrutia, The Rise of the Colombian Labor Movement (New Haven: Yale University Press, 1969).
   4. Hubert Herring, op. cit., p. 529.
   5. Ibid.
   6. Ibid., p. 532.
   7. Ibid., p. 529.

8. Ibid.
9. Lillo Linke, Ecuador, Country of Contrasts (London: Royal Institute of International Affairs, 1954), page 36
10. Hubert Herring, op. cit., page 532
11. Alipio Valencia Vega, Desarrollo del pensamiento político en Bolivia (La Paz, 1953), p. 71.
12. Ibid., p. 75.
13. Ibid., p. 76.
14. Hubert Herring, page 556.
15. Alberto Cornejo, Programas políticos de Bolivia (Cochabamba: Imprenta Universitaria, 1949), p. 26.
16. Hubert Herring, op. cit., page 578
17. Huberto Herring, op. cit., page 587
18. Maurice H. Hervey, Dark Days in Chile (New York: Macmillan & Co., 1892), p. 105. This is a study of the revolution against Balmaceda.
19. Hubert Herring, op. cit., page 701
20. George Pendle, Paraguay (London: Royal Institute of International Affairs, 1954), p. 30.
21. Anyda Marchant, "Politics, Government and Law," in T. Lynn Smith and Alexander Marchant, eds., Brazil: Portrait of Half a Continent (New York: The Dryden Press, 1951), Ch. 16, p. 55.
22. For an extensive discussion of these events see John Martz, Central America: The Crisis and the Challenge (Chapel Hill: University of North Carolina Press, 1959), Ch. 4.
23. Hemisphérica, March 1965., Page 2
24. Interview with Luis Quesada, a leader of Partido Liberal Independiente, ex-minister of finance, Managua, August 3, 1948.
25. Interview with Juan Manuel Gutiérrez, Partido Liberal Independiente deputy, Managua, June 28, 1967.
26. The best résumé of Gaitán's ideas is to be found in Luis Emiro Valencia, ed., Gaitán: Antología de su pensamiento social y económico (Bogotá: Ediciones Surmericana Ltda., 1968).
27. For an extensive and enlightening discussion of Colombian party politics, see James Payne, Patterns of Conflict in Colombia (New Haven: Yale University Press, 1969).
28. Linke, op. cit., p. 36
29. José Fellman Velarde, Víctor Paz Estenssoro: El hombre y la revolución (La Paz: E. Burrillo & Cia., 1955), p. 196.
30. Ibid., p. 243.
31. Ibid., p. 259.
32. Hubert Herring, op. cit., page 591
33. For this controversy, and a generally unfavorable picture of Alessandri, see Ricardo Donoso, Alessandri: Agitador y

demoledor, II (Mexico City: Fondo de Cultura Económica, 1954); Donoso had made a similar kind of attack on Alessandri in his volume contributing to Ricardo Lavere's HISTORIA DE AMERICA, VOLUME IX, to which Alessandri issued a reply: see Arturo Alessandri, Rectificaciones al tomo IX (Santiago: Imprenta Universitaria, 1941).

34. For a more extensive study of Arturo Alessandri, see Robert J. Alexander, Prophets of the Revolution (New York: Macmillan 1962), Ch. 4.

35. Dece (Santiago), February-March 1965.

36. For a fuller discussion of Batlle, see Alexander, op. cit., Ch. 2; and Russell/Fitzgibbon, Uruguay: Portrait of a Democracy (New Brunswick, N.J.: Rutgers University Press, 1954).

37. For a discussion of the Pacheco government program, see Robert J. Alexander, "Uruguay's Future Dim, not Dead," Los Angeles Times, September 29, 1968.

38. A good discussion of the Uruguayan parties can be found in Fitzgibbon, op. cit., Ch. 10.

39. Pendle, op. cit, p. 36.

40. Ibid., p. 37.

41. Ibid., p. 41.

42. Daniel M. Friedenburg, "Report from Paraguay," New Leader, November 8, 1965, pp. 5-7.

CHAPTER 3

1. Hubert Herring, A History of Latin America (New York: Alfred Knopf, 1964), p. 312.

2. Ibid., p. 313. For an extensive discussion of the protectionism of Alamán and the early Mexican Conservatives, see Robert Potash, The Banco de Avio of Mexico, a Study of Government Efforts to Develop Industry 1821-1946 (Cambridge, Mass.: Harvard University Press), p. 165.

3. Acción Nacional, Acción Nacional: Principios de doctrina (Mexico City, 1959), p. 9.

4. Ibid., p. 10.

5. For an extensive argument on these lines, see interview with PAN President Adolfo Christleib, Excelsior (Mexico City), May 22 and 23, 1963.

6. Partido Acción Nacional, Partido acción nacional: XIV convención nacional (Mexico City, 1959), pp. 10-11.

7. Howard Cline, Mexico: Revolution to Evolution: 1940-1960 (New York: Oxford University Press, 1963), p. 169.

8. Robert Scott, Mexican Government in Transition (Urbana: University of Illinois Press, 1959), p. 182.

9. Ibid., p. 183.

10. Ibid.

11. Ibid., p. 184.
12. Latin American Digest, April 1969.
13. Herring, op. cit., p. 453. A fascinating account of Carrera can be found in John L. Stephens, Incidents of Travel in Central America, Chiapas and Yucatan (New Brunswick, N.J.: Rutgers University Press, 1949).
14. Herring, op cit, p. 453
15. John Martz, Central America: The Crisis and the Challenge (Chapel Hill: University of North Carolina Press, 1959), p. 115.
16. Ibid., pp. 115-16.
17. Interview with Tiburcio Carías Andino, Tegucigalpa, June 23, 1967.
18. Martz, op. cit., p. 123.
19. Ibid., p. 147.
20. Hemisphérica, October 1963., p. 3
21. Ibid., February 1965, p. 1
22. Ibid., March 1965, p. 1
23. Herring, op. cit., p. 463.
24. Ibid., p. 503.
25. Ibid., p. 507.
26. Ibid., p. 512.
27. The most authoritative study of "la violencia" is that of Germán Guzmán Campos, Orlando Fals Borda, and Eduardo Umana Luna, La violencia en Colombia, 3 vols. (2d ed.; Bogotá: Tercer Mundo, 1963-64).
28. Hubert Herring, op. cit., page 530
29. Hubert Herring, op. cit., page 530
30. Hubert Herring, op. cit., page 531
31. Lillo Linke, Ecuador, Country of Contrasts (London: Royal Institute of International Affairs), page 34
32. Interview with Francisco Salazar Alvarado, president of Partido Conservador, Quito, July 4, 1966.
33. Linke, op. cit., p. 35.
34. Alipio Valencia Vega, Desarrollo del pensamiento político en Bolivia (La Paz, 1953), p. 71.
35. Ibid., p. 74.
36. Ibid., p. 87.
37. Ibid., p. 88.
38. Hubert Herring, op. cit., page 557
39. Hubert Herring, op. cit., page 578
40. Alberto Edwards Vives, La fronda aristocrática (Santiago: Editorial del Pacífico, 1945), p. 56.
41. Ibid., p. 41.
42. Ricardo Donoso, Arturo Alessandri: Agitador y demoledor, I (Mexico City: Fondo de Cultura Económica, 1952), p. 93. This volume has an extensive survey of these party groupings and re-groupings.

NOTES 487

43. Ibid., II, p. 121.
44. See José Luís Romero, El desarrollo de las ideas en la sociedad argentina del siglo XX, (Mexico City: Fondo de Cultura Económica, 1965), Ch. 1 for a discussion of the "Generation of 1880."
45. For the political evolution of Argentina before 1890 see Rodolfo Puiggrós, Pueblo y oligarquía (Buenos Aires: Jorge Alvarez, Editora. 1965).
46. For a discussion of this controversy, see Rodolfo Puiggrós, El trigoyenismo, (Buenos Aires: Jorge Alvarez, Editora, 1965).
47. George Pendle, Paraguay (London: Royal Institute of International Affairs, 1954), p. 30.

CHAPTER 4

1. See Rodolfo Puiggrós, El yrigoyenismo, (Buenos Aires: Jorge Alvarez Editora, 1965), for a discussion of this controversy.
2. Interview with Juan Perón, Madrid, September 1, 1960.
3. For an extensive discussion of the policies of the Frondizi government, see Robert J. Alexander, An Introduction to Argentina (New York: Frederick A. Praeger, 1969).
4. For a discussion of this election, see Hispanic American Report, September 1963, pp. 716-17.
5. For a full-length study of the Argentine Radicals, see Peter Snow, Argentine Radicalism (Iowa City: University of Iowa Press, 1965).
6. For a discussion of the origins of the Chilean Popular Front, see Eudosio Ravines, The Yenan Way (New York: Charles Scribners Sons, 1951), written by the man most responsible for organizing this alliance.
7. This version of events was given to the author by Gabriel González Videla in an interview, Santiago, July 5, 1968.
8. Interview with Jaime Olivares Silva, member of national executive of Democracia Radical, Bogotá, January 1, 1970.
9. Interview with Rene Abeliuk, Sub-Secretary General of Partido Izquierda Radical, in Santiago, June 26, 1972.

CHAPTER 5

1. For a severe criticism of Justo's ideas on this, from a nationalist point of view, see Rodolfo Puiggrós, Las izquierdas y el problema nacional (Buenos Aires: Jorge Alvarez, Editora, 1967).
2. Jacinto Oddone, Historia del socialismo argentino (Buenos Aires: Talleres Gráficos "La Vanguardia," 1934), II, p. 293.
3. Ibid., p. 316.
4. Ibid., pp. 89-172.
5. Ibid., pp. 385-404.

6. Ibid., pp. 334-337.
7. Ibid., pp. 166-171.
8. Ibid., pp. 400-403.
9. For detailed information on this strike and the origins of the Federación Agraria Argentina, see Placido Grela, El grito de Alcorta: Historia de la rebellión campesina de 1912 (Rosario: Editorial Tierra Nuestra, 1958).
10. A discussion of this split is to be found in the Communist Party's Esboso de historia del partido comunista de la Argentina (Buenos Aires: Editorial Anteo, 1947); and in Puiggrós, op. cit.
11. Leandro A. Reynes, "Cuarenta años de acción," in Anuario socialista 1937 (Buenos Aires, 1937), p. 182.
12. An extensive discussion of the background of this split can be found in Joaquín Coca, El contubernio (Buenos Aires: Ediciones Coyacán, 1961).
13. Robert J. Alexander, Labor Parties of Latin America (New York: League for Industrial Democracy, 1942), p. 26.
14. Reynes, op. cit., p. 193.
15. For a more extensive discussion of Perón's capture of organized labor, see Robert J. Alexander, The Perón Era (New York: Columbia University Press, 1951); and Labor Relations in Argentina, Brazil and Chile (New York: McGraw-Hill, 1962).
16. Hispanic American Report, September 1963, p. 717.

CHAPTER 6

1. For an excellent biography of Recabarren and a study of his attitudes toward the Russian Revolution and the Communist International, see Julio César Johet, Recabarren: Los orígenes del movimiento obrero y del socialismo chileno (Santiago: Presna Latinoamericana, 1955).
2. Partido Comunista (Trotskyite faction), En defensa de la revolución—informes, tesis y documentos presentados al congreso nacional del partido comunista à verificarse el 19 de marzo de 1933 (Santiago: Editorial Luís E. Recabarren, 1933), p. 49.
3. John Reese Stevenson, The Chilean Popular Front (Philadelphia: University of Pennsylvania Press, 1942), p. 65.
4. Ibid., p. 71.
5. Ibid., p. 73.
6. Ibid., p. 74.
7. Ibid., p. 75.
8. Ibid., pp. 108-09.
9. Ibid., p. 101.
10. Partido Socialista de Trabajadores, El camino del pueblo—resoluciones del tercer congreso general del partido socialista de trabajadores, 1 al 3 de mayo de 1942 (Santiago, 1942), p. 15.

NOTES 489

11. Boletín del Buro coordinador de la Interacional socialista en América Latina, 2d trimester, 1964, p. 37.
12. Interview with Raul Ampuero, Santiago, June 25, 1971.

CHAPTER 7
1. The Call (New York), January 23, 1911.
2. For a more extensive discussion of the transformation of the first Socialist Party of Uruguay into the Communist Party, see Robert J. Alexander, Communism in Latin America (New Brunswick, N.J.: Rutgers University Press, 1957), pp. 136-37.
3. American Labor Year Book 1931 (New York: Rand School of Social Science, 1931), p. 314.
4. International Information, January 5, 1932.
5. Political Handbook of the World 1934 (New York, 1934), p. 193.
6. International Information, June 23, 1934.
7. Ibid., December 22, 1933.
8. Ibid., September 12, 1936.
9. New York Times, March 29, 1938.
10. Hugo Fernández Artucio, Nazis en el Uruguay (Montevideo, 1941.
11. New York Times, December 31, 1940.
12. Labor Action, December 19, 1955.
13. El partido socialista contesta al partido comunista (Montevideo, June 1956), pamphlet.
14. Informe del Comité administrativo del Centro León Blum a sus afiliados, à la militancia socialista y à la opinion pública (Montevideo, July 25, 1961).
15. Boletín del Buro coordinador de la Internacional socialista en América Latina, 2d, 3d, 4th trimesters, 1964.
16. Interview with Juan Acuña, ex-secretary-general, Confederación Sindical Uruguaya, Montevideo, June 4, 1968.
17. "Orientación," organ of Centro Socialista León Blum, June 1963.
18. Humberto Maiztegui in Boletín del Buro coordinador de la Internacional socialista en América Latina, 4th trimester, 1966, p. 245.
19. Russell Fitzgibbon, Uruguay: Portrait of a Democracy (New Brunswick, N.J.: Rutgers University Press, 1954), p. 149.

CHAPTER 8
1. For details on the earliest Partido Socialista see Robert J. Alexander, Communism in Latin America (New Brunswick, N.J.: Rutgers University Press, 1957), pp. 237-38.
2. Napoleón Humberto Saa, Informe que el compañero Napoleón Humberto Saa, secretario general del partido socialista ecuatoriano,

presenta al V congreso del partido (Quito: Editora Moderna, 1938), pp. 15, 20.

3. Interview with Hugo Larrea Benalcazar, ex-leader of Partido Socialista Ecuatoriano and of Partido Socialista Revolucionario, Quito, July 4, 1966.

4. For origins of the Communist Party see Alexander, op. cit., pp. 235-37.

5. Interview with Luís Emiro Valencia, secretary-general, Partido Popular Socialista, Colombia, Bogotá, September 12, 1956.

6. Interview with Antonio García, founder of Colombian Socialist Party, Bogotá, July 10, 1947.

7. Interview with Luís Emiro Valencia, Bogotá, July 8, 1964.

8. Interview with Antonio García, in La Paz, July 11, 1957.

9. For example, see Antonio García, Gaitán y el problema de la revolución colombiana (Bogota: M.S.T., 1955); and Antonio García and Luís Emiro Valencia, Presencia del socialismo colombiano (Bogota: Editorial Los Andes, 1954).

10. Le mouvement socialiste (Paris), October 15, 1899, p. 473.

11. La revue socialiste (Paris), March 1891, p. 360.

12. Le mouvement socialiste, October 15, 1899, pp. 474-75.

13. Ibid., September 1, 1902, p. 474.

14. Interview with Astrogildo Pereira, founder and historian, Brazilian Communist Party, Rio de Janeiro, October 19, 1965.

15. Interview with Heroclinio Cascardo, former Tenente, national secretary of Partido Socialista Brasileiro in the 1930s, Rio de Janeiro, February 3, 1966.

16. Res Pereigão, Manifesto do partido socialista brasileiro (Rio de Janeiro, 1933), p. 66.

17. Interview with Heroclinio Cascardo, Rio de Janeiro, February 3, 1966.

18. Interview with Mario Pedrosa, editor, Vanguarda socialista, Rio de Janeiro, August 14, 1946.

19. For an extremely favorable study of the peasant movement led by Francisco Julião, which greatly overrates its importance, see Irving Horowitz, Revolution in Brazil (New York: E. P. Dutton, 1964).

20. Interview with Alejandro Freitas and Ramón Mayora, secretary of organization and secretary-general, respectively, partido Socialista de Trabajadores, Caracas, August 1, 1947.

21. La república (Caracas), September 4, 1961.

22. El nacional (Caracas), May 27, 1968.

23. Ibid., July 29, 1968.

24. Venezuela Up-to-Date (Washington, D.C.), Winter 1968-69, p. 3.

25. Interview with José Brouwer, Panamanian Socialist deputy, Caracas, July 24, 1947.

26. Interview with Diógenes de la Rosa, former secretary-general, Panamanian Socialist Party, Panama City, July 26, 1948.
27. Interview with Domingo Barría, secretary-general, Federación Sindical de Trabajadores de Panamá, Panama City, July 7, 1967.
28. Interview with José Brouwer, Caracas, July 24, 1947.
29. Ibid.
30. Interview with José Brouwer, Panama City, July 26, 1948.
31. Interview with Demetrio Porras, former head, Panamanian Socialist Party, member of Supreme Court, Panama City, July 7, 1967.
32. Interview with Lucio Mendívil, senator for Partido Obrero Revolucionario, La Paz, May 28, 1947.
33. Interview with Gustavo Navarro (Tristán Marof), La Paz, May 26, 1947.
34. Interview with Francisco Lazcano Soruco, leader, Partido de la Unión Republicana Socialista, La Paz, June 3, 1947.
35. Antonio Correa, "Boceto histórico del socialismo en Cuba," El folleto (Havana), October 1916.
36. New Leader (New York), September 4, 1926.
37. See Alexander, op. cit., p. 278.
38. New York Times, February 9, 1941.
39. See Acción socialista (Havana), May 1952.
40. The Call (New York), April 26, 1912.
41. See Alexander, op. cit., pp. 319-22, for a detailed discussion of this split.
42. Robert Reischauer, "The Rise and Fall of the Partido Laborista Mexicano" (1964), unpublished manuscript.
43. Acción social (Mexico City), June 1937.
44. Ibid., November-December 1949.
45. One can best follow the activities of the Grupos Socialistas de la República Mexicana through its magazine Acción social, published from the late 1930s to the early 1950s.
46. Santiago Iglesias, "Porto Rican Masses Reach to Socialism for Freedom," New Leader (New York), February 20, 1926.
47. Santiago Iglesias, "The Workers of Porto Rico Build a Great Socialist Party," ibid., January 21, 1933.
48. Ibid.
49. New York Times, November 15, 1936.

CHAPTER 9

1. For a biography of Víctor Raúl Haya de la Torre, see Felipe Cossio del Pomar, Víctor Raúl (Mexico City: Editorial Cultura, 1961).
2. For an extensive study of the Aprista ideas, see Harry Kantor, The Ideology and Program of the Aprista Movement

(Cambridge, Mass.: Harvard University Press, 1954). For a summation of Aprista ideology see Víctor Raúl Haya de la Torre, Treinta años del Aprismo (Mexico City: Fondo de Cultura Económica, 1956).

3. Translated by the author from the Spanish version of Kantor's book, Ideologia y programa del movimiento aprista (Mexico City: Ediciones Humanismo, 1955), p. 39.

4. Interview with Mariano Echegaray and Cleofe Tupac Yupanque de Saenz, national secretary and head of Women's and Children's Section, Secretariat of Indian and Peasant Affairs, Partido Aprista Peruano, respectively, Lima, June 21, 1947.

5. Interview with Armando Villanueva, secretary-general, Partido Aprista Peruano, Lima, July 11, 1966.

CHAPTER 10

1. For details on the early history of Acción Democrática, see John Martz, Acción Democrática (Princeton: Princeton University Press, 1966), pp. 17-55.

2. For an extensive description of the accomplishments of the 1945-48 Acción Democrática government, see Rómulo Betancourt, Venezuela: Política e Petróleo (Mexico City: Fondo de Cultura Económica, 1956), pp. 207-460.

3. For an extensive discussion of the 1948-58 dictatorship, see ibid., pp. 461-754.

4. For an extensive discussion of the fall of Pérez Jiménez, see Tad Szulc, Twilight of the Tyrants (New York: Henry Holt and Co., 1959), pp. 241-304.

5. For an extensive discussion of the provisional regime, see Robert J. Alexander, The Venezuelan Democratic Revolution: A Profile of the Regime of Rómulo Betancourt (New Brunswick, N.J.: Rutgers University Press, 1964), pp. 51-61.

6. República de Venezuela, VI mensaje presidencial presentado por el ciudadano Rómulo Betancourt, presidente constitucional de la república, el 7 de marzo de 1964 (Caracas, 1964), pp. 32-33.

7. Ibid., p. xli.

8. Ibid., p. xxix.

9. For a more extensive discussion of the Betancourt administration, see Alexander, op. cit.

10. For a description of this phase of the Venezuelan guerrilla effort, see Norman Gall, "The Continental Revolution," New Leader, April 12, 1965.

11. For an extensive discussion of the rise and fall of the Venezuelan guerrilla effort, see D. Bruce Jackson, Castro, the Kremlin and Communism in Latin America (Baltimore: The Johns Hopkins Press, 1969.

NOTES

12. Interview with Raúl Ramos Giménez, secretary-general, Acción Democrática (Oposición), Caracas, August 2, 1962.

CHAPTER 11

1. Partido Social Demócrata, Estatuto constitucional del partido social demócrata, fundado el 11 de marzo de 1945 (San José, n.d.).
2. See José Figueres, Palabras gastadas—Democracia, socialismo, libertad (San José, 1943). For a description of the origins of the PSD see Hugo Navarro Bolandi, La generación del 48 (Mexico City: Ediciones Humanismo, 1957). For a sympathetic treatment of José Figueres, see Robert J. Alexander, Prophets of the Revolution (New York: Macmillan, 1962), Ch. VI; and for an unsympathetic one, see John Martz, Central America: The Crisis and the Challenge (Chapel Hill: University of North Carolina Press, 1959), pp. 241-59.
3. See Martz, op. cit., pp. 212-15, for a description of this incident.
4. Joaquín Maurín, "Costa Rica y su presidente Figueres," Cuadernos (Paris), April 1955, p. 88.
5. Harry Kantor, "The Struggle for Democracy in Costa Rica," South Atlantic Quarterly, January 1956, pp. 12-18.
6. José Figueres, Mensaje del señor presidente de la república don José Figueres y contestación del señor presidente de la asamblea legislativa, lic. don Otto Cortes Hernández, 1 de mayo de 1956 (San José, 1956).
7. José Figueres, Estos diez Años, discurso pronunciado por el señor presidente de la república don José Figueres de día 29 de enero 1958 (San José, 1958).
8. José Figueres: Mensaje del señor presidente de la republica don José Figueres y contestacion del senor presidente de la asamblea legislativa lic don Otto Cortes Hernández, 1 de Mayo de 1957 (San José, 1967).
9. José Figueres, Los problemas de la paz y de la guerra, discurso pronunciado por el presidente de Costa Rica, José Figueres, en la reunión de presidentes de América celebrada en Panamá el 22 de julio de 1956 (San José, 1956).

CHAPTER 12

1. Harold Osborne, Bolivia, a Land Divided (London: Royal Institute of International Affairs, 1954), p. 63.
2. See Richard Patch, "Bolivia: U.S. Assistance in a Revolutionary Setting," in Council on Foreign Relations, Social Change in Latin America Today (New York: Harper and Row, 1960), ch. 3.

3. For a sympathetic treatment of the first Paz Estenssoro administration, see Robert J. Alexander, The Bolivian Nacional Revolution (New Brunswick, N.J.: Rutgers University Press, 1958); for a hostile view of the same period, see Alberto Ostria Gutiérrez: A People Crucified: The Tragedy of Bolivia (New York: The Prestige Book Co., 1958). For a firsthand description of the events of the first year of the revolution, and sketches of some of the principal leaders, see Alicia Ortiz, Amanecer en Bolivia (Buenos Aires: Editorial Hemisferio, 1953).

4. For an extensive and intriguing account of the 1956-57 stabilization program, see George Jackson Eder, Inflation and Development in Latin America: A Case History of Inflation and Stabilization in Bolivia (Ann Arbor: Program in International Business, Graduate School of Business Administration, University of Michigan, 1968).

5. Boletín del Buro coordinador de la Internacional socialista en América Latina, 4th trimester, 1967. pp. 91-92.

6. These observations are based on the author's conversation with leaders of various MNR factions, La Paz, July 1968.

7. For the best overall survey of the strengths and weaknesses of the MNR-led Bolivian national revolution, see Cornelius Zondag, The Bolivian Economy 1952-1965: The Revolution and Its Aftermath (New York: Frederick A. Praeger, 1966).

CHAPTER 13

1. For a biography of Luís Muñoz Marín, see Thomas Aitken, Jr., Luís Muñoz Marín, Poet in a Fortress (New York: New American Library, 1964.

2. For a thorough discussion of Muñoz Marín's connection with the New Deal, see Thomas Mathews, Puerto Rican Politics and the New Deal (Gainesville: University of Florida Press, 1960).

3. For a highly personal account of Tugwell's role, see his book The Stricken Land (New York: Doubleday, 1947).

4. Commonwealth of Puerto Rico, Department of the Treasury, Economy and Finances of Puerto Rico 1967 (San Juan, 1968), p. 6.

5. Sergio Camero, "Diversification New Springboard to Growth in Puerto Rico," Investment Dealer's Digest, July 22, 1968; republished in Government Development Bank for Puerto Rico, Quarterly Report to Investors in Puerto Rican Securities, San Juan, September 1968. pp. 1-2.

6. Commonwealth of Puerto Rico, op. cit., p. 9.

7. Ibid., p. 6.

8. Government Development Bank for Puerto Rico, A Special Report on the Commonwealth of Puerto Rico, February 1965 (San Juan, 1965), p. 19.

9. Commonwealth of Puerto Rico, op. cit., p. 7.
10. For an extensive and very favorable picture of the early accomplishments of the PPD government, see Earl Parker Hanson, Puerto Rico; Land of Wonders (New York: Alfred Knopf, 1960); and the same author's Transformation: The Story of Modern Puerto Rico (New York: 1955). Alfred Knopf.

CHAPTER 14

1. Robert Scott, Mexican Government in Transition (Urbana: University of Illinois Press, 1959), pp. 130-44.
2. For a study of the political role of Mexican army officers, see Franklin Margiotta, "The Mexican Military: A Case Study in Nonintervention" (Washington, D.C.: Georgetown University, 1968), unpublished M.A. thesis.
3. Scott, op. cit., pp. 154-56. For a strong argument by an old advocate of the agrarian reform for the abolition of the ejido, see Rodrigo Garcia Treviño: Precios, salarios y mordidas (Mexico City: Editorial America, 1953).
4. Ibid., p. 154.

CHAPTER 15

1. For a more extensive discussion of the Communists' attitudes and behavior toward the Machado and Batista dictatorships, see Robert J. Alexander, Communism in Latin America (New Brunswick, N.J.: Rutgers University Press, 1957), ch. 8.
2. Interview with Carlos Prío Socarras, Havana, January 12, 1959.
3. These observations are the result of a visit by the author to Cuba about 10 days after Batista's seizure of power, and interviews conducted at that time.
4. Partido del Pueblo Cubano (Ortodoxo), Doctrina del partido ortodoxo—independencia, económica, libertad política, justicia social (Havana, 1951), pp. 7-17.
5. Hispanic American Report, March 1963, p. 39.
6. Ibid., April 1963, p. 135.
7. Probably the best day-to-day account of the 1965 Dominican civil war and the U.S. intervention is Tad Szulc, Dominican Diary (New York: Delacorte Press, 1965).
8. Socialist International Information, May 10, 1969, p. 107.
9. Partido Acción Revolucionaria, "Declaración de principios y bases fundamentales del programa político del 'PAR' aprobados en sesión plenaria de la convención nacional Celebrada el 16 de noviembre de 1946." (Guatemala City, 1946). Mimeographed.
10. For extensive discussions of the Guatemalan parties of the Arévalo-Arbenz period, see Ronald Schneider, Communism in

Guatemala 1944-1954 (New York: Frederick A. Praeger, 1958); and Daniel James, Red Design for the Americas: Guatemalan Precedent (New York: The John Day Co., 1954).

11. Interview with Isaac Monterosa Méndez, member, National Directorate, Partido Revolucionario, Guatemala City, June 17, 1967.

12. Interview with Julio César Méndez Montenegro, president of Guatemala, Guatemala City, June 16, 1967.

13. For a quite hostile version of the Partido Revolucionario's administration, see Eduardo Galeano, Guatemala: Occupied Country (New York: Monthly Review Press, 1969).

14. Most information on MOP before 1952 was gathered in visits to Haiti in 1948, 1949, and 1952, and interviews with Daniel Fignolé, Port-au-Prince, June 25, 1948, August 23, 1949, and July 20, 1952; New York, June 19, 1957, and May 5, 1959. On the post-1957 period most information is drawn from the MOP exile periodical Construction: Journal haïtien.

15. Interview with Elpidio Yegrós, former secretary-general of Partido Revolucionario Febrerista, La Catalina, Costa Rica, July 3, 1967.

16. For a discussion of this period, see George Pendle, Paraguay (London: Royal Institute of International Affairs, 1954), pp. 36-44.

17. Tribuna Febrerista, February 17, 1952, p. 16.

18. Pendle, op. cit., p. 43.

19. Tribuna Febrerista, February 17, 1952, pp. 3-5.

20. Elpidio Yegrós, "Frente a la tiranía." (Unpublished article.)

21. Interview with Carlos Aguero, departmental agent, Instituto de Bienestar Rural, Pedro Juan Caballero, Paraguay, November 26, 1965.

22. Interview with Elpidio Yegrós, La Catalina, Costa Rica, July 3, 1967.

CHAPTER 16

1. Ernst Halperin, Nationalism and Communism in Chile (Cambridge, Mass.: The MIT Press, 1965), pp. 182-92.

2. Interview with Jaime Rojas Fraga, trade union secretary, Falange Nacional, Santiago, January 19, 1947.

3. Roger S. Abbott, "The Role of Contemporary Political Parties in Chile," American Political Science Review, June 1951, p. 453.

4. Interview with Luis Quiroga, Falangista member, Executive, Central Unica de Trabajadores de Chile, New Brunswick, N.J., February 17, 1954.

5. Interview with Padre Rafael Larraín, head, Instituto de Educación Rural, Santiago, July 19, 1968.

NOTES 497

    6. Halperin, op. cit., p. 193.
    7. Ibid.
    8. Ibid.
    9. Eduardo Frei, Chile, 1964-1970 (Santiago, 1964).
   10. Halperin, op. cit, pp. 218-19.
   11. Eduardo Frei: Quinto mensaje del presidente de la república, don Eduardo Frei Montalva, al inaugurar el período de sesiones ordinarias del congreso nacional, 21 de marzo de 1969 (Santiago, 1969).
   12. Joseph R. Thome, "A Brief Survey of the Chilean Agrarian Reform Program," Land Tenure Center Newsletter (University of Wisconsin, Madison), September 1968-February 1969.
   13. These observations on rural unionism and its effects, socially and politically, were drawn from the writer's experiences in June and July 1968, when he made a survey of rural unionism for the United States Agency for International Development (AID). For the rural unionization law, see Diario Oficial de la República de Chile, Sindicación campesina (Santiago, 1967).
   14. Unión de Trabajadores de Chile, "Resumen de la declaración de principios y plataforma de lucha" (Santiago, 1968). (Mimeographed.)
   15. See "Dólares y dolores de Hector Alarcon," El siglo, July 5, 1968; and "Respuesta al llamado divisionista de UTRACH," ibid., July 13, 1968.
   16. El mercurio (Santiago), July 7-13, 1969. (International edition.)
   17. Ibid., February 24-March 2, 1969.

CHAPTER 17
    1. John Martz, Acción Democrática (Princeton: Princeton University Press, 1966), p. 316.
    2. Ibid., p. 317.
    3. Ibid., p. 69.
    4. Interview with Rafael Caldera and Edecio La Riva, leaders, Partido Copei, Caracas, July 28, 1947.
    5. Martz, op. cit., p. 74.
    6. Interview with Rafael Caldera, Caracas, July 22, 1952.
    7. Interview with Rafael Caldera, Caracas, June 25, 1954.
    8. Partido Copei, Por qué Copei no asiste a la constituyente (Caracas, January 9, 1953). (Throwaway.)
    9. Interview with Elio Aponte González, secretary-general, COFETROV, Caracas, July 22, 1952.
   10. Interview with Rómulo Betancourt, leader, Acción Democrática, Piscataway, N.J., August 11, 1957.
   11. Interview with Rómulo Betancourt, New York City, November 11, 1957.

12. Martz, op. cit., p. 105.
13. For a fuller discussion of Copei participation in the Betancourt government, see Robert J. Alexander, The Venezuelan Democratic Revolution (New Brunswick, N.J.: Rutgers University Press, 1964.
14. Martz, op. cit., p. 335.
15. Venezuela Up-to-Date, Winter 1968-1969, p. 2.
16. Ibid., Spring 1969, p. 4.
17. Interviews with Ramón Silva, director, Instituto Nacional de Estudios Sindicales, New Brunswick, N.J., May 9, 1962; Caracas, August 4, 1952.

CHAPTER 18
1. Hispanic American Report, May 1963, p. 292.
2. Ibid., August 1963, pp. 611-14.
3. Ibid., September 1963, pp. 716-17.
4. Ibid., September 1964, p. 840.
5. Interview with José Pineiro Cortés, member, state executive committee, Partido Demócrata Cristão of São Paulo, São Paulo, July 17, 1954.
6. Interview with María Luisa Viegas de Mederos, Partido Demócrata Cristão member, Pernambuco state legislature, Recife, February 22, 1956.
7. Boletín informativo demócrata cristiano (New York), October 1963, p. 8.
8. Ibid., November 1963, p. 5.
9. Dece (Santiago, Chile), April 1965, p. 7.
10. Joaquín Secco-Illa, Historia de la Unión cívica, quoted in Edward J. Williams; Latin American Christian Democratic Parties (Knoxville: University of Tennessee Press, 1967), p. 12.
11. Williams, op. cit., p. 133.
12. Interview with Sotuyo, member, National Executive Committee, Partido Demócrata Cristiano, Montevideo, June 3, 1968.
13. Interview with Romeo Pérez, member, International Secretariat, Partido Demócrata Cristiano, Montevideo, June 3, 1968.
14. Interview with Ismael Bielich, Partido Demócrata Cristiano deputy in Peruvian parliament, Maracay, Venezuela, April 25, 1960.
15. Interview with Hector Cornejo Chávez, leader, Partido Demócrata Cristiano, Peru, Madison, Wisconsin, March 15, 1963.
16. Interview with Patricio Ricketts, founder, Partido Popular Cristiano, Peru, New Brunswick, N.J., April 9, 1968.
17. Interview with Luís Napoleón Duarte, leader, Partido Demócrata Cristiano, El Salvador, San Salvador, June 20, 1967.

18. Interview with José García Bauer, founder, Guatemalan Christian Democratic Party, Guatemala City, July 20, 1953.
19. Interview with René Armando de León Schlotter, member, National Executive Committee, Movimiento Demócrata Cristiano, Guatemala City, June 15, 1967.
20. Latin American Digest, May 1970, p. 2.
21. Boletín informativo democrata cristiano, March 1963, p. 5.
22. Interview with Antonio Rosario, president, Partido Revolucionario Social Cristiano, Santo Domingo, July 11, 1964.
23. Interview with Rafael Martínez González, press secretary, Partido Revolucionario Social Cristiano, Santo Domingo, March 13, 1967.
24. Interview with Hipólito Martínez, assistant press secretary, Partido Revolucionario Social Cristiano, Santo Domingo, March 13, 1967.
25. Interview with Manuel Peralta, student leader, Partido Revolucionario Social Cristiano, Santo Domingo, July 31, 1968.
26. Interview with Caonabo Javier, secretary-general, Partido Revolucionario Social Cristiano, Santo Domingo, August 18, 1970.
27. Dece (Santiago, Chile), November 1964, p. 3.
28. Boletín informativo demócrata cristiano, March 1963, p. 6.
29. Información democrática cristiana (New York), July 1960, p. 3.
30. Ibid., May-June 1956, p. 3.
31. Boletín informativo demócrata cristiano, December 1963, p. 5.
32. Ibid., March-April 1964, p. 5.
33. Interview with Francisco de Paula Jaramillo, leader, Partido Social Democrático Cristiano, Bogotá, July 28, 1968.
34. Información democrática Cristiana, June 1959, p. 4.
35. Dece (Santiago, Chile), June 1964, p. 3.
36. Latin American Digest, March 1970, p. 3.
37. Información democrática cristiana, January-February 1958, p. 2.
38. Boletín informativo demócrata cristiano, September 1963, p. 7.
39. Ibid., May 1964, p. 6.
40. Ibid., January-February 1964, p. 8.
41. Interview with Paul Cassagnol, president, Parti Populaire Social Chrétien, Haiti, Port-au-Prince, August 29, 1949.
42. Boletín informativo demócrata cristiano, March 1963, p. 6.
43. Información democrática cristiana, July 1960, p. 2.

CHAPTER 19

1. See Daniel James, Red Design for the Americas: Guatemalan Prelude (New York: John Day, 1954).

2. Osvaldo Peralva has a description of such training in O retrato (Rio de Janeiro: Editora O Globo, 1962).

3. For an extensive discussion of the experience of the Venezuelan Communist Party in guerrilla war, see D. Bruce Jackson, Castro, the Kremlin and Communism in Latin America (Baltimore: Johns Hopkins Press, 1969); and Robert J. Alexander, The Venezuelan Communist Party (Stanford: Hoover Institution Press, 1969).

4. For more extensive discussion of the orthodox Communist parties, see Robert J. Alexander, Communism in Latin America (New Brunswick, N.J.: Rutgers University Press, 1957); and Rollie Poppino, International Communism in Latin America, a History of the Movement, 1917-1963.

CHAPTER 20

1. For the most complete study of Maoist parties in Latin America yet to appear, see Cecil Johnson, Communist China and Latin America 1959-1967 (New York: Columbia University Press, 1970).

2. Communist International, April 5, 1934.

3. Interview with Gustavo Navarro, La Paz, May 26, 1947.

4. The so-called Pulacayo thesis can be found in Alberto Cornejo, Programas políticos de Bolivia (Cochabamba: Imprenta Universitaria, 1949), pp. 314-40.

5. Interview with Jorge Salazar, Partido Obrero Revolucionario leader, La Paz, August 13, 1952. Also see Lucha Obrera (organ of the Partido Obrero Revolucionario), June 12, 1952.

6. International Socialist Review (New York), March-April 1968.

7. The Newsletter (London), February 4, 1969, p. 4.

8. La mañana (Montevideo), March 16, 1969.

9. For example, see Intercontinental Press, September 16, 1968.

10. Yugoslav Facts and Views (New York), Yugoslav Information Service, March 16, 1969.

11. Robert J. Alexander: "Dual Communism in Latin America," New Leader, New York, October 13, 1952.

12. For an extensive analysis of the three Mexican Communist parties, see Karl Schmitt, Communism in Mexico (Austin: University of Texas Press, 1965).

13. For an extensive analysis of Venezuelan dual Communism, see Robert J. Alexander, Communism in Latin America (New Brunswick, N.J.: Rutgers University Press, 1957), ch. 7.

NOTES 501

14. See Alexander, op. cit., pp. 172-76.
15. Osvaldo Peralva, O retrato (Rio de Janeiro: Editora O Globo, 1962), pp. 272-74.
16. See the list of participants in Che's guerrilla band in Bolivia in Jay Mallin, "Che" Guevara on Revolution (Coral Gables: University of Miami Press, 1969), pp. 229-34. See also Oscar Zamora, "Bolivian CP (M-L) Rebuts Castro," World Revolution (New York), January-March 1969.
17. Peking Review, the English-language publication issued weekly in Peking, has frequent reports on parties in Latin America that are sympathetic to the Chinese.

CHAPTER 21

1. For details on this trial, see Robert J. Alexander, 'Old Quarrels in Havana," New Politics, Summer 1964, pp. 67-75.
2. For details on this trial, see World Outlook, New York, February 23, 1968, pp. 155-167.
3. For an important study of Guevara's relations with Castro, see Ricardo Rojo, My Friend Ché (New York: The Dial Press, 1968).
4. For details on the Tricontinental Conference, see D. Bruce Jackson, Castro, the Kremlin and Communism in Latin America (Baltimore: The Johns Hopkins Press, 1969).
5. See Ernst Halperin, Nationalism and Communism in Chile (Cambridge, Mass.: The MIT Press, 1965).
6. See Jackson, op. cit., for extensive information on this.
7. See Eduardo Galeano, Guatemala: Occupied Country (New York: Monthly Review Press, 1969).
8. For a detailed discussion of this, see Jackson, op. cit.
9. See the interview with Castro in Intercontinental Press.
10. See Régis Debray, Revolution in the Revolution? Armed Struggle and Political Struggle in Latin America (New York: Monthly Review Press, 1967).
11. See Jay Mallin, "Che" Guevara on Revolution (Coral Gables: University of Miami Press, 1969).
12. For an extensive analysis of the incentives controversy in Cuba, see Carmelo Mesa-Lago, The Labor Sector and Socialist Distribution in Cuba (New York: Frederick A. Praeger, 1969).
13. For an extended discussion of the Guatemalan guerrilla war, see Galeano, op. cit.
14. See Ernesto Guevara's Diary, two versions of which have been published in the United States. These are listed in the bibliography.
15. See Rojo, op. cit.

16. Interview with Juan Román Díaz, a leader of Movimiento Politico 14 de Junio, Dominican Republic, Caracas, September 12, 1961.

CHAPTER 22
1. For a description of the origins of the Integralista Movement, see Plinio Salgado, Despertamos a nação (Rio de Janeiro: Livraria José Olympio Editor, 1935).
2. See Alzira Vargas, Getúlio Vargas, meu pai (Rio de Janeiro: Editora O Globo, 1960).
3. Ibid., pp. 91-116.
4. John Reese Stevenson, The Chilean Popular Front (Philadelphia: University of Pennsylvania Press, 1942), p. 77.
5. Ibid., p. 86.
6. Ibid., and Ricardo Donoso, Alessandri: Agitador y demoledor, II (Mexico City: Fondo de Cultura Económica, 1954), ch. 15.
7. Alberto Cornejo, Programas políticos de Bolivia (Cochabamba: Imprenta Universitaria, 1949), pp. 133-34.
8. Ibid., p. 135.
9. Ibid., p. 137.
10. Ibid., p. 135.
11. Ibid., p. 136.
12. New York Times, August 12, 1940.
13. New Masses, May 30, 1944.
14. Howard Cline, The United States and Mexico (Cambridge, Mass.: Harvard University Press, 1953), pp. 293-94.
15. James Allen, Daily Worker (New York), January 4, 1944.
16. Cline, op. cit., p. 318.
17. Hispano Americano (Mexico City), February 4, 1949.
18. Robert Scott, Mexican Government in Transition (Urbana: University of Illinois Press, 1959), pp. 182-83.
19. Ibid., p. 184.
20. Cline, op. cit., p. 320.

CHAPTER 23
1. For an extensive discussion of this consensus government, see Paulo Mercadante, a consciencia conservadora no Brasil (Rio de Janeiro: Editora Saga, 1965).
2. For a discussion of the role of the coroneis, see Marcos Vinicius Vilaca and Roberto de Albuquerque, Coronel, coroneis (Rio de Janeiro: Tempo Brasileiro, 1965).
3. For an extensive discussion of the São Paulo Democratic Party, see Paulo Norgueira Filho, O partido democrático e a revolução de 1930 (Rio de Janeiro: José Olympio Editora, 1965).

4. For a discussion of the Borges de Medeiros regime, see Joseph Love, "Rio Grande do Sul as a Source of Political Instability in Brazil's Old Republic 1900-1932," Ph.D. dissertation (Columbia University, 1967).

5. The best available general survey of Brazilian politics between World War II and the 1964 revolution is to be found in Thomas Skidmore, Politics in Brazil 1930-1964; An Experiment in Democracy (New York: Oxford University Press, 1967).

CHAPTER 24

1. For perhaps the best description of this early period of Peronismo, see Robert J. Alexander, The Perón Era (New York: Columbia University Press, 1951).

2. For the best description of the role of Evita in the early years of Peronismo, see María Flores, The Woman with the Whip (Garden City, N.Y.: Doubleday and Co., 1952).

3. For an extensive description of Justicialismo, see George Blanksten, Perón's Argentina (Chicago: University of Chicago Press, 1953), chs. 8-12.

4. Hispanic American Report, August 1963, pp. 608-12.

5. Ibid., September 1963, pp. 716-19.

6. Ibid., September 1964, pp. 651-52.

7. Ibid., October 1964, p. 745.

8. Interview with Augusto Vandor, Buenos Aires, June 22, 1966.

9. See CGT, organ of Ongaro faction of Confederación General del Trabajo, May 30, 1968.

10. Hispanic American Report, March 1964, pp. 75-76.

BIBLIOGRAPHY

Much of the contents of this book is drawn from the author's nearly quarter of a century of contact with Latin American parties and politicians. These contacts have involved attending numerous party meetings, including sessions of national executive committees. They have included interviews with thousands of national and local political leaders in all of the republics of the hemisphere. In the present bibliography only those interviews cited directly in the text or in the notes are listed.

The written sources for this book are extremely varied. They include books, pamphlets, official party and government documents, and newspapers and magazines. Again only those written sources cited in text or notes are listed.

The list that follows should be of some help to readers interested in further study of the political parties of Latin America.

BOOKS

Aitken, Thomas, Jr. *Luís Muñoz Marín, Poet in a Fortress*. New York: New American Library, 1964.

Alessandri, Arturo. *Rectificaciones al tomo IX*. Santiago: Imprenta Universitaria, 1941.

Alexander, Robert J. *The Perón Era*. New York: Columbia University Press, 1951.

―――――. *Communism in Latin America*. New Brunswick, N.J.: Rutgers University Press, 1957.

―――――. *The Bolivian National Revolution*. New Brunswick, N.J.: Rutgers University Press, 1958.

―――――. *Labor Relations in Argentina, Brazil and Chile*. New York: McGraw-Hill, 1962.

―――――. *Prophets of the Revolution*. New York: Macmillan, 1962.

———. The Venezuelan Democratic Revolution: A Profile of the Regime of Rómulo Betancourt. New Brunswick, N.J.: Rutgers University Press, 1964.

———. An Introduction to Argentina. New York: Frederick A. Praeger, 1969.

———. The Venezuelan Communist Party. Stanford, California: The Hoover Institution Press, 1969.

Belaúnde Terry, Fernando. Peru's Own Conquest. Lima: American Studies Press, 1965.

Betancourt, Rómulo. Venezuela: Política e petróleo. Mexico City: Fondo de Cultura Económica, 1955.

Blanksten, George. Perón's Argentina. Chicago: University of Chicago Press, 1953.

Cline, Howard. The United States and Mexico. Cambridge, Massachusetts: Harvard University Press, 1953.

———. Mexico: Revolution to Evolution: 1940-1960. New York: Oxford University Press, 1963.

Coca, Joaquín. El contubernio. Buenos Aires: Ediciones Coyoancán, 1961.

Cornejo, Alberto. Programas políticos de Bolivia. Cochabamba: Imprenta Universitaria, 1949.

Cossio del Pomar, Felipe. Víctor Raúl. Mexico City: Editorial Cultura, 1961.

Council on Foreign Relations. Social Change in Latin America Today. New York: Harper and Brothers, 1960.

Cressweiler, Robert. Trujillo: Life and Times of a Caribbean Dictator. New York: Macmillan, 1966.

Debray, Régis. Revolution in the Revolution? Armed Struggle and Political Struggle in Latin America. New York: Monthly Review Press, 1967.

Donoso, Ricardo. Alessandri: Agitador y demoledor. Two volumes. Mexico City: Fondo de Cultura Económica, 1952, 1954.

Eder, George Jackson. Inflation and Development in Latin America: A Case History of Inflation and Stabilization in Bolivia. Ann Arbor: Program in International Business, Graduate School of Business Administration, University of Michigan, 1968.

Edwards Vives, Alberto. La fronda aristocrática. Santiago: Editorial del Pacífico, 1945.

Facio, Rodrigo. Estudio sobre economía costarricense. San José: Editorial Surco, 1942.

Fellman Velarde, José. Víctor Paz Estenssoro: El hombre y la Revolución. La Paz: E. Burillo & Cia., 1955.

Fernández Artucio, Hugo. Nazis en el Uruguay. Montevideo, 1941.

Fitzgibbon, Russell. Uruguay: Portrait of a Democracy. New Brunswick, New Jersey: Rutgers University Press, 1954.

Flores, María (Mary Main). The Woman with the Whip. Garden City, N.Y.: Doubleday & Co., 1952.

Galdames, Luis. Historia de Chile. Santiago: Empresa Editora Zig Zag, 1945.

Galeano, Eduardo. Guatemala: Occupied Country. New York: Monthly Review Press, 1969.

Galíndez, Jesús de. La era de Trujillo. Santiago: Editorial del Pacífico, 1957.

García, Antonio. Gaitán y el problema de la revolución colombiana. Bogotá: M.S.T., 1955.

García, Antonio, and Luís Emiro Valencia. Presencia del socialismo colombiano. Bogotá: Editorial Los Andes, 1954.

García Treviño, Rodrigo. Precios, salarios y mordidas. Mexico City: Editorial América, 1953.

Grela, Placido. El grito de Alcorta: Historia de la rebellión campesina de 1912. Rosario, Argentina: Editorial Tierra Nuestra, 1958.

Guevara, Ernesto "Che": The Complete Bolivian Diarias of Ché Guevara. Edited with introduction by Daniel James. New York: Stein & Day, 1968.

──────. The Diary of Che Guevara, Bolivia: November 7, 1966- October 7, 1967. The authorized text in English and Spanish, with introduction by Fidel Castro. Edited by Robert Scheer. New York: Bantam Books, 1968.

Guzman Campos, Germán, Orlando Fala Borda, and Eduardo Umana Luna. La violencia en Colombia. Second edition. Two volumes. Bogotá: Tercer Mundo, 1963, 1964.

Halperin, Ernst. Nationalism and Communism in Chile. Cambridge, Massachusetts: The MIT Press, 1965.

Hanson, Earl Parker. Transformation: The Story of Modern Puerto Rico. New York: Alfred Knopf, 1955.

──────. Puerto Rico; Land of Wonders. New York: Alfred Knopf, 1960.

Haya de la Torre, Víctor Raúl. Treinta años del Aprismo. Mexico City: Fondo de Cultura Económica, 1955.

Herring, Hubert. A History of Latin America. New York: Alfred Knopf, 1964.

Hervey, Maurice H. Dark Days in Chile: An Account of the Revolution of 1891. New York: Macmillan and Co., 1892.

Horowitz, Irving. Revolution in Brazil. New York: E. P. Dutton, 1964.

Jackson, D. Bruce. Castro, the Kremlin and Communism in Latin America. New York: The John Day Co., 1954.

James, Daniel. Red Design for the Americas: Guatemalan Precedent. New York: The John Day Co., 1954.

Johet, Julio César. Recabarran: Los orígenes del movimiento obrero y del socialismo chilenos. Santiago: Prensa Latinoamericana, 1955.

Johnson, Cecil. Communist China and Latin America 1959-1967. New York: Columbia University Press, 1970.

Kantor, Harry. The Ideology and Program of the Aprista Movement. Berkeley: University of California Press, 1953.

Linke, Lillo. Ecuador, Country of Contrasts. London: Royal Institute of International Affairs, 1954.

Mallin, Jay. "Che" Guevara on Revolution. Coral Gables: University of Miami Press, 1969.

Martz, John. Central America: The Crisis and the Challenge. Chapel Hill: University of North Carolina Press, 1959.

_____. Acción democrática. Princeton: Princeton University Press, 1966.

Mathews, Thomas. Puerto Rican Politics and the New Deal. Gainesville: University of Florida Press, 1960.

McBride, George McCutcheon. Chile: Land and Society. New York: American Geographical Society, 1936.

Mercadante, Paulo. A consciencia conservadora no Brasil. Rio de Janeiro: Editora Saga, 1965.

Mesa Lago, Carmelo. The Labor Sector and Socialist Distribution in Cuba. New York: Frederick A. Praeger, 1969.

Navarro Bolandi, Hugo. La generación del 48. Mexico City: Ediciones Humanismo, 1957.

Nogueira Filho, Paulo. O partido democrático e a revolução de 1930. Rio de Janeiro: José Olympio Editora, 1965.

Oddone, Jacinto. Historia del socialismo argentino. Two volumes. Buenos Aires: Talleres Gráficos "La Vanguardia," 1934.

Ornes, Germán. Trujillo: Little Caesar of the Caribbean. New York: Thomas Nelson & Sons, 1958.

Ortiz, Alicia. Amanecer en Bolivia. Buenos Aires: Editorial Hemisferio, 1953.

Osborne, Harold. Bolivia, A Land Divided. London: Royal Institute of International Affairs, 1954.

Ostria Gutiérrez, Alberto. A People Crucified: The Tragedy of Bolivia. New York: The Prestige Book Co., 1958.

Partido Comunista de la Argentina. Esboso de historia del partido comunista de la Argentina. Buenos Aires: Editorial Anteo, 1947.

Payne, James L. Patterns of Conflict in Colombia. New Haven: Yale University Press, 1968.

Pendle, George. Paraguay. London: Royal Institute of International Affairs, 1954.

Peralva, Osvaldo. O retrato. Rio de Janeiro: Editora O Globo, 1962.

Poppino, Rollie. International Communism in Latin America, a History of the Movement, 1917-1963. New York: Free Press, 1964.

Potash, Robert. The Banco de Avio of Mexico, A Study of Government Efforts to Develop Industry 1821-1846. Cambridge, Massachusetts: Harvard University Press.

Puiggrós, Rodolfo. Pueblo y oligarquía. Buenos Aires: Jorge Alvarez Editora, 1965.

_____. El yrigoyenismo. Buenos Aires: Jorge Alvarez Editora, 1965.

_____. Las izquierdas y el problema nacional. Buenos Aires: Jorge Alvarez Editora, 1967.

Ravines, Eudosio. The Yenan Way; The Kremlin's Penetration of South America. New York: Charles Scribners Sons, 1951.

Rojo, Ricardo. My Friend Ché. New York: The Dial Press, 1968.

Romero, José Luís. El desarrollo de las ideas en la sociedad argentina del siglo XX. Mexico City: Fondo de Cultura Económica, 1965.

Salgado, Plinio. Despertemos a nação. Rio de Janeiro: Livraria José Olympio Editor, 1935.

Schmitt, Karl M. Communism in Mexico. Austin: University of Texas Press, 1965.

Schneider, Ronald. Communism in Guatemala 1944-1954. New York: Frederick A. Praeger, 1958.

Scott, Robert. Mexican Government in Transition. Urbana: University of Illinois Press, 1959.

Siso Martínez, J. M. Historia de Venezuela. Caracas: Editorial Yocoíma, 1956.

Skidmore, Thomas. Politics in Brazil 1930-1964: An Experiment in Democracy. New York: Oxford University Press, 1967.

Smith, Lynn, and Alexander Marchant. Brazil: Portrait of Half a Continent. New York: The Dryden Press, 1951.

Snow, Peter. Argentine Radicalism. Iowa City: University of Iowa Press, 1965.

Stephens, John L. Incidents of Travel in Central America, Chiapas and Yucatán. New Brunswick, N.J.: Rutgers University Press, 1949.

Stevenson, John Reese. The Chilean Popular Front. Philadelphia: University of Pennsylvania Press, 1942.

Szulc, Tad. Twilight of the Tyrants. New York: Henry Holt and Co., 1959.

_____. Dominican Diary. New York: Delacorte Press, 1965.

Tannenbaum, Frank. Mexico: The Struggle for Peace and Bread. New York: Alfred Knopf, 1950.

Tugwell, Rexford Guy. The Stricken Land. New York: Doubleday & Co., 1947.

Urrutia, Miguel. The Rise of the Colombian Labor Movement. New Haven: Yale university Press, 1969.

Valencia, Luis Emiro, editor. Gaitán: Antología de su pensamiento social y económico. Bogotá: Ediciones Suramericana Ltda., 1968.

Valencia Vega, Alipio. Desarrollo del pensamiento político en Bolivia. La Paz: 1953.

Vargas, Alzira. Getúlio Vargas, meu pai. Rio de Janeiro: Editora Globo, 1960.

Vilaca, Marcos Vinicius, and Roberto de Albuquerque. Coronel, Coroneis. Rio de Janeiro: Tempo Brasileiro, 1965.

Williams, Edward J. Latin American Christian Democratic Parties. Knoxville: University of Tennessee Press, 1967.

Zondag, Cornelius. The Bolivian Economy 1952-1965: The Revolution and Its Aftermath. New York: Frederick A. Praeger, 1966.

PAMPHLETS

Alexander, Robert J. Labor Parties of Latin America. New York: League for Industrial Democracy, 1942.

Figueres, José. Palabras gastadas—democracia, socialismo, libertad. San José, 1943.

──────. Los problemas de la paz y de la guerra, discurso pronunciado por el presidente de Costa Rica, José Figueres, en la reunión de presidentes de América celebrada en Panamá el 22 de julio de 1956. San José, 1956.

Frei, Eduardo. Chile, 1964-1970. Santiago, 1964.

GOVERNMENT AND OFFICIAL PUBLICATIONS

Commonwealth of Puerto Rico, Department of the Treasury. Economy and Finances Puerto Rico 1967. San Juan, 1968.

Diario Oficial de la República de Chile. Sindicación campesina. Santiago, 1967.

Figueres, José. Mensaje del señor presidente de la república don José Figueres y contestación del señor presidente de la asamblea legislativa, lic. don Otto Cortes Hernández, 1 de mayo de 1956. San José, 1956.

———. Mensaje del señor presidente de la república don José Figueres y contestación del señor presidente de la asamblea legislativa, lic. don Otto Fernández, 1 de mayo de 1957. San José, 1957.

———. Estos diez años, discurso pronunciado por el señor presidente de la república don José Figueres de dia 29 de enero de 1958. San José, 1958.

Frei, Eduardo. Quinto mensaje del presidente de la república, don Eduardo Frei Montalva, al inaugurar el período de sesiones ordinarias del congreso nacional, 21 de marzo 1969. Santiago, 1969.

Government Development Bank for Puerto Rico. A Special Report on the Commonwealth of Puerto Rico, February 1965. San Juan, 1965.

República de Venezuela. VI mensaje presidencial presentado por el ciudadano Rómulo Betancourt, presidente constitucional de la república, el 7 de marzo de 1964. Caracas, 1964.

ARTICLES

Abbott, Roger S. "The Role of Contemporary Political Parties in Chile," American Political Science Review, June 1951.

Alexander, Robert J. "Old Quarrels in Havana," New Politics, Summer 1964.

———. "Uruguay's Future Dim, not Dead," Los Angeles Times, September 29, 1968.

Camero, Sergio. "Diversification New Springboard to Growth in Puerto Rico," Investment Dealers' Digest, July 22, 1968. Republished in Government Development Bank for Puerto Rico, Quarterly Report to Investors in Puerto Rican Securities. San Juan, September 1968.

Correa, Antonio. "Boceto histórico del socialismo en Cuba," El polleto (Havana), October 1916.

Friedenburg, Daniel. "Report from Paraguay," New Leader, November 8, 1965.

Gall, Norman. "The Continental Revolution," New Leader, April 12, 1965.

Iglesias, Santiago. "The Workers of Porto Rico Build a Great Socialist Party," New Leader, January 21, 1933.

⎯⎯⎯⎯. "Porto Rican Masses Reach to Socialism for Freedom," New Leader, February 20, 1936.

Kantor, Harry. "The Struggle for Democracy in Costa Rica," South Atlantic Quarterly, January 1956.

Kruning, Martin. "Cost Rica's Elections," Latin American Times, August 16, 1965.

Maiztegui, Humberto. "Las elecciones en Uruguay," Boletín del Buro coordinator de la Internacional socialista en América Latina, Fourth Trimester 1966.

Maurín, Joaquín. "Costa Rica y su presidente Figueres," Cuadernos (Paris), April 1955.

Reynes, Leandro A. "Cuarenta años de acción," in Anuario socialista 1937. Buenos Aires, 1937.

Thome, Joseph R. "A Brief Survey of the Chilean Agrarian Reform Program," Land Tenure Center Newsletter (University of Wisconsin, Madison), September 1968-February 1969.

Zamora, Oscar. "Bolivian CP (M-L) Rebuts Castro," World Revolution (quarterly of Progressive Labor Party, New York), January-March 1969.

PARTY PUBLICATIONS

Acción Nacional. Acción nacional: Principios de doctrina. Mexico City, 1939.

⎯⎯⎯⎯. Partido acción nacional: XIV convención nacional. Mexico City, 1959.

Partido Accion Revolucionaria. "Declaración de principios y bases fundamentales del programa político del 'PAR' aprobados en sesión plenaria de la convención nacional celebrada el 16 de noviembre de 1946. Guatemala City, 1946. (Mimeographed.)

Partido Comunista (Trotskyite faction in Chile). En defensa de la revolución—informes, tesis y documentos presentados al congreso nacional del partido comunista a verificarse el 19 de marzo de 1933. Santiago: Editorial Luís E. Recabarren, 1933.

Partido del Pueblo Cubano (Ortodoxo). Doctrina del partido ortodoxo— independencia económica, libertad política, justicia social. Havana, 1951.

Partido Demócrata Cristiano. Su compromiso con Chile: Síntesis de El programa. Santiago, 1964.

_____. Ud. decide. Santiago, 1964.

Partido Liberación Nacional. "Programa ideológico del Partido liberación nacional." Undated. (Mimeographed.)

Partido Social Demócrata. Estatuto constitucional del partido social Demócrata, fundado el 11 de marzo de 1945. San José, n.d.

Partido Socialista. Anuario socialista. Annual publication of Argentina Socialist Party in 1920s and 1930s.

Partido Socialista de Trabajadores. El camino del pueblo—resoluciones del tercer congreso general del partido socialista de Trabajadores, 1 al 3 de mayo de 1942. Santiago, 1942.

Pereigão, Res. Manifesto do partido socialista brasileiro. Rio de Janeiro, 1933.

Saa, Napoleón Humberto. Informe que el compañero Napoleón Humberto Saa, secretario general del partido socialista ecuatoriano, presenta al V congreso del partido. Quito: Editora Moderna, 1938.

NEWSPAPERS AND PERIODICALS

Acción Social. Monthly publication of Grupo Socialista de la CTM, and subsequently of the Grupo Socialista de la república Mexicana. 1930s to early 1950s.

Acción Socialista. Socialist monthly in Havana. 1920s through early 1950s.

American Political Science Review. Quarterly periodical of American Political Science Association.

Boletín del Buro coordinador de la Internacional socialista en América Latina. Published in Montevideo under official auspices of the Socialist International. Humberto Maiztegui, editor. 1950s and and 1960s.

Boletín informativo demócrata cristiano. Monthly publication of Centro de Acción Demócrata Cristiana, New York. 1960s.

CGT. Organ of Confederción General del Trabajo of Paseo Colón, Buenos Aires. After 1968.

Communist International. Official publication of the Communist International. 1920s until dissolution of Comintern in 1943.

Construction—journal haïtien. Official publication of Mouvement d'Organization du Pays, New York. 1950s and 1960s.

Daily Information Bulletin of Office of Coordinator of Inter American Affairs. Organ of U.S. agency delaing with Latin America during World War II.

Daily Worker. Official organ of the Communist Party of the United States.

Dece. Organ of Latin American Christian Democratic parties, Santiago. 1960s.

El mercurio. Daily newspaper (more or less) of Liberal Party orientation, Santiago.

El nacional. Daily newspaper of Caracas, independent but on Left.

El siglo. Daily newspaper of Communist Party of Chile, Santiago.

Excelsior. Largest daily newspaper of Mexico City.

Hemisphérica. Monthly newsletter of Inter American Association for Democracy and Freedom, New York. 1950s and 1960s.

Hispanic American Report. Excellent monthly survey of events in Latin America, published by Institute of Hispanic-American and Luso-Brazilian Studies of Stanford University. Suspended publication in 1964.

Hispano Americano. Weekly news magazine, Mexico City.

Información democrática cristiana. Monthly periodical of Christian Democratic Union of Central Europe, New York. 1950s and early 1960s.

"Intercontinental Press." Trotskyite (Socialist Workers Party) weekly mimeographed newsletter on international affairs. 1960s.

"International Information." Mimeographed newsletter of Labor and Socialist International. 1920s and 1930s.

International Socialist Review. Magazine of Trotskyite Socialist Workers Party of United States, New York. 1950s.

Izquierda. Weekly publication issued by Uruguayan Socialist Party after suppression of El sol in December 1967.

La mañana. Daily newspaper of Montevideo.

La república. Pro-Acción Democrática daily newspaper, Caracas. 1960s.

La revue socialiste. French Socialist monthly, before World War I, founded by Benoit Malon.

Labor Action. Weekly paper of Workers Party and subsequently of Independent Socialist League, dissident U.S. Trotskyite group. 1940s and 1950s.

"Land Tenure Center Newsletter." Mimeographed publication of Land Tenure Center of University of Wisconsin.

Latin American Digest. Published by Latin American Center at Arizona State University.

Le mouvement socialiste. French Socialist publication before World War I.

New Leader. At first Socialist, then liberal, weekly, New York. After 1925.

New Masses. Weekly magazine of U.S. Communist Party. 1930s and 1940s.

New Politics. Independent Socialist quarterly, New York. 1960s.

New York Times. New York City daily newspaper.

"Orientación." Mimeographed bulletin of Socialismo Auténtico, Montevideo. 1960s.

Peking Review. English-language weekly issued in Peking, carrying extensive information on pro-Peking Communist parties in Latin America.

Revista marxista. Official organ of pro-Chinese Partido Comunista Revolucionario of Chile, Santiago. 1960s.

Socialist International Information. Newsletter of Socialist International, London. After 1951.

The Call. Daily newspaper of U.S. Socialist Party, New York. Suspended in 1924.

The Newsletter. Organ of Socialist Labor League, "Healyite" faction of Fourth International, London. 1960s.

Tribuna febrerista. Official organ of Partido Revolucionario Febrerista of Paraguay, published in Montevideo.

Venezuela Up-to-Date. Official publication of Venezuelan Embassy, Washington, D.C.

World Revolution. Periodical of U.S. Progressive Labor Party dealing particularly with pro-Chinese Communist parties in various parts of the world.

"Yugoslav Facts and Views." Mimeographed periodical of Yugoslav Information Service, New York.

UNPUBLISHED MATERIAL

Hewitt, Ashley Cooper, Jr. "Ecuadorean Political Parties." Manuscript written at Columbia University, 1964.

Love, Joseph LeRoy, Jr. "Rio Grande do Sul as a Source of Political Unstability in Brazil's Old Republic, 1909-1932." Ph.D. dissertation, Columbia University, 1967.

Margiotta, Franklin. "The Mexican Military: A Case Study in Non-intervetion." M.A. thesis, Georgetown University, Washington, D.C., June 1968.

Reischauer, Robert. "The Rise and Fall of the Partido Laborista Mexicano." Manuscript written at Columbia University, 1964.

Yegrós, Elpidio. "Frente a la tiranía," n.d. (Mimeographed.)

YEARBOOKS

American Labor Year Book. Socialist-inclined annual publication of Rand School Press. World War I until early 1930s.

Political Handbook of the World. Annual publication of Council on Foreign Relations.

THROWAWAYS

Al pueblo de Bolivia. Manifesto of Falange Socialista Boliviana, signed by Mario Gutiérrez. March 1957.

El Partido socialista contesta al Partido comunista. Montevideo, 1956.

Informe del Comité administrativo del Centro León Blum a sus afiliados, a la militancia socialista y a la opinión publica. Montevideo, July 25, 1961.

Por qué Copei no asiste a la constituyente. Issued by Partido Copei to explain why it did not participate in Pérez Jiménez' constitutional assembly. Caracas, January 9, 1953. .

Unión de Trabajadores de Chile. "Resumen de la declaración de principios y plataforma de Lucha." Santiago, 1968. (Mimeographed.)

INTERVIEWS

Acuña, Juan. Former secretary-general, Confederación Sindical Uruguaya. Montevideo, June 4, 1968.

BIBLIOGRAPHY

Aponte González, Elio. Secretary-general, of Comité Pro-Federación de Trabajadores Organizados de Venezuela (CONFETROV), Copei trade union group during Pérez Jiménez dictatorship. Caracas, July 22, 1952.

Aramburu, Pedro E. Former president of Argentina. Buenos Aires, June 7, 1968.

Barría, Domingo. Secretary-general, Federación Sindical de Trabajadores de Panamá. Panama City, July 7, 1967.

Betancourt, Rómulo. Twice president of Venezuela. Piscataway, New Jersey, August 11, 1957; New York, November 11, 1957.

Bielich, Ismael. Partido Demócrata Cristiano member of Peruvian Chamber of Deputies. Maracay, Venezuela, April 25, 1970.

Brouwer, José. Socialist member of Panamanian National Assembly. Caracas, July 24, 1947; Panama City, July 26, 1948.

Caldera, Rafael, and Edecio La Riva. Leaders of Partido Copei. Caracas, July 28, 1947. With Caldera, secretary-general of Copei and subsequently president of Venezuela. Caracas, July 22, 1952; July 25, 1954.

Caonabo, Javier. Secretary-General, Partido Revolucionario Social Cristiano. Santo Domingo, August 18, 1970.

Carías Andino, Tiburcio. Former president of Honduras. Tegucigalpa, June 23, 1957.

Cascardo, Heroclinio. Former Tenente, national secretary, Partido Socialista Brasileiro in 1930s. Rio de Janeiro, February 3, 1966.

Cornejo Chávez, Hector. President, Partido Democrático Cristiano, Peru. Madison, Wisconsin, March 15, 1963.

Cortés, José Pinhairo. Member, São Paulo state executive committee, Partido Demócrata Cristão. São Paulo, July 7, 1954.

De la Rosa, Diógenes. Socialist member, Panamanian National Assembly. Panama City, July 26, 1948.

De Leon Schlotter, René Armando. Member, Executive Committee, Movimiento de Democracia Cristiana, Guatemala. Guatemala City, July 15, 1967.

Echegaray, Mariano, and Cleofe Tupac Yupanque de Saenz. National secretary and Head of Women and Children's Section, Secretariat of Indian and Peasant Affairs, Partido Aprista Peruano, respectively. Lima, June 21, 1947.

Fignolé, Daniel. President of Haiti, 1957. Port-au-Prince, June 25, 1948; July 20, 1952; New York, June 19, 1957; May 5, 1959.

Freitas, Alejandro, and Ramón Mayora. Secretary of organization and general secretary, respectively, Partido Socialista de Trabajadores. Caracas, August 1, 1947.

García, Antonio. Founder of Partido Popular Socialista, Colombia. Bogotá, July 10, 1947.

García Bauer, José. Early leader, Guatemalan Christian Democratic Party. Guatemala City, July 20, 1953.

Gassagnol, Paul. President of Parti Populaire Sociale Chrétien, Haiti. Port-au-Prince, August 29, 1949.

Gutiérrez, Juan Manuel. Partido Liberal Independiente member of Nicaraguan Chamber of Deputies. Managua, June 28, 1967.

Jaramillo, Francisco de Paula. Leader of Partido Social Democrático Cristiano, Colombia. Bogotá, July 28, 1968.

Larraín, Padre Rafael. Director, Instituto de Educación Rural. Santiago, July 19, 1968.

Larrea Benalcazar, Hugo. Former leader, Partido Socialista Ecuatoriano and Partido Socialista Revolucionario. Quito, July 4, 1966.

Lazcano Soruco, Francisco. Leader of Partido de Unificación Republicana Socialista. La Paz, June 3, 1947.

Martínez, Hipólito. Assistant press secretary, Partido Revolucionario Social Cristiano, Dominican Republic. Santo Domingo, March 13, 1967.

Mederos, Luisa Viegas de. Partido Demócrata Cristão member of state legislature, Pernambuco. Recife, February 22, 1956.

Méndez Montenagro, Julio César. President of Guatemala. Guatemala City, June 16, 1967.

Mendivil, Lucio. Partido Obrero Revolucionario member of Senate. La Paz, May 28, 1947.

Monterosa Méndez, Isaac. Member, Directiva Nacional, Partido Revolucionario. Guatemala City, June 17, 1967.

Navarro, Gustavo (Tristán Marof). Precursor of Trotskyism in Bolivia, head of Partido Socialista Obrero Boliviano. La Paz, May 26, 1947.

Olivares Silva, Jaime. Member, National Executive, Partido Democracia Radical, Chile. Bogotá, January 1, 1970.

Pedrosa, Mario. Editor, Vanguarda socialista. Rio de Janeiro, August 14, 1946.

Peralta, Manuel. Student leader, Partido Revolucionario Social Cristiano, Dominican Republic. Santo Domingo, July 31, 1968.

Pereira, Astrogildo. Historian, Communist Party, Brazil. Rio de Janeiro, October 19, 1965.

Pérez, Romeo. Member, International Secretariat, Partido Demócrata Cristiano, Uruguay. Montevideo, June 3, 1968.

Péron, Juan. Former president of Argentina. Madrid, September 1, 1960.

Polas Aguero, Carlos. Departmental agent, Instituto de Bienestar Rural. Pedro Juan Caballero, Paraguay, November 26, 1965.

Porras, Demetrio. Former head, Panamanian Socialist Party and member of Supreme Court. Panama City, July 7, 1967.

Prío Socarras, Carlos. Former president of Cuba. Havana, January 12, 1959.

Quesada, Luís. Leader, Partido Liberal Independiente, Nicaragua, and former minister of finance. Managua, August 3, 1948.

Quiroga, Luís. Falange Nacional member, Executive Committee, Central Unica de Trabajadores de Chile. New Brunswick, N.J., February 17, 1954.

Rámos Giménez, Raúl. Secretary-general, Acción Democrática (Oposición), Caracas, August 2, 1962.

Ricketts, Patricio. One of the founders of Partido Popular Cristiano, Peru. New Brunswick, N.J., April 9, 1968.

Rojas Fraga, Jaime. Trade union secretary, Falange Nacional. Santiago, January 19, 1947.

Román Díaz, Juan. Leader, Movimiento Político 14 Junio, Dominican Republic. Caracas, September 12, 1961.

Rosario, Antonio. President, Partido Revolucionario Social Cristiano, Dominican Republic. Santo Domingo, July 11, 1964.

Salazar, Jorge. Leader, Trotskyite Partido Obrero Revolucionario. La Paz, August 13, 1952.

Salazar Alvarado, Francisco. President, Partido Conservador, Ecuador. Quito, July 4, 1966.

Silva, Ramón. Director, Instituto Nacional de Estudios Sindicales, Venezuela. New Brunswick, N.J., May 9, 1962; Caracas, August 4, 1962.

Sotuyo. Member, National Executive Committee, Partido Demócrata Cristiano, Uruguay. Montevideo, June 3, 1968.

Valencia, Luís Emiro. Leader, Partido Popular Socialista, Colombia. Bogotá, September 12, 1956; July 8, 1966.

Vandor, Augusto. Secretary-general, of Unión Obrera Metalúrgica. Buenos Aires, June 22, 1956.

Villanueva, Armando. Secretary-general, Partido Aprista Peruano. Lima, July 11, 1966.

Yegros, Elpidio. Former secretary-general, Partido Revolucionario Febrerista, Paraguay. Caracas, March 11, 1964; La Catalina, Costa Rica, July 3, 1967.

INDEX OF PEOPLE AND PARTIES

AAA. See Frente Democrático AAA
Ação Integralista Brasileira, 429-32, 441, 445, 461
Acción Democrática (Costa Rica), 219
Acción Democratica (Venezuela), xviii, 32-34, 162-64, 177-78, 197-216, 259-60, 280, 290, 338-51, 399-400, 411, 419-20, 423
Acción Democrática en Gobierno, 213
Acción Democrática en Oposición, 213, 346
Acción Nacional (Chile), 42
Acción Nacional (Mexico). See Partido Acción Nacional
Acción Popular, 9-11, 191-94, 358
Acción Sindical Chilena, 320, 322
Acción Social Demócrata, 366
Acción Socialista Group, 167-68
Acuña, Juan, 145-47
AD. See Acción Democrática
Agramonte, Roberto, 283, 289-90
Agrarian Labor Party. See Partido Agrario Laborista
Agrupação Renovadora Nacional, 463-64
Agrupación Revolucionaria Nacionalista Ecuatoriana, 13
Agrupación Socialista Obrera, 145
Aguilar, Andrés, 345
Aguilúz, Marcial, 229
Aguirre, Francisco, 285
Aguirre Cerda, Pedro, 41, 72, 96, 98-99, 128-29, 131, 319, 327, 432-33
Alamán, Lucas, 49
Albizu Campos, Pedro, 256
Alcantara Herrán, Pedro, 59
Alem, Leandro, 82
Alemán, Miguel, 52, 267-68, 271, 275, 438
Alende, Oscar, 93, 477
Alessandri, Arturo, 25, 40-42, 71, 96-99, 124-25, 127-28, 132, 135, 319, 321, 323, 329, 432-33
Alessandri, Fernando, 41, 72, 132, 320
Alessandri, Jorge, 42, 101-02, 135, 323-24, 329, 335-36

Alfaro, Eloy, 23, 27
Alfonso, Pedro, 101, 321
Alianza Liberal, 71
Alianza Nacional Popular, 63
Alianza Popular Revolucionaria Americana. See Partido Aprista Peruano
Alkmin, José María, 450, 453
Allende, Salvador, 42, 101-02, 124, 131, 134-37, 321, 323-28, 335-37, 425-26
Almazán, Juan Andreu, 51, 274
Almeida, Clodomiro, 136
Alonso, José, 477-81
Altamirano, Carlos, 136
Alvarez, Luís, H., 52
Alvear, Marcelo T. de, 84, 86, 113
Alvim, Hugo Panasco, 297
Alzate Avendaño, Gilberto, 62-3
Ampuero, Raúl, 133-37
ANAPO. See Alianza Nacional Popular
Andrade, Víctor, 249
APRA. See Partido Aprista Peruano
APRA Rebelde, 424
Aprista Party. See Partido Aprista Peruano
Aramburu, Pedro, 18, 89, 121, 473-75
Arana, Francisco, 222, 303
Arana, Osorio, Carlos, 306, 361
Araujo Hidalgo, Manuel, 13
Araya, Bernardo, 132, 320
Arbenz, Jacobo, 54, 302-04, 360-61, 376, 383
ARENA. See Agrupação Renovadora Nacional
Arévalo, Juan, 168
Arévalo, Juan José, 222, 301-04, 360-61
Arguello, Fernando, 58
Arias, Arnulfo, 14-15, 165
Arosemena, Carlos, 13, 66, 154
Arroyo del Río, Carlos, 11-12, 37-38, 152, 378
ARS. See Acción Democrática en Oposición
Arze, José Antonio, 39, 235
Asociación National de Ex-Combatientes, 309
Avalleneda, Nicolás, 75, 80, 108
Avalos, Eduardo, 86
Avila Camacho, Manuel, 51, 267, 271, 274-75, 377, 438
Ayala, Eusebio, 46

523

Báez, Cecilio, 26
Bakunin, Michael, 107, 140
Balaguer, Joaquín, 291-92, 298-300, 362-63
Balbín, Ricardo, 87-90, 474
Baldomir, Alfredo, 16, 44, 77, 144
Balmaceda, José Manuel, 25, 40, 70, 96
Ballivian Rojas, Hugo, 238
Banzer, Hugo, 249, 364, 437
Baptista, Mariano, 67
Barrientos, René, 247-50, 363, 436
Barrios, Gonzalo, 34, 164, 212, 348
Barrios, Justo Rufino, 20-21, 54
Barros, Adhemar de, 17-18, 455-56, 463
Barros Borgoño, Luís, 71
Batista, Fulgencio, 168, 229, 281-86, 289, 368, 376-79, 391, 402-03, 413
Batlle Berres, Luís, 16-17, 44-45
Batlle y Ordóñez, José, 16-26, 43-45, 77-78, 140-41
Batlle Pacheco, César, 16-17, 45
Beaujon, Andrés, 349
Bedoya Reyes, Luís, 194, 358-59
Belaúnde Terry, Fernando, 9-11, 186, 189-94, 358
Benavides, Oscar, 185-86
Benn, Brindley, 407
Bernardes, Arturo, 462
Bernardes, Arturo, Jr., 462
Betancourt, Rómulo, 33-34, 163, 197-200, 202-16, 260, 293, 339, 343-47, 350, 399, 400, 415, 419-20, 423
Bilbao, Francisco, 96, 123
"Black" Communists. See Union Popular (Venezuela)
Blanco, Hugo, 395
Bolívar, Simón, 21-22, 65
Bordaberry, Juan María, 150
Borges de Madeiros, Augusto, 444
Borges, Mauro, See Teixeira, Mauro Borges
Borghi, Hugo, 15-16, 460
Borlenghi, Angel, 471
Borregales, Germán, 210, 212
Bosch, Juan, 260, 290-301, 362, 425
Bossay, Luís, 101
Braga, Ney, 355-56
Braendler-Thalheimer Group, 396
Bravo, Douglas, 420, 426
Bravo, Mario, 113
Brizola, Leonel, 458-59, 461
Brouwer, José, 165

Bukharin, Nicholas, 396
Bulnes, Manuel, 70
Burelli, Miguel Angel, 34, 212, 348
Busch, Germán, 39, 68, 234, 236, 391
Bustamante y Rivero, José, 186-88
Bustamante, William Alexander, 293

Caamaño, Francisco Alberto, 297, 299, 362
Caballero, Bernardino, 79
Caballeros, Jorge Lucas, 361
Café Filho, João, 451-52, 455
Caffrey, Jefferson, 281
Caldera, Rafael, 34, 164, 205, 210, 212, 338-40, 342-46, 348, 419-20
Calderón Guardia, Rafael, 218, 220-22, 226, 229-30
Calles, Plutarco Elías, 51, 169-70, 264-65, 437
Camargo Neto, Affonso, 355
Camero, Sergio, 255
Camisas, Doradas, 437
Campa, Valentin, 397-98
Campos, Francisco, 431
Campos, Milton, 355, 457
Capanema, Gustavo, 450
Cárdenas, Lázaro, 51-52, 170, 264-68, 274-75, 377, 394, 398-99, 437
Cardoso, José P., 144
Carias Andino, Tiburcio, 5, 28, 54-56
Carnevali, Alberto, 202
Carranza, Venustiano, 269
Carrera, Rafael, 53-54
Carrillo Puerto, Felipe, 168
Casals, Pablo, 257
Casanova, Baudillo, 136
Castelo Branco, Humberto, 17-18, 160, 355-56, 449, 453-54, 459, 462-63
Castilhos, Julio de., 444
Castillo Armas, Carlos, 304, 361
Castillo, Jaime, 335
Castillo, Luciano, 155-56
Castillo, Ramón, 291
Castillo, Ramón S., 76, 86, 235, 476
Castro Cervantes, Fernando, 221, 227
Castro, Cipriano, 22
Castro, Fidel, 28, 62, 121, 135-36, 139, 147-49, 154, 156, 158, 191, 212, 216, 229, 270, 275, 285-87 289-90, 318, 368, 373, 378-79, 386-87, 390-91, 406, 412-27

Centro Leon Blum, 148
Cerro, Francisco, 354
Cespedes, Carlos Manuel de, 280
Chamorro, Emiliano, 58
Charnaud Macdonald, Augusto, 302
Chaves, Federico, 46, 79
Chávez, Ñuflo, 242, 243
Chibás, Eduardo, 288-89
Chinese Communists, 136, 139
Chonchol, Jacques, 335
Cline, Howard, 51-52, 437-38
Club La Gloria, 167
Codovilla, Victorio, 113, 385, 401-02
Comintern. See Communist International
Comité de Organización Revolucionario, 310
Communist Information Bureau, 385
Communist International, 125, 127, 129, 140-41, 151-52, 155, 166, 169, 182-83, 197-98, 338, 373-76, 384-85, 387, 389, 396-98, 419
Communist Party, China, 404-09
Communist Party, India, 169
Communist Party, Soviet Union, 383, 388
Communist Party, United States, 396
Communist Party, Yugoslavia, 396
Comonfort, Ignacio, 49
Concentración de Fuerzas Populares, 38, 280
Concentración Patriótica Nacional, 165
Concentración Revolucionaria Febrerista, 310
Concentration of Popular Forces. See Concentración de Fuerzas Populares.
Concha, Malaquias, 123
Concordancia, 76
Contreras Labarca, Carlos, 389
Cooke, Juan William, 87
Copei. See Partido Social Cristiano Copei
Cordova, Andrés, 13
Cornejo Chávez, Hector, 357-59
Cortes, León, 218
Costa e Silva, Arthur, 463-64
Crespo Toral, Jorge, 13
Crispim, José María, 397
Cristeros, 437
Cruz, Coke, Eduardo, 41, 72-73, 320, 323
Cruz, Ramón, 30, 57
Cuban Socialists, 167-68
Cunha, Pedro da., 159

Dantas, San Thiago, 458
Dávila, Carlos, 126
Debray, Régis, 409, 416-19, 422, 425
De Gaulle, Charles, xv
Dejoie, Louis, 308
Delgado Chalbaud, Carlos, 33, 201, 341
Democracia Radical, 102
Democratic Front. See Frende Democrático.
Democratic Party. See Partido Democrático (Costa Rica).
Díaz, Adolfo, 58
Díaz, Martínes, Juan, 127
Díaz Ordaz, Gustavo, 268, 273, 275-78
Díaz, Porfirio, 20-21, 50, 168
Directorio Liberal National, 37
Directorio Liberal Revolucionario, 37
Directorio Revolucionario, 413
Di Tella, Guido, 353
Domenech, José, 117-18
Donoso, Ricardo, 71
Duarte, Luis Napoleón, 360
Duhalde, Alfredo, 99, 132
Durán Cano, Ricardo, 148
Durán, Julio, 40, 101-02, 325-27
Dutra, Eurico Gaspar, 446-47, 450, 455-56, 460
Duvalier, François, 308, 369

Echandi, Mario, 226, 229-30
Echeverria, Esteban, 107
Echeverria, Luis, 53, 278
Ecuadorean Liberals. See Partido Liberal Radical
Eder, George, 242
Edwards, Alberto, 70
Eguigueren, Luis Antonio, 185
Eisenhower, Dwight, xv
Ejercito de Liberación Nacional, 423, 425
Elio, Tomás Manuel, 39, 69
Encina, Dionisio, 397
Escalante, Anibal, 413
Escalante, Diógenes, 199
Escovar Salom, Ramón, 163
Esquerda Democrática, 160
Estigarribia, José Félix, 46
Estimé, Dumarsais, 306-07, 367
Estrada Cabrera, Manuel, 21
Ewert, Arthur, 385

Facio, Rodrigo, 218, 220
Falange Española Tradicionalista, 428-29, 433-34

Falange Nacional, 72-73, 319-23, 356
Falange Nacional Conservadora, 318-19
Falange Socialista Boliviana, xviii, 241, 249, 363, 369, 429, 433-37
FAR. See Fuerzas Armadas Revolucionarias
Farrell, Edelmiro, 86
Fascist Party, 428-29
Federación Indígena, 152
Federación Libre, 171
Federación Obrera Regional Peruana, 180
Federación Socialista, 168
Federales (Argentina), 74-75
Fernández Artucio, Hugo, 144
Fernández, Lorenzo, 340, 345, 349
Ferrari, Francisco, 355, 457, 459, 461
Ferré, Luis, 257, 261
Fiallo, Viriato, 293
Fidanza, Alfredo, 118
Fignolé, Daniel, 306-08
Figueres, José, 220-22, 224, 226-29, 231, 259-60, 293, 366, 411, 424
First International. See International Workingmen's Association
Fitzgibbon, Russell, 150
Fiuza, Yeddo, 447
Flores, Juan José, 22, 65
Flores, Luis A., 185
Fortun Sanjines, F., 247-48
Fortuny, José Manuel, 302
14th of June Movement. See Movimiento 14 de Junio
Fourth International, 391, 394-395
Framini, Andrés, 471, 476, 481
France e Silva, Dr., 158
Francia, José Gaspar Rodriguez de., 26
Franco, Francisco, 339
Franco, Montoro, André, 356
Franco, Rafael, 46, 309-11
Frei, Eduardo, 42, 73, 101, 124, 136, 316, 318-19, 323, 325-37
Freire, Ramón, 24
Freitas, Alejandro, 163
Frente Cívico, 359
Frente Democrático AAA, 284-86
Frente Democrático (Chile), 42
Frente Democrático (Peru), 186. See also Partido Aprista Peruano.
Frente Democrático Popular, 210, 212
Frente Electoral Independiente, 201-02, 341

Frente de Izquierda, 97
Frente Izquierda Revolucionaria, 395
Frente Nacional, 36-37, 62-64
Frente Nacional Democrático, 34, 163, 211-12
Frente Popular, 41
Frente Popular Libertador, 301-03
Frente Popular Velasquista, 13
Frigerio, 353
Frondizi, Arturo, 88-95, 121, 353, 474-78, 482
Frugoni, Emilio, 140, 142-45, 148
Fuenmayor, Juan Bautista, 399-400
Fuentes Pieruccini, Mario, 361
Fuerzas Armadas de Liberación Nacional, 420
Fuerzas Armadas Revolucionarias, 421, 425

Gaitán, Gloria, 157-58
Gaitán, Jorge Eliécer, 35, 60, 157-58
Galich, L. F., 304
Gallego Anda, Elías, 13
Gallegos, Rómulo, 33, 199, 201, 340, 400
Gálvez, Juan Manuel, 28, 55-56
García, Antonio, 156-58
García Bauer, José, 360
García Godoy, Hector, 298, 362
Garcia Moreno, Gabriel, 23, 53, 65
Garreton, Manuel, 318
Gay, Luís, 468
George, Henry, 156
Gestido (General), 45
Ghioldi, Américo, 116
Ghioldi, Rodolfo, 385
Giménez Landínez, Vicente, 340, 345
Godoy Urrutia, César, 130-31
Goes Monteiro, Pedro Aurelio, 446
Gomes, Eduardo, 446-47, 451
Gómez, Alejandro, 89, 92
Gómez, Alvaro, 62
Gómez, Eugenio, 142
Gómez, Juan Vicente, 5, 22, 27-28 32, 163, 177, 197-98, 200, 338
Gómez, Laureano, 36, 60-63, 157
Gómez, Luís, 397
Gómez Morín, Manuel, 51-52
González Hinojosa, Manuel, 51
González Luna, Efraín, 51-53, 438
González Moscoso, Hugo, 394
González, Natalicio, 46, 79
González Prada, 183
González Videla, Gabriel, 41-42, 72, 99-100, 132-34, 320, 327

González von Maree, Jorge, 432-33
Goulart, João, 17, 161-62, 355, 383, 395, 405, 449, 452-53, 456-60
Grabois, Mauricio, 405
Gracidas, Carlos, 170
Grau San Martín, Ramón, 168, 177, 281-88, 390-91
Grechko, Andrei, 426
Grove, Marmaduque, 72, 97-98, 126-31, 389
Grupo Socialista de la CTM, 170
Grupo Socialista de la República Mexicana, 170
Grupo Tupac Amaru, 391
Guachalla, Fernando, 39
Guarello, Angel, 123
Guevara, Ernesto "Che", 215, 268, 406, 409, 414, 416, 418, 421-22, 425
Guevara Arce, Walter, 234, 244-45, 249
Guido, José Maria, 76, 92-93, 476
Gumucio, Rafael, 335
Gutiérrez Guerra, Jose, 68
Gutiérrez Gutierrez, Mario R., 436
Guzman Blanco, Antonio, 22

Haberman, Robert, 168-169
Hamilton, Alexander, 49
Haya de la Torre, Víctor Raúl, 10, 181-89, 192-95, 260, 282
Henríquez Guzmán, Miguel, General, 275
Hernández, Alejandro, 164, 212
Hernández Colón, Rafael, 261
Herrera, Campins, Luis, 349
Herrera, Luis Alberto, 78, 144
Herring, Hubert, 21-25, 37, 40, 49, 53, 57, 65, 68-69
Hertzog, Enrique, 39, 69, 237
Hevia, Carlos, 283, 287
Hewitt, Ashley, 11, 13
Hidalgo, Manuel, 124, 389-90
Hurtado Cruchaga, Alberto, 320, 322

Ibáñez, Bernardo, 72, 99, 127, 129, 131-32, 320
Ibáñez, Carlos, 40-42, 71-72, 97-99, 101, 125-26, 128, 134-35, 318-19, 321, 323, 325, 388-89, 432-33
Iberlucea, Enrique, 112
Iglesias, Santiago, 171-73
Illia, Arturo, 18, 93-94, 122, 354, 477, 479

Imbert, Antonio, 299
Independent Nationalists, 146
Independent Socialists (Argentina), See Partido Socialiste Independiente
Insular Labor Party, 171
International Workingmen's Association, 140
Intransigencia Nacional, 88
Intransigencia y Renovación, 88-89
Intransigentes (Argentina). See Union Civica Radical Intransigente
Irigoyen, Hipólito, 75-76, 82-85, 112, 114
Iturralde, Abel, 68

James, Daniel, 382
Jaunarena, Mario, 145
Johnson, Lyndon, 293
Juárez, Benito, 20, 49-50, 438
Juárez Celman, Miguel, 82
Julião, Francisco, 162
Junco, Sandalio, 390
Justo, Augustín, 76, 85, 115
Justo, Juan B., 107-09, 111, 113, 116

Kantor, Harry, 186
Kelly, Guillermo Patricio, 478
Khrushchev, Nikita, 136
Kropotkin, Peter, 107
Kruning, Martin, 229
Kubitschek, Juscelino, xx, 354, 447-48, 452-53, 457-58

Labor and Socialist International. See Socialist International
Labor Party, Great Britain, 146
Laborde, Hernán, 397-98
Lacerda, Carlos, 447, 449
Laferte, Elias, 389
Lanusse, Alejandro, 93, 122, 481
Lara Lena, José, 339
La Riva, Edecio, 341
Larrain, Rafael, 322
Larralde, Crisólogo, 88
Larrázabal, Wolfgang, 33, 203, 205, 210, 212, 344-45
Latcham, Ricardo, 130
Lavalle, Hernán, 189-90
Lazcano Sorruco, Francisco, 166
League of Communists of Yugoslavia, 397
Lechín, Juan, 234, 236-37, 239, 243-49, 392-93

Mosca, Enrique, 87
Moscoso, Teodoro, 260
Mosquera (archbishop), 21
Mosquera, Tomás Cipriano de, 21, 59
Mouvement d'Organization du Pays. See Mouvement Ouvrier Paysan
Mouvement Ouvrier Paysan, 280, 306-08
Mouvement Républicaine Populaire, 340
Movimento Democrático Brasileiro, 463-64
Movimento Trabalhista Nacional, 457, 461
Movimiento Acción Popular Unitaria, 335
Movimiento Cívico Cristiano, 356
Movimiento de Acción Nacional, 210, 212
Movimiento de Democracia Cristiana, 360-61
Movimiento de Integración y Desarrollo, 94
Movimiento de la Izquierda Revolucionaria (Chile), 136, 425
Movimiento de la Izquierda Revolucionaria (Peru), 156, 191, 422, 424
Movimiento de la Izquierda Revolucionaria (Venezuela), 119, 208-09, 212-13, 215, 345, 350, 414-15, 419-20, 423-24
Movimiento de Liberación Nacional (Tupamaros), 357
Movimiento Demócrata Cristiano (Cuba), 368
Movimiento Demócrata Cristiano (Panama), 366
Movimiento Democrático Pradista, 8
Movimiento Democrático Progresista, 8
Movimiento Electoral del Pueblo, 34, 164, 212, 215, 348
Movimiento 14 de Junio, 292, 425
Movimiento Nacionalista Revolucionario, xvii, 27, 39-40, 68-69, 167, 177-78, 233-50, 280, 363, 392-94, 435-37
Movimiento Obrero Comunista, 402
Movimiento Popular Demócrata Cristiano, 366
Movimiento Pro Independencia, 259
Movimiento Republicano Progresista, 163
Movimiento Revolucionario Pazestenssorista, 249
Movimiento Revolucionario Peronista, 478
Movimiento Social Demócrata Cristiano (Mexico), 367
Movimiento Social Democrático Cristiano (Paraguay), 364-65
Movimiento 26 de Julio, 229, 285, 289, 412-13
Muñoz Marín, Luís, 172, 251-53, 257, 259-62, 293, 368
Muñoz Rivera, Luis, 251-52
Musalem Saffie, José, 321, 323

National Democrats (Argentina). See Partido Demócrata Nacional
National Republican Party. See Partido Republicano Nacional
National Socialist German Workers Party, 428-29
Nationalist Party. See Partido Nacionalista (Puerto Rico)
Navarro, Gustavo. See Tristán Marof
Negrão de Lima, Francisco, 454
Negrón Lopez, Luis, 261
Neves, Tancredo, 453
Nicaraguan Liberals. See Partido Liberal (Nicaragua)
Nueva Acción Política, 126
Nuevo Partido Progresista, 48, 261
Núñez, Benjamin, 222
Núñez, Rafael, 22, 59-60

Obregón, Alvaro, 169, 263-64, 271
Ocampo, Salvador, 127
Oddone, Jacinto, 109
Odría, Manuel, 8-9, 188-93, 357, 401, 403-04
Oduber, Daniel, 230
Olaya Herrera, Enrique, 34, 60
Ongania, Juan Carlos, 18, 94, 122, 354, 476, 479, 482
Ongaro, Raimundo, 480-81
Ordóñez, Manuel, 353
Organización Demócrata Cristiana de América, 356, 368-69
Oribe, Manuel, 25, 77
Orlich, Francisco, 220, 228-30, 293
Ortiz, Roberto, 85-86
Osborne, Harold, 237
Ospina Pérez, Mariano, 35, 60-64
Ovando, Alfredo, 248, 250, 436

Leguía, Augusto, 155, 177, 181, 183-84
Leighton, Bernardo, 318
Lemus, José María, 359
Lenin, Vladimir, 215, 268
Leonardi, Eduardo, 121, 473
Leoni, Raúl, 34, 205, 209-12, 214-15, 346-47, 350-51, 419-20
Lescot, Elie, 306, 367
Levingston, Roberto, 94
Liga Operaria, 158
Lima, Hermes, 460
Lima, Negrão de, 454
Linhares, José, 447
Linke, Lillo, 12-13, 65-67
Lleras Camargo, Alberto, 35-36, 60, 62, 64
Lleras Restrepo, Carlos, 36-37, 64
Lombardo Toledano, Vicente, 394, 398-99, 402-04
López, Alfonso, 34-35, 60, 64
López, Carlos Antonio, 26
López Contreras, Eleazar, 197-98, 200, 339
López, Francisco Solano, 25-26, 77
López, José Hilario, 21
Lopez Mateos, Adolfo, 52, 268, 271 275
López Michelson, Alfonso, 37
López, Osvaldo, 29, 57
Lora, Francisco Augusto, 363
Lora, Guillermo, 392, 394
Lott, Henrique Teixeira, 162, 452-53, 462
Lovestone, Jay 396
Lozano, Julio 28-29, 56
Ludovico, Pedro. See Teixeira, Pedro Ludovico
Luna, Juan P., 185, 401, 403-04
Luz, Carlos, 452

Machado, Christiano, 451
Machado, Eduardo, 399-400
Machado, Gerardo, 28, 168, 280-81, 390
Machado, Gustavo, 399-401
Madrazo, Carlos, 277
Magalhães, Juracy, 447
Magalhães Pinto, José, 447
Magalhães, Sergio, 459-60
Magloire, Paul, 307-08, 368
Magaño, Ruben, 170
Maia, Prestes, 354
Maiztegui, Humberto, 146
Mao Tse-tung, 268, 417-18

Mapai, Israel, 148
MAPU. See Movimiento Acción Popular Unitaria
Marchant, Anyda, 26
Marianetti, Benito, 116
Mariategui, José Carlos, 155
Marieda, Manuel Maria, 156
Marinello, Juan 168, 378
Maritain, Jacques, 318
Marof, Tristán, 166, 391
Marquez Sterling, Carlos, 282
Marris, Florencio, 165
Martz, John 54-55
Marx, Karl, 140
Matera, Raúl, 353, 477
Matos, Huber, 412
Matte Hurtado, Emilio, 126
Matte Larrain, Arturo, 42, 72, 101, 321
Maximilian (emperor), 50
Mayora, Ramón, 163
Medici, Emilio Garrastazú, 464
Medina, Angarita, Isaias, 32, 198-200, 399
Medrazo, Carlos, 277
Mejía Colindres, T., 55
Melgarejo, Mariano, 23
Méndez Montenegro, Julio César, 305-06, 361, 415, 421
Méndez Montenegro, Mario 303, 306
Mendieta, Carlos, 281, 390
Mendivil, Lucio, 236, 392
Mexican Socialism, 168-70
Miolán, Angel, 290-91, 293, 300
Miquilena, Luis 399
MIR. See Movimiento de Izquierda Revolucionaria (particular countries)
Mitre, Bartolomé, 75, 80, 108
MNR. See Movimiento Nacionalista Revolucionario
Molina Ureña, José Rafael, 297
Molino, José A., 366
Moncada, José María, 58
Monge, Jorge, 366
Monge, Luis Alberto, 230
Monje, Mario, 406
Monteiro, Goes, 431
Montero, Juan Estéban, 41, 72, 97
Montt, Manuel, 70, 123
Mora, Manuel, 217
Morales Carrión, Arturo, 260
Morazán, Francisco, 53- 97
Moreno Martinez, Alfonso, 363
Moreno, Higinio, 46, 79, 310
Morones, Luis N., 169-70, 264-65

Pacheco, Gregorio, 67
Pacheco, Jorge, 45, 150
PADENA. See Partido Democrático Nacional (Chile)
Padilla, Ezequiel, 275
Paez, Federico, 152
Pagán, Boulívar, 172
Paixão, Murcio, 158
Palacios, Alfredo, 110, 113, 121, 166
Palmer, Bruce, 297
PAN. See Partido Acción Nacional (Mexico)
Pando, José Manuel, 24, 68
Paredes, Ricardo, 152
Parodi, Delia de, 477
Parti Social Chrétien, 306-07, 367-68
Parti Socialiste Populaire, 306-07, 376
Partido Acción Cristiana, 368
Partido Acción Nacional (Mexico), xviii, 48, 50-53, 270, 273, 367, 369, 438
Partido Acción Revolucionaria, 301-03
Partido Acción Unitaria, 403
Partido Agrario (Mexico), 263
Partido Agrario Laborista, 321
Partido Aprista (Cuba), 282
Partido Aprista Peruano, xix, 8-11, 155-56, 177, 180-96, 233, 260, 280, 357-58, 411, 424
Partido Aprista Rebelde, 191. See also Movimiento de la Izquierda Revolutionaria
Partido Auténtico (Cuba). See Partido Revolucionario Cubano
Partido Blanco. See Partido Nacional (Uruguay)
Partido Bolchevique Leninista, 390-91
Partido Colorado (Paraguay), 26 46-47, 78-79, 309-10, 312
Partido Colorado (Uruguay), 16-17, 25-26, 28, 43-45, 47, 77-78, 140-43, 150, 357
Partido Colorado Baldomirista, 16
Partido Batllista, 5, 16, 45, 146, 150
Partido Colorado Blancoacevedista, 16
Partido Colorado Riverista, 16
Partido Communista (Argentina), 113, 116-17, 119-20, 382, 385, 396, 401-02, 480
Partido Comunista (Bolivia), 235 241, 248, 378, 405-06, 408, 422, 436
Partido Comunista (Brazil), 4, 16, 27, 161, 375, 382-83, 385, 395-97, 404-05, 429, 441, 445-47, 453-55, 460-61
Partido Comunista (Chile), 41-42, 72, 98-102, 125-36, 138-39, 318-23, 325, 328, 331-36, 375-77, 384, 388-90, 397, 407-08, 414, 432
Partido Comunista (Colombia), 35, 62, 156, 376, 378, 382, 406-07
Partido Comunista (Costa Rica), 197, 217-18, 220-22, 226, 230, 375, 378, 382
Partido Comunista (Cuba, Pre-1961), 167-68, 281-83, 375, 377-78, 382, 390-91, 411
Partido Comunista de Cuba (Post-1965), xx, 407, 413, 446
Partido Comunista (Dominican Republic), 294, 376
Partido Comunista (Ecuador), 12, 38, 151-54, 376, 378, 382, 406
Partido Comunista (El Salvador), 375-76
Partido Comunista (Guatemala), 301-03, 360, 375-76, 382, 383, 414-15, 420
Partido Comunista (Honduras), 375-76
Partido Comunista (Marxista-Leninista), 407
Partido Comunista (Mexico), 170, 375-76, 382-84, 394, 397-99, 404
Partido Comunista (Nicaragua), 376, 378
Partido Comunista (Panama), 164, 166, 376, 378
Partido Comunista (Paraguay), 46, 79, 310
Party Comunista (Peru), 155, 185-86, 191, 375-76, 402, 403, 406
Partido Comunista (Uruguay), 140-50, 357, 375, 378, 382
Partido Comunista (Venezuela), 34, 198, 203, 208-09, 211-13, 338, 342-44, 376, 378, 382, 386, 399-401, 414-15, 419-20, 423-24
Partido Comunista Brasileiro, 405
Partido Comunista do Brasil, 405
Partido Comunista Revolucionario, 407
Partido Concentración Obrera, 396

Partido Conservador (Argentina), 73-75. See also Partido Democrata Nacional
Partido Conservador (Bolivia), 67-69
Partido Conservador (Brazil), 26-27, 48, 442-45
Partido Conservador (Chile), xxi, 24-25, 40-42, 48, 69-73, 96-98, 100-02, 128, 135, 318-20, 323, 326, 330
Partido Conservador (Colombia), xvii-xviii, 21-22, 34-37, 48, 59-64, 365
Partido Conservador (Ecuador), 11-13, 23, 38, 48, 53, 64-67, 152-53
Partido Conservador (Guatemala), 53-54
Partido Conservador (Mexico), 48-50
Partido Conservador (Nicaragua), 30-32, 48, 57-58, 366-67
Partido Conservador Popular, 76, 353, 466-67
Partido Conservador Social Cristiano, 72-73, 320-21, 323
Partido Conservador Tradicionalista, 72-73, 320-21, 323
Partido Cruzada Nacional, 17
Partido de Acción Renovadora, 360
Partido de Fuerza Popular, 438
Partido de Izquierda Christiana, 336
Partido de Izquierda Radical, 102
Partido de Izquierda Revolucionaria, 39, 69, 235, 238, 241, 243-44, 435
Partido de Reconciliación Nacional, 360
Partido de Representação Popular, 431, 445, 461
Partido de Unificación Republicana Socialista, 69
Partido del Pueblo. See Partido Aprista Peruano.
Partido del Pueblo Cubano. See Partido Popular Cubano
Partido de la Revolución Guatemalteca, 303
Partido de la Revolución Mexicana, 50, 265-67
Partido de la Unidad Revolucionaria, 304
Partido Democracia Cristiana. See Movimiento de Democracia Cristiana
Partido Demócrata (Chile, 1930s), 124, 128
Partido Demócrata Cristiano (Argentina), 352-54, 476-77
Partido Demócrata Cristiano (Bolivia), 363-64
Partido Demócrata Cristiano (Chile), xviii, xx, 42, 72-73, 101-02, 124, 135-37, 315-16, 318-37, 352, 357
Partido Demócrata Cristiano (Costa Rica), 230-231, 366
Partido Demócrata Cristiano (El Salvador), 359-60
Partido Demócrata Cristiano (Dominican Republic), 316
Partido Demócrata Cristiano (Panama). 366
Partido Demócrata Cristiano (Uruguay), 315, 356-57
Partido Demócrata Cristiano Revolucionario, 364
Partido Demócrata Nacional (Argentina), xxi, 48, 75-76, 85-87, 102, 108, 112, 114-15, 118, 352, 401, 479
Partido Demócrata Nacional (Ecuador), 12
Partido Demócrata Progresista, 87, 115
Partido Democrático (Brazil), 443
Partido Democrático (Chile), 71, 123-24 127, 129, 132
Partido Democrático Cristiano (Brazil), 354-56, 441, 447, 457, 461, 463
Partido Democrático Cristiano (Chile), 72-73, 321, 323
Partido Democrático Mexicano, 275
Partido Democrático Nacional (Chile), 124
Partido Democrático Nacional (Honduras), 54, 325. See also Partido Nacional
Partido Democrático Nacional (Venezuela). See Accion Democrática
Partido Dominicano, 6-7, 374
Partido Febrerista. See Partido Revolucionario Febrerista
Partido Federal (Argentina), 353
Partido Federal (Brazil), 444-45, 461
Partido Guatemalteco del Trabajo, 303, 415, 421
Partido Independentista Puertorriqueño, 358-59
Partido Independiente, 468
Partido Integralista, 27
Partido Justicialista, 477-78
Partido Laborista (Argentina), 468-69
Partido Laborista (Chile), 125
Partido Laborista Mexicano, 169-70, 264
Partido Laborista Nacional, 7

Partido Liberacion Nacional, 224-32, 259, 280, 290, 306, 366, 411
Partido Liberal (Bolivia), 23-24, 27-28, 39-40, 47, 67-69, 435
Partido Liberal (Brazil), 26-28, 442-45
Partido Liberal (Chile), xvi, xviii, xxi, 24-25, 28, 40-42, 47, 70-73, 96-101, 128, 133, 135, 320, 323, 325-26, 330, 334, 432-33
Partido Liberal (Colombia), xvii-xviii, 21-22, 34-37, 59-64, 156-58, 365
Partido Liberal (Cuba), 28
Partido Liberal (Guatemala), 20-21, 27
Partido Liberal (Honduras), xvi, 28-30, 47, 55-57
Partido Liberal (Mexico), 20, 27, 49-50
Partido Liberal (Nicaragua), xvi, 30-32, 57-58
Partido Liberal (Panama), 165
Partido Liberal (Paraguay), 26, 28, 45-47, 79, 309, 311-12
Partido Liberal (Uruguay). See Partido Colorado (Uruguay)
Partido Liberal (Venezuela), 22, 27
Partido Liberal Independiente, 31, 58
Partido Liberal Nationalista, 31-32
Partido Liberal Puertorriqueno, 252, 257
Partido Liberal Radical, xvi, 11-12, 22-23, 37-38, 65-66, 152
Partido Liberatador, 445, 461-62
Partido Nacional (Chile), 42, 71, 73, 102, 334-35
Partido Nacional (Honduras), 28, 48, 54-57
Partido Nacional (Uruguay), xxi, 16, 25-26, 43-44, 77-78, 141-44, 149, 357
Partido Nacional Democrático, 7
Partido Nacional Republicano, 218, 226, 366
Partido Nacional Revolucionario, 169, 170, 264-65
Partido Nacionalista, 29-30, 253
Partido Nacista, 126, 128, 429, 432-33
Partido Obrero (Puerto Rico), 261
Partido Obrero y Campesino de México, 398-99

Partido Obero Revolucionario (Bolivia), 236, 241, 243-44, 391-94
Partido Obrero Revolucionario (Cuba), 391
Partido Obrero Revolucionario (Trotskista) (Chile), 390
Partido Obrero Revolucionario (Trotskista) (Peru), 395
Partido Obrero Revolucionario (Trotskista) (Uruguay), 395
Partido Operario Revolucionario (Trotskista), 395
Partido Ortodoxo. See Partido Popular Cubano
Partido Panameñista, 14-15
Partido Peronista, xx, 5-6, 87, 94, 121, 196, 352-53, 441, 465-80
Partido Peronista Feminino, 469-71
Partido Popular (Mexico). See Partido Popular Socialista (Mexico)
Partido Popular Cristiano, 194, 358
Partido Popular Cubano (Orthodoxo), 282-83, 288-90
Partido Popular Democratico, 172-73, 178-79, 251, 262, 280, 290, 388
Partido Popular Socialista (Colombia), 156-58
Partido Popular Socialista (Mexico), 398-99, 403
Partido Proletario (Comunista), 400-01
Partido Radical (Argentina), See Unión Civica Radical
Partido Radical (Chile), xix, 41-42, 71-72, 80, 96-102, 127-29, 133, 137, 319-20, 324-26, 335, 337, 432
Partido Radical Democrático, 99
Partido Radical Socialista, 127
Partido Reformista (Dominican Republic), 298, 362
Partido Reformista (Honduras), 56
Partido Renovacion Nacional, 301-03
Partido Republicano (Bolivia), 24, 39, 48, 68-69, 167
Partido Republicano (Brazil), 27, 443-45, 447, 461-62
Partido Republicano (Puerto Rico), 48, 172, 257, 259, 261
Partido Republicano Estadista. See Partido Republicano (Puerto Rico)

Partido Republicano Genuino, 68
Partido Republicano Nacional, 230
Partido Republicano Socialista,
    166-67
Partido Republicano Trabalhista, 16,
    445, 460
Partido Revolucionario, 304, 361,
    415, 421
Partido Revolucionario Auténtico
    (Bolivia), 245, 248-49
Partido Revolucionario Auténtico
    (Guatemala), 304
Partido Revolucionario Cubano
    (Auténtico), 168, 177, 179, 280-88,
    290
Partido Revolucionario Dominicano,
    179, 280, 290-301, 362-63
Partido Revolucionario Febrerista,
    46, 79, 280, 308-12
Partido Revolucionario Febrerista
    Auténtico, 311
Partido Revolucionario Institucional,
    xviii, 50, 177, 197, 263-80,
    398
Partido Revolucionario de Izquierda
    Nacionalista (Bolivia), 247, 249
Partido Revolucionario de Izquierda
    Nacionalista (Venezuela), 215, 338
Partido Revolucionario Social
    Cristiano, 362-63, 369
Partido Revolucionario de Unificación,
    Nacional, 274
Partido Social Cooperativista, 151
Partido Social Cristiano (Bolivia), 437
Partido Social Cristiano (Ecuador),
    13, 67, 153
Partido Social Cristiano (Nicaragua),
    58, 366-67
Partido Social Cristiano Copei, xviii,
    33-34, 164, 200-05, 208-10, 212,
    216, 334-52, 362
Partido Social Demócrata (Chile), 325
Partido Social Demócrata (Costa
    Rica), 219-24
Partido Social Democrático (Bolivia),
    363-64
Partido Social Democrático (Brazil),
    xvi, xx, 441, 445, 447, 449-57,
    459, 462-63
Partido Social Democrático (Chile),
    124
Partido Social Democrático (Peru—
    1930s), 185
Partido Social Democrático (Peru—
    1960s), 9, 194

Partido Social Democrático
    Cristiano, 365
Partido Social Progresista, 17
Partido Social Republicano, 127
Partido Social Trabalhista, 16, 445,
    460
Partido Socialista (Argentina), 75-76,
    87, 105, 107-122, 124, 151, 166,
    352, 401, 411, 480
Partido Socialista (Bolivia), 166-67
Partido Socialista (Chile), xviii,
    41-42, 72, 97-102, 123-39,
    151, 319, 323, 325, 328,
    332-36, 377, 389-90, 425,
    432-33
Partido Socialista (Costa Rica), 424
Partido Socialista (Ecuador), 11-13,
    38, 151, 154-55
Partido Socialista (Panama), 164
Partido Socialista Agrario, 163
Partido Socialista Argentino, 113,
    121-23, 375, 470
Partido Socialista Argentino de la
    Vanguardia, 121
Partido Socialista Auténtico, 131
Partido Socialista Brasileiro, 105,
    158-62, 354, 441, 444-45, 447,
    461, 463
Partido Socialista Colomibano. See
    Partido Popular Socialista
    (Colombia)
Partido Socialista de Chile (1930s),
    126, 165
Partido Socialista de Chile (1950s),
    133-34, 136, 318, 320-21
Partido Socialista de Cuba, 105, 167
Partido Socialista de Guatemala,
    302-03
Partido Socialista de Trabajadores
    (Chile), 130, 375
Partido Socialista de Trabajadores
    (Venezuela), 163
Partido Socialista de Yucátan,
    168-69
Partido Socialista del Peru, 155-56
Partido Socialista del Pueblo, 136
Partido Socialista del Uruguay, 105,
    140-51, 357, 375
Partido Socialista Democrático
    (Argentina), 121-22, 396
Partido Socialista Democrático
    (Chile), 325-26
Partido Socialista Democrático
    (Venezuela), 164-66, 212

Partido Socialista Independiente (Argentina), 85, 114-17
Partido Socialista Independiente (Bolivia), 167
Partido Socialista Internacional, 126
Partido Socialista Marxista (Chile), 126
Partido Socialista Marxista (Panama), 164-66
Partido Socialista Mexicano, 169
Partido Socialista Obrero (Argentina), 116
Partido Socialista Obrero (Chile), 124-25, 375
Partido Socialista Obrero (Cuba), 168
Partido Socialista Obrero (Puerto Rico), 171
Partido Socialista Obrero Boliviano, 391
Partido Socialista Popular (Chile), 133-34, 321, 397
Partido Socialista Popular (Cuba), 402, 413. See also Partido Comunista (Cuba)
Partido Socialista Popular (Dominican Republic), 375
Partido Socialista Puertorriqueno, 171-73, 253, 257, 259
Partido Socialista Revolucionario (Brazil), 395
Partido Socialista Revolucionario (Colombia), 156
Partido Socialista Revolucionario (Ecuador), 154
Partido Socialista Unificado (Bolivia), 69, 166
Partido Socialista Unificado (Chile), 126
Partido Socialista Unificado (Ecuador), 154
Partido Socialista Venezolano, 163-64
Partido Trabalhista, 159-60
Partido Trabalhista Brasileiro, 5, 15-16, 161, 355, 441, 445, 447, 449, 451, 464
Partido Trabalhista Nacional, 16, 445, 460-61
Partido Unico de la Revolución, 469
Partido Unificado de la Revolución Socialista Cubana, 413
Partido Unión Federal, 353
Partido Unión Republicana Socialista, 120, 167, 237, 435

Pasqualini, Alberto, 457, 459
Pastrana Borrero, Misael, 37, 62
Patrón Costas, Robustiano, 86, 465
Payne, James, xvii-xviii, 26, 36-37, 62-63
Paz Baraona, Miguel, 55
Paz Estenssoro, Víctor, 39, 234, 236-37, 239, 241, 243-50, 393, 436
Paz, Galarraga, Jesús, 214-15
Paz, Luis, 68
Pedro II (emperor), 26
Pelligrini, Carlos, 82
Peña Chavarría, Antonio, 220
Peñaranda, Enrique, 39, 68, 166-67, 235
Pendle, George, 46, 79
Penelón, José, 396
People's Progressive Party, 407
Peralta Arzadua, Enrique, 305, 361, 415
Pérez, José Joaquín, 70
Pérez Jiménez, Marcos, 17, 33, 163, 201-03, 207-09, 213, 228, 260, 290, 341-44, 349-51, 401, 403-04, 423
Pérez Leiros, Francisco, 113, 117-18
Perón, Eva Duarte de, 469-71
Perón, Juan Domingo, 18, 76, 86-96, 118-22, 135, 189, 352-53, 396, 401-02, 404, 465-82
PGT. See Partido Guatemalteco del Trabajo
Picado, Teodoro, 221-23
Piedra, Julio de la, 9, 194
Pila, Raúl, 461-62
Piña Soria, Rodolfo, 170
Pinedo, Federico, 115
Piñero, Jesús, 258
Pinheiro, Israel, 454
Pinto, Francisco, 24
Pizarro, Francisco, 181
Plaza Lasso, Galo, 12, 38, 153-54
PLM. See Partido Laborista Mexicano
Ponce Henriquez, Camilo, 13, 66, 153
Popular Democratic Party. See Partido Popular Democrático
Popular Party. See Partido Popular (Puerto Rico)
Porras, Demetrio, 164-65
Portales, Diego, 69-70
Posadas, J., 390, 394-95, 421
Pradistas, xviii

Prado, Manuel, 8-9, 185, 189-92, 358, 401, 424
Prat, Jorge, 325-26
Prato, Agelvis, 164
Prestes, Luiz Carlos, 4, 161, 383, 385, 404-05
Prialé, Ramiro, 189
Prieto, Joaquin, 70
Prieto Figueroa, Luis Beltrán, 164, 212, 214-15, 348
Primo de Rivera, José Antonio, 434
Primo de Rivera, Miguel, 85
Prio Socarras, Carlos, 283-87, 402
PRM. See Partido de la Revolución Mexicana
Progressive Democratic Party. See Partido Demócrata Progresista
Puiggrós, Rodolfo, 82, 401-04

Quadros, Jânio, 161-62, 354-55, 447, 453-58, 461
Quijano, Horacio, 87, 468
Quintero, Rodolfo, 401, 403

Radical Labor Party, 167
Ramírez, Domingo, 68
Ramirez, Pedro, 235
Ramos Giménez, Raúl, 210, 213
Rangel, Domingo Alberto, 213
Ravines, Eudocio, 155, 385
Razón de Patria (RADEPA), 235
Recabarren, Luis Emilio, 124-25, 375, 389
"Red" Communists, 200, 399-401, 404. See also Partido Comunista (Venezuela)
Regules, Dardo, 356
Reid Cabral, Donald, 296, 362
Remón, José, 14, 165
Renterria, Ramon Leon, 168
Repetto, Nicolas, 116, 121
Resck, Luis, 364
Reyes, Cipriano, 468-69
Riesco, Germán, 71
Rios, Juan Antonio, 41, 72, 97-99, 131-32, 319-20, 327
Rivera, Diego, 394
Rivera, Fructuoso, 25
Rivera, Julio, 360
Rivera Parga, Augusto, 72
Rivera, Primo de, 85
Robles, Marcos, 15, 165
Roca, Julio A., 80, 82
Rocafuerte, Vicente, 22

Rodas Alvarado, Modesto, 29
Rodriquez, Carlos Rafael, 378
Rodriquez de la Sotta, Horacio, 72
Rodriquez, Nicolas, 437
Rojas Contreras, J., 163
Rojas Pinilla, Gustavo, 36, 61-63, 157-58
Ronin, José Maria, 364
Roosevelt, Franklin, 253
Rosa, Diógenes de la, 164-65
Rosario, Antonio, 362
Rosas, Juan Manuel de, 74-75, 77, 80
Ross Santa María, Gustavo, 41, 72, 97, 128, 319, 432
Rossi, Jorge, 229
Roy, M. N., 169
Ruiz Cortines, Adolfo, 268, 271, 275
Ruiz Pineda, Leonardo, 202

Saad, Pedro, 153, 406
Saavedra, Bautista, 68-69, 166
Sabattini, Amadeo, 88-89
Sabroso, Arutro, 185, 191
Sacasa, Juan B., 30
Sáenz Peña, Roque, 75, 83, 92, 112
Sáez Merida, Simon, 204
Salamanca, David, 68-69
Salgado, Plinio, 429-32
Sánchez Arango, Aureliano, 284-85
Sánchez Cerro, Luis, 184-85
Sánchez, Ismael, 165
Sánchez Vilella, Roberto, 260-61
Santibañez, Adolfo, 169
Santos, Eduardo, 35
Santos Zelaya, José, 58
Saravia, Aparicio, 77
Sarmiento, Domingo Faustino, 75, 80-81, 83, 108
Schick, René, 31
Schnake Vergara, Oscar, 129
Schneider, Ronald, 21
Scott, Robert, 52
Segadas Viana, Jose, 459
Selemé, Antonio, 239
Seoana, Manuel, 142
Seoane, Edgardo, 10, 194
Seregni, Liber, 150, 357
Siles, Hernán, 234, 237, 239-40, 242-44, 247-49, 435-36
Siles, Hernando, 68
Siles, Luis Adolfo, 249
Silfa, Nicolás, 291
Social Democratic Party, Germany, 116

Socialismo Auténtico, 148-49
Socialist International, 124, 146, 156, 159, 164, 170, 178, 299
Socialist Party, France, 148
Socialist Party, United States, 169, 171, 394
Sociedad de Iqualdad, 96, 107, 123
Solano Lima, Vicente, 76, 477
Somoza, Anastasio, 30, 58
Somoza de Bayle, Anastasio, 31-32, 58, 367
Somoza de Bayle, Luis, 31
Somoza family, xvii, 30-32, 58
Sosa, Rubén, 480-81
Soulez Baldo, 342
Stalin, Joseph, 145-47, 268, 377, 389, 394, 396-97
Stevenson, John Reese, 128, 130, 433
Stroessner, Alfredo, 46, 79, 311, 364-65
Suárez Flamerich, German, 341
Sueldo, Horacio, 353-54
Sylvestre Regnis, Carlos, 477

Tabón, Benjamin, 170
Tamborini, José P., 87, 468
Tarso, Paulo de, 355
Távora, Juárez, 159, 161, 354-55, 447, 452
Tefel, Reynaldo Antonio 366-67
Teixeira, Mauro Borges, 453
Teixeira, Pedro Ludovico, 450
Tejeda Solorzano, 168
Tejera, Diego Vicente, 167
Terra, Gabriel, 44, 77, 143-44
Thayer, William, 332
Thomas, Norman, 298
Titoism in Latin America, 134, 139, 396-97
Toledano, Vicente Lombardo, 170
Tomic, Radomiro, 318, 335-36
Toro, David, 39, 68, 233, 236
Torre, Lisandro de la, 115
Torres, Camilo, 317
Torres, Juan José, 249-50, 364, 436
Transformación Social, 151-52
Trejos Fernández, José, 230
Troitiño, Liber, 142-43
Trotsky, Leon, 391-94
Trotskyites, Bolivia, 249, 391-95
Trotskyites, Chile, 126-27, 389-90
Trotskyites, Cuba, 282, 390-91
Trotskyites, Mexico, 394-95
Trotskyites, Panama, 164
Trotskyites, Peru, 191

Trotskyites, Uruguay, 357
Trujillo, Rafael Leónidas, xxii, 6-7, 179, 201, 290-93, 295-96, 298, 300, 362, 374, 425
Trujillo, Rafael Jr., 291-92
Truman, Harry, 258
Tugwell, Rexford Guy, 253, 258
Tupamaros, 425
Turcios, Luís, 421
26th of July Movement. See Movimiento 26 de Julio

Ubico, Jorge, 21, 27, 54, 301
UCR. See Unión Cívica Radical
UCRI. See Unión Cívica Radical Intransigente
UDELPA. See Unión del Pueblo Argentino
UDN. See União Democrática Nacional
Ulate, Otilio, 218, 221-24, 226, 229-30
União Democrática Nacional, 160-61, 354-55, 441, 445-49, 452-53, 456-57, 461-62
Unified Socialist Party. See Partido Socialista Unificado
Unión Cívica (Uruguay), 142-43, 356
Unión Cívica Nacional, 292-95, 362
Unión Cívica Radical, 75-76, 80-96, 107-08, 111-13, 115, 120-21, 128, 352, 401-02, 468
Unión Cívica Radical Antipersonalista, 84-86, 88, 114-15
Unión Cívica Radical del Pueblo, 18, 90, 92-94, 121, 474, 477, 481
Unión Cívica Radical Renovadora, 87, 468
Unión del Pueblo Argentino, 18
Unión Democrática Popular, 13
Unión Nacional, 56, 71, 221, 223, 226, 230, 266
Unión Nacional Odriísta, 8-9, 191-92
Unión Nacional Sinarquista, 429, 437-38
Unión para Avanzar, 420
Unión Popular (Argentina), 353, 476
Unión Popular (Uruguay), 149
Unión Popular (Venezuela), 198, 399-401, 403-04
Unión Republicana Democrática, xviii-xix, 32-34, 164, 200-16, 341-45, 351
Unión Revolucionaria (Cuba), 168

Unión Revolucionaria (Peru), 185
Unión Revolucionaria Comunista, 168
Unión Revolucionaria Democrática, 304
Unión Socialista, 130, 432
Unión Socialista Feminina, 470
Unión Socialista Popular, 137
Unionist Radicals, 87-89, 95
Unitarios, 25, 74
UNO. See Unión Nacional Odriista
URD. See Unión Republicana Democrática
Uribe Uribe, General, 156
Uriburu, José, 85
Urquiza, Justo José de, 74
Urriolagoitia, Mamerto, 39, 237-38
Uslar Pietri, Aruturo, 34, 163, 210-12
USP. See Unión Socialista Popular

Valadares, Benedito, 450
Valencia Guillermo León, 36-37, 62
Valencia, Luis Emiro, 157-58
Valencia Vega, Alipio, 23-24, 50 67-68
Vandor, Augusto, 477-81
Vanguardia Revolucionaria Socialista, 152
Vanguarda Socialista group, 160, 433
Vargas, Alzira, 430
Vargas, Getúlio, 15-17, 159-62, 354-55, 395, 429-32, 441, 444-60, 464

Velasco, Ibarra, José María, 11-15, 38, 66, 152-54, 427
Velasco, Juan, 194-95, 359, 426-27
Velasquista Committees, 11-13
Villagrán Kramer, Francisco, 304
Villalba, Jóvito, 32, 34, 164, 210, 339, 343-44
Villalón, Hector Orlando, 478
Villarroel, Guilberto, 39, 68, 167, 235-36, 392
Villeda Morales, Ramón, 28, 56-57, 293
Viña, Ramón, 144
Vives del Solar, Fernando, 318

Waiss, Oscar, 136-37, 397
Welles, Sumner, 280-81
Williams, Abraham, 56
Workers and Peasants Party of Mexico. See Partido Obrero y Campesino de Mexico
World Christian Democratic Movement, 368

Ydígoras Fuentes, Manuel, 304
Yon Sosa, Marco Antonio 420-21

Zapata, Emiliano, 263
Zuloaga, Félix, 49

ABOUT THE AUTHOR

ROBERT J. ALEXANDER is Professor of Economics and Political Science at Rutgers University, where he has taught since 1947. He has been Visiting Professor at Columbia University, the New School for Social Research, Atlanta University and the University of Puerto Rico.

Dr. Alexander is the author of 14 books, the latest of which were An Introduction to Argentina, and a study of the Communist Party of Venezuela. He has also written more than seven hundred articles and reviews.

Dr. Alexander did all of his university work at Columbia University, where he received his B.A., M.A. and Ph.D., the latest in 1950.

DATE DUE